Also by
JEFF BENEDICT

Tiger Woods (with Armen Keteyian)

QB: My Life Behind the Spiral
(with Steve Young)

Make a Choice:
When You Are at the Intersection
of Happiness and Despair

My Name Used to Be Muhammad:
The True Story of a Muslim Who
Became a Christian (with Tito Momen)

The System: The Glory and Scandal of
Big-Time College Football (with Armen Keteyian)

Poisoned: The True Story
of the Deadly E. coli Outbreak
That Changed the Way Americans Eat

Little Pink House:
A True Story of Defiance and Courage

How to Build a Business Warren
Buffett Would Buy: The R. C. Willey Story

The Mormon Way of Doing Business:
Leadership and Success through Faith and Family

Out of Bounds:
Inside the NBA's Culture of Rape,
Violence, and Crime

No Bone Unturned: Inside the
World of a Top Forensic Scientist and His Work
on America's Most Notorious Crimes and Disasters

Without Reservation:
How a Controversial Indian Tribe Rose to Power
and Built the World's Largest Casino

Pros and Cons:
The Criminals Who Play in the NFL

Public Heroes, Private Felons:
Athletes and Crimes Against Women

THE
DYNASTY

Jeff Benedict

AVID READER PRESS

New York   London   Toronto   Sydney   New Delhi

Avid Reader Press
An Imprint of Simon & Schuster, Inc.
1230 Avenue of the Americas
New York, NY 10020

First Avid Reader Press hardcover edition September 2020

AVID READER PRESS and colophon are
trademarks of Simon & Schuster, Inc.

For information about special discounts for bulk purchases,
please contact Simon & Schuster Special Sales at
1-866-506-1949 or business@simonandschuster.com.

The Simon & Schuster Speakers Bureau can bring authors to
your live event. For more information or to book an event,
contact the Simon & Schuster Speakers Bureau at
1-866-248-3049 or visit our website at www.simonspeakers.com.

Interior design by Lewelin Polanco

Manufactured in the United States of America

1   3   5   7   9   10   8   6   4   2

Library of Congress Cataloging-in-Publication
Data has been applied for.

ISBN 978-1-9821-3410-5
ISBN 978-1-9821-3412-9 (ebook)

To Art Taylor, the man who was most responsible for my becoming a writer. In 1992, when I was fresh out of college, he invited me to Boston and offered me a research internship. This opportunity exposed me to influential writers. At that point, I had never considered writing as a career choice. Art changed that. More important, he believed in me and took a personal interest in my future. It's amazing how far a little encouragement can take you.

Over the years, Art read every one of my books, but he was particularly thrilled about this one. I was still working for him when Robert Kraft purchased the Patriots franchise in 1994. Art loved the Patriots, and when I told him in 2018 that I was writing a book on the Patriots' dynasty, he told me that he could not be prouder. He couldn't wait to read it. But in June 2019, Art passed away.

Art, this one's for you and your lovely wife, Ann-Louise. Thank you for believing in me. Thank you for giving me a chance. I will always love you.

Contents

Prologue

Wearing a surgical mask, a gown, and latex gloves, Dr. David Berger stood over Drew Bledsoe and made a careful incision in his chest. It was the evening of Sunday, September 23, 2001, and high-intensity ceiling lights in a trauma bay at Massachusetts General Hospital illuminated the thirty-seven-year-old surgeon's steady hands. Bledsoe, the starting quarterback for the New England Patriots, had an oxygen cannula in his nose and IV fluids flowing into his veins to resuscitate him. The twenty-nine-year-old had lost over a third of his blood through a partially severed artery that was pulsing into his chest cavity and preventing his left lung from expanding. Berger needed to get the internal bleeding under control or Boston's most famous athlete would die. But first, he had to remove the blood from Bledsoe's chest.

Inserting a slim tube in the incision, Berger gingerly snaked it under Bledsoe's skin, over a rib, and into the space between the lung and the chest wall where the blood was pooling. Within moments, blood began flowing from Bledsoe's chest through the tube into a machine equipped with filters that removed clots and other impurities. The machine then re-transfused the clean blood back into Bledsoe through a second tube that flowed into one of his veins.

As soon as Bledsoe's lung started working again, Berger turned his attention to the sheared artery. When a patient loses a liter and a half of blood, standard medical protocol calls for surgery to stop the bleeding. But Bledsoe wasn't a standard patient—he was the most talented quarterback in team history and had just signed a ten-year, $103 million contract that made him the highest-paid player in the National Football League.

Reluctant to operate, Berger talked to Bledsoe and his wife, Maura, together. The injury, he explained, was to Drew's left chest. When a right-handed thrower like Drew brought the ball back, cocked his arm, and then extended it forward, he was rotating around on his left chest, using all of

those muscles to generate the torque to throw. "I will have to cut at least some of those muscles," Berger told Drew. Then Berger turned to Maura. "The procedure could potentially end his football career," he told her.

Bledsoe was adamant that he didn't want surgery.

Berger explained that sometimes an artery will stop bleeding on its own, averting the need for surgery. Under the circumstances, Berger recommended keeping the chest tube in and closely monitoring Bledsoe. If the bleeding didn't stop within a few hours, he'd have no choice but to go in.

Two hours earlier, Berger had been at home enjoying a quiet dinner with his family when he received a call from Dr. Tom Gill, a New England Patriots team physician. Berger and Gill were friends. At Gill's urging, the Patriots had started using Berger as a surgical consultant a couple of years earlier. Berger had a reputation for being the "busiest surgeon" at Mass General, where he performed about eight hundred operations a year. The moment he heard Gill's voice, Berger knew this wasn't a social call.

"Can you meet Drew over at the MGH emergency room?" Gill said in an urgent tone.

Berger asked what was going on. Gill said he wasn't sure. Late in the fourth quarter, he explained, Bledsoe had been running with the ball toward the Patriots sideline when he was blasted by New York Jets linebacker Mo Lewis. The hit was so violent that players along the Patriots sideline compared the sound of the collision to a car crash. Bledsoe went airborne, and his face mask bent. After lying on the turf for a minute or so, he finally got up and made his way to the bench. He returned to the field on the Patriots' next possession. But coach Bill Belichick replaced him moments later when it became apparent that Bledsoe couldn't remember the plays. When the game ended, he was taken to the locker room to be examined. X-rays were inconclusive, but his vital signs were troubling. High heart rate. Faint pulse. Shallow breathing. He was complaining of pain in his left chest and was beginning to be short of breath.

"I think he has an internal injury," Gill told Berger, wondering aloud if Bledsoe might have ruptured his spleen.

Berger knew that Bledsoe was the linchpin of the Patriots team, the face of the franchise.

"He's on his way to the hospital?" Berger asked.

"We're putting him in an ambulance now," Gill said.

"I'll be there."

The Patriots' backup quarterback, Tom Brady, used the locker next to Bledsoe's in the team locker room. While changing out of his uniform after the game, Brady watched the medical staff escort Bledsoe from the training room. Brady was twenty-four and had just begun his second season in the NFL. He'd seen some big hits in college, but nothing like the one Bledsoe had sustained. And the sight of his friend and mentor being placed on a gurney and loaded into the back of an ambulance had him deeply concerned. Brady and Bledsoe were close. Brady often hung out at Bledsoe's home, and Maura frequently cooked him dinner. He felt like he was part of the family.

Brady quickly got dressed and drove straight from the stadium to the hospital. It was his first trip to Mass General. Unrecognizable in Boston, he had trouble getting past security at the nurse's station outside the trauma unit. He had to convince the hospital staff that he was Drew Bledsoe's backup. Eventually, he talked his way in and followed signs to the waiting room, where he discovered Maura, alone and crying.

Brady put his arms around her. "What's going *on*?" he asked.

Wiping her eyes, Maura brought him up to speed. "They're deciding whether to go in and repair the artery," she said. "If it doesn't stop bleeding on its own, it could be career-ending."

Brady couldn't believe what he was hearing.

Down the hallway, Robert Kraft huddled with one of the team doctors who were closely monitoring the situation. Kraft wanted to know the prognosis. The doctor was direct. Mo Lewis's hit, he explained, had resulted in an injury unlike anything he'd ever seen in a professional athlete. When Lewis hit Bledsoe he broke a number of his ribs, despite the fact that Bledsoe was wearing a flak jacket. The jagged edges of the broken ribs tore an artery in Bledsoe's chest, causing internal bleeding. The official medical diagnosis was that Bledsoe suffered a hemothorax—a collection of blood in the space between the chest wall and the lung. Roughly 50 percent of the blood circulating through Bledsoe's body ultimately leaked into his chest and needed to be drained. He also had a pneumothorax—a collapsed lung. Apparently, one of his broken ribs had poked a hole in it.

The doctor told Kraft that Bledsoe could have died.

Stunned, Kraft had trouble keeping his emotions in check. Bledsoe was like a son to him. Kraft doubted he'd ever play football again. Gathering himself, he briefed Belichick, who had also come straight from the stadium. Belichick had seen his fair share of serious injuries. But Bledsoe's situation was the worst. In that moment, he wasn't thinking about football. He was just hoping Bledsoe would pull through.

Determined to stay until Bledsoe was stable enough to have visitors, Kraft and Belichick ducked into a waiting area. It was going to be a long night.

At around midnight nurses told Kraft, Belichick, and Brady that they could see Bledsoe. He slept as they quietly filed into his room and took their places beside his hospital bed. Blood was still flowing from the tube in his chest through the machine and back into one of his veins. He had an IV in his arm. Maura sat beside him, gently stroking his right hand. Kraft, Belichick, and Brady stood shoulder-to-shoulder over Bledsoe's left side.

After a few minutes, Bledsoe opened his eyes. Groggy and disoriented, he first spotted Maura. She smiled and squeezed his hand. Then he turned his head to the left and looked up to see Mr. Kraft, Coach Belichick, and Tommy gazing down at him. Confused and still experiencing the effects of powerful pain medication, he wasn't sure what they were doing there. To him, they looked like a vision from another time and place.

At that moment, Kraft owned a franchise that had never won a championship. Belichick's overall record with the Patriots was 5-13. Brady had never started an NFL game. It was unimaginable to think that Bledsoe was staring up at the nucleus of the greatest sports dynasty of the modern era.

one

END GAME

G illette Stadium was deserted. The goalposts had been removed, the scoreboards turned off. Under sunshine and blue sky, the home of the greatest sports dynasty of the twenty-first century was as serene as Walden Pond. Wearing jeans, a white T-shirt, and sneakers, Tom Brady was in his luxury box. Standing alone in the place where his family sat on game days to watch him perform, the most celebrated quarterback in NFL history gazed down at the field and the 65,000 empty seats surrounding it. It was just before noon on Sunday, September 1, 2019, one week before the New England Patriots franchise would unveil its sixth Super Bowl banner prior to kicking off the season opener against the Pittsburgh Steelers. In a rare moment of solitude, Brady contemplated that this would likely be his last season in New England.

A month earlier, Brady had turned forty-two, making him the oldest football player in modern history to lead a championship team. On the day after his birthday, he signed a new three-year contract with the Patriots. He'd long said that he planned to play until he was forty-five. But his new deal had an unusual provision that caused the contract to automatically void after the upcoming 2019 season. At that point, Brady would become a free agent with the option to re-sign with the Patriots, retire, or join another team. Uncertainty about Brady's plans beyond the upcoming season loomed large over the organization. The consensus among sportswriters, football fans, and team officials throughout the NFL was that Brady would never leave New England for another team. Yet Brady and Patriots owner Robert Kraft had negotiated an exit clause that enabled him to do just that.

Brady viewed Kraft as a mentor, a confidant, and a father figure. His relationship with Kraft was the reason he had remained a Patriot for so long. For Kraft's part, he had long treated Brady like a son. His emotional

connection to his quarterback was so deep that once Brady reached his thirties, Kraft had spent the next decade doing whatever it took to deter head
coach Bill Belichick from moving on from him. Although Belichick and
Brady were the greatest coach-quarterback duo in history, they had become
distant. They were the NFL's version of Lennon and McCartney. Belichick
was the introverted genius who spoke few words and intimidated people
with his stare. Brady was the perfectionist who outworked everyone and
needed approval. They rarely spoke to each other away from the stadium.
But when Belichick put on a headset and Brady put on a helmet, they were
on their own wavelength, enabling them to reach heights that everyone else
could only gape at. In nineteen seasons together they won an unprecedented
sixteen AFC East division titles, went to nine Super Bowls, and won six
championships. They didn't have to be friends to establish the Patriots as
the envy of the league and the gold standard by which every future sports
team would be measured.

The last thing Kraft wanted was for Brady and Belichick to break up and
for Brady to finish his career in another uniform. But it was Kraft's decision
to give Brady the leverage to leave the Patriots at the end of the 2019 season.
After such an epic run, he knew that the game's two biggest stars were tired
of playing on the same stage. The only hope of keeping the band together
beyond 2019, Kraft felt, was to give Brady the power to dictate his own future.
Maybe when he was free to walk away, he'd decide not to.

But Brady had already laid some of the groundwork for his departure.
Earlier in the summer, he and his wife had gone through the process of finding a Realtor, signing a broker agreement, having a market analysis performed
on their home, getting the property photographed, and preparing the listing.
Less than twenty-four hours after Brady signed his one-year extension with
the Patriots, his Boston area home went on the market.

Standing in his box, Brady swelled with gratitude. When he was a little
boy, his hero had been Joe Montana. In New England, he'd gone places
Montana had only dreamed about. Along the way, Brady got married,
raised three children, built a home, started his own business, and won
more championships than anyone in NFL history. Pondering, he took one
more look at the empty stadium where he had evolved from a recent college graduate to a middle-aged man. "How did all of this happen?" he wondered.

He checked his watch. It was time to get ready for practice. Turning his
back on the field and shifting his focus to the Steelers, he left his box and

headed for the locker room. He was eager to start his twentieth season in New England.

Heading into the 2019 season, Bill Belichick was focused on one thing—winning the next championship. He liked his team's chances. The roster was rich with mentally and physically tough guys who understood what it took to win. But Belichick, who was now sixty-seven, never stopped looking for players who could make the Patriots better. And on Saturday, September 6, 2019, he saw one who immediately piqued his interest. That morning, Oakland Raiders wide receiver Antonio Brown went on Instagram and called on the team to release him from his contract. Within hours, the Raiders obliged. And by 11:00 a.m., the league confirmed that Brown would be eligible to sign with another team at four that afternoon. Belichick immediately started working the phones to gather information.

Brown was considered the most talented wide receiver in the league. For six consecutive seasons in Pittsburgh, he caught more than one hundred passes and racked up more than 1,200 receiving yards, making him the most prolific receiver in Steelers history. But by the end of the 2018 season, he was openly feuding with quarterback Ben Roethlisberger and had become such a disruptive presence in the locker room that the team traded him to Oakland in 2019. After the Raiders offered Brown a three-year contract worth $54 million, he announced he'd be a "good force" in Oakland. Then he showed up for the first day of training camp in a hot-air balloon. Things went downhill from there. He started missing practices. He got into a feud with the league over his desire to wear a helmet that had been banned for safety reasons. The team fined him multiple times over absences. Eventually, things devolved to the point that Brown got into an altercation with the team's general manager, prompting the Raiders to suspend him for the season opener. That's when Brown took to social media, saying he wanted out of his $54 million contract.

Belichick recognized that Brown had a mercurial personality. In the space of one summer he'd worn out his welcome with two franchises. But the Patriots' biggest weakness heading into 2019 was its receiving corps. Brady's favorite target, tight end Rob Gronkowski, had retired in the offseason. And although they still had Julian Edelman, there were a lot of question marks beneath him on the depth chart. The addition of Brown would be a game changer that could make the Patriots' offense all but unstoppable.

Normally, Belichick had full autonomy to make player personnel decisions. But in certain instances he knew he needed the owner's blessing. Signing the most controversial player in the NFL certainly fit that category.

Belichick reached for his phone.

Although it was a Saturday and the Patriots front office was closed, seventy-eight-year-old Robert Kraft was at his desk. With just over twenty-four hours until the home opener, he was catching up on correspondence and making phone calls. The bank of television monitors on his wall was tuned to a variety of news, business, and sports channels. Antonio Brown's image appeared on ESPN and the NFL Network as commentators for both outlets speculated on where the receiver might end up. Kraft muted the sound. The moment that the Raiders cut Brown, Kraft expected he'd get a call from Belichick. After being together for so long, he knew how Belichick rolled.

Belichick's first game as head coach of the Patriots was against the Tampa Bay Buccaneers at Foxboro Stadium on September 3, 2000. That morning, Belichick gave Kraft a gift—a vintage photograph of Ted Williams and Babe Ruth. It came with a handwritten note.

Robert,

Thanks for giving me the opportunity to coach your team. Let's hope we will be as successful as these two fellas.

Bill

The Patriots lost that day. They lost again the next week. And the week after that. And the week after that. It was October before Belichick got his first coaching victory in New England. His debut season didn't exactly go as planned. The Patriots went 5-11 and finished in last place in the division. Both Belichick and Kraft came under fire. "I wouldn't hire Belichick to run a Burger King," a popular Boston talk show host said at the time. A top sports columnist wrote, "If the Pats owner cannot see why Belichick is wrong for his franchise, the team is doomed."

Kraft stuck with Belichick. Over the ensuing nineteen years, Belichick established the highest overall winning percentage (.683) of all time among professional football coaches and became the only head coach to win six Super Bowls. During that eighteen-year span, the other three teams in the

Patriots' division—the Jets, Bills, and Dolphins—went through a combined twenty-four head coaches. The continuity and efficiency that stemmed from the Kraft-Belichick partnership had enabled the Patriots to always remain a step ahead of the competition.

The picture of Williams and Ruth still hung from Kraft's office wall, although the ink on the note had faded. Kraft was staring at the image when his cell phone rang at 2:00 p.m.

Belichick cut to the chase. He thought he could sign Brown to a one-year contract. It would cost $15 million—a $10 million signing bonus and $5 million in base salary. But if he was going to do it, he had to act fast. Other teams were in the hunt.

"He obviously would help us a lot," Belichick told Kraft.

Kraft brought up Brown's erratic behavior.

"I don't think he's really that bad to deal with," Belichick said. "Look, he hasn't worked out much in the preseason. But he would help us. Believe me."

"Do you know him?" Kraft said.

"I don't have any direct relationship," Belichick said.

"So that's the risk," Kraft said.

"I'm not really worried about that," Belichick said.

"I believe he had a domestic-violence accusation in the past," Kraft said. "How did that play out?"

"He's a pretty good kid," Belichick said. "Doesn't drink. Doesn't smoke. I'm not aware of any domestic violence."

Belichick had another call coming in. It was from Raiders general manager Mike Mayock. "Let me take this," he told Kraft. "I'll call you back."

Kraft sat at his desk, weighing the pros and cons of putting Brown on his payroll. In his mind, Brown's pattern of behavior didn't fit the Patriots' brand. But there were other factors to consider. Uncertain whether Brady would leave in one year or two, Kraft knew that once he was gone it would be impossible to ever match what had gone on in Foxborough over the previous nineteen years. His priority was to extend the magic for a little longer.

Kraft called Brady.

Brady was home watching the Michigan-Army football game. He turned down the volume when he saw Kraft's name on his caller ID. He listened intently as Kraft told him that he and Belichick were considering signing Antonio Brown.

"What do you think?" Kraft said.

Brady appreciated being asked. One of his biggest frustrations in recent years had been the way key personnel decisions that affected the offense were made without input from him. A week earlier, Belichick had cut backup quarterback Brian Hoyer and veteran receiver Demaryius Thomas. Brady had great chemistry with Hoyer, who was thirty-three and had a wife and kids. Brady considered him an important asset to the offense. And with the Patriots lacking depth at wide receiver, Brady would have preferred to keep an experienced receiver like Thomas on the roster as well. It aggravated him that after two decades as the team's quarterback, he still wasn't a part of the conversation before important moves were made. So he appreciated the fact that Kraft was seeking his input on whether to sign Antonio Brown.

"I'm all for it," he told Kraft. "One hundred percent."

"So you support it one hundred percent?" Kraft said.

"A thousand percent!" Brady said.

The last time he had a wide receiver with Brown's talent was when Belichick traded to get Randy Moss in 2007. That year, Brady set an NFL record for touchdown passes and Moss set an NFL record for touchdown receptions. For Brady, the prospect of throwing to Brown gave him something to look forward to.

"Well, you deserve it," Kraft said.

Brady was so thrilled that he couldn't wait to get on the practice field with Brown.

"All right," Kraft said. "Here we go. I love you."

Kraft immediately called his fifty-five-year-old son, Jonathan. Savvy and fiercely loyal, Jonathan Kraft oversaw the Kraft Group's business operations and had been the Patriots team president since his father purchased the franchise in 1994. He was to his father what Bobby Kennedy was to JFK—his most trusted confidant. The Krafts had talked earlier in the day about the likelihood of Belichick pursuing Brown. Now, Jonathan listened as his father explained that it was in motion and that he had already looped in Brady.

"This is risky," Robert said. "Bill doesn't know Brown. If Tom was ambivalent, I wouldn't support it."

Jonathan agreed that Brady being on board was important. He also shared his father's concerns about Brown's unpredictability. But Belichick was the mitigating factor. He had a long track record of bringing controversial players to New England and getting them to conform.

Minutes later, Belichick called Kraft back. He had talked to the Raiders. The Patriots, he assured Kraft, were free to strike the deal with Brown.

"Are you prepared to do it?" Kraft said.

"Yeah," Belichick said.

Kraft hesitated. He was still uneasy about signing Brown. But he desperately wanted to keep Brady in New England beyond 2019. And the clock was ticking.

"Make the deal," he told Belichick.

The next day, Antonio Brown arrived in New England, a sixth Super Bowl banner was raised at Gillette Stadium, and the Patriots blew out the Steelers to start the season. But things went sideways with Brown, as we'll see. The season—the twentieth that Kraft, Belichick, and Brady spent together—was filled with frustration. Six weeks after it ended, the quarterback of the greatest sports dynasty of the twenty-first century left the Patriots and joined the Tampa Bay Buccaneers. The departure of the most revered athlete in Boston's storied history marked the end of a golden era the likes of which the football world has never witnessed. The way it ended brought bigger meaning to Brady's question from the luxury box: *How did all of this happen?* How was the dynasty built? How did it survive for two decades? As Belichick and Brady split up, the sports world would also be asking: Why did it end this way?

The answers proved to be complex. And when retracing the origins of an epic journey, the best place to start is the very beginning.

two

BOBBY

———————

T he Peppermint Twist" by Joey Dee & the Starliters was playing on the radio and astronaut John Glenn was on the cover of *Life* magazine when twenty-year-old Robert Kraft ducked into Ken's Coffee Shop in the Back Bay section of Boston a little before midnight on February 2, 1962. Home from Columbia University for the weekend, he was with three college buddies who went by nicknames—Moose, Pig, and Snake. Kraft was simply "Bobby." He was the ringleader. Despite the late hour, the coffee shop was hopping. While the other guys looked up at the menu board, Kraft couldn't take his eyes off the girl standing ahead of them in line. Her dark hair was in a band and she wore a cable sweater and a mid-length skirt with knee socks and a pair of Weejuns penny loafers. She was with a guy and another couple. When the boy with her got out of line to use the restroom, Kraft tried to strike up a conversation.

"Do you go to Barnard?" he said.

She looked at him. "No, I go to Brandeis."

The girl in the preppy clothes seemed uninterested in his small talk.

Kraft watched her and her friends crowd into a booth, and he led his friends to an adjacent one. After making eye contact with the Brandeis girl a couple of times, Kraft whispered in Moose's ear, "Find out her name."

A burly football player, Moose was also gregarious. He leaned over the booth and made the ask. Then he scribbled *MYRA HYATT* on a paper napkin and pushed it across the table. Kraft slipped it into his pocket.

When Myra stood up to leave, Kraft winked at her, and she winked back.

The next morning, Kraft telephoned the main switchboard at Brandeis and asked to be connected to Myra Hyatt's room. He spelled her last name for the operator.

"I'm sorry," the operator said. "There's no one here with that last name."

Kraft figured that Moose must have misspelled her name.

"Well, her first name's Myra," he told the operator. "Maybe start at the top of the H's and see if you see a Myra."

"There's a Myra Hiatt, spelled H-*I*-A-T-T," the operator said.

"That's it," Kraft said.

She connected him. Moments later, Hiatt's roommate answered. She told Kraft that Myra was studying at the library. He thanked her and hung up.

None of the girls he had dated would have been found in the library after being out late on a Friday night. Despite being the president of his class at Columbia and an accomplished student, he couldn't help wondering if Myra Hiatt was too serious for him.

Undeterred, he talked his uncle into letting him borrow his car for the day and drove to Brandeis, located the library, and searched all the study areas. No Myra. Discouraged, Kraft headed for the door. On the way out, he ran into a friend who attended Brandeis. He asked him if by chance he knew a girl named Myra. The friend nodded and motioned for Kraft to follow him to the one area he hadn't checked—the stacks, where Hiatt had her face buried in a book.

Kraft thanked his friend and approached Hiatt.

"Hi," he said.

She looked up and immediately recognized him.

He introduced himself as a junior at Columbia. She volunteered that she was a sophomore.

"I'd like to take you out tonight," he said in a hushed voice.

"I can't," she whispered.

"Why not?"

"My boyfriend is coming home from a ski trip today, and we're going out tonight."

Kraft paused. Suddenly, he was getting the picture. Her boyfriend could afford to go skiing in Vermont on weekends. Myra Hiatt was out of his league and already spoken for. Those were two big strikes against him. The safe play was to bow out gracefully and move on.

But what happened next in the Brandeis library foreshadowed how and why Robert Kraft would one day pull off a series of unthinkable feats—acquiring the New England Patriots at the end of a ten-year legal and financial odyssey, choosing Bill Belichick as a head coach despite repeated warnings that doing so would be a grave mistake, and convincing Tom Brady to remain in New England for an unprecedented twenty consecutive years as his quarterback. Perseverance, instinct, and persuasiveness—the three

qualities that enabled Kraft to build and sustain the longest-running dynasty in American team sports history—were part of his DNA long before everyone knew his name.

Kraft pulled up a chair, sat down, and faced Hiatt. "Look," he told her, "I went through a lot of trouble and effort to get here and to find you. I'd really like to go out tonight."

For Hiatt, it wasn't so much what he said, but how he said it that won her over. He wasn't forceful. His tone was soft. The entire time he spoke, he looked her in the eyes. And despite being unabashedly direct, he came across as refreshingly sincere, to the point of appearing vulnerable.

As Kraft spoke, Hiatt's mind raced. She had been dating the same boy for four years. They'd been a couple since midway through high school. But she sensed that the guy who had winked at her the night before in the coffee shop and who was now staring into her eyes was different. There was something charming about his persistence. *I mean, he tracked me down in the library! Who does that?*

Intrigued, Hiatt went back to her dorm and telephoned her mother, who agreed to call the boyfriend and make up a phony story for why Myra couldn't go out that night.

Kraft returned later that evening and took Hiatt to a pizza place in Cambridge, where they spent two hours talking. Kraft peppered her with questions. *Where did you grow up? What are you studying? Do you have plans after college? What about your family?*

Born in 1942, Hiatt grew up in Worcester. Her father, Jacob Hiatt, was fluent in five languages and had been a district judge in Lithuania. Two years after Adolf Hitler was appointed chancellor of Germany, Jacob immigrated to the United States, where two of his brothers were already living. Jacob's parents, his sisters, and one other brother remained in Lithuania and were later killed in the Holocaust. After settling in Massachusetts, Jacob took a job making shoe boxes for his brother's store. Later, he borrowed the money to purchase a small paper box company, which supplied the boxes for his brother's shoe business. Jacob's company ultimately became the Rand-Whitney Corporation.

As a result of her father's success, Myra had grown up with the trappings of privilege. She attended private schools, was well read, and loved the theater. She had an eye for fashion and a taste for fine food. At the same time, she was saddled with her parents' high expectations, especially when it came to education. Her father was a trustee at Brandeis. Myra was probably heading to law school.

Listening to Hiatt, Kraft couldn't help thinking how different his up-bringing had been from hers. Born in June 1941, Kraft was the middle child in a tightly knit, conservative-orthodox Jewish family. They lived on the second floor of a three-story walk-up in a blue-collar neighborhood in Brookline, Massachusetts. His aunt Zelda and her family occupied the first floor. The Hamburgers, Jewish immigrants from Germany, lived on the third floor. Robert's father, Harry Kraft, scratched out an honest living selling plus-size women's clothing out of a shop near Chinatown in Boston. Outside of work, Harry dedicated all of his time and resources to his role as president of the most prominent Jewish synagogue in town. Harry studied the Torah every morning and the Bible every night. He never watched television. Never owned a car. And throughout his life he insisted on tithing, meaning he gave 10 percent of his income to his synagogue for charitable purposes. "A good name is more important than oil or gold," he frequently reminded his children.

Despite being a devout Jew, Harry Kraft married Sarah Webber, a petite, blue-eyed, blond woman from Nova Scotia who was born Jewish but was raised in a non-observing family. Webber attended a school run by nuns and grew up singing "God Save the King." A voracious reader who smoked two packs a day and liked to sit home alone on the Jewish Sabbath and listen to opera, Sarah managed the Kraft family finances and stressed to her children the importance of frugality, manners, and education. She kept a sign in the kitchen that read: "Hard work, savings, and perseverance are the main things in life." Growing up, little Bobby Kraft looked at that sign every morning while eating breakfast.

It wasn't until Kraft was a teenager that he started to appreciate the significance of his father, who was so religious, marrying someone who was not observant. From his father's example, Kraft learned the importance of loving unconditionally and that people who profess to be religious are sometimes the most judgmental. "My father's the one who instilled spirituality in me," Kraft would later say. "My mother was the tough one. My successes in business stemmed from the lessons she taught me. I lucked out having parents like them."

After pizza, Kraft drove Hiatt back to Brandeis and parked the car outside Hiatt's dorm. "So what about you?" she said. "What's your story?"

Rather than mention that his parents didn't own a home or a car, Kraft talked about his ambitions. He had been president of his class at Brookline

High School and was elected by his peers to the same position at Columbia. President John F. Kennedy was a role model. Kraft had even volunteered on Kennedy's presidential campaign. Politics appealed to Kraft, but his father wanted him to become a rabbi. It was a burden that weighed heavily on him. He explained that his father was a beloved figure in the Jewish community who taught hundreds of children at Temple Kehillath Israel Religious School every week. The children's parents compared him to Julie Andrews with the Trapp family.

The last thing Kraft wanted to do was disappoint his father. "He's the greatest man I know," he told Hiatt. But Kraft wasn't drawn to spending his life as a Jewish religious leader. His two biggest passions were sports and business. He told Myra he was planning to attend Harvard Business School after he graduated.

They ended up talking for nearly three hours. At times, he put the engine on to heat the car. He also turned on the radio. When Hiatt heard the opening chords to "Moon River," she said, "I *love* this song," and reached for the volume nob.

Breakfast at Tiffany's was in theaters, and Audrey Hepburn's character, Holly Golightly, performed an acoustic version of the romantic ballad in the film. The hit topped the charts and would go on to win an Academy Award and a Grammy for Song of the Year. As the music crackled through the car radio, Hiatt knew all the words and wasn't afraid to sing them.

> *Oh, dream maker, you heart breaker*
> *Wherever you're goin', I'm goin' your way*

Smitten, Kraft saw a little Holly Golightly in Hiatt. Beautiful. Clever. Worldly. Sitting there, watching Hiatt's lips move, he felt as if *he* were in a movie. It was a feeling that he didn't want to end.

Leaning against the passenger door and staring back at him, Myra could not foresee that Bobby Kraft would become infinitely more successful than her father. Nor was it imaginable that the boy who had to borrow his uncle's car for a date would go on to rub shoulders with presidents and prime ministers, and form close friendships with some of the world's greatest entertainers from the industries of sports, music, and film. Rather, she was just going off what she felt in the moment—that the guy behind the wheel had a certain flair, like a man who knew where he was headed in life. She looked at him and said: "Marry me."

Kraft was speechless. Earlier that day he'd just been trying to figure out

how to get her to say yes to a date, and suddenly she was proposing marriage. And she didn't pose the idea as a question; her tone was matter-of-fact. At the time, Kraft was dating a number of girls, one of whom he'd been seeing for some time. But no girl had ever made him question himself the way Myra did. *Am I good enough for her? Do I measure up?* He wasn't sure. But he knew he'd never felt so enamored of a girl.

Nonetheless, the notion of committing to marriage on a first date seemed completely irrational. Everything about the proposition—right down to the fact that it came from her, not him—was unconventional. Yet a voice inside him was telling him, *Do it.* He decided not to hesitate.

That night they made a pact not to tell their parents that they were getting married. Not yet, at least. In the meantime, Kraft handed Hiatt his fraternity pin to commemorate their informal engagement. She pinned it to her bra, where it remained for six months, until Kraft cashed in the savings bonds he had received for his bar mitzvah when he was thirteen. He used the money to purchase an engagement ring. Then, in June 1963, a little over a year after they met, they married, right after Kraft graduated from college. For a wedding song, they chose the one they'd heard on the radio on their first date.

With family and friends looking on, Robert and Myra Kraft danced while she whispered along in his ear:

Two drifters, off to see the world.
There's such a lot of world to see.

three

FATHERS AND SONS

S tanding at the kitchen sink, looking out the window, Myra Kraft saw her husband pull into the driveway of their Brookline home. It was late in the afternoon one day in the spring of 1971.

"Dad's home!" she yelled to her sons.

Seven-year-old Jonathan, the eldest of four, ran to the front door, threw his arms around his father's neck, and kissed him on the cheek.

"Come here," Kraft said softly, taking his son by the hand and leading him to the parlor. "I want to show you something."

Sporting thick sideburns and a gray Brooks Brothers suit, Kraft placed his briefcase on a small end table and manipulated the gold-plated, three-digit combination locks on each side of the handle. Jonathan's eyes widened as the case popped open. Peering inside, he spotted perforated strips of shiny white paper. Each one was embossed with a miniature Patriots football helmet.

"These are season tickets to the Patriots in their new home," Kraft said.

His mouth open, Jonathan ran his fingers over the glossy tickets, touching the helmets of the opposing teams: Oakland Raiders, Detroit Lions, Baltimore Colts, New York Jets.

Just one year earlier, the Boston Patriots had joined the National Football League. Although the team finished with the league's worst record at 2-12, Kraft was optimistic about the upcoming '71 season. Awarded the number one pick in the draft, the Patriots had just selected Stanford quarterback Jim Plunkett. The team had also changed its name to the New England Patriots, and they were moving into the newly constructed Schaefer Stadium in Foxborough.

"We have *season tickets* to the *Patriots*?" Jonathan said.

Kraft nodded.

For Jonathan, the best part was that he and his brothers were going to get to spend Sunday afternoons at Dad's side, watching Dad's favorite team play Dad's favorite sport.

That night, Jonathan and his six-year-old brother, Danny, couldn't sleep. A recent issue of *Sports Illustrated* with Jim Plunkett on the cover was atop their dresser. In their beds with the lights out, they were talking about what it was going to be like to see Plunkett play up close.

Suddenly, their whispers were interrupted by yelling.

"Buying tickets to *football games*?" Myra shouted. "What were you thinking?"

Robert tried to explain.

"We can't afford it!" she said.

"We'll be fine," he insisted.

"And the games are on *Sunday*," she continued. "The boys have to go to Hebrew school on Sunday."

"Myra, I'll take them to the games after Hebrew school ends."

Myra had looked at the tickets. The game times conflicted with the school schedule. "C'mon, Robert," she said.

Whenever Myra started calling him Robert, he knew he was in trouble.

Jonathan was too young to know anything about the family finances or how Hebrew classes might be affected. All he knew was that the situation sounded pretty serious. He had never heard his mother yell at his father. Neither had Danny.

"I guess Dad really messed up," Danny whispered.

The first football game was played at Schaefer Stadium on August 15, 1971. It was an exhibition contest against the New York Giants. The game produced what was generally regarded as one of the worst traffic jams in Massachusetts history. The only two-lane road to the new stadium was so snarled that thousands of fans never made it in time to see the game. Still, the Patriots' 20–14 victory was witnessed by tens of thousands of people. Kraft and his two eldest sons were among them, sitting on aluminum benches in row 23 of section 217, cheering so loudly that they nearly lost their voices.

The stadium's eight hundred toilets stopped flushing that day. Drains overflowed and hideous odors wafted through the stands. The drinking fountains failed. And it took four hours to make the thirty-mile drive home afterward. Kraft didn't mind. As a thirty-year-old father, he was focused on the priceless memories. The expression on his sons' faces as they entered an NFL stadium for the first time. The way they held the game program as if it were a treasure. And the feeling of their little arms around his waist when the Patriots scored a touchdown. Kraft was working seventy-hour weeks,

traveling back and forth to Canada, trying to build a business. Patriots games with his boys, he knew from the outset, would be a great escape from everything else he had going on in his life.

Right after finishing business school, Kraft had gone to work for his father-in-law at the Worcester-based Rand-Whitney Corporation, which manufactured corrugated boxes and fancier packaging, such as cosmetic boxes. Three years later, Kraft struck out on his own, starting a small box factory in Chelmsford, Massachusetts. He soon figured out that the real money in the paper and packaging industry was in the commodity itself, not in converting it to packaging. One day he read in the *Wall Street Journal* about a government-backed, state-of-the-art paper mill being constructed in Newfoundland and Labrador, the easternmost province of Canada. The Labrador Linerboard mill promised to feature "the latest advances in mechanization, process technology, and pollution control." Upon completion it would convert black spruce lumber into brown paper known as "linerboard," the very product that Rand-Whitney relied on in its Worcester plant to make corrugated boxes. Kraft decided to bid against a number of big companies, such as International Paper, that were competing to become the sales agent to market the new mill's output.

Aware that the Labrador Linerboard mill was capable of producing a thousand tons of brown paper per day, Kraft pledged to either sell two hundred thousand tons per year or pay the Canadian government for what he couldn't sell. His bold "take or pay" offer, which none of the big paper companies would match, convinced Newfoundland's premier to choose Kraft as the mill's exclusive sales agent. After getting the contract in Canada, Kraft formed International Forest Products (IFP) to buy and sell the raw materials coming out of the mill.

Within six months of Kraft starting his commodities trading company, President Richard Nixon instituted price freezes on paper milled in the United States. At the time, the United States was the biggest producer of linerboard in the world. With foreign importers suddenly scrambling to find alternative sources, Kraft started getting calls from all over the world. Soon he was exporting paper from Newfoundland to London, Korea, and Iran. He eventually added customers in Spain and Portugal. He expanded his business to include shipping raw materials and extending credit to manufacturers in developing countries. By the end of the seventies, he became the first independent exporter of brown paper to China.

Kraft had so much success at IFP that he bought out his father-in-law

and took over Rand-Whitney Packaging Corporation. By age thirty-one, he owned two companies doing business in the global economy.

Since her husband was away so much on business, Myra Kraft eventually came around to the idea of her sons spending Sunday afternoons in the fall with their father at Schaefer Stadium. "My dad, in his unique way of salesmanship, convinced her that it was okay," Dan Kraft said. "Because of his upbringing, religion was a pillar of his life. He knew it was important. But he also knew how hard we were working to prepare for our bar mitzvahs, and he recognized that we needed time to have fun, too."

On the Saturday night prior to each home game, Kraft would handwrite notes to his sons' Hebrew class teachers and slip them under the boys' pillows before bedtime.

Dear Mrs. Cohen, please excuse Daniel at 11:30. He has a family commitment. Sincerely, Mr. Kraft

On Sundays they had the routine down to a science. At 11:15 sharp, Kraft would enter Provisers deli around the corner from the school and order "the usual"—four sandwiches on bulky rolls; two corned beef and two roast beef with mustard. Minutes later, he'd emerge with a brown paper bag and pull up to the school in his dark green Porsche 911S. At 11:30, Jonathan, Daniel, and Josh would run out of the building and cram into Dad's sports car as if they were breaking out of jail. While Kraft sped to Foxborough, the boys tore into the brown bag. By the time they reached the stadium, the only available parking spots were a mile away. But the parking attendant at the lot closest to the stadium entrance always reserved a spot for Kraft. The attendant loved his Porsche because it reminded him of the model that Steve McQueen drove in the 1971 film *Le Mans*. Just before kickoff, Kraft would approach the LOT FULL sign, slip the attendant a twenty-dollar bill, and pull into the space reserved just for him. Moments later, he'd push his boys through the ticket turnstile and away they'd escape for three hours of cheering alongside fellow New Englanders. It felt like belonging to one giant family.

When Kraft's youngest son, David, was old enough, he went to the games, too. By then, Kraft had expanded his business ventures by building a manufacturing plant in the Alborz Mountains in Iran and investing in a packaging company in Israel. Despite the frequent travel abroad, his commitment to

making it back home in order to be in Foxborough with his sons for every Patriots home game only intensified. Those dates were hallowed like Jewish holidays on the Kraft family calendar.

Kraft even flew with his sons to Houston on one occasion in 1980 to see the Patriots play the Oilers in the Astrodome on *Monday Night Football*. Danny Kraft, who was fifteen by that time, had proposed the idea to his father, and Kraft turned it into a weekend adventure. On the day of the game, Kraft and his four boys visited the Houston Galleria Mall, where they ran into Patriots star tight end Russ Francis in a men's clothing store. For the boys, the encounter was as thrilling as the game.

"Ranking the highlights of my youth, going to Houston is right up there as one of my best memories," Jonathan reflected. "The Oilers had Earl Campbell, who was this mythical figure. The Astrodome, if you were a kid and a sports fan, was the coolest thing ever. And we met Russ Francis, who was as big as Gronk at the time, and he was really nice to us. The trip caused us to miss a couple days of school, and my mother was apoplectic about that, but this was my father with his boys, doing what he enjoys most."

For a man who had grown up in a very religious family, with a father who had hoped his son would become a rabbi, Robert Kraft appeared to have ended up in a faraway place. Occupationally, that was certainly true. But Kraft's connection to his sons through football was an outgrowth of his close relationship with his own father. Much later in his life, after he had owned the Patriots for twenty-five years, Kraft was asked: "What was your favorite thing to do with your dad when you were a little boy?" After some reflection, he replied, "Study the Old Testament. We used to go to services on the Sabbath, have lunch, and then afterwards, study." Pondering that memory for a few moments, Kraft added: "I didn't really like it at the time, but it was very good. I didn't realize it then, but the lessons I was learning would later help me in all types of situations both personally and professionally." In retrospect, Kraft revered his father for the way he lived his life and for instilling in him a set of ethical and spiritual beliefs.

Like most young boys, however, Kraft didn't get a thrill out of scripture study. His passion was playing and watching sports, but sports were not encouraged in his home. Although Kraft grew up within walking distance to Braves Field and attended a lot of Braves games as a kid, he never went with his father. It wasn't until he had his own sons that he finally got to combine his two favorite pastimes—sports and spending time with family.

In that respect, the Patriots represented something bigger than football in the Kraft home.

"For us, family was real important," said Jonathan Kraft. "But our family wasn't geared around religion. Not that we weren't religious. We were. But it wasn't the centerpiece of our lives. I think my father chose sports. The Patriots really were the 'religious' centerpiece for our family. It started with him getting us out of Hebrew School early to go to Patriots games."

If we only had a chance to own the team. Kraft said that to himself countless times while watching the Patriots suffer through losing seasons. As the years wore on, it became more and more evident that the team he and his boys loved was poorly managed. "Sitting in the stands," Kraft said, "I would dream of what our family could do with the team."

The problem was that the team was in the hands of another Boston family with designs on controlling it for generations. William "Billy" Sullivan had been the Patriots' owner since the inception of the American Football League in 1959. That year, Sullivan had put up $25,000 and been awarded the franchise rights to enter the Boston Patriots in the newly formed league. He'd been at the helm ever since. Eventually, he promoted his son Chuck to be the Patriots' executive vice president and his other son, Patrick, to be the general manager.

Kraft got to know Billy Sullivan and from time to time would tell him the same thing—if you ever decide to sell the team, I hope you'll call me and give me a shot at it.

Sullivan never called. He simply had no incentive to sell. Plus, his sons were waiting in the wings to succeed him.

Kraft couldn't help thinking he'd never get his shot. Then he got some unexpected help from a most unlikely source. At the end of 1982, Michael Jackson released *Thriller*. It sold a staggering 100 million copies and propelled him to global superstardom, cementing him as the "King of Pop." Soon thereafter, Jackson announced he was going on tour with his brothers. The Victory Tour, as it was billed, was projected to be the highest-grossing concert tour in history.

By this point, Schaefer Stadium had been renamed Sullivan Stadium. When Billy Sullivan's son Chuck, who ran Sullivan Stadium, heard about the tour, he saw an opportunity to help his father. At the time, the Patriots were in deep financial trouble and were considered to be the weakest link in the NFL chain of franchises. The Sullivan family was paying several million

dollars a year in interest just to service the loans that they were relying on to meet the team's payroll and keep the lights on at the stadium. Hoping to persuade the Jacksons to perform three shows in Foxborough, Sullivan flew to Los Angeles to meet with their representatives. It was a fateful trip that would end up changing the fortunes of the Sullivans, the Krafts, and the National Football League.

Chuck Sullivan got what he was after. The Jacksons agreed to perform a series of concerts in Sullivan Stadium. If Sullivan had stopped there, things might have turned out very differently. But after talking with a representative from the Jacksons' record label, Sullivan learned that the tour's promoter had unexpectedly backed out. Jackson was looking for a replacement. That gave Sullivan another idea. While running the Patriots with his father, he had been the promoter for a number of big concerts at their stadium. He figured that if he could get himself named as promoter of the Jackson tour, he'd score a big enough windfall to wipe out his father's debts altogether and put the Patriots organization on firm financial footing. So he made the Jacksons an offer they couldn't refuse—an up-front advance of $41 million and 75 percent of anticipated gross revenues from ticket sales. Those numbers were naively outlandish. The industry standard for performers at that time was closer to 50 percent of gross ticket revenues. Sullivan was effectively guaranteeing that the Jacksons would be paid as if every show had sold out, whether or not they actually did.

Again, Sullivan got his wish. In 1984 he was named promoter of the Victory Tour and placed in charge of booking dates and venues throughout the United States. To bankroll the tour, he had to borrow money. His initial installment of $12.5 million was due to Jackson at the start of the tour. To cover the loan, Sullivan put up Sullivan Stadium as collateral. It seemed like a safe bet. After all, he had Michael Jackson.

But Sullivan was in way over his head. First, he vastly underestimated what it would cost to transport not one but two 175-ton stages from city to city, where they had to be constructed and then disassembled at each venue. Second, his expectation of profiting from his status as an NFL owner backfired. He had been counting on discounted terms for stadium rentals at other pro football venues, but instead he ended up paying premium rates. Finally, on top of everything else, Foxborough officials inexplicably denied Sullivan's permit for the Jacksons to perform in Sullivan Stadium. All three shows were quashed, forcing the Sullivan family to forfeit their big payday.

Chuck Sullivan had intended for his Victory Tour gambit to rescue his father from financial peril and enable him to hold on to the Patriots, but it did just the opposite. While Jackson's tour did indeed finish up as the highest-grossing in history, Chuck Sullivan personally lost at least $20 million, which, according to published reports, amounted to virtually all of the Sullivan family's net worth.

One year after becoming the tour's promoter, Billy Sullivan engaged the Wall Street investment banking firm Goldman Sachs to help him sell the franchise.

The moment that Kraft heard that the Patriots were going up for sale, he sprang into action, tasking lawyers, accountants, and bankers to help him determine the value of the team.

Finally, the Patriots were in play.

four

THE LONG GAME

R obert Kraft's favorite sport to watch had always been football, but his favorite sport to play was tennis. In the mid-1970s, he had his first venture in sports-team ownership when he bought the Boston Lobsters, which competed in the newly formed World Team Tennis league. Shortly after he took over the team, eighteen-year-old high school student Martina Navratilova defected from communist Czechoslovakia while she was in America to participate in her first US Open. Eager to establish a following for his fledgling team, Kraft put up the most money ever paid for a female athlete for the rights to Navratilova. He also brought in tennis legend Roy Emerson to coach the team. In the context of World Team Tennis, these were very expensive investments, especially considering that Navratilova had not yet won a Grand Slam singles title.

But from the moment Navratilova arrived, the stands at Boston University's Walter Brown Arena, where the Lobsters played, were packed. Then Navratilova won Wimbledon, within a year of joining the Lobsters. Suddenly, Kraft had the hottest tennis star in the world playing on his team. In 1978, Navratilova was named Most Valuable Player of World Team Tennis and led the Lobsters to the best overall record in the league. Over the ensuing fifteen years, she went on to win eighteen Grand Slam singles titles and would be ranked number one in the world for an unprecedented 332 weeks.

Kraft's experience with Navratilova taught him an important truth—fans turn out to see stars, and the brighter the star, the bigger the draw. But to get beyond box-office success and actually establish a winning culture, Kraft also recognized the critical component of superior coaching. "Roy Emerson knew how to bring out the best in Martina," Kraft said.

When it came to owning a professional sports team, Kraft's underlying philosophy rested on the notion that winning over a sustained period of time requires the coexistence of a superior athlete and a superior coach. One is not more important than the other; you need both to achieve greatness. That

notion, which initially took shape from his experience with Martina Navratilova and Roy Emerson, would one day guide his managerial approach to Tom Brady and Bill Belichick.

But as Kraft first set out to buy the Patriots in the summer of 1985, he wasn't yet thinking that far down the road. Rather, he was focused on another, equally important lesson that he learned in his Team Tennis days, about economics. When Kraft owned the Lobsters, he did not own the arena where the team performed. As a result, even though he put up all the money to bring in the star player who filled the arena and attracted the sponsorships, Kraft's revenue was limited to ticket sales.

"I paid for all the advertising to promote the matches, and I paid the players' and coaches' salaries," Kraft said. "But the venue collected all the profits from parking, concessions, and the sponsorships. That showed me the importance of controlling the venue and all the revenue that came with it."

That realization became more pronounced once Kraft performed his due diligence on the Patriots franchise. The way the Sullivan family had structured their ownership, the team and the stadium were separate entities. Billy Sullivan owned the Patriots. His son Chuck owned Sullivan Stadium through a company called Stadium Management Corporation (SMC). The Patriots paid rent to SMC for use of the facility. Under the lease, the team controlled all the game-day revenues from ticket sales, concessions, sponsorship signage, and so on.

However, after the Sullivan family got mixed up in the Jackson tour, they tore up the lease between the team and the stadium and drafted a new one. Under the new terms, the Sullivans redirected the bulk of the cash flows—concessions, luxury seats, advertising in the stadium—away from the team to the stadium. Only ticket sales and the proceeds from the sale of game-day programs continued to flow to the team. This was done to satisfy the banks that had lent the money to Chuck Sullivan to finance the Jackson tour. Since Sullivan had put up the stadium as collateral, the banks wanted to make sure that the stadium had adequate revenue streams to meet its loan obligations. Furthermore, the banks insisted that the lease between the stadium and the team contain a fifteen-year operating covenant that obligated the Patriots to play their home games in Sullivan Stadium through the 2001 season. If the banks were lending money to the stadium, they wanted to be sure the team wasn't going to move.

The situation presented a conundrum. The team's entire cash flow was being drained by the lease and diverted to the stadium. Yet without the team, the stadium was worthless. Under the circumstances, Kraft decided he wouldn't buy the team unless he also owned the stadium.

Then there was a third piece of the puzzle: the land. Although the stadium was owned by the Sullivans, the land under the footprint of the stadium was owned by the town of Foxborough. Nor did the Sullivans own the 330 acres that surrounded the stadium, which consisted mainly of parking lots. Those were owned by Foxboro Associates, a partnership composed of roughly a dozen local businessmen. The stadium had a parking lease with Foxboro Associates that governed home games. So the team didn't control the parking; Foxboro Associates did.

Just as it would have been imprudent to buy the team without owning the stadium, Kraft determined it made even less sense to buy the stadium without controlling the parking lots. It was another wrinkle that had to be factored into Kraft's bid.

On paper, the team was valued at $75 million. The stadium was appraised at approximately $15 million. After taking into account the land lease governing the use of the parking lots, Kraft was preparing to offer $100 million for everything.

But while Kraft was finalizing his bid, the Patriots did the unexpected— they went on a run in the fall of 1985 that took them all the way to the Super Bowl in January 1986. For the first time in franchise history, Billy Sullivan and his family finally had a championship contender. Even though New England went on to lose the Super Bowl to Chicago, the euphoria of success and the lure of getting back to the Promised Land was too powerful. With Kraft ready to buy the team, Sullivan developed second thoughts about selling, and the sale was put on hold.

For Kraft, it was a letdown. Nonetheless, it was apparent that Sullivan's financial problems weren't going away. Even after the most successful season in franchise history, the organization was still bleeding money. Despite charging the highest ticket prices in the league and selling out every game during the 1985 season, the team still lost nearly $10 million that fiscal year. Shortly after the Super Bowl, the Sullivans defaulted on their lease on the land around the stadium.

It was at this juncture that Kraft put his finger on something that none of the other prospective buyers had figured out. Compared to the team and the stadium, the parking lots were by far the least expensive part of the overall acquisition, yet they controlled the economics of the deal. Without the parking lots, there was no way to guarantee that you could actually open

the stadium on game day. The last thing Kraft would have done was let that lease lapse.

Recognizing that Sullivan had made a critical mistake, Kraft partnered with a real estate developer and approached the landowners in Foxborough, offering them a $2 million advance and $1 million per year in rent for a ten-year option on the land surrounding the stadium. With the option, Kraft and his partner got the right to operate the parking lots. They also had the right to purchase the 330 acres outright for $17 million at any point during the ten-year contract period.

The unconventional move was Kraft's first strategic step to acquiring the Patriots. Finally, he had some leverage.

The same year that his father took control of the land around Sullivan Stadium, Jonathan Kraft graduated from college and took a job with Boston-based Bain & Company, a fast-growing global consulting firm whose brightest star was thirty-nine-year-old Mitt Romney. Right before Kraft got to Bain, a twenty-nine-year-old Harvard Business School grad named Andy Wasynczuk joined the firm as well. Kraft and Wasynczuk sat next to each other in an open bay. One day Wasynczuk overheard Kraft talking on the phone about Martina Navratilova. A tennis fan, Wasynczuk was impressed that Kraft was carrying on as if he were personally acquainted with the top female tennis player in the world.

"What's your connection to Navratilova?" Wasynczuk asked after Kraft hung up.

Kraft tried to downplay it. "Well, my family was involved with the Boston Lobsters," he said.

Wasynczuk stared at him blankly. He was from Chicago and had never heard of the Boston Lobsters.

Kraft filled him in on the history. "Martina was one of the people who played for us at the time," he explained.

That led to a big discussion of tennis. At the end of it, Kraft invited Wasynczuk to his family's home to play. A couple of weeks later, they were about an hour into a match when Robert Kraft exited the house and walked toward the court with a small cooler containing a six-pack of beer. An early investor in Bain Capital, Kraft was well aware of the high-caliber talent that gravitated to Bain. After introducing himself, Robert offered Wasynczuk a beer.

While Wasynczuk took a sip, Kraft began peppering him with questions

about his background and what he was doing at Bain. Wasynczuk's answers impressed Kraft, who then volunteered that he had his sights set on buying the New England Patriots.

Looking around the estate, Wasynczuk had no doubt that Kraft probably had the resources to pursue such a venture.

"Bain's got talented people," Kraft told him before returning to the house. "If you ever run into folks that we should consider for areas in our family business, let me know so we can think about whether we should hire them."

Wasynczuk made a mental note.

Early in 1988, *Sports Illustrated* published a lengthy special report on Billy Sullivan's financial woes titled "The $126 Million Fumble." The $126 million figure represented the combined debt of the team, the stadium, and individual members of the Sullivan family. Remarkably, just two years after reaching the Super Bowl, the Patriots were "a financially emaciated team." In addition to losing three separate lawsuits filed by shareholders, the Sullivans were also being sued by creditors and foreclosed on by banks. Circumstances got so dire that Sullivan had to beg the NFL to release emergency funds so he could pay his players. No longer able to put off the inevitable, he was desperate to find a buyer.

Kraft was the most obvious candidate, and he knew it. He'd been Billy Sullivan's special guest at Super Bowl XX against the Bears in New Orleans. He had been given VIP treatment at the Patriots' annual "media day," where he mingled with players and was introduced by Patrick Sullivan to some of the family's creditors as a "potential buyer." And there had been ample discussion between the Patriots' chief financial officer and Kraft's representatives. Even the Boston press had declared Kraft the "leading contender" to be the team's next owner. After circling for three years, Kraft was finally poised to land the prize he'd long desired. But when discussions progressed toward doing a deal, Sullivan insisted he wanted some add-ons. Most notably, Sullivan wanted to remain involved as a minority shareholder, retain his position as club president, receive a guaranteed lifetime salary, and have the organization maintain his family's pension plans and health insurance. He also wanted his son Patrick to remain the team's general manager.

Kraft decided to walk away.

"One of the reasons I chose not to buy the team at that point was that I didn't like that you had to pay for all these sidebar things," Kraft explained. "Paying people for life. Having people from the previous ownership group

weighing in on business matters and football decisions. I knew how to run an operating business, but I didn't want to be fettered. Plus, I don't do big things on impulse. I do things that feel right and that I know I can handle."

Shortly after Kraft bowed out, Stadium Management Corporation declared bankruptcy, with debts exceeding $52 million. Fearing that Billy Sullivan and the team might also declare bankruptcy, the NFL approved a hastily arranged sale of the Patriots to Connecticut businessman Victor Kiam for $80 million on October 6, 1988. The stadium was not part of the purchase.

Given what little Kraft knew about Kiam's background, the transaction didn't make sense. As the chairman of Remington Products Company, Kiam had distinguished himself from other CEOs by writing and starring in his company's commercials. In the very first one, he introduced himself to the world this way:

> Hello, I'm Victor Kiam. I used to be a dedicated wet shaver until my wife bought me this Remington M3 electric shaver. They said its two incredibly thin micro-screens and one hundred and twenty cutting edges shave as close as a blade or they'd give her money back.
>
> I was delighted and impressed. So impressed, I bought the company.

The TV ad was a stroke of marketing genius. Remington went from being in the red to capturing 20 percent of the global market in shaving products with $160 million in annual sales, and Kiam became known throughout the world as "the man who bought the company."

Apparently, Kiam was so impressed with the opportunity to own an NFL team that he bought the Patriots without doing his due diligence. He reportedly told more than one person that just forty-eight hours after meeting Sullivan he signed an offer sheet. Under the terms, Kiam became the controlling partner, but Billy Sullivan remained a minority shareholder, became team president, and had a lifetime salary. And his son Patrick remained the team's general manager in charge of football operations.

Convinced that Kiam had no idea what he'd gotten himself into, Kraft turned his sights to Sullivan Stadium. It was going to be sold to the highest bidder through a foreclosure auction overseen by the US Bankruptcy Court. Thanks to all of his previous due diligence and his deal on the land, Kraft viewed the stadium as the linchpin to gaining control of the team. The lease

that assigned all of the revenue from the team to the stadium was still in effect, including the operating covenant that kept the Patriots tethered to the stadium through 2001. Whoever took possession of the stadium would effectively control the team's destiny for the next twelve years. From that perspective, Kraft wasn't just bidding on a run-down, bankrupt stadium. He was bidding for something much more valuable—leverage.

Kiam, on the other hand, viewed Sullivan Stadium as a "dump." He hoped to soon construct a new stadium in Connecticut, closer to Remington's global headquarters. In the interim, he didn't want to overpay for what he envisioned would be a temporary home for the Patriots.

Blind bids were due by October 31, 1988, just three weeks after Kiam took control of the team. A week later, they were unsealed and made public:

Kraft—$25 million
Kiam—$19.85 million

Along Robert Kraft's odyssey to own the Patriots, the most critical move he made was acquiring the stadium. To use a chess analogy, securing the parking lots a couple of years earlier was check. Outbidding Kiam for the stadium amounted to checkmate. On November 23, 1988—precisely 1,200 days after Kraft initially emerged as the first bidder to buy the Patriots franchise from Billy Sullivan—Chief Justice James N. Gabriel of the US Bankruptcy Court in Boston determined that it was in the best interest of the creditors to award the stadium to Kraft, not Kiam. With the stroke of a judicial pen, Kraft became the owner of Sullivan Stadium and the Patriots' landlord.

The implications of the new landlord-tenant relationship were on display at the Patriots' next home game. As the new owner of the stadium, Kraft suddenly had a suite on the fifty-yard line. As the tenant, Kiam didn't have a seat. He ended up watching the game from the back of the press box. By the time the two men met for the first time, the significance of the stadium lease was no longer lost on Kiam.

"This lease is a piece of shit!" Kiam complained, clenching a copy of the lease in his hand.

"Victor, have you read it?" Kraft said.

Kiam didn't appreciate the question. After calming down, he admitted that he hadn't known about the lease when he bought the team. His lawyer had since informed him that thanks to the document, the stadium held the team captive.

"We have to do something about this," Kiam complained.

The point of the lease was that Kraft didn't *have* to do *anything*. Although he didn't own the team, he essentially owned the owner. Kraft controlled the parking. Kraft controlled the stadium. Kraft controlled almost all of the revenue that the team was generating. And he had the power to keep the Patriots anchored in Foxborough as his tenant through 2001. The operating agreement was Kraft's trump card. He wasn't about to give it up.

"You should have read the lease before you bought the team," he told Kiam.

It was a frosty start to their relationship.

Jonathan Kraft had left Bain and enrolled at Harvard Business School. But he stayed in close contact with his colleague Andy Wasynczuk, who remained at Bain as a consultant. "Andy is ridiculously smart," Jonathan said in response to his father's request for an honest assessment. "Smarter than even he knows. And he has no ego." One of the first things that Robert did after being awarded the stadium was reach back out to Wasynczuk. Reiterating that he remained on track to buy the Patriots, he told Wasynczuk that the task at hand was to do everything possible to improve the stadium and its profitability during the interim.

"I'd love to have you join us," Kraft said.

"In what capacity?" Wasynczuk said.

"Well, you'd run the stadium."

Wasynczuk was speechless. *Run the stadium?* He wouldn't know where to begin. His expertise was in preparing profit-and-loss statements. He was also adept at breaking down revenues, costs, and expenses. But he had no managerial experience.

Kraft wasn't concerned. He was running his global commodities company and he and a business partner had recently taken over a television station in Boston. In both cases, Kraft had hired talented people to work beneath him on the operational side. With the stadium, he was looking for someone with competence who could come in at the beginning and work with him over the long haul. His instincts told him that Wasynczuk was a wise choice.

"Look, we're going to be learning this business together," Kraft reassured him. "And we'd love to get some good people on the team to help us think creatively."

"But I've never run a stadium or a retail project or anything like that."

"I don't want somebody who has been in that area," Kraft said. "I want someone who will think outside the box."

Both flattered and intrigued, Wasynczuk confessed that he'd never even been to the stadium. And everything he'd heard about the place was negative.

Kraft confirmed that the stadium wasn't very good. "I don't want to convince you or give you the VIP treatment," he told Wasynczuk. "Why don't you go and experience what fans see? Take a real honest look at what goes on there. Then we can talk again."

Only one home game remained on the Patriots' 1988 schedule. Wasynczuk bought a ticket and went. Being there verified every negative thing he'd heard about the venue. The aluminum-bench seating was cold and uncomfortable. The restrooms were deplorable. Aspects of the construction clearly needed upgrading. It reminded Wasynczuk of a glorified high school stadium. Yet he came away convinced that he wanted to work for Kraft.

Months later, he took an office at the stadium and became its chief operating officer. The first item of business was to change the facility's name from Sullivan Stadium to Foxboro Stadium, which was accomplished in 1989.

A couple of years before buying the Patriots, Victor Kiam wrote a bestselling book called *Going for It*, about how to succeed as an entrepreneur. It was full of catchy phrases and inspiring quotes. One of his most well-known quotes was "An entrepreneur assumes the risk and is dedicated and committed to the success of whatever he or she undertakes." It rankled Kiam that he bore all of the risk as the owner of the team but virtually all of the revenue that the team generated went to Kraft. On top of the $1.5 million base rent for the stadium, the team was paying Kraft 100 percent of the game-day concessions; 100 percent of the sponsors' signage inside the stadium; all of the profits from luxury-seat sales; and 30 percent of the team's share of ticket revenues. Plus, Kraft collected 100 percent of the parking revenues.

Undoubtedly, what irritated Kiam most was that he looked foolish. Midway through his first season of ownership, he showed up for a home game wearing an expensive topcoat made of cashmere. It was raining that day, and while Kiam was walking through a lower corridor in the stadium, sporting his year-round tan and perfectly coiffed silver hair, rainwater gushed through a hole in the roof and soaked his head. Later on, mustard splatted on the shoulder of his new coat. It had apparently fallen from a hot dog being eaten by a fan seated in the deck above him.

By the time Kiam entered Patrick Sullivan's office for a prescheduled meeting with him and Kraft following the game, he was fuming.

"This place is a pigsty!" Kiam shouted.

It was all Kraft could do to keep a straight face. Kiam had hair spray in one hand and a mirror in the other. His wet hair looked like a mud pie. His coat had a big yellow blot on it.

"You've got to do something about this damn stadium," Kiam insisted.

Soon enough, Kiam had a much bigger problem on his hands than a run-down stadium. In September 1990, at the beginning of Kiam's second season of ownership, *Boston Herald* reporter Lisa Olson entered the Patriots' locker room to interview a player. While Olson sat on a stool talking to the player at his locker, four or five players emerged from the shower area. Naked, they approached Olson. One of them positioned his penis inches from her face and dared her to touch it. "This is what you want," he said. "Do you want to take a bite out of this?"

Disgusted and humiliated, Olson looked away.

"Give her what she wants," a second player yelled, generating laughter.

Olson kept her head down.

"Make her look," a third player yelled. "That is what she's in here for."

Another player, also naked, approached Olson from behind and positioned his genitals near her in a suggestive way.

Surrounded, Olson wasn't sure whether to scream or cry.

That afternoon, Olson reported the encounter to her editor. Appalled, he notified Patriots GM Patrick Sullivan. Expecting that the team would discipline the players and take steps to ensure a safer and more professional work environment, the *Herald* made no mention of the players' behavior. Olson, in particular, had been adamant that she didn't want the humiliating ordeal reported in the paper.

Days passed, but the team took no action. During that time, the rival *Boston Globe* got wind of what had happened and published a story about it. In response, Victor Kiam defended his players. "I can't disagree with the players' actions," Kiam said.

His statement, combined with the team's inaction, raised the ire of the *Herald*, which contacted Kiam seeking an explanation for his response. Kiam lashed out. "Your paper's asking for trouble sending a female reporter to cover the team," he said. "Why *not* stand in front of her [naked] if she's an intruder?"

A day after making that statement, Kiam traveled with the team to Cincinnati for the third game of the season. Determined not to be intimidated, Olson traveled to Cincinnati as well. New England got crushed. Afterward, Olson entered the locker room, along with all of the other members of the press corps, to conduct postgame interviews. But three Patriots officials trailed her, making it impossible for Olson to interview anyone. Miffed, she spotted Kiam in the locker room and sarcastically asked if he wanted to follow her as well. As she turned to leave, Kiam said: "She's a classic bitch. No wonder the players don't like her."

The utterance of those two words—*classic bitch*—marked the beginning of the end of Victor Kiam's tenure as owner of the Patriots. Two sportswriters overheard the sexist slur and reported it, prompting *Washington Post* media critic Howard Kurtz to liken Kiam's words to "pouring gasoline on a campfire." Within forty-eight hours, newspaper editors throughout the country weighed in on Olson's behalf. The NFL was deluged with demands to suspend the Patriots owner. The *Boston Herald* urged fans to boycott the Patriots' next home game. And the Boston chapter of the National Organization for Women called on women everywhere to boycott Lady Remington razors. A decade after female sportswriters had gained access to male locker rooms, Victor Kiam managed to reignite a debate over the appropriateness of that practice. By doing so, he thrust his team and the NFL into the epicenter of a national conversation about sexual harassment in the workplace.

Paul Tagliabue, a highly accomplished lawyer in one of Washington, DC's most prestigious firms, had barely been installed as the NFL's new commissioner when Lisa Olson's sexual harassment allegation landed on his desk. The Patriots initially denied Olson's locker room account, and Kiam denied calling her a bitch. Meanwhile, Patriots fans chanted "Lisa Olson" and knocked around an inflated rubber woman in the stands during a home game against the Jets, and the words CLASSIC BITCH were spray-painted on Olson's apartment house. The *Herald* reassigned her to cover the Boston Celtics and the Boston Bruins. Switching her assignment did no good. Fans at a Celtics exhibition game chanted at her, taunting her to show them her breasts. And everyone from Oprah to Geraldo on the television networks wanted to talk to her.

Amid the public furor, Tagliabue hired Harvard Law School professor Philip Heymann to conduct an investigation, which ultimately concluded that Olson had told the truth and had been "degraded and humiliated."

Tagliabue fined three Patriots players who were the main culprits. He also fined the team $50,000 for conduct degrading to a female reporter. And in a letter, he chastised Kiam, calling the episode "distasteful, unnecessary, and damaging to the league and others."

More than anything, Tagliabue wanted to put the entire sordid affair in the league's rearview mirror. But not long after the commissioner disciplined the Patriots, Kiam reignited the controversy while speaking at a men-only athletic association banquet in his hometown of Stamford, Connecticut. The First Gulf War had just begun, and Kiam wisecracked: "What do those Iraqi Scuds and Lisa Olson have in common? They've both seen Patriot missiles up close."

His punch line was reported in the *New York Times*, which put the NFL back in the spotlight. "It should go without saying that this office does not condone offensive comments of any type," a league spokesman told the *Times*. The National Organization for Women extended its boycott to all Remington products. As Remington's sales plummeted and its cash flow tightened, the Patriots' debts were simultaneously mounting.

Facing a personal financial crisis, Kiam decided to sell the team.

LEVERAGE

T he Lisa Olson controversy and an extreme losing streak brought the New England Patriots franchise to its nadir. The team was 1-1 before Olson was accosted in the locker room. After the incident, the team lost all fourteen remaining games that year to finish at 1-15, which marked the worst record in team history. Fans turned away in droves. By midseason, 60 percent of the seats at home games were empty. After the season, General Manager Patrick Sullivan resigned. The head coach was fired. Victor Kiam's reputation was in tatters. And the team's finances were in worse shape than when Billy Sullivan owned the team.

Robert Kraft watched the self-destruction of Victor Kiam and the subsequent implosion of the team from a unique vantage point. In addition to being the Patriots' landlord, Kraft controlled one of the media outlets that covered the Lisa Olson incident. Shortly before acquiring the stadium, Kraft had purchased New England Television Corporation, which owned CBS's Boston-affiliate, WNEV-TV, Channel 7. Kraft served as president of the television station while the news division was reporting on Kiam's troubles.

During that period, Kraft did not interact with Kiam. Nor was he privy to the league's internal conversations about the state of affairs in Foxborough. He had, however, heard rumblings that the league might be forced to take control of the team. Those rumors turned out to be true.

The NFL's constitution contained a provision that empowered the league to take the franchise away from Kiam. It was essentially a "nuclear option" reserved for worst-case scenarios, and it had never been exercised in league history. But in the aftermath of the Lisa Olson scandal, Paul Tagliabue and his top deputy, Roger Goodell, were facing the prospect of asking the league's owners to vote on whether to purchase the Patriots franchise. "New England, as a region of the country, was a critical market for us size-wise," explained Goodell. "The team was in constant turmoil. There was no stability

in ownership. The team was mired in litigation. And the franchise was about to go bankrupt."

In an initial step to prevent the team from declaring bankruptcy, the league stepped in on October 10, 1991, and took control of the organization's board of directors. Then, without, Kraft's knowledge, the league began reviewing a proposal that would transfer ownership from Victor Kiam to James Busch Orthwein in St. Louis. Under the circumstances, the sixty-seven-year-old executive possessed one very appealing quality in the eyes of the league—significant personal wealth that far exceeded the Patriots' previous ownership group's. As an Anheuser-Busch heir, Orthwein was the brewing company's second-largest shareholder. His offer to buy the Patriots was rooted in his desire to help the city where his family's company had long been headquartered.

After the St. Louis Cardinals football team left town for Phoenix in the late eighties, Orthwein became chairman and CEO of an investment group called St. Louis NFL Partnership. The group's purpose was to restore pro football to Orthwein's hometown. With that in mind, Orthwein's group played an important role in convincing the city to draw up plans for a publicly financed, state-of-the-art, domed stadium. The proposed stadium positioned St. Louis as the front-runner when the NFL announced in 1991 that it was expanding by adding two new franchises. The other cities in the running for an expansion franchise were Memphis, Baltimore, Jacksonville, and Charlotte.

The NFL's expansion announcement coincided with Victor Kiam's financial meltdown. In an effort to bolster St. Louis's bid for an expansion franchise, Orthwein offered to step into the breach in New England and buy the Patriots on an interim basis. His interest, he said at the time, was "to ensure I get a team in St. Louis." He figured that by taking the mess in New England off of the NFL's hands, he'd build goodwill with the league.

"My goals were to stabilize the franchise, to resolve the stadium issue, and to sell to proper, local ownership," Orthwein said. "As everyone knows, my involvement in the NFL came about due to my efforts to help St. Louis, my hometown, get a team."

NFL owners liked Orthwein's approach. By taking over the debt-heavy Patriots, Orthwein spared the NFL the likelihood of expensive litigation and assured that the team would remain in New England, at least for a few more years. In March 1992, the league approved the sale of the Patriots to Orthwein for $106 million.

"I want to be completely clear on two points," Orthwein said on the day the sale was announced. "I do not want to remain the owner of the New England Patriots on an indefinite basis, nor do I have plans to move the Patriots to St. Louis. I only want to resolve the present difficult situation."

Despite how badly he wanted to buy the team, Kraft never had an opportunity to bid before Orthwein bought out Kiam. Nonetheless, Kraft liked Orthwein's statement. And he really liked some of the moves that Orthwein made in his first year of ownership, as they added real value to the franchise—especially his game-changing decision to lure legendary New York Giants head coach Bill Parcells out of retirement to coach New England. In addition to a multimillion-dollar salary, Orthwein promised Parcells a great deal of latitude to run the team's football operations.

Parcells, known by his nickname, Tuna, was formally announced as the new head coach of the Patriots on January 21, 1993. The impact on the franchise was sudden and dramatic. The following day, the Patriots set the franchise record for tickets sold in a twenty-four-hour period. For the first time in a long time, football fans in New England had something to cheer about.

"Bill was a very important part of what Jim was trying to do," said Patriots vice chairman Michael O'Halloran, who worked directly for Orthwein. "We had to improve the marketing of the team. We had to get the financial part together. Jim was going to eventually sell the team, and hiring Bill, who had won Super Bowls before, was a key part of the entire plan to improve the value."

Three months later, the franchise got another shot in the arm. Since New England had the worst record in the league the year prior, it had the first pick overall in the 1993 NFL Draft. Parcells selected quarterback Drew Bledsoe. Suddenly, the Patriots had a bona fide star-in-the-making at quarterback to go along with a renowned coach.

Overnight, it seemed, New England's fortunes had changed. That was the sense throughout the NFL. Investors felt that way, too. Before Parcells coached his first game or Bledsoe threw his first pass, Orthwein started receiving unsolicited offers from numerous parties interested in buying the Patriots. So in September 1993, as the Patriots' inaugural season under Parcells kicked off, Orthwein asked Goldman Sachs to handle the sale of the team for him. In consultation with Orthwein and his advisors, the investment bank decided to attempt something that had never been done in league

history—hold an auction. Eric Grubman, a specialist in Goldman's Mergers and Acquisitions Department, was tapped to lead the effort.

Kraft reached out to Grubman's office right away and let it be known that he intended to bid on the Patriots. He also put Grubman on notice that he had a lease with an operating covenant that he planned to enforce. In other words, anyone else who intended to bid on the Patriots should be made aware that the team had a contractual obligation to play in Foxboro Stadium until 2001.

Orthwein was fully aware when he bought the team that he was inheriting a very restrictive lease. At the time, he wasn't concerned because he considered himself a short-term tenant. But now that Orthwein was eager to sell the team, Kraft's call came across like a brush-back pitch, thrown high and tight with the intent of scaring off other prospective buyers.

Goldman Sachs, however, recognized that Kraft was raising a legitimate point. Every other bidder was going to have to reckon with the fact that Kraft had the team in a vise grip until 2001, when the lease expired.

"Robert very much wanted to be taken seriously as a bidder," Grubman said, "even though he expected he might be competing against people who were far better known than he was and far wealthier than he was."

Kraft's competition included actor Paul Newman, novelist Tom Clancy, Hall of Fame football player Walter Payton, and a handful of financial backers who had joined forces in an effort to acquire the team and move it to Hartford, Connecticut. Other bidders included Hollywood filmmaker Jeffrey Lurie, a well-heeled group from Baltimore, and St. Louis–based real estate developer Stan Kroenke, who was married to Wal-Mart heiress Ann Walton.

All of the other prospective buyers may have had more money than Kraft. But none of them was best friends with the NFL's closest thing to a kingmaker. Kraft picked up the phone and called the most-connected man in league circles.

Will McDonough, known as Willie by friends, began his career as a reporter for the *Boston Globe* in 1960. His first beat assignment was the Boston Patriots. McDonough spent decades covering the team and the NFL. An Irish Catholic, McDonough had grown up in a housing project in South Boston in what friends described as "a tribal whirl of street-corner life and sports." His neighbor, William "Billy" Bulger, was one of McDonough's closest childhood friends. Bulger rose to become the president of the Massachusetts State Senate, while his brother, James "Whitey" Bulger, became a mobster and was

eventually found guilty for his involvement in eleven murders. One of Mc-Donough's journalism colleagues jokingly said that Willie "could get you a papal blessing or your legs broken . . . probably in the same phone call."

In the early eighties, McDonough became an NFL analyst for CBS and later NBC, becoming one of the first journalists to simultaneously cover the NFL in print and on television. Right before transitioning into television, McDonough achieved legendary status among sportswriters throughout the country for decking Patriots defensive back Raymond Clayborn. Following a Patriots victory, reporters had gathered around the locker of a player who had just scored three touchdowns. Some of the reporters apparently encroached on the space in front of Clayborn's locker. In a bad mood, Clayborn yelled at the writers to essentially get out of his way so he could get dressed. It wasn't the first time that Clayborn had yelled at a reporter. When McDonough refused to budge, Clayborn reportedly pointed at him and said, "I'm gonna bury you, motherfucker." Making a fist, McDonough said, "You're not going to bury anybody." Then the balding forty-four-year-old writer punched the twenty-four-year-old cornerback in the face, knocking him into his locker. A melee ensued. Before it was over, Patriots owner Billy Sullivan "ended up in a laundry bin," according to one report. The NFL promptly fined Clayborn, and sportswriters dubbed McDonough "Will of Iron."

Kraft and McDonough met in 1977, two years before the locker room incident. They became so close that by the time Kraft turned fifty in 1991, he chose McDonough to emcee his fiftieth birthday party. At that point, Kraft recognized that his friend had the ear of almost every person of influence in the NFL. By virtue of the friendships he'd formed with owners and coaches throughout the league, McDonough routinely got calls from them. No one called McDonough more often than Bill Parcells. The two of them had been best friends for almost as long as Kraft had known McDonough.

With Orthwein trying to sell the team, it was dicey for his head coach to meet with a prospective buyer. It was even more precarious for a journalist who was reporting on the team and the sale process to arrange such a meeting. But McDonough didn't let that stop him. After all, McDonough had initially introduced Parcells to Orthwein and brokered the meeting between them in Florida that resulted in Parcells taking the Patriots job.

One day in the fall of 1993, McDonough drove Kraft to a cheap hotel near Foxboro Stadium. Parcells was waiting inside. When Kraft entered Parcells's room, he couldn't help noticing that the place was unusually dark, cramped, and cold. But Parcells was gregarious. When they shook hands,

Kraft had no trouble imagining how great it would be to own the team with Parcells at the helm.

All three men had mutually aligned interests. Parcells had joined the Patriots to bring a championship to New England, not St. Louis. He had no interest in relocating. Kraft had been on a decade-long quest to acquire the team and was emboldened by the prospect of working with Parcells. McDonough wanted the team to stay in New England and wanted to see his two friends join forces.

Kraft thought it was important to introduce himself to top league officials. McDonough agreed. When Kraft said he had reached out to people in the commissioner's office, McDonough insisted it was better to go straight to the top. With one phone call, he told Kraft, he would arrange a face-to-face with Commissioner Tagliabue. "I'll take care of it," he told Kraft.

On a warm fall afternoon in 1993, Kraft and McDonough exited a car on the corner of Madison Avenue and East Seventy-Seventh Street in New York and ducked into the restaurant at the Mark Hotel. Paul Tagliabue, who lived a block way, liked to dine there. Not with NFL owners, though. Tagliabue preferred to avoid any appearance of favoritism or chumminess. It was even more unusual for him to meet with a prospective owner. But the Patriots presented an unusual situation. Long before becoming commissioner, Tagliabue had spent the better part of two decades as the league's outside counsel. During that period, he spent a disproportionate amount of time dealing with legal problems pertaining to the Patriots. He was intimately aware of how badly the organization needed a financially stable, long-term owner. At the same time, the league desperately wanted to keep the team in New England to preserve a presence in one of the country's largest television markets. Privately, Tagliabue was hopeful that Kraft might be an answer to all of these headaches.

Yet the commissioner knew virtually nothing about Kraft when he sat down across from him and McDonough at a table in the back corner of the restaurant. Over dinner, Kraft asked Tagliabue a series of questions about the league's television contracts, its labor deal with the players' union, and a host of other economic issues. It was clear to Tagliabue that McDonough's friend was extremely well informed. He also made it clear that he was not like any of the other individuals looking to buy the Patriots. "This will be our family business," Kraft told Tagliabue. "And we will keep the team in the Boston area. Boston is our home."

As Tagliabue listened, he formed a favorable impression. "Willie was touting Kraft as a really good local guy who could be a great owner," Tagliabue recalled. "I came away thinking he was a solid businessman who was younger and who had kids who were going to be working for the organization."

But what really struck Tagliabue were Kraft's peculiarities: he had business partners in countries throughout the world; he used to own a professional tennis team; he controlled a television station; and he was on the board of the Boston Symphony. In each instance, Tagliabue could see how Kraft's experiences could be leveraged to help the league. For instance, there was no one on the league's broadcast committee who possessed the background of owning a television station.

"That fact that he was involved in a lot of things both domestically and internationally gave him a broader perspective," Tagliabue said. "Many of the other owners had one company or very little interest in subjects other than sports."

Publicly, the commissioner couldn't endorse or support one prospective owner over another. But privately, he came away thinking that McDonough had introduced him to the ideal person to take over the Patriots.

On October 26, 1993, the NFL owners unanimously voted to award one of the new expansion franchises to a group of investors from Charlotte, North Carolina. The Carolina Panthers would become the league's twenty-ninth team and would commence play in 1995. The league's decision to overlook St. Louis, which had been widely regarded as the presumptive front-runner, was a clear indication that Orthwein's hometown was in trouble. With the city nearing completion of its new stadium, the pressure on Orthwein to move the Patriots to St. Louis mounted.

Seeing what was happening, Kraft reiterated that he intended to enforce his stadium lease.

Goldman Sachs knew it had a problem. All of the potential bidders were asking what it would cost to buy out the lease with Kraft. But Goldman Sachs had no answer. Kraft, acting on his lawyer's advice, refused to provide one. Under the legal doctrine of specific performance, the courts would require the Patriots to perform at Foxboro Stadium as long as Kraft refused to accept money in lieu of the team's honoring its lease. "Don't give them any number, no matter how high," Kraft's lawyer told him. "Because once you quantify your damages then you don't get to enforce the specific performance anymore."

Kraft's stance frustrated Orthwein's camp. In response, Goldman Sachs denied Kraft access to the team's financial statements, which had been shared with every other prospective buyer. The move put Kraft at a disadvantage. Without the ability to evaluate the amount and duration of the team's contracts with coaches and players, not to mention review the organization's profit-and-loss statements, Kraft was effectively prevented from preparing a bid. With the submission deadline fast approaching, the message being communicated was clear: *No matter what, don't sell to Kraft.*

Objecting to Goldman's tactics, Kraft received an invitation to meet with Eric Grubman in New York. Thinking he was finally going to get access to the financials, Kraft traveled to Manhattan on the day after Thanksgiving in November 1993. With his son Jonathan at his side, Kraft sat down for lunch with Grubman at the Pierre Hotel.

"We're going to let you in the bidding process," Grubman told him.

Those were the words Kraft wanted to hear.

"But," Grubman continued, "we still need a number."

Kraft put down his napkin and pushed back from the table. "I'm not putting a value on the lease," he said. "Either you let me in the data room or not."

Then he walked out. Jonathan followed.

That night, Kraft telephoned his friend Stephen Friedman, the chairman of the board at Goldman Sachs. They served together on Columbia University's board of trustees. Kraft didn't waste time with pleasantries.

"You guys are screwing me," he said.

Friedman wasn't involved in the deal and didn't have personal knowledge of the details. Kraft filled him in and insisted he'd been denied access to the Patriots' financials, which essentially blocked him from the bidding process.

"Your firm won't let us in the room," Kraft said. "And I think it's illegal."

Kraft never used the words *racketeering* or *antitrust*, but he didn't have to. Shortly after Kraft's conversation with Friedman, Jonathan and two of Robert's associates spent a day at the Goldman Sachs headquarters in New York, poring through financial documents pertaining to the Patriots franchise.

On December 1, 1993, NFL owners voted 26–2 to award the final expansion franchise to Jacksonville, Florida. Naturally, Orthwein was one of the two owners who voted against the decision. His plan of doing the league a favor by steadying the ship in New England in hopes of ensuring an expansion team in St. Louis had failed. Perturbed, Orthwein sent a strongly worded

letter to Commissioner Paul Tagliabue. In it he warned the league not to interfere in his efforts to sell the Patriots. His message was clear—now that an expansion franchise was out of the question, the push was on to bring the Patriots to St. Louis. At the same time, Tagliabue started hearing from people at Anheuser-Busch who wanted the Patriots in St. Louis.

Tagliabue had to decide whether to respond to the letter from Orth-wein. One of the individuals he turned to for advice was Frank Hawkins, the league's senior vice president of business affairs. Previously, Tagliabue and Hawkins had worked in the same law firm. When Tagliabue became commissioner, he convinced Hawkins to come with him to the NFL. Among other responsibilities, Hawkins reviewed all of the documentation related to league transactions. When he studied Kraft's stadium lease and operating agreement, Hawkins concluded that unless Kraft was willing to let the Patriots move, Goldman Sachs would end up with a busted auction. "In my judgment, Kraft won the team when he bought the lease out of bankruptcy in 1988," Hawkins said. "Unless Kraft agreed to a lease buyout, the team would be sold to him."

The other lawyers in the league office agreed with Hawkins. Collectively, they passed along their analysis to Tagliabue, with a recommendation that if he let the situation play out on its own, Kraft would end up owning the team. "We told him that if Kraft doesn't want the team to move, it will not move," Hawkins explained.

Tagliabue opted to let the situation play itself out.

Robert and Jonathan Kraft were discouraged and angry when they arrived at Foxboro Stadium on January 2, 1994. After starting out 1-11, New England had won its last three games to improve to 4-11. As the Patriots got set to play their final regular season game against Miami, signs of promise were evident. Yet the press was reporting that the team was probably headed to St. Louis. The game was billed as the last time the Patriots would play a home game in New England. Nearly fifty-four thousand fans—more than twice the attendance at the previous home game—turned out to see Parcells and Bledsoe one more time and bid farewell to the team.

Robert looked out from his suite at the crowd and contemplated his situation. Goldman Sachs still hadn't asked for his bid. Yet everyone else's bids were in. And rumors were rampant that Orthwein was going to sell to Missouri businessman Stan Kroenke. It was hard not to feel pessimistic.

"Maybe this just isn't going to happen," Robert said to Jonathan.

New England played its best game of the season that day, going toe-to-toe with a Miami team that was competing for a playoff berth. The Patriots led until the final minutes, when the Dolphins finally surged ahead, 24–20. But Bledsoe drove his team seventy-five yards, capping off the drive with a dramatic touchdown pass to Ben Coates to put his team back up, 27–24. Miami countered with a last-second field goal to send the game to overtime. Rarely had New England fans witnessed so much drama.

With four minutes and forty-four seconds remaining in overtime, Bledsoe was hit and driven to the ground just as he lofted a high-arching spiral toward the end zone. Receiver Michael Timpson raced thirty-six yards and caught the ball in stride, sending the crowd into a frenzy. "You could not comprehend the crowd noise here," NBC announcer Don Criqui said on the air.

New England had won their fourth straight, knocking off heavily favored Miami, 33–27, and eliminating them from playoff contention.

Kraft thrust his fists in the air and gave Jonathan a bear hug, nearly knocking him over. Chants of "Drew, Drew, Drew" echoed through the stadium. The Patriots had finished the season 5-11. But with the presence of Parcells and the emergence of Bledsoe, the future of the franchise had never looked brighter.

A full ten minutes after the game ended, the stands were still largely full. Robert and Jonathan were in the steel-framed elevator that went from the suite level to the ground level outside of Foxboro Stadium. Thousands of fans were still inside, chanting, "Don't take our team! Don't take our team! Don't take our team!" In the twenty-two years that Kraft had been a season ticket holder, he had never witnessed such emotion. With the cold evening wind whipping through the metal elevator frame, he turned to Jonathan. "There's no fucking way we're not buying this team," he said.

six

SOLD!

A s president of Bank of Boston, Charles "Chad" Gifford had many responsibilities, one of which was to establish and maintain relations with customers who meant the most to the bank's shareholders. Robert Kraft was one such customer. His paper and packaging businesses had been clients of Gifford's bank for years. Kraft also maintained numerous personal accounts there. Early on, he approached Gifford about a loan from Bank of Boston to buy the Patriots.

After looking at the team's balance sheet and financial disclosures, Gifford and a team of bankers and analysts determined that the market value of the Patriots franchise was about $115 million. Kraft agreed, but figured he'd need to bid upwards of $150 million to get the team. At first, Gifford was a little uneasy. The Patriots were arguably the worst team in the NFL; they were losing money; and they were badly in need of a new stadium. But Kraft made a compelling case that the Patriots were still a very important asset to the region, which would be lost if the bank didn't step up.

It helped that Kraft had a track record of taking depressed or underperforming companies and making them profitable. He'd done it in manufacturing, shipping, media, and entertainment. The arrival of Parcells and Bledsoe also contributed to a sense of security about the team's future.

Confident that the franchise would turn around with Kraft at the helm, Gifford's group spent weeks running numbers. It was a stretch, but the bank ultimately approved a financing package that enabled Kraft to bid $158 million.

In mid-January 1994, Kraft received a call from Eric Grubman at Goldman Sachs. Without tipping his hand, he let it be known that he possessed several competitive bids. He wouldn't disclose the amounts of the other bids. Nor did he say where Kraft's bid ranked in the mix. He simply suggested that Kraft come back with his best shot.

To Kraft, it sounded like a bluff. "Why should I raise my price now?" he said. "I already put in a good price."

"I can't tell you what to do," Grubman said. "I can only ask you to put your best price forward. If you've done that, then fine. But if not, now is the time."

Incredulous, Kraft spent the rest of the day figuring out his next move. He knew his offer was solid. He also knew that his lease gave him a tremendous advantage over the other bidders. Perhaps Orthwein had finally resigned himself to the fact that he was going to have to sell to Kraft. And perhaps the call from Goldman Sachs was simply a last-ditch effort to drive Kraft's purchase price a little higher. Under this scenario, Kraft would basically be bidding against himself by raising his offer.

But what if Grubman wasn't bluffing? It was certainly conceivable that the group in St. Louis had outbid him. It was also possible that the guys in St. Louis were so hell-bent on getting a team that they were willing to overpay for the Patriots, despite the fact that Kraft had a lease saying they couldn't move until 2001.

Those were risks Kraft wasn't willing to take. He called Grubman back and said he might consider increasing his offer. But he also told Grubman in no uncertain terms that he was tired of screwing around. He wanted a target—a number—for what it was going to take to get his bid where it needed to be to win the day. No more shooting in the dark. After some back-and-forth, Kraft hung up with a clear sense that he needed to raise his bid by about $15 million.

Unlike the other bidders, Kraft didn't have endless resources. He had already committed everything he had to offer toward the purchase price. To go any higher, he needed help.

Kraft's office was one block from Bank of Boston. He telephoned Chad Gifford and said he was walking over. "I need to see you right away," he said. "It's urgent."

The tension in Kraft's voice was palpable. Fearing the worst, Gifford told his secretary to clear his afternoon calendar and hold all his calls. "I felt like Robert was about to say, 'Fuck it! I've had it with these people.'"

The short walk from his office to Gifford's did little to calm Kraft's nerves. As soon as he took a seat on Gifford's yellow couch, Kraft unloaded. Goldman Sachs was playing dirty pool. He didn't know how much other bidders had bid. But he was being forced to bid higher.

Gifford cut to the chase. "What's the bottom line?"

"I need another $15 million," Kraft said.

"Ho-lee *mackerel*," Gifford said. "We've already stretched it to the limit, Robert."

Kraft knew that. But he needed the bank to stretch further or the deal could be lost.

"Son of a bitch!" Gifford shouted.

Kraft and Gifford were both angry at the situation. But they were yelling at each other. "It was a real mano-a-mano, eyeballs-to-eyeballs moment," Gifford recalled.

After about an hour of intense back-and-forth, one thing was clear— both men were determined to make one final push to get the team. Gifford, however, was going to have to make sure Kraft's loan could be structured to ensure the bank could get a bigger return in exchange for the additional capital.

"Chad," Kraft said in a soft but firm voice, "you will never get hurt from this loan. You have my word. We'll pay you back every penny. I promise."

Gifford said he'd be back to him with an answer as quickly as possible.

Over the next twenty-four hours, Gifford had a lot of internal conversations with his group. The numbers they were looking at simply didn't justify paying what would amount to roughly $173 million for the team. Yet Gifford felt confident that over time, NFL franchises only went up in value. And deep down, he sensed that going into business with Kraft was ultimately going to pan out well for the bank and its shareholders.

"The most important part of a loan is the person you're lending to," Gifford explained. "The borrower's integrity and what he will do to pay you off if there are challenges are critical. You wouldn't do something like this if you don't develop a sense of trust, especially with entrepreneurial loans. Robert did a tremendous job in my mind of earning that trust."

Less than forty-eight hours after the meeting in Gifford's office, he called Kraft with the news. "We'll do it," Gifford told him.

"Chad, I will not let you down," Kraft told him.

Kraft called Grubman back and told him he was prepared to raise his offer by $15 million. But he had one condition—he wanted to meet face-to-face with Orthwein, and he was willing to fly to St. Louis to make that happen. "I'm sick of dealing with intermediaries," Kraft said.

A meeting with Orthwein wasn't possible, Grubman indicated.

No meeting, no offer, Kraft countered.

Grubman said he'd see what he could do.

At that moment, Kraft knew that if he got the meeting with Orthwein, he was getting the Patriots. Conversely, if Orthwein didn't agree to the meeting, the Patriots were likely going to be sold to someone else.

Later that day, Kraft got his answer. Grubman called back and told him: "Get on a plane."

The law firm Bryan Cave represented James Orthwein. The firm's senior partner Walter Metcalfe personally handled Orthwein's legal affairs. Metcalfe was a power broker in St. Louis. Due to his dealings, there was perhaps more pressure on him than on Orthwein to deliver an NFL team to their city. It was Metcalfe who had negotiated the pact to build the domed stadium in St. Louis. It was Metcalfe who had convinced Orthwein to buy the Patriots and then written the sales contract that transferred ownership from Kiam to his client. And it was Metcalfe whom the *St. Louis Post-Dispatch* had credited for pulling off the "crafty move that aimed to leverage the team for an expansion franchise in St. Louis."

Robert and Jonathan Kraft arrived at Metcalfe's office in midmorning. They were accompanied by two lawyers, one of whom was Richard McGinnis, a tax law expert who would end up running Coopers & Lybrand's global corporate tax practice. With the exception of Kraft, all of McGinnis's clients were multinational corporations. He was accustomed to minimizing tax exposure on multibillion-dollar deals. His presence gave Kraft peace of mind.

Metcalfe, Orthwein, and Orthwein's right-hand man, Michael O'Halloran, were ready for them. After exchanging pleasantries, Kraft and Orthwein went into a private room.

"You know," Orthwein began with a wry smile, "you are a tough landlord."

"I thought I was a pussycat," Kraft said.

Both men had a laugh. It had been a long, hard-fought negotiation. But now that a deal appeared imminent, they both turned on the charm. As they spent a few minutes getting acquainted, it was apparent that they were heading in opposite directions. At fifty-two, Kraft was a self-made millionaire who was ascending to the pinnacle of his business career. Orthwein, on the other hand, was about to turn seventy and was the heir to 1.6 million shares

of stock in Anheuser-Busch. He had no appetite for owning a professional football team; he'd just wanted a team in St. Louis.

"Well," Orthwein told Kraft, "you came through with your offer for the team."

Kraft's offer, it turned out, was approximately $25 million less than St. Louis real estate mogul Stan Kroenke's. But Kroenke's offer came with strings. He wanted Orthwein to absorb the $20 million fee imposed by the league for moving the team to St. Louis. More important, his offer required Orthwein to pay the legal fees and damages associated with terminating the team's stadium lease and operating agreement with Kraft. The sky was the limit on those costs. Selling to Kraft, on the other hand, was much cleaner. No moving costs. No legal fees. No mitigating damages. Just a quick sale and a hefty profit.

Kraft found Orthwein to be both forthcoming and personable. At one point, Orthwein conceded that it was better for the Patriots to remain in New England. And he said how pleased he was that the organization would be in such good hands. That's when Kraft knew deep down that Orthwein hadn't been the obstacle to selling the team to him. The pressure had come from elsewhere.

After working out some final aspects of their deal, Kraft and Orthwein rejoined their lawyers and advisors in a conference room, where Kraft signed a binding letter of intent to purchase the Patriots for approximately $173 million.

Kraft and Orthwein looked each other in the eye and shook hands. One was ecstatic, the other relieved. They had a deal. Kraft instructed his lawyer to trigger a $15 million wire transfer—the cash down payment—from his account to Orthwein's law firm.

Not everyone in the room was thrilled, though.

"We're going to announce this in Boston tomorrow," Walter Metcalfe said matter-of-factly. "We're *not* going to announce it here."

Metcalfe was torn. Although his client was satisfied, his city was taking a hit. St. Louis was about to become home to a brand-new, *empty* domed stadium. News of the sale to Kraft, Metcalfe explained, was going to generate backlash, much of which would be directed at Orthwein. So his client would be flying to Boston to sign the purchase-and-sale agreement and announce the sale of the team the following morning.

Privately, Kraft was thrilled. Boston, in his mind, was the *only* place a deal like this should be announced.

"In the meantime," Metcalfe said, "this can't leak. If word leaks out, the deal is off."

By the time Robert and Jonathan boarded a commercial flight back to Boston that afternoon, they had the urge to thrust their fists in the air and shout, "Yesssss!" But thanks to Metcalfe's threat, they were afraid to even whisper to each other about what had just transpired. The possibility of the press learning about the deal before the closing documents were signed the next day could upend everything. Robert worried that Metcalfe might leak it himself just to sabotage the sale.

Jonathan had his own concerns. The realization that they had just spent $173 million was overwhelming him. How will we cover so much debt? How many suites do we have to sell? How much can we charge? How many season tickets can we sell? What's the price point? There was so much to do.

At home, Myra had spaghetti with her famous homemade sauce warming on the stove when Robert and Jonathan arrived. The three of them had barely sat down to eat when the phone rang. Robert answered and was surprised to hear Walter Metcalfe's voice on the line. Bracing for bad news, Kraft listened as Metcalfe made an eleventh-hour offer designed to get him to back out of the deal. The group in St. Louis would pay Kraft $75 million for letting Orthwein out of the stadium lease. Instead of taking on $173 million in debt, Kraft would receive $75 million in cash for essentially doing nothing other than being willing to step aside and allow the team to move to St. Louis. It was easy money.

"Thanks, but we've worked too hard for this," Kraft said politely. "I'm not interested."

He hung up and bit into a meatball. "Can you imagine they're trying to bribe us not to buy the team?" he said.

Jonathan wanted details.

In between bites, Robert summarized the call.

"You were too polite," Jonathan told him.

"You should always be polite," Robert said. "Pass me the Parmesan."

"Wait a minute," Myra interjected. "They were going to pay you $75 million for a stadium you paid $25 million for?"

His mouth full, Robert nodded.

"And you would still own the stadium?" she said.

He nodded again.

"And you didn't *take it*?" she said.

Robert put down his fork. "Let me explain something."

Kraft's first job as a boy had been selling newspapers outside Braves Field in Boston. After the games started, he'd sneak in and watch from the cheap seats. He knew every player's name, number, and position. He particularly admired third baseman Sid Gordon, the team's only Jewish player, and centerfielder Sam "the Jet" Jethroe, the team's first black player. In the early 1950s, Braves Field was probably the only place in Boston where everyone would come together to cheer on a Jew and an African American.

"That was my team," Kraft said as Myra and Jonathan listened. "After the Braves left town, a part of me died. I was heartbroken. I still remember that feeling. It never leaves you. So this isn't about money."

The phone rang again. This time Robert recognized the number—it was McDonough from the *Boston Globe*. No doubt his friend was calling for confirmation on whether the Patriots were heading to St. Louis or staying in New England. There was no way Kraft was taking that call.

Instead, after finishing his food, he stepped into his study and placed a call to Massachusetts governor William Weld at his home. That weekend, Kraft was supposed to travel to Israel on a trade mission with members of Weld's administration. He told the governor he was going to have to cancel. Something big had come up.

"I'm about to buy the team," Kraft told him.

Elated, Weld couldn't believe it. He had already been preparing himself for the fact that the Patriots were leaving for St. Louis. He was also convinced that fans and the media would blame him for not doing more to keep the team in Massachusetts. "You saved my butt," Weld said.

The two men exchanged verbal high-fives over the phone and Kraft invited him to the press conference in the morning. Weld said he wouldn't miss it for the world. Then Kraft got down to the real reason for his call.

"I'm going out on a limb here," Kraft told him. "We can't survive and compete in the NFL market if we don't have a new stadium in Boston."

Weld said he totally understood.

"I need your commitment that you're going to help me get one," Kraft continued.

Weld gave his word.

Kraft and Orthwein were set to sign the closing documents in a private room at the Ritz-Carlton hotel in Boston early in the morning on Friday, January

21, 1994. The press conference announcing the sale was scheduled for immediately afterward. Robert's son Dan was afraid he might miss the big event because he had an even more important event going on—his wife was pregnant with their first child, though they hadn't broken the news to their parents yet. His wife was scheduled to have an ultrasound shortly before the start time of the press conference. There was no way Dan was going to miss the ultrasound.

As soon as they were finished at the hospital, Dan and his wife sped to the hotel, arriving just a few minutes before the press conference was set to start. Dan rushed inside with an ultrasound picture and showed it to his father.

"What's this?" Robert said.

"Your first grandchild," Dan said.

Robert's eyes welled up. "I have a *grandchild*?"

With tears in his eyes, Dan nodded.

Robert stared at the image for a moment before handing it back to Dan. "And I just bought the Patriots," he said, hugging Dan and his daughter-in-law. "Now, let's go close this deal."

It finally dawned on Dan that his father was holding a bottle of Dom Pérignon. "What's that for?" Dan said.

"It's for Orthwein."

"Why are you giving him vintage champagne?" Dan asked.

"Because it's the right thing to do."

"Dad, you're giving him $170 million. He should be giving *you* champagne."

Seated at a table with stationary microphones, Orthwein and Kraft faced the media. Smiling and looking like a man who had just escaped a bad marriage, Orthwein spoke first. "Thank you all for coming," he began. "I appreciate it. In May of 1992 when I purchased the New England Patriots I said that I would be an interim owner." He proceeded to outline all that he had done since then to keep his word. Hiring Bill Parcells and drafting Drew Bledsoe, he said, had given the team "a solid foundation for the future." Insisting he had accomplished what he had set out to do, he thanked the city and introduced Kraft.

Before addressing the press, Kraft invited his family and Chad Gifford to join him. As they lined up behind him, Kraft thanked Orthwein. "This is a great day for my family and, I hope, for all the fans in New England," he

began. Then he started talking about the day the Braves left Boston and when the Dodgers left Brooklyn.

"Some people think it's pretty silly to spend so much money just for a game," he said. "But for those of you who are fans, let me tell you, this game holds the attention of this community and communities throughout this country from August to January in a way that's hard to explain if you're not into it. And it really impacts the psyche and the fabric of the community."

As Kraft spoke, Orthwein looked at him and nodded.

"This is my hometown," Kraft continued. "And I just believe this hometown wouldn't have been the same if this team had left here. . . . If this team had left, I think it would have had a long-term damaging effect."

His boys beamed. So did Myra. The amount of money her husband had paid for the team made her nervous. But as she stood over his shoulder and looked at all the reporters, cameras, and politicians from the governor to members of the Massachusetts congressional delegation looking back at her husband, she couldn't help feeling an immense sense of pride over his achievement. At one point, she leaned over and whispered in Gifford's ear: "Chaddie, are we going to be all right?" He smiled and nodded.

"In closing," Kraft said, "I would just like to say that my objective in doing this is to help bring a championship to New England. We didn't do this to be a doormat for any other teams."

Twenty-three years after becoming a season ticket holder, Kraft had finally realized his dream. He owned the Patriots. It felt as though he'd been sprinkled with stardust. This, he felt, was going to be the most fun he'd had in his life.

Or so he thought.

seven

MEET THE NEW BOSS

H ours after the press conference with Orthwein, Kraft took his family to Boston Garden to see a Celtics game. It was their way of celebrating. Later that evening, Myra was in bed reading and Robert had just come to the bedroom when the phone rang, around 10:30. He answered it and sat down on his side of the bed. It was Bill Parcells. Speaking in an urgent tone, he said a situation had come up that required immediate attention.

"We need to re-sign Bruce Armstrong," Parcells said.

"How much is that going to cost?" Kraft said.

"A four-year deal will cost $10 million."

Kraft took a deep breath. He was already in the hole for $173 million.

"Ten million is a lot of money," he said.

"Yeah, well, he's our left tackle," Parcells said. "He protects Bledsoe's blind side. So he protects the franchise."

Kraft listened as Parcells made his case. It was a moment that crystallized Kraft's new reality—the most revered head coach in the NFL was calling him at home to discuss how to protect one of the brightest future stars in the game. Kraft suddenly occupied the catbird seat. The figures being tossed around were mind-boggling. But he was living a boyhood dream.

"Okay, Bill," he said. "Go ahead. Ten million for four years."

As Robert hung up, Myra looked up from her book and glared over the frame of her reading glasses. "Is the summer house in my name?" she said.

Under the financing package that Kraft negotiated with Bank of Boston, he put down $15 million. The remaining $158 million was borrowed. The percentage of debt made it the most leveraged loan in league history. Before approving the sale to Kraft, the NFL's finance committee, which was composed of various team owners, wanted to hear from him and his lender. Kraft and

bank president Chad Gifford were summoned to Atlanta just days before Super Bowl XXVIII.

In a hotel conference room, Kraft faced a group of NFL owners. As he spoke, one member of the finance committee—San Francisco 49ers team president Carmen Policy—sized him up. A lawyer by training, Policy served as proxy for 49ers team owner Eddie DeBartolo. Policy had been on the finance committee long enough to see the Patriots ownership change hands three times. He was also intimately familiar with the team's financial problems and its inferior facility. His main question was whether Kraft was committed to owning the team for the long haul. The league was fed up with all of the uncertainty surrounding the Patriots.

"I want to be a good partner," Kraft said. "I'm not buying with the idea of building up my equity so I can sell. I'm buying because this is going to be part of my life. And hopefully my legacy."

Sensing sincerity, Policy said nothing more.

It fell to Gifford to break down the details of the loan and field questions about the bank's financing package. His detailed, straightforward presentation impressed the committee. At the conclusion of his remarks, Gifford looked around the room, making eye contact with each owner. "I can guarantee members of this committee we would have never made the loan if we didn't think Bob was going to follow through and be good for it," he told them. "The bottom line is that we made this loan because of confidence in Bob Kraft."

Gifford's endorsement extinguished any lingering concerns.

Afterward, Kansas City Chiefs owner Lamar Hunt approached Kraft. Back in the seventies, when Kraft had owned the Boston Lobsters tennis team, Hunt had owned a rival tennis team.

"You know," Hunt said, "I still think that lobster was the best sports logo I've ever seen."

Kraft thanked him, and Hunt extended his hand and welcomed Kraft to the NFL.

That afternoon, Kraft and Gifford went for drinks at the hotel bar in Buckhead. O. J. Simpson entered the bar with a strikingly beautiful blond woman at his side. Heads turned as the couple approached Kraft's table. When Kraft stood, Simpson flashed a big grin, put his arm around him, congratulated him, and cracked a joke about Parcells. The woman never said a word. Nor did Simpson introduce her. Five months later, when Simpson was charged with murdering his ex-wife, Nicole Brown Simpson, Kraft

and Gifford recognized her picture on television as the woman who had been with O. J.

Later that evening, Kraft joined his son Jonathan for a nightcap in the bar. They were joined by NBC's Bob Costas and Bryant Gumbel, former Redskins head coach Joe Gibbs, and actor Kevin Costner.

"You did a great thing," Gumbel told Kraft.

It was strange to think they were having drinks with one of Hollywood's biggest stars. Costner's last film, *The Bodyguard*, with Whitney Houston, had been a box-office hit. His next film, *Wyatt Earp*, was due out in months. And he was about to start filming *Tin Cup*. After everyone drifted off to their rooms, Jonathan Kraft found himself alone with Costner, who had to fend off more than one young woman.

"We're going to have to make you a Patriots fan," Jonathan said.

"You can't *make* me anything," Costner said. "But you can earn my support."

The Super Bowl scene was eye-opening. Celebrities were everywhere. And, suddenly, Kraft was being treated like one. The author George Plimpton walked up and said, "I'm your biggest fan." Musician Charlie Daniels introduced himself and offered to sing the national anthem at a Patriots game. Feature writers from *Sports Illustrated* to the *New York Times* wanted to interview Kraft.

But the most illuminating aspect of the experience was Kraft's encounters with Dallas Cowboys owner Jerry Jones. When the two men first met during a private dinner for NFL owners at the home of Atlanta Falcons owner Rankin Smith, they were at opposite ends of the spectrum. Kraft was the newcomer, the guy just trying to put names with faces. Jones was on top of the football world. Just four years after buying the Cowboys, Jones was the envy of the league. Flamboyant and outspoken, he had his team on the verge of winning back-to-back Super Bowls. Yet, despite being the center of attention, Jones went out of his way to spend time with Kraft and make him feel welcome. Then, while at a party hosted by Commissioner Tagliabue on the eve of the Super Bowl, Jones approached Kraft again. This time he invited Kraft and his son Jonathan to watch the Super Bowl with him from his private box.

"We can't do that," Kraft said. "It's your day."

"I insist," Jones said, confiding that he wasn't extending an invite to any other owner.

Eager to learn as much as he could about how Jones ran his team, Kraft

joined him in his suite at the Georgia Dome on January 30, 1994. Led by head coach Jimmy Johnson and his superstar trio of Troy Aikman, Emmitt Smith, and Michael Irvin, Dallas dismantled the Buffalo Bills for the second consecutive year, giving Jones his second Super Bowl championship. As Kraft looked on, he could scarcely envision that just over a decade later, he and Jones would each possess three Super Bowl championships, and the two of them would be recognized as the two most influential owners of the NFL's modern era.

On the flight back to Boston the following morning, Kraft couldn't wait to get to work.

In his first day on the job as owner, Robert Kraft signaled that the days of business as usual in New England were over. Alone on the hook for $173 million, Kraft wasn't about to trust the management of the franchise to anyone else. Determined to learn and master the business of professional football, he stepped down as CEO of International Forest Products in order to fully immerse himself in his new role as chairman and CEO of the Patriots. While his second-eldest son, Dan, stepped in to run IFP, Kraft rounded out the executive team of the Patriots by appointing Jonathan Kraft president and Andy Wasynczuk chief operating officer.

At twenty-nine, Jonathan was by far the youngest senior executive in the NFL. Wasynczuk, in his mid-thirties, was right behind him.

Their appointments revealed a lot about the new direction Kraft wanted to take. Neither Jonathan nor Wasynczuk had any experience operating a professional sports teams. But they had both been educated at Harvard Business School and trained at Bain, where they were expected to figure out how complex companies across diverse industries could improve performance. Weeks before his purchase of the team went through the formal approval process by the league, Kraft and Wasynczuk were tasked with learning everything there was to know about two new concepts that promised to change the league's landscape: the salary cap and free agency. There was a lot to figure out.

Prior to Kraft's purchasing the Patriots, the NFL owners and the players' union agreed that starting in 1994, teams would be limited to spending $34.6 million on player salaries. This new limit—referred to as a salary cap—was intended to bring parity to the game by preventing the more dominant teams in bigger markets—such as the New York Giants, San Francisco 49ers, Chicago Bears, and Dallas Cowboys—from gaining an unfair advantage over

teams in smaller markets simply by outspending the competition. This was a change that Kraft thought would help the Patriots.

Free agency, on the other hand, came about after the league's top defensive player, Reggie White, and others sued the league, resulting in a historic labor settlement that enabled players with at least five years of experience to become unrestricted free agents. During the litigation, an NFL lawyer told the court that free agency "would be the destruction of the National Football League that we know today." The owners feared that they'd lose control over players, the salaries for top players would get out of control, and that roster turnover would become like a revolving door. But Kraft welcomed free agency as an opportunity to gain a competitive advantage through sound business practices and financial discipline, particularly as it pertained to evaluating personnel and managing payroll.

Right after returning from the Super Bowl in Atlanta, Kraft called a meeting with Bill Parcells and General Manager Patrick Forte. By then, Wasynczuk and Jonathan Kraft had begun creating spreadsheets and plugging in numbers based on analytics designed to determine a free agent's value on the open market: age, years in the league, position, average salary, and so on. At Kraft's invitation, they joined the meeting with Parcells and Forte.

At the outset, Kraft said he wanted to begin by discussing free agency. The conversation quickly turned to the decision to re-sign offensive lineman Bruce Armstrong. At Kraft's request, Parcells reiterated why he thought $10 million over four years was the right price.

"Bill," Jonathan interjected, "where does Armstrong rank among the twenty-eight left tackles in the league?"

Parcells gave him a blank stare.

"Is he top five?" Jonathan continued. "Top ten? Top fifteen? And what's the average salary for left tackles?"

His tongue forming a ball in his cheek, Parcells glared at Jonathan.

"The salary cap is going to be $34 million," Jonathan said. "What percentage of the cap do we think should be going to the offensive line? And how much of that number needs to go to left tackle?"

Parcells had heard enough.

"Look, Harvard boy," he boomed. "I don't know what the fuck you're talking about. But let me tell you how it's done in the NFL. You call the agent up and you throw out a number. And you know the number's low, and that's okay. And the agent's going to throw out a number, and it's going to be high, and that's okay too. But then you meet in the middle. That's the way it's done in the NFL. You got it, Harvard boy?"

"First of all," Kraft said, "I didn't go to Harvard. I went to Harvard Business School. There's a difference. Second, the system you just described is the way it *used to be* done in the NFL. There's a salary cap now, and you have to start thinking about—"

"Patrick," Parcells said, looking at Forte, "teach this kid how this fucking works! I don't have time for this nonsense."

The contentious exchange exposed a culture clash between the way Bill Parcells was used to running his football teams and the way Robert Kraft was used to running his businesses. Although they were the same age, Kraft and Parcells looked at the business of football from very different perspectives. Parcells wore a whistle and a headset. His domain was the locker room and the sideline. His job was to lead and motivate men in a game of violent conflict. Intimidation and confrontation were his methods of operation. He was the public face of the franchise, the dominant personality in the room. He made decisions purely on instinct and ruled with an iron fist.

Kraft dressed in a suit and tie and operated from behind a desk. He was at home in boardrooms. His role was to oversee and manage large, complex organizations. His trademark traits were forming relationships of trust with people of influence and finding ways to differentiate his business from his competitors. He thrived behind the scenes. His name appeared on the lower right-hand corner of the checks. He was data driven and liked to lead with a velvet touch.

Kraft followed through on his commitment to offer Bruce Armstrong a $10 million contract extension. But he informed Parcells that Armstrong's contract would include a provision requiring him to make a minimum of ten appearances each year at Boston-area charities.

Parcells wasn't thrilled about telling Armstrong he had to do charity work.

This wasn't going to be unique to Armstrong, Kraft informed him. He planned to put the same provision in every player contract the Patriots negotiated going forward.

"Why are we telling the players they have to go out in the community?" Parcells groused.

Kraft had his reasons. On the night that he returned from St. Louis and informed Myra that he had spent $173 million on the Patriots, she was angry. She was even angrier when he turned down $75 million in cash to walk away from the deal. Her life revolved around philanthropy. The $75 million, she insisted, would have enabled them to do a lot more for the needy. "Forget about the $75 million," Kraft told her that night. "If we do a good job running this

franchise, we will have a bigger impact on the community than if we gave $1 million a week to charity." She made him promise. "With this team, we will bring this community together," he told her. "I promise."

Kraft didn't bother trying to explain all of that to Parcells.

Nor did Parcells try to explain where he was coming from. A creature of the pro football world, he'd spent his entire adult life in the business and he knew how to navigate it. Kraft, on the other hand, was new to the game and didn't yet understand how it was played. While the new owner was finding his way, Parcells figured that things between them weren't going to be smooth.

While attending his first NFL owners meetings in March 1994, Kraft said very little. The good news for him was that none of the league business discussed behind closed doors seemed particularly complicated. He was more surprised by the chaotic scene he witnessed outside the room. On the second day of the conference, when the owners recessed for lunch, Kraft stepped out with Jerry Jones and got on an escalator. As they started to descend, Kraft spotted a throng of television cameramen and reporters waiting below. Kraft wondered what was going on.

It turned out that the night before, Jones had said something provocative. It had started when Jones proposed a toast and subsequently felt snubbed by his head coach, Jimmy Johnson. Later that night, well after midnight, Jones was in the hotel bar when he let slip to reporters that he "should have fired [Johnson] and brought in Barry Switzer." He added: "There are five hundred coaches who could have won the Super Bowl with our team." It was no secret by that point that the relationship between Jones and Johnson was frayed. But when word of Jones's comments got to Johnson on the morning of the second day of meetings, Johnson stormed out.

As Jones reached the bottom of the escalator and was instantly surrounded by lights and microphones and shouts of "Jerry," Kraft made a mental note about the new world he was in. As the CEO of a global commodities company, Kraft had spent years attending trade organization meetings with other leaders in the forest products industry. Never once had he emerged from a meeting and encountered members of the media. Never once had he been interviewed about something he'd said or done in his capacity as the owner of a paper mill or a manufacturing plant. Nobody outside the industry cared what paper and lumber executives had to say about anything.

Watching Jones get bombarded with questions about an offhand comment he'd apparently made to a couple of people over drinks was a stark

reminder that the entertainment business was a big change from selling commodities. Professional football was a fishbowl.

The experience convinced Kraft that the Patriots organization needed
a highly skilled communications executive to manage the organization's
day-to-day interactions with the press and the community. He specifically
wanted someone he already knew and trusted. Back when Kraft owned the
CBS affiliate in Boston, he had been impressed with television journalist Don
Lowery and promoted him to be the head of the station's editorial board.
Lowery was the first African American to hold the position, and he worked
closely with Myra Kraft, who was also on the editorial board, to make a positive impact on minority communities throughout Boston. After Kraft sold
the station, Lowery went on to have a successful career working in PR for
corporate clients.

Days after returning from the NFL meetings, Kraft attended a black-tie
fund-raiser in Boston, where he ran into Lowery. The two men embraced.

"I've been trying to get a hold of you," Kraft told him. "What are you
doing tomorrow morning at eight?"

"Sleeping."

"You're going to go meet Parcells."

"What do you mean?" Lowery said.

"I'm going to see Parcells. You'll come. And if he trusts you, you'll get the
job."

"What job?"

"We'll talk about it on the way down to Foxborough. I'll pick you up a
little before eight."

Lowery had no idea what Kraft had in mind. But he agreed to go along
because of their relationship. While Kraft owned the station, Lowery's mother
suffered a massive stroke. She survived, but some of her health-care costs
fell to him. Unable to manage under his salary, he explained the situation to
his station manager and requested a pay raise. The humiliating conversation
ended with his boss telling him that the station wasn't in a position to increase his salary. Distraught over the prospect of having to quit his job and
find new employment, Lowery got a call from Kraft. "Donny, I heard about
the money," Kraft told him. "Don't worry about it. It's taken care of." When
Lowery tried to thank him, Kraft cut him off. "You don't need to thank me,"
he said. "You deserve it."

That phone call changed the path of Lowery's life. He stayed in Boston
and went on to have a very fulfilling career. But it was that unforgettable

feeling of being appreciated and understood in a time of crisis that prompted Lowery to hop in Kraft's car on a Sunday morning and head off to a meeting with Bill Parcells—without even knowing what Kraft had in mind. During the drive, Kraft explained how badly he wanted to improve the team's public perception, as well as its relationship with the community. "I want the team to form a deeper connection with the people of New England," Kraft told him. "You are the ideal person to help us do that."

But the role Kraft had in mind for Lowery would also include working with Parcells to manage the PR side of the team. "That's why I want to get Parcells to buy in before offering you the job," Kraft told him. "This is only going to work if Parcells trusts you."

"Any suggestions?" Lowery asked.

"Just do what you have to do to make him feel comfortable with you," Kraft said.

Lowery wasn't sure exactly what that meant.

"Listen," Kraft said. "Parcells will come at you. Don't be intimidated. He just wants to see how you react."

Parcells was at his desk when Kraft knocked and entered. Parcells stood up and Kraft introduced Lowery. Then Kraft ducked out.

Lowery knew little about Parcells's background, other than the fact that he was from New Jersey. Lowery had nearly gone to college in New Jersey on a football scholarship.

"I got recruited to play at Rutgers," Lowery told him.

"Rutgers?" Parcells said. "Who was the coach?"

"John Bateman."

"Bateman! Oh, he's a great guy. Had some good players."

Parcells spent the next twenty minutes pontificating about Rutgers football. He never got around to asking Lowery about his experience in PR. He decided Lowery was a nice enough fellow.

On the drive back to Boston, Kraft congratulated Lowery. He was the new Director of Public and Community Relations for the New England Patriots.

Only three teams had a worse record than the Patriots in 1993. That meant the Patriots had the fourth overall pick in the 1994 draft. Prior to the draft, Parcells invited a few top pro prospects to Foxborough for one-on-one meetings. One of the invitations went to Willie McGinest, an All-American

linebacker at the University of Southern California, where he had earned a reputation as a ferocious pass rusher and punishing tackler. He reminded Parcells of the greatest player he'd ever coached—linebacker Lawrence Taylor.

When McGinest arrived in Foxborough, Parcells showed him two sets of film clips. One was a series of plays from McGinest's worst game, against UCLA. The other clips were from his best game, against Penn State.

"If I was to draft you, which Willie McGinest would I get?" Parcells said.

"The one you saw in the Penn State game," McGinest said.

After the visit, McGinest never heard another word from Parcells. Nor did his agent. But McGinest's agent got a barrage of calls from Dallas. Owner Jerry Jones coveted McGinest. The Cowboys informed McGinest's agent that they were trading a top player to the Rams in exchange for the Rams' fifth-overall pick, which they were going to use to select McGinest.

Confident he was headed to the Super Bowl champion Cowboys, McGinest had a number of representatives from the Cowboys organization with him on draft day. But Parcells chose McGinest with the fourth pick. McGinest was elated. He had grown up watching Parcells coach the New York Giants to two Super Bowls. There was no one he would have rather played for.

Kraft was eager to meet the first player drafted under his tenure of ownership. When McGinest arrived in Foxborough for a press conference, Kraft scheduled some time alone with him. After telling him how thrilled he was to have him join the Patriots, Kraft let it be known that he expected him to be involved in community service. "It's important to give back," Kraft told him. "And you are being given a big platform to make change."

It was the first time anyone in the football world had talked to McGinest that way. Kraft also introduced McGinest to Myra. She immediately started talking about the Boys and Girls Clubs of Boston. She told McGinest that she wanted him to go with her to spend time with troubled and less fortunate children. The Krafts' message resonated with him. He had grown up in Long Beach, where gangs and neglect and poverty had landed many children in his neighborhood in trouble.

McGinest's introduction to Parcells went a little differently. That summer in training camp, Parcells was abrasive toward him. Yelling. Swearing. Getting in his face. "He talked to everyone the same way," McGinest said. "Whether you were a first-round draft pick or a third-string lineman, he yelled at you and embarrassed you and singled you out for criticism. He didn't care about your status. He treated everyone the same way, which I respected."

McGinest quickly figured out how to survive under his new coach. "You

can't take shit personally with Parcells," he said. "You have to have a shield around you mentally to deal with it. You couldn't be sensitive or emotional."

Prior to the Patriots' first preseason road game, Don Lowery produced a list of every staff member who was expected to make the trip. That list ended up on Bill Parcells's desk for final approval. He scanned it and called Lowery to his office. Parcells was holding up the list when Lowery walked in.

"Lowery, what are you doing?"

"What do you mean?" Lowery said.

Parcells pointed to the name of a female staff member on Lowery's travel list. "No broads on the plane!" Parcells said.

"Excuse me?" Lowery said.

"We don't have women on the plane," Parcells said. "We don't need any kind of nonsense going on."

Nonsense? Lowery wasn't sure what that meant. But it wasn't his place to question Parcells. That afternoon, Lowery had an awkward conversation with the female staff member, explaining to her that she could not go on the trip because the coach didn't want her on the plane. Despite being insulted and humiliated, she didn't protest.

Lowery figured he'd better inform Robert and Jonathan, both of whom were planning to bring corporate sponsors—some of whom were women—on the team plane. When Robert heard what had happened, he rolled his eyes. "He doesn't want *women* on the plane?" Robert said.

Lowery nodded.

Jonathan grinned, but he wasn't amused. Everyone walked on eggshells around Parcells. Except Jonathan. He saw Parcells as a bully. And Jonathan's attitude toward bullies had been heavily influenced by his mother. Back in 1983, Myra and her sons had accompanied Robert on a business trip to South Africa, when apartheid was still in force. Shortly after checking into a hotel in Johannesburg, Robert headed off to a meeting, telling nineteen-year-old Jonathan, "Don't let your mother get in any trouble." That afternoon, Myra and her sons went for a walk. Not far from the hotel they encountered a group of white police officers rounding up black men and forcing them into a police van. Appalled, Myra confronted one of the officers, who explained that the men were being arrested for not having proper identification. Apartheid laws required black men to carry papers authorizing them to be in certain urban areas.

"I don't have the proper ID, either," Myra said. "So arrest me, too."

The officer turned to walk away.

Myra stepped in front of him and held out her hands to be handcuffed. "Arrest me!" she demanded.

"Mom, c'mon," Jonathan said, stepping between his mother and the officer. "Let's go."

She stepped around her son and again demanded that the officer arrest her.

With the officer getting agitated, Jonathan picked up his mother and carried her away from the scene. Myra wasn't arrested. But her actions that day were an instructive moment for her sons, especially her eldest. From that day forward, Jonathan never shied away from confrontation when he encountered a bully.

Not long after Lowery told him about Parcells's no-women-on-the-plane policy, Jonathan was walking past the head coach's office when he heard Parcells yell his name. Kraft backed up and stepped in.

Wearing a team-issued polo shirt and shorts, Parcells stood and faced the much shorter and slimmer Kraft, who stared back at him in a white shirt, skinny tie, and wire-rimmed glasses with circular frames. For Parcells, Jonathan came off like Lieutenant Daniel Kaffee—the young, cocky, Ivy League JAG lawyer played by Tom Cruise in *A Few Good Men*. Kaffee investigates decorated US Marine colonel Nathan Jessup, a crass, foul-mouthed character played by Jack Nicholson. When it becomes clear that Kaffee is going to be a thorn in his side, Jessup says to him: "What I do want is for you to stand there in that faggoty white uniform and with your Harvard mouth extend me some fucking courtesy."

This was that moment for Jonathan. Parcells stood up from behind his desk. "So I got a few rules we gotta get straight," Parcells said, looking down at Jonathan.

"Okay."

"First rule. No broads on the team plane."

"Bill, what exactly does that mean, 'No broads on the team plane'?"

"It means no women on the team plane."

"Why?"

"Because they're a distraction."

"So *no women* can come on the team plane?"

"That's right."

Kraft folded his arms and took a step closer to Parcells. "So if my mother wants to come on the team plane, she can't come?"

"That's right. Women are a distraction."

Kraft grinned.

Parcells didn't appreciate that.

"You know, people say you're a great football coach," Kraft said. "If you're such a great football coach, you've got to explain something to me."

"What's that?"

"How does a fifty-two-year-old, ninety-five-pound woman act as a distraction to twenty-two-year-old men?"

Parcells's eyes narrowed.

"If my mother's a distraction, you can't be much of a coach."

Parcells glared at Kraft.

"Anything else, Bill?"

"No!"

Kraft turned and walked out.

Later that day, Jonathan told his father about the encounter and how incredulous it made him.

"Jonathan, of course we're going to put women on the plane," he said.

Quarterback Drew Bledsoe was the Patriots' most prized player. But his relationship with Parcells was scarred even before Bledsoe joined the team. In 1993, Parcells and the Patriots had been sitting on the number one overall pick in the NFL Draft. Parcells had every intention of using it on Bledsoe, then a twenty-one-year-old All-American at Washington State University. At six five and 238 pounds, Bledsoe was durable and tough, capable of absorbing hits. But what really impressed Parcells was Bledsoe's arm. In just twenty-eight college games, Bledsoe had racked up nearly 7,500 passing yards. A leading football writer described Bledsoe's arm as "awe-inducing." Parcells had never seen a quarterback with such a strong arm.

Yet, when Bledsoe flew coast to coast to visit with members of the Patriots organization prior to the draft, Parcells repeatedly insulted him, prompting Bledsoe to wonder, *Why am I here?* Nonetheless, Parcells picked him and subsequently agreed to a contract that made Bledsoe the highest-paid player on the team. When Bledsoe arrived for rookie camp a few weeks later, Parcells got in his face.

"Just remember one thing," Parcells told him. "I don't want a celebrity quarterback on my team. I hate celebrity quarterbacks. You understand?"

Bledsoe nodded. But he never really understood or liked Parcells. Mainly, he had no use for the mind games and the constant needling. Once, during a practice session, Parcells blew his whistle because he didn't like how long it

took Bledsoe to recognize a blitz. "Bledsoe!" he yelled. "You don't have time to stand back there and order lobster thermidor for dinner." In another instance during Bledsoe's rookie season, the Patriots were on the opponent's one-yard line with seconds to play. Trailing by three, Parcells called a quarterback sneak. Bledsoe plowed ahead for the one yard, but didn't extend the ball over the goal line. When Bledsoe came off the field, Parcells shouted, "*Anybody* has enough sense to do that." The game ended with New England inches short of victory.

Things were so bad during Bledsoe's rookie year that his mother paid a visit to Parcells. "I don't think you should talk to Drew the way you do," she told him. "It's not going to help him perform better."

"Well, Mrs. Bledsoe, what you need to do is not watch the games," Parcells told her. "Because this isn't high school football. This is professional football. And this young man is getting paid to win games. That's what we're doing here."

Rather than ease up on Bledsoe, Parcells threatened him. "You were the fair-haired boy in the NFL going into this year," he told him. "But next year there will be another fair-haired boy coming out of college. And the year after that, there will be another one, and you'll be the guy who's forgotten unless you wake up and turn yourself around."

Robert Kraft's first interaction with Drew Bledsoe took place on the practice field. As Kraft approached, the second-year quarterback wasn't sure what to expect. Kraft put his hand on Bledsoe's arm and started asking him questions. He answered, "Yes, sir," and "No, sir."

At the end of the conversation, Kraft invited Bledsoe and his fiancée to come to his home for dinner with him and his wife. Flabbergasted, Bledsoe readily accepted.

For Kraft, this was an obvious and natural thing to do. He had just bought a business and Bledsoe was the highest-paid person on the payroll. He was also the team's on-field leader. Kraft expected him to be in the fold for a long time, and he wanted to build a relationship with him that extended beyond the field.

For Bledsoe, being invited to dine with the owner was surreal. He had never even seen the previous owner. On the drive to the Krafts' home, Bledsoe and his fiancée, Maura, envisioned an elaborate setting with a catered meal served by servants in tuxedos. Instead, they found Myra in the kitchen preparing a home-cooked meal. Then the four of them sat around a modest

kitchen table and talked about family, parenting, and marriage. Football never came up.

Numerous times during the meal, Bledsoe noticed that Robert reached over and held Myra's hand. "Maura and I were engaged at that point," Bledsoe recalled. "We were kids—twenty-two years old—and a long way from home. I was young with a lot of pressure on me. To have a home that we were welcomed into by this wonderful guy who happened to be my boss was a great thing. It was also eye-opening to see such an amazingly successful couple be so respectful and in love with each other."

The bond that began to form between Kraft and Bledsoe that summer disturbed Parcells. He thought it demonstrated naïveté on Kraft's part. "That was a major mistake to show preferential treatment," Parcells later explained. "The problem was not knowing any better, and thinking, 'Well, this is my franchise.'"

The Patriots opened the 1994 season by losing their first two games. The third game was in Cincinnati. Robert Kraft invited Bank of Boston president Chad Gifford to fly with the team and sit with him in the visiting owner's box. It was the least he could do to show appreciation for the man who had pulled together the financing to buy the team.

Gifford, tall and distinguished looking, trailed Kraft onto the team plane. As soon as they entered the cabin, they encountered Parcells. He took one look at Gifford and said, "What the *fuck* is he doing here?"

Everyone within earshot stared blankly at the president of Boston's most prestigious bank. "I felt like shit," Gifford recalled.

Embarrassed for his friend, Kraft motioned for Gifford to take his seat. "He can be like that," Kraft whispered. "Don't pay any attention."

The rest of the experience turned out great for Gifford. He got to see New England win, in Kraft's first victory as an owner. Afterward, the Krafts rushed down to a waiting area near the visitors' locker room beneath Riverfront Stadium. Although Kraft owned the team, Parcells made him wait outside until he gave the go-ahead. So Kraft stood by the locker room door, leaning against the exterior wall, trying to listen to what was being said on the other side. A pool of reporters was also standing nearby, awaiting access to the locker room for postgame interviews. One of them said to Kraft: "That's the 'classic bitch' wall right there," referring to the wall where previous owner Victor Kiam was standing when he infamously referred to Lisa Olson as a classic bitch.

"Really?" Kraft said. "Victor was standing right here when he said *that*?"

The reporter nodded and other reporters laughed.

"I don't want to be anywhere near it," Kraft said, backing up. "This is a better day."

Moments later the locker room door opened and Parcells stuck his head out. "Could Bob Kraft come in here for a minute?" he yelled.

Wearing a blue suit and red tie, Kraft entered and took his place amid the sweaty, bloodied players.

"I've never given a game ball to anybody but a player," Parcells began.

All eyes shifted to Kraft as Parcells handed him the ball.

Tears welled up in Kraft's eyes as the players broke into raucous cheers. Clutching the ball, he put his arms around Parcells. Towering over him, Parcells gave him a bear hug, causing the players to cheer even louder.

"I waited a long time for this moment," Kraft said, choking up. "I hope this is the first of many wins for this team."

After the players showered, dressed, and headed for the bus, Kraft continued to linger in the locker room, taking it all in. A reporter approached and asked him about the moment. "I got emotional, to be honest," Kraft told him. "To have a bunch of guys act spontaneously like that. Nothing like this has ever happened to me before."

eight
THIS GUY IS DIFFERENT

N ew England closed out the 1994 season on a roll, winning its final seven games to wind up 10-6. The strong finish qualified the Patriots for the playoffs for the first time since 1986. Kraft was giddy. Heading into the postseason, the Patriots were the hottest team in the NFL. But their hopes of advancing past the first round were dashed by the Browns, a team coached by forty-two-year-old Bill Belichick, the youngest head coach in the league.

Severely disappointed that his team had lost, Kraft nonetheless made his way to the Browns' locker room area afterward. Stadium security guards were surprised to see the opposing team's owner waiting to talk to the Browns' head coach. Belichick was surprised, too. He was even more astonished when Kraft extended his hand and congratulated him and his team for a job well done. The interaction lasted less than thirty seconds. But it left a lasting impression. In his entire career, Belichick had never had a losing owner from an opposing team seek him out to congratulate him.

A few minutes later, Kraft took an upbeat approach when he addressed reporters about his thoughts on the season. "I thought we had one of the best coaches in the game and one of the great quarterbacks of the future," he told them.

Two years earlier, New England had tied Seattle for the worst record in the NFL. Suddenly, the team was respectable. The quick turnaround earned Parcells Coach of the Year honors. Meanwhile, Bledsoe set a number of records, including pass attempts (691, the most in league history) and passing yards (4,555, the most in franchise history). At twenty-two, he became the youngest quarterback ever to be named to the Pro Bowl.

Bledsoe had played so well in his second season that Kraft feared he might lose him to free agency. After scrutinizing Bledsoe's contract, Jonathan Kraft and Andy Wasynczuk shared that opinion. Back on draft day in 1993, Parcells had signed Bledsoe to a six-year contract. In theory, that meant

Bledsoe had four years remaining in New England. But Bledsoe's contract had been negotiated by Leigh Steinberg.

Steinberg was the most powerful agent in professional football. In 1994, he represented ninety players, eighty-two of whom had been to the Pro Bowl. His clients included half of the starting quarterbacks in the league, including future Hall of Famers Troy Aikman, Steve Young, and Warren Moon—three players who kept leapfrogging each other as the highest-paid player in the league. He was known to say, "Show me the money." And for eight consecutive years, he represented the number one pick in the NFL Draft. Put simply, he had more stars in his orbit than any team in the league.

Generally, owners and front office executives had a very low opinion of agents. In the case of Steinberg, they respected him the way you would a shark if you were swimming in the deep. He was a formidable foe. Kraft, however, had taken a different tack. He decided to become Steinberg's friend.

Back in January 1994, just days after buying the Patriots, Kraft showed up at Steinberg's annual Super Bowl party in Atlanta. There were lots of Super Bowl parties. But Steinberg's was akin to the annual *Vanity Fair* party at the Oscars—the one that attracted the movers and shakers from Hollywood, Wall Street, and DC, and, of course, the biggest names in sports.

When Kraft arrived at the party, which was held at the Fox Theater in Atlanta, he bumped into his old friend Ted Kennedy. Kraft had run the Democratic Party in his town, and he had worked on Kennedy's US Senate campaigns in the sixties and seventies. The two embraced and Kennedy introduced Kraft to a number of the sixteen US senators who stopped by Steinberg's party that evening.

Eventually, Kraft made his way to Steinberg. At the time, there were published reports that Tom Cruise had agreed to play the character Jerry Maguire in a forthcoming film, which was loosely based on Steinberg's life. But it was Steinberg, suntanned in January and sporting a perfectly pressed gray suit, who looked like the movie star.

With Myra at his side, Kraft greeted him and struck up a conversation that went on for nearly half an hour. Steinberg was instantly disarmed by Kraft. He also found Myra charming. As he observed them throughout the evening, he was impressed with how easily the two Krafts worked the room, mingling with actors, musicians, athletes, and politicians.

That night marked the beginning of a business relationship that blossomed into something deeper. Thanks in large part to their shared Jewish heritage, the two men held a lot of common priorities. Their conversations frequently covered Israel, world politics, religion, and philanthropy. Kraft

respected Steinberg's football expertise so much that he asked him all kinds of questions about the business side of the game. And Steinberg reciprocated by telling Kraft things he wouldn't say to any other owner. Early on, Steinberg emphasized that the key to winning in the NFL was a quality organization. It was a belief that resonated with Kraft.

Kraft had plenty of experience running big companies, but football was a unique business; only thirty organizations were permitted to compete and only one reached the top each year. Kraft was interested in what differentiated the teams that reached the top the most—such as the San Francisco 49ers—from everyone else. Steinberg was uniquely qualified to weigh in, given that he did business with the front office of every team in the league. But he enjoyed an unusually close working relationship with the 49ers. "The players go round and round," Steinberg said. "The key is strong, stable ownership that has the intelligence to hire a strong coach and talented front office people who can evaluate talent."

Kraft never took notes. But he absorbed everything. "Most powerful men have forgotten that the key skill in life is listening," Steinberg recalled. "Bob would listen intently. I had never encountered an owner like that."

When it came to Drew Bledsoe's contract with the Patriots, Steinberg had inserted a number of clauses intended to void the agreement after three years. For instance, if Bledsoe was on the field for more than 40 percent of the offensive plays or started more than six games, he could get out of his contract after his third season. It was a concept that Steinberg had come up with called "voidable years." He took this approach with all of his quarterbacks' contracts. The objective was to accelerate the path to free agency by including performance benchmarks that were easily achieved by elite players, assuming they remained healthy.

The bottom line was that if Bledsoe played even modestly well in his third season, he'd become a restricted free agent, making him eligible to entertain offers from other teams. *Restricted*, as opposed to *unrestricted*, meant the Patriots would have the right to match any offers that Bledsoe received. But Steinberg had also inserted a number of "poison pills"—conditions that were impossible for the Patriots to match—to ensure that his player could change teams.

"It was painful to us," Wasynczuk said. "Bledsoe's contract basically gave him a ticket out of town."

Determined not to let that happen, Kraft reached out to Steinberg shortly after the playoff loss in Cleveland and told him he wanted to negotiate a new contract for Bledsoe. Steinberg's first thought was that owners don't negotiate

contracts. Kraft made it clear to Steinberg that when it came to Bledsoe, he'd be handling the contract himself. While he had no intention of getting personally involved in any other player contracts, Kraft viewed the quarterback position differently. He suggested a simple approach: Both he and Steinberg would come up with terms that seemed fair and appropriate. Then they'd get together and compare notes. They would proceed on a good-faith basis.

Knowing Kraft as he did, Steinberg agreed.

Bledsoe's contract situation reinforced what Kraft was already thinking—the organization needed a better system, one with checks and balances to oversee spending and manage player personnel decisions. Specifically, Kraft felt the need to curtail some of Parcells's authority. Parcells was in charge when all of those disadvantageous provisions were inserted in Bledsoe's contract. But that wasn't what was driving Kraft's thinking. He was much more unsettled by something Parcells had told him—that at the end of each year, he retreated to Florida, where he'd unwind and decide whether he wanted to continue coaching.

Parcells had a five-year contract. But he had told Kraft that he coached year to year. That didn't set well with Kraft. Through free agency, Parcells had signed a fair number of older players to four- and five-year contracts. Whether they performed well or not, Kraft was obligated to pay them. Yet, Kraft feared, the coach who signed them might leave this year or the next simply because he felt like it.

Owners rarely had to worry about coaches walking away from a job. Typically, it's coaches who fret about being fired by owners. But Parcells was an enigma. Months after coaching the New York Giants to their second Super Bowl championship, he'd abruptly walked away from what many people saw as the most coveted job in the NFL. If he'd walk away from the Giants when they were on top, Kraft reasoned, he was certainly capable of walking away from the fledgling Patriots.

Parcells's contract had been negotiated by James Orthwein. Kraft had his lawyers scrutinize it to see if it expressly gave the coach authority over all personnel decisions. Turns out it didn't. The contract expressly required Parcells to get "prior approval of the chairman or his designee" on personnel moves. In other words, the way Orthwein structured his deal with Parcells, the head coach needed the owner's consent before signing a high-priced free agent or agreeing to a trade. Those approval powers passed to Kraft when he inherited Parcells's employment contract.

Additionally, when Kraft purchased the team he inherited General Manager Patrick Forte. Normally, GMs oversee personnel matters. Under Orthwein, Forte was on the payroll, but Parcells functioned as both head coach and GM, largely due to the fact that he had no faith in Forte's abilities. Forte had no real football experience. Parcells didn't understand how he even got the job.

Kraft saw eye to eye with Parcells when it came to Forte, so firing him would be the easy part. The challenge was going to be hiring a new general manager and empowering him with the authority to make football personnel decisions. Parcells was sure to interpret the move as an infringement on his turf. Kraft knew he had to find someone he could trust to make sound football personnel decisions and who wouldn't shrink in the withering shadow of Bill Parcells.

But who?

Kraft's preference was Bobby Grier, who had been with the Patriots organization since 1981, working as both an assistant coach and a scout. Kraft had a lot of faith in Grier's abilities. More important, he knew that Parcells trusted Grier. When Parcells had become head coach, he promoted Grier to director of pro scouting. So Grier was someone Parcells already liked working with.

While Kraft mulled over whether to promote Grier, he received some unsolicited advice from a highly respected figure in the NFL: Be careful if you hire black people because they're very hard to fire if it doesn't work out.

As a new owner, Kraft wasn't sure how prevalent that view was throughout the league. But the individual who made that remark to Kraft knew that he was considering Grier, who is black, as his new GM. The comment was made right as a report on the hiring practices of the NFL, NBA, and Major League Baseball was published by the Center for the Study of Sport in Society, a Boston-based think tank at Northeastern University. It revealed that African Americans were virtually nonexistent in front-office positions in the NFL. Conversely, an overwhelming majority of the players on NFL rosters were African American. The year after Kraft bought the Patriots, for example, 68 percent of the players in the league were black, yet there wasn't one black general manager. Nor had there ever been. Since the inception of the Super Bowl era in the mid-1960s, the front-office position most responsible for evaluating player talent and overseeing personnel moves for NFL teams had never been occupied by a person of color.

The complexion of the Patriots' front office had instantly begun to diversify under Kraft. Within a month of purchasing the team, he'd hired Don Lowery and put him in charge of public affairs and community relations. A

month later, Kraft offered a senior position to Patriots linebacker Andre Tippett. At the time, Tippett had played twelve seasons in New England and was contemplating retirement. "Robert came to me and said, 'If you don't want to play and would rather retire, here is an opportunity to come into the front office,'" Tippett recalled.

Tippett had only known Kraft for a short time. But one of the things that Kraft had told him on multiple occasions was that the key to Kraft's success was having good people around him. The fact that Kraft was offering him the chance to come into the front office and be one of those people made it an easy call. "Not many faces like mine were in those positions," Tippett said. "We were all wearing helmets. But he looked at me as someone who was credible, hardworking, loyal, and reliable."

Tippett was named Director of Player Resources, where he oversaw all player-related off-the-field matters. Kraft often sought Tippett's input on issues involving players and frequently brought him along on business trips. Their friendship quickly deepened. At one point, Kraft confided to Tippett that he'd been warned not to hire black people because they were hard to discharge. They discussed the statement and its implications.

Tippett ended up laminating the racist advice on a piece of paper the size of a business card and sticking in his wallet. He would end up working in the Patriots front office for twenty-five years. The statement remained in his wallet the entire time. "I carry that quote with me as a reminder that I can never let my guard down," Tippett said in 2019. "And never stop working hard and never think that we're all on the same level. Because it is not a level playing field. I tell my kids, 'It's not what you know. It's who you know.'"

On February 6, 1995, the Patriots announced that Bobby Grier had been hired as the team's new director of player personnel, effectively making him the first African American GM in the NFL. The history books recognize Ozzie Newsome, who was appointed by the Baltimore Ravens in 2002, as the first African American GM in league history. He is in fact the first man to hold that title. But Grier performed the same job with the same responsibilities seven years prior. The only difference was that Kraft gave him a different job title, in large part to minimize the pushback from Parcells.

Parcells liked Grier, but he still groused about Kraft's decision to promote him. His complaint had less to do with Grier than Kraft. "He didn't want me to be the show," Parcells would later explain. "A couple of owners told him, 'Some of these coaches get too big for their britches. You've got to put them in their place.' So that was what he was doing."

Nonetheless, at the outset, Parcells and Grier worked well together. That

spring at the 1995 NFL Draft, they chose defensive back Ty Law in the first round, linebacker Ted Johnson in the second round, and running back Curtis Martin in the third round. It was one of the best draft classes in the history of the franchise. Law and Martin would both end up in the Hall of Fame. And Johnson would develop into a core member of the team for a decade and end up being a critical member of the franchise's first three Super Bowl championships.

After the draft, Grier immediately started working on Director of Player Resources Andre Tippett, trying to persuade him to work alongside him in the GM's office. With Kraft's support, Tippett made the move. "For Bobby to get the opportunity to be GM was awesome," Tippett said. "I knew that because he was African American, he had eyes on him. So I went in there with a determination to work hard and never do a half-ass job. I didn't want to let him down."

The historical significance of Kraft's decision to promote Grier and give him the latitude to make executive decisions received little fanfare. But Grier and Tippett soon started showing up at league meetings and representing the New England Patriots. The commissioner's office and owners throughout the league took notice. During the nearly thirty-year span between the first Super Bowl, following the 1966 season, to when Kraft purchased the Patriots in 1994, only two African Americans—Art Shell and Dennis Green—had been head coaches in the NFL. The hiring climate for minority general managers was even worse. In 2003, the NFL adopted what's known as "the Rooney Rule," which required teams to interview ethnic minority candidates when there were head coaching vacancies. It wasn't until 2009 that the league expanded the policy to apply to job openings in senior football operations.

The negotiation between Robert Kraft and Leigh Steinberg over Drew Bledsoe's new contract broke off fast. When Kraft presented his preliminary offer, Steinberg balked at the number. When Steinberg countered, Kraft walked away. It wasn't a tactic. They were simply too far apart.

The two men didn't talk for a few months. Then Steinberg negotiated a series of record-setting signing bonuses for a number of the top players in the 1995 draft. In the midst of those signings, Kraft reached back out to Steinberg and invited him to come to Boston. On a warm evening in mid-June, they met over dinner at an Italian restaurant in the city's North End. As Steinberg coated his Italian bread with olive spread, Kraft said, "I guess you like that stuff."

"I *love* olive spread," Steinberg told him.

Kraft made a mental note.

After three hours of negotiations, they moved to Kraft's home. Over wine, they settled on the basic terms for Bledsoe's new contract: $42 million over six years, with a substantial percentage of the money—$11.5 million— payable in the form of a signing bonus. The deal would make Bledsoe the highest-paid player in the league.

There were just two sticking points. One of them stemmed from an off-hand comment that Bledsoe had made the first time he visited Kraft's office. Spotting a photograph of Kraft and his family on a ski slope, Bledsoe volunteered that he had just taken his father helicopter skiing. Unfamiliar with the term, Kraft asked what it meant. Bledsoe explained that it referred to skiing down mountains that can't be accessed by a ski lift. A year later, Kraft insisted on a clause in the new contract that forbade Bledsoe from helicopter skiing.

"How can you reasonably expect me to put all this money up only to have my quarterback get hurt doing something crazy?" Kraft told Steinberg.

Steinberg agreed to talk to Bledsoe about it.

"You're about to become the highest-paid player in football," Steinberg told Bledsoe. "He just wants one little alteration in your offseason."

Bledsoe wished he'd never mentioned the skiing.

The other issue had to do with philanthropy. Kraft believed that where much is given, much is expected. While every Patriots player's contract included a provision requiring ten appearances at charities or hospitals each year, Kraft wanted Bledsoe to also donate $2 million of his salary to charity. He talked directly with Bledsoe to make his point. "This is really important to me personally," Kraft told his quarterback.

Without putting it in writing, Bledsoe pledged $1 million to the Kraft Family Foundation and $1 million to another charity of his choosing.

To celebrate, Kraft invited Steinberg to the Krafts' summer home on Cape Cod. With the television tuned to *SportsCenter*, Kraft and Steinberg sipped wine in a hot tub on the back patio. Suddenly, an image of Steinberg appeared on the screen as ESPN anchor Chris Berman read off all of the deals that he had done in the past week.

"Leigh, time to take a vacation," Berman joked on the air.

Kraft and Steinberg laughed and raised their glasses. If ESPN only knew.

When Steinberg arrived back home in Los Angeles a couple of days later, he discovered a small crate at his front doorstep. It held boxes of jars containing gourmet olive spread. The card was from Kraft.

nine

NOT SO FAST

J ust before the start of training camp in the summer of 1995, Robert
Kraft announced that the team had signed Drew Bledsoe to a new contract that represented the highest average salary and the highest signing
bonus in NFL history.

"This is one of the best investments of any kind that I have ever made,"
Kraft said. "This solidifies the future of this organization for many years to
come with one of the best young talents of the game."

Bledsoe could not have been happier. When reporters asked for his
thoughts on the deal, he smiled and said: "I can't even do the math."

One thing was abundantly clear. After just two seasons, the twenty-three-
year-old quarterback had the full faith and confidence of the owner. The
same thing could not be said, however, about the head coach. Bill Parcells
already resented the relationship between the owner and the quarterback,
and the new contract only deepened his displeasure. It wasn't just the fact
that Kraft and Steinberg had torn up the deal Parcells had given Bledsoe two
years earlier. What really bugged Parcells was that the pecking order within
the organization was shifting. By crowning Bledsoe with the highest salary
in the NFL, Kraft had clearly elevated the up-and-coming quarterback as the
designated face and future of the franchise.

But Parcells still maintained complete control in the places that more
directly influenced the outcome on the field—the team meeting rooms, the
practice field, and the sideline. In those domains, Parcells sometimes treated
Bledsoe more like an underling than the team's on-the-field leader. It was
a dynamic that some felt played out to the detriment of the team. Heading
into the 1995 season, the Patriots were projected to compete for a Super Bowl
championship. Instead, New England went 6-10 and didn't come close to
returning to the playoffs. After taking one big step forward in '94, the team
took two steps backward in '95.

No one felt worse than Bledsoe. After signing the big contract, he threw

more interceptions (sixteen) than touchdowns (thirteen) in 1995 and barely completed 50 percent of his passes. By every measure, it was the worst year of his career. The convenient narrative that formed around the situation was that Bledsoe wasn't playing up to his potential. *Sports Illustrated* summed it up this way:

> The bonus baby played like a bust within twenty yards of the end zone. He bickered with Parcells on the sideline and didn't throw a TD pass until the fifth game of the season (by comparison, he threw 11 touchdowns in the same span in '94). The offense flopped inside the red zone, scoring touchdowns on only 24 of 62 chances.

The same piece quoted Bill Parcells saying this about Bledsoe: "He had some mechanical problems, choice problems, read problems, and accuracy problems. We have to have a better performance from that position."

Everything that Parcells said was true. But there was more to the story. Early in the 1995 season, the Patriots were 1-1 when they traveled to San Francisco to play the defending Super Bowl champions on September 17, 1995. Midway through the first quarter, 49ers' linebacker Ken Norton Jr. hit Bledsoe and slammed him to the turf right after Bledsoe released the ball. Bledsoe landed hard on his left shoulder. Clearly hurting, he went to the sideline, where he sat out the next series. After talking to the team doctor, Bledsoe said he wanted to play, and on the Patriots next possession, Parcells sent him back out. But it was immediately apparent that something was wrong. His throwing mechanics were off and he seemed uncharacteristically unsure in the pocket. Niners defenders would later say that since they knew he was injured, they stepped up the pressure by blitzing more often. During halftime, Bledsoe's shoulder was heavily taped so he could play the second half.

Robert and Jonathan Kraft were watching the action that afternoon from the visiting owner's box at Candlestick Park. Leigh Steinberg joined them. He was furious with Parcells for leaving Bledsoe in the game. Of course Bledsoe was going to say he could play, Steinberg reasoned. He was a competitor. And every football player was programmed to play through pain.

By the middle of the fourth quarter, the 49ers held a commanding 28–3 lead and Bledsoe had taken a brutal beating. He was relentlessly hit, knocked down, and sacked four times. The way the Niners' defense was teeing off on him, he was at risk of being seriously injured.

"You can't let this happen!" Steinberg said to Kraft.

Steinberg also represented Niners quarterback Steve Young. One year

earlier, the Niners had faced a similar situation. Early in that season they'd been getting trounced by the Eagles and Young had been pummeled. In that case, Young hadn't sustained an injury—Niners coach George Seifert pulled him out of the game to preserve him. Young had returned the following week and led the Niners to ten straight victories.

Bledsoe wasn't just getting pummeled as Young had been; Bledsoe was injured, which, Steinberg felt, made it all the more irresponsible to keep him out there. Yet when the Patriots got the ball back with just three minutes remaining and trailing by four touchdowns, Parcells again sent Bledsoe onto the field. Moments later, a defensive lineman broke through, wrapped up Bledsoe, and slammed him to the turf. Steinberg pounded the counter. Even the television announcers were questioning why Parcells was leaving Bledsoe in the game. A couple of plays later, Bledsoe took yet another shot, this time to his knees, causing him to land awkwardly. The Patriots' final drive stalled moments later on the Niners' eight-yard line.

In the locker room afterward, Bledsoe had glassy eyes and a noticeably red shoulder heavily coated in analgesic. Parcells faced the press. One reporter questioned why he'd left Bledsoe in to finish such a one-sided game. "The doctor said he was able to play," Parcells said. "That's why he played." He added: "He was well enough to finish the game, obviously, or I wouldn't have put him in there."

It turned out Bledsoe wasn't all right. A postgame exam revealed that Bledsoe had probably suffered a separated shoulder. The extent of the ligament damage was unclear.

Steinberg and the Krafts left Candlestick Park together after the game. During the car ride to the airport, the conversation about Bledsoe's injury and Parcells's judgment continued.

"Look, this is your franchise," Steinberg told Kraft. "The long-term health of your quarterback is as high of a priority as you have."

Kraft didn't disagree.

"Parcells has got to be managed," Steinberg continued. "He's a legendary coach. But just like anyone else, he needs to be managed."

Back in Boston, medical tests confirmed that Bledsoe had indeed suffered a mild separation of his nonthrowing shoulder. Two days later, Parcells announced that Bledsoe would not miss any action. "We will probably rest him for a couple of days, and he should be okay for the next game," he told reporters.

His handling of the situation caused a stir. He even got into a shouting match with a television reporter for reporting a true statement—that Bledsoe had been put back in the 49ers game despite being in obvious pain.

"Players play," Parcells said. "That's what they do. I'm not into worrying about protecting players. I didn't feel we were jeopardizing him any further by letting him play, or he wouldn't have been in there to begin with."

Statements like that infuriated Steinberg. So he intervened. In the area of sports medicine, Dr. James Andrews was considered the leading orthopedic surgeon for knee, elbow, and shoulder injuries. His patients included Michael Jordan, Jack Nicklaus, Roger Clemens, and Bo Jackson. Andrews had also performed shoulder surgery on a number of Steinberg's clients, including quarterback Troy Aikman. Days after Parcells declared Bledsoe fit to play, Steinberg insisted Bledsoe see Dr. Andrews. Fortunately, Andrews felt that Bledsoe didn't need surgery to repair his ligaments, but he advised that Bledsoe should sit out the next game. Otherwise, he would be at risk of further aggravating the injury.

Armed with that prognosis, Steinberg held a press conference and essentially put Parcells on notice. His client, he said, shouldn't be expected to play "because the pain level has been so intense . . . and because there would be some awkwardness in some throwing situations. He would be less protected and could get hurt in another way."

After the Patriots had a bye week, Parcells sat Bledsoe for one game. Then, three weeks after being injured, Bledsoe returned to the starting lineup for a home game against Denver. That week, Parcells asked Bledsoe whether he should start Troy Brown or rookie Kevin Lee at receiver. It was unusual for Parcells to seek Bledsoe's opinion.

Without hesitation, Bledsoe chose Brown. "He's always open and I trust him," Bledsoe told Parcells.

An important ingredient to a quarterback's success is having receivers he can trust. Nonetheless, Parcells started Lee, saying he was faster than Brown.

In the Denver game, Bledsoe threw a strike to Lee that bounced off his shoulder pads and into the hands of a defender. On the stat sheet, the play was recorded as an interception to Bledsoe when in fact it was the result of a rookie mistake that the sure-handed Brown wasn't prone to making. Fed up after the interception, Bledsoe walked off the field and said to Parcells: "There's your boy. Good choice."

Although few people on the sideline had witnessed the sarcastic comment, Parcells was pissed. After his team was trounced by Denver, Parcells

publicly critiqued Bledsoe in front of the media. "With the number of games that he's played, things should be going a little more smoothly for him than they are right now," Parcells said. "He's going through a rough spot. Some quarterbacks emerge from these kinds of things and gain confidence and go on to develop further, and some don't. He's still a young player and teams are taking a certain approach toward him and he's got to learn to deal with it."

Bledsoe played the rest of the season with a separated shoulder. Certain throws—especially on deep routes—triggered significant pain. To work around it, he altered his throwing motion, which threw off his mechanics. That was the primary explanation for the drop-off in his accuracy.

During that period, Parcells didn't make things any easier. Most notably, as Bledsoe continued to play through the injury, Parcells hinted at the one thing players fear most—being replaced.

"He's my starting quarterback," Parcells said near the midway point of the season. "So I'm going to stay with him as long as he can play, until such point in time I think I should try someone else."

Kraft was in a bind. On one side he had the game's most powerful agent leaning on him to protect his client. On the other he had a head coach who was as obstinate as he was revered. But as the team's 1995 season was melting down, Kraft faced a more perilous situation: lawmakers in Massachusetts seemed to be backing off the plan to build a new football stadium in Boston. Without a new stadium, Kraft would never be able to meet his loan obligations to Bank of Boston. He was on edge.

Before purchasing the team, Kraft had been given assurances that a new domed stadium for the Patriots would be part of a comprehensive redevelopment plan in Boston known as the Megaplex, which also included a new convention center. "Within the last two weeks, the assurances and support from the governor, senate president, and the house Speaker has convinced me and others that regardless of the length of the legislative process that the Megaplex will become a reality," James Orthwein had said at the press conference on the day he sold the team to Kraft.

The promise of the stadium had factored into Kraft's decision to take on so much debt to buy the team. Foxboro Stadium was one of the oldest, most dilapidated facilities in the league. Even NFL commissioner Paul Tagliabue was adamant in his belief that the Patriots needed a new home to survive. In addition to its deteriorating condition, Foxboro Stadium had an outdated design that made it virtually impossible for the Patriots to compete on the

same financial footing as other teams. For example, it had only forty-two luxury boxes and no club seating. By contrast, Cowboy Stadium had four hundred luxury suites and thousands of premium club seats. As a result, in 1994 alone, Cowboys owner Jerry Jones pulled in an additional $30 million in stadium revenue over and above what he was required to share with the league.

Kraft, on the other hand, couldn't make the Patriots profitable, despite the fact that he was selling out every game for the first time in franchise history. Due to the antiquated stadium, the team was still losing money. In Kraft's first year of ownership, the Patriots reported a loss of $48 million.

What angered Kraft the most was the inaction of Governor William Weld, who had promised his support for a new stadium. In the interim, the governor had also pledged support for immediate funding to upgrade roads and make other improvements around Foxboro Stadium. The idea was to make the old stadium safer and more accessible while plans for a new stadium were approved and carried out.

But a full year after Kraft bought the team, the state had failed to make meaningful progress. The Megaplex plan was languishing in legislative committees and appeared nowhere near being approved. Nor had the legislature appropriated the promised money for the highway improvements around Foxboro Stadium. Fed up, Kraft called out the governor and the legislature in an interview with the *Boston Globe*, hinting that if they didn't step up soon, he might be forced to move the team out of the state. "Commitments were made to me," Kraft told the *Globe*. "Those commitments were part of what induced me to do such a non-economical deal."

His comments caused a stir. Legislators interpreted them as a threat. Two days after Kraft spoke out, a state senate committee dropped the $35 million appropriation for highway improvements in the area of Foxboro Stadium. The move was clearly intended to deliver a message to Kraft. "There are other residents in the commonwealth besides him," said a spokesman for the state's secretary of transportation.

Other high-ranking political leaders chimed in. Most important among them was Thomas Finneran, chairman of the powerful House Ways and Means Committee. Finneran controlled the purse strings on Beacon Hill. Without his support, the idea of a domed stadium in Boston would go nowhere. When he read Kraft's comments, he came out swinging. "The state is not around to immunize people from unintelligent decisions," Finneran said. "The whole premise is absurd."

A year earlier, Patriots fans had viewed Kraft as a hero for buying the

team and keeping it in Massachusetts. But now he was dealing with a different crowd—lawmakers on Beacon Hill and the press corps that covered the State House. Some of them resented Kraft. "Bob, if you really want some free money, pronto, there is one guaranteed way to get it," wrote *Boston Herald* political columnist Howie Carr. "Move to Mexico."

Even a polling firm that normally tracked political races weighed in with a public opinion poll. The results showed that Massachusetts residents were overwhelmingly against state aid for the Patriots. The poll also showed that people largely would blame Kraft if he moved the team out of Massachusetts for a better deal.

The reality was that the last thing Kraft wanted to do was move the team out of Massachusetts. Nor was he looking for a better deal. His objective was to build a better stadium, preferably in Boston, and he was willing to invest his own money to make it happen. But a stadium in Boston would require a substantial investment from the state for all of the surrounding infrastructure, and without it, the Patriots might have little choice but to relocate the team to a neighboring New England state. Both Rhode Island and Connecticut had sent signals that they would welcome the team and build a new stadium.

Determined to make it work in Massachusetts, Kraft hired one of the most powerful lobbyists on Beacon Hill and tasked him with jump-starting the Megaplex initiative within the legislature. Then, during the summer of 1995, Kraft stepped up the pressure, pledging $215 million in payments and annual rent in hopes of prodding the legislature to approve the domed stadium in the Megaplex plan.

But the harder Kraft pushed, the more he rankled Tom Finneran. Shortly after Kraft made his $215 million pledge, Finneran's Ways and Means Committee decided to drop the Megaplex plan altogether.

Kraft was up against envy and resentment. At its core, politics is a popularity contest. Since buying the Patriots, Kraft had become the man of the town, his name recognition eclipsing that of the powerful political leaders he needed to win over. Flattering headlines such as "Kraft Now a Star in His Own Right," which appeared in the *Boston Globe* in the fall of 1995, weren't helping his cause.

It also didn't help that Kraft continued to publicly chastise the politicians. "They're playing poker," he told the *Globe*. "What they need to understand is, eventually the game ends." In a separate interview, Kraft criticized

the governor for having promised to support a stadium and failing to deliver. "The point is, the commitment was made and I believed it," Kraft said. In a private letter to Weld, Kraft was much more direct, saying that his inaction would "lead to an unfulfilled vision for a world-class facility and cost this region an important source of both economic and psychic benefit."

The letter ended up in the hands of the press, which pushed the standoff to another level. Referring to it as a "shoot-yourself-in-the-foot letter," the *Globe*'s State House bureau chief, Joan Vennochi, pointed out that the governor was still pushing for a stadium. "It may sound harsh," Vennochi wrote, "but Kraft is his own worst enemy. . . . One of Kraft's biggest problems on Beacon Hill has been Robert Kraft."

By this point, even the sportswriters were weighing in. "Raise your hand if you're sick of Bob Kraft whining about how much money he's losing on the Patriots," sports columnist Dan Shaughnessy wrote. "Enough with the I'll-take-my-team-and-go-elsewhere antics. Pul-eeeze. We'd love you to stay, Bob. But if the Pats have to go because we won't help build you a new stadium, then go."

In the midst of this political climate the Patriots traveled to Indianapolis for the final game of the 1995 season. It was two days before Christmas and New England was 6-9. Bledsoe was hurting. Parcells was brooding. And Kraft was fuming. Everyone was ready for the offseason.

On the eve of the game, Parcells called Kraft to his hotel room. The moment he entered, Kraft knew something was up. Parcells's shoulders were slumped and he had a forlorn expression on his face.

"Are you all right?" Kraft asked.

"Bob, I don't know if I want to coach beyond one more year," Parcells began.

Kraft sat down. "Why?" he asked.

"You know," he said, "it's hard work. The kids are different than they used to be. The system is different."

The system had in fact changed. Free agency and the salary cap had added new layers of complexity to the job. Plus, the 1995 season had been a grind and the results were demoralizing.

"I may be getting too old for this," Parcells told Kraft.

Humility wasn't one of Parcells's qualities. But in this moment he appeared vulnerable as he admitted his uncertainty. Earlier that season, Kraft and Parcells had been running side-by-side on treadmills at the stadium one afternoon when Parcells suddenly stepped off and bent over, resting his hands

on his knees and laboring to breathe. "Bill, are you okay?" Kraft had said to him. In that instance, Parcells had waved Kraft off, saying he just needed a minute. But as they faced each other in his hotel room, Parcells admitted that his health wasn't good and he had concerns.

Kraft had his differences with Parcells, but this wasn't the time to dwell on them. He had a coach who was pouring his heart and soul into the team. Parcells, Kraft told himself, had given his all.

That night, they agreed that Parcells would coach one more season, after which Kraft would let him out of the final year of his contract and waive the $1.2 million penalty for not fulfilling his obligation.

Just to be clear, Kraft raised the question: What if Parcells changed his mind and wanted to coach in 1997? Parcells said that wasn't going to happen. He was finished.

Kraft promised to have his lawyer draft an amendment to his employment contract. Parcells thanked him, and they both agreed that neither of them would discuss their agreement publicly until the end of the 1996–97 season.

The Patriots general counsel, Richard Karelitz, seldom attended road games. But he happened to be traveling with Kraft for the final regular season game in Indianapolis. When Kraft left Parcells's hotel room, he went to see Karelitz and filled him in on the situation.

No one had been at Kraft's side longer than Karelitz. He'd started working for Kraft in 1975, shortly after Kraft started International Forest Products. Since then, Karelitz had performed complex legal work for Kraft all over the world. Sophisticated and shrewd, Karelitz had a knack for getting to the core of an issue quickly. As he listened to Kraft recount his conversation with Parcells, he distilled it down to the two most salient points—the coach was essentially saying he didn't feel up to coaching beyond one more season due to health reasons and on that basis the owner was willing to let him out of the final year of his contract without penalty. He immediately anticipated a potential problem. He told Kraft: "What if Parcells has a change of heart and decides he wants to coach after the 1996 season?"

The prospect of Parcells trying to coach another team didn't set well with Kraft.

"Why don't we say that if he decides that he wants to coach again, he would coach for the Patriots and not for anyone else?" Karelitz said.

"That's a good idea," Kraft said.

When he got back to Boston, Karelitz drafted an amendment to Parcells's contract. One sentence of that amendment would lay the groundwork for one of the biggest feuds in NFL history:

> In the event that the Employee desires to continue as an NFL head coach or other comparable position after January 31, 1997, and the Employer desires to continue to employ the Employee as its Head Football Coach for an additional year through January 31, 1998, then the parties agree to extend the Employment Agreement for the Extension Year.

He faxed the amended agreement to Parcells in Florida. Without showing it to his agent, Parcells signed it on January 12, 1996.

Kraft had never expected it to be easy to turn the Patriots into a winning organization. But by the end of the 1995 season, he couldn't help thinking that he hadn't exactly gotten what he had bargained for when he purchased the franchise. At the time of the purchase, Parcells was arguably the most attractive asset—along with a budding star quarterback—on the payroll. Kraft had figured the two of them would lead the franchise for many years to come. He'd also thought he'd be moving into a new stadium in Boston. A little over a year into his ownership tenure, the stadium looked like a pipe dream and Parcells was on his way out the door.

Suddenly, he had a new priority at the top of his to-do list—find a new head coach. Before he started formulating a list of prospects, the Cleveland Browns fired head coach Bill Belichick, on February 14, 1996. Kraft immediately got a call from Parcells saying he wanted to add Belichick to his coaching staff. He also said that he had already broached the idea with Belichick, who was open to the possibility. But Belichick had already been offered a defensive coordinator position with the Miami Dolphins. In hopes of convincing Belichick to come to New England instead, Parcells wanted Kraft to get on a plane and go meet with him at once.

"Tell me how this makes sense," Kraft said. The Patriots didn't need a defensive coordinator. In fact, all of their coaching positions were filled. And they were already over budget on coaches' salaries.

"Look," Parcells said, "I worked with this guy. He's really good. If we don't get him, he's going to go to Miami."

As Parcells pushed, Kraft agreed that it wasn't in the Patriots' best interest to have Belichick become the defensive coordinator in Miami. The Dolphins were a division rival, and New England faced them twice a year.

"What's your relationship like with Belichick?" Kraft asked.

"We have a good relationship professionally," Parcells said.

It was a telling response. Kraft perceived that the two men might not be particularly close off the field.

"Look," Parcells said, "you won't really be his friend. He's not going to embrace you. But I think you'll like this guy. He'll be good for us."

Intrigued, Kraft flew to Indianapolis, where Belichick was attending the NFL Scouting Combine. They met off-site so no one would spot them. Kraft began by telling Belichick how much he admired his success as a defensive coordinator with the Giants. Belichick fondly recalled Kraft's unusual display of sportsmanship after the Browns knocked off the Patriots a couple of years back. The two of them then launched into a conversation that lasted several hours.

"We talked about a lot of things," Belichick recalled. "I was most impressed by our conversations about the football organization and really from a big picture standpoint. It wasn't a lot of X's and O's and coaching. It was about building a team, contracts, support staff, development of players. Just philosophically how to build a team, which I felt pretty well versed in because that's what I had been doing for the previous five years in Cleveland."

For Kraft, it was a new experience. In three years' time, Bill Parcells had never sat down with him for several hours to brainstorm about how to build a team. The opportunity to have that kind of discussion with Belichick enabled Kraft to see that he was different. Kraft found Belichick's approach appealing. So much so that despite the fact that the team really couldn't afford and certainly didn't need him, Kraft offered him a job.

Two days after Kraft returned from Indianapolis, Belichick joined the coaching staff in New England. His title was Assistant Head Coach.

ten

SHE

A t around 5 p.m. on the day before the 1996 NFL Draft, Robert Kraft was at his desk in his downtown office when his secretary told him Will McDonough from the *Globe* was on the line. Kraft had an idea what the reporter wanted. For more than twenty years, McDonough had spent a few weeks prior to the draft trying to, as he put it, "get a fix on what the first round would look like." He'd call teams in advance and obtain information directly from coaches and GMs. Then he'd publish a draft-day story projecting whom each team was going to pick. It never made sense to Kraft that teams would disclose in advance what they were going to do on draft day.

Nonetheless, Kraft took his friend's call. In his head, he quickly determined what not to say—that Bobby Grier coveted Ohio State wide receiver Terry Glenn. Given that Parcells was vehemently opposed to using a first-round pick on a receiver and that Glenn might get chosen before the Patriots made their selection, Kraft planned to stay away from that prospect altogether.

McDonough asked Kraft straight up whom the Patriots were picking in the first round.

"Well, it all depends on who is there," Kraft said. "But my boys tell me we're going to take a defensive lineman."

McDonough knew that *boys* was a reference to Parcells and Grier.

"There's three guys we're interested in," Kraft continued. "Cedric Jones, Duane Clemons, or Tony Brackens. We'll have a shot at one of those three."

McDonough didn't speak to Grier. But after hanging up with Kraft, he called Parcells and told him what Kraft had said.

"That's right," Parcells responded. "One of those three defensive linemen. That's where we need help."

McDonough then told Parcells that two people had told him that Kraft wanted to draft Ohio State's Terry Glenn.

"We're not taking a receiver with that pick," Parcells told him. "We're

going to get the defensive lineman first, then get the receiver at the top of the second round. There will still be some good ones left."

That evening, McDonough turned in his story to sports editor Don Skwar, who informed him that Patriots football writer Ron Borges was writing a separate story reporting that Terry Glenn would be the Patriots' first pick. Convinced that Borges had talked to Kraft, McDonough informed his editor what Kraft and Parcells had told him. "I wonder why Kraft is giving Borges a bad story," McDonough said to Skwar.

McDonough's prediction that the Patriots were taking a defensive lineman in the first round appeared the following morning in the *Boston Globe*. Hours later, Parcells and Grier filed into the war room at Foxboro Stadium, where they were joined by Robert Kraft, Jonathan Kraft, Andy Wasynczuk, and a handful of scouts. The first four picks were not a surprise. But then things got interesting. With the fifth pick, the Giants chose Cedric Jones, the lineman that the Patriots had rated as their top choice. Then the Rams used the sixth pick to take Lawrence Phillips, Nebraska's supremely talented running back who had assaulted more than one woman in college. As a result, Terry Glenn was still on the board when it was the Patriots' turn to pick at the seventh spot.

Suddenly, Grier had a dilemma. There was no question in his mind that they should take the speedy receiver. When Bledsoe had set passing records in 1994, he had had track star Michael Timpson, who caught seventy-four passes for nearly 1,000 yards. Timpson's ability to outrun defenders had given the Patriots' offense a deep threat that opened up the field for other receivers, enabling Bledsoe to pick defenses apart. After Timpson left through free agency, Bledsoe had no one who could run the deep routes in 1995, which changed the way defenses schemed against Bledsoe. Terry Glenn would give the Patriots another deep threat.

But Grier knew Parcells was dead set against taking Glenn. The Patriots' defense was badly in need of pass rushers, and that was Parcells's top priority.

The Patriots had fifteen minutes to make their decision.

With the clock ticking, Kraft asked Grier and Parcells to step out for a private conference. Irritated, Parcells followed him and Grier into another room. There Kraft asked Grier his opinion. Grier cut to the chase: Bledsoe was one of the highest-paid players in the league. It didn't make sense to spend that kind of money on a top-tier quarterback and not surround him with adequate weapons. Talent-wise, he added, Glenn was the best receiver on the board; the Patriots' scouting reports had unanimously reached that conclusion.

Aggravated, Parcells pushed back. He wanted defensive lineman Tony Brackens.

Kraft did not want to decide whom to draft. That wasn't his role. But he had taken the time to read the scouting reports and they clearly put Glenn ahead of Brackens.

"We spend two million dollars a year on scouts and scouting reports and we do all this analysis," Kraft said. "If we're not going to go by their conclusions, let's get rid of the system and start a new system."

He was looking at both men, but his words were clearly directed at Parcells.

"I'm trying to build a system for the long term that makes us excellent year in and year out," Kraft continued. "I don't think you can do it on intuition."

Parcells bristled.

Kraft turned to Grier. "Bobby, you're ultimately the guy who is going to make the decision," he said. "You make the call."

Grier repeated that he thought the best choice for the Patriots was Glenn.

Kraft looked at Parcells. "We're going with Glenn."

"O-*kay*," Parcells said, as he headed out the door. "If that's the way you want it, you got it."

Moments later, Commissioner Paul Tagliabue announced that the New England Patriots had selected Ohio State's Terry Glenn. That sentence signaled stormy weather ahead in Foxborough. Later that day, Parcells called his assistant coaches together and told them that Kraft had acted deliberately to publicly humiliate him. He vowed he would never forget it.

Parcells wasn't the only one seething. McDonough was also furious. "My embarrassed chin was hanging on the ground," he would later say of the moment.

Thirty minutes after Glenn was selected, McDonough tracked down Kraft, led him into a men's room at Foxboro Stadium, closed the door, and lit into him, demanding to know what Kraft was "trying to pull" with his bullshit story about taking a defensive lineman.

Kraft insisted he wasn't trying to pull anything.

McDonough quickly cut him off. "What do think, I'm stupid?" McDonough said. "That I don't know what you told me yesterday?"

Kraft didn't want to argue.

"You're lying," McDonough said.

McDonough tended to see things in black and white. With Willie, you were either right or wrong. But Kraft operated in gray. Accustomed to knowing things that no one else knew he knew, Kraft practiced discretion like an art form. McDonough had never asked him about Glenn, and Kraft had his reasons for not volunteering that information on the night before the draft. Nor was he about to explain those reasons in a bathroom.

Instead, he reiterated that the team had in fact been looking at drafting a defensive lineman in the first round. "But when we looked at our board," he said, "Glenn was the highest-rated player."

McDonough wasn't buying it.

Kraft apologized for any "misunderstanding."

"You just made a colossal mistake," McDonough said, insisting that Kraft had made Parcells look like a fool. "There isn't a chance in hell this guy stays here."

When the second day of the draft got under way, Kraft was back in the war room with Parcells and Grier. The draft had moved to the fifth round and Kraft was puzzled as he studied the board. A highly rated six-foot-three, 304-pound defensive lineman named Christian Peter was still available. But all of the linemen that the Patriots had rated below Peter had been drafted. Usually that indicated that the undrafted player was a risk due to off-the-field problems. But the Patriots had a color code for high-risk players, and Peter's name wasn't color coded. Kraft didn't get it. Peter had been the anchor of the defense for the two-time defending national champion Nebraska Cornhuskers.

"Why hasn't he been picked?" Kraft asked.

"He's had some problems," one of the scouts said.

Kraft wanted specifics.

Someone in the room described a situation where Peter had been at a bar and tried to feel up a girl.

"We met with him," one of the scouts added. "We feel good about him."

Both Grier and Parcells wanted Peter. And Parcells had spoken directly to Nebraska's head coach, Tom Osborne, who had vouched for Peter.

After all of the tension around the Terry Glenn pick the previous day, there was no serious debate over whether to take Peter. New England selected him with the 149th pick. Parcells telephoned Peter at home with the news. "You're a Patriot," Parcells told him.

After announcing the pick, Parcells talked about Peter to the press. More than one reporter was aware that Peter had off-the-field problems at Nebraska.

"I think once he gets in a good, solid structure, everything will be fine," Parcells told reporters.

Grier concurred. "Peter understands what this organization stands for," Grier said, "that we're not going to stand for any shenanigans off the field or anything that's going to put a bad light on the franchise or the community."

Within a few hours, Don Lowery was in his media relations office when a fax came through from one of the Patriots' beat writers. On the cover sheet, the reporter had scribbled: "You should see this."

The fax consisted of two articles about Peter's run-ins with the law. One was a short piece in *Sports Illustrated*. The other was a longer, more detailed story from a local paper in Nebraska. Peter, it turned out, had a litany of arrests in college. Some of the charges—trespassing, disturbing the peace, failure to appear—were less serious and ultimately dismissed, while others, such as urinating in public and possession of alcohol by a minor, had resulted in convictions. The more serious cases involved women. After being arrested for twice grabbing Miss Nebraska by the crotch in a bar, Peter pleaded no contest to third-degree sexual assault and was sentenced to eighteen months' probation. Then, just one month before the draft, he was arrested again and charged with assault after allegedly grabbing a woman by the throat at a bar. He was convicted of disturbing the peace. There was also a civil suit filed against the university by a Nebraska student who claimed Peter had raped her on two occasions. Peter claimed the sex was consensual. The case was eventually resolved when the university reached an out-of-court settlement with Peter's accuser.

Lowery immediately took the articles to Kraft. "You need to see these," Lowery told him.

Seated behind his desk, Kraft read them in silence. Stunned, he looked up at Lowery with a blank expression. "Did you know about this?"

"No."

"How did we not know about this?" Kraft said.

"I don't know."

Dismayed, Kraft looked back down at the articles. He hated it when he felt critical information had been withheld from him.

Deeply offended, Kraft went to see Parcells, demanding to know why they had drafted a player with a documented history of violence against women.

Parcells downplayed the situation, reiterating that he had talked to Coach Osborne at Nebraska. Peter was not a bad kid, Parcells insisted.

Parcells genuinely believed what Osborne had told him. He also believed

that the NFL wasn't full of choir boys. Some guys come, he liked to say, a little rough around the edges.

Kraft knew he had a problem.

Myra Kraft was incensed when she learned of Christian Peter's record by reading about it in the paper. One of Myra's signature causes had been combating violence against women. No one had donated more money to the ROSE Fund, a Boston-based nonprofit dedicated to ending domestic violence, than Myra and Robert Kraft. In partnership with the Massachusetts Eye and Ear Infirmary, the organization enabled battered women to erase the scars of violence by undergoing facial reconstructive surgery. At Myra's urging, the Patriots had become a sponsor of the ROSE Fund right after Robert bought the team, making New England the first team in the NFL to acknowledge the seriousness of violence against women and actively work to reduce it. Many of the Patriots players' wives also got involved, attending ROSE Fund events with Myra and helping to raise awareness about a social problem that was seldom discussed in public.

When facing difficult decisions, Robert Kraft would always consult his wife. But in the case of what to do with Christian Peter, that wasn't necessary. Kraft knew what Myra's answer would be. But it wasn't that easy, and over the next forty-eight hours, he wrestled with what to do. No NFL team had ever drafted a player and then promptly relinquished the rights to him on the basis of prior acts of violence against women. The idea was so unheard-of that Kraft called the league office seeking guidance. At the time, the NFL was starting to face scrutiny for the first time in league history for turning a blind eye toward players charged with crimes against women. Back in October, retired running back O. J. Simpson had been acquitted of murdering his ex-wife. And in late February, a jury in Texas had acquitted Minnesota Vikings quarterback Warren Moon of spousal abuse. A handful of other active players were under investigation in 1996 for alleged violent crimes against women.

The fact that the league had no policy in place for dealing with active players who had been formally charged with violence against women made Kraft's question about how to handle a draft pick who had been convicted in college more complicated. With no policies or precedent to point toward, the commissioner told Kraft that it was his call. The conversation drove home the realization that Kraft was going to be out there all by himself on this one.

Kraft decided he didn't want to add a player with a recent history of abusing women to his team. Doing so, he felt, sent the wrong message. At the

same time, Kraft wanted to drive home the point to Parcells that the owner was the one who signed the checks, and therefore he needed to be fully informed before making draft picks that were questionable.

Two days after Peter was selected, Kraft went to see Parcells again.

"We're cutting him," Kraft said.

Parcells was incredulous. They weren't going to have a football team if this was the new standard.

"I don't give a shit," Kraft said. "You should have disclosed this to me."

Later that day, Kraft got a call from Nebraska head coach Tom Osborne.

"You're making a mistake," Osborne told him.

Kraft didn't put any stock in Osborne's words.

Exasperated, Parcells informed Kraft that the Kansas City Chiefs were offering a seventh-round draft choice in the following year's draft for Peter. But Kraft vetoed that idea, too, saying he didn't want to profit from the mistake of drafting Peter in the first place. Instead, he gave the green light for Don Lowery to issue a press release announcing that Christian Peter had been released. It read, in part: "Based on information we obtained in the last 48 hours following a review of his past actions, we concluded this behavior is incompatible with our organization's standards of acceptable conduct."

Parcells fumed.

When contacted by a reporter seeking comment, Peter lashed out, saying that he "wouldn't want to play for someone without enough guts to defend a player he selected, who then comes up with some cockamamie story he wants to give the public. I feel hurt and somewhat betrayed."

After reading Peter's comments, Kraft wrote him a letter, apologizing for the way the Patriots had mishandled the situation at the outset. He told Peter that he meant him no ill will.

Peter later signed with the New York Giants.

The 1996 NFL Draft was a watershed moment in the history of the New England Patriots franchise. Kraft's decision to back Bobby Grier and overrule Parcells in the selection of Terry Glenn reset the power structure in Foxborough and established a clear chain of command that would eventually become a hallmark of the Patriots dynasty. Separately, Kraft's decision to cut Christian Peter over his mistreatment of women marked the establishment of a new identity for the organization. It was a 180-degree turn away from the way the organization had handled the Lisa Olson sexual harassment incident six years earlier.

Both of these seismic shifts in the culture of the organization also acceler-ated the departure of Bill Parcells and permanently damaged the long-standing friendship between Kraft and McDonough. After the confrontation in the bathroom on draft day, McDonough stopped talking to Kraft. At the same time, the personal relationship between Parcells and McDonough tightened.

A couple of weeks after the draft, McDonough and Parcells played golf together on Cape Cod. Over lunch inside the Oyster Harbors clubhouse, they talked about Kraft. Parcells said he had almost resigned after the draft. "For about twenty-four hours, I made up my mind I was finished here," Parcells told McDonough. "I didn't want any more to do with this guy."

At that point, McDonough felt the same way about Kraft.

A month later, Parcells and McDonough golfed together again. This time they were in New Jersey. And once again, they talked about Kraft. Parcells confided in McDonough that he and Kraft had reached a confidential agree-ment earlier that year. "If I want to come back, I come back," Parcells told McDonough. "If I don't, I'm out of here free and clear. That's the deal."

That wasn't actually the deal that Parcells signed. But that's what he rep-resented to McDonough. Parcells then revealed that the upcoming season would definitely be his last year coaching. "I don't need the money," Parcells told him. "I got a house here. I got a house in Florida. I'm going to sell my house in Foxborough, spend winters in Florida and summers here."

McDonough couldn't blame him.

The falling-out with Will McDonough gnawed at Kraft. After three months of being incommunicado, Kraft finally picked up the phone one day and di-aled McDonough's work number. Hoping to revive their friendship, he asked if they could talk. McDonough was still pissed. Nonetheless he agreed to lis-ten. Kraft drove to the *Globe*, picked him up, and took him to Castle Island in South Boston. Sitting on a bench that faced the ocean, they had a heart-to-heart that lasted over two hours.

McDonough spoke first, telling Kraft that he was no longer the guy Mc-Donough had known before he bought the Patriots. He cited Kraft's treat-ment of Parcells as Exhibit A.

It was hard listening to McDonough's perspective. From Kraft's vantage point, Parcells was the wedge between him and McDonough. It felt like his friend had sided with Parcells without hearing Kraft's side of the story.

When it was his turn to speak, Kraft confided to McDonough that he was losing a lot of money and was not happy. Parcells, he explained, was

the source of his unhappiness. The man he was paying $1 million per year to coach his team was "two-faced," constantly talking behind his back, and stirring up problems for him in the media.

"Then fire Parcells," McDonough said. "You own the team. You spent all that money, and you're unhappy. Fire him."

"I almost fired him right after the draft," Kraft said, raising his hand to his chin. "I had it up to here with that guy. It just isn't any fun to go down there. I'm not having any fun.

"You keep telling me he won't come back," Kraft continued. "I'm telling you it's not his decision. It's my decision. I own this team. He works for me. With me, it's a matter of respect. We give him everything he wants, and still he shows no respect for me."

McDonough had known Kraft for a long time. The sincerity he heard in Kraft's voice as he stared at the water quelled McDonough's anger. It was obvious that his old friend was hurting.

"The only thing I want from you is the truth," McDonough said quietly. "I just don't want any more fast ones like the one you pulled in the draft."

"I didn't lie to you," Kraft said. "I just wasn't forthright. I thought if I told you about Glenn, you would tell Parcells, and he would tell some other team, and we would lose Glenn."

When training camp opened in the summer of 1996, rookie Terry Glenn wasn't on the field due to an injury. After a couple of days, Parcells faced reporters.

"Is Terry Glenn still hurt?" one writer asked.

"Well, he missed again today," Parcells said. "So, we'll see. She's making progress. Shouldn't be too much longer."

The reference to Glenn as a "she" was no slip of the tongue. And it drew a few grins and chuckles within the media pool. It also ended up in the newspaper the next morning. Don Lowery had barely reached his office when he received a call from Myra Kraft. She was indignant.

"Did he really say that?" she said.

"Yeah, he did," Lowery told her.

Myra hated sexism in any form, and she didn't find anything funny about the suggestion that a player who needed time to heal was weak like a woman.

That afternoon, Myra was approached by a reporter at the Patriots' kick-off luncheon. When asked about Parcells comment, she called it "disgraceful," adding: "I hope he's chastised for that."

When Parcells got word of Myra's comments, he was beside himself. Flummoxed, he tracked down Lowery. "What did I do wrong?" Parcells asked.

Lowery wasn't sure what to say. But he was struck by the fact that Parcells actually cared how Myra felt. Parcells typically didn't give a damn what people thought about him.

Her comments at the luncheon ended up being published by the Associated Press. The AP also asked Robert to respond to Parcells's reference to Glenn as a woman. "That's not the standard we want to set," Kraft said. "That's not the way we do things. It's just like there was a player last year that gave the finger to the crowd. He's not here anymore."

Parcells saw the AP story and again went to Lowery.

"Why is everybody making a big deal out of this?" Parcells asked.

Again, Lowery wasn't sure what to say.

It had never occurred to Parcells that his tongue-in-cheek remark would be interpreted as offensive. He'd been saying stuff like that his entire career and no one had ever complained. The difference was the presence of an assertive woman and an NFL owner who shared her view.

At Parcells's next press conference, reporters wanted his reaction to Kraft's statement.

"Coach, yesterday the Associated Press reported that the owner had chastised you."

Parcells laughed, but he didn't find the question funny.

"Would you comment on that?" the reporter pressed.

"Yeah, I'll comment on that," Parcells said, his voice rising. "I've never had a better relationship with Bob Kraft. And I don't know what's going on here. I'm getting a little tired of it. I'm sure he is also. And, ah, we haven't spoken about that issue." By this point, Parcells was practically yelling. "You guys were there when I made the comment. You know in what context that comment was made. Okay? And now you see what's been fabricated out of it. It was just in jest. I've said that for twenty years, those kinds of references. It was a lighthearted thing. And everyone who was in the room when I said it knows it."

That afternoon, a television reporter cornered Kraft at training camp and asked about the Terry Glenn situation.

"Is there a rift?" the reporter asked.

"It's much ado about nothing," Kraft said. "Bill told me that he's happy we drafted him. He realizes he can help us win games. Bill's style is to just needle players who have injury time. It's what's worked for him. Whether it's right in the modern age, I don't know."

"You and Parcells, no problems whatsoever?" the reporter asked.

"None at all. Matter of fact, I think we've never gotten along better. We've had to establish certain boundaries and understanding. Both of us are committed to winning as many games as we can."

The Patriots played solid football in 1996. Lost in all the controversy was the fact that Parcells and Grier chose some exceptional defensive players in the '96 draft—safety Lawyer Milloy and linebacker Tedy Bruschi. Early in the season, Kraft spent a lot of time on the practice field. One thing he observed was the way the defensive players were responding to newcomer Bill Belichick. In particular, the young defensive backs like Milloy and second-year cornerback Ty Law were like sponges around Belichick. He had them playing like seasoned veterans.

After practice one afternoon, Kraft telephoned Jonathan to rave about Belichick. "This guy is a helluva teacher," he said. "I mean you should watch this guy coach. The players just suck up everything he says. They listen to him."

Kraft also told his son that he had talked with Belichick a couple of times about the salary cap and was impressed with his knowledge and perspective.

Jonathan never attended practices. So he hadn't personally observed the kinds of things his father was describing about Belichick. But in the sixth week of the season, when the Patriots were in Baltimore to face the Ravens, Jonathan was working out in the hotel gym around 5:00 a.m. on the morning of the game when Belichick walked in. No one else was around. They ended up talking for thirty minutes, and most of the conversation centered on the salary cap. Later that morning, Jonathan told his father: "Now I know what you mean about his take on the salary cap. He totally gets it. And that kind of understanding could be a real competitive advantage for a coach."

On October 27, New England knocked off the Buffalo Bills to improve to 5-3. The team was starting to gel. Three days later, Kraft called McDonough.

"Your boy wants to coach again," Kraft told him.

"You're kidding me. He always told me he's finished when the season is over."

"See how this guy changes?" Kraft said. "He does it all the time. Now he wants to coach again."

McDonough called Parcells, who confirmed that he indeed had changed his mind and wanted to continue coaching the Patriots beyond the 1996 season. McDonough was shocked.

But Kraft wasn't sure he wanted Parcells to come back. He preferred to wait until after the season to figure that out.

New England finished the regular season in dramatic fashion, coming back from a 22–0 halftime deficit to knock off the Giants in the Meadowlands, 23–22. It was a gritty, hard-fought win that gave the Patriots an 11-5 record. They had won their division and earned a first-round bye in the playoffs.

No one had been tougher in the second half of the game than rookie receiver Terry Glenn. He led the way with eight catches for 124 yards and he scored the team's first touchdown. But the thing that stood out most to Parcells was his willingness to play hurt. Midway through the second half, Glenn took a direct blow to the pelvis that caused a contusion and forced him out of the game. Despite admitting afterward that it "really hurt," Glenn returned to the field and made a couple of crucial catches to set up the game-winning score—a Bledsoe touchdown pass on fourth-and-7 to tight end Ben Coates, who dragged two defenders toward the end zone before barely stretching the ball across the goal line.

As the final seconds ticked off the clock, Parcells turned to the crowd behind the Patriots bench and triumphantly put his fist in the air. He hugged Bledsoe. He even hugged Kraft. But he really let go in the locker room. With tears in his eyes, he called on Terry Glenn to step forward.

"You showed me today that you're a player!" Parcells said.

The eyes of his teammates on him, Glenn struggled to hide his emotions. He knew Parcells hadn't wanted him initially, and he'd endured his barbs during training camp. Yet Glenn had gone out and set an NFL record for rookies with ninety receptions, racking up 1,132 yards and scoring six touchdowns. He drew so much attention from defenses that other Patriots receivers found it easier to get open, enabling Bledsoe to have one of the best seasons of his career, passing for over four thousand yards and throwing twenty-seven touchdown passes. Everything had turned out the way Bobby Grier had hoped. "The bottom line is that without Terry Glenn, we don't make the playoffs," Bledsoe said. "He was that big of a difference maker."

But to be singled out by Parcells for praise in the locker room was bigger than any compliment from Grier, Bledsoe, or anyone else. Validation from Parcells was the proudest moment of Glenn's season. All he'd ever wanted was to be wanted by one of the game's greatest coaches.

Parcells put his arms around him.

eleven

THE TROUBLE WITH CONTRACTS

Momentum from the dramatic come-from-behind victory in New York propelled New England through the playoffs. In the first round, the Patriots hosted their first playoff game in eighteen years, knocking off the Steelers, 28–3. Then, on January 12, 1997, for the first time ever, Foxboro Stadium was the site of the AFC Championship game. That morning, the *Boston Herald* ran a story reporting that an agreement existed between Kraft and Parcells that gave the Patriots the right to block Parcells from coaching for another team the following season unless the Patriots were adequately compensated.

Will McDonough was scheduled to tape a television interview with Bill Parcells that would run during NBC's pregame show that afternoon. When McDonough arrived at the stadium at 8:30, Parcells was livid.

"Imagine, we're here today playing for the Super Bowl, and Kraft is planting this garbage in the paper," Parcells told McDonough. "This is unbelievable. This never stops."

McDonough was also convinced that Kraft had planted the story in the *Herald*. "Listen," he told Parcells. "I'll grab Kraft when he gets here, bring him into your office, and straighten this thing out. He told me all along he wants to take the high road. Let's see what the deal is."

By late morning, tailgaters packed the parking lots leading to Foxboro Stadium. Despite subfreezing temperatures, New Englanders were in a festive mood. But as Kraft drove past them, his mind was preoccupied with his relationship with Parcells. It was dominating the conversation on sports talk radio. The story in the *Herald* in particular aggravated Kraft to no end. It made him look like the bad guy, like he was the one pushing Parcells out the door.

When Kraft reached the stadium, McDonough was waiting for him. He reported that Parcells was fuming about the story.

"Yeah, well, I had nothing to do with it," Kraft told McDonough. "I never talked to the guy."

Together, they went to Parcells's office. McDonough closed the door and Kraft took a seat opposite Parcells. Standing, McDonough started the meeting by reminding both of them that they had previously talked about "taking the high road." After some back-and-forth, Parcells looked Kraft in the eye. "Bob, this is what I'm going to do," he said. "When the season is over, I say that it is time for me to move on. That I've enjoyed my time here. The fans were great. You treated me well. I wish you the best, and I even give you a plug for a new stadium. And the next day, you notify Tagliabue that I am free and clear with no further obligations to the New England Patriots."

Parcells reached across the desk to shake Kraft's hand.

Kraft started to extend his hand but quickly withdrew it. "We shouldn't even be having this conversation," he said. "Our agreement is to talk when the year is over."

In Kraft's mind, the meeting that McDonough had brokered was nothing more than a ploy to get him to undo the written contract that Parcells had signed. Kraft interpreted Parcells's words "free and clear with no further obligations to the Patriots" as code for free and clear to go coach another team.

As Kraft withdrew his hand, McDonough couldn't believe what he was seeing. It didn't look to him like the high road.

Parcells turned to McDonough. "I want to talk to Bob alone."

McDonough stepped out.

As soon as the door was closed, Parcells and Kraft had it out. Parcells was furious—in part at himself—that he had signed an amended contract that prohibited him from coaching for another team in 1997 without Kraft's consent. He had a lot of pent-up frustration toward Kraft and he desperately wanted out of Foxborough. Kraft was indignant over the fact that they were even discussing Parcells's future plans hours before the most important game in franchise history. Although he couldn't prove it, he was convinced that the New York Jets wanted Parcells, which was creating the sense of urgency in Parcells to find a way out of his contract in New England. It also galled Kraft that McDonough seemed to be in cahoots with Parcells. It felt like he had lost one of his best friends. And he blamed Parcells for that.

Thirty minutes later, Kraft emerged. McDonough was still waiting outside Parcells's office. "I'm glad you saw that," Kraft told him. Then he walked off. It was the last time Kraft and McDonough ever spoke.

That evening, amid freezing temperatures and mounds of snow forming a ring around the outer edge of the field, New England was clinging to a 13–6

lead with two minutes to play and Jacksonville at midfield with the ball. Moments later, Patriots defensive back Otis Smith recovered a fumble and raced forty-seven yards for the game-clinching score. Robert and Myra Kraft embraced and wept as sixty-thousand-plus fans celebrated the most emotional moment in the stadium's history. When the game ended minutes later, Patriots players jogged along the edge of the stands. Fans slapped their hands and kissed their sweaty heads. Fireworks lit up the nighttime sky. The Patriots were headed to the Super Bowl.

On a makeshift stage hurriedly erected on the field, Parcells and the Kraft family assembled for the televised trophy ceremony. The cheering was so loud it was hard to hear league president Neil Austrian, who said, "I'd like to present to Bob Kraft and his family the Lamar Hunt Trophy, emblematic of supremacy in the AFC."

As Kraft gripped the trophy, NBC broadcaster Greg Gumbel stood between him and Parcells. "For a guy who's been a season ticket holder since 1971," Gumbel said, "this has to be an awfully nice moment, Bob."

"This is for all the fans out here who have waited *thirty-seven years!*" Kraft shouted, hoisting the trophy as the fans roared. "Thank you! Thank you! Thank you!"

Kraft turned to Parcells. "And to the greatest coach in the history of the game in modern times," Kraft said. "Thank you."

"Thank you, Bob," Parcells said.

Chants of "TU-NA! TU-NA! TU-NA!" boomed through the stadium.

The ovation for Parcells was so loud that Gumbel had to wait ten seconds—an eternity on live television—before speaking.

"That's quite an accolade, coach," Gumbel finally said. "The 'greatest coach in the history of the game.'"

Overwhelmed by a mix of emotions, Parcells didn't know what to say.

Patriots fans knew what was at stake. They chanted "Four more years!" as Parcells left the field and headed to the locker room. Only one other coach in NFL history had led two different teams to a Super Bowl. Surrounded by his players, Parcells tried to treat the occasion as just another victory. As he addressed his team, he tried to get them to focus on getting ready for the next game.

"Be here at nine thirty tomorrow to run," he told them.

It was barely 6:00 a.m. the following morning. Paul Tagliabue and his wife were asleep in their Manhattan apartment when the phone rang. Mrs.

Tagliabue lifted the receiver, listened to the caller, then turned to her husband with her hand over the phone. "He says it's Bill Parcells," she whispered. "I don't know if it is or not."

Skeptical and irritated, Tagliabue took the phone and said hello.

"I have something that you need to start thinking about," Parcells said from his office at Foxboro Stadium.

Immediately recognizing the voice, Tagliabue interrupted him. "I don't need to start thinking about it at six o'clock in the morning unless it's really important," he said.

"Well, it's really important," said Parcells, launching into his dispute with Kraft over his amended employment contract.

"Look," Tagliabue said, cutting him off, "I don't know anything about it. And I can't make a determination at this point."

"I'm just giving you a heads-up," Parcells said. "Once we get through the Super Bowl, you're going to have a dispute between the Patriots and me."

Parcells had been up all night. The victory had been satisfying. But his exchange with Kraft before the game was all he could think about. Unable to sleep when he got home after the game, he had returned to his office at the stadium around 3:00 a.m. Stewing, he called and woke up more than one friend, including Lawrence Taylor, before placing the call to the commissioner.

Tagliabue could hear in Parcells's voice that he was extremely worked up.

"Call me after the Super Bowl," Tagliabue told him. "We'll do whatever we have to do."

Parcells finally calmed down.

"And one more thing," Tagliabue said. "You don't have to call me at six in the morning to find me."

Later that day, Parcells hired an attorney.

New England fans were in ecstasy—their team was heading to New Orleans to face the Green Bay Packers in Super Bowl XXXI. But inside the executive offices at Foxboro Stadium, there was nothing but tension. In the days immediately following the AFC Championship, Kraft and Parcells had a series of heated conversations. Now lawyers were involved and demand letters had been sent.

While all of that was going on behind closed doors, McDonough telephoned Parcells hours before the team was scheduled to attend a send-off rally with fans at Boston City Hall. Then, at Parcells's direction, McDonough

called Parcells's agent. The next day, right after the Patriots touched down in New Orleans, McDonough's story appeared in the *Boston Globe* under the headline "Parcells to Leave." Citing unidentified sources, McDonough wrote that Parcells was finished and that the situation between Parcells and Kraft was so acrimonious that it could end up in court.

The McDonough story laid bare the fact that the Super Bowl was the last game Bill Parcells would coach for New England. The story also placed the blame squarely on the irreparable relationship between the owner and the coach.

Kraft was furious. Not only did McDonough's story essentially point the finger at him, but it was so explosive that it overshadowed the game. "The organization is not speaking about any of this stuff until after the Super Bowl," Don Lowery told the press. But there was no stemming the tide. The feud between Kraft and Parcells had managed to eclipse the one between Jerry Jones and Jimmy Johnson. There was no precedent for a coach leading his team to a Super Bowl and letting it be known before the game was played that he would be walking away after the game.

The situation was so absurd that even the players got dragged into it. When Drew Bledsoe spoke to the national media, he was asked about his personal relationship with Parcells. "Personal relationship?" Bledsoe said. "We don't have a personal relationship." He added: "Whether Bill is here or not, this team is going to be successful. We've got good players. A great nucleus. A great owner."

Assistant coach Bill Belichick had a front-row seat to the feud between Parcells and Kraft. But he managed to avoid the fray. Privately, he disagreed with the way Parcells had conducted himself leading up to the Super Bowl. "I can tell you firsthand, there was a lot of stuff going on prior to the game," Belichick later confided to journalist Michael Holley. "I mean, him talking to other teams. He was trying to make up his mind about what he wanted to do. Which, honestly, I felt [was] totally inappropriate. How many chances do you get to play for the Super Bowl? Tell them to get back to you in a couple of days. I'm not saying it was disrespectful to me, but it was in terms of the overall commitment to the team."

Belichick made those comments years after the fact. At the time, he kept his feelings tightly under wraps. One luxury of being an assistant coach was that he could lie low. Instead of getting drawn into the fracas, on the day before the Super Bowl, Belichick talked privately with his good friend Jon Bon

Jovi during the Patriots' final practice at the Superdome. One of the things Belichick appreciated about Bon Jovi was that he never asked probing questions about the inner workings of the organization.

Bon Jovi's presence at a practice that was otherwise off-limits to friends and the press caught Kraft's eye. He had no idea how or why Belichick appeared to be close friends with the rock star.

The friendship dated from Belichick's days on the Giants. Born and raised in New Jersey, Bon Jovi was a die-hard Giants fan. About six years after forming his rock band, he ran into Giants punter Sean Landeta one night in a New Jersey nightclub. It was 1989 and Landeta was wearing his Super Bowl ring from 1987, the same year that Bon Jovi's *Slippery When Wet* went platinum and was the top-selling rock-and-roll album in the United States. Both twenty-seven at the time, Bon Jovi and Landeta immediately hit it off, talking music and football, and by the end of the night, Landeta said he'd see if he could get Bon Jovi into a Giants practice session.

Landeta approached Parcells about it when Bon Jovi's "I'll Be There for You" was the number one hit in the country. Even Parcells, who listened to Elvis Presley and doo-wop music, knew of Bon Jovi, and he told Landeta he could invite the rocker to a practice. But when Bon Jovi pulled up in a Ferrari and strolled in with his flowing long hair, faded jeans, and leather boots, Parcells lit into him.

"Gee-zuz *Christ*," Parcells bellowed as soon as he spotted him. "What are you doing here?"

All the players stopped and stared at Bon Jovi.

Rather than be intimidated, Bon Jovi was simply deferential to Parcells. He put his hair in a ponytail, tucked it up under a hat, and stood quietly on the sideline. At one point, he even cracked a joke with Parcells that brought a smile to the coach's face. Afterward, Bon Jovi got invited back. And before long he was shagging punts in practice in his boots, and Parcells was yelling: "Gee-zuz Christ, get off the field!" It was a sign that Parcells liked him.

While Bon Jovi got along well with Parcells, the singer was much closer in age to Bill Belichick. Plus, Belichick was really into Bon Jovi's music. The two of them became close. So when Belichick became head coach of the Browns, Bon Jovi started trekking to Cleveland to watch practices and attend home games there. And when Belichick reunited with Parcells in New England, Bon Jovi started hanging out in Foxborough.

Kraft had seen Bon Jovi around, but they had never been formally introduced. Now, once Belichick stepped away from Bon Jovi and returned to working with the players, Kraft approached and introduced himself.

"Tell me about your friend," Kraft said.

"Belichick?" Bon Jovi asked.

Kraft nodded.

Bon Jovi paused and then said, "Well, he's a defensive genius."

Kraft had already arrived at that conclusion. He wanted to know what Bon Jovi thought of Belichick as a human being. As soon as the Super Bowl ended, Kraft would be officially in the market for a new head coach. But he had been gathering intelligence for a while, and most NFL insiders that he talked to about Belichick said negative things about his personality. During his tumultuous coaching tenure in Cleveland, the press had deemed him a "cold-fish coach" and compared him to Napoleon. *Sports Illustrated* opined, "If *Bill Belichick: The Movie* were ever made, Belichick would be played by Harrison Ford: aloof, rumpled, preoccupied by things the rest of us will never fully understand."

But none of the people who were saying all of these things had a personal relationship with Belichick. Bon Jovi did. So Kraft pressed him to elaborate.

Savvy enough to recognize what was going on, Bon Jovi discreetly shared a couple of anecdotes that put Belichick in a different, more favorable light.

Bon Jovi told Kraft that Belichick was a great individual, someone he admired and respected. Kraft thanked him and told him he was always welcome around the Patriots.

When practice ended, Bon Jovi met up with Belichick. Rather than ride the team bus back to the hotel, the two decided to walk back with John Mellencamp's longtime drummer Kenny Aronoff and Bon Jovi's sound engineer Obie O'Brien. Along the way they stopped for drinks. As they sat on a New Orleans curb sipping hurricanes and exchanging stories, Belichick could have easily passed for a member of the band. Comfortable and at ease, he fit right in.

New England played Green Bay tough. At one point in the third quarter it even looked like the Patriots might have a shot at winning when the team scored a touchdown to pull within six points. But the Packers' Desmond Howard returned the ensuing kickoff ninety-nine yards for a touchdown, and the Patriots never recovered. Green Bay won 35–21.

Before the game ended, NBC Sports chairman Dick Ebersol paid a visit to Robert Kraft's suite. Although Kraft wasn't saying a word to anyone about whom he was eyeing to be the Patriots next head coach, Parcells had told McDonough that the Patriots were already talking to San Francisco 49ers

defensive coordinator Pete Carroll about the job. The *Globe* then reported the story in the paper, which irked Kraft. But there were also rumors that Kraft might go after Belichick.

As an executive at a network that was spending millions to televise AFC games, Ebersol had a vested interest in Kraft's decision. Among AFC teams, the Patriots were in the third-largest television market in the country. From a ratings standpoint, it was vital to NBC that New England bring in a head coach who was capable of building on the winning foundation that Parcells had established.

At one point, Ebersol pulled Jonathan Kraft aside for a word in private. "People tell me your father will listen to you," Ebersol said. "Well, don't let him hire Belichick when Parcells leaves."

Jonathan was familiar with the case against Belichick. His record as a head coach in Cleveland was 36-44. On top of a losing record, he had routinely sparred with the media and infuriated fans by unceremoniously cutting quarterback Bernie Kosar, who was the city's favorite son.

"Tell him to consider Pete Carroll," Ebersol continued.

Jonathan knew his father's thinking on the matter—that his head was telling him to go with Belichick, but his gut was telling him he had to clean house first. He also knew that no one else's opinion—not even someone whom Robert respected as much as he did Ebersol—was going to have any sway whatsoever on whom he hired to succeed Parcells. Nonetheless, Jonathan passed along Ebersol's comments after the game. "For what it's worth," he told his father.

Bill Parcells had a reputation for being "as sentimental as a traffic ticket." Outwardly, he relished that image. Inwardly, he brimmed with affection for his players. "I see these faces on these players," he said days before the Super Bowl. "I remember the faces of the players I had that went before. That's the priceless thing in this business. Those faces are the faces that you remember. You see those kids, and there is a bond that never leaves. It's always there because we did this together. It's special. It's a little corny, but it's special."

Of all the "kids" on the Patriots roster, linebacker Willie McGinest and running back Curtis Martin, whom Parcells called "Boy Wonder," were two that Parcells had a soft spot for. Likewise, both players revered Parcells and felt indebted to him for taking a shot on them, mentoring them, and teaching them what it meant to be a professional football player. As the final seconds ticked off the clock at the Superdome, McGinest wept as Parcells put his arms

around him and hugged him. McGinest's mother said she'd never seen her son cry like that.

When the Patriots' chartered jet left New Orleans for home, Bill Parcells wasn't aboard. His absence sent a clear message to his players: *What you've been reading and hearing all week is true; I'm not coming back.* Plenty of guys were confused. They felt he should want to share in what he had helped build.

The situation was particularly disorienting for younger players. Seated in the rear of the plane, rookie linebacker Tedy Bruschi was quietly reflecting on the season and all that had transpired when he looked up and noticed Bill Belichick coming toward him. Belichick crouched down, looked Bruschi in the eye, and started talking about how well he had played throughout the season. Belichick also praised Bruschi for his two sacks on Brett Favre during the Super Bowl. Pretty impressive for a rookie, Belichick told him.

At first, Bruschi didn't know how to respond. He'd been on the team for a year and this was the first time that Belichick had said a word to him. When Bruschi had arrived in Foxborough for rookie mini-camp the previous spring, he attended his first meeting for the defensive players. They were looking at a film of a screen play in which a lumbering offensive lineman was able to get downfield and make a block on a speedy defensive back. Bruschi recalled: "I heard this voice chime in, 'I can't believe he let this fat expletive, expletive, expletive lineman cut him down in the open field.' I looked back and I see Bill standing there talking, animated. I thought to myself, 'Oh, that's the Cleveland guy.' My first impression of him was a profanity-laced coaching point on how to beat a fat offensive lineman in space on a screen pass if you're a defensive back or a linebacker."

But as Belichick remained crouched in a catcher's stance beside Bruschi on the team plane, he struck a much more encouraging tone.

"There are going to be good things in the future," Belichick reassured Bruschi.

"Okay, coach," Bruschi said. "I appreciate that."

Belichick then moved down the aisle and had a similar conversation with rookie Lawyer Milloy. Then he crouched down beside second-year player Ty Law. One by one, he was trying to lift up the players, who had just suffered a heartbreaking defeat and the loss of a revered coach in the same day.

"I guess he's our next head coach," Bruschi thought.

twelve

NEW ENGLAND VERSUS NEW YORK

T wo days after the Super Bowl, Commissioner Paul Tagliabue convened a hearing to determine whether Parcells had the right to terminate his employment contract with the Patriots and seek employment with another NFL team for the upcoming 1997 season. Both Kraft and Parcells testified, and the hearing was contentious throughout. Twenty-four hours later, Tagliabue issued a seven-page letter outlining his decision.

"If Mr. Parcells elects to coach in the NFL in 1997, he must do so for the Patriots if the Club so desires," Tagliabue wrote. "In the alternative, he may refrain from coaching in the NFL or take another, non-comparable position for the 1997 season."

The ruling was a clear victory for Kraft. The contract amendment that Parcells had signed was deemed binding.

Hours after the decision, Parcells huddled with his lawyer, Joel Kozol, in the attorney's Boston office. Parcells felt trapped. He'd have to either sit out or coach one more year in New England, which would require Kraft's consent.

Kozol tried to talk him into calling Kraft's bluff by telling him that he wanted to fulfill his contract and continue coaching in New England. That would force Kraft to either live with Parcells for another year or fire him. But Parcells wanted no part of that. Nor did he want to go to court to challenge the commissioner's decision. What he wanted was to coach a different team. His only option, it seemed, was to sit out a year and bide his time.

Kozol suggested there might be a third option.

Parcells didn't follow.

Kozol reread Tagliabue's decision and homed in on the words *non-comparable position*. Tagliabue had opened the door for Parcells to take a position that wasn't comparable to coaching for the 1997 season.

Kozol told Parcells he could be a consultant.

They telephoned Robert Fraley, Parcells's longtime agent. Fraley agreed with Kozol's interpretation. There was nothing stopping Parcells from going to work for another team right away as a consultant.

Suddenly, Parcells was encouraged. A plan was coming together.

The Patriots brass had long suspected that Parcells and the Jets were communicating through back channels prior to the Super Bowl. Team officials said an internal audit of in-room service charges billed to the Patriots by the New Orleans Marriott during the week of the Super Bowl revealed a series of calls placed from Parcells's room to a number in Hempstead, Long Island, the town where the Jets were headquartered. But Parcells denied this, saying the notion that he had called the Jets from his hotel room was "total horseshit." He added, "If I talked to the Jets, do you think I'm stupid enough to talk on Patriots phones?"

Nonetheless, within hours of Tagliabue's ruling, the Jets organization contacted the Patriots to gauge their interest in discussing a trade for Parcells. The Patriots were noncommittal. Later that day, after praising Tagliabue's decision, Kraft talked to the media. He used the opportunity to send a message to the Jets. "I'm speaking now to the Jets," he said. "If you have an interest in Bill, please don't trade the number one pick. That must be part of the solution." The Jets were sitting on the first overall pick in the draft.

Jets owner Leon Hess didn't appreciate Kraft's tactics. A day after Kraft talked to the press, the Jets notified the Patriots that Hess wasn't about to give up a first-round pick for Parcells.

When facing big decisions, Robert Kraft lived by a rule: *Measure nine times and cut once.* It stemmed from a Russian proverb that referred to carpenters taking preparations to prevent errors. Kraft had ignored his rule on only three occasions: accepting Myra's marriage proposal, making the deal for the mill in Newfoundland that gave rise to his first company, and agreeing to put up more than anyone had ever paid for an American sports franchise to acquire the Patriots. He had no intention of putting the selection of the Patriots' next head coach to that short list of exceptions.

For months, Kraft had been considering names, and in his mind, one was head and shoulders above the rest—Bill Belichick. Kraft had had the advantage of observing him up close for an entire year, and Belichick was the greatest teacher and motivator Kraft had ever seen. He also had a sophisticated

approach to the challenges presented by the salary cap. Most important, Kraft knew that Belichick was looking for a long-term home.

But Belichick had one giant strike against him—he was one of Parcells's longtime assistants, which made him guilty by association. Kraft was convinced that Belichick would be a great head coach and he felt he was the right guy for the Patriots. But he didn't trust anyone with ties to Parcells. Jonathan Kraft felt the same way. He liked Belichick, but the organization needed to rid itself of anyone connected to Parcells.

The number two name on Kraft's list was Pete Carroll, the defensive coordinator for the San Francisco 49ers. Kraft decided to call 49ers team president Carmen Policy to discuss his dilemma.

Policy was one of the few people in the league who understood and appreciated what Kraft was going through with Parcells. Policy's biggest achievement was deftly managing the famously complicated and combustible relationship between 49ers owner Eddie DeBartolo and 49ers head coach Bill Walsh.

Kraft began the call by telling Policy that he was thinking of hiring Carroll. He asked Policy for his candid assessment.

"He's not of the Walsh-Seifert mold," Policy told Kraft. "He'll be more contemporary in terms of his approach to coaching. But he's pretty smart. Very savvy." Policy had nothing but good things to say. One of Carroll's best attributes, he said, was the way he got along with personnel. "The younger players are going to like his style," Policy said.

The bottom line, Policy told him, was that Carroll would make a fine head coach.

"Thank you, Carmen. Now I need to ask you something else."

"Shoot."

"If you were in my shoes, would you hire Bill Belichick?"

Policy hesitated. Right after Kraft had bought the Patriots, he and Jonathan had flown to San Francisco and spent a day with Policy at the 49ers team headquarters. Kraft had told Policy at the time that he viewed the 49ers as the gold standard of the NFL and he wanted to learn as much as Policy would share about how they had built their dynasty. Policy had been forthcoming that day. He knew how much Kraft trusted his judgment, so he wanted to be honest. But he also wanted to be measured.

"I would not," Policy finally said.

"Why?" Kraft asked.

"You're coming off this situation with Parcells," Policy said. "I don't know that you can take a risk like hiring Belichick."

Two days after Paul Tagliabue issued his decision, Bill Parcells handed Robert Kraft his resignation letter and called a press conference at Foxboro Stadium. A throng of national writers and correspondents from *Sports Illustrated*, the *New York Times*, ESPN, and CNN jammed into a press room with dozens of journalists from Boston and New York. After reading from the letter he had given to Kraft, Parcells got peppered with questions about why he was leaving. He went back and forth with reporters for fifteen minutes. Finally, Parcells insisted: "It's not about power. It's really not."

Looking on from the back of the room, Kraft thought to himself: "It's all about power. Power and trust."

"Look," Parcells continued, "it's just . . . it's just . . . A friend of mine told me something. I'm gonna quote and I'm not tryin' to be cute here. I'm just gonna say it. 'They want you to cook the dinner. At least they ought to let you shop for some of the groceries.'"

It was a direct parting shot at both Robert and Jonathan.

Kraft seethed. For three years, he had let Parcells spend tens of millions of dollars on free agents who hadn't panned out. For three years he'd gone deeper and deeper into debt while supporting Parcells's efforts to build a winning team. During that time in only two instances out of more than one hundred had Kraft told Parcells no. One was when Parcells wanted to draft a lineman over Terry Glenn, who had turned out to be essential to getting the team to the Super Bowl. The other was Christian Peter.

Kraft had heard enough, and there was no way he was going to let Parcells get the last word. As Parcells stepped off stage, Kraft walked up and sat in the chair that Parcells had just vacated. In a conciliatory tone, Kraft updated the press on where things stood and assured them that he was in the process of forming a list of coaching candidates.

The press wanted to talk about Parcells. "Bill said if they want you to cook the dinner, at least they ought to let you shop for some of the groceries," a reporter said.

Kraft grinned.

"Do you acknowledge," the reporter went on, "that there was a fundamental lack of getting together on the same page as far as who would be making decisions regarding personnel?"

"Well, first of all, if you look at Bill and I, we don't lack for adequate groceries."

The reporters cracked up.

"And I think our groceries are pretty good," Kraft said. "They're fresh."

More laughter.

"But apparently you do the shopping," a reporter said.

"I don't do any shopping," Kraft said. "We have an organization that shops. One other part of the organization is to make sure we're paying the right price for the groceries. Because we're on a limited budget. We have a cap."

Before stepping down, Kraft again used the opportunity to talk directly to the Jets. "Guys," he said, "if you want Bill as your coach in '97, make sure your first-round draft choice is there in its current position."

Bill Belichick's future was up in the air. Throughout the 1996 season, he had cultivated a good relationship with Kraft. Immediately after Belichick had arrived in Foxborough he had talked with Kraft about free agency and discussed what to do with specific players. By training camp, they were talking about player contracts. And as the year went on, their conversations extended to organizational structure and the management of the team. It was clear that Kraft valued his knowledge and respected his judgment. But would Kraft hire him?

As soon as Parcells and Kraft finished their press conferences, Belichick met with Kraft in his office. Then the two men left in Kraft's car. That evening they joined their wives at the Capital Grille in Chestnut Hill, right around the corner from Kraft's home. It was Kraft's restaurant of choice when celebrating momentous occasions with friends. But this dinner wasn't Kraft's idea. It was Debby Belichick's. She really wanted her husband to get the Patriots job.

The life of a coach's wife is one of uncertainty. Being uprooted often and on sudden notice is the norm. Bill had coached in Baltimore, Detroit, Denver, New York, and Cleveland before landing in New England. After just one season, she could see that the organization and the atmosphere in Foxborough were different: the Krafts' leadership provided a sense of stability and direction. Myra had befriended her. There was an unusual sense of belonging. And New England was an ideal setting to put down roots and raise children. Bill wanted the same thing—a stable place that his family could always call home.

When what you've longed for is finally in reach, the prospect of its slipping away creates an anxious sense of foreboding. Kraft knew the feeling, and he cared a great deal for Debby. But he had measured nine times. It was time to cut.

"I feel a tremendous affection for you both," he told the Belichicks over dinner. "But in life, the timing has to be right."

Belichick knew what that meant—he wasn't going to be the next head coach in New England. No point in trying to change Robert's mind.

Debby, however, remained convinced that her husband was the best man for the job. She went to bat for him, highlighting his experience and qualifications, and making the case for why he would be a good fit for the Patriots.

Kraft agreed with everything she said, and he told her as much.

"But I think it's better we each go our own ways," Kraft told them.

It was a hard sentence for Debby to hear. But Bill didn't push back. He understood the situation. After dinner, he shook Kraft's hand and thanked him for everything.

That night, Kraft couldn't sleep.

The next morning, the Jets telephoned Belichick and asked him if he'd like to be their head coach for one year until Parcells could assume the role. Belichick packed his bags and headed for New York.

On February 3, 1997, Robert Kraft introduced forty-five-year-old Pete Carroll as the team's new head coach at a press conference. In a preview of things to come, the New England sportswriters did not respond kindly. And the criticism had little to do with Pete Carroll. Bill Parcells had been popular among the Patriots beat writers. Some of them blamed Kraft for driving out the best coach in the history of the franchise. And they took the opportunity to unload on Kraft, a hands-on owner who had tried to build a rapport with fans by doing things like tailgating with them on game days.

"For better or worse, it's Kraft's show now," *Providence Journal* writer Bill Reynolds wrote. "Kraft has been drawn to the camera like a moth to the light. . . . Maybe all you have to know is that he's become infamous for driving through the stadium parking lots on game days in a golf cart shaking hands, as if some benevolent despot bestowing favors on the huddled masses. Please."

"Why doesn't Bob Kraft just get it over with and name himself coach of the Patriots?" wrote *Boston Globe* columnist Dan Shaughnessy. "Kraft signed Carroll to a five-year contract and Carroll gave every indication that he'll be able to do what Bill Parcells never could do: bow at the feet of an owner who is rapidly spinning out of control."

On the same day that the papers in New England were ripping Kraft, the New York Jets held a press conference of their own, announcing that Bill Belichick would be the team's new head coach for one season, and that Bill Parcells would join the organization as a "consultant." After one season, the

Jets said, Belichick would slide back into an assistant role and Parcells would become the head coach.

Commissioner Paul Tagliabue was in Los Angeles when he read the Jets' press release. "That's ridiculous!" he told a colleague. "You can't sign a coach to be a consultant." He called league headquarters in New York and instructed his staff to get a message to the Jets right away. "Tell them to forget about it," he said.

Hours later, the league issued an official statement: "The Jets are neither denied nor given permission to make a consulting agreement with Parcells for 1997. If asked to review the agreement between the Jets and Parcells as it may affect the Patriots' contract rights for 1997, the Commissioner will review the matter, including holding a hearing if necessary."

Jets team president Steve Gutman was furious. So was Parcells's lawyer, Joel Kozol. They had talked to people in the league office and felt they had obtained tacit consent for their approach. But the commissioner said he hadn't been part of those discussions.

On the heels of the league statement, the Patriots issued their own, publicly calling on the commissioner to review the Jets' agreement with Parcells and to determine if it violated his agreement with the Patriots.

For Kraft, it was a fight worth waging. Parcells had built the Patriots' roster. He knew everything about the team. Its strengths. Its weaknesses. Its playbook. Now he'd be taking Belichick to New York and essentially pulling all of the levers as a "consultant." That put New England at a distinct competitive disadvantage. The Jets were a division rival that the Patriots had to face twice each season. The commissioner, Kraft felt, had an obligation to level the playing field.

The Boston sports media continued to pound Kraft. As soon as he challenged Parcells's becoming a consultant for the Jets, Kraft was compared by *Globe* columnist Bob Ryan to "a kid in need of some Ritalin." Ryan wanted Kraft to put up or shut up. "Stop babbling about some perceived 'competitive disadvantage' with a Parcells-coached Jets team and get a player, a draft pick, or whatever, for his departed coach," he wrote.

His colleague Dan Shaughnessy was even more critical. "Kraft goes down in history as the man who drove Bill Parcells out of town," he wrote. "Let's see how the Patriots do now that Kraft is back in control of the football operation, and has rid himself of the Tuna."

The same week that the Jets announced they were hiring Belichick and

Parcells, a group of Boston's most powerful politicians attacked Kraft's plan to build a sixty-nine-thousand-seat open-air stadium in South Boston. Rekindling some of the animosity from Kraft's previous push to get a new stadium built in Boston, Speaker of the House Tom Finneran and Boston mayor Tom Menino both publicly criticized Kraft and his idea. And residents in South Boston actively rallied against Kraft's plan. The opposition culminated in protests, one of which took place at the Polish American Citizens Club. The next day, the *Boston Globe* quoted a response from Kraft: "The people in the Polish Hall don't know the facts. It's like South Boston. They're uneducated."

As soon as the article appeared, Don Lowery called the *Globe* to complain that Kraft had been quoted out of context; Kraft's full statement had been "They're uneducated about the stadium and the economic benefits it will bring to the area." By cutting the quote short, Lowery argued, the paper had altered its meaning.

The damage was already done. The South Boston community was in an uproar. "I have received two hundred calls today from people who are outraged at the arrogance of Bob Kraft," City Council president James M. Kelly, who represented South Boston, told the *Globe*. "We may not be quite as educated as Bob Kraft, but we have more class and character."

State senator Stephen F. Lynch, a South Boston Democrat who opposed Kraft's stadium plan, also jumped in. "He has never impressed me with his public relations skills," Lynch told the press. "This is not slick PR. This is common courtesy. You don't have to criticize or look down upon the people you are working with."

The Patriots had a brand-new head coach, but Pete Carroll's arrival was completely overshadowed by the feud between the Patriots and the Jets over Parcells and by the controversy over whether to build a new stadium in South Boston.

Days after the Patriots challenged the Jets' decision to hire Parcells as a consultant, Commissioner Tagliabue scheduled a hearing. Kraft stepped into a conference room in the midtown Manhattan law offices of Skadden Arps. He was accompanied by Andy Wasynczuk. The two of them took a seat opposite Jets owner Leon Hess and team president Steve Gutman. A court reporter was on hand to create an official transcript of the proceedings. The Patriots and Jets had talked beforehand about a possible trade to resolve the matter.

But Kraft reiterated that he would let Parcells go only if the Jets gave up their first-round draft choice, and Hess had balked at that. Commissioner Tagliabue reminded both sides that the purpose of the hearing was to remedy the ongoing dispute between the two franchises. The commissioner planned to act as a facilitator. But if push came to shove, he would intervene and make a ruling that both sides would be forced to live with.

Fifty-six-year-old Kraft and eighty-two-year-old Hess were a contrast in styles.

At the outset, Hess attempted to set the tone. "I've faced far more threatening circumstances in my negotiations than fearing that the commissioner will come in and rule against me," Hess told Kraft. As the CEO of a petroleum company that was one of the largest producers of crude oil in the United States, Hess had decades of experience dealing with oil suppliers in the Middle East. He let Kraft know that his Arab counterparts would often start negotiations off by placing a loaded gun on the table.

Kraft smiled. He had also done a lot of business in the Middle East and was used to dealing with formidable adversaries. When the Ayatollah Khomeini took power in the Iranian Revolution in 1979 and seized control of Kraft's manufacturing plant there, Kraft went to The Hague to take on the Iranian leader in international court to protect his business interests. But he made no mention of his experiences to Hess.

Instead, he introduced Wasynczuk, who outlined the Patriots' position. There was no precedent to establish the trade value of a head coach, but under the collective bargaining agreement negotiated by the players' union and NFL owners, when Team A took Team B's designated franchise player in a trade, Team B was entitled to Team A's first-round draft choice for two years. "Parcells," Wasynczuk argued, "is way more valuable than a franchise player."

"That's just crazy," Gutman said.

It went downhill from there. Two hours later, Tagliabue determined they were getting nowhere.

"Everyone can go to lunch except for me and Mr. Hess and Mr. Kraft," Tagliabue said. "We'll stay here in the conference room. I'm going to get us some sandwiches. And we'll have a conversation. Just the three of us."

Tagliabue excused the court reporter as well. This was going to be an off-the-record discussion.

"Look, if the two of you can agree on how to get this resolved, fine, we can forgo further testimony and it'll be done," Tagliabue told them. "If you

can't agree, I think the way for us to proceed is for the two of you to put down on paper what would be satisfactory to you. If the two pieces of paper don't cross, I'll go back to my office and split the difference."

Kraft and Hess agreed to Tagliabue's approach.

But they didn't agree on anything else. As soon as Tagliabue gave them the floor, they started arguing over Parcells.

"You knew what you were agreeing to," Hess insisted. "You knew he could leave. And the only reason you're blocking him is because we're in your division."

"I told him he could leave, but he couldn't take another job for a year," Kraft countered. "Now we're letting him take another job. So I deserve to get something after going through this traumatic and unsatisfying era."

"We're taking a problem off your hands," Hess said. "*You* should be paying *us*."

Kraft protested.

"It couldn't have been that bad," Hess snapped. "You got to the goddam Super Bowl! I can take chest pains like that myself."

Tagliabue had heard enough. It was clear that Kraft and Hess weren't going to find common ground. He told them to each put down their terms in writing and he'd make his decision.

Kraft wrote that he wanted the Jets' first-round draft choice in the upcoming April draft. But as it was his tendency to always look for other ways to find value in a deal, he also asked for the Jets to make a $500,000 donation to a Patriots charity. He figured that if the commissioner didn't give him everything he wanted on the draft choice, he'd be more inclined to placate him by throwing in the charitable contribution.

Hess held firm on no first-round draft choices under any circumstances. He proposed a package of late-round picks.

Less than an hour later, Tagliabue rendered his decision: The Jets could hire Parcells as a head coach for the 1997 season. In return, the Patriots would receive the Jets' third- and fourth-round draft picks in '97, the Jets' second-round pick in '98, and the Jets' first-round pick in '99. The Jets also had to pay $300,000 to a Patriots charity.

Neither Kraft nor Hess was pleased. Tagliabue interpreted this to mean he had found the middle ground. Former president George H. W. Bush, who had been keeping an eye on the dispute, was so impressed with the outcome that he sent a handwritten letter to his nephew, Joe Ellis, who worked in the commissioner's office. "I was proud of Tagliabue working out the Parcells deal," Bush wrote. "I wish baseball had an effective Commissioner like 'Tag.'"

The following day, Bill Belichick's tenure as head coach of the Jets came to an end after just six days. With Leon Hess making a rare public appearance, the Jets held a press conference to announce that Bill Parcells had signed a six-year, $14.4 million contract to be the team's new head coach. Parcells was all smiles.

"I just want to be the little boy that goes along with him and pushes the cart in the supermarket and lets him fill it up," Hess said. "He's going to run the show, and it's not going to be two or three cooks in the kitchen. It will just be him."

It was another shot at Kraft.

The rivalry between the New England Patriots and the New York Jets was officially on.

thirteen

YOU KNOW ME

The Denver Broncos were in town to play a preseason game against the Patriots, but on the eve of the exhibition contest Robert Kraft and Broncos owner Pat Bowlen had other places to be. On a hot, sunny afternoon in August 1997, a helicopter dispatched by NBC's parent company, General Electric, touched down next to Kraft's summer home on Cape Cod and he climbed aboard. A second helicopter picked up Bowlen in Boston. This was no vacation retreat. Kraft and Bowlen had been invited to have dinner at the Martha's Vineyard home of NBC Sports president Dick Ebersol.

Commissioner Paul Tagliabue had recently appointed Kraft to the NFL Broadcast Committee, which Bowlen chaired. The third member was Jerry Jones. The committee was responsible for negotiating the league's television contracts with its network partners—the largest source of revenue to the league and its teams. And at the end of the upcoming season, the contracts with NBC, Fox, and ABC were up for renewal. Although that was still five months away, the networks were already jockeying for position.

Recently named the most powerful person in sports by the *Sporting News*, Ebersol was NBC's point person in the forthcoming negotiations with the NFL. Since taking over at NBC, Ebersol had systematically acquired the broadcast rights to NBA games, Notre Dame football, Major League Baseball, and both the Winter and Summer Olympics. But the crown jewel in the NBC Sports portfolio was its contract with the NFL to broadcast AFC games on Sundays. And New England and Denver were two of the most important markets in the AFC package. Determined to remain in business with both owners, Ebersol graciously welcomed Kraft and Bowlen to his place overlooking Edgartown Harbor. Moments later, a third helicopter carrying GE's CEO, Jack Welch, and NBC's CEO, Robert Wright, arrived. Over dinner, Kraft and Bowlen regaled their hosts with stories about their two teams, and Welch dispensed pearls of wisdom about economics.

While the top brass at NBC wined and dined Kraft and Bowlen, the network executives at CBS were angling to get in on the action. For decades, CBS had held the broadcast rights to all of the NFL's NFC games televised on Sundays. But in 1993, Rupert Murdoch's upstart Fox network shocked the television industry when it outbid CBS by $100 million for the coveted NFC package, which included teams in the five largest television markets in the United States. The shakeup brought an end to CBS's forty-year relationship with the NFL, and for CBS, the consequences were immediate. Viewership on Sunday afternoons fell off a cliff. As a result, CBS lost its most effective platform—the commercial spots during football games—for advertising and promoting its prime-time lineup of sitcoms and dramas. Before long, the CBS network went from number one to last place.

When Sean McManus was named president of CBS Sports at the end of 1996, his job description didn't include figuring out how to bring the NFL back to the network. Not a day went by, however, that McManus didn't think about that prospect. Yet it seemed like a pipe dream—until a media mogul named Mel Karmazin sold his radio empire, Infinity Broadcasting, to Westinghouse for $3.8 billion. Westinghouse was CBS's parent company. It was an all-stock transaction, and it made Karmazin Westinghouse's largest individual shareholder. With CBS doing so poorly, Karmazin was named president and CEO of the network, in hopes of turning it around.

One of Karmazin's top priorities was to help Les Moonves, the recently hired president of CBS Entertainment, revamp the prime-time lineup with new shows. Karmazin's other priority was to get back in business with the NFL. "The problem was nobody was watching CBS," Karmazin explained. "So it was very difficult to launch TV shows. If you're now going to blow up your lineup because the lineup's not working, how do you tell people that you have these new shows? One of the biggest ways of doing it was with the NFL."

Karmazin and McManus agreed that it made no sense for CBS to make a play for the NFC package that it had lost to Fox. No one was going to be able to outbid Rupert Murdoch. Nor was CBS interested in the prime-time *Monday Night Football* package held by ABC. The obvious choice was to target NBC's AFC package. The problem was that NBC had seen how losing the NFC package back in 1992 had devastated CBS. It seemed unthinkable that NBC would make the same mistake.

To put CBS in the best possible position, Karmazin was prepared to authorize McManus to make an exorbitant bid on behalf of the network.

But Karmazin suspected that there were people at NFL headquarters who wanted the AFC package to stay at NBC. He wanted to make sure the league wouldn't simply use CBS's bid to leverage more money out of NBC. So Karmazin wanted to open back-channel communications with the team owners in hopes of protecting the integrity of the process.

Karmazin knew many of the owners on a first-name basis, but there was none that he trusted more than Kraft. Three years earlier, the two men had bonded during a negotiation that put the Patriots on one of Karmazin's radio stations, and since then they had become close friends—so close that they started spending time at each other's homes and going out together with their wives. It helped that Kraft and Karmazin had so much in common, starting with the fact that they were both self-made millionaires who had worked their way out of blue-collar Jewish neighborhoods and climbed to the top of corporate America. Since they became friends, Kraft had also introduced Karmazin to other NFL owners, a number of whom had gone on to make radio deals with Infinity Broadcasting. None of those deals directly benefited Kraft, but his role in facilitating the transactions had further demonstrated to Karmazin that Kraft was an honest broker.

Kraft was pleased to get the call from Karmazin. He was also encouraged to hear that there had been a sea change within CBS in terms of what the network was prepared to pay to get the NFL back on its network.

"You know me," Karmazin told him. "This is very important for CBS. We have a history. We're not new. We're CBS."

Kraft did indeed know him. He considered Karmazin one of the smartest, most trustworthy people he'd ever done business with. Kraft also appreciated CBS's long relationship with the league. "How can I be helpful?" Kraft asked.

"I'd like to have a shot at getting back in," Karmazin told him. "But I don't want to be a stalking horse."

Kraft understood.

Not long after the call, Karmazin brought Sean McManus to Foxborough to introduce him to Kraft as the executive who would be taking the point position for CBS in the negotiations. McManus used the opportunity to plant the seed that it would be beneficial to the NFL to have CBS back as a partner. Kraft asked a lot of probing questions.

"His job was to get the best deal that he could for the NFL from the various networks," McManus said. "He wasn't there to do an inside deal or give us an unfair advantage. He was there to say to us, 'If you guys can get to this level monetarily and in nonmonetary terms, we think you have

a shot of getting the NFL.' He was aboveboard, honest, and transparent. There was no BS."

Pete Carroll and his staff had dubbed Bill Parcells and the New York Jets the Evil Empire. The feud between Kraft and Parcells had turned the rivalry between the Patriots and the Jets into the most emotionally charged one in the league. When the two teams met in New England in the third week of the 1997 season, it marked the first time in NFL history that a coach who had just led a team to a Super Bowl was coaching against that same team the following season. Hyped as the "Tuna Bowl," the contest was one of the most anticipated regular season NFL games of all time. Roughly five hundred media credentials were issued, quadrupling the normal allotment. More than two hundred extra police officers were brought in to provide security for the game. And the NFL featured the game in the Sunday night prime-time slot, giving it maximum national exposure.

Parcells seemed to relish being cast in the role of Darth Vader as he led his team into Foxboro Stadium amid a chorus of boos and expletives. The stands were filled with signs—on bedsheets, on poster board, on fans' bare bellies:

TUNA SUCKS
BILL PAR SELL OUT
CAN THE TUNA
BAD TUNA TURNS GREEN

Both teams fed off the energy. For a lot of the Patriots players, competing against their former coach was personal. Drew Bledsoe wanted to throttle the Jets. No one, however, was more determined to send a message to Parcells than running back Curtis Martin. Every time he was tackled near the Jets' sideline, Martin looked at Parcells with a death glare.

The game lived up to the hype. There were in-your-face jawing, unsportsmanlike-conduct penalties, jarring hits, three ties, and multiple lead changes. It took an overtime field goal by Patriots kicker Adam Vinatieri to give New England the victory. Running back Curtis Martin, who had racked up what was then a career-high 199 yards on forty carries, was named Player of the Game. Afterward, he tracked down Parcells on the field.

"I love you," Martin told him.

His lips quivering, Parcells said, "I love you, too, Boy Wonder."

Paul Tagliabue had met Mel Karmazin on an occasion or two, but they weren't close. At Kraft's suggestion, Tagliabue agreed to meet with the new president of CBS, to hear what he had to say. It was in the best interest of the NFL, Kraft assured him. Tagliabue said he'd follow Kraft's lead in the meeting.

A strategy was coming together at CBS. There was talk within the industry that Disney, ABC's parent company, wasn't going to step up to hold on to *Monday Night Football*. As a result, NBC was supposedly eyeing that opportunity. CBS believed that this created an opening to acquire the AFC package.

When Karmazin showed up for the meeting with Tagliabue and Kraft, he cut to the chase. "I want your word that I'm going to have a legitimate shot," he told them. "Because if I have a legitimate shot, not only will I have an influence on the package that I'm bidding on, I assure you that I will be so bizarre in what I'm going to pay that the other packages are going to go up in value."

"Well, what is that?" Kraft asked.

"We're basically prepared to pay you $500 million a year," Karmazin said.

There was a long pause. Tagliabue was stunned. He did the quick math in his head. NBC was currently paying $217 million per year. Karmazin was talking about a 130 percent annual increase. The potential financial ramifications for the league and all thirty-one teams were staggering. If CBS paid $500 million for the AFC package, Fox would undoubtedly have to exceed that amount for the NFC package. The league would have $1 billion per year just for the Sunday packages.

Kraft said little. He'd been talking with Karmazin for some time and had been encouraging him to come in strong. He wasn't surprised by Karmazin's figure.

The important thing to Karmazin was timing. He wanted the NFL to put the AFC package out to bid first. NBC held a right of first refusal, which meant it could keep the package if it matched CBS's offer. But Karmazin hoped the richness of CBS's offer would discourage NBC from matching and drive it toward the ABC *Monday Night Football* package instead.

From Kraft's perspective, the NFL had nothing to lose by putting the AFC package out for bid first. In fact, it would be to the league's advantage.

Tagliabue agreed.

After starting out 5-1 under Pete Carroll, New England finished the 1997 season 10-6, making the playoffs. But after knocking off Miami in the wild-card

round, New England fell to Pittsburgh 7–6 in the divisional round on January 3, 1998. Extremely disappointed, Kraft turned his attention to the negotiations between the NFL and the networks. He headed to his New York City apartment to prepare.

For Kraft, it was a moment of introspection. He had grown up in a home where his father never watched television. Yet Kraft was now at the head of the table in discussions with the leaders of the television industry: Rupert Murdoch, Michael Eisner, Bob Iger, Dick Ebersol, Sean McManus, and Mel Karmazin. Billions of dollars were at stake. And Paul Tagliabue believed that the most qualified person to steer the NFL and its thirty-one teams through the high-stakes process was Kraft.

On Friday evening, January 9, 1998, Kraft telephoned Sean McManus and asked him to fax over CBS's bid for the AFC package.

Sitting at his desk, McManus slid a piece of letterhead in his typewriter. The basic terms were $500 million per year for eight years. Moments later, he stood at the fax machine and punched in Kraft's number. Right after he hit the send button, the fax machine spat out a fax from a nearby pizza restaurant that McManus frequently ordered from.

Panicked, he looked at his colleague. "Do you think we just faxed our offer to the pizza shop?" McManus said. He quickly reached for the phone and called Kraft.

"I got it," Kraft told him. "We'll call you if NBC matches."

NBC had until noon on Monday. McManus spent the weekend at his home in Connecticut. Every time the phone rang, he jumped. The situation became unbearable on Sunday during NBC's broadcast of the AFC Championship. His closest colleague at CBS Sports telephoned him four times during the game. Finally, McManus told him, "Stop calling me! Every time the phone rings I have a heart attack."

But the call McManus feared never came. Instead, on Monday, shortly after noon, Tagliabue telephoned and invited McManus back to NFL headquarters to finalize the contract. NBC had decided not to match CBS's offer.

Pinching himself, McManus immediately headed across town. On his way to Park Avenue, he stopped by St. Patrick's Cathedral on Fifth Avenue. McManus, a practicing Catholic, figured it wouldn't hurt to thank the Lord and ask for His guidance through the final step.

His prayer was answered. Twenty-four hours later, a representative from the league office showed up at CBS headquarters with a fully executed contract. "Congratulations," he told McManus. "You've got a deal."

Moments later, McManus sat at his desk listening to the excitement in

the office. People on his floor screamed at the top of their lungs: "We got the NFL back!"

"It was so life-changing, not only for CBS Sports, but for the CBS Television Network," McManus said. "It's hard to overestimate just how important it was to the division."

McManus called Kraft to thank him personally.

Kraft appreciated the gesture and told McManus that he was looking forward to a long partnership between the NFL and CBS.

"I love you, Robert," McManus said.

"I love you also," Kraft told him.

The next morning, under the headline "CBS Guarantees Billions to Get N.F.L. Back," the *New York Times* reported that pro football had just inked "by far the richest sports television contract ever." Thanks to CBS's astronomical bid for the AFC, Fox paid even more—$550 million per year—for the NFC package. Combined with the prime-time package, the league was due to take in more than $15 billion over an eight-year span.

fourteen

DEAR JOHN

J ay Malcynsky was the most politically connected lobbyist in Connecticut. One of his clients was Governor John Rowland. In the spring of 1998, Governor Rowland was running for reelection, and Malcynsky was his senior advisor. Aware that the Kraft family owned a paper mill in Montville, Connecticut, Malcynsky contacted the Patriots and asked if the governor could tour the facility.

Jonathan Kraft facilitated the governor's visit and was on hand to welcome him. After Rowland met with workers and posed for a photo, he and Malcynsky met privately with Kraft. The conversation quickly turned to the team's failed attempts to construct a new stadium in Massachusetts.

"You've having a hard time up there," Rowland told Jonathan. "If I get reelected, would you guys be willing to think about building a stadium in Connecticut?"

"We're getting near our wits' end," Kraft told him. "At this point, my father would be willing to think about anything as long as it's in New England."

Indicating that Connecticut's door was open, Rowland extended an invitation for Robert to meet with him.

The last thing Robert Kraft wanted to do was contemplate moving the New England Patriots to Connecticut, but he felt compelled to explore the possibility. After years of political opposition to building a publicly financed stadium in Boston, the Patriots organization had been working closely with Massachusetts Senate president Thomas Birmingham on legislation that would result in a new privately financed stadium in Foxborough. Under the proposed bill, the Patriots would spend $225 million to construct a new facility on land adjacent to Foxboro Stadium. For its part, the state would appropriate $72 million to go toward transportation infrastructure

improvements on the state highway that abutted the stadium. The state senate voted 36–1 in favor of the plan. But the legislation was defeated in the House of Representatives. "We're not going to have taxpayers offer cash assistance just simply to retain a business here in Massachusetts," House Speaker Tom Finneran said.

So Kraft traveled to Hartford and met with Governor Rowland.

"Listen, I've exhausted my opportunities up in Boston," he told Rowland in a face-to-face conversation in the spring of 1998. "Quite frankly, I wouldn't be here but for that. I can't get anything done up there, so here I am. Let's talk."

Over the ensuing six months, Kraft and Rowland talked a lot. They met in Hartford. They met in Boston. They had dinners together. They even visited each other's homes. While the two of them were cultivating a relationship, officials from the governor's office and the Patriots' front office jointly studied the feasibility of constructing a new stadium for the Patriots in Hartford. By the time Governor Rowland was elected to a second term, on November 3, 1998, he and Kraft were close to formalizing a deal. Under the terms, the state of Connecticut would:

- Construct a $350 million, sixty-eight-thousand-seat, open-air stadium with six thousand club seats and 125 to 150 luxury boxes.
- Finance the construction with state bonds to be repaid with a 10 percent ticket tax.
- Lease the stadium to the Patriots for thirty years.
- Complete construction in time for the Patriots to play home games there starting in the fall of 2001.

The Patriots would:

- Finance a $50 million hotel adjacent to the new stadium.
- Move the team's training and practice facilities to Connecticut.
- Relocate the team's headquarters to Hartford.

The deal was contingent on approval by the Connecticut General Assembly. Rowland planned to convene a special legislative session in December in hopes of getting a bill passed before Christmas. The first step, however, was to formally announce and sign a memorandum of understanding between the Patriots and the state of Connecticut.

A few days before the scheduled announcement, Kraft telephoned Rowland's top political advisor, Jay Malcynsky. It was apparent that the key to the stadium deal was going to be getting it through the legislature. It was also clear that Malcynsky's lobbying firm, Gaffney Bennett, was the largest government-relations outfit in Connecticut. Kraft told Malcynsky he wanted to hire him to represent the Patriots during the legislative process.

Stunned, Malcynsky hesitated. He was flattered by the request, but he nonetheless wanted to first make sure this wouldn't be a conflict of interest. After all, he represented the governor.

The next day, Malcynsky spoke with Rowland, who was all for the idea. As far as he was concerned, the fact that Kraft wanted to hire the most influential lobbyist in the state was great news. It meant that Kraft was serious about getting the new stadium built in Hartford.

On November 17, 1998, Malcynsky registered with the State Ethics Commission as a lobbyist for Robert Kraft. That same day, news outlets in Boston reported that the announcement of a stadium deal in Hartford was imminent. The political ramifications of losing the Patriots to Connecticut finally started to sink in. Governor Paul Cellucci issued a warning aimed directly at House Speaker Tom Finneran. "It's going to fall squarely on the House. They have not supported what is needed."

Senate president Thomas Birmingham also sounded the alarm bell. "It's not my function to try to influence the legislature in the House," he said. "But this is not rocket science. And one way that people express their views about public policy issues is to call their elected officials. The ball is now clearly in the court of the House."

Finneran hit back hard. "I'm going to give tax [breaks] to some fat-assed millionaire and screw our kids?" he said.

Finneran's widely published personal shot at Kraft exasperated Senator Birmingham. The senator felt that it made sound economic sense to keep the Patriots in the state—they were a big employer and they paid a lot of taxes. Birmingham also felt that the Patriots were seeking modest allowances for infrastructure, which the state provided to businesses and other employers on a routine basis. Finneran, in Birmingham's view, was being intransigent.

To seal the deal in Connecticut, Governor Rowland agreed that the Patriots would not have to pay any rent for use of the stadium. And 90 percent of the tickets sales would go to the Patriots, along with all of the revenue from stadium concessions and parking. Rowland even agreed to buy back any luxury suites that went unsold and to pay the team whatever it lost on

local sponsorship deals due to playing in a smaller market. With all of these additional concessions, the deal assured that the Patriots would be the top revenue earner in the NFL.

Robert Kraft received a standing ovation when he entered the state capitol with Governor Rowland on November 19, 1998. Hundreds of lawmakers, legislative staffers, and capitol employees cheered and clapped and whistled as Kraft joined with the governor to announce and sign their historic agreement. Tears streamed down Jonathan Kraft's face as he watched his father. It had saddened him to hear the things that Finneran and others had said about his father. All the applause from the people of Connecticut was a refreshing change. Despite being happy for his father, Jonathan knew he didn't want to be there.

"This is a historic day for the Hartford community," Rowland told the gathering. "If we are successful . . . as we think we will be, the Patriots in the fall of 2001 will play their first home game here."

The banner headline on the front page of the *Hartford Courant* the following day read "TOUCHDOWN!" "The Patriots are coming," wrote the *Courant*'s political writer.

Kraft sent a letter to all season ticket holders, informing them of the relocation plan and assuring them that they would not have to pay extra fees to retain their seats in Hartford. He also published a full-page letter of apology in the *Boston Globe* and *Boston Herald*. "Make no mistake," it read. "This decision was not easy. . . . I love Massachusetts. It has been home to my family all our lives. I wanted nothing more than to keep the Patriots here. It was simply impossible to do so and fulfill my obligation to continue to put a championship caliber team on the field."

For Massachusetts officials, the Patriots' leaving the state was no longer hypothetical. You don't hire the top lobbyist in Connecticut, enter into an agreement with the governor, sign away your right to talk with any other states about a stadium deal, and send formal notices to season tickets holders unless you are actually planning to change your address.

It took less than a month for the Connecticut legislature to pass a bill authorizing the construction of a new stadium in Hartford. Shortly after the vote, on December 15, 1998, Governor Rowland addressed the media outside the state capitol. "It's official," he announced. "The New England Patriots are coming to Connecticut and they are coming to Hartford." The governor was going full steam ahead.

But a number of unforeseen challenges had cropped up. One was the discovery of coal tar—a toxic pollutant—buried deep in the soil on the site designated for the new stadium. The extra time needed to excavate the contaminated soil and remediate the site was estimated to delay the opening of the new stadium to the fall of 2002. Even more concerning was a breakdown in negotiations between the state and the owners of a giant steam plant currently in operation on the designated stadium site. The state was in a stalemate with the plant's operator, who wanted a lot more money to relocate than the governor was willing to pay.

Kraft knew from his experience as the owner of a global paper business that deals hit snags. Especially complex deals with government entities. To protect himself, he always insisted on having an exit clause, enabling him to walk away cleanly without having to go through a litigation process. In his agreement with Connecticut, Kraft had until May 1, 1999, to withdraw without penalty. Knowing he had that option, Kraft reluctantly agreed to the state's request to push back the stadium completion date by one year. But he told Rowland that he expected progress reports in the upcoming months. Rowland agreed.

At 6:15 on a cold Saturday morning in January 1999, Jonathan Kraft entered the Starbucks around the corner from his Brookline home. He wore sneakers, gray sweatpants, a gray sweatshirt, and a baseball cap. While ordering a coffee for his wife, he bumped into Senate president Tom Birmingham, who lived forty minutes away on the other side of Boston.

"Hey, Tom, what are you doing here?" Jonathan said.

It turned out that Birmingham's daughter attended a private school in the neighborhood. Birmingham had an hour to kill before picking her up for a family commitment.

"Well, good seeing you," Kraft said, ready to go on his way.

Birmingham asked if they could talk for a minute.

"About what?"

Birmingham nodded toward the door, and Kraft followed him outside.

Birmingham lit a cigarette and took a drag. "Look," he said, "if we did something, is there any chance?"

Kraft knew what he was getting at. "I can't talk to you about that," he said, looking Birmingham in the eye.

A skilled politician, Birmingham homed in on what Kraft didn't say—no. He interpreted that to mean yes, there might be a chance. He took another

drag on his cigarette. "Politically," he said, "I can't do anything unless I know the league is really going to get behind it."

"If you want to talk to somebody, the guy to call at the NFL is Roger Goodell."

"Ga-dell?"

"G-O-O-D-E-L-L. And by the way, we didn't have this conversation."

As Commissioner Tagliabue's top deputy, Roger Goodell had oversight of stadium construction throughout the league. He was also the league's point person anytime a team tried to relocate from one state to another. Personally, he wasn't keen on the idea of the Patriots' moving to Hartford. It was a great deal for the Patriots, one that would put them in position to become the richest franchise in the league. But it was a bad move for the league, and numerous NFL owners were voicing concerns to the commissioner. The owners of the New York Giants and New York Jets, in particular, didn't want the Patriots encroaching on their respective fan bases in Connecticut. More broadly, owners like Dan Rooney in Pittsburgh felt it was critical, especially in light of the NFL's new blockbuster television contract with CBS, that the AFC maintain a team in the Boston market. With 2.2 million television households, Boston was the sixth-largest market in the United States. Hartford, on the other hand, ranked twenty-seventh.

Goodell agreed with Rooney. But he was at a loss over what to do. Massachusetts had kicked the Patriots to the curb, and Connecticut had rolled out the red carpet. A deal had been signed. A law had been passed. Public money was being appropriated, and architectural designs of the new stadium were complete. The Patriots' move to Connecticut seemed like a fait accompli.

Then Goodell got an unexpected call from the 617 area code. After introducing himself, Senator Tom Birmingham explained that he had sponsored the bill in the state senate that would have enabled the Krafts to build a new stadium in Foxborough. Distraught over the situation in Connecticut, Birmingham told Goodell he was prepared to make a last-ditch effort to keep the Patriots in Massachusetts, and he believed the governor would go along.

"Is it worthless at this point?" Birmingham asked. "Is there any hope for us?"

Goodell tried not to sound ecstatic. "For sure," he told Birmingham. "But we need to know what you guys can do."

Encouraged, Birmingham promised to get back to him shortly.

After hanging up, Goodell talked to Tagliabue. "This is our obligation," Goodell said. "We need to do our due diligence and determine if there is really an opportunity in Massachusetts."

Tagliabue agreed. There was just one complicating factor: Kraft had signed an agreement with Connecticut that prevented him from talking to officials in Massachusetts.

"I could evaluate whether there is something in Massachusetts," Goodell said.

Tagliabue liked that approach. He promptly dispatched Goodell to Boston to carry out a stealth effort they dubbed Operation Team Back. Using an alias to avoid drawing attention to himself, Goodell checked into a hotel and linked up with a longtime Boston political insider whom the league hired to help him navigate the state capitol. At the same time, Steelers owner Dan Rooney put Goodell in touch with his influential Catholic friends in Boston's business community.

While the NFL put on a full-court press to resurrect stadium plans in Massachusetts, Governor Rowland was losing his patience in Connecticut. Despite signing into law a bill that authorized $374 million in state spending for a new stadium and training facility, he couldn't persuade the owner of a steam plant to relocate in order to make way for site cleanup and stadium construction. Furious, Rowland held a press conference at the state capitol and threatened to tear down the steam plant. "We're in worse shape now in negotiations than we were when we began," he said.

There were other problems too. A team of experts working for Kraft had been sifting through the latest progress reports provided by Connecticut officials. Buried in the details were more red flags: Due to delays, soil tests still had not been taken from the proposed site. Without that information, it was unclear how long it would take to complete the environmental cleanup. And the current design for the stadium called for part of it to be built over a highway, which might not be able to be completed with the funding allocated by the state legislature.

Kraft had already extended the initial completion deadline from 2001 to 2002. Now it was looking like it would be 2003, which, in his mind, was simply too far off. Nonetheless, on April 23, 1999, the Patriots filed their formal application with the league office to relocate to Hartford. But in the back of his mind, Kraft was feeling unsettled.

Kraft knew the NFL was engaged in talks with officials in Massachusetts, and the suspense was keeping him up at night. He wasn't used to being on the outside looking in.

A little before midnight on April 27, he was pacing in his living room when he got a phone call from Roger Goodell, who had just stepped out of a marathon negotiation with Senator Birmingham, House Speaker Finneran, and Governor Cellucci. They were offering to provide $70 million in infrastructure spending to improve the roadways and install sewer lines in Foxborough, all of which would be reimbursed over time by the Krafts. The cost to construct the stadium would rest entirely on Kraft. And the plan would still have to be ratified by the legislature. But Birmingham and Finneran were cautiously optimistic that they could get a bill through their respective chambers without significant amendments.

From Goodell's perspective, this was a breakthrough that was cause for celebration.

But for Kraft, the call was a big letdown. After three months of lobbying on the part of the league, Massachusetts had done little more than resurrect the same deal that Finneran had blocked a year earlier. Plus, they still had to get it through the legislature, where it was susceptible to being watered down and possibly even defeated. The bottom line was that their offer was worlds away from Connecticut's. If Kraft chose Massachusetts, he paid for everything and assumed all the risk. If he chose Connecticut, everything was paid for and the Patriots were guaranteed to be among the top three revenue-generating teams in the NFL for thirty years.

"It's the best we're going to be able to do," Goodell said.

Kraft was torn. Deep down, he wanted to keep his team in his home state. Massachusetts was finally coming around, but there was still a great deal of uncertainty on that front. Connecticut, on the other hand, had guaranteed a much more lucrative deal, but the delivery date was in question. Kraft was also feeling pressure to do what was in the best interest of the league. And the clock was ticking. The deadline for pulling out of the Hartford plan without forfeiting $100 million was four days away.

Kraft was scheduled to meet with Governor Rowland in Hartford at 4:00 p.m. on April 29. Early that morning Kraft telephoned his lobbyist Jay Malcynsky and summoned him to Boston. When Malcynsky arrived, Kraft told him that he wanted Rowland to extend the penalty-free withdrawal deadline

by sixty days. That would give state officials more time to figure out whether they could meet the agreed-upon completion date for the stadium.

Malcynsky didn't think Rowland would go for that, especially given what was going on in Massachusetts.

Kraft wondered aloud whether there was any point in going to Hartford to meet with the governor if he was unwilling to negotiate on a deadline extension.

Malcynsky advised him to keep the face-to-face appointment and use it as an opportunity to share his reservations with the governor.

Publicly, Governor Rowland had been downplaying all of the efforts on the part of the NFL to work out a stadium deal in Massachusetts. Privately, however, he was seething. He'd gone as far as to telephone Commissioner Tagliabue and threaten legal action.

Already on edge, Rowland was in a foul mood when he and his lawyer, Brendan Fox, sat down at a conference table with Robert and Jonathan Kraft and Jay Malcynsky. Kraft spoke first, outlining his concerns that the state wouldn't be able to complete the stadium in time for the 2002 season.

"As the governor of the state of Connecticut," Rowland told him, "I commit to you that I will get this done."

Kraft wasn't persuaded.

"I'll get it done, Robert," Rowland repeated. "I guarantee it. I'll give you my left nut."

Instead of a verbal guarantee, Kraft asked Rowland for a sixty-day extension to make up his mind on whether he wanted to go forward.

Rowland didn't like that idea. Politically, he thought an extension would create the wrong impression. It would signal that the deal was in trouble. "I can't do that," he told Kraft.

Kraft countered by asking for a thirty-day extension.

"Look, I'm hanging out here politically," Rowland said. "I cannot delay or give you guys any more assurances about timing."

Kraft wasn't pleased.

"We've stepped up," Rowland said. "Now is the time. You're either with us or against us."

"You can't guarantee when the site will be ready," Kraft said. "And if you won't extend the deadline for us to make an informed decision, I might have to pull out."

Rowland pounded the table with his fist. "What's the worst that can happen?" he said. "The stadium opens in 2003 instead of 2002."

"We're just executing our right in the agreement," Jonathan chimed in.

Rowland was incredulous that Kraft would exercise his right to withdraw.

"Well, you put that in the agreement," Jonathan reminded him.

"I put it in because I never thought you'd take it," Rowland said. "This deal is too good."

Robert said nothing in response.

"Do you see that chair?" Rowland said, pointing across the room.

Everyone turned to look.

"I'm going to go bend over that chair right now," Rowland continued, glaring at Kraft, "and you can shove anything you want up my ass. But don't back out of this deal!"

Kraft's eyes narrowed as he met Rowland's glare.

"After all we've been through, you owe me an answer," Rowland said.

"Give me until tomorrow night and I'll give you an answer," Kraft said.

"Get back to me by five o'clock tomorrow," Rowland said.

When Rowland and Kraft emerged from their closed-door meeting, a pack of reporters and a dozen television cameras were waiting outside.

"My goal and the Patriots' goal is to open the 2002 season here in Hartford," Rowland told the press. "As I've said so many times before, it will happen. Failure is not an option."

Standing beside Rowland, Kraft looked like a man at a funeral. "Our goal has always been to play in a new stadium in downtown Hartford in the year 2002," he told the press. "That was the spirit of our discussion tonight. And as usual, it was very frank and candid."

Rowland and Kraft did not take questions, and they exited the capitol through separate doors.

Afterward, Rowland asked his attorney what he thought.

"I think if they were going to walk away," Fox said, "they would have done it just now."

Rowland agreed. The Krafts weren't leaving Hartford. There was too much money on the table.

The Krafts' flight back to Boston that night was quiet. When they touched down, Robert turned to Jonathan and said, "He doesn't know us."

That night, lying awake in the dark, Kraft made his decision. Rowland was offering him the most lucrative stadium deal in the history of professional sports. Without investing any money, the Patriots were guaranteed to be one of the top three teams in revenue in the NFL for the next thirty years. Along

the way, Kraft would personally become a billionaire. Yet it didn't feel right. At the end of the day, he made deals with people. And the way Rowland had operated was making Kraft uncomfortable. When he did what Rowland wanted, the governor embraced him. When he didn't do what the governor wanted, Rowland was petulant.

The next day, Kraft penned a letter that began: "Dear John." In it, he informed the governor that he was exercising his legal right to withdraw from the stadium deal in Hartford. Then he telephoned the governor, informing him of his decision and telling him that his letter was en route.

"Let me get this straight," Rowland fumed. "Those politicians up there dumped shit on you for years and gave you a lousy deal. We put a billion dollars on the table down here. You and your kids will never have to worry again. Everything would be in place for another thirty years. And you're worried about delaying this thing for just *one more year*?"

Kraft tried to be conciliatory.

"I don't understand it," Rowland said.

Shortly after hanging up, Rowland addressed more than one hundred members of the press assembled at the state capitol. "You can expect legal action, not only with regard to the Kraft family, but presumably with the NFL as well," he said. "No one walks away from a year's planning and a $374 million package because of concerns the schedule would not be met. I'm sure he has some other plans in the works, and I'm sure we'll find out about those in the near future."

At the end of his remarks, he flashed a devious grin. "It's official," he said. "I'm a New York Jets fan now. And probably forever."*

The banner headline in the following morning's *Hartford Courant* read: "DEAR JOHN." "Shame on Robert Kraft," wrote one of the *Courant*'s most decorated columnists. "He is a ruthless businessman. As a man, he is no better than a common tenement rat; his word, no better than used toilet paper."

---

* Connecticut governor John Rowland and Massachusetts house Speaker Tom Finneran both resigned from office in 2004. After being snared in a corruption investigation, Rowland pleaded guilty to conspiracy to commit mail fraud and tax fraud. He served ten months in federal prison. After his release he became a radio talk show host in Connecticut. Finneran pleaded guilty to obstruction of justice after federal authorities accused him of lying about his role in a redistricting plan that discriminated against black voters. He was disbarred and stripped of his state pension. He ended up being a radio talk show host in Massachusetts.

The Boston press depicted Kraft as a hero. "With yesterday's decision to choose Massachusetts over Connecticut, Kraft did more than simply select a home for the team," the *Boston Globe* editorialized. "He also took a giant step in defining his public image, emphasizing soft-hearted public citizen over the hard-nosed businessman."

Even *Globe* sports columnist Will McDonough, who hadn't spoken to Kraft since their friendship ruptured two years earlier, praised Kraft. "He deserves all the credit he can get," McDonough wrote. "At the end of the day, Kraft stayed here for short money. The Massachusetts deal is just about the worst any owner has had to accept to stay put in the National Football League."

He added: "Whether you like him personally, or whether you like the way he has run his football team, it shouldn't make any difference. He deserves all the credit he can get for passing on the money, and for the way he did it. Kraft could have carried it out, gone to the league meeting, and made the NFL owners vote him down, which would have taken some of the heat off him. But he didn't."

Days later, Kraft was the guest of honor at a business roundtable at the Boston Harbor Hotel in Boston. More than 250 of the city's top executives had gathered. Shortly before it started, Kraft was at the head table when Tom Finneran approached. All eyes were on Kraft to see how he'd respond to the man who had hurled personal insults at him while repeatedly blocking him from building a new stadium.

When Kraft saw him, he smiled and shook his hand.

"There'll be a hearing and then a vote on Tuesday," Finneran told him with a smile.

A week later, behind closed doors at the NFL owners meetings, Steelers owner Dan Rooney took a moment to say something to his colleagues about Kraft. "He has done a tremendous service to the league by keeping the team in the Boston area," Rooney said. "He gave up a lot to do it, but it is very important to all of us that he did."

fifteen
GETTING BELICHICK

L ong before the start of the 1999 season, Robert Kraft was kicking himself for not hiring Bill Belichick after the '96 season. "He regretted it
from the day he didn't do it," Jonathan Kraft said. "He would say it
to me all the time. And I would remind him it wouldn't have worked. The
timing wasn't right."

But as the 1999 season evolved, Robert became convinced that the time to
bring in Belichick had arrived. After starting out 6-2, the Patriots imploded.
Key players started showing up late to practices and meetings. Two starters got
into a fistfight in the locker room. A star player got arrested and suspended. As
the off-the-field problems mounted, the cohesion in the locker room unrav-
eled. During a seven-week stretch, the team lost six games to fall to 7-8. For
the first time since 1995, the Patriots were going to miss the playoffs.

Kraft liked Pete Carroll immensely, but in each of the three years that
Carroll had been the head coach, the team's record had gotten progressively
worse. Things came to a head after a late season beat-down at the hands of
the lowly Philadelphia Eagles. The loss eliminated the Patriots from playoff
contention and marked the single worst performance by the team since Kraft
had purchased the franchise six years earlier. Guys simply quit playing. After
that game, Kraft had tears in his eyes when he left the locker room.

Linebacker Willie McGinest had had it. Aware that some of his teammates had partied at a nightclub the night before the flight to Philadelphia,
McGinest erupted in the locker room, calling out teammates in a profanity-
laced tirade for being "party animals" who didn't understand what it takes to
win in the NFL. "I'm tired of fucking losing!" he shouted.

The scene was a snapshot of a team in disarray.

New York Jets head coach Bill Parcells was keeping tabs on the situation in
New England. Will McDonough was a primary source. Toward the end of the

season, McDonough told Parcells that Kraft definitely planned to fire Carroll. He also had it on good authority that Kraft was going to pursue Belichick as the Patriots' next head coach and that he was prepared to offer him up to $2 million per year in salary.

Parcells had already been thinking about stepping down after the 1999 season and moving into the Jets' front office. His conversations with McDonough helped clarify his decision. The Jets held their final practice of the season on January 1, 2000. Afterward, Parcells met with Belichick and told him "there was a 99 percent chance that this was going to be my last game."

The prospect of Parcells stepping down had contractual implications for Belichick. A year earlier, during a meeting with Parcells, Jets owner Leon Hess, and team president Steve Gutman, Belichick was informed that Parcells might step aside at the end of the 1999 season. "What I'd like to do is make this my final season and then I'll turn it over to you and I'll ride off into the sunset," Parcells said in that meeting. Belichick confirmed to Hess that he wanted to succeed Parcells as head coach of the Jets in 2000, and that in the interim he'd remain on staff as an assistant. After the meeting, Gutman provided Belichick with a letter, memorializing the succession plan and stating that Belichick would receive a $1 million bonus to remain in New York as an assistant until Parcells retired.

As Belichick and Parcells stood face-to-face on the day before the final game of the 1999 season, it sounded as though Belichick's turn had finally arrived. All that remained was for Parcells to inform Jets team president Steve Gutman of his decision to step down. "As soon as I do that," he told Belichick, "you're the head coach. And I plan to do it right after the game."

Belichick showed no emotion.

"Are you ready to take this on?" Parcells said.

"I've been planning on it for a year," Belichick said.

The next day, New England won its final game to finish tied with the Jets for last place in the division at 8-8. Then Kraft fired Carroll. In New York, the Jets also won their final game. Afterward, Parcells invited Gutman into his office and submitted his resignation. Around 4:15 p.m., Gutman notified Leon Hess.

That evening, Jonathan Kraft sent a fax to the Jets headquarters, seeking permission, per league rules, to speak with Belichick about becoming the head coach and general manager of the Patriots. On Monday morning, a member of the Jets staff brought it to Parcells. After reading it, Parcells balled it up and chucked it in the garbage. He never mentioned it to Belichick.

That same morning in Foxborough, Robert Kraft announced the dismissal of Pete Carroll, telling the media: "I must say up front he is someone I have great respect for. But this is a business of accountability. And two years ago we won the division. Last year we barely made the playoffs. And this year we're 8-8. We need a momentum change. Is it solely Pete Carroll's fault? No, I think we have to reassess the whole organization."

At the same time, Parcells gathered his players and coaches to inform them that he was retiring and that Belichick was taking over. The news came as a surprise to the players and left them feeling disconcerted. Belichick did little to reassure them. At one point, Parcells looked at Belichick and asked if he had anything he wanted to say to the team. "No," Belichick replied.

Shortly after the meeting, Jets public relations director Frank Ramos talked to Parcells about his ideas for a farewell news conference, suggesting that Parcells could use the opportunity to introduce Belichick as his successor. "It would be like a perfect pass, one coach to another," Ramos said.

"Why don't you go talk to Bill about it," Parcells told him.

But Belichick declined Ramos's invitation to appear with Parcells at a joint press conference. "No, let Bill have his day," he told Ramos. "He deserves the day. Let him have that. I'll do it tomorrow."

Belichick's reluctance was driven by the fact that he wasn't sure what he wanted to say. He was unsettled by the situation. Unaware how his protégé felt, Parcells addressed the media by himself, formally announcing his retirement.

"By contract arrangement," Parcells told reporters, "Bill Belichick immediately ascends to the head coach of the Jets and I'm going to continue in the operations end for an undisclosed period of time."

Parcells made sure there was no ambiguity in his plans. "I'm not going to coach any more football games," he said. "This is definitely the end of my football career."

That afternoon, the Jets formally declined the Patriots' request to speak to Belichick, citing the fact that he had already become the head coach of the Jets. The Patriots protested the Jets refusal to the league office. After reviewing Belichick's contract with the Jets, Commissioner Tagliabue advised the Patriots that the Jets had acted properly by refusing permission. Teams may not contact head coaches of other teams.

Meanwhile, Belichick spent his first day as the Jets' head coach holding a number of meetings. He met with the team doctors. He met with the strength and conditioning coach. He met with Gutman. He met with his director of player personnel. But as the day wore on, it became harder and

harder to focus. Around 6:00 p.m. he tracked down Parcells in the coaches' locker area and asked him point blank if the Patriots had asked permission to speak with him.

Parcells confirmed that they had.

Belichick didn't appreciate the fact that he wasn't told.

Parcells reminded him that he was already the head coach of the Jets. "So it was a moot point," he said.

Belichick said he would have liked to have heard what the Patriots had to say.

Parcells didn't particularly care. Belichick had signed a contract with the Jets. He was the head coach. Furthermore, Leon Hess had given him a king's ransom to stick around long enough to become the coach.

But things had changed, Belichick pointed out. Leon Hess had died earlier in the year. A new owner still hadn't been named. There was uncertainty about who the next owner would be and what it would be like working under him.

Parcells didn't like what he was hearing. Impatient, he told Belichick he'd better rethink things. "If you feel that undecided, maybe you shouldn't take this job," he said.

According to Parcells, the remark wasn't intended to be taken literally. It was more of a brush-back pitch, punctuated by Parcells's repeating that he would not allow Belichick to talk to the Patriots.

Belichick pushed back. He had coached for Parcells for a mighty long time. He felt he had earned the right to at least hear what the Patriots were offering.

Parcells disagreed. "A deal's a deal," Parcells told him.

Done talking, Belichick left and headed home.

Unbeknownst to Belichick, Parcells was keeping a written record of important events in his final season as head coach for a book he planned to write later that year with Will McDonough. Shortly after the testy exchange with Belichick, he described what transpired:

> He tried to tell me that after eighteen years of being with me, he felt I owed him that opportunity to go coach in New England if that is what he wanted to do. I wasn't going to do that. . . .
>
> When he left, I thought it was just a conversation with a guy trying to review all his options, and nothing more. I thought he was still going to want to coach the Jets.

Despite having known Belichick for more than twenty years, Parcells didn't really understand him. That was partly due to Belichick's personality. He could be introverted, extremely guarded, and unusually prone to suppressing his emotions. The bigger problem was that Parcells had been taking Belichick's loyalty for granted for too long. In Parcells's system, Belichick was the ultimate lieutenant commander. Parcells gave the orders; Belichick executed them. And they both got rewarded—Parcells by being glorified as one of the greatest coaches of all time, Belichick by being credited as a defensive genius. Belichick's desire to meet with the Patriots was a clear signal that the discrepancy in power and credit between him and Parcells had gotten old. The fact that Parcells thought he could strong-arm Belichick into staying in New York was an indication that he didn't realize what his protégé was capable of.

Belichick had his own vision for what an ideal football team would look like and how it should be run. It was based on a lifetime of applied learning. He also had devoured books on coaching, leadership, management, and the military. He had a firm handle on the complexities of the salary cap and had ideas on how to leverage it to his advantage. All of this was part of his own system that he was champing at the bit to implement.

Most of all, though, Belichick was possessed by a determination to prove his naysayers wrong. Mickey Corcoran, a mentor and longtime confidant to Parcells, summed up Belichick's coaching career as follows: "Parcells made [Belichick's] career. After he fell on his ass in Cleveland, he grabbed him right up. Without Parcells there is no Belichick."

Belichick was familiar with Corcoran, and he knew that Parcells confided in him. The undercurrent of superiority that flowed from Parcells only fueled Belichick's obsession to win on his own terms. The notion that what had transpired in the Jets coaches' locker room after Belichick's first day as head coach was "just a conversation with a guy trying to review all his options," as Parcells described it, could not have been further from the mark.

That night, Belichick thought a lot about what Parcells had said. *"If you feel that undecided, maybe you shouldn't take this job."* Deep down, Belichick knew where he wanted to be, and it wasn't New York. He knew whom he wanted to work for, and it wasn't Parcells and some yet-to-be-determined owner. But the Jets were effectively telling him it was too late for all that now. He'd taken the money. He'd signed the contract. He was the team's head coach. All that remained was his press conference, a perfunctory event scheduled for the following day.

Facing the biggest decision of his career, Belichick went to the Jets facility early the next morning to work out and clear his head. While running on a treadmill, he considered the ramifications to what he was contemplating. Litigation was likely. Unemployment was certainly possible. A media firestorm was guaranteed. If he walked away from the Jets, it would make Parcells's departure from New England seem like a tempest in a teapot. But in the final analysis, it boiled down to the fact that Belichick had a relationship with Kraft and he believed that New England provided a better situation for success than New York.

As Belichick's workout was winding down, his friend Carl Banks, the Jets' director of player development, approached. "Congratulations," Banks said. "Do you need me to do anything today?"

"No, I won't need anything," Belichick said "Thanks, Carl."

After his workout, he showered, put on a suit and tie, and handwrote a characteristically minimalist resignation letter:

> Due to various uncertainties surrounding my position as it relates
> to the team's new ownership, I've decided to resign as the HC of the
> NYJ.

He added two more lines, one thanking the organization and another wishing them well. Then he walked into Parcells's office ten minutes before his scheduled press conference and told him he was resigning.

Furious, Parcells told him the Jets would stop him from interviewing anywhere else.

Belichick was undeterred.

Parcells told him he'd better tell team president Steve Gutman.

Belichick walked out, grabbed longtime Jets PR man Frank Ramos, and asked him to summon Gutman, who was already inside the auditorium, awaiting the start of the press conference. Moments later, Belichick and Gutman had a tense exchange in Gutman's office. After reading Belichick's resignation letter, Gutman said words to the effect of: "I hope you fully realize the ramifications of what you are about to announce to the media."

Belichick didn't flinch.

Gutman told him that if he resigned, he'd be through as a coach in the NFL. He'd never coach again. Anywhere.

Belichick said he wasn't interested in being threatened.

Gutman said it wasn't a threat. It was an opportunity to think before going through with his plan.

"Let's go," Belichick said.

Trailed by Gutman, Belichick walked into the auditorium and stepped to the lectern. Tugging at the knot in his tie, he read the statement he had just handed Gutman. The moment he uttered the words "I've decided to resign," camera shutters started clicking. The dozens of writers on hand were dumbfounded. Photographers scurried to the front of the room in order to get closer. Everyone recognized that they were witnessing something unprecedented. With four simple words, Belichick had become the first head coach in NFL history to quit two days after being handed the job. He spent the next forty minutes trying to explain his decision. A reporter asked if his decision had been influenced by the coaching vacancy in New England. Belichick downplayed that.

Moments later, he thanked everyone and walked off the stage.

Furious, Gutman stepped to the lectern and addressed the media. "We should have some feelings of sorrow and regret for him and his family," Gutman said. "He obviously has some inner turmoil."

Belichick left the building. It was a defining moment, one that would alter the course of his life, dictate the fortunes of two franchises, and profoundly shape the future of the NFL.

More immediately, though, things got very ugly very fast. Bill Parcells believed that Belichick would have been a great head coach for the Jets. And he had been looking forward to being the general manager with Belichick at the helm. The prospect of Belichick coaching the Patriots gnawed at him. Parcells told Gutman he had no intention of allowing Belichick out of New York. "He's not going to coach anywhere unless we let him," Parcells said. "His excuse about things changing with the death of Mr. Hess was weak." Gutman agreed and promptly contacted league headquarters. That afternoon, the commissioner released a statement advising teams that they were not permitted to speak to Belichick or his representatives about employment unless further notified by the NFL. Not about to back down, Belichick, through his agent, promptly filed a grievance with the league, contesting his inability to interview with other teams. Belichick and Parcells were digging in.

The headlines in the New York papers the next morning weren't kind. "BELICHICK ARNOLD." "BELICHICKEN." The Boston sportswriters were even more harsh. Belichick was called "duplicitous pond scum," a "lying sack of swill," a "disingenuous rambling nincompoop," and an "unprincipled opportunist." By this point, the worst-kept secret in football was that Kraft

wanted Belichick as his coach, and the football writers who covered the Patriots weren't on board with that idea. "This will be a disaster of hideous proportions," wrote *Boston Herald* columnist Michael Gee. "Three years after Belichick gets here, Pete Carroll's gonna look like Knute Rockne. . . . If the Pats owner cannot see why Belichick is wrong for his franchise, the team is doomed."

The media wasn't the only camp weighing in on Belichick. Kraft got barraged with unsolicited advice from fellow owners and league executives. Former Cleveland Browns owner Art Modell was one of the first people who called. Publicly, Modell was on record describing Belichick as "impossible" and "having difficulty with people." He even called Belichick "the most difficult man I've ever known in a PR sense." But in his private conversation with Kraft, Modell went further. "If you hire Bill Belichick, it will be the biggest mistake of your life," Modell warned.

Longtime New York Giants general manager George Young painted an even more ominous picture of Belichick. He had dealt with both Belichick and Parcells in New York. When he found out that Kraft wanted to hire Belichick, he sent him a simple message: "You had trouble with Parcells. This guy is ten times worse."

Kraft asked Tagliabue for his thoughts on Belichick. Tagliabue was reluctant to weigh in.

"Look, I don't normally get involved in this," he told Kraft. "I don't know these coaches. All I hear is secondhand information."

Kraft pressed him.

"From everything I heard from everybody I've spoken to over the years," said Tagliabue, "he's been a great coordinator, but he'll never be a great coach."

Tagliabue emphasized that he didn't know Belichick personally. But the only things he had heard about him were negative: that he was too intellectual and didn't connect with players; that he had lost the support of his team in Cleveland; and that he was adversarial with the press. A lot of what Tagliabue had been told came from former Giants executive George Young.

The only individuals Kraft could find who were in favor of hiring Belichick were players. Defensive backs Lawyer Milloy and Ty Law were practically begging him to bring him in as head coach. The one season they had with him in 1996 had been transformational. They told Kraft that Belichick was the best coach they had ever played for. Even Drew Bledsoe was lobbying for Belichick. Bledsoe considered Belichick a defensive nemesis. Taking him away from the Jets and bringing him to New England seemed like a brilliant

move. "I'm firmly in favor of having Belichick come in and coach the team," Bledsoe told Kraft.

His mind settled, Kraft nonetheless reached out to his trusted friend Carmen Policy, who had resigned as president of the San Francisco 49ers and had become a minority owner of the Cleveland Browns. At the outset, Policy said he was sorry that things didn't work out with Pete Carroll.

But Kraft hadn't called to discuss Pete Carroll. He wanted to talk about Belichick. Unlike the more measured tone Policy had taken when they talked about Belichick three years earlier, this time he was more specific.

"Robert, you saw what happened when he was here in Cleveland," Policy said. "He's supposed to be this mad genius. But you never know how he's going to react. He's a different personality. It's risky putting this guy in as your head coach."

"It is a risk," Kraft said. "And by the way, every single person I talked to says the same thing you're saying. But I gotta tell ya, I really, really think this guy can be a special coach. I think he was put on this earth to coach football."

"That's a big statement, Robert."

"I really mean that."

"Look, there's no question the guy is smart," Policy said. "But you can talk about the X's and O's. What about his personality and the mentality of fitting in in the NFL? Does his personality fit the kind of franchise you want to build?"

There was a long pause.

"You know, Carmen, I just feel strongly about him."

"Well, you're the boss," Policy said. "And you have good instincts. So if you feel that strongly, well . . ."

Kraft shared all of the Belichick feedback with Jonathan.

"What do you think?" Robert asked.

"I think Bill's smart," Jonathan said. "And I agree with you that he gets the cap. But you've watched him coach the players. I haven't."

It was true that Robert had spent a tremendous amount of time on the practice field, observing Belichick. But that wasn't what was driving his obsession to hire him. Kraft's conviction that Belichick was put on earth to coach was a gut feeling. It wasn't something he could quantify or support

with data. Yet his conclusion flew in the face of everything that every experienced NFL executive was telling him.

Jonathan didn't put much credence in what everyone else was saying about Belichick. "Dad," he said, "if your gut is telling you something is right, I'm deferring to your gut."

In an attempt to resolve the contract dispute between Belichick and the Jets, Commissioner Tagliabue scheduled an evidentiary hearing for January 13, 2000. Both sides would be given the opportunity to present evidence, including witnesses. Belichick retained high-profile antitrust lawyer Jeffrey Kessler, who notified the league in a letter: "We wish to call Bill Parcells as an adverse witness, and we request the League to require Mr. Parcells's attendance at the hearing."

The hearing deepened the rift between Parcells and Belichick. Under questioning, Belichick testified that Parcells's resignation was part of a "scheme" to deny him the opportunity to discuss coaching positions with other teams, particularly the Patriots.

The hearing also caused a schism between Parcells and his assistant Charlie Weis, who testified that Parcells had told him back in late December that the Patriots would be interested in talking to Belichick. When Weis pointed out that under league rules, Belichick would be free to talk to the Patriots while he was still an assistant coach with the Jets, Parcells replied: "Yeah, but alls I'd have to do is resign and he would become the head coach."

A lot of dirty laundry got aired. But in the end, Tagliabue ruled that Belichick had improperly breached his contract with the Jets. As a result, Belichick could not seek employment with the Patriots or any other club without the Jets' consent. At the same time, Tagliabue rejected the Jets' legal argument that Belichick should be barred from seeking employment in any role with any other NFL club for the full three-year term remaining on his contract. He gave the Jets a week to provide written answers to a series of legal questions, such as whether the team's contract rights to Belichick should remain in place in the event Bill Parcells reassumes the team's head coaching position.

Unwilling to wait, Belichick filed an antitrust suit against the Jets and the NFL. Attorney Jeffrey Kessler asked a federal judge in Newark, New Jersey, to issue a temporary restraining order, hoping to enable Belichick to pursue employment elsewhere. "The league's directive requiring all clubs to stop dealing with Coach Belichick is a classic group boycott," Kessler argued.

Tagliabue was more than irritated. Kessler had previously brought antitrust suits against the league alleging the NFL was functioning like a monopoly and should not be exempt from federal antitrust laws. The most frustrating thing about the Belichick suit was that it could have been avoided. Before it was filed, Tagliabue had called the Jets and the Patriots in hopes of persuading them to work out a trade. But neither side would budge. Belichick's willingness to take the league to court was clear and convincing evidence that he wasn't afraid to play hardball.

On January 25, 2000, a federal judge denied Kessler's request for a temporary restraining order. In doing so, the court ruled that Belichick's contract with the Jets was valid. Hours later, Belichick withdrew his antitrust suit. There was no getting around the fact that he wasn't leaving New York without the Jets' say-so.

Once the federal court weighed in, Bill Parcells knew he had the leverage. The Jets had Belichick under contract for three years. But as a practical matter, Parcells also understood better than anyone that it was pointless to try to compel Belichick to coach in New York when his heart was in New England. Parcells had been in the same shoes three years earlier when he wanted out of New England so he could coach in New York.

Parcells thought about calling Kraft to see if they could work out a trade. That, however, would require swallowing his pride. The last time the two of them had spoken was the day Parcells resigned. On the way out the door, Parcells had delivered a personal blow, chiding Kraft about wanting him to cook the meals while not letting him shop for the groceries. Since then it had been a three-year cold war between them. There were a lot of hard feelings.

Deep down, though, Parcells wanted to make the call.

It was 7 p.m. and Kraft was still at his desk when his secretary told him that Bill Parcells was on the line. Shocked, Kraft stopped what he was doing and picked up the phone.

"This is Darth Vader," Parcells said.

Kraft chuckled.

So did Parcells. He was calling, he said, to see if they could put the past behind them and get on with the future. The "border war" between the Jets and Patriots, he said, had gone on long enough. If they could air their differences, then perhaps they could talk about Bill Belichick.

Kraft agreed that it would be in the best interest of both franchises and the league to resolve things and move on.

Parcells went first, acknowledging that he had regrets about some of his actions. "I did some things leaving New England that I would not have done if I had a chance to do it over again," he said.

"If I knew then what I know now as an owner, I would have done some things differently too," Kraft said. "When my family bought the team in '94, you brought respectability to this franchise. I will forever be grateful for that."

Both men were magnanimous. The conversation then shifted to Belichick.

"Bob, do you want this guy to be your head coach?"

Kraft said he did.

"Okay," Parcells said. "There's going to be some compensation involved."

After some back-and-forth, Kraft offered a third-round draft pick in April and a fourth-round pick in 2001.

The Jets were not interested, Parcells told him, unless the trade included a first-round draft choice in the upcoming draft.

Kraft wanted to think about it.

They agreed to talk again in the morning.

It bothered Kraft that the price the Jets wanted for Belichick was higher than the price the Jets had been willing to pay for Parcells. It didn't seem fair. Parcells had won two Super Bowls and had been only the second coach in NFL history to lead two teams to the Super Bowl. Belichick was unproven as a head coach. He had an overall losing record. There was no way he was higher than Parcells in trade value.

Yet Kraft was convinced that Belichick was going to be a great head coach.

Jonathan was more concerned about timing. Free agency was about to start. The draft was right around the corner. And construction for the new stadium was under way. "Dad, the clock is ticking," Jonathan said. "We have to hire someone. If your gut is telling you something that strongly, then we just have to do it. We've got to get going."

Robert, however, remained methodical. The next morning, he called Parcells with an improved offer: a second-round pick in April and a third-round pick in 2001.

"Bob, we are not going to make a deal unless we get a first this year."

"I don't want to give up a first for Belichick."

Parcells held his ground.

"Then I'm going to go in a different direction," Kraft told him.

The conversation was amicable. But it was clear that they were not going to have a meeting of the minds.

Parcells hung up, convinced that Bill Belichick was not going to New England.

It was late by the time Robert got home. Mulling the situation over, he couldn't escape the thought that life seldom offers you a do-over. He considered his decision not to hire Belichick three years earlier the biggest mistake he'd made since buying the Patriots. And he had a chance to get it right this time. He telephoned Jonathan and said, "I'm going to call Parcells."

It was 10:30 p.m. when Parcells answered his phone. He was surprised to hear Kraft on the other end.

"I'm going to make a decision here that I don't want to make because I want this guy as my head coach," Kraft said.

"We can work this out," Parcells said. "Let's do this."

"If we're going to do a deal," Kraft said, "we need to do it now. Otherwise, I'm going in a different direction."

"You give me the one this year and a four next year," Parcells said. "Then I give you back a five the next year. Then I would like to have a seventh-round choice from you the year after that."

Kraft told Parcells to put down the terms in writing and fax them to him in the morning.

Bill Belichick was restless. He had quit his job with the Jets and he'd been told by the commissioner and a federal judge that he couldn't coach anywhere else for three years without the Jets' consent. Three years was the equivalent of a death sentence for his career. Coaching was the only thing he knew, the only thing he'd ever done. Without it, what would he do? How would he occupy his time? His mind?

He'd been up for a couple of hours when the phone rang at his Long Island home at 7:00 a.m.

"We've made a tentative deal to let you go to New England," Parcells told him.

Belichick didn't know what to say.

Both sides still had to sign the paperwork, and the league had to sign off as well. But Parcells was optimistic. "Stay by the phone," he told Belichick.

It was hard for Belichick not to be skeptical. But a couple of hours later, Parcells called again. "You have permission to call Kraft," he said.

Belichick knew what that meant. He told Parcells that he appreciated what had just happened.

"Good luck," Parcells told him.

Many years later, Parcells would reflect back on this period of friction between him and Belichick. "Football is not for well-adjusted people," he said in 2020. "And I'm being serious. It's only for maladjusted sons of bitches like us."

Right after Belichick hung up with Parcells, his phone rang again. This time it was Kraft.

"How fast can you get to Foxborough?" he said.

That evening at 6:00 p.m., Robert Kraft introduced Bill Belichick to a throng of journalists packed into the media room at Foxboro Stadium.

"Thank you," Belichick said. "Hopefully, this press conference will go a little better than the last one I had."

The press broke out in laughter.

Belichick laughed at himself.

"I'm tremendously excited to be here," Belichick continued. "To be part of the New England Patriots organization. This is a first-class operation. I had an outstanding experience in 1996 when I was here with the Patriots and with Robert. I'm thrilled to be part of this organization and to be able to have the opportunity to lead this team."

The reporters had a lot of questions. In response to one of them, Belichick said: "That's all I really am about is trying to win football games."

Truer words had never been spoken at a Belichick press conference.

sixteen

TOMMY

A s soon as he arrived in Foxborough, Bill Belichick began assembling
his staff. For the most senior positions, he chose accomplished men
that he'd known and trusted for a long time: Scott Pioli as assistant director of player personnel, Dante "Scar" Scarnecchia as assistant head
coach, and Charlie Weis as offensive coordinator.

Even his position coaches—such as Pepper Johnson, working with the
linebackers, and Eric Mangini, working with the defensive backs—were guys
who had played for Belichick or coached under him previously. But the most
pivotal personnel move Belichick made in his first days on the job in Foxborough was his decision to hire forty-four-year-old Richard "Dick" Rehbein as
his quarterbacks coach. Rehbein was an unconventional choice. He had never
coached quarterbacks. Nor had he evaluated them. He had, however, been an
All-American center at Division II Ripon College. So he had some firsthand
experience working with quarterbacks. Belichick figured it wouldn't hurt to
have a fresh perspective at that position.

Rehbein was perhaps the most unheralded member of Belichick's new
staff. He was immediately tasked with scouting and evaluating the college
quarterback prospects for the upcoming draft. The Patriots had serious deficiencies at nearly every position on the roster, but quarterback was one position where they were solid. They had a bona fide superstar in Bledsoe. And
behind him were two solid backup quarterbacks, veteran John Friesz and
second-year standout Michael Bishop. Nonetheless, Rehbein had his marching orders. He was handed a list of four campuses to visit. One of them was
Michigan.

When Tom Brady was seventeen years old, he viewed the Michigan Wolverines as the gold standard in college football. But in 1994, as he prepared to
enter his senior year at Serra High School in San Mateo, California, Brady

didn't expect to get recruited to play quarterback for the University of Michigan. Never mind that he'd written the words "If you want to play with the big boys, you gotta learn to play in the tall grass" beneath his yearbook picture. Privately, Brady was just hoping for an opportunity to play quarterback *somewhere*. After all, he was considered much better at baseball than football. He was a standout catcher at the same high school that Barry Bonds had attended, and the Montreal Expos had already drafted him.

Brady's heart, however, was set on football, a sport he'd only been playing for a few years. When he was a high school freshman, Brady saw no action. Unofficially designated the backup quarterback on a team that went the entire season without scoring a touchdown, Brady didn't play a single down. As a sophomore, he became the starting quarterback on the junior varsity team by default when the kid ahead of him quit the team. It wasn't until his junior year that Brady finally got noticed and started every game—on a mediocre team. Serra High barely won half of its games in Brady's junior and senior seasons. College scouts weren't exactly beating down his door.

To help his son land a scholarship, Tom Brady Sr. created a highlight reel for him and sent it to fifty-four colleges and universities. Michigan wasn't on the list of recipients.

One day, Brady asked his dad about sending a tape to Michigan.

"Sure," his father said.

Tom quickly second-guessed his own idea. "We can send this, but it's pretty much a waste of tape," he said.

As he predicted, Michigan didn't respond to the reel. A number of schools did, however. Two, in particular, showed the most interest—the University of Illinois and the University of California. Brady was turned off by the weather when he visited the Illini campus in December of his senior year. It was cold and dreary, a stark contrast to the Bay Area. At the same time, Cal was promising Brady that he'd be the starter after his freshman year.

There seemed to be little question where Brady would end up, and the prospect of his son playing college ball thirty miles from home thrilled Tom Brady Sr. Then, very late in the recruiting process, Michigan unexpectedly invited Brady to visit the campus. He arrived on a frigid, gray day in January. That night he called home and said, "Dad, this place is fabulous." He returned home two days later with a scholarship offer.

"You know they've got six quarterbacks," his father told him.

Tom was aware.

"Cal says you'll start as a sophomore, junior, and as a senior," his father reminded him.

Tom was aware of that, too. But Cal wasn't Michigan.

Brady faced the first major decision of his life. His father's wishes were evident. But Brady was determined to sort this out on his own.

"I knew I wanted to go to Michigan," Brady recalled. "But it was an easier choice to go to Cal. That was the dilemma. Do I take the harder, more unknown, bigger challenge? Or do I take the sure thing that's closer to home?"

The pull of family and familiarity was significant. Brady's three older sisters were in the Bay Area. He was particularly close to his mother, Galynn. If he went to Cal he'd be able to go home on weekends, eat Mom's home cooking, get his laundry done, and play golf with his father. Plus, the whole family would be able to see him play on Saturdays in a climate that was warm and sunny.

Brady's exceptional home life, however, was what ultimately convinced him to head east. "I needed to grow up," Brady said. "I was a California kid, surrounded by three sisters. I needed to toughen up. There wasn't a lot of adversity in my life. So I decided, 'I have to go away for school.'"

When Tom signed his letter of intent to attend Michigan, his father cried for two days.

Tom Brady's climb to the top of the football mountain did not begin on a field. It started with the simple recognition that he needed adversity to grow. Very few teenagers are mature enough to recognize the importance of opposition in life. It's even rarer for a celebrated high school athlete to turn down the chance to be the big man on campus and submit to being seventh on the depth chart. But that was exactly where Brady found himself when he arrived at Michigan in the fall of 1996. With six quarterbacks ahead of him, he couldn't see light at the end of the tunnel. Michigan promptly redshirted him, meaning he'd be ineligible for the active roster his freshman year. It was the coach's way of saying that Brady needed to develop his skills and learn the offense without using up a year of his football eligibility. In other words, he was on the five-year plan.

In Brady's second year at Michigan, he was considered a freshman in terms of his football eligibility. His parents flew out for nearly every home game. But there was nothing to see. Tom appeared only briefly in two games, throwing a total of five passes on the season. Discouraged, he had a talk with his dad while sitting in a car near the stadium.

Brady told his dad that he didn't think he'd ever get a chance to start at Michigan. His dad agreed. At that point, Tom Brady Sr. didn't see his son as a

future NFL quarterback. He simply wanted him to have a good college experience, one that he'd be able to look back on with a sense of accomplishment and happiness. In that moment, however, Tom Brady Jr. wasn't very happy. Nor did he appear to be accomplishing anything in Ann Arbor. They talked seriously about the possibility of transferring. Cal, it turned out, still needed a quarterback.

But Brady couldn't shake the feeling of wanting to prove that he belonged at Michigan. If nothing else, he wanted to prove it to himself. With his father's support, he opted to stick it out and work harder in the upcoming offseason.

But in the summer between his sophomore and junior years he developed a severe case of appendicitis that landed him in the hospital, where he lost thirty pounds. The illness not only set him back physically but caused him to doubt himself even more. Feeling desperate, he went to see counselor Greg Harden in the Michigan athletic department.

"I need help," Brady said as soon as he entered Harden's office.

Looking across his desk, Harden saw a kid who was mentally beaten down and emotionally fragile. As he listened to Brady, he could tell he was going through a dark time. "All I could tell him was the truth," Harden recalled. "He had to decide for himself that he was going to be the best quarterback on the team and that he would have to do it for himself."

It was a lonely proposition. But Brady took to Harden and started meeting with him regularly. He was slotted as the third-string quarterback entering his sophomore season of eligibility. Then, in camp, he clearly outperformed everyone and appeared poised to become the starting quarterback. Even his teammates viewed him as the preferred starter. But head coach Lloyd Carr instead chose Brian Griese, whose father had been a star quarterback in the NFL. That year, Michigan went 12-0 and won the national championship. Again, Brady barely played, throwing just fifteen passes. And again, Brady seriously considered transferring to Cal. After the 1997 season, Coach Carr was even telling his staff: "Tom's going to leave."

The way Brady handled his college experience was evidence of his staying power and a harbinger of his NFL experience. Virtually everyone associated with the Michigan football program figured Brady wouldn't come back, and given his experience in Ann Arbor, he certainly would have been justified in leaving. But he decided to return to Michigan for his junior season. That offseason, Brady trained harder than ever, and Carr designated him as the starter heading into the 1998 season.

But that year, Michigan had recruited a local phenom named Drew Henson, a high school quarterback who had already signed a $4.5 million contract to play for the New York Yankees after his college days were over. Upon Henson's arrival, Carr called him "without question the most talented quarterback I've ever been around." The statement undercut Brady and fueled calls from Michigan boosters who preferred Henson as Michigan's starter.

With Brady at the helm, Michigan lost the first game of the 1998 season to Notre Dame. A week later, Brady threw an interception early against Syracuse. Carr immediately benched him and sent in Henson. Brady returned as the starter the following week. But Carr's actions sparked a quarterback controversy that dragged on for two seasons. It reached a point early in Brady's senior year where Carr was playing both quarterbacks on a weekly basis. Every time Henson entered the game, he'd get an ovation. Then Michigan would fall behind, and Brady would go back in and lead them to victory.

Brady's father called Carr's approach "bullshit."

Brady felt betrayed. But rather than lashing out, he internalized his anger. A formidable chip appeared on his shoulder. The presence of Henson, coupled with the lack of appreciation Brady felt from Carr, drove home the feeling that he was the man nobody wanted. "These experiences helped me grow and helped me learn and figure out a lot of things about myself," Brady said many years later. "A lot of those lessons were things I needed to apply as I moved forward in the rest of my life."

In the midst of all that adversity and uncertainty, Brady set school passing records in his junior year and led the Wolverines to a string of comeback victories during his senior year. He capped off his career at Michigan in dramatic fashion at the Orange Bowl on January 1, 2000. That day, he led his team back from a two-touchdown deficit to beat Alabama in overtime, 35–34. He was no longer content to prove that he belonged at Michigan. His sights were clearly set on the NFL.

When Dick Rehbein reached Ann Arbor in the early spring of 2000, he knew almost nothing about Brady's background or what he'd been through in his five years as a Wolverine. Rehbein put Brady through a workout and was impressed with the sharpness of his mechanics, his concentration, and his work ethic. Then, while talking one-on-one with him, Rehbein sensed that the kid from San Mateo that everyone affectionately called Tommy possessed

an unusual degree of maturity and mental toughness. His conclusions were supported by what he heard from Brady's coaches. Lloyd Carr put it most succinctly: "This game is a struggle. Tom Brady embraced that struggle more than anybody I've ever known."

Upon returning home from his scouting trip, Rehbein told his wife, Pam, that people would one day know the name Tom Brady.

Bill Belichick knew Tom Brady's name in the spring of 2000. He had watched his Orange Bowl performance. But Belichick hadn't paid a great deal of attention to Brady until Rehbein told him that he liked Brady more than any other quarterback in the draft.

More than any other quarterback in the draft?

That was pretty high praise from a guy who wasn't known for hyperbole.

Rehbein emphasized Brady's leadership capabilities. "Tommy's clearly the one," he told Belichick. "Everyone wants to follow him."

The conviction in Rehbein's voice was persuasive.

"He's the best fit for the Patriots system," he told Belichick.

Belichick decided to take a closer look. He sifted through every scouting report available on Brady. They could be distilled down to two categories:

PROS: "Very poised and composed . . . smart and alert . . . can read coverages."
CONS: "Looks like a rail . . . frail . . . lacks mobility . . . lacks a really strong arm."

Belichick also looked at Brady's performance at the NFL scouting combine, where he ran the forty-yard dash in 5.3 seconds. To put that in perspective, between 2000 and 2018, a total of 308 college quarterbacks were timed in the forty-yard dash at the NFL combine. Three hundred and five of them ran faster than Tom Brady.

But one sentence about Brady in a pre-draft report prepared by *Pro Football Weekly*'s expert Joel Buchsbaum caught Belichick's eye: "Produces in big spots and big games."

Belichick considered Buchsbaum to be a solid analyst. At one point, when Belichick was the head coach in Cleveland, he had even tried to hire Buchsbaum as a scout. Essentially, Buchsbaum's analysis of Brady echoed a lot of what Rehbein was saying. He noted that Brady "is not what you're looking for in terms of physical stature, strength, arm strength, and mobility, but he has the intangibles."

Intangibles were hard to measure, but they were so often what distinguished the great ones. And when it came to quarterbacks, there was perhaps no greater intangible than the ability to produce under pressure.

Belichick knew little about Brady's backstory or what he'd overcome at Michigan. He could only go on what he could see. The more film he saw of Brady, the more apparent it became that the bigger the stage, the better he performed. The 2000 Orange Bowl was a case in point. In the biggest moment of his college career, he had his greatest performance, throwing for 369 yards and four touchdowns. In overtime, when everything was on the line, Brady never flinched.

Coolness under pressure is something that can't be taught. A player either has it or he doesn't. But it's an absolutely essential quality for a quarterback to succeed in the NFL. Dick Rehbein thought Tom Brady had it. Belichick thought Rehbein might be right.

"We talked a lot about his production his senior year at Michigan, when they rotated Henson in, and there was a problem, and they ended up bringing Brady back," Belichick recalled. "Most of the time he'd fix the problem and move the team into position where it could win. The way he handled it was good, but I think what was better was what he did with the opportunities he had."

Nevertheless, the Patriots didn't need a quarterback. They were three deep at that position. So despite how intriguing Brady appeared, all that predraft analysis was probably for naught. The draft would be in the very late rounds before the Patriots could think about taking a chance on a quarterback. By that time, Belichick figured, Brady would be long gone.

As the 2000 NFL Draft got under way on April 15 at Madison Square Garden, Tom Brady gathered with his family around the television at his parents' home in San Mateo. Everyone was excited. It was hard not to dream about the possibility that Tom would be drafted by the San Francisco 49ers. The family had had season tickets since Tom was a baby. When Tom was four, his parents had taken him to his first 49ers game, on January 10, 1982. That day, San Francisco beat Dallas in the NFC Championship game when Joe Montana and Dwight Clark connected on "The Catch," perhaps the most iconic play in league history. For the NFL, that game was a watershed moment in more than one respect. It ended the Cowboys' reign as the most dominant team in the NFC, and it marked the commencement of the 49ers' dynasty,

which would end up extending all the way until the mid-nineties. Separately, the dramatic, last-minute touchdown pass to Clark catapulted Montana to stardom.

The Catch also had an important place in Brady family lore. Tom Brady was too young to remember much about the play, but he'd literally had a front-row seat for it. Montana became his childhood idol. By the time Brady was in high school, his favorite player was Montana's successor, Steve Young. Rooting for the 49ers was a family affair in the Brady household. And like everyone else in the Bay Area, they knew that San Francisco was now in the market for a new quarterback. Young had suffered a season-ending injury in 1999 and was expected to announce his retirement shortly after the 2000 draft. Seeing Tommy in a Niners uniform would be a dream come true, and the Brady family couldn't help thinking about it.

Brady, on the other hand, just wanted to be wanted. He was looking for a place to get his foot in the door, an organization that would give him an opportunity to work his way into a job. He told himself that he was going to devote his all to the team that picked him.

He watched in silence as Marshall University's Chad Pennington became the first quarterback to get his number called. Bill Parcells and the New York Jets selected Pennington in the first round, with the eighteenth overall pick.

The first round dragged on for hours. No other quarterbacks were chosen. Restless, Brady left the house and went to Candlestick Park to see a Giants baseball game.

Inside the war room at Foxboro Stadium, Bill Belichick and his staff waited.

Due to the trade Robert Kraft had made to get Belichick, the Patriots didn't have a first-round pick. When it finally came their time to make a selection, halfway through the second round, they chose an offensive lineman, Adrian Klemm out of Hawaii.

The 49ers, meanwhile, had four picks in the first two rounds. They used all four selections on defensive players. At the start of the third round, San Francisco decided to take a quarterback. With the sixty-fifth overall pick, they selected Giovanni Carmazzi, prompting one of Brady's sisters to ask: "Who's he?" Carmazzi was a superior athlete who stood six foot three and weighed 224 pounds. He played at Hofstra. Bill Walsh, who had recently rejoined the 49ers front office, loved Carmazzi. Walsh thought he was a lot like Steve Young, only bigger.

Tom Brady Sr. couldn't believe the Niners had taken Carmazzi over

Tommy. "We had season tickets for the 49ers for twenty-five years and we were just hurt," said Tom Brady Sr. "We kinda took it personally."

Brady got back from the baseball game just as the first day of the draft was winding down. He was dejected. He hadn't expected to be a top pick, but he certainly thought he'd get drafted on the first day.

Dick Rehbein was puzzled. He hadn't expected Brady would still be available on the second day of the draft. Belichick was surprised, too. At one point, Belichick even blurted out, "Brady's still on the board," causing everyone in the Patriots war room to look up at the team's board and take note that among the remaining players who were eligible to be drafted, Belichick and his staff had ranked Brady above all of them.

Still, New England continued to draft players for positions where the team had deficiencies. A running back. An offensive tackle. A tight end. A defensive tackle. But when the New Orleans Saints drafted quarterback Marc Bulger out of West Virginia with the 168th overall pick in the sixth round, Belichick couldn't help wondering aloud.

"Brady's still on the board," he said. "Why is he still there?"

No one in the war room had an answer.

There was one nagging red flag for Belichick—the fact that Michigan kept trying to replace Brady with Drew Henson. It signaled to Belichick that they didn't really want Brady as their starter. He wondered what the problem was.

Robert Kraft, meanwhile, couldn't figure out why Belichick was so fixated on a quarterback.

Tom Brady was worried. The draft was well into the sixth round and he still hadn't been picked. It was looking more and more like no one was going to take him.

The Cleveland Browns were one of the teams that he thought might genuinely have an interest in him. Dwight Clark, the former 49ers player who was Cleveland's director of football operations, was in the market for a quarterback. But with the 183rd pick, Clark chose quarterback Spergon Wynn from Texas State University.

"I don't understand this," Tom seethed. "I do *not* understand this."

The family was crushed. "Dwight Clark—unbelievable," said Tom Brady Sr.

Brady couldn't take it anymore.

"I gotta get out of here," he said, storming off.

His parents looked on with concern as Tom went upstairs to his room, grabbed a baseball bat, came back down, and headed out the door. The draft had sent him a clear message—nobody wanted him.

After a while, Brady's parents went looking for him. When they found him, he had tears in his eyes. Galynn put her arms around him. Tom Sr. patted him on the back. Together they walked around the block with him. He'd read the scouting reports. He knew what they said about him. "Basically, they're saying that I don't look like an NFL quarterback," Brady said.

Depressed, Brady had one overwhelming question weighing heavily on his mind: "What am I going to do with the rest of my life?"

With the 187th pick in the sixth round, the Patriots chose a cornerback named Antwan Harris. By this point, six quarterbacks had been selected, and Brady was still on the board.

"Brady's too much value," Belichick said to his staff. "Why's he still there?"

No one in the Patriots war room knew Bill Belichick better than Scott Pioli. When Belichick kept raising questions about Brady, Pioli knew that it was because Belichick was convinced there was something there.

"What are we doing?" Pioli said, looking at Belichick.

Dick Rehbein's position was clear. If it had been up to him, he would have taken Brady much sooner.

Robert and Jonathan Kraft remained silent. But they knew the analytics, which clearly showed that good NFL quarterbacks are not found in the sixth round. Good quarterbacks are taken in the early rounds. Plus, they had three quarterbacks on the roster.

Belichick had only one concern—the inexplicable fact that Michigan didn't seem to want him. With the clock ticking, he resigned himself to the fact that he might never know the answer. All he could do was evaluate what he could see. And what he saw was that time after time in his senior year, Brady came in and rescued his team from defeat. And he did it against the best teams in the country.

Belichick turned to his personal assistant, Berj Najarian, and told him to get in touch with Brady.

Tom Brady was still outside in the yard, crestfallen, when the phone rang at his home. Tom Sr. answered. The caller said he was from the New England Patriots.

Tom Sr. ran to get his son. The family gathered around as Tom put the receiver to his ear.

"Tom, this is Berj Najarian with the New England Patriots. We're about to draft you. I'll pass you over to Bill."

Before Brady could utter a word, Belichick was on the line. "Good to have you," he said in a monotone voice. "Looking forward to getting you here. We're gonna work hard."

Brady tried to speak, but he was too excited. The only thing he could think to say was thank you.

"See you soon," Belichick said.

In less than thirty seconds, the call of a lifetime was over.

Tom Brady Sr. ran into the room and popped a bottle of champagne. Surrounded by his parents and his sisters, Tom took in the moment.

"With the one hundred and ninety-ninth pick in the draft," the commissioner announced, "the New England Patriots select Tom Brady."

Brady had trouble controlling his emotions.

In the Patriots war room, Robert and Jonathan Kraft looked at each other in silent disbelief. They were both wondering the same thing: *Why are we drafting a quarterback?*

seventeen

BUILDING THE CORE

When Bill Belichick arrived in 2000, the New England Patriots franchise didn't have an identity. The team had existed for forty years, but it had never won a championship. Robert Kraft was counting on Belichick to change that. To help him succeed, Kraft gave Belichick a lot more control than he had given to Parcells or Carroll.

"You don't really know anything before you buy a team," Kraft recalled. "You think you do. But you don't. Parcells was a good learning curve for me."

One of the things that Kraft learned was the importance of delegating decision-making authority in football operations to a head coach who was capable of functioning like a general manager.

"In some ways, I was unfair to Pete Carroll," Kraft said. "I handicapped him. I gave Bobby Grier final say. So I think Pete was not happy with personnel decisions.

"I was still learning," Kraft continued. "When Parcells was the coach, I knew I couldn't trust him to make long-term commitments. I had confidence at the time in Bobby Grier."

The first real sign that the culture in New England was about to change occurred right after the 2000 draft, when Bill Belichick fired Bobby Grier. Grier was a longtime Patriots employee who had been loyal to the Kraft family.

"This is an unpleasant thing for me to do," Belichick said in a formal statement issued by the team. "I recognize that Bobby Grier has made significant contributions to the New England Patriots over many years. This decision is unrelated to any specific event, performance, or personal relationship. It is more a reflection of my general feeling to proceed in a new direction with regard to the structure and operation of our personnel department."

Grier's dismissal was controversial. The *New York Times* reported: "There were some black coaches who were outraged that Grier, one of the few black general managers in the National Football League, was not allowed to exit with grace."

Belichick ignored the criticism. His decision to fire Grier had nothing to do with race. It had to do with control.

"Kraft assured me that I would have everything that I needed and wanted to be successful," Belichick had told the press back on the day he was hired. "If I felt like somebody was going to be coming in here, or was going to be here, and making lots of decisions for me, then I wouldn't be sitting here. I don't have that feeling at all."

Belichick added: "Now, do I want to join into a marriage with someone else to help make decisions? Possibly. It depends. If it's the right person, sure. If it's not, no. But I feel that I'm going to have a big say in that one way or the other. And he [Kraft] has expressed that to me."

Despite how much Kraft liked and appreciated Grier, he backed Belichick. Kraft recognized that in order to have the best chance of building a winning team, Belichick needed his own right-hand man—someone he trusted—to help him carry out his vision. And that guy was thirty-four-year-old Scott Pioli, whom Belichick had known since Pioli had started helping out with the New York Giants while still a student at Central Connecticut State University. Pioli was a workaholic who followed Belichick to Cleveland and then to the Jets. He intuitively understood what Belichick was looking for in players, especially when it came to intangible qualities such as leadership, discipline, and toughness.

The second sign that the culture in New England was about to change appeared as soon as Pioli arrived in Foxborough. That week, Belichick cut two of the most beloved players in Patriots history—fourteen-year veteran offensive lineman Bruce Armstrong and nine-year veteran tight end Ben Coates. Both had played their entire careers in New England. But their best days were behind them, and removing their multimillion-dollar salaries created cap space. New England had the third-highest payroll in the league, and they were $10.5 million over the salary cap. Bill Parcells was famous for offering generous salaries to veteran players. It was a by-product of his sense of loyalty to guys who had played long years for him. Belichick had a very different approach.

The decision to start paring down the Patriots roster went deeper than Belichick's determination to control player spending. He wanted to overhaul most of the roster. In his estimation, only about a dozen of the fifty-three players on New England's payroll fit his definition of an ideal football player.

"A quarter of the team couldn't pass the conditioning run," Belichick said. "So that wasn't a very good start. I don't think there was a lot of commitment with that group."

Days after the NFL Draft, Brady flew to Ann Arbor, picked up his vehicle, and headed for Boston. Alone on the road for eleven hours, the twenty-two-year-old had plenty of time to think.

This was a chance, he told himself. At least he knew he wasn't going to be an insurance agent. He could shift all of his attention to the Patriots. It was a realization that got him wondering about a lot of things:

What was it like in New England?
What was the Patriots organization like?
How would Drew Bledsoe be toward him?
Who was Bill Belichick, and what would it be like playing for him?

Brady didn't know what to expect. Nor did he know about the circumstances that had landed Belichick in Foxborough or the rest of the complicated history that had preceded his arrival. Brady knew nothing about Robert Kraft or what he had endured to acquire the team. He didn't even know a new stadium was in the works. And he had no sense of how he might fit into the picture. He just told himself to focus on the one thing he could control—his effort. Determined to prove to everyone that he belonged in the NFL, he couldn't wait to get to work.

"I had no backup plan," Brady recalled. "I was just going to play pro football."

Cruising toward Boston on the Massachusetts Turnpike, he cranked up his radio. He had a feeling he was going to like it in New England.

In order to make the Patriots successful, Belichick was convinced he had to completely change the culture in the locker room. The first player he met with after coming to Foxborough was linebacker Willie McGinest. McGinest was precisely the kind of leader he wanted. Back when he'd been head coach of the Browns, Belichick had wanted to draft McGinest. He'd even flown out to the University of Southern California and interviewed him. During that session, McGinest was stunned to discover how much Belichick knew about his background, including things McGinest had done in elementary school. Belichick even knew things about McGinest's father.

The Patriots picked ahead of Cleveland that year, so Belichick never had the chance to select McGinest. But he got to coach him in 1996 when Belichick joined Parcells's staff in New England. That year, McGinest got in a fight with a teammate. A defensive lineman who was much bigger than

McGinest swung first, and McGinest hammered him. That lineman never messed with McGinest again. No one did. Belichick liked guys like that.

When Belichick met with McGinest in the spring of 2000, he got right to the point. "We want to use you like Lawrence Taylor," Belichick told him.

Those eight words touched and inspired McGinest. LT was his role model. All through high school and college, McGinest had tried to emulate the legendary Giants linebacker. Plus, McGinest was aware that Belichick had been Taylor's defensive coordinator with the Giants, and that he considered Taylor the greatest player he'd ever coached. Belichick's willingness to put McGinest in the same sentence as Taylor instilled instant loyalty.

Without saying a derogatory word about Pete Carroll or even referencing what had transpired under his predecessor's tenure, Belichick convinced McGinest that things were about to change in New England. Guys like him and linebacker Tedy Bruschi, linebacker Ted Johnson, and defensive backs Lawyer Milloy and Ty Law were the core players whom Belichick planned to retain and build the team around. They were all defensive guys who were mentally tough, hard-nosed, and hypercompetitive.

The summer of 2000 was a hectic time for Robert and Jonathan Kraft. With the new stadium under construction, they were bouncing back and forth between their downtown offices and their offices at Foxboro Stadium. Days after the rookies arrived for rookie mini-camp, Robert arrived at the stadium around five in the afternoon. Heading up the stairwell to the executive offices, he encountered a tall, skinny player carrying a pizza box.

"Hey, Mr. Kraft," the player said. "I'm Tom Brady."

"I know who you are. You're our sixth-round draft choice out of Michigan."

"Yeah, that's me," Brady said, smiling and looking Kraft in the eye. "I just want you to know I'm the best decision your franchise has ever made."

Speechless, Kraft stopped and stared at Brady as he continued down the stairs, got into his vehicle, and drove off.

"I was just a confident kid," Brady said when recalling that moment many years later. "At Michigan I had played in front of 110,000 people. It wasn't like I was coming from Middle Tennessee State. I was at a big program where there were a lot of expectations and a lot of exposure."

The encounter left such an impression on Kraft that he couldn't stop thinking about it. Two hours later, he called Jonathan back at the office in Boston and told him about the conversation.

Jonathan was amazed. "Did he sound *cocky*?" he asked.

Kraft paused. "No. And you wanna know something? This will sound crazy, but there was something about the way he said it that made me believe him."

A few weeks later, Brady signed his rookie contract. The occasion seemed so insignificant that the team issued a simple two-sentence statement to the press: "The New England Patriots announced the signing of two sixth-round draft choices from their 2000 draft class today. The signings of Virginia cornerback Antwan Harris and Michigan quarterback Tom Brady."

In his first team meeting with the Patriots players, Belichick faced a jam-packed room and began to speak. A few minutes later, linebacker Andy Katzenmoyer, the team's first-round draft choice from the previous year, strolled in late. Instead of finding a seat in the back, Katzenmoyer made his way down front. Belichick stopped talking and glared at him.

"Who in the hell do you think you are?" Belichick snapped.

Unaccustomed to being called out, Katzenmoyer didn't know what else to say. He took a seat.

"We're not gonna start this program off with you walking in whenever you fucking feel like walking in," Belichick said. "Now get your ass outta here!"

The rest of the players sat up in their seats. The room was as quiet as a morgue.

Tom Brady immediately realized he wasn't at Michigan anymore, and Bill Belichick was not Lloyd Carr. In college, Brady had been sacked by Katzenmoyer, who had been a decorated player at Ohio State. He had won the Butkus Award, which is given to the nation's top college linebacker. But the hulking player looked sheepish as he exited the room.

Willie McGinest liked what he saw. "Andy was a good dude," McGinest said. "But we had so much of that going on in the previous regime, as far as guys not being disciplined. Guys not being accountable. Guys not holding each other accountable. You could walk into a meeting late. You might get fined. But 'Okay, I'm still gonna play.' I was fed up with that. And we had some guys who were immature, and Andy was one of them."

Katzenmoyer's dismissal made one thing instantly clear—Belichick didn't care about what players had done in college or how heralded they'd been or whether they'd been drafted in the first round. He reiterated that point in one of the next team meetings, when he singled out another first-round draft choice, defensive back Tebucky Jones. "You ran a four-point-four-three at the

combine," Belichick said to him, "but you really run a five-point-oh because you don't know where the fuck you're going."

Parcells had used to browbeat players and ridicule them. But Belichick was different. No one laughed when he criticized a player. His critiques were withering. And no one was immune from them. Brady learned that early on. In training camp, Belichick rode him hard.

"I can't stand it!" Belichick shouted during one play as Brady made an incorrect decision. "Run it again. Huddle up and *run it again*, Brady!"

The more Belichick carped at him, the harder Brady worked.

Each summer, the Pro Football Hall of Fame in Canton, Ohio, inducts a new class of members. The induction ceremony is followed by a preseason game after which the new NFL season starts. On July 30, 2000, Joe Montana and Ronnie Lott, the respective leaders of the San Francisco 49ers team that won four Super Bowls in the eighties, were inducted into the hall. The next evening, the 49ers played the Patriots in the annual Hall of Fame Game.

The exhibition game had no bearing on the standings. But Brady had a score to settle. The 49ers had skipped over him in the draft, and he was itching to show them they had made a mistake.

On the opposite sideline, Joe Montana was watching rookie quarterback Giovanni Carmazzi warm up. Carmazzi was on record saying how honored he felt to be the potential heir to Montana and Young.

The Niners had high expectations for Carmazzi. "The kid had all the measurables," said 49ers head coach Steve Mariucci. "He was fast. He was athletic. He was strong. He was smart."

Belichick and the Patriots, on the other hand, had put almost no expectations on Brady. They were just trying to determine if he could make the roster. All of the pressure on Brady to perform well was self-generated.

The first two times Carmazzi dropped back to pass, New England put ferocious pressure on him, sacking him both times. In each instance he got hit hard, and the hits unnerved him. He ended up completing just three of his seven passes for a total of nineteen yards. "It became evident in the first preseason game," Mariucci said, "the stage was maybe a little too big. The lights might be a little too bright for him."

When Mariucci pulled Carmazzi out of the game, he looked dazed and overwhelmed.

"When you get out on the field and the other team wants to knock your head off, you have to be able to handle that mentally and emotionally,"

Mariucci said. "Some do. And with some, it makes them very nervous and they lose some confidence. To this day, I believe that Gio got off on the wrong foot against the Patriots in a preseason game and I think some doubt crept in."

Belichick saw the same things in Carmazzi that day that Mariucci saw. Belichick also saw that Brady played with great composure and completed some difficult passes. The main thing was that he wasn't afraid to stand in the pocket.

"We walked out of that game feeling that we had taken the right guy," Belichick said.

Giovanni Carmazzi never appeared in a regular season game for the 49ers. He was released by the team after two seasons.

At the end of the preseason, Belichick had to pare his roster down to fifty-three players. He faced a decision that hardly seemed momentous at the time: whether to cut Tom Brady. The Patriots already had three healthy quarterbacks. Most NFL teams carried two healthy quarterbacks during the regular season. A few teams carried three. It was unheard-of, however, for a team to carry four healthy quarterbacks. Roster spots were simply too valuable.

But Belichick was convinced that Brady was worth making an exception. He worked exceptionally hard and was hypercompetitive. Plus, Belichick felt that in game management situations—especially in tight games against good competition—Brady could handle pressure. Belichick didn't want to cut Brady and risk seeing another team pick him up. So he gave the final roster spot to the rookie from Michigan and told him that he wanted him to spend time in the weight room getting stronger.

"Look," Belichick told him, "you're skinny. You don't have enough lower body strength to power the ball."

Brady took it all in stride.

"I was not ready," Brady said. "I was overwhelmed by everything. Pro football is very different than college football. There were different responsibilities. Different levels of expectation."

At the start of the 2000 season, Bill Belichick had more pressure on him than anyone. Including the playoffs, he'd gone 37-45 in his five seasons as the Browns head coach. The adage in the NFL is that a head coach is allowed

to fail once. A coach who fails with two teams is finished. Belichick was extremely grateful to Kraft for giving him a second chance. But he was acutely aware of how much heat Kraft had taken for hiring him.

"Giving up a number one [draft pick], I think, is a lot," said NFL analyst Ron Jaworski at the time. "Belichick is one of the game's outstanding defensive coaches, but as a head coach he didn't prove much. I would think there were other qualified coaches out there so you don't have to give up a number one."

Among the national media, Jaworski was hardly alone in his thinking. "I am in a way surprised Kraft went for the deal, and at the steep price of a number one," said television broadcaster John Dockery. "A number one is an awfully steep price, especially for an assistant coach." *New York Post* columnist Steve Serby went as far as to mock Kraft, writing, "Bill Parcells killed Bob Kraft with kindness, and gets the last laugh on his way out the door." Especially in New England, the consensus among sportswriters was that Parcells had "snookered" Kraft and that Belichick was not, as one Patriots beat writer put it, "worth the tariff the Patriots surrendered to Parcells."

Belichick got off to a rough start. A month passed before he finally got his first win. After ten weeks, New England was 2-8, and as the losses mounted, Kraft was taking a beating in the media. The naysayers were all saying the same thing—"We told you so."

Tom Brady spent the 2000 season in awe. "When I got here," Brady said, "there were all these marquee players. Bruschi. Law. Milloy. I was just trying to fit in."

The biggest marquee player of all was Drew Bledsoe. And no one did more than Bledsoe to help Brady fit in. From day one, Bledsoe went out of his way to make Brady feel welcome. Knowing that Brady was single, Bledsoe often invited him to his home for dinners cooked by Bledsoe's wife, Maura. After dinner, Bledsoe and Brady would hit golf balls in the backyard. Brady became like an extension of the Bledsoe family.

"We had a great relationship," Brady said. "He was a great family man and a great friend. He'd drive me. But we weren't competitive because everyone knew he was the starter."

Punter Lee Johnson also took Brady under his wing. Like Bledsoe, he had a locker next to Brady's. The first time Johnson saw Brady, the rookie was wearing oversized khaki pants and a baggy shirt, his hair was matted, and he looked way too frail to survive in the NFL. Then Johnson observed him on

the practice field. His feet were slow, and his passes were off target. Johnson turned to kicker Adam Vinatieri and said: "Oh, man, who's *this guy*?"

Johnson had been in the league for more than fifteen years. Brady was drawn to the fact that he always had a smile on his face and a contagiously positive attitude about everything. Plus, Brady knew that Johnson had played college ball at Brigham Young University, which gave them something in common. Brady had been courted by BYU and he followed the program. When they got on the subject, they discovered they had another connection: Johnson and Steve Young had been college teammates and had roomed together for four years. Young remained one of Johnson's closest friends.

"For real?" Brady said to Johnson. "I love Steve Young. He was my favorite player. Him and Joe. I loved Steve's game."

Brady started asking Johnson lots of questions. Knowing that Johnson had played for three other teams—including an eleven-year stint in Cincinnati—before joining the Patriots, he was curious.

"What's it like being in the NFL and traveling around so much?" Brady asked him one day.

"It's a crazy, amazing time," Johnson told him. "My wife loves it. My kids love it."

"How many kids do you have?"

"Five."

"You have *five* kids?"

Johnson smiled. He was a Mormon, and he knew Brady was a Catholic—two religions known for big families. "Lemme tell ya, bro," Johnson told Brady. "We got you guys beat."

Brady laughed. "How does that work?" he asked.

It was a serious question that changed the way Johnson looked at Brady.

"Tom was genuinely interested in me as a person," Johnson said. "He would ask me the kind of questions that a lot of people never asked. And I was impressed by that. I was married with children and he wanted to know what it was like trying to balance football with being a family man. These were things he was thinking about. Life issues. The stuff that really matters."

The Patriots finished in last place in their division in 2000. The team's 5-11 record marked their worst showing since Kraft had acquired the franchise. From the outside, all those predictions about Belichick lacking what it took to be a successful head coach appeared to be on target. But Kraft was never

influenced by the critics. He spent a lot of time in the locker room, and he saw it was a changed environment. Leaders were emerging, and a sense of discipline was taking root. When authorities in New York discovered a small amount of the illegal drug ecstasy in Ty Law's luggage after a late-season game in Buffalo, Belichick came down hard, suspending his star defensive back for the final game. The suspension cost Law nearly $100,000 in salary. It also sent a message.

Kraft liked Law a great deal. But he also liked the fact that Belichick was putting down boundaries. "In my mind it was poor judgment [by Law]," Kraft told the *Boston Globe*. "When we sign anyone to a big contract, we make it clear what we expect. . . . We're trying to stand for something on the field and off of it."

Kraft's confidence in Belichick was unwavering.

Belichick, meantime, didn't dwell on the 5-11 record. As soon as the season ended, he held one-on-one meetings with a number of the players whom he considered critical to the future. Willie McGinest was one of the guys who got called in. Before they went their separate ways in the offseason, Belichick made a simple plea. "Look, trust me," Belichick told McGinest. "I'm putting together the core."

"There was a group of men that Belichick recognized as the core group," McGinest explained. "We didn't care about our record in 2000 because we were just an average football team when Belichick arrived. What we cared about was what was being built within the walls of the locker room. We knew we were on our way. The football operational part of it was looking for a prototype player that fit Bill's vision."

McGinest was so motivated that he spent the offseason recruiting players to come to New England. His primary target was his friend Roman Phifer, a tough, hard-charging linebacker who had spent ten seasons in the league. McGinest and Phifer spent the offseason working out together in Southern California. A free agent, Phifer talked about how badly he wanted a Super Bowl ring. He had his mind set on joining the Oakland Raiders, who had gone 12-4 and made it to the AFC Championship game that year. And they had a great young head coach in Jon Gruden. Most experts projected them to be the front-runners to win the Super Bowl in 2001.

"You should check out New England," McGinest told Phifer one day during a weight-lifting session.

Phifer didn't bite.

"We're putting something special together," McGinest continued.

"Man, I don't know," Phifer said.

Phifer didn't want to insult McGinest. But during his ten years in the league Phifer had yet to win a playoff game. He was tired of playing for losers.

McGinest knew Phifer was hoping to sign with Oakland. He also understood the appeal. Still, he insisted that Phifer should at least consider Belichick before signing with Gruden.

"Look, go meet with Bill," McGinest told his friend. "Trust me."

eighteen

IN AN INSTANT

A t twenty-nine years old, Drew Bledsoe had played eight seasons with
the Patriots. During that period, he had established himself as the
franchise's all-time leading passer with 4,452 attempts, 2,504 completions, and 29,257 yards. In the history of the NFL, only Dan Marino had
thrown for more yards in his first eight seasons.

With each passing year, Robert Kraft's affection for Bledsoe grew deeper.
In addition to developing into one of the game's elite quarterbacks, Bledsoe
was the face of Kraft's franchise and was beloved throughout New England.
He also fully bought in to Kraft's emphasis on philanthropy and charitable
giving. It meant the world to Kraft that his brightest star was such a great
ambassador for the Patriots organization.

Kraft believed that Bledsoe was on track to go down in history as one of
the biggest sports icons in Boston, alongside Ted Williams, Bill Russell, Larry
Bird, and Bobby Orr. Williams, Russell, and Bird had played their entire careers in Boston. Orr had played his final two seasons in Chicago, and that
had never felt right to Kraft. Tradition and loyalty were very important to
him, and he was devoted to those who were true to him and the organization.
All of this factored into his decision at the end of the 2000 season to reward
Bledsoe by offering him the biggest contract in NFL history—a ten-year extension worth $103 million. He and Bledsoe were on such good terms that
they worked out the deal through a series of one-on-one conversations.

Then, on March 7, 2001, Kraft invited Belichick to join him and Bledsoe
at a press conference at the Fleet Bank Building in downtown Boston, where
Kraft announced Bledsoe's new blockbuster deal. "I remember feeling sad
when Bobby Orr left," Kraft told the press. "I saw this as an opportunity to
sign one of the greatest Patriots for the rest of his career."

At the completion of Bledsoe's new contract, Kraft figured, the Patriots' quarterback would be thirty-nine years old and he would have spent
eighteen seasons in New England. "I think that is only fitting," Kraft said.

"Because he came here and was part of the resurgence of football in the New England region."

Bledsoe could not have been happier. "I have expressed over and over again through the years my desire to play my entire career for the New England Patriots organization," Bledsoe said as Kraft and Belichick looked on. "I am excited that with this contract it looks like that is a very real possibility."

Belichick was not directly involved in Bledsoe's contract or the decision to make him the highest-paid player in the league. But he understood the situation. Kraft's bond with Bledsoe was obvious, as was the fact that Bledsoe's value to the franchise went beyond his arm. With the new stadium being constructed in Foxborough, the franchise was under tremendous financial pressure to sell all the tickets for the club seating and luxury boxes, and Bledsoe was the biggest draw.

Weeks after Bledsoe signed his new deal, Kraft took him to the "topping off ceremony," a tradition in the construction industry that marks the completion of a new building's inner structure. More than three hundred construction workers in hard hats and steel-toed boots chanted, "Drew, Drew, Drew," as Bledsoe signed a forty-two-foot-long steel girder that weighed nearly six thousand pounds. It was the last beam to be erected in the new stadium.

Kraft also signed the beam. Then he invited Commissioner Paul Tagliabue to say a few words.

"I came up here ten years ago to try to talk up the need for a new stadium," Tagliabue told a gathering of public officials and business executives. "I was called 'a good man on a fool's errand.' Well, as things have turned out, I was a good man, I hope, on a good errand. This isn't just a new stadium. This is going to be the home of a future Super Bowl champion."

While everyone cheered, Kraft pointed at Bledsoe and smiled, signaling that he would be the one to quarterback them to the championship. Bledsoe couldn't wait. The new sixty-eight-thousand-seat, state-of-the-art stadium was on schedule to open in time for the start of the 2002 season.

Belichick was focused on the upcoming 2001 season, and his emphasis was on overhauling the roster. He started with the draft, where he used his first-round pick to choose Georgia's standout defensive end Richard Seymour, and his second-round pick to take Purdue's left tackle Matt Light. Both were players who Belichick felt could make an immediate impact, one as a pass rusher, the other protecting Bledsoe's blind side.

At the same time, Belichick cut a bunch of players and declined to re-sign a number of others who were eligible for free agency. Anyone whose on-field performance wasn't on par with his salary was gone. For instance, Belichick declined to re-sign nose tackle Chad Eaton, who ended up taking a $3.5 million signing bonus to go to Seattle. During the 2000 offseason, Belichick signed eighteen new players to lower annual salaries than what Eaton had received.

The players Belichick brought in through trades and free agency were seasoned veterans, many of whom were defensive players. They included defensive lineman Anthony Pleasant and linebackers Mike Vrabel, Larry Izzo, Bryan Cox, and Roman Phifer—who had taken his friend Willie McGinest's advice, met with Belichick, and chosen the Patriots over the Raiders. These five players had forty years of experience in the NFL, but not one of them had ever won a championship. They showed up in Foxborough hungry and determined to do whatever it took to bring a title to New England.

Belichick also made a couple of critical personnel moves at the quarterback position that reflected his conviction that Tom Brady was a unique talent. First, Belichick released both backup quarterbacks and signed free agent quarterback Damon Huard, a proven veteran who had played behind Dan Marino in Miami. But he also kept Brady and was determined to have him compete head-to-head against Huard for the number two position behind Bledsoe.

During the offseason, most players scattered to other parts of the country. But rather than returning home to California, Brady spent his first offseason in Foxborough and practically took up residence at the stadium. During the day, he lifted in the weight room, ran stairs in the stadium, or did passing drills. When he wasn't working out, he was studying film in a cramped room that the coaches referred to as "the dungeon." Over the spring and summer of 2000, Brady logged hundreds of hours alone in that room. It wasn't uncommon for assistant coaches or staff members to find him in there at ten or eleven at night.

"Why are you here?" one of the coaches asked him late one evening.

"I'm just trying to learn," Brady told him.

His answer caused the coach to shake his head and chuckle.

As the team's senior vice president and chief operating officer, Andy Wasynczuk spent a lot of time at the stadium over the summer. He occasionally made small talk with the assistant coaches. One morning they started

talking about Brady. "This kid is a crack-up," one told Wasynczuk. "We find him in the film room all the time."

Wasynczuk had never understood why Belichick drafted Brady. He was even more surprised that Brady made the team as a rookie. But Wasynczuk couldn't help noticing that the kid worked extremely hard. "The commitment level he was showing was pretty unusual," Wasynczuk said. "Here's a fourth-string quarterback, sitting there looking at film, studying tendencies, searching for ways to improve. No one else was doing that."

One afternoon that summer, Brady was alone in the quarterback room when he discovered coach Dick Rehbein's notebook on the table. It read "QUARTERBACKS" on the cover. Curious, Brady opened it and flipped through the pages until he found Rehbein's evaluation of him:

> Slow on reads. Slow to react. Doesn't deliver the ball on time. Needs to do everything quicker.

On it went. Brady stared at the words. He could have taken the criticism personally or dismissed it. But he revered Rehbein. Without him, Brady wouldn't have been a Patriot. Rehbein was the one who had lobbied Belichick so passionately on his behalf. One of the things that motivated Brady to push himself so hard was his desire to reward Rehbein for believing in him.

He closed Rehbein's notebook and put it back where he found it. If that was what his coach thought of him, Brady determined he had to do a better job. He started by adding more drills to his workout routine. He spent more time studying the playbook. He also stepped up his physical training.

None of this went unnoticed by Belichick, the one guy who spent more time at the stadium than Brady. In addition to what his assistant coaches were telling him, Belichick also observed that Brady was in the weight room a lot. By the time training camp opened in late July, Brady had put on fifteen pounds, most of which was muscle. Unlike Rehbein, Belichick didn't praise Brady. But he made a mental note that in addition to looking stronger, Brady was more confident in his decision making. His reaction time was faster. And he was making better reads.

Through the first two weeks of training camp in 2001, Brady clearly outperformed veteran Damon Huard, whom Belichick had initially penciled in to be the number two quarterback. Brady's play quickly changed Belichick's mind.

Thrilled, Rehbein continued to encourage Brady. Then, on August 6, Rehbein didn't show up for camp. The previous day he had been admitted to

the hospital after blacking out while running on a treadmill. Tests revealed that his loss of consciousness had been caused by a preexisting heart condition. That night, Rehbein called assistant coach Charlie Weis and assured him he'd be back to work the next day. But the following morning, after undergoing a stress test, Rehbein blacked out during the recovery period and never regained consciousness. The cause of death was cardiomyopathy. He was forty-five.

The shocking news cast a pall over the entire team. Belichick canceled practice that afternoon. Brady, in particular, was heartbroken. That night he went to Bledsoe's house. The two of them commiserated together until well past midnight. It was hard to come to grips with the fact that their quarterback coach was suddenly gone.

In one of the last days of training camp, Belichick did something noteworthy— he singled Brady out after a particularly impressive series of plays.

"Right there," Belichick said. "Good! Way to see it, Brady."

Encouraged, Brady turned and walked toward him.

"That's the best series you've had in camp right there," Belichick told him.

It was a rare outward expression that hinted at what Belichick was thinking privately—that Dick Rehbein had been right when he returned from Ann Arbor in the spring of 2000 and said, "He's the best fit for the Patriots system." Although Brady still hadn't proven himself in game situations, Belichick was encouraged by the fact that the youngster was so malleable. He truly wanted to be coached. He responded affirmatively to constructive criticism. And he never made the same mistake twice.

With the Patriots scheduled to open the 2001 season in Cincinnati, Belichick met with Robert Kraft on the eve of the season opener. They were joined by Jonathan Kraft and Scott Pioli. Belichick briefed Kraft on the status of the team. Robert Kraft asked a lot of questions, and Belichick outlined the areas where he felt the team still needed to improve. As the meeting wound down, Belichick looked at the owner and said: "I just want you to know if I was going to start the best quarterback on the football team this weekend, I'd be starting Tom Brady. Not Drew Bledsoe."

Belichick did not elaborate. Nor did Kraft ask him to. He had just re-signed Bledsoe to a record-breaking deal. Bledsoe was one of the two or three most talented quarterbacks in the game. Brady, on the other hand, was an unproven backup who had spent his rookie season on the practice squad. It

was hard to take Belichick's comment at face value. Yet Kraft knew full well that Belichick was not a man who made hyperbolic statements. So why, Kraft wondered, did he say that?

New England lost 23–17 in Cincinnati to start the season 0-1. Two days later, terrorists hijacked four planes and flew two of them into the World Trade Center in lower Manhattan, one into the Pentagon in Washington, and one that crashed in a field in Pennsylvania. Suddenly, football seemed inconsequential.

That night, a lot of the Patriots players gathered at Drew Bledsoe's home. No one knew what to say. One of their teammates, center Joe Andruzzi, was the son of a New York City cop, and all three of Andruzzi's brothers were New York City firemen. They had been on duty when the twin towers came down. One of Andruzzi's brothers had been in Tower I. He'd barely made it out alive. Some of his comrades hadn't.

Wondering what the future held, Bledsoe's teammates hung out at his place until after midnight. Brady ended up spending the night. It was clear that none of the guys felt like playing football. That was the sentiment of players throughout the league. For the first time in history, commissioner Tagliabue suspended all games for the upcoming weekend. Major League Baseball promptly followed suit.

At the urging of political leaders from President George W. Bush to New York City mayor Rudolph Giuliani, the NFL resumed play on Sunday, September 23, 2001. For the Patriots, it was their home opener against the New York Jets. Before the singing of the national anthem, the chants of more than sixty thousand fans—all waving miniature American flags that had been distributed at the ticket turnstiles—reverberated like thunder under the sunny, blue sky: "U-S-A. U-S-A. U-S-A."

It was approaching 4:00 p.m. in New England. And as on previous occasions following national tragedies, Americans were looking to sports for a diversion from sadness and to restore some semblance of normalcy.

"Good afternoon, ladies and gentlemen," NBC announcer Dick Enberg said over the public address system. "And welcome to Foxboro Stadium. The events of September eleventh have changed the world. Let us now take a moment to remember and to move forward in a new spirit of unity and determination."

In a stadium engulfed in an emotional outpouring of grief, patriotism, and unity, the contest between New England and New York took on a subdued tone. Neither team scored a touchdown in the first half. After a Patriots

fumble, the Jets scored a touchdown in the third quarter to go up 10–3. The score remained unchanged as the game slogged toward the final minutes. The early-season contest between two 0-1 teams seemed destined to be a forgotten footnote in the larger post-9/11 narrative.

But sports have an uncanny ability to upend destiny with surprise. When you least expect it, something unprecedented and unforgettable can happen. Undoubtedly, no one inside Foxboro Stadium or watching from home on television that evening could have imagined that they were about to witness something so seismic that it would shift the course of NFL history.

With just over five minutes remaining, Drew Bledsoe dropped back to pass on third-down-and-ten from the Patriots' nineteen-yard line. Finding no open receivers and feeling pressure from his blind side, he scrambled to his right, then turned upfield. With his eyes locked on the red first-down marker at the twenty-nine-yard line, he angled toward the Patriots sideline as a defender gave chase from behind. At the last second, instead of running out of bounds, Bledsoe hesitated just long enough for the pursuing defender to reach him and push him in the back, propelling him forward as 258-pound linebacker Mo Lewis plowed head-on into Bledsoe at full speed, planting his shoulder into the quarterback's chest. Bledsoe's feet left the ground and his head whiplashed like a rag doll's. He crash-landed out of bounds, near the feet of Patriots punter Lee Johnson.

The hit was so violent that Johnson flinched as if he himself had been hit.

"I had been in the league for eighteen years and that was the worst hit I ever saw," Johnson said. "I'll never forget the noise it made. It was like a truck hit him. I literally felt it. I thought it killed Drew."

Team medical personnel rushed to Bledsoe, who remained down while the Patriots punt unit took the field and kicked the ball back to the Jets. Dazed, Bledsoe finally got up and staggered to the bench. His face mask was crooked and loose. When Belichick asked how he felt, Bledsoe said he was all right.

He had in fact sustained a concussion, but it went undiagnosed in the immediate aftermath of the hit. As Bledsoe sat on the bench for a few minutes, the Jets barely managed to burn a minute off the game clock before being forced to punt the ball back to New England. With 3:46 remaining in the game, Bledsoe went back in. In the huddle, his teammates immediately knew something was wrong. Bledsoe had trouble remembering the plays. He also couldn't distinguish right from left. "I couldn't think straight," Bledsoe would later say. "I got my bell rung pretty good."

On the third play of the series, running back Marc Edwards fumbled,

turning the ball back over to the Jets. When Bledsoe came back off the field, Brady and Damon Huard approached. Both quarterbacks were concerned.

"Hey, you sure you're all right?" Brady said.

Bledsoe looked confused. "What are the check-with-me plays?" he said.

Brady and Huard looked at each other. "Check-with-me" is when a quarterback calls two plays in the huddle and then decides at the line of scrimmage which one to run, based on the defensive formation. The fact that Bledsoe couldn't remember the plays was disconcerting.

"This isn't right," Huard said to Brady.

"We gotta get him out of the game," Brady said.

Huard went to Charlie Weis. Moments later, Belichick found Brady. "Drew is out and you're in," he told him.

Brady put on his helmet and started warming up on the sideline. Shocked by the severity of Mo Lewis's hit on Bledsoe, Brady nevertheless blocked out what he had seen and heard—the loudest hit he'd ever witnessed, Bledsoe's bent face mask, Bledsoe's blank stare and inability to remember plays. This wasn't the time to dwell on that stuff.

When the Jets failed to get a first down and punted the ball back to New England with 2:16 remaining, Brady buckled his chinstrap and jogged onto the field.

The Patriots were all the way back on their own twenty-six-yard line. They had to score a touchdown—something they'd been unable to do all day—just to tie the game. And Brady had no time-outs to work with. Still, he fully expected to lead his team to victory.

Up to this point, Brady had made one brief appearance in a game during the previous season, throwing a grand total of three passes. His sudden appearance was immediately noted by NBC announcer Dick Enberg.

"Tom Brady, the second-year quarterback from the University of Michigan," Enberg said on the air. "This is his first duty of 2001. Apparently, Bledsoe was knocked around a little more than it appeared. And Brady is in charge."

Over the next two minutes, Brady threw seven passes and completed six of them. He also ran the ball once for nine yards. He drove New England all the way to the Jets' twenty-nine-yard line. It was the best drive of the day. The crowd was into it. With fourteen seconds left, Brady had the Patriots in striking range. But for the final two plays, the Jets packed the end zone with defenders, making it impossible for the Patriots receivers to get open. New England fell to 0-2.

Rather than focusing on the loss, Belichick noted that Brady had moved

the team all the way downfield without any time-outs. Belichick also noted that Brady was furious with himself when they didn't score at the end. That was a good sign.

Walking off the field, Drew Bledsoe was complaining of shoulder pain, which got the attention of Patriots physician Thomas Gill. Bledsoe never groused about pain. Gill took him directly to the X-ray room.

The X-rays of Bledsoe's shoulder were negative. So were the X-rays of his abdomen. Other than a pretty severe concussion, there were no visible signs of injury. But something was amiss. Bledsoe had shortness of breath and his heart rate was high. Gill consulted with team internist Jim Dineen, telling him that he thought something was going on with Bledsoe's abdomen.

While the doctors talked, Bledsoe told his brother, Adam, who was in the locker room, that he just wanted to go home and lie down. They were getting ready to leave when the Patriots medical staff headed them off.

"Wait a minute," Gill said. "Let's just settle down and figure out what's going on."

Patriots lead physician Bertram Zarins joined the discussion. The biggest red flag was Bledsoe's vital signs. His faint pulse and shallow breathing were disconcerting. There was no way the doctors could let him go home under the circumstances. Gill telephoned Dr. David Berger, the lead trauma surgeon at Massachusetts General Hospital. Berger was at home. After being briefed on Bledsoe's situation, he agreed to go directly to the ER.

Minutes later, Bledsoe was placed on a gurney and loaded into an ambulance. His brother got in with him. It normally took about forty minutes to make the thirty-mile drive from Foxboro Stadium to Mass General in Boston. But on game days it could take two hours just to get out of the stadium parking lot. State troopers on motorcycles led the way, pounding on car windows and ordering motorists to clear a path. By the time Bledsoe's ambulance reached the outskirts of Boston, he was moaning and slipping in and out of consciousness. Fearing his brother was dying, Adam banged on the ambulance cab window with his fist and screamed at the driver: "Get there! Get there!"

Maura Bledsoe was in the stands during the Jets game. From afar, she saw her husband get hit by Mo Lewis. She also saw him return to the game a few minutes later. Seeing her husband get knocked down was so routine that she

never suspected he was injured, and after the game, she did what she always did at the conclusion of home games—made her way to an area beneath the stadium where wives and girlfriends waited for their husbands and boyfriends. And she waited. And waited. And waited. Eventually, every player had come out except Drew. "Where is he?" she said to no one in particular.

She was pretty irritated by the time the Patriots' head of security showed up.

"Maura, we've been looking for you," he said.

"Me? Why?" she said.

He explained that Drew had left the stadium in an ambulance. "C'mon," the security chief said. "We've got a police escort to take you to the hospital."

"A *police escort*?" she said.

"Yeah. We gotta get you to the hospital as fast as possible."

Before she had a moment to process what was happening, Maura was hustled into the backseat of a sedan being driven by a retired cop who worked security for the team. A Massachusetts state trooper in a police cruiser turned on his lights and led them away from the stadium. Maura felt anxious. "There's no way this is just a concussion," she told herself as the red glare of the police lights illuminated the way.

When Robert Kraft arrived at Mass General, he huddled with one of the team doctors. He wanted a detailed rundown on Bledsoe's condition. The doctor walked him through the whole catalog of injuries—the broken ribs, the lacerated artery, the blood pooling in the chest, the punctured lung. A chest tube, he explained, had been inserted to remove blood from Bledsoe's chest and circulate it through filters before re-transfusing it through one of his veins. It was still unclear whether Bledsoe would need surgery to stop the internal bleeding.

Kraft was overwhelmed to learn how close Bledsoe had come to dying. Fortunately for Bledsoe, the injury happened at the end of the game and the team rushed him to one of the top hospitals in the United States, where he was put in excellent hands. If Bledsoe's injury had taken place in another city, the outcome could have been very different. By the time he woke up in the ICU to find Kraft, Belichick, and Brady standing over his bed, he realized he was lucky to be alive.

For Maura, it was a struggle to control her emotions. It was hard to see her husband looking so vulnerable.

Before leaving, Kraft hugged Maura and encouraged her to try to get some rest.

It was well after midnight when she finally got home and crawled into bed. It seemed empty without Drew. Alone in the dark, she bawled into her pillow. "He was bleeding out," she told herself. "If he hadn't come out of the game when he did . . . If he had taken one more hit . . ."

She didn't want to go there.

nineteen

CHANGING PLACES

R obert Kraft could look out of his office window at Foxboro Stadium and see the new stadium taking shape before his eyes. Each day, it got a little bigger. Each day, his longtime quest to erect a world-class facility for his team and the fans of New England got closer to being realized. The construction was actually ahead of schedule, meaning 2001 would definitely be the team's final season in the old stadium.

But instead of being excited, Kraft was anxious. Only about one-third of the six thousand premium club seats and fewer than half of the stadium's eighty-eight luxury suites had been sold. Under normal circumstances, that wouldn't be cause for alarm one year ahead of the opening. But in a post-9/11 world, it was hard not to wonder whether corporations and wealthy individuals would become more skittish about investing in luxury stadium seating. That concern wasn't unique to the Patriots. Stadium operators throughout the country were suddenly confronting a new reality—venues that drew large numbers of people were potentially attractive targets for terrorists.

Kraft also had other reasons to worry. He had personally guaranteed the $53 million needed to purchase the 6,300 blue steel girders that formed the new structure. The best way to mitigate the risk was to establish a winning team before the stadium opened. That had been the plan when Kraft hired Belichick. "I believe he's the most capable person at this point in time to help us win next year," Kraft had said at Belichick's introductory press conference in February 2000. "We want to win next year, and I believe we have the man that's going to help us do that."

But the team didn't win under Belichick in 2000. And with the loss of Bledsoe, Kraft didn't see how the team was going to win in 2001.

In fact, Kraft was so shaken up about Bledsoe's medical condition that winning had become an afterthought. He got emotional every time he contemplated how close Bledsoe had come to losing his life. And the prognosis

that Bledsoe might never play again was even more depressing. For Kraft, the prospect of life in Foxborough without Bledsoe was a melancholic proposition.

Yet the good news coming out of Mass General was that Bledsoe's damaged artery had stopped bleeding on its own, which enabled him to avoid potentially career-ending surgery. Although Bledsoe would need to remain hospitalized for weeks while the hole in his lung healed, the doctors were suggesting that Bledsoe might be able to return to action later in the season. Relieved that Bledsoe had stabilized, Kraft nonetheless put the brakes on talk about his playing again, before Bledsoe got his hopes up. Kraft made it clear that when the time came, he was going to insist that Bledsoe be examined by top lung specialists who were unaffiliated with the team or Mass General. He wanted an independent examination to determine whether it was safe for Bledsoe to play football again.

One of Bill Belichick's nicknames was Doom. Bill Parcells had given it to him when Belichick was his defensive coordinator for the Giants. "We used to call him Doom because every time he walked around it was the end of the world," ex-Giants linebacker Lawrence Taylor said. "'Ah, you didn't make this play.' 'Ah, you didn't go over here.' It was the end of the world."

The nickname fit Belichick's dour demeanor, which fed into his tendency to focus on and prepare for scenarios that most coaches overlooked. "Looking at the negative side and preparing for the negative has made him a better football coach, because he prepares for all of the things that can go bad," said Patriots defensive coordinator Romeo Crennel. "And to tell you the truth, I think he kind of halfway liked the idea that people were calling him Doom because that way, he didn't have to be nice to anybody."

With Drew Bledsoe hospitalized, Belichick had a legitimate reason to project doom and gloom. But for once, he didn't. Instead, he exuded confidence, wasting no time in naming Tom Brady as the starter in week three against the Indianapolis Colts. In doing so, Belichick cited Brady's performance at the end of the Jets game. "I thought he did okay with what he had there," Belichick told the press. "All things considered, I thought in that situation he threw the ball pretty accurately and made good decisions."

Some writers who covered the team had expected Belichick to start Damon Huard, who was considerably more experienced and had compiled an impressive 5-1 record while filling in for an injured Dan Marino the previous year in Miami. But Belichick had made his mind up about Brady very

early on. "Tom was special his rookie year even though he didn't play," Belichick said. "His leadership with the other rookies in the class—we had a big rookie class. Tom took them every day after practice and would run them up and down the field in their offensive plays. He was clearly a leader on the field and had a very good training camp in 2001."

If it had been up to Belichick, Brady would have been his starter at the beginning of the 2001 season. He had said as much to Kraft when they met at the end of the preseason, but Belichick had known that he wasn't in a position to push the issue then, when Bledsoe was the face of the franchise and Belichick was coming off a 5-11 season. Although Kraft had given him tremendous latitude over personnel decisions, benching the greatest quarterback in franchise history in favor of an unproven rookie right after Kraft had made Bledsoe the highest-paid player in the league would have been a bridge too far.

But Bledsoe's injury had enabled Belichick to start the quarterback he had wanted all along. Publicly, however, Belichick went out of his way to lower people's expectations for Brady. On the same day that he announced Brady would be the team's starter, Belichick told the press: "I don't think we're talking about John Elway here."

Members of the Patriots defense certainly didn't have a lot of faith in Brady.

"Bledsoe had the ability to carry a team and throw for four hundred–plus yards," said linebacker Tedy Bruschi. "We didn't think Brady could come in and do that. Everyone believed it was going to be harder. Tom had shown us nothing except for good practices. He was still learning."

When linebacker Willie McGinest learned that Bledsoe would be sidelined indefinitely, he warned his defensive colleagues that they'd have to shoulder the load. "Our mentality on defense at the time was that we were the catalyst for the team," said McGinest. "It wasn't as if our offense had been scoring forty-five points a game anyway. So when Drew went down, we were like: 'Fuck it. If our offense only scores fourteen, we can only give up ten. We really gotta shut teams down.'"

The first team that New England faced with Brady under center was not going to be easy to shut down. Led by fourth-year quarterback Peyton Manning, the Colts had the number one offense in the AFC. They had blown out their first two opponents of the season, putting up forty-five points against the Jets and forty-two against Buffalo. Belichick's defensive game plan was simple—manhandle Manning and disrupt his wide receivers by jamming them when they came off the line of scrimmage. Just prior to the game,

Patriots linebacker Bryan Cox put it more succinctly: "I'm looking to knock Peyton's head off," Cox said.

Hands on his hips, chinstrap dangling from his helmet, Tom Brady stood at the edge of the tunnel in one corner of Foxboro Stadium with his fifty-two teammates bunched up behind him. From the moment he'd been drafted by the Patriots, he had repeatedly told himself that when he got his shot, he would be ready. With a miniature play sheet taped to his left wrist and eye black beneath his eyes, Brady stared ahead in stony silence.

In the opposite corner of the stadium, Peyton Manning jogged onto the field as the announcer introduced him. If there was such a thing as blue blood in the NFL, Manning was it. The son of All-Pro quarterback Archie Manning and the first player chosen in the 1998 NFL Draft, Peyton had signed a $46 million deal that included an $11.6 million signing bonus. In his rookie year he passed for more than 3,700 yards and set five rookie passing records. Now, in just his fourth season, Manning was considered the most elite passer in the game.

Conversely, Brady was a commoner. The son of an insurance salesman, he was the quarterback no one had wanted. He earned $231,500 in his rookie year and threw just three passes, completing one of them. His own team-mates considered him "a skinny little pretty boy named Tom." The best thing he had going for him was the monumental chip on his shoulder.

With fog hovering over Foxboro Stadium and Ozzie Osbourne's "Crazy Train" blaring through the sound system, Brady ran out of the tunnel with his teammates, for the first time as a starter in the NFL. Too young to appreciate the pressure on Belichick to start winning and too aloof to fully understand how much was riding on his own performance, Brady had one objective—to make no mistakes.

On the Colts' second offensive play of the game, Manning threw over the middle to receiver Jerome Pathon. Waiting for him, linebacker Bryan Cox lowered his shoulder and leveled Pathon. The hit was so hard that it prompted the CBS announcer to say: "Bryan Cox almost took his head off."

Cox's hit set the tone. The Colts' offense never got in sync, and Manning ended up throwing three interceptions. Two of them were returned by the Patriots for touchdowns. Meantime, Brady executed Belichick's game plan to perfection. The Patriots ran the ball twice as much as they threw it, chewing up the clock and keeping Manning off the field. Although Brady passed for just 168 yards and threw no touchdown passes, he threw no

interceptions. New England won 44–13, causing ESPN to declare: "Drew-less Patriots stun Colts."

The next day, reporters started asking Belichick how Brady's performance would impact Bledsoe's status when he returned.

"We'll take care of that when he's ready," Belichick said. "Right now, Tom's the quarterback."

Pressed to clarify his position, Belichick resisted getting drawn into a controversy when one didn't exist. "We're trying to get ready for Miami," he said. "Tom will be the quarterback against the Dolphins."

In Tom Brady's second start, Miami thrashed New England 30–10. The loss dropped the Patriots to 1-3. It also lowered Belichick's overall record in New England to 6-14. Whispers about his job security were getting louder. If it had been up to the countless Patriots fans who called in to the city's popular sports talk radio stations, Belichick would have been gone already.

Belichick was under no illusions about what would happen if the team didn't start winning. He once advised his friend Scott Pioli: "You're going to get fired in this business. This just isn't a business where you last. Sometimes it's in your control, but most of the time it's not."

One of Belichick's strengths, however, was his ability to focus on things within his control and ignore circumstances outside his control. He also made a point of constantly driving that mentality into his players. If he was sweating, he wasn't going to let his players see it.

When the Patriots returned to the practice field after losing in Miami, they discovered a large hole that had been hand-dug. Belichick was standing next to it, with a football in one hand and a shovel in the other.

"You guys see this ball?" he said. "This is the ball from the game yester-day."

The players nodded.

"And this is what I think of it," he said, tossing it into the hole.

The players watched as Belichick shoveled dirt on top of the ball. When he finished, he stuck the shovel in the ground.

"That game's over," Belichick told them. "We're burying it and moving on."

The imagery of Belichick burying the past had an impact on the entire team. The message especially got through to Brady. After everyone else walked away from the interred ball, Brady stomped on the dirt. "It's over!" he said under his breath.

Six days later, New England played at home against San Diego. Trailing by three points in the fourth quarter, the Patriots were forced to punt from deep in their own territory. Punter Lee Johnson mishandled the snap, giving a defender time to reach him. Despite being in the defender's grasp, Johnson still tried to get the punt off. In doing so, he fumbled and the defender scooped up the ball and rumbled into the end zone to put the Chargers up 26–16.

Belichick fumed. It looked like the game—as well as the season—was lost.

But in just his third start, Brady orchestrated two late scoring drives. He capped off the second one by throwing a touchdown pass to tie the game with thirty-six seconds remaining. Then he put New England in position for a game-winning field goal by Adam Vinatieri in overtime. Miraculously, the Patriots won 29–26.

Brady completed thirty-three of fifty-four passes for 364 yards and two touchdowns. These were Bledsoe-esque numbers. And once again, Brady threw no interceptions.

"You never know what you're going to get from a young quarterback, but Tom's been pretty consistent all season, starting from training camp," Belichick told reporters. "He runs the team well and doesn't make a lot of mistakes, like letting the play clock run down or missing the checks at the line of scrimmage."

After the Chargers game, Brady's teammates started to see him in a different light. He had demonstrated an ability to perform under pressure. In the following morning's paper, a *Boston Globe* writer dubbed Brady "Cool-hand Tom."

The day after the Chargers game, punter Lee Johnson had a bad feeling when he was told that Coach Belichick wanted to see him in his office. Johnson took a seat on the other side of Belichick's desk.

"Lee, we're letting you go," Belichick told him matter-of-factly. "You're slipping."

There was awkward silence. *That's it?* Johnson thought. *I'm gone?*

Belichick had nothing more to say.

Johnson couldn't believe it. He was one of the best punters in league history. In sixteen seasons, he had racked up more than fifty thousand career punting yards. Only one punter was ahead of him on the all-time list. And since joining the Patriots, he'd flubbed punts in only two games, and one of

those games was during a snowstorm. He wanted to say, "Look, Bill, I know why I'm getting fired—the mishandles; you don't think I want to be a football player anymore, that I'm too interested in other things. But let's look at my stats."

Instead, Johnson kept his mouth shut.

When the Patriots had signed Johnson in 1999, he relocated his family to Massachusetts. For the first time in his career, he and his wife had purchased a home. They liked New England so much they planned on retiring there. His children were in the school system. They had friends. The family was settled. Johnson wasn't ready to give up his job with the Patriots. But he was intimidated by Belichick and wasn't about to argue with him. He went straight from Belichick's office to the locker room and cleaned out his stuff.

Things were changing fast in Foxborough. In a three-week span, Tom Brady's two locker mates had disappeared, one due to a freak injury and one because he made a mistake in a key situation. Brady kept reminding himself to focus on what he could control, make the most of his opportunity, work hard, and, most of all, try not to make mistakes.

Over the next four weeks, Brady led the team to three wins and one loss. The team was 5-2 since he took over and 5-4 overall.

Fifty-one days after Bledsoe suffered a life-threatening injury, on November 13, 2001, he joined doctors at a press conference at Massachusetts General Hospital. A few weeks earlier, Bledsoe had been cleared to start throwing and working out. During the games, he'd been on the sideline in street clothes, encouraging Brady. The purpose of the press conference was for the Patriots medical team to declare Bledsoe medically fit to return to football. "We have also had Drew evaluated by five specialists in lung injuries," the Patriots lead physician said. "All the consultants who have seen him agree that his current injury has healed and that there is no residual problem."

The press was eager to hear from Bledsoe.

"Do you see yourself playing Sunday?" a reporter asked. "Is Sunday too quick?"

"Put it this way," Bledsoe said. "I am going to do everything in my control to be on the field on Sunday."

"In light of the success the team has had, do you still feel like this is your team?" another reporter asked.

"Yeah, I think so," Bledsoe said. "I think that the guys still look to me and I still have the presence in the locker room and with the team and so on. The

team's done great. Brady's played excellent football and I'm ecstatic about that, but at the same time it is bittersweet because I want to be on the field while it is going on."

Bledsoe was itching to play. In five days, the Patriots would be hosting the Rams in a nationally televised Sunday night game. It would be New England's toughest test of the season. St. Louis had the best record in the league and the number one offense. Driving home from the press conference, Bledsoe telephoned Belichick to let him know he was raring to go.

"Good to hear," Belichick said.

Bledsoe waited for Belichick to say more. But he didn't. Instead, the call ended awkwardly. After Bledsoe hung up, he worried for the first time that he might not get his job back.

Now that Bledsoe was healthy, Belichick faced the most perilous decision of his career—whether to stick with Brady. He had played admirably in Bledsoe's absence. But the point was that Bledsoe was no longer absent and there was an unwritten rule that starters—especially elite quarterbacks of Bledsoe's stature—didn't lose their jobs to injury. A lot of veterans in the locker room definitely subscribed to that philosophy. "No disrespect to Tom," said Adam Vinatieri. "But without Drew getting hurt, he would've never seen the field. At that point, Drew Bledsoe was our franchise."

Perhaps most important, Belichick couldn't ignore the fact that Kraft was partial to Bledsoe. If Belichick mishandled the situation, he ran the risk of creating friction in the locker room and possibly even putting his own career in jeopardy. Whichever way he went, the most important thing was to win.

As soon as Bledsoe returned to practice, Belichick had him and Brady split the number of snaps they took with the first team. But a few days before the Rams game, Belichick called Bledsoe into his office. The conversation was very one-sided: Belichick talked and Bledsoe listened. The message was blunt—Brady was starting against the Rams.

It was all Bledsoe could do to keep his composure. There was no loyalty in the NFL anymore, he told himself. There just wasn't. If you do your job on the field and do it well, hey, look out if you get hurt. Don't leave the field. Do whatever you have to do to stay out there.

But he didn't say any of that to Belichick. Pissed, he just walked out.

With Bledsoe on the sideline, New England lost to St. Louis 24–17 to fall to 5-5. In the locker room after the game, the Patriots players were frustrated

and angry. Robert Kraft paid close attention as Belichick brought the team together and told them how proud he was of their performance. Then he put things in perspective.

"That's the best team in the league," Belichick told them. "You played them very tough."

As he spoke, the players' demeanor changed.

"Remember this game," Belichick continued. "We very well might see them again."

The players knew what Belichick was suggesting. The Rams were in the NFC. The only way the Patriots could see them again was in the Super Bowl. He was telling his team that he felt they were good enough to go toe-to-toe with the best team in the league. In a moment of defeat, Belichick had managed to motivate everyone to work harder.

When Belichick addressed the media the following morning, the primary thing that reporters wanted to talk about was the one thing he didn't care to discuss—who was going to start at quarterback in the upcoming game against New Orleans.

"I don't see any change this week," Belichick said.

Under the circumstances, the press felt some explanation was in order. After all, he had one of the most elite quarterbacks in the game at his disposal, and he wasn't using him. Meantime, Brady had thrown a couple of interceptions in the Rams game. Statistically, it wasn't one of his better games.

Belichick recognized that Brady had made some mistakes in the Rams game. But one of his interceptions bounced off his receiver's hands and into the hands of a defender. That had nothing to do with Brady. Moreover, the Rams had a fierce defense, yet Brady still completed nineteen of twenty-seven passes for 185 yards and a touchdown. If Brady hadn't been as sharp as usual, Belichick blamed himself. It would be hard for anyone to play well after only getting half the reps in practice the week before, he reasoned.

Rather than making a change at quarterback, Belichick decided to change how he was going to handle Bledsoe and Brady in practice going forward. A few hours after talking to the media, Belichick met with both quarterbacks and told them how it was going to be. "We're going with Tom," he said, looking at Bledsoe. "He's going to get all the reps. And he's going to play."

Bledsoe wasn't pleased.

But Belichick had his reasons. From his perspective, Tom was game ready. He was in rhythm. Drew, through no fault of his own, hadn't played in more than two months. With six regular season games remaining, Belichick didn't think it made sense to upset the chemistry.

Bledsoe didn't buy Belichick's explanation. And he considered it bullshit that he wasn't even going to get a chance to compete for his job. Livid, he decided to talk to Kraft.

Kraft and Bledsoe had a lot of one-on-one conversations over the years. But the one in Kraft's office in the week leading up to the New Orleans game stood out. Kraft mainly listened as Bledsoe pleaded his case. Prior to his injury, he had started 111 of 114 regular season games. Other than Brett Favre, he'd been the most durable quarterback in the league. From the day he'd arrived in Foxborough, he'd done everything the organization had asked of him. Never once had he complained. But he couldn't keep quiet any longer. The fact that he had lost his job over a hit that nearly cost him his life was hard to accept.

Empathetic to Bledsoe's plight, Kraft faced a dilemma. Up to this point, he had firmly backed every personnel move that Belichick had made. When Belichick had cut popular players, including ones who had spent their entire careers in New England, Kraft had supported him. Even when Belichick had decided to fire Bobby Grier, Kraft had refrained from intervening. But Bledsoe was different. He was in a class by himself. He was practically a fifth son.

Kraft told Bledsoe he'd talk to Belichick.

The situation presented a defining moment for Kraft. As the owner, he certainly had the power to tell Belichick to restore Bledsoe to the starting lineup. From a business standpoint, it would not be an unreasonable demand. Kraft wasn't paying Bledsoe $103 million to stand on the sideline and hold a clipboard. Yet Kraft had never told a coach who should play and who should sit. Doing so in this instance would clearly alter the dynamic with Belichick.

When Kraft went to see Belichick, he decided to ask questions rather than advocate. The situation was a defining moment for Belichick as well. Although Kraft didn't say a word about his preference, it was clear where his allegiance lay. They wouldn't have been meeting if Bledsoe had been playing. From a self-preservation standpoint, Belichick could have told Kraft what he thought his boss wanted to hear. Instead, he was unequivocal. Brady, he insisted, was the right leader at the right time for this team. As the head coach, Belichick believed that having Brady on the field put the team in the best position to win.

Kraft went back to his office to consider his next move. He could side with his head coach or he could side with his franchise quarterback. Either

way, there was going to be tension. In his other businesses, Kraft had been consistently successful by hiring good managers and empowering them to make decisions. His definition of a good manager was someone who was bold, willing to take risks, and unafraid to fail. By going with Brady, Belichick had certainly demonstrated all three elements of the definition.

The other thing that Kraft expected from his managers was execution and accountability. But if he didn't give his business managers authority, he couldn't expect to hold them accountable. If he wanted accountability from Belichick, he had to allow him to make the decision.

Kraft met again with Bledsoe. After summarizing his conversation with Belichick, Kraft told Bledsoe that Brady would remain the starting quarterback.

"I feel horrible," Kraft told him. "But I'm leaving this decision to Bill."

Bledsoe didn't hide his disappointment.

"Look, I could force it," Kraft told him. "But if I do that, it would not be good for you."

A few days before the Saints game, the press learned that Brady was going to be the permanent starter. One reporter asked Belichick to characterize Bledsoe's reaction to the news.

"You'll have to ask Drew that," Belichick said.

When reporters cornered Bledsoe in the locker room, he wasn't in the mood to talk about his reaction to Belichick's decision.

"Next question," Bledsoe said.

"Are you frustrated?" another reporter asked.

"Next question," Bledsoe said.

A reporter asked how he could get ready to compete if he didn't get reps in practice.

"Next question."

Another reporter asked about his emotional state.

"Next question."

It was clear that Bledsoe was fuming. "I look forward to getting the chance to compete for my job," he said flatly.

The next day, *Boston Globe* sportswriter Ron Borges accused Belichick of lying. "He lied to Drew Bledsoe about what the competitive situation would be when the quarterback regained his health," Borges wrote. "That was no miscommunication. There was no misunderstanding. There was no hedging of the bet. He fibbed."

Under fire, Belichick held a press conference and defended his decision to stick with Brady. "That's what Mr. Kraft is paying me to do," he said. "And that's what I'm gonna do. I'm gonna make the decisions that I think are best for the football team. T-E-A-M, as in team."

Tom Brady didn't want any friction with Bledsoe. "I've been on both sides of something like this," he told the press. "I empathize with him, of course. Those are the feelings you fight. It's the feeling that one of your best friends and teammates isn't as happy as he normally is."

Although Bledsoe's injury had afforded Brady a chance to play, Belichick was now extending him the opportunity to keep his job. It was a simple proposition—if Brady continued to play well, he would be the Patriots' starting quarterback for the future. At the same time, the situation also put Brady in a position to undermine Belichick's job security. By hitching his wagon to an unproven, sixth-round draft choice, Belichick had put his own job at risk. If Brady didn't pan out, there would be consequences. A lot was riding on what Brady did next.

Three days after Belichick faced down reporters, Brady played his best game to date, tossing four touchdown passes and completing nineteen of twenty-six pass attempts. New England walloped New Orleans 34–17 and Brady was named the NFL's Player of the Week. After the game, he wrote the following words on the game ball:

To Dad,

A huge win!! Wish you were here. This ball is for my idol.

Love,
Your Son

For Belichick, the trademark of a great quarterback is his ability to bounce back after a poor performance. Brady did that against New Orleans. It was, in Belichick's eyes, a turning point in the 2001 season. The players felt that way, too.

"When Bledsoe came back, my question was: 'Is Belichick going to walk the walk?'" said linebacker Tedy Bruschi. "He did a lot of talking about 'Do your job.' And he'd say, 'Week-to-week, how good are you?' Well, when Drew came back, Tom was playing pretty well and we were starting to become a

good football team. I was thinking: 'You tell us all this stuff about winning football games and giving us the best chance to win. Well, who do you think gives us the best chance to win? Because right now, this Brady kid is doing a good job and we're getting better as a team.'

"We had a feeling that we were on to something," Bruschi continued. "If Bill interrupted that, it would not have been consistent with what he'd been preaching to us since he was hired. So that was a moment for me. When he left Tom in, it made me feel legitimacy in terms of what Bill had been preaching."

Even Bledsoe made a conscious decision to support Brady. The next week, when New England faced the first-place Jets in New York, Bledsoe was standing next to Belichick when Brady came to the sideline with 1:46 remaining in the game. Clinging to a one-point lead, New England faced a critical third down. If the Patriots were forced to punt, the Jets would have a chance to kick a field goal and win the game. Belichick could see that Brady was in a lot of pain from a previous blow to his ribs and chest. Nonetheless, Belichick called a quarterback sneak.

"That's the one you want, huh?" Brady said, wincing.

Belichick nodded.

"Just run the ball," Bledsoe chimed in. "Get the first down and win the game."

"All right," Brady said. "Let's do it."

Needing a yard and a half, Brady put his head down and barreled forward, disappearing into a sea of wide bodies. He went down so close to the first down marker that the officials had to measure. By less than the length of a football, he'd made the first down.

"Yes!" Belichick yelled, pumping his fist in the air.

The Patriots never looked back. With Brady at the helm, they beat the Jets and every team left on the schedule.

twenty

THE PERFECT STORM

O n January 6, 2002, New England closed out the regular season in Carolina by beating the Panthers 38–6. With an 11-5 record, they had won the AFC East division title. During the flight home, the mood was celebratory. Then the pilot came on the loudspeaker and announced that the Jets had upset the AFC West division champion Raiders. Cheers filled the cabin. The Raiders' loss dropped them to 10-6, allowing the Patriots to leapfrog them in the playoff seeding. It meant the Patriots would have a bye in the wild-card round and have home-field advantage in the divisional round.

Amid the jubilation, Robert Kraft placed an urgent call to his contractor. Foxboro Stadium was scheduled to be demolished the next day, but that would have to be postponed. There would be one more game at Foxboro Stadium.

The unexpected turn of events gave Kraft an idea. No NFL playoff game had ever been televised during prime time. CBS and the NFL had decided to change that by televising one of the four divisional round playoff games in a prime-time slot on Saturday, January 19, 2002. It was a bold experiment that would entail bumping the popular dramas *Touched by an Angel* and *The District*. Kraft requested that the Patriots game be the one that got the prime-time nod.

Kraft got his wish. CBS Sports president Sean McManus felt confident that a clash between the notoriously intimidating and rebellious Oakland Raiders and the underdog, Cinderella-like New England Patriots held the promise of great theater. Kickoff was set for 8:05 p.m. on the East Coast.

Tom Brady recognized the significance of playing in his first playoff game as a New England Patriot. Although the twenty-four-year-old had lived in the region for only eighteen months, Brady knew that Boston sports fans

were among the most fervent in the country. Yet the Patriots had never won a championship. Now, millions of people throughout the six New England states would be tuning in and rooting for the Patriots to upset the Raiders. As the Patriots' starting quarterback, Brady had a chance to do for New Englanders what his boyhood idols Joe Montana and Steve Young had done for San Franciscans—foster a deeper sense of community by establishing a winning tradition.

On the day of the game, the sky was blue and the sun was shining in Foxborough. The temperature was near forty degrees. For mid-January in New England, the conditions could not have been more balmy as Brady set out for the stadium. But he'd been in the car only a few minutes when the sky darkened and snow started falling. He had never played football in the snow, not even in Ann Arbor. *This could be fun*, he told himself.

Mindful of Belichick's requirement that players arrive three hours before kickoff, Brady had left his house in plenty of time. He lived near the stadium, and taking the back roads to avoid game-day traffic, he usually made the trip in ten minutes. But this time he found his normal route snarled. Brady tried another road in hopes of getting to the rear of the stadium. But as he approached Route 1—the primary thoroughfare to Foxboro Stadium—he ran right into the biggest traffic jam he'd ever seen. All roads leading to and from the stadium were gridlocked. Boxed in, he shifted the car into park and surveyed the situation. He realized it could take him an hour or more to go just a mile. And Belichick didn't tolerate tardiness.

With the snow picking up and his wiper blades working to keep the windshield clear, Brady reached for his cell phone.

Frank Mendes had spent thirty years as a Massachusetts state trooper. During that time, he worked hundreds of hours at Foxboro Stadium on traffic details, on foot patrols, and escorting visiting teams to and from the facility on game days. He became such a familiar face to Patriots officials that Mendes was eventually hired as director of team security. One of his job responsibilities was making sure logistics went smoothly on game day. He was almost to the stadium when he got the call from Brady.

"I'm stuck, Frank," Brady told him.

Mendes lived for moments like this. It was suddenly his responsibility to get the starting quarterback to the game.

"Where are you?" Mendes said.

"Pine Street, near Route One," Brady told him.

"What are you driving?"

"My yellow Jeep."

Fortunately, Mendes still had a lot of friends at the local barracks. He called dispatch and told the officer on duty about the situation. "Brady's stranded," he said. "We gotta get him to the stadium."

Within fifteen minutes, Brady heard a siren approaching. A state trooper pulled up, rolled down his window, and said: "Follow me."

With police lights flashing and a siren wailing, vehicles packed with Patriots fans inched onto the shoulder, creating a narrow lane for Brady and his police escort. Patriots running back Antowain Smith was stuck in the same jam as Brady. Scared that he would face Belichick's wrath for being late, Smith was elated when he looked in his rearview mirror and recognized Brady's jeep approaching. As the trooper and Brady passed, Smith pulled out behind them and joined the escort. The closer Brady got to the stadium, the more players ducked in line behind him. Before long, the trooper was leading a motorcade of players while fans along the route honked and cheered.

The incident was emblematic of the kind of leader Brady had already become. When the unexpected happened, he figured out a solution. And other players got in line behind him.

When he finally made it to the stadium, Brady quickly changed and hustled out to the field to get loose. The snow was coming down hard. Wearing shorts and a T-shirt, he marveled at the giant flakes dropping from the sky. The field resembled a winter carnival. To play a game in these conditions was a California boy's dream.

Despite how eager he was to open the new stadium, Robert Kraft had a soft spot for Foxboro Stadium. It was the place where he and his sons had fallen in love with the Patriots, the place where his dream to own the team had been born. The opportunity to host a playoff game before the building was torn down felt like a last hurrah.

For such a momentous occasion, Kraft invited his good friend Sanford "Sandy" Weill to be his guest for the Raiders game. At the time, Weill was chairman and CEO of Citigroup, the largest and most profitable financial institution in the world. He was also a New Yorker and a longtime Jets fan.

Weill's ties to the Jets went all the way back to team founder Sonny Werblin, the entertainment executive, who named the franchise and chose their uniform colors in the mid-sixties. With a background in show business, Werblin helped turn Jets quarterback Joe Namath into "Broadway Joe," the NFL's

first bona fide celebrity. After the quarterback achieved superstardom by famously guaranteeing that the Jets would upset the heavily favored Colts in Super Bowl III, Weill provided investment and banking advice to Namath, at Werblin's request. That was the start of Weill's long and close association with the Jets organization and its founder.

Weill had never been to Foxborough. Nor did he have any interest whatsoever in the Patriots. Nonetheless, he was flattered when Kraft invited him and his wife to such an important game.

About twenty minutes before kickoff, Kraft and Weill stood on the Patriots sideline in matching blue Patriots winter parkas and white Patriots division-champion baseball caps, chatting privately in near-blizzard conditions. Kraft's decision to lobby for the Patriots to play at night rather than at 4:00 p.m. suddenly looked like a stroke of genius. Oakland was a warm-weather team with a corps of receivers that possessed track-star speed. Since four o'clock, the temperature in Foxborough had dropped twenty degrees and an unforeseen snowstorm had moved in and blanketed the field. A small army of groundskeepers was using leaf blowers to expose the yard lines. The snow would take away the Raiders' speed advantage. "Ideal conditions," Kraft told Weill.

About twenty yards away from where they stood, Brady threw his final warm-up passes as Nelly's "#1" pulsed through the stadium sound system. *You better watch who you talkin' bout . . . running your mouth like you know me.* Brady knew the words well enough to mouth them. One hundred and ninety-eight players had been picked before him in the 2000 draft. He was determined to show everyone that the experts who had said he was too slow and too weak to play quarterback in the NFL didn't know him.

Through the driving snow, Brady spotted Kraft and jogged over to him. Undoing his chinstrap, he said: "We're gonna get this one."

"Promise?" Kraft said.

"I promise that," Brady said.

Kraft smiled and pointed at Brady just as Nelly's song hit its signature line: *I am number one.*

A little ways away, Drew Bledsoe stood in silence, looking at Kraft looking at Brady.

At thirty-eight, Raiders head coach Jon Gruden was considered the best up-and-coming head coach in the NFL. The year before, he had led Oakland to the AFC Championship game. When Gruden learned that Brady was starting

for the Patriots, he figured that his team's chances of getting back to the AFC Championship had just gone up. Oakland's imposing defense was loaded with veterans. Gruden couldn't believe that Belichick wasn't starting Bledsoe.

In the first half, Brady looked overmatched, completing just six of thirteen passes for seventy-four yards with one interception. With Oakland leading 7–0 at the half, Bledsoe was champing at the bit for a chance to play. But Belichick declined to make a change. The Patriots didn't fare any better in the third quarter. By the fourth quarter, with Oakland leading 13–3, the fans were restless. When Brady threw an incomplete pass on third-and-eighteen, the booing was noticeable.

If Belichick had changed quarterbacks at this point, no one would have been surprised. Instead, he changed the tempo. With 12:29 remaining in the game, he had Brady go with the no-huddle offense. Over the next five minutes, Brady drove his team sixty-seven yards, completing nine consecutive passes in virtual white-out conditions. He capped off the best drive of his young career by scampering six yards, eluding three would-be tacklers, and diving into the end zone. It was the first rushing touchdown of his career. Springing to his feet, he spiked the ball so hard that he lost his balance and fell face-first into the snow. With 7:57 to play, the score was 13–10. New England was alive, and Foxboro Stadium was rocking.

Over the next six minutes, Oakland failed to put the game away. With no time-outs left and 2:06 remaining, New England got the ball back on its own forty-six-yard line. Moments later, Brady ran for a first down and was shoved out of bounds along the Patriots' sideline at the Raiders' forty-two-yard line. After Brady got up, he walked toward offensive coordinator Charlie Weis to get the next play.

"Three by one. Trips right. Throw the slant the back side," Weis told him.

It was a play that called for three receivers to line up on the right side, while a lone receiver lined up to Brady's left, or back side. Weis wanted Brady to throw to the lone receiver on the back side.

As Weis instructed Brady, Raiders defensive back Eric Allen lingered along the Patriots' sideline and overheard the play call. Allen quickly ran to the Raiders huddle and told his teammates what was coming. He specifically told a linebacker to take away the slant pass to the back side. This set the stage for the most momentous and controversial play in NFL history.

With 1:50 to go, Brady stood four yards behind the line of scrimmage, his knees slightly bent, a layer of fresh snow atop his silver helmet. Taking the snap, he cocked his arm, preparing to throw to the lone back-side receiver running a slant pattern to his left. Anticipating the play, a Raiders defender

obstructed the passing lane, causing Brady to discontinue his throwing motion. His one-second hesitation was just enough time for Raiders cornerback Charles Woodson, who was blitzing from Brady's right, to get airborne and hit Brady just as he was about to re-cock his arm to throw to a different receiver. The ball came loose as Woodson drove Brady to the ground.

Referee Walt Coleman was twelve yards away from Brady and lost sight of the ball, which rested atop the snow, not far from Brady's feet. Raiders linebacker Greg Biekert quickly pounced on it.

Flat on his back, Brady brought both hands to his helmet. "NO!!!!!" he thought.

Coleman ruled the play a fumble.

Raider defenders jubilantly jumped up and down.

Furious with himself for fumbling, Brady walked off the field, convinced the game was over. Belichick thought it was over, too. Everyone did. Up in the owner's box, Robert Kraft dropped his head and closed his eyes. Fans started heading for the exits.

As Raiders players danced in the snow, a replay appeared on the giant screen in the stadium. The crowd suddenly went into an uproar. It appeared that Brady's arm was in motion when the ball was knocked free, meaning it might have been an incomplete pass rather than a fumble. However, the Patriots had no way to challenge the on-the-field ruling. On his own, Walt Coleman made his way to the sideline, put on a headset, and ducked his head under a blue tarp. As Coleman peered at the instant-replay monitor, Phil Collins's "In the Air Tonight" started playing on the stadium sound system.

Belichick and Charlie Weis got on the phone with Ernie Adams, who was up in the booth. Adams was the team's rules guru. After watching television replays, Adams told them that he believed the play should be ruled an incomplete pass, not a fumble. He referenced NFL Rule 3, Section 22, Article 2, Note 2:

> When a Team A player is holding the ball to pass it forward, any intentional forward movement of his hand starts a forward pass, even if the player loses possession of the ball as he is attempting to tuck it back toward his body.

Referred to as the "Tuck Rule," it had been added to the rulebook only two years earlier. Most players and coaches were unfamiliar with it. But Adams knew the rule verbatim. And Belichick and the Patriots had some personal experience with the rule. Back in the second game of the season,

Jets quarterback Vinny Testaverde had fumbled and the Patriots recovered, but the call was reversed and the ball was given back to the Jets by virtue of the Tuck Rule.

Under the rule, a forward pass starts with the forward motion of the quarterback's hand, so if a quarterback suddenly decides to discontinue a pass—in other words, if he starts the throwing motion but doesn't release the ball—the initial forward-passing motion doesn't conclude until the quarterback's arm comes to a complete stop. This is evidenced either by a quarterback's tucking the ball against his body or by his arm's otherwise coming to a complete stop, such as when he takes off running.

Standing next to Weis, Brady wanted to know what Adams was saying.

"What do you think?" Brady said.

"I think we got a shot," Weis told him. "Your arm was going forward. It could be an incomplete pass."

After less than one minute, Coleman removed his headset, turned on his microphone (which enabled his voice to carry through the stadium's public address system), and spoke fifteen words that would alter the course of NFL history: "After reviewing the play, the quarterback's arm was going forward. It is an incomplete pass."

The end of Coleman's sentence was drowned out by the deafening roar of more than sixty thousand fans.

On the Raiders sideline, Jon Gruden was bewildered. Raiders owner Al Davis was furious. "It's my opinion, and almost everybody in the world, that the play was a fumble," Davis said later. "It should have been called a fumble. That someone would reverse it without conclusive, indisputable evidence is just unbelievable."

Mike Pereira, the NFL's vice president of officiating, had anticipated the backlash. "I knew the call was right," Pereira said. "I also knew that it was not going to be accepted by the majority of the people because they would read clear intent here that [Brady] was not trying to pass the ball when the ball came loose."

With the reversal, the Patriots had new life. But Oakland still had the lead. And with just over a minute and a half to play and no time-outs remaining, New England's season remained in peril.

Returning to the field, Brady promptly completed a thirteen-yard strike to David Patten, advancing the Patriots to the Raiders' twenty-nine-yard line. Three plays later, with twenty-seven seconds remaining, Belichick sent out kicker Adam Vinatieri for what seemed like an impossible forty-five-yard field goal attempt in driving snow. The field conditions were so bad that

Vinatieri had to modify his approach to avoid losing his footing. Unable to get much lift, he booted a low line drive that barely got over the outstretched hands of Raiders defenders. Visibility was so poor that people watching the game on television couldn't see the ball as it disappeared into the snowy sky. Even those inside the stadium were in the dark until the referees beneath the goalpost raised their arms.

"It is good! It is good!" shouted Patriots radio announcer Gil Santos. "Forty-five yards! Adam Vin-A-Terry kicks it through the snow. And we're tied at thirteen to thirteen."

Snow-covered Patriots fans screamed and jumped up and down. In a ninety-second span, they had gone from despondency to euphoria. It was as if Vinatieri had beaten Mother Nature with his foot. A sense of destiny enveloped Foxboro Stadium.

Belichick sent Drew Bledsoe out to midfield for the overtime-period coin toss, which New England won. Moments later, Brady took the field and drove the Patriots sixty-one yards by completing all eight passes he threw. Then, on fourth down, Adam Vinatieri trotted back out to attempt a game-winning twenty-three-yard kick. "It is going to be a chippy field goal," said Santos. "The crowd will tell you whether he makes it or not."

It was 11:35 p.m. Helmet in hand and snow falling on his head, Brady stood directly behind Belichick on the Patriots sideline, holding his breath.

"Set to go," Santos said. "Snap. Ball down. Kick is up . . ."

Sixty thousand fans let out a collective "YEAH!" that seemed to shake the stadium.

"Patriots win in overtime!" Santos shouted.

In a scene reminiscent of George Bailey running through snow-covered streets in *It's a Wonderful Life*, shouting "Hello, Bedford Falls!" after discovering that he was still alive, Tom Brady and Bill Belichick threw their arms around each other and shouted for joy.

"Sixteen to thirteen!" Santos yelled on the air. "We're going to the AFC Championship game."

It was absolute bedlam in Foxboro Stadium. Something magical had just happened, and those in attendance didn't want it to end. Neither did the players. They lay in the snow and made snow angels. They cried. They looked heavenward and thanked God Almighty. And they ran around the stadium hugging fans. The greatest game ever played at Foxboro Stadium was the final one, and the players and fans reveled in being part of it.

In the owner's box, Kraft jumped up and down, embracing his wife and sons. In that moment, Sandy Weill did something he never dreamed he'd

do—converted to being a Patriots fan. "I was a Jets fan," Weill said. "But I witnessed how Bob behaved when Brady lost the ball and it appeared they had lost the game. Here was a guy whose team had a chance to go to the AFC Championship game and it suddenly seemed it was 99.9 percent sure that he had lost it. Yet Bob was a very gracious loser and a very good sport. He reacted much better than if I were Bob Kraft. Then, moments later, I witnessed maybe the most exciting moment in Bob's life. I said, 'I am now going to be a Patriots fan.'"

Kraft invited Weill to accompany him to the locker room. When Kraft found Brady, he kissed him on the cheek and gave him a bear hug. It had been twenty months since Brady had first bumped into Kraft on the stadium steps and boldly proclaimed: "I'm the best decision your franchise has ever made." Kraft was now a full-fledged believer.

"I want you to meet a dear friend," Kraft told Brady. "This is Sandy Weill."

Weill nodded admiringly and extended his hand.

The locker room was a scene of joyous chaos. But for a moment, Brady treated Weill as if they were the only two people in the room, extending his hand and saying, "Hi, I'm Tom Brady."

Moments later, Weill marveled as the precocious quarterback descended into a sea of lights, cameras, and reporters. Brady's confidence and charisma reminded Weill of something his old friend Sonny Werblin had told him after Joe Namath delivered on his prediction that the Jets would upset the heavily favored Colts: "A real star lights up a room when he comes in. Namath has the presence of a star."

"Isn't Tommy something?" Kraft said to his friend.

"He has the presence of a star," Weill told him.

twenty-one

WE ARE ALL PATRIOTS

F or CBS and the NFL, the experiment of broadcasting a playoff game at night was a ratings bonanza. Nearly thirty million viewers watched the Patriots defeat the Raiders, making it the network's third-most-watched prime-time show of the entire 2001–2 television season. Only the CBS Sunday Movie *9/11* and the Carol Burnett special drew larger audiences that year. "It was as memorable a broadcast as I can remember," said CBS Sports president Sean McManus. "Thanks to the snow, we had incredible pictures. With the call going against the Raiders we had great controversy. And the two Vinatieri kicks provided great drama."

New England was the biggest beneficiary of the prime-time broadcast. For the rest of the country, the game served as an introduction to an enterprising team led by a stern, taciturn coach and a precocious quarterback. Foxboro Stadium resembled a winter wonderland. The optics, combined with the most controversial replay review in NFL history and the greatest kick in NFL history, created a sense that supernatural forces had propelled the Patriots that night. "Suddenly there was magic in Foxborough," said long-time NFL Films president Steve Sabol. "And suddenly the Patriots were the storybook team of the year."

But the experts and NFL insiders didn't expect the storybook season to continue. A week later, the Patriots traveled to Pittsburgh to face the heavily favored Steelers for the right to advance to the Super Bowl. During CBS's pregame broadcast, analyst Deion Sanders was asked to predict the outcome. "Tom Brady and the Brady Bunch have had a wonderful season," he said, drawing laughs. "But I've just been informed by Sean McManus that this will be the final episode of *The Brady Bunch*."

With just over two minutes remaining in the first half and New England clinging to a 7–3 lead, a Pittsburgh defender lunged at Brady's knees just as he completed his throwing motion. Brady's body twisted like a pretzel as

he fell to the ground, where he writhed in pain and clutched his left ankle. Moments later, unable to put weight on his left leg, Brady hobbled off the field.

While doctors attended to Brady, Drew Bledsoe trotted out with 1:40 left in the half. It had been 106 days since Bledsoe had last taken a snap. He fired a completion on his first play. Then on his second play from scrimmage, Bledsoe scrambled to his right and took off running. Just as he reached the Patriots sideline, a Steelers defensive back came speeding up and hammered him, sending him sprawling out of bounds. The play was eerily similar to the one that had knocked Bledsoe out of action back in September. This time the hit drew penalty flags for unnecessary roughness. Pissed that Bledsoe had been hit out of bounds, Brady got off the bench, hopped over on one leg, and started jawing with Steelers defenders. Despite a laceration on his chin, Bledsoe sprang to his feet. Yelling and clapping his hands, he ran back onto the field. He slapped his teammates' helmets. Moments later, he threw a touchdown pass that put New England up 14–3.

Pittsburgh never recovered and Brady never returned. Behind a gritty effort by Bledsoe, New England upset Pittsburgh 24–17. As the game clock expired, tears streamed down Bledsoe's face and his teammates mobbed him. Then Bledsoe spotted his father. As their eyes met, Bledsoe came undone.

Robert Kraft could not have been happier for Bledsoe. After hugging the quarterback and telling him how much he appreciated him, Kraft stepped onto a platform, taking his place beside Belichick for the trophy presentation. "Mr. Kraft," said CBS broadcaster Jim Nantz, "this is the anniversary date of when you hired Bill Belichick. Can you tell me what he's meant to your franchise?"

"Well, I think we stole him, giving up a first-round pick. It's the cheapest deal I've ever done. One of the best deals, too."

Belichick beamed.

"Bill, what does this moment mean for you, in your second year to take the Patriots to the Super Bowl?" Nantz said.

"Well, it's a great thrill and an honor to represent the AFC in the Super Bowl," he said. "But this is all about our team. The New England Patriots."

"They really epitomize team," Nantz said. "Players rooting for each other. Bledsoe, all season long, really rooting for Brady. And now you might have a little quarterback controversy this week. Who will start?"

Belichick avoided the question. With Brady injured, Belichick was in no rush to publicly announce who would be starting. There was an advantage to keeping New England's opponent in the dark for as long as possible.

But less than forty-eight hours after the AFC Championship game, Belichick talked to Bledsoe and Brady, informing them that Brady would start in the Super Bowl, provided he'd be able to practice on Wednesday, Thursday, and Friday.

"That's what I expected you to do," Bledsoe told Belichick.

Super Bowl XXXVI was destined to be different from previous Super Bowls. In the aftermath of 9/11, Commissioner Paul Tagliabue felt the NFL had a responsibility to do more than simply stage another entertaining spectacle. Determined to capitalize on the fact that more than 100 million Americans would be tuning in, he wanted to scrap the standard pregame and halftime entertainment and replace it with patriotic themes that would inspire unity and pay homage to the victims of the terror attacks and the emergency responders who had died trying to save them. At Tagliabue's request, Robert Kraft reached out to the Boston Pops and invited them to become the first orchestra to perform at a Super Bowl. Under the direction of Keith Lockhart, the Pops agreed to play composer Aaron Copeland's "Lincoln Portrait" during the pregame show while Presidents Gerald Ford, Jimmy Carter, George H. W. Bush, and Bill Clinton and First Lady Nancy Reagan read aloud the words of President Lincoln. Fox, which was televising the game, produced a stirring ten-minute video with images of the Statue of Liberty, Arlington National Cemetery, the World Trade Center coming down, Gettysburg, and other moving backdrops that would air as the Pops played.

With such a powerful pregame lineup in the works, the NFL and Fox were struggling to come up with a halftime performer with sufficient gravitas. By October 27, 2001, the league still had no one in mind. That night, John Collins, the NFL's vice president of marketing and sales, attended a U2 concert at Madison Square Garden. During the show, from above the stage, U2 unfurled a giant scroll that listed the names of everyone who had died in the twin towers. It was a solemn moment. People around Collins were crying.

The next morning at NFL headquarters on Park Avenue, Collins told his colleagues what he had witnessed.

"All of a sudden, you'd hear, 'Oh my God, there's my brother,'" Collins said.

At one point, Bono, wearing a blue NYFD shirt and an NYPD cap, invited

scores of New York City firemen and police officers onstage to sing along with the band. The scene was mesmerizing. It lifted the entire audience.

"That's what we're trying to do," Collins said. "They have the vision. And we have the platform."

Tagliabue liked the idea. So did television executives at Fox. "A lot of thought went into it," Tagliabue said. "It was to show that as a nation we were unified and resilient and determined, but to do it in a way that would above all respect those who had lost their lives."

The invitation was extended in late November and U2 readily accepted.

On the Wednesday prior to the Super Bowl, U2 was scheduled to hold a press conference at the Superdome to preview their halftime show. A league official who knew that Jonathan Kraft was a huge U2 fan invited him to attend. Beforehand, Kraft spent some time talking with Bono and the Edge about the time he attended the band's first performance in Boston at a small club back in 1980. The subject soon shifted to football and the upcoming game. Bono and the Edge were well aware of the Patriots' quarterback controversy and the fact that Coach Belichick had yet to announce whether Brady or Bledsoe would be starting.

"Tell me," Bono said, "who's going to play quarterback?"

Kraft hesitated. He was one of only a handful of people within the organization who knew the answer. Belichick was scheduled to make the announcement later that day. Until then, mum was the word. But this was Bono asking!

"Brady," Kraft said in a hushed voice.

Bono raised his eyebrows and nodded.

A few minutes later, Brian McCarthy from the NFL stepped to a podium in a special-events room beneath the Superdome to welcome the media and introduce the band. Before turning the stage over to U2, McCarthy told the press: "Jonathan Kraft was actually backstage and the only person aside from the coach of the Patriots who knows who's starting is Bono. So, uh, that may be one of the questions you may want to ask here."

A knot formed in Kraft's stomach as the band approached the podium.

"Bono, are you going to tell us who the starting quarterback is going to be?" McCarthy asked.

"Oh, fuck," Kraft said to himself.

Bono hesitated. "That's a very sore subject in our band," he said, glancing at the Edge.

"There's been a lot of nonsense written about the whole Brady versus Bledsoe issue over the last few days," the Edge said playfully. "And we are not

here to add to that controversy today. So, we're not going to be fielding any questions on that issue, okay?"

The Edge then glanced back at Bono and grinned. "It's up to Coach Belichick," he continued. "However, it does have to be said that Bledsoe has a superior long pass, and I think that Brady's sore ankle is a bit of a problem. I've had one myself, and it lasted for a good deal longer than one week. Anyway, we are not here to get into that. We are here to bring peace."

"We're here to bring peace," Bono repeated. "We want to bring peace between Bledsoe and Brady."

The press laughed.

Kraft finally exhaled.

The Super Bowl wasn't expected to be much of a contest. The St. Louis Rams had the number one defense in the league. And the Rams offense, known as the "Greatest Show on Turf," was considered one of the best in NFL history. The oddsmakers in Las Vegas listed the Rams as fourteen-point favorites, a huge margin for a championship game.

Before the Patriots left for New Orleans, Belichick had a stern message for his team. "*Everybody's* fucking riding the plane back home," Belichick said. "So don't make plans."

On the surface, it sounded like Belichick was referring to the time when Bill Parcells had chosen not to fly back from New Orleans with the team after the Patriots lost to Green Bay in Super Bowl XXXI. Although that incident had rubbed Belichick the wrong way, he had something else in mind when telling the players not to make plans. He was sending his team a message: *Don't make plans for the day after the Super Bowl because we are going to win, which will require us to be in Boston for a victory parade.*

"When you talk about parades and let everyone know that you are planning on winning the game," Willie McGinest said, "you give the other team motivation. Bill was more genius about it. He just enforced a rule that had been in place all season long—we travel back together. Everyone."

Another team rule that had been in place all season long was that prior to games, the players were introduced as a team, not as individuals. It was another way for Belichick to emphasize the importance of team over individuals. Doing that in the regular season was one thing. "The Super Bowl was a different story," linebacker Tedy Bruschi said. "For a player, that's your 'Look at me' moment. They say your name. They say your college. They say your position. You run out and have your 'Look, Mom, I made it' moment.

That year it was supposed to be the defense that was introduced. So for us to give that up was a big deal. But it was a conscious decision on our part. We decided: 'We're going out as a team.'"

One reason that Belichick got his players to fully embrace a selfless approach was that he led by example. Right after the team arrived in New Orleans, team captain Lawyer Milloy complained to Belichick that his hotel room was so small that it felt claustrophobic. A number of other team captains, Milloy insisted, were in the same boat. In response, Belichick gave his spacious suite to Milloy and moved into Milloy's room. He also convinced a number of his assistant coaches to trade rooms with players.

Word of Belichick's decision to trade rooms with a player didn't just ripple through the locker room; it reached Kraft. So did Belichick's plan to ignore the Super Bowl protocol of introducing players individually. Once the league got wind of what the Patriots were planning, Kraft got a call from the commissioner's office. A league representative reminded Kraft that television sponsors paid top dollar for the advertising slot associated with pregame introductions. It was essential, the league said, for the Patriots to be introduced the traditional way.

As Kraft listened, he thought about the fact that one of the highlights of an NFL player's career is the opportunity to hear his name called on Super Bowl Sunday and run out of the tunnel during the introductions. Guys dream of that moment from childhood. The fact that Belichick got his starting defensive players to forgo that privilege in favor of running onto the field as a team was evidence of a new culture taking root in New England.

Kraft told the league he was backing his coach.

Frustrated, the league threatened to fine Kraft if his team didn't comply.

"So fine me," Kraft said.

Announcers Pat Summerall and John Madden called the game for Fox. Summerall handled the player introductions.

"Good evening, ladies and gentlemen, and welcome to Super Bowl Thirty-Six," he said over the Superdome's public address system. "And now, ladies and gentlemen, choosing to be introduced as a team, here are the American Football Conference champions—the New England Patriots."

In an unprecedented scene, all fifty-three Patriots players emerged from the tunnel at once, led by a kicker, a linebacker, and a receiver.

"When we ran out as a team, that summed it all up," Brady said. "No one had ever done that before. But that was important to us and what we'd been doing the whole year."

Meantime, as the Rams' offensive players were introduced, receiver Ricky

Proehl looked into a television camera and declared: "Tonight, the dynasty is born, baby." Proehl was right. He just had the wrong team.

Belichick wasn't thinking dynasty. He was focused on disrupting the Rams' offense. When New England had played St. Louis earlier in the year, the defensive game plan had centered on stopping quarterback Kurt Warner. This time around, Belichick decided to put the focus on running back Marshall Faulk. The plan was simple—pound him every time he touched the ball, and pound him every time he didn't touch the ball. "Knock the shit out of him," Belichick said.

His message got through. "We knew they weren't physical," said Willie McGinest. "We knew they didn't want to get hit. My job was to knock the shit out of anybody that passed me. Break their will. Make them quit."

Belichick felt that if they took Faulk out of the flow of the offense, Warner would not be nearly as effective. In the first half, the strategy worked. Faulk never got going and Warner got flustered. In the second quarter, he threw an interception that Ty Law returned forty-seven yards for a touchdown to put New England up 7–3. The Rams turned it over again with just over a minute left before halftime. Brady then drove the Patriots forty yards in under fifty seconds, throwing a touchdown pass to put his team up 14–3.

The score stunned the audience. Even the announcers didn't know what to say.

"Who would have thought that if someone was going to explode on offense it was going to be the New England Patriots in Super Bowl Thirty-Six?" Madden said.

"This is Shock-Dome Thirty-Six," Summerall said.

Robert Kraft wasn't shocked that his team was up at the half. In his mind, at least six or seven teams in the NFL had more talented rosters than the Patriots. But New England had demonstrated all season long what can be accomplished with teamwork and everyone pulling together. That was exactly what the country needed—everyone pulling together.

Looking down from his suite, he couldn't get over the fact that his team's red, white, and blue uniforms matched the colors of the American flag. It dawned on him that if New England won, he'd have an opportunity to address the nation during the Lombardi Trophy presentation. As workers speedily erected a stage for U2's halftime performance, he turned to his son Jonathan.

"What am I going to say if we win?" he whispered in his ear.

"Dad, I don't know."

"Well, what do you think I should say?"

"Let's go talk about it," Jonathan said.

They ducked into the bathroom for privacy. For the next few minutes, Robert expressed his view that this Super Bowl was different from any other. If the Patriots won, he insisted, he didn't want to take a victory lap. Everyone, not just Patriots fans, needed to feel a part of the victory. He wanted to tap into the nation's sense of unity and patriotism. His words needed to transcend the game of football.

"All right," Jonathan said. "Let me write something."

As soon as Robert walked out, Jonathan put down the toilet lid, took a seat, and started scribbling down words on a miniature notepad: *Faith. Hope. Democracy. Country. Patriots.* He had to come up with a speech that would weave together these themes. But it had to be a speech that could be delivered in under twenty seconds. That was about how much time Fox would allocate for his father's remarks. So he had to get it down to a paragraph.

Bright white lights lit up the darkened Superdome as Bono stepped onto a heart-shaped stage and belted out the words "It's a beautiful day. . . . Sky falls, you feel like it's a beautiful day." The spirited rendition of a song about finding joy after losing everything had the audience jumping up and down, shouting euphorically. When it ended, the house lights went dark again and a spotlight shone on a gigantic banner titled "September 11, 2001" as it unfurled from high above the field. The names of the victims, starting with those who were aboard American Airlines Flight 11, followed.

"Sleep, sleep tonight," Bono sang. "And may your dreams be realized." As the band worked its way through "MLK," the thousands of 9/11 victims' names continued to scroll under headings: "The Pentagon," "FDNY," "NYPD," "United Airlines Flight 175," and so forth. So many names.

U2's halftime performance at Super Bowl XXXVI is considered the greatest in Super Bowl history. One league official called it "the most important event ever held in the National Football League." At that time, most Americans had stopped traveling by air. People weren't going to big venues. There was tremendous fear and trepidation about what might happen.

U2 ended its historic, eleven-minute performance with "Where the Streets Have No Name." Bono once said: "We play 'Where the Streets Have No Name' whenever we need God to walk through the room." When the Edge struck the song's instantly recognizable opening chords, the screams in

the Superdome reached a fever pitch. With the names of victims still scroll-
ing, Bono shouted "America!" as he sprinted around the stage and launched
into some of the most well-known lyrics in pop music: "I want to run. I want
to hide. I want to tear down the walls that hold me inside."

Still holed up in the bathroom, Jonathan Kraft feverishly penned a victory speech for his father. He was missing an epic performance by his favorite band, but he knew how important it was to get the words just right. His
father might have an opportunity to speak to the country. The tone had to
be pitch perfect.

As he scribbled down the final sentence, he heard Bono sing "We're
beaten and blown by the wind."

"Shit! It's over," he said to himself. He stuffed the speech into his suit coat
pocket and burst through the bathroom door, nearly knocking over a couple
of people as he rushed to the front row of the suite just in time to hear Bono
sing the final lines: "We go there with you. It's all we can do."

He got chills as Bono opened his leather jacket, revealing an American
flag stitched into the lining. While Bono held his pose, the Edge strummed
the final chords and Jonathan cried.

"God, we have to win this game," he said to himself.

The Patriots' offense sputtered in the second half, managing just a field goal.
Meanwhile, the Rams' high-octane offense finally started clicking, scoring
two fourth-quarter touchdowns. The second one tied the game at 17–17 with
1:21 remaining. The momentum had clearly shifted.

After the Rams kicked off, New England was pinned back on its seventeen-
yard line. With no timeouts remaining, Belichick faced a decision—take a
knee, run out the clock, and try to win the game in overtime, or attempt to
get into field goal range. The second option came with a big risk: a turnover
might hand the game to the Rams.

Brady approached Weis. "What's our plan?" he said.

Weis and Belichick were weighing the options.

Fox color commentator John Madden chimed in on the air. "With no
time-outs, I think the Patriots, with this field position, have to just run the
clock out," he said. "You have to play for overtime now. . . . You don't want to
force anything here. You don't want to do anything stupid."

Most likely, any head coach in the NFL would have agreed with Madden in this situation, especially with Brady being a first-year starter. But one
didn't. Belichick was concerned about his defense. They'd been on the field

for most of the second half and they were exhausted. If the game went into overtime and the Rams won the coin toss, Belichick feared they'd march right down the field and win the game. To give his team the best chance to win, he wanted to try to get within field goal range now.

"Let's go for it," Belichick said.

Weis agreed. "We're going," he told Brady.

The plan was to have Brady run the two-minute offense. But the number one priority was make certain that he did nothing that would turn the ball over to the Rams.

"Make sure you take care of the ball," Weis told Brady.

Brady nodded.

"Hey!" Bledsoe yelled at Brady. "Just go out there and fuckin' sling it!"

Determined, Brady jogged toward the huddle. After all that had gone on, Bledsoe's support at that critical moment was a huge confidence booster to Brady. He got a charge out of Bledsoe's call to "sling it."

But Brady was not a gunslinger. He was more of a game manager who had fully embraced a philosophy that Belichick constantly preached: "You can't win until you keep from losing." In other words, avoid the mistakes that lose games.

Belichick trusted Brady's ability to make decisions under pressure. *Going for the win is not that dangerous,* Belichick thought, *because Brady's not going to make a mistake.* With barely more than one minute left to play, Belichick wasn't afraid to put the outcome of the Super Bowl in Brady's hands.

The pressure was palpable when Brady entered the huddle. Most players would have wilted under the weight of the moment. But Brady relished it. With more than 100 million people watching on television, the Patriots' season hung in the balance. While his teammates looked at him for direction, Brady listened as Charlie Weis spoke to him through the tiny wireless transmitter in his ear: "Okay, Tommy. Gun F. Left 51. Go O-PECK. Look for Patten versus man. If not, Troy or J. R. Be careful with the ball."

Brady relayed the play to the offense.

Receiver David Patten was Brady's primary target. Second and third options were Troy Brown or running back J. R. Redmond coming out of the backfield. "Let's go do this thing," Brady told his teammates.

The Rams rushed four linemen, immediately collapsing the pocket. Brady barely escaped before dumping the ball off in traffic to Redmond, who was quickly pounced on by a pack of defenders. He gained five yards.

"I don't agree with what the Patriots are doing right here," Madden said on Fox.

On the next play, Brady again threw quickly to Redmond, who scampered for a first down. Hustling to the line of scrimmage, Brady spiked the ball, stopping the clock. Moments later, he completed another pass, and the receiver ran out of bounds at the Patriots' forty-one-yard line.

Thirty-three seconds remained.

After Weis sent the next play in to Brady, Belichick looked on as the Rams brought eight defenders to the line of scrimmage. A blitz was coming. It was a dangerous moment for a young quarterback to make a mistake. If he held the ball too long, he'd get sacked for a loss, virtually ensuring that they wouldn't get into field goal range in time. If he tried to force the ball while under pressure, he'd risk throwing an interception.

As Brady took the snap, he was immediately forced from the pocket. Rolling to his right, he quickly threw the ball out of bounds, stopping the clock. Statistically, it was recorded as a mere incomplete pass and a loss of down. But from a decision-making standpoint, it may have been the most important play of the drive. Rather than getting sacked for a big loss by staying in the pocket too long or trying to make a play by forcing a pass that had a high likelihood of getting intercepted, Brady quickly got rid of the ball. The move validated the trust that Belichick had placed in him.

With twenty-nine seconds remaining, Brady got back in the shotgun. This time the Rams didn't blitz, and Brady completed a twenty-three-yard strike to Troy Brown, who ran out of bounds at the Rams' thirty-six-yard line, just barely out of field goal range.

"This is amazing," Madden said on the air. "This is something—and I'll admit that as a coach and as an analyst—I don't think they should have done. But they had the guts. They have a young quarterback. . . . They're not only *calling* these plays but *making* these plays!"

Twenty-one seconds remained. Brady dumped a short pass over the middle. The receiver got dragged down at the thirty-yard line. The clock continued to run as the referee tried to recover the ball from the bottom of the pile.

:14

:13

"They've gotta hurry," Fox announcer Pat Summerall said as the crowd noise rose.

:12

:11

Brady sauntered to the line of scrimmage.

:10

:09

"Maybe he can spike it right here and stop the clock," Summerall said.

:08

:07

Brady took the snap and calmly tossed the ball down at the turf. As if on a string, it bounced back into Brady's hand. Amid the commotion, Brady gently tossed the ball to the referee.

"What Tom Brady just did gives me goose bumps," John Madden said on the air.

Up in the owner's box, Robert Kraft exhaled. In silent awe, he stared through binoculars at Brady. "Who does that?" Kraft thought. Most quarterbacks in that situation would have frantically run to the line of scrimmage, taken the snap, and hurriedly fired the ball at the ground. It's an adrenaline thing. But Brady managed the clock as if he barely had a pulse. And his cool demeanor clearly rubbed off on the rest of the offense, making it easier for them to concentrate.

Seemingly emotionless, Brady strode slowly to the sideline while Adam Vinatieri and the field goal unit took the field. Once again, the outcome rested on Vinatieri's foot. This time, weather wouldn't be a factor. Facing goalposts that were forty-eight yards away, Vinatieri powered his foot through the ball. As the kick sailed through the air, Pat Summerall made the final call of his illustrious career broadcasting Super Bowls: "And it's right down the pike," Summerall said as the ball split the uprights and the Superdome filled with cheers. "AD-DUM VIN-A-TARRY! No time on the clock. And the Patriots have won Super Bowl Thirty-Six. Un-bee-*liev*-able!"

Belichick and Brady practically tackled each other.

"How 'bout that?" Brady yelled.

Belichick rubbed the top of Brady's head the way a father would after his son hit his first home run in Little League.

Then Brady found Bledsoe. "Way to go, twelve," Bledsoe said. "You *are* the man."

The Rams were stunned. So were the experts. The Brady Bunch had beaten the Greatest Show on Turf. Ron Jaworski, ESPN's top NFL analyst, said that in his twenty-nine years playing and analyzing football, Belichick's coaching performance was "the best coaching job I've ever seen."

With confetti filling the air, Tom Brady crowded onto a makeshift stage for the trophy presentation. Wearing a backward baseball cap, he looked into the sea of delirious Patriots fans in the end zone stands behind the platform.

They were pointing at him and screaming his name. The kid that no one had wanted on draft day had just become the youngest quarterback to win a Super Bowl and be named Super Bowl MVP. He spotted his sisters in the crowd, waving at him. The magnitude of the achievement finally sinking in, Brady raised his hands to his head and mouthed the words: "Holy shit!" His sisters, who had fumed with him when Michigan's head coach had jerked him around and cried with him when he'd been passed over in round after round in the NFL Draft, had tears streaming down their cheeks as they mimicked in unison the words "Holy shit" back at their kid brother.

A few feet away, Robert Kraft was about to be awarded the Lombardi Trophy. Bursting with pride, he told himself this was no time to gloat.

Fox broadcaster Terry Bradshaw handed him the microphone.

"Fans of New England have been waiting forty-two years for this day," Kraft said on national television. "Spirituality, faith, and democracy are the cornerstones of our country. We are all patriots. And tonight, the Patriots are world champions."

Cheers filled the Superdome. In four simple sentences, Kraft had tapped into the mood of the nation, framing his team's inspiring achievement as something that belonged to fans throughout the country.

It was after midnight and victory parties had been going for a couple of hours when Tom Brady popped into Bill Belichick's hotel room, where the coach was drinking a Corona with family members. "Have a beer," Belichick said, handing Brady a bottle.

Brady needed a word with his coach. As the MVP of the Super Bowl, he'd been offered the "I'm going to Disney World" television spot, which required him to be in Orlando later on Monday. But he hadn't forgotten what Belichick told the team before heading to New Orleans—"Everybody's fucking riding the plane back home, so don't make plans."

"Is it okay for me to miss the team flight in order to go to Disney World?" he asked.

Puzzled by the question, Belichick looked at him and grinned. "Of *course* you can go!" he said. "How many times do you win the Super Bowl?"

twenty-two

GROWING PAINS

Tom Brady wasn't the only player skipping the team flight home after the Super Bowl. Drew Bledsoe wasn't getting on board, either. And he could not have cared less how Belichick felt about it.

Bledsoe was the unsung hero of the Patriots' 2001 season. Had he handled things differently after losing his job to Brady, he could have divided the locker room, which undoubtedly would have derailed the season. Instead, he accepted the role of Brady's backup and did his part to support him. In that respect, Bledsoe epitomized Belichick's mantra of putting team over individual more than anyone else on the roster.

Not one bit of that was easy. To go from being the franchise player, to suffering a life-threatening injury, to coming back, to becoming the designated clipboard holder while his team was on one of the most thrilling rides in sports history had been emotional vertigo.

Brady sympathized with Bledsoe's situation. "When you're the backup quarterback," Brady said, "you don't even feel like you're on the team. You feel like a fan. You always feel that you're just taking up space." Inevitably, the situation put a strain on Brady and Bledsoe's friendship.

Even before the Patriots got to New Orleans, Bledsoe figured his career in New England was over. The improbable victory over the Rams only confirmed his thinking: *It's Tommy's team now.*

Mentally drained, Bledsoe couldn't wait to get out of his pads and head to Whitefish, Montana, where he maintained a second home in the mountains. He planned to do some skiing and clear his mind. He was thinking he might even do some helicopter skiing.

Leaving the locker room at the Superdome, he encountered one of his best friends, Scott Zolak. Before Brady had come along, Zolak had been Bledsoe's backup. Zolak had since taken a television job at WBZ Channel 4, Boston's CBS affiliate, and his first assignment was to cover the Super Bowl. After the game, he was tasked with getting a comment from Bledsoe about

his future. Microphone in hand, Zolak asked: "Are you excited for your next venture?"

"You're such an asshole for asking that question," Bledsoe said.

Zolak felt bad. The interview lasted about five seconds.

A little while later, Bledsoe boarded a private plane and took a seat opposite his wife and two little boys. Silent, Bledsoe stared out the window into the darkness. Maura knew what he was feeling.

"It's a weird sensation," she said. "You're happy for your teammates, but yet disappointed in not being able to participate in the game. I just remember being quiet on that flight. Then as time went on, the realization set in that we were going to Montana—his happy place. He started to decompress a little bit."

By the time Bledsoe's plane touched down in snowy Whitefish, his focus had turned to his family and he no longer looked so glum. "It's pretty easy to change your way of thinking when you are looking at what is most important," Bledsoe said.

On the morning after the Super Bowl, Bill Belichick and Tom Brady got into the back of a limo outside the team hotel in New Orleans. They'd barely slept, and the magnitude of their achievement still hadn't fully registered. In just their second season together, they had delivered the first championship in the franchise's forty-two-year history and reached the top of the football world. The *New York Times* called the Patriots' victory over the heavily favored Rams a "stunning, magical . . . upset" that "rocked pro football." The Boston media was already comparing Brady to sports legends Larry Bird and Bobby Orr.

As the limo drove off, Belichick turned to Brady.

"Tom, just want to let you know you had a pretty good year."

Brady smiled. "Thanks, coach."

The two of them were embarking on what would end up being one of the most epic rides in sports history. At the outset, Belichick had some words of wisdom for Brady. Pleased that his quarterback had been named the Super Bowl MVP, Belichick reminded him that the Patriots' success was the result of an exemplary team effort. The more individual attention Brady received, Belichick warned, the greater the threat to the team dynamic.

After that discussion, Brady turned down multiple endorsement opportunities that offseason. He politely declined when his home town back in California proposed a Tom Brady Day in his honor. And he said no to a number of things that he felt would be a distraction, such as an invitation

to attend *Vanity Fair*'s exclusive Academy Awards party. He was determined not to lose the respect of his teammates. He also didn't want to end up like so many guys who had one great season and then played poorly the next. His biggest fear was to end up being a one-hit wonder. As a result, Brady cut his offseason vacation short and returned to Foxborough in the spring to start training for the upcoming season.

Robert Kraft felt all along that Bill Belichick had it in him to become one of the game's greatest coaches. But now he was also thinking that Tom Brady was equally capable of developing into one of the all-time greats at his position. "I knew it when I saw the way he responded after it looked like we'd lost that game," Kraft said. "After he lost the ball and the Raiders recovered, all hope appeared to be gone. Then the call got reversed and we got a second chance. That was the moment when Brady really convinced me that he was different."

Football, like life, is a game of second chances. At the same time, luck is meaningless if you don't capitalize on it. The Patriots may have been lucky when the referee reversed the fumble call. But that decision by no means assured them a victory. They still needed two scores. "What Brady did in that situation showed me a great deal about him as a football player and as a human being," Kraft said.

The Patriots' victory in New Orleans solidified Kraft's thinking that his franchise had the league's most formidable duo. Belichick was the architect of what was being labeled one of the greatest Super Bowl upsets in NFL history. And Brady executed the game plan with machinelike precision. The high-risk game-winning drive was a testament to the unique bond of trust that had formed between the coach and the quarterback.

The implications of all of this for Drew Bledsoe weighed heavily on Kraft's mind. He put Bledsoe's situation at the top of his list of offseason priorities, and he and Belichick discussed Bledsoe's future shortly after they got back from New Orleans.

For Belichick, it was a simple calculus. "A football team can have only one starting quarterback," Belichick said. "In the end, it can only be one guy."

Kraft agreed. Still, the thought of parting with the player he viewed as one of his sons left him feeling melancholy. Bledsoe had done so much for the franchise. Plus, Bledsoe's family was part of the fabric of the Boston community. Trading him would uproot everything.

Belichick, on the other hand, removed all of the emotional factors from

the equation. "He's not afraid to get rid of anybody, no matter how important a person is, no matter how valuable people on the street might think he
is," his offensive coordinator Charlie Weis explained. "He's never afraid to go
ahead and make a change or a move that might be perceived as unpopular."
Football writer Peter King put it more colorfully, saying that when it came
to cutting players loose, Belichick had the emotional detachment of Paulie
Walnuts, a fictional Mafia underboss on *The Sopranos*.

Reluctantly, Kraft gave Belichick the green light to shop Bledsoe, and the
Buffalo Bills soon offered New England a first-round draft pick for him. Before pulling the trigger on the deal, Belichick needed Kraft's approval. Kraft
gave it. When the trade was announced, Kraft issued a statement: "Let me
speak as a Patriots fan. Drew Bledsoe is a special player. I have great respect
for all he has done for this franchise, not only for his contributions on the
field, but also his contributions off the field. He gave our fans some of the
greatest memories in the franchise's history, and there will always be a special
place reserved for him in the hearts of Patriots fans. For many reasons, and at
many levels, this was a difficult trade to make."

One year after signing a $103 million contract, Drew Bledsoe was gone.

Louisville wide receiver Deion Branch gathered with some friends at an
apartment to watch the 2002 NFL Draft on television. A senior, Branch was
waiting to learn his future. One of the topics of conversation in the room was
Tom Brady, who appeared shirtless and hugging a football on the cover of
that week's edition of *Sports Illustrated*. The headline read: "THE NATURAL:
A Whirlwind Off-Season for the New Prince of the NFL."

The prospect of playing for the defending Super Bowl champs and
catching passes from Brady was all Branch could think about. Weeks earlier,
a scout from the Patriots had visited Louisville and promised him: "We're
going to take you." But Branch had heard the same thing from a handful of
other teams. Midway through the second round, Branch's name had yet to be
called, and the anticipation and uncertainty were getting to him. He told his
friends he was going for a walk.

Branch was an exceptional college receiver and the brightest star on the
Louisville team. The biggest knock against him as an NFL prospect was his
size. He stood just five feet nine inches tall. But he possessed exceptional
speed and a tireless work ethic, which he credited to his mother. She worked
two or three jobs to provide for her children. He poured the same level of
commitment into football. He was thinking about her as he made his way

through a residential neighborhood not far from campus and his phone rang. The call was coming from a blocked number.

"Hey, Deion, this is Coach Belichick."

Branch took a deep breath.

"What do you think about joining the Patriots?" Belichick continued.

"This is what I've been waiting for," Branch said. "I would love to be part of this organization."

"That's exactly what we want to hear," Belichick said, who told him to be prepared to work hard.

When Branch arrived in Foxborough that spring for rookie camp, he was surprised to see Tom Brady at the facility. It was the offseason for veterans, but Brady was there working out on his own. At one point, Brady introduced himself to Branch. "Just come in and do your job," Brady told him. "We're expecting big things."

Brady embraced his new leadership role. Over the summer, Belichick extended Brady's contract through the 2006 season. Under the new deal, Brady maintained the $375,000 salary from his rookie contract for the 2002 season. Then his salary jumped to $3.1 million in 2003, $5.5 million in 2004, $5.5 million in 2005, and $6 million in 2006. Although this represented a substantial pay increase for Brady, it was a far cry from the ten-year, $103 million deal that Kraft had offered Bledsoe a year earlier. But Brady didn't complain. Although he had led the team to its first championship, he felt that he still needed to prove himself.

By the end of the offseason, Brady had spent a lot of time throwing one-on-one with Branch. He liked Branch's work ethic and thought the kid from Louisville was going to be a good fit in the Patriots' scheme. Branch, meanwhile, still hadn't gotten over the fact that he was working out with Tom Brady and getting coached by Bill Belichick.

The Patriots kicked off the 2002 season on September 9 in Foxborough, playing against the Steelers on *Monday Night Football*. The game was the first in the team's new stadium. In an elaborate pregame ceremony that featured live music, fireworks, Minuteman re-enactors firing muskets, and a visit from President George H. W. Bush, Robert Kraft unveiled the team's first Super Bowl banner. "We've been waiting together for this night for forty-two years," he said to sixty-eight thousand cheering fans. "I want to welcome you to your new home—Gillette Stadium."

Heading into the new season, the consensus around the NFL was that the

Patriots' 2001 season had been a fluke. When ESPN published its preseason predictions, not one of the network's eighteen experts picked the Patriots to win the Super Bowl again. Only four of them thought New England would win its division, prompting ESPN's Chris Mortensen to quip: "The most underrated team just might be the defending Super Bowl champion Patriots."

Pittsburgh was considered the top team in the AFC. But New England thumped them 30–14 in the opener, behind a huge effort by Brady, who threw for nearly three hundred yards and three touchdowns. During one stretch of the game, Brady threw twenty-three consecutive passes without calling a running play. His favorite target was rookie Deion Branch, who caught six passes for eighty-three yards and scored his first NFL touchdown.

The presence of a speedster at the wide-out position added a new dimension to New England's offense. The next week the Patriots dominated the Jets 44–7. Brady once again put up big numbers and Branch caught a forty-nine-yard bomb for his second touchdown. In week three, Brady threw for over four hundred yards for the first time in his career and New England won 41–38.

But Belichick wasn't pleased. He was convinced that the team couldn't win consistently the way they were playing. The defense was too porous, and the offense needed a more balanced attack. He was right. After starting 3-0, New England dropped four straight and ended up going 9-7 on the season. The Patriots' defense finished the year ranked twenty-third, making it one of the worst in the league. One year after winning the Super Bowl, New England failed to make the playoffs.

Long-term, New England's failure to qualify for the playoffs in 2002 may have been the best thing that happened to the franchise. While the rest of the league wrote the Patriots off as a flash in the pan, New England's veteran players started focusing on the 2003 season as soon as the 2002 season ended. Under the league's labor agreement, offseason workouts were considered voluntary; teams couldn't require players to participate. But the leaders in New England's locker room, starting with Willie McGinest and Mike Vrabel, decided that in Foxborough, *voluntary* meant *mandatory*. The message got through. The Patriots had one hundred percent attendance for offseason workouts. The commitment level set the tone for the upcoming season.

For his part, Bill Belichick used the offseason to shore up his defense. He signed pass-rushing specialist Rosevelt Colvin, a Bears linebacker who was considered one of the most prized free agents, and Broncos cornerback

Tyrone Poole, who promised to improve New England's pass coverage. But the guy Belichick coveted the most was someone he felt would elevate the team's overall toughness and intensity.

One of the teams that New England had lost to in 2002 was the San Diego Chargers. During pregame warm-ups at that match-up, Belichick noticed that Chargers safety Rodney Harrison got into a fight with one of his teammates, and Belichick made a mental note. Harrison had spent his entire nine-year career in San Diego. During that time, he developed a reputation as one of the hardest hitters in the league. He also racked up more than $100,000 in fines and became known as a dirty player. The reputation stemmed from a series of hits, including a helmet-to-helmet collision in 2002 that drew one of the biggest fines in league history and a blow he delivered to Jerry Rice in 2002 that led to a suspension for what the NFL deemed "a simply gratuitous effort to punish your opponent."

Harrison resented being labeled a dirty player, but he embraced the role of villain. "Anybody I played against I would wanna hurt," Harrison later told NFL Films. "I don't wanna injure you. Because I would want you to be able to have your career, take care of your family. But anyone that I try to tackle I want to hurt you. Yes, I do, and I'm not gonna apologize for that."

Belichick saw enough of Harrison to recognize what he was about. "He wasn't a cheap player," Belichick said. "He was an aggressive player. And he was a great player. When they're on your team, you appreciate them and you love their toughness. You love their competitiveness. When they're on the other team, you can be a little bit offended by it."

Toward the end of the 2002 season, Harrison started hearing that the Chargers management thought he was "washed up" and "couldn't run anymore." His production had in fact fallen off that year, but the decline was largely because he had played almost the entire season with a severely torn groin. When San Diego cut him, Harrison felt betrayed.

From Belichick's perspective, the fact that Harrison had played hurt said a lot about his mentality. After tracking down his number, he called Harrison. When Harrison answered his cell phone, he was sitting in the office of Raiders owner Al Davis, preparing to sign with his team. Harrison stepped out so he could speak to Belichick in private.

"I remember when we played you guys," Belichick told him. "In warmups I saw you hit one of your defensive backs and knock his helmet off."

Harrison was astonished. "You remember that?" he said.

Belichick convinced Harrison to fly to New England and meet with him before making a decision on his future. Then, when they met in Foxborough,

Belichick looked Harrison in the eye and told him: "I need you for this defense. I want you to be a leader."

The combination of being needed and wanted was persuasive. Harrison called his agent and told him he wanted to play for the Patriots.

Rodney Harrison's arrival in Foxborough raised some eyebrows. He was a strong safety, and New England already had Lawyer Milloy, one of the most accomplished strong safeties in the league. Milloy was also a team captain, an immensely popular presence in the locker room, and one of the hardest hitters on the defense.

But everyone immediately discovered that Harrison hit even harder. And he brought a certain edginess that Belichick thought had been lacking. Some of that edginess was directed at Tom Brady. In training camp, Harrison went after Brady, taunting him, getting in his face, knocking him down. His approach got under Brady's skin.

"I just had never seen Tom get rattled that badly," said receiver Troy Brown. "Not even in games."

But Harrison didn't only go after Brady. He nailed every offensive player who touched the ball. When Troy Brown came across the middle on a passing patter, Harrison leveled him. He hammered running back Kevin Faulk so hard on a routine scrimmage play that Faulk threw the ball at him, which led to a brawl involving more than a dozen guys. "There were fights," Harrison said. "Linemen pushing me and shoving me and punching me."

Belichick relished Harrison's aggressive play in practice. He called Harrison "the best practice player, probably ever. Ruffled a few feathers, not in a dirty way. Just in a highly competitive way. He made everybody else better."

With Harrison on the field, New England's practices became much more combative. "I carried a lot of anger with me because I was always pissed off," Harrison said. "I was pissed off because people didn't believe in me. I always wanted to hit people."

Harrison's attitude toward football was rooted in his upbringing. As a child, he had a stuttering problem, and other kids mercilessly made fun of him. When he wanted to play peewee football at age six, his mother couldn't afford the forty-dollar registration fee. Every penny she could scrounge went toward his speech therapy. She told him she simply didn't have the money for football. But he begged her. Ultimately, his mother decided not to pay her light bill so she could sign Rodney up for football. He was so good that he

eventually got a chance to attend a Catholic school, where the student body was 98 percent white. "I had to bring Rodney to school every day," his mother recalled. "I had a car that wasn't what you call a good car. Sometimes the car would break down. The kids would throw stuff at our car and laugh."

Harrison internalized all of the ridicule. "I saw my mom work three jobs," he said. "I saw my mom on welfare. I saw my mom struggle when my father didn't want to be there. I saw people make fun of us. And it brought me to tears. That's why I play with so much passion and emotion. Because I just got tired of people laughing at us."

The tension that Harrison was generating between his teammates reached a point toward the end of training camp where Willie McGinest finally had to pull him aside.

"Rodney, we know that you can play," McGinest told him. "We respect you. But you can't knock guys out during practice."

"I'm good now," Harrison told him. "I'm good."

While Rodney Harrison was making an impression in Foxborough, Belichick asked strong safety Lawyer Milloy to take a pay cut. Milloy was in the fourth year of a seven-year, $35 million contract. In an effort to get below the salary cap, Belichick wanted to reduce Milloy's annual salary from $4.4 million to around $2.5 million. Milloy's agent balked. At twenty-nine, Milloy was in his prime. He had started in 106 consecutive games and played in four of the previous five Pro Bowls. He didn't think Milloy should have to take a pay cut.

Milloy's agent wasn't posturing. But neither was Belichick. As much as he liked Milloy as a football player, he was unwilling to continue paying him $4.4 million per year. Not when he had Rodney Harrison locked up for six years at $14.5 million. And not when he had two very impressive rookie defensive backs who were itching to play. One of them—Eugene Wilson, a hard-hitting cornerback who had the ability to play safety as well—was showing all the signs of becoming a Pro Bowl player in his own right. And Wilson had a four-year, rookie contract. His salary was a small fraction of what the team was paying Milloy.

On September 2—just five days before the 2003 season opener—Belichick cut Milloy. The players had figured something was up when Belichick showed up uncharacteristically late for a scheduled team meeting. But they were stunned when he began the meeting by informing them in a matter-of-fact tone that Milloy had been released. Looking and sounding

uncomfortable, he praised Milloy's contribution and referred to him as a casualty of the system. Guys were going to be upset, Belichick acknowledged. But they were going to have to get over it.

The room was silent when Belichick momentarily paused before transitioning to a discussion of their upcoming opponent. The players were too shell-shocked to focus. Some scowled in silence. Some just shook their heads, thinking: "What the fuck just happened?"

Belichick had informed Kraft right before he broke the news to his players. Kraft felt horrible. He liked Milloy immensely. He was one of the best players on the team, and he had been instrumental in them winning the Super Bowl. After stewing over Belichick's decision for a couple of hours, Kraft headed to Belichick's office to discuss the situation further. On his way, he ran into Brady, who glared at him.

"How could you let him do that?" Brady said.

Kraft was speechless. It was the first time he'd ever seen Brady furious at him.

Instead of talking to Belichick, Kraft went back to his office and called Milloy. He wanted to personally express his appreciation for all he'd done for the Patriots and tell him how much he regretted the fact that he'd no longer be with the team. But Milloy was too pissed to talk and hung up on him.

Brady drove straight from practice to Milloy's home. He brought Ty Law with him. They were a tight-knit trio. Their friendship had taken hold during the summer after Brady's rookie year. At the start of training camp in 2001, Milloy and Law noticed that Brady's physique had changed over the offseason. "Man, you really worked hard," Milloy told him. "You're doing a good job, man," Law added. "Keep it up." The praise and recognition from two of the best defensive backs in the league was a tremendous boost to Brady's self-confidence. After Brady stepped in for Bledsoe, Milloy and Law ruthlessly taunted him in practice, dancing in his face every time they intercepted him, talking trash about his mama. But Brady never backed down, which endeared him to Milloy and Law even more. The friendship solidified as Brady quarterbacked the team to a Super Bowl championship. Since then, the three of them had socialized a lot away from the field.

Sitting in Milloy's living room, trying to console him, Brady and Law had a hard time coming to grips with the fact that he was no longer on the team. It wasn't fair. It was Milloy who had lobbied Kraft the most to hire Belichick in 2000. When Adam Vinatieri kicked the game-winning field goal to beat the Rams in Super Bowl XXXVI, Milloy was the first player to run to Belichick and hoist him up. He was one of Belichick's staunchest supporters.

Milloy felt the same way Rodney Harrison had when San Diego cut him—betrayed.

"The NFL is a cold business, bro," Law said.

Later that day, Belichick informed the Boston media.

"Today is a day that nobody is happy about," he said. "This isn't the way we wanted this story to end. This is the hardest player that I have had to release. It was the hardest situation that I've had to go through like this, here or anywhere else."

Locally, the reaction was swift and in some quarters quite harsh. Patriots beat writer Kevin Mannix wrote, "Bill Belichick is pond scum again."

Perhaps no one took the loss of Milloy more personally than Tedy Bruschi. He and Milloy had a special bond. They had come into the league together. During their rookie year, they were roommates at the End Zone Motor Inn. When asked by Peter King from *Sports Illustrated* how he felt about Milloy's departure, Bruschi didn't mince words: "I'm not as fully committed to the Patriots as I was to my team at Arizona or Roseville High," Bruschi said. "[The Patriots] took a franchise player and kicked him to the curb five days before the season." Bruschi struggled to express how angry he felt. "I wish . . . I wish . . . it was the old days in this game," he continued, "and I could put my heart on the line for something. But how do you do that in a place where guys who've established what this team is about just come and go?"

Milloy immediately signed with Buffalo. New England's division rival offered him a $5 million signing bonus and a four-year contract that paid him more than Belichick had been offering. Asked how he felt about his former coach, Milloy said, "I couldn't care less about him. I'm all about the Buffalo Bills now."

Days later, New England traveled to Buffalo for the season opener. The team was so bitter toward Belichick that communication between the players and the coaching staff had shut down. Before the game, Milloy made an emotional visit to his former teammates. Few words were spoken. But there were a lot of embraces. "You could see the love in his eyes for all the guys in our locker room," said Deion Branch.

The game, however, was a different story. Reunited with former Patriots quarterback Drew Bledsoe, Milloy played with fury, registering five tackles and sacking Brady once. New England, on the other hand, was listless. The Bills embarrassed them 31–0. It was the worst opening-day loss in Patriots history.

Afterward, Milloy was blunt. "I miss my teammates," he told the press.

"I miss the fans. It's unfortunate that they're stuck with an organization that deals away players, good players. There's no loyalty there."

Eighteen months removed from the emotional high of winning a Super Bowl, the Patriots were a team in turmoil. Standing in the locker room after the Bills game, linebacker Larry Izzo shouted: "We've got to get our shit together!"

twenty-three
ALL IN THE FAMILY

B ill Belichick's decision to cut Lawyer Milloy was the kind of move that would have wreaked havoc on most teams. But the Patriots weren't built like most teams. The franchise's quintessential characteristic over the past two decades has been its resiliency. During the Belichick-Brady era, no team in any sport has consistently rebounded from humiliating losses and excelled amid controversy the way the Patriots have. After the Bills game, Belichick tore into his players during a film session, angrily pointing out mistake after mistake. "Bill yelled at us and screamed at us," said Harrison. "And we went out there Wednesday and we had one of the most physical practices we've ever had."

Everyone was still in a foul mood when the Patriots traveled to Philadelphia to face the Eagles on September 14, 2003. That morning on ESPN's popular pregame show *Sunday NFL Countdown*, former Pro Bowl linebacker-turned-television-analyst Tom Jackson talked with his cohost Chris Berman about the loss of morale in the Patriots' locker room.

"I want to say this very clearly," Jackson said on the air. "They hate their coach. And their season could be over, depending on how quickly they can get over this emotional devastation they suffered because of Lawyer Milloy."

Shaken, Belichick went to Kraft right after the broadcast. Jackson's words had wounded Belichick, and he was at a loss over what to do.

Kraft had never seen Belichick look vulnerable.

Pissed, Kraft called the president of ESPN and unloaded. "That crossed the line," Kraft told him.

Jonathan Kraft was angry, too. During the pregame, he found ESPN's Sal Paolantonio on the field and lit into him.

"Don't yell at me," Paolantonio told him. "I don't make the editorial decisions for ESPN."

Jackson's incendiary remarks were a flashpoint in the Patriots' locker room. The players viewed his words like an attack on a family member. "Even

though there may have been a little bit of truth to what he said, when I heard someone else say that about Bill it made me upset," Tedy Bruschi said. "It's like talking about my brother. 'I'm pissed off at you right now, but I still love you.' There is only a small group of people who can say and feel that, and that was us as players. We were going through a tough time, and we may have had certain feelings about Bill at that moment. But we were the only ones who could have those feelings. People outside our locker room had no right to be talking about that because they were not a part of us."

Inadvertently, at a critical moment when Belichick and his players were not seeing eye to eye, Jackson helped unify them. Suddenly, all of the negative emotions that players felt toward Belichick were channeled toward New England's opponent. That afternoon, the Patriots destroyed the Eagles 31–10. The victory in a road game against the best team in the NFC helped New England turn the page. "It told us, 'We're still a good team and it's time to just let it go,'" said Bruschi. "Wins help you do that. Winning without Lawyer. Winning with Rodney. It opened our eyes to the fact that we were going to be okay."

After the Eagles game, reporters wanted Belichick's reaction to Tom Jackson's pregame comments. Seething, Belichick said, "I am not going to dignify the comments with any type of response." Privately, he wanted to knock Jackson's teeth out, one tooth at a time.

His players were more outspoken about Jackson. "He was flat wrong," Harrison said. "He wasn't in that locker room. So how can he say that we hate our coach? A helluva a lot of us were pissed off at Bill Belichick. But we don't hate him."

Galvanized by the win in Philadelphia, the Patriots manhandled the Jets a week later. Two weeks after that they put up thirty-eight points and knocked off a very tough Tennessee Titans team. Then, over a span of three weeks, the Patriots defense held opponents to six, thirteen, and three points. When the 7-2 Cowboys came to Foxborough in the middle of the season, the Patriots shut them out 12–0.

Part of the team's newfound sense of urgency was attributable to Harrison's emergence as a team leader. His take-no-prisoners approach to the game and his punishing style of play helped the 2003 Patriots develop an identity that was very different from the 2001 Cinderella team's. Another contributing factor was Brady's increasing ability to drive his teammates and effectively lead them on the field and in the locker room. "He has a knack for

getting on guys in a way that they don't take personally," Belichick said. "It's hard to sum up his natural leadership, but he's got it. It's like pornography—even if you can't define it, you know it when you see it."

But the biggest change in the team had to do with mind-set, which was directly attributable to Belichick. "Lawyer was our captain," said Deion Branch. "His departure struck a lot of us like, 'Man, this is crazy. You're releasing the captain!' It made us realize—this could happen to *anybody*. From that point on, my youthful attitude about having fun changed. My new mind-set was: 'This is a business. I'm going to come here, do my business, and let the chips fall where they may.'"

Whether he intended it or not, Belichick's decision to unceremoniously cut a team captain had instilled fear in his players. It made everyone realize that no one was safe and that in order to keep your job you had to perform at a very high level week in and week out. As linebacker Mike Vrabel put it: "You play for Belichick and every week's a tryout."

The more New England won, the more palatable Belichick's approach became to the players. On November 30, the Patriots faced the Colts in Indianapolis. Both teams entered the game 9-2. The Colts had the top-rated offense in the league. The Patriots had the NFL's stingiest defense. After Brady and Manning dueled all afternoon, the game came down to four plays on the Patriots' goal line.

With forty-five seconds to play and New England leading 38–34, Colts running back Edgerrin James rumbled his way to a first down at the Patriots two-yard line. With the clock ticking, Manning hustled his team to the line of scrimmage in an attempt to run the next play before the Patriots had time to reset. He handed off to James, who was met head-on by Bruschi and Vrabel. They dropped James at the one-yard line.

Facing second-and-one, Manning again hustled his team to the line without using a time-out. Again he handed off to James. And again he was met at the line of scrimmage by Bruschi, who was joined by Rodney Harrison and Ted Washington. They stuffed James for no gain, forcing Manning to call time-out with eighteen seconds to play.

On third-and-goal from the one, Manning threw an incomplete pass, stopping the clock with fourteen seconds. The Colts were down to a final play.

On fourth-and-one, Manning handed off to James. This time Willie Mc-Ginest came off the edge and dropped James for a one-yard loss.

The Patriots' sideline erupted and the defensive players on the field mobbed McGinest. Belichick, however, remained expressionless. In four consecutive plays his defense had stopped the most potent offense in the league from advancing two yards. It was a Herculean effort that preserved a victory. But in Belichick's mind, they had simply done their job. "You guys haven't done anything yet to compare yourselves to the last Super Bowl team," Belichick told his players afterward. The next day, he put together film of every mistake they made in the Colts game—missed tackles, blown coverages— and angrily pointed them out. Players were looking at each other as if to say, "I thought we just won." Belichick was establishing a standard of excellence in New England, one that measured success by Super Bowl championships. Victories during the regular season were not cause for celebration. The Patriots were *supposed* to win those games. And they weren't supposed to pat themselves on the back for it.

The Patriots closed out the 2003 regular season at home against the Buffalo Bills. Still smarting from the humiliating 31–0 loss in Buffalo in week one, Belichick told his team: "You don't always get a chance to settle a score in season. We got this one. We need to take advantage of this week." Brady threw four first-half touchdown passes and the Patriots defense battered Drew Bledsoe, ultimately knocking him out of the game in the third quarter. In the final quarter, with his team leading 31–0, Belichick pulled many of his starters. But in the closing seconds, the Bills drove to the Patriots' goal line. Determined to preserve the shutout, the starters on the Patriots' sideline strapped on their helmets, demanding to go back in the game. Then, with thirteen seconds on the clock, linebacker Larry Izzo intercepted the ball in the end zone, sending the Patriots' sideline and the Gillette Stadium crowd into a frenzy. "It meant a lot," Izzo said. "I know all fifty-three guys on this team wanted to keep that zero on the scoreboard."

At midfield, Tom Brady and Ty Law found Lawyer Milloy and hugged him. The Bills were 6-10. Their old teammate's season was over. Milloy congratulated Brady and Law. At 14-2, New England had the best record in the league and had locked up home-field advantage for the playoffs. Grateful to be Patriots, Brady and Law turned and jogged off the field, each holding his index finger in the air.

The Patriots' fourteen-win season was the best in franchise history. It was also the first time the team had gone 8-0 at home. Heading into the playoffs, they were riding a twelve-game winning streak. Yet when asked after the Bills game to assess his team's season, Belichick said, "Not bad." He told

the press the same thing he told his team: "Right now we're headed into the second season, and everyone is 0-0. It's how you fare from here that matters."

The players echoed his sentiments.

"I don't think we have very grand illusions of ourselves," Brady said. "I don't think we put ourselves on this pedestal of being unbeatable, or being great players. I think we pride ourselves on our humility, on being a good player, and contributing in whatever your role on the team is. And because of that, nobody is ever satisfied."

The top brass at CBS could not have been happier. The New England Patriots were the hottest team in the NFL, and Tom Brady was the league's brightest star, making the network's AFC package increasingly valuable. Robert Kraft didn't have to lobby very hard for the network to feature the Patriots-Titans divisional-playoff game in the coveted 8:00 p.m. prime-time slot on January 10, 2004.

It was four degrees and the windchill made it feel like minus ten, making it the coldest game in Foxborough history. Belichick told his players that the Titans would be the toughest challenge they had faced all season. Quarterback Steve McNair was the top-rated passer in the league and had just been named NFL Co-MVP. Determined, Brady started the game by driving the length of the field and throwing a forty-one-yard touchdown pass to put his team up 7–0. After Tennessee tied the game on the next possession, Brady eventually led the team on another scoring drive. From there, both defenses stiffened. The score remained 14–14 until the final minutes, when Adam Vinatieri kicked a game-winning forty-six-yard field goal.

The clutch victory in freezing conditions was New England's thirteenth straight win, and it propelled them to the AFC Championship. But the attitude in the locker room afterward remained all business. "We're not jumping for joy in here," Bruschi said. "We know what we want to do. We're just one step closer."

Eight days later, the Patriots hosted the Colts, a team that had steamrolled through the first two rounds of the playoffs behind the NFL's other Co-MVP, Peyton Manning. In two playoff games, Manning had thrown eight touchdown passes and no interceptions. Belichick instructed his defense to be especially physical with Manning's receivers. "Forget about the guy throwing the ball and focus on those trying to catch it," he said. The message got through. "This is probably the most simple game plan we had," Ty Law said. "Just go out there and stick them and beat them up at the line of scrimmage. If you watch those guys all through the season and postseason putting up big

numbers, you see a lot of guys running through the secondary. We said we are not going to let them do that to us."

To get ready for New England, the Colts practiced outdoors all week, proclaiming they were "immune to the New England chill." It was snowing at game time, and Patriots fans held up signs that read: "This is not Peyton's Place."

For the second straight week, Brady started the game by driving his team down the field and throwing a touchdown pass to put his team up 7–0. On Manning's first drive, he was picked off in the end zone by Rodney Harrison. On Manning's second possession, he was intercepted by Ty Law. By the end of the first half, the field was blanked in slushy snow and New England led 15–0.

"Listen," Belichick told his team at halftime, "we've been in this position before. They exploded on us in Indianapolis. We have to stay with our game plan. Be physical. And more importantly, take care of the football."

In the second half, New England continued to rough up the Colts receivers, and Ty Law intercepted Manning two more times. "It was all about being physical, physical, physical with their receivers," Harrison said. "We wanted to hit these guys in the mouth and let them know we are here."

New England won 24–14. Furious, Colts team president Bill Polian chased the officials off the field, sarcastically shouting: "Great game!" He later complained to the league's competition committee, arguing that the Patriots defenders had repeatedly gotten away with grabbing Colts receivers five yards beyond the line of scrimmage.

The Patriots were the only team in the past ten years to make a third trip to the Super Bowl. As Brady left the field, the fans chanted: "M-V-P, M-V-P, M-V-P."

In the locker room, Kraft pulled Brady aside and informed him that the White House had called. President George W. Bush had extended an invitation for Brady to sit with First Lady Laura Bush during the State of the Union address before Congress. The president was going to call for sports figures to be good role models by staying away from steroids.

Enthused, Brady said he'd go.

Kraft told him he could fly down with Jonathan, who had been invited by a member of Congress from Massachusetts.

Two days after knocking off the Colts, the Patriots returned to Gillette Stadium to start preparing for their Super Bowl opponent—the Carolina Panthers. It was January 20, 2004, and as soon as practice ended, Brady hustled off to the airport with Jonathan Kraft and boarded a private plane

bound for Washington, DC. During the flight, Brady and Kraft talked about the Patriots' chances against Carolina. Kraft spoke with caution. Brady was definitive.

"We're gonna win," he said.

The conversation then shifted to how hard it is to win in the NFL over a sustained period of time.

"The problem is quarterbacks," Brady said. "I've looked at it. When quarterbacks get in their thirties and they get married and have kids, you can see how they all decline."

Kraft hadn't thought much about that. But Brady's point made sense. Eventually, quarterbacks start to lose some of their competitive drive. Life demands, such as being a father and a husband, contribute to that. But so does age.

"Eventually, nature takes its course," Kraft said.

"Well, not with me," Brady said.

Brady's teammates were stunned to see him on television that night, dressed in a suit and tie, seated between Joyce Rumsfeld and Alma Powell in the first lady's box, applauding as President Bush spoke. The next day at practice, everyone razzed him. McGinest nicknamed him "Little Bush."

But the team was all business by the time it got to Houston. After bullying their way through the playoffs, the Patriots were preparing to face a Panthers team that thrived on the same brand of smash-mouth football. Belichick was expecting the Super Bowl to be like a heavyweight title fight—two teams going toe-to-toe for sixty minutes. On the day of the game, he gathered his players and staff in a large meeting room at the team hotel. Standing before them in a suit and tie, he bent down, reached into a box, retrieved the Lombardi Trophy that the Patriots had won two years earlier, and placed it on a table.

"Look, guys," Belichick said, "this is what we're playing for."

He paused while the players stared at the glimmering sterling silver football atop a three concave-sided stand.

"Let's put this week in perspective," he said. "It's not about the parties. It's the trophy. Only thirty-seven teams can say they've owned this. You guys can be the thirty-eighth."

Everyone nodded. Everyone was locked in.

Looking on from the back of the room, Robert Kraft liked what he saw. Heading into the biggest game of the year, the team was in perfect harmony.

Rodney Harrison, in particular, had emerged as an ideal leader on defense and an exceptional teammate. Brady had really bonded with him. The two of them brought a remarkable amount of intensity and focus to work each day. It got Kraft thinking about Belichick's unpopular decision at the beginning of the season to cut Lawyer Milloy. It was the right move, Kraft felt.

Cutting a player—especially one who is beloved by his teammates and has been a big contributor to the team's success—is tough. Kraft had the self-awareness to recognize that he was emotionally invested in his players. Belichick, on the other hand, took an analytical approach to personnel decisions. His discipline, Kraft thought, had served the team well. Although he would have preferred a more empathetic touch in terms of timing and communication, Kraft recognized that Belichick's willingness to part with players—especially ones he particularly admired, such as Milloy—would put the Patriots in a position to excel year in and year out in the salary cap era.

"If you think back on our season," Belichick told the players, "no matter what tough spot you've been in, the reason why you won is because you identified the situation, heard the call, and you *did . . . your . . . job*." He paused and refocused their attention on the trophy. "There's one champion," he continued. "It'll be us if we play well. Good luck today, men. Play like champions."

On the opening kickoff of Super Bowl XXXVIII, two players exchanged blows after the whistle and the head official got his hat knocked off when members of both teams joined the scrum and started pushing and shoving. It was a precursor of things to come. The hitting was ferocious. Ball carriers were leveled. Helmets were knocked off. There was pushing and shoving after the whistle. And skirmishes that had to be broken up by the referees. The defenses were dominating. Through the first twenty-seven minutes of play, neither team scored.

Then, while sacking Panthers quarterback Jake Delhomme from behind, Mike Vrabel tomahawked Delhomme's throwing arm, jarring the ball loose. Richard Seymour recovered the fumble for the Patriots on Carolina's twenty-yard line. Moments later, Brady hit Deion Branch for a touchdown.

It was as if a switch had flipped. Over the final four minutes of the first half, the two teams combined for twenty-four points. New England led 14–10 at the half.

As soon as the first half ended, Commissioner Paul Tagliabue ducked out of his suite and headed to the CBS booth for a radio interview. Afterward, he got back to his suite as the second half was about to start. His

thirty-two-year-old daughter, a high school teacher in Baltimore who had traveled to Houston to attend the game with her father, greeted him with a disgusted look on her face.

"What's wrong?" Tagliabue said.

"Did you see the halftime show?" she said.

He hadn't.

"It was awful," she said. "It was horrible. It was offensive."

Normally unflappable, Tagliabue struggled to maintain his composure. A month earlier, he had been driving to Kennedy Airport to catch a flight when he received an urgent call from Roger Goodell, who voiced serious concerns about the Super Bowl halftime entertainment. CBS was allowing MTV, one of its flagship properties, to produce the halftime show. But MTV hadn't been forthcoming with the NFL about the performers, and Goodell didn't like being in the dark about the show's content and lyrics. He urged Tagliabue to call CBS president Les Moonves right away. "Tell him to rein in MTV," Goodell told Tagliabue. "And tell him we're not going to have someone else produce the halftime show unless he guarantees that we'll be fine." Tagliabue immediately reached out to Moonves and expressed his reservations about turning the halftime show over to MTV. "Our people are very concerned that this is not going to work out well," he told Moonves. "It's going to take your personal engagement to make sure it works out satisfactorily." Moonves had assured Tagliabue that he didn't need to worry.

But now Tagliabue was hearing that the show had featured crotch grabbing and sexually explicit lyrics by rappers P-Diddy and Nelly, and an obnoxious performance by the notoriously misogynistic Kid Rock, who had come onstage wearing an American flag for a shirt, which he later flung off while two scantily clad women danced behind him, waving American flags. Then, to top it off, Justin Timberlake and Janet Jackson had performed "Rock Your Body," and while singing the song's closing line—"I bet I'll have you naked by the end of this song"—Timberlake had torn off Jackson's bra, exposing her breast.

Tagliabue couldn't believe what he was hearing.

"When I go back to school on Tuesday," his daughter told him, "it's not going to be possible for me to explain how a halftime show that offensive could go on the air under your supervision."

Tagliabue's wife agreed with their daughter. The entire halftime show was a disgrace.

Embarrassed and fuming, Tagliabue found Goodell, who had seen the halftime show and was already getting an earful about it. Every guest in the

NFL's suite was appalled. And the league's PR people were being inundated with calls. Goodell was so livid he wanted to go find Justin Timberlake and deck him. Instead, Tagliabue dispatched Goodell to track down Moonves. CBS had a lot of explaining to do.

While executives from the NFL and CBS scrambled, New England built a 21–10 lead and appeared to be pulling away. But in the fourth quarter, Carolina mounted two quick scoring drives. The second one came on an eighty-five-yard pass play that put Carolina up 22–21. With just under seven minutes to play, the Patriots were behind in a game for the first time since November.

On the Patriots' sideline, trepidation gripped some of the players. Ty Law could see that Rodney Harrison feared the game was slipping away from them. "Rodney, we're not gonna lose this game," Law told him. "You know why? Because we have Tom Brady."

It took Brady four minutes to drive his team the length of the field. With 2:51 to play, he threw a one-yard touchdown pass to linebacker Mike Vrabel. Then New England executed the two-point conversion to go up 29–22.

But Carolina drove eighty yards in ninety seconds and tied the game.

With 1:08 to play, Brady remained calm. Facing a scenario nearly identical to the one at the end of the Super Bowl against the Rams, he huddled the offense and told them matter-of-factly that they had this. Over the next fifty-nine seconds, he methodically completed passes for thirteen, twenty, thirteen, four, and seventeen yards to advance the Patriots to the Panthers' twenty-three-yard line. Then, with nine seconds left, he called time-out and Belichick sent out the field goal unit. As Brady and Adam Vinatieri passed each other, their eyes met and they touched hands. But neither of them said a word. Brady had done his job. Now it was Vinatieri's turn.

On the Patriots' sideline, players knelt in a circle and bowed their heads. In the owner's box, Kraft clasped hands with his wife and sons and pulled them close. With flash bulbs flickering throughout Reliant Stadium, Vinatieri booted the ball. As it sailed toward the goalpost, Vinatieri raised his arms in triumph. With four seconds left, his forty-one-yard kick split the uprights, putting New England up 32–29. His teammates mobbed him. Coaches jumped up and down. And Kraft's family smothered him.

Brady, however, remained stoic, showing no expression. Belichick didn't celebrate, either. The moment he knew the kick was good, he turned and called for the kickoff team to get ready. New England still had one more play. It wasn't until after the Patriots' special teams players gang-tackled the

Panthers' kick returner a few moments later that Belichick finally raised his arms and let out a yell.

Brady raced onto the field with his teammates, his arms extended wide, a jubilant expression on his face. At twenty-six, he had become the youngest starting quarterback to win two Super Bowls. He had completed thirty-two of forty-eight pass attempts for 354 yards and three touchdowns. But it was his coolness under pressure during that flawless game-winning drive that earned him his second Super Bowl MVP award.

Belichick tracked down Harrison, hugged him, and told him how glad he was that the Patriots got him. Harrison's eyes welled up. Before he signed with New England, Belichick never asked him "Are you hurt?" or "Can you still run?" or "Can you still play?" He simply looked him in the eye and said: "I know what you can do." No one, other than his mother, had showed so much faith in him. With confetti landing on him and tears streaming down his face, Harrison was overcome with affection for his coach. To Harrison, the moment felt like a fairy tale. "I've waited ten years for this," he said.

Belichick was hounded by reporters seeking interviews, including two different people who approached him from ESPN. He said no to both of them. He hadn't forgotten what ESPN's Tom Jackson had said about him back in the first week of the season. But when Chris Berman personally appealed to him, Belichick didn't want to say no to a friend. The two of them walked across Reliant Field toward ESPN's stage, where Jackson was already on set. As Belichick approached, Jackson extended his hand.

Belichick glared at him and said, "Fuck you."

Jackson walked off. Belichick sat for a one-on-one with Berman.

twenty-four

LEAGUE OF THEIR OWN

On the morning after the Super Bowl, Sean McManus was in his hotel room in Houston waiting for the game's television ratings to come in when he got an unexpected call from Mel Karmazin. Karmazin had become the president of Viacom when the media conglomerate purchased CBS, and he'd been up most of the night dealing with fallout from the Super Bowl halftime show. Federal Communications Commission chairman Michael Powell called the exposure of Jackson's breast a "classless, crass, and deplorable stunt" and was threatening to investigate and potentially levy fines on every CBS-owned station and affiliate in the country. Meanwhile, the president of MTV Networks blamed the situation on "a renegade mistake by a performer." Justin Timberlake wasn't talking. And Janet Jackson claimed through a spokesman that her breast-baring was the result of a "wardrobe malfunction."

"I just need to know," Karmazin said to McManus, "what did you know? And when did you know it?"

"I had zero idea," McManus said. "And I can't imagine that anybody at MTV would ever have any knowledge of this and allow that to happen."

"Okay, that's all I wanted to know," Karmazin said. "By the way, good job on the game."

A little while later, McManus got word that the television ratings were off the charts. A record audience of 143.6 million viewers had tuned in. It was great news. But it aggravated him that the most thrilling Super Bowl ever played was being overshadowed by controversy. Paul Tagliabue was so incensed that he vowed he'd never allow a network to produce a halftime show again.

Later that day, Kraft called McManus to congratulate him and the rest of the team at CBS Sports. As chairman of the NFL's broadcast committee, Kraft was concerned about any controversy involving the league and its television partners. But it wasn't clear to him why the FCC was making such big deal

out of the Janet Jackson incident. Her breast was visible for no more than one second of air time. It happened so fast that if you blinked, you missed it. To Kraft, the situation was being overblown and would soon fade.

On the other hand, the impact his team was having on the NFL was transformational. With two Super Bowl victories in three years and a cast of characters headlined by Tom Brady and Bill Belichick, the Patriots had become the league's marquee team. And from a broadcasting perspective, the Patriots had emerged as the crown jewel of CBS's AFC television package. Starting with the controversial snow game against the Raiders, Patriot games consistently produced superior ratings. It was clear to league officials and senior executives at CBS that the balance of power in the NFL had shifted to Foxborough.

Back in New England, Kraft was riding high. In a region long dominated by the Red Sox, the Patriots were the new kings. On February 3, 2004, an estimated 1.5 million people lined the streets of Boston in wintry weather for the team's Super Bowl victory parade. It was the busiest day in the history of the state's public transportation system. Hundreds of thousands of fans jammed City Hall Plaza for a rally at the end of the parade route. As the team arrived, AC/DC's "For Those About to Rock" blared while highlights of the 2003 season played on a giant jumbo screen.

"We're baaaack!" Brady told the cheering crowd from a platform outside City Hall.

The roar of the crowd echoed off the downtown buildings.

"There was no way we were coming back out here without that Lombardi Trophy," Brady continued. "One was nice. Two's a lot nicer. But I need number three!"

The fans went wild.

When Belichick tried to speak, the delirious crowd was so loud that his voice was drowned out. Ty Law took the microphone and called on Belichick to join the team in a hip-hop dance. "Give me some!" Law yelled at Belichick. "Give me some. Give me some."

With his players egging him on, Belichick raised his arms over his head and started awkwardly bobbing up and down.

"We're the first people in history to see Bill Belichick dance!" said Patriots radio announcer Gil Santos, who was the emcee of the festivities.

Brady and Kraft joined in, sending the audience into a frenzy.

It was a party unlike anything ever witnessed in Boston.

The following night, Belichick appeared on *The Late Show with David Letterman*. Ostensibly there to talk about the Super Bowl, Belichick didn't

miss a beat when Letterman asked if he had had any knowledge of Janet Jackson's "wardrobe malfunction" during the halftime show. "Nobody kept us abreast of that," Belichick quipped.

Between the Tuck Rule game and the Super Bowl halftime fiasco, the Patriots were associated with both of the NFL's biggest controversies since the turn of the century. Yet the organization managed to remain above the fray. When the team assembled in the Rose Garden at the White House, President George W. Bush treated them as if they were America's team.

"The mighty New England Patriots have returned," Bush said, looking at Kraft. "Just like you told me they would. It's such an honor to welcome the team back here. I'm especially glad to see Tom Brady. I'm trying to figure out what it's like to be around a real celebrity."

Praising the team for performing so well under pressure, Bush singled out kicker Adam Vinatieri. "I also appreciate so very much the coach," he continued, looking at Belichick. "I don't know what it's like in the locker room, but I remember when you were here two years ago and you said you were going to say a few words and you said like four words."

Everyone in the Rose Garden laughed.

"I got carried away," Belichick said.

The audience laughed even louder.

"Here's what I like about this team," Bush said, looking at Kraft. "They had a thousand hours of volunteer service to communities in Massachusetts and New England. That is an unbelievably important example for champions to set for others. I know you supported the Boys and Girls Club and the Dana-Farber Cancer Institute, the Massachusetts 9/11 Fund, the ROSE Fund to end domestic violence. I really want to thank you for that."

Kraft beamed.

"My hope, of course, is that I'm back here again to see you next year," Bush said, generating laughter. "Your hope is that you come back."

At the start of the 2004 offseason, one question loomed large over Robert Kraft's franchise: Could the New England Patriots become the first NFL dynasty in the twenty-first century?

Since the start of the Super Bowl era, the NFL had had four dynasties: the Green Bay Packers in the sixties, the Pittsburgh Steelers in the seventies, the San Francisco 49ers in the eighties, and the Dallas Cowboys in the

nineties. Each of those teams won at least three championships in the same decade. But since the league had introduced a salary cap and implemented free agency in the mid-nineties, no NFL team had managed to win three Super Bowls. Kraft was counting on Belichick to change that.

With the same goal in mind, Belichick took a quick trip to Hartford, Connecticut, days before the 2004 NFL Draft. He brought along Scott Pioli. At a restaurant, they met with Cincinnati Bengals running back Corey Dillon. He was only the fourth player in NFL history to rush for over a thousand yards in each of his first six seasons. But in his seventh season, he had suffered an injury and the Bengals had relegated him to a backup role. Fed up and feeling unappreciated, Dillon hurled his helmet, shoulder pads, and cleats into the stands at Paul Brown Stadium while walking off the field after the last game of the 2003 season. He also called out Bengals owner Mike Brown, telling the press: "We will never win with the Brown family in Cincinnati."

Belichick considered Dillon the missing piece that New England needed to establish a powerful ground game. Brown, who wanted to offload Dillon, had given Belichick permission to talk to him.

Pioli gave Dillon the bottom line. "Look, if we're going to trade for you, you're going to have to take less money," he told Dillon, who was due to earn $3.3 million and $3.85 million in the remaining two years on his contract in Cincinnati. "We can't tie up that much money in the running back position," Pioli added.

Belichick chimed in: "What are your motivations?"

"Coach, I've been in the league seven years," Dillon said. "And I've never been to the playoffs. Never mind win a championship. I've never been to the *playoffs.*"

Belichick liked what he heard.

"I want to win," Dillon continued. "You trade for me, just tell me what you want me to take."

When Belichick returned to Foxborough, he informed Kraft that he had worked out a deal with Cincinnati that would bring Corey Dillon to New England in exchange for a second-round draft pick. Dillon had agreed to take a $1.55 million pay cut to play for the Patriots.

Kraft loved the idea of adding an elite running back to the offense. Brady had guided them to two championships without a thousand-yard rusher behind him. With Dillon in the backfield, Brady's passing game would open up even more, making it near impossible for defenses to stop New England's offense. Regarding Dillon's reputation as a malcontent, Kraft wasn't concerned. Belichick's genius was that he saw things in players that everyone else

overlooked. In Dillon, Belichick saw a tenacious competitor who was tired of playing for an organization that wasn't committed to winning. He was so hungry for a championship that he'd do anything to win. In other words, Dillon would fit in perfectly in the Patriots' locker room.

When the trade was announced in mid-April, one NFL beat writer described it this way: "The Bengals get rid of a major source of headaches in the perpetually disgruntled Dillon."

After the FCC received more than 200,000 complaints about the Super Bowl halftime show, Congress convened hearings to determine whether the Timberlake-Jackson stunt had violated indecency laws. Paul Tagliabue and Mel Karmazin were called to testify. Tagliabue told Congress that he had a problem with all aspects of MTV's halftime entertainment. Taking responsibility for the league's not having retained adequate control over the "character, contents, lyrics, choreography, and other critical elements of the show," he pledged that this would never happen again. Karmazin limited his testimony to "the incident of Janet Jackson." Calling it "regrettable," he nonetheless told lawmakers that he had personally interviewed fifty witnesses and reviewed hours of rehearsal tapes and found no evidence that anyone at CBS or MTV had advance knowledge of what transpired. He also told lawmakers that Jackson and her choreographer had met with Timberlake an hour before the performance to discuss modifications to the choreography.

Still, Republican lawmakers chastised Karmazin. "You knew what you were doing," Representative Heather Wilson of New Mexico told him. "You know that shock and indecency creates a buzz that lines your pocket. . . . But the American people are fed up with indecency, and you just don't seem to get it."

The NFL was not sanctioned. But after the hearing, the FCC slapped CBS with the highest fine ever levied on a television network. A US appeals court eventually overturned the fine.

Kraft appreciated the way Karmazin had absolved the NFL of all responsibility and dealt with the situation head-on.

Earlier, when Karmazin was preparing his congressional testimony, Kraft had called him to request a personal favor. Kraft explained that very few entertainers really mattered to Jonathan. One of them was Howard Stern. He listened to him every morning. Although Jonathan never asked for anything, Kraft wanted to surprise his son on his fortieth birthday by arranging a private dinner with Stern.

Considered the "King of All Media," Stern was notorious for being a recluse. The idea of going out to dinner with strangers was anathema to him.

"Howard hates that kind of thing," Karmazin told Kraft.

Kraft knew that about Stern. He also knew that he was putting Karmazin in an awkward position. Stern was so close to Karmazin that he'd do anything he asked.

"I hate to ask you," Kraft said. "But it's for my son. It would really mean a lot to him."

A short time later, Jonathan got a voice mail from Karmazin, inviting him and his wife, along with Robert and Myra, to a celebratory dinner at Jean-Georges in New York. Jonathan assumed they were celebrating the Super Bowl victory. When they arrived at the restaurant overlooking Central Park, Jonathan noticed there was an empty chair. Karmazin said that Tagliabue might be joining them. A few minutes later, Jonathan felt a tap on his shoulder. He turned around and was momentarily blinded by a mass of long black hair.

"Hi, I'm Howard Stern. Happy birthday. Mind if I sit down for a minute?"

Everyone in the restaurant was staring at Stern. He too was under investigation by the FCC and earlier that week he had made national headlines when Viacom's subsidiary Clear Channel Communications suspended him for "vulgar, offensive, and insulting" content. Stern sat down and spent an hour with the Krafts. A relationship was struck up. It was the best birthday present Jonathan had ever received.

Kraft returned the favor by presenting his friend with a Super Bowl ring with "KARMAZIN" inscribed on it. When Kraft had ordered Super Bowl rings studded with thirty-two diamonds for each of his coaches and players, he had an extra one made for Karmazin. It was his way of saying thank you to a dear friend.

The bond between Kraft and Karmazin—and by extension, the Patriots and CBS—was deepening.

The Patriots opened the 2004 season by beating the Colts. Brady outshone Manning again, throwing for 335 yards and three touchdowns. And Corey Dillon carried the ball fifteen times for eighty-six yards. It was the team's sixteenth consecutive victory.

In the locker room afterward, Tedy Bruschi huddled his teammates for what had become his postgame locker room ritual.

"How do we feel about a vic-tor-ee?" he said.

"Ooooh, yeah!" the team yelled in unison.

That fall was rapturous in New England. The Boston Red Sox were en route to winning their first World Series since 1918 and the Patriots were rewriting history on a weekly basis. On October 3, New England defeated Buffalo, becoming just the fourth NFL team to win eighteen consecutive games.

Yet Belichick railed against his team's mistakes—a fumble on a punt and a ninety-eight-yard kick return for a touchdown by the Bills. "We can't go on like this if we want to be any good," he told his players.

A week later, the Patriots knocked off the Dolphins 24–10 to become the first team in the eighty-five-year history of the NFL to win nineteen consecutive games. "How do we feel about nineteen in a row?" Bruschi said afterward, provoking the familiar locker room chorus: "Ooooh, yeah!" The feat landed Brady on the cover of *Sports Illustrated* for the second time in less than two months. "Think how long it's been since we lost," Kraft told the magazine. "Britney Spears has been married twice since then."

Next New England beat Seattle.

Then the Patriots ground out a 13–7 win in Foxborough against the 5-0 Jets, extending the winning streak to twenty-one. Running off the field to the cheers of fans, Brady looked like a kid on a giant playground as he exuberantly fired a football into the upper deck of Gillette Stadium.

The Patriots finally lost a game in Pittsburgh on Halloween. But they immediately resumed a new winning streak. With three games to play in the 2004 regular season, the Patriots were 12-1 when they traveled to Miami for a *Monday Night Football* game against the Dolphins, a team with the worst record in the AFC at 2-11. Leading by eleven points with under four minutes to play, New England appeared to have another victory well in hand. In the final minutes, however, Brady threw two interceptions, Miami rallied, and New England lost 29–28. It was the biggest upset of the season and generated headlines in papers across the country. Statistically, Brady, who threw a total of four interceptions on the night, had the worst performance of his career.

It was after 3:00 a.m. by the time the Patriots landed back in New England and took shuttle buses to Gillette Stadium. Exhausted, sore, and in foul moods, the players stepped into the dark winter air, found their vehicles in the player lot, and motored home. Furious with himself, Brady instead headed into the stadium. In a film room, he spent an hour looking at what he'd done wrong in Miami and another three hours watching film on the Patriots' upcoming opponent.

"I threw four picks in the Miami game," Brady said. "As a player, I never want to be the reason why we lose. I never have to be the reason why we win. I just don't want to be the reason why this team loses the game.

"The way I look at it, they give me the ball," he continued. "Everyone who cheers for you—all the coaches and all the players, their wives, their families—it's all about the ball. If I throw four picks in a game, we have no shot. It's just over. I rarely have one of those games. But when I do, those hurt to the core. Those games change me as a player. Because I don't want to be that. I just want to do my job. Be a good leader, a very great, dependable player that the team knows they can count on."

You learn a lot about a man by knowing what he chooses to do when no one is watching. Perhaps more than any other player on the Patriots' roster, Brady spent a lot of time alone. Much of that time was spent in the dark, pushing the play and rewind buttons over and over, studying his mistakes and studying his upcoming opponent.

Brady never made it home on the night after the Dolphins game. As the sun came up on Tuesday morning, he napped briefly at the stadium and was up and ready to go by the time his teammates returned for team meetings later that day.

"After that loss, I wanted to learn and move on," Brady said. "It wasn't like the season was over. We had a *great* season. We had a great *team*. We just shouldn't have lost that game. And the reason we lost was because I played the way I played. I just didn't want that to happen again."

The Patriots won their final two regular season games and finished 14-2 for the second year in a row. Corey Dillon was finally going to the playoffs. In 2004, his 345 carries for 1,635 yards and twelve touchdowns were all career highs. Like Rodney Harrison, he never regretted the fact that he'd taken a considerable pay cut to play in New England.

The Colts returned to Foxborough for a playoffs rematch on January 16, 2005. Despite New England's superior record, Indianapolis was favored by a point to win. The Colts had one of the most prolific offenses in recent history, and Peyton Manning had thrown a record-setting forty-nine touchdown passes and been voted league MVP for the second straight year. A week earlier, in the wild-card playoff game against Denver, the Colts had scored thirty-five points in the first half alone, and Manning had thrown for 458 yards and four touchdowns.

Meantime, New England's secondary was decimated by injuries. Manning's nemesis Ty Law broke his foot, and two other starters were also sidelined, forcing Belichick to enlist receiver Troy Brown to play defense. Patriots players were bombarded all week with questions about whether they'd be able to slow down Manning. The lack of respect for the Patriots' ability permeated the locker room. But it motivated the players. The whole team fed off it.

Before the game, Colts coach Tony Dungy didn't want his players to focus on the weather and the conditions at Gillette Stadium. But as Manning tossed warm-up passes to his receivers, he could see his breath emanating through his face mask. It was twenty-five degrees, and the windchill was sixteen. Patriots fans held up signs that read: "YOU CAN'T WIN HERE." By game time, snow was falling.

Belichick told his defense to hit every Colts receiver and running back on every play. He even wanted the blockers hit. New England relentlessly hounded and hammered Manning's receivers, and for the first time all year, the Colts were held without a touchdown. While Manning struggled, Brady picked apart the Colts defense with short-range passes and Dillon battered his way to 144 bruising yards on 23 carries. Up 13–3 at the start of the final period, the Patriots drove ninety-four yards before Brady barreled into the end zone from one yard out to put the game away 20–3.

Nobody fed off disrespect as much as Brady. After spiking the ball and head-butting teammates, he stalked the Patriots' sideline. "That was ninety-four yards!" he screamed at his offensive line. "You boys are kicking some fucking ass today. I love that!"

It was the kind of fiery outburst that endeared him to his teammates and distinguished him from Manning and every other quarterback in the league. For the second consecutive year, the Colts' Super Bowl aspirations were dashed in the snow in Foxborough.

To get back to the Super Bowl, the Patriots were going to have to go through Pittsburgh, where they had lost earlier in the year. The Steelers had lost only one game all season. Since Belichick had become the head coach of the Patriots, there had been fourteen occasions when his team had faced an opponent that had beaten them previously in the season. Belichick's record in second-chance encounters was 14-0. But on the eve of the AFC Championship game, Belichick was faced with the fact that this time he might have to manage without Brady.

Shivering with a 103-degree temperature, Brady had an IV in his arm and a bowl of soup beside his bed in Room 304 of the Four Points Sheraton in Pittsburgh. He had a serious case of the flu. Other than the team doctors, only Belichick and Kraft knew how badly Brady was struggling. The next day, on the bus ride from the hotel to Heinz Field, Brady lay across two seats and curled up in the fetal position. With the windchill factor the temperature was minus one. This would be the coldest game in Pittsburgh in Steeler history. Nonetheless, when Brady took the field for pregame warm-ups, he wore only shorts and a T-shirt. He felt like hell, but he was determined not to let Pittsburgh or even his own teammates know that he was ill.

When Belichick gathered the team in the locker room before the game, he kept it brief. "Gentlemen, take a good hard look around the room," he said. "All you have tonight against these Steelers and this home crowd is each other."

At the seven-minute mark of the first quarter, Pittsburgh faced a fourth-and-one situation at the New England thirty-nine-yard line. When the Steelers elected to go for it, Belichick motioned linebackers Tedy Bruschi and Ted Johnson to the sideline. "Roscoe Lena nose!" he told them. It was football speak that meant, "Move the nose tackle to the side of the ball where we anticipate the Steelers are going to run." The Patriots shifted 337-pound Keith Traylor to the gap between the center and the right guard. It was the gap that Steelers fullback Jerome Bettis planned to run through.

On the snap, Traylor filled the gap while Bruschi and Johnson stuffed Bettis, stopping him behind the line of scrimmage as another defender stripped the ball. The Patriots recovered the fumble. On the next play, Brady threw a sixty-yard touchdown pass to Deion Branch. A few minutes later, New England scored again. Then with just over two minutes remaining in the first half, Rodney Harrison intercepted Roethlisberger and ran the ball back eighty-seven yards for a touchdown. By halftime, New England led 24–3 and went on to defeat Pittsburgh 41–27. Brady was too weak to exhibit his typical intensity on the sideline. But he had played one of the biggest games of his career.

After such a gritty performance, Brady was standing on a makeshift stage when CBS's Greg Gumbel handed him the Lamar Hunt Trophy. Brady immediately passed it to Belichick. "That's for you," Brady told him.

Brady was always looking for Belichick's approval. He'd play with the flu in frigid temperatures to earn Belichick's praise. But even when Brady delivered him a trophy, Belichick couldn't bring himself to tell Brady he was proud of him. Prodded by a reporter in a postgame press conference to comment on Brady, Belichick said, "Not every play is perfect, but most of them

are pretty good. Seems like he's always ready to play. He's always prepared. He's always on top of the game plan. He sees things well on the field. I don't think the magnitude of the game or the crowd noise bothers him. He's able to just focus on what he needs to do. And usually does a pretty good job of it. There's no quarterback I'd rather have. He's a terrific football player."

The Patriots were headed back to the Super Bowl to face the Philadelphia Eagles.

On the morning of Super Bowl XXXIX, Belichick gathered his team in a dimly lit ballroom at their hotel in St. Augustine, Florida. After going over the game plan, he stood beside an overhead projector at the head of the room, holding a copy of an email that an Eagles employee had sent to a Red Sox employee. "Let me just read a little something here," Belichick said. "I thought this was kind of interesting. At first, I couldn't believe it. But it's actually true. I'm talking about the Philadelphia parade after the game, all right? It's eleven o'clock in case any of you want to attend that."

Pen in hand, Tom Brady looked up from his notepad. He couldn't believe the Eagles had already planned a victory parade. That pissed him off.

"It's gonna go from Broad Street up to Washington Avenue," Belichick continued. "Past City Hall, then down the Benjamin Franklin Parkway and will end up at the Art Museum. And the Eagles will be in double-decker buses."

As Belichick paused for effect, Willie McGinest rocked back in his chair, nodding his head, chewing his gum. Tedy Bruschi felt insulted. Rodney Harrison couldn't wait to belt someone.

"And the Willow Grove Naval Air Station is gonna fly over with their jets, too," Belichick continued, "in case you're interested in that."

Pushing the right buttons was an important part of Belichick's coaching philosophy. So was staying on message. "Do . . . your . . . job," he told them. "Do . . . your . . . job. Just take care of your assignment. *Know* what it is. *Execute* it. And get it taken care of.

"This is over six months we've been working at this. And today you've got a chance to do something very special. It all comes down to your performance tonight.

"Do your job. Be physical. And you'll be champions again tonight. Okay?" Everyone nodded.

"Good luck tonight, men."

His chin strap dangling, Brady strode slowly onto the field at Alltel Stadium in Jacksonville as his teammates rushed past him and formed a huddle. The Patriots were about to run their first series of plays. With more than 78,000 fans looking on, Brady looked at running back Corey Dillon, who was trying not to think about the magnitude of the moment. Brady knew that Dillon had struggled throughout his entire career with nervousness at the start of games. He also knew that all season long Dillon had looked to him in the huddle as a calming influence.

Snapping his chin strap, Brady dispassionately called a passing play. Then, licking the fingers on his throwing hand, he approached the line of scrimmage and surveyed the defense. He pointed at the Eagles' middle linebacker, a cue to Dillon that it was his responsibility to pick him up if he blitzed.

On the snap, Brady dropped back and the linebacker stormed untouched into the Patriots' backfield. Dillon stepped up, lowered his shoulder, and up-ended him while wide receiver Deion Branch modified his route, running over the middle into the open space vacated by the blitzing linebacker. Brady delivered a perfect strike and Branch hauled it in for a thirteen-yard gain. Dillon got up, dusted himself off, and returned to the huddle as Brady nodded at him, acknowledging his block. It was clear that Dillon's anxiety had left him.

Dillon went on to carry the ball eighteen times for seventy-five yards and a touchdown. The only offensive player on the Patriots who outshone him was Branch. Throughout the season, Branch had been Brady's favorite target. In private workouts, he would make Branch run routine patterns over and over and over, telling him, "I want to be able to throw this ball with my eyes closed and know you're going to be there." The chemistry between them was on display against the Eagles. Brady targeted Branch twelve times, completing eleven of the passes for 133 yards. Branch's eleven receptions tied the Super Bowl record and propelled the Patriots to a comfortable fourth-quarter lead.

The Patriots' first two championships had been won on last-second field goals, leaving no opportunity for Belichick to experience the ritual of being showered with ice water in the waning moments of the Super Bowl. This time, when Rodney Harrison intercepted quarterback Donovan McNabb with nine seconds remaining, sealing New England's 24–21 victory over Philadelphia, Tedy Bruschi was determined to give Belichick his due. With television cameras focused on Belichick, Bruschi sneaked up behind him and dumped a Gatorade bucket of ice water over his head. When Belichick wheeled around to see who had nailed him, Bruschi threw his arms around him.

"If you knew Bill Belichick when he was coaching with the Cleveland

Browns," said Fox color commentator Cris Collinsworth, "they had one winning season there. And to now say that his record in the playoffs would be
better than the great Vince Lombardi, I don't know if there's a person in
Cleveland that's not scratching their head a little and saying, 'Are you believing what we're seeing?'"

"There's no better coach in the game today than Bill Belichick," said announcer Joe Buck.

It was after 3:00 a.m. and the Patriots' victory party at World Golf Village
in St. Augustine was still going full tilt when Brady cruised through the VIP
area with the Lombardi Trophy, posing for pictures with teammates. He was
especially thrilled that Deion Branch had been named Super Bowl MVP. "It's
awesome to see a guy like Deion win it," Brady told a reporter. "The guy has
done everything he can for this team. And this is a team full of guys who
cheer for one another."

In all of the revelry, Jonathan Kraft congratulated Belichick. Days earlier,
Jonathan had received an email from Howard Stern's producer. If the Patriots
prevailed, Stern was hoping Belichick would call in to his radio show for a
few minutes on Monday morning. Kraft had showed the email to Belichick,
who never did that sort of thing. But this was a personal request through
Kraft, who assured Belichick that Stern wouldn't ask obnoxious questions.

After being up all night, Belichick called in just before 8:00 a.m. "It's a big
thrill to be on with you," Belichick said. "I'm a big fan of the show and I've
followed you for years."

Belichick answered a series of questions about his coaching style and the
Patriots' Super Bowl victory. Then Stern asked if he made love to his wife
after the game. Belichick took it in stride, indicating there really hadn't been
time for that. Stern followed that up by offering to take him to the strip club
Scores the next time Belichick was in New York.

Afterward, Stern was inundated with emails from listeners across the
country who were convinced that he had had an actor call in pretending to
be Belichick. "If that was Belichick then I'm the queen of England," one lis-
tener said. Stern's producer issued a public statement, saying: "Really, it was
Bill Belichick."

Belichick could afford to laugh about it. He had become the first coach
in NFL history to win three Super Bowls in four years, and the New England
Patriots were officially a dynasty.

twenty-five

A DAY IN THE LIFE

T om Brady had become the soul of the New England Patriots. Tedy
Bruschi was the heart. After another victory parade through the
streets of Boston, the two of them jetted off to Hawaii on a private
plane to play in the Pro Bowl on February 13, 2005. Brady had been there before, but it was Bruschi's first invitation to the NFL's all-star game. Reclined
in leather seats at thirty thousand feet, the two of them took stock of their
friendship.

From the moment he had arrived in New England, Brady had tried to
emulate the way Bruschi played the game—never acting cocky or gloating
after victories, always letting his play speak for him. And early on, Bruschi
recognized leadership qualities in Brady and was particularly drawn to his
relatability. Connected by their California roots and their Catholic faith, they
told each other things about themselves that they didn't divulge to anyone
else on the team.

Their time together in Honolulu was a nice respite. After the Pro Bowl,
Brady had something to discuss. Over a meal at their hotel, he brought up
how cool it was that they had won three Super Bowls in four years. The only
other team to have pulled that off was the Cowboys in the early nineties.
Then Brady flashed a mischievous grin.

"What?" Bruschi said.

"Three-peat," Brady said.

"*Three-peat?*" Bruschi said.

The New York Yankees had won three straight World Series championships between 1998 and 2000. The Los Angeles Lakers had won three straight
NBA championships between 2000 and 2002. But dating all the way back to
the inception of the Super Bowl in the mid-sixties, no NFL team had ever
won three straight Lombardi Trophies. Brady leaned forward in his chair.

"We need to be the team that does it," Brady said.

"Ma-a-an," Bruschi said, "that would be pretty amazing."

Thirty-six hours later, Bruschi was back home, asleep in his bed, dreaming that Steelers running back Jerome Bettis was barreling toward him. Bracing for the collision, Bruschi suddenly woke up. His fists were clenched, his arms extended, his muscles contracted. He felt a pins-and-needles sensation in his left arm and left leg. It was 4 a.m. and his wife, Heidi, was asleep beside him. After repeatedly making a fist in an effort to increase blood flow to his arm, Bruschi got out of bed to use the bathroom. As soon as he stood, his left leg was so numb that he lost his balance and had to grab the bedpost to prevent himself from crashing to the floor.

The commotion woke up Heidi. "What are you doing?" she said.

"I think I slept on my arm wrong or something," he said.

Unable to walk, Bruschi crawled to the bathroom.

Heidi was accustomed to seeing her husband so banged up after games that he could barely walk without moaning and groaning. But this was different. After getting back in bed and sleeping until ten, Bruschi woke up in even worse shape. His head ached. He was disoriented when he tried to stand. And the left side of his body was increasingly numb.

Concerned, Heidi called Patriots trainer Jim Whalen, who advised her to get Bruschi to the hospital.

Bruschi wasn't convinced that was necessary; he wasn't experiencing a great deal of pain. Then he heard his five-year-old son, TJ, scurry into the bedroom from the left. Although he could hear him, Bruschi couldn't see his son until he entered the right side of Bruschi's field of vision and said, "Good morning, Daddy." Suddenly scared, Bruschi turned to Heidi and said, "Call 911."

A neighbor came over to stay with the kids while EMTs placed Bruschi on a stretcher and wheeled him out of the house, his little boys trailing him as Heidi fought back tears. "Daddy's just going for a ride," she told them.

Crying, Bruschi pulled his sons close, repeatedly kissed them, and told them he loved them. Once the ambulance doors closed and he was en route to the hospital, Bruschi frantically called Jim Whalen again.

"What's wrong with me, Jim? What's going on?"

Bruschi had suffered a mild stroke. Doctors at Massachusetts General Hospital discovered that he had been born with a small hole in his heart. The stroke had occurred when a blood clot passed through the hole, obstructing blood flow to the brain. He was lucky. If the clot had been a couple of millimeters in a different direction, he could have died. As it was, the left side of his face

had drooped, he'd lost his coordination on the left side, and had practically no vision in his left eye.

The hospital kept him on round-the-clock observation to make sure he didn't have an aneurism before the clot dissipated. Once he stabilized, he'd be put on blood thinners in preparation for surgery to repair his heart. Then there would be a long period of physical rehabilitation. It was a lot to absorb.

The Patriots were tight-lipped about Bruschi's medical condition. But his hospitalization quickly became the top story in New England and generated headlines across the country. On the day he was released to go home, a throng of television cameramen and news photographers camped outside the hospital. When Bruschi exited and saw them, he insisted on getting out of his wheelchair and walking to the car. "Hold my hand so I don't fall," he told Heidi. That night on the evening news, footage of him moving robotically and meekly waving at the press was jarring. Pale and unsteady, the player who epitomized the Patriots' fighting spirit looked feeble.

Bruschi's situation added to the state of flux in Foxborough. Right after the Super Bowl, Belichick's two top assistant coaches were hired away. Offensive coordinator Charlie Weis took the head coaching job at Notre Dame. Defensive coordinator Romeo Crennel left to become head coach of the Cleveland Browns. Both were exceptional lieutenants who had been at Belichick's side since he arrived in New England. In their absence, Belichick promoted a couple of significantly younger assistants—Josh McDaniels and Eric Mangini.

At the same time, Belichick faced difficult roster decisions. A number of veteran players who had been instrumental in the Super Bowl championships were eligible for free agency. Additionally, the Patriots needed to shed a couple of big salaries in order to remain under the salary cap. Although Belichick was consistently portrayed in the media as making personnel calculations "without sentiment" and was perceived by his own players as having little emotional attachment to them, cutting team members was the aspect of coaching that he found most vexing. "Guys who have played and won for you," Belichick said, "and do everything you ask them to do—run, lift weights, train, be tough, make personal sacrifices. Then you say, 'You're not going to be on the team.' There's nothing worse."

Yet in order to stay ahead of the competition and consistently put the Patriots in a position to win, he had to remove sentimentality from the

equation. At the start of the offseason, Belichick opted not to re-sign veteran offensive lineman Joe Andruzzi, and he cut a number of key defensive players, including linebacker Roman Phifer and lineman Keith Traylor. But the hardest decision was to part ways with star cornerback Ty Law. Law had spent his entire ten-year career in New England and held several team records, including most career interceptions. He was generally considered the greatest cornerback in team history. Partway through the 2004 season, Law had broken several bones in his foot and badly torn the ligaments. With one year remaining on his contract, Law was on track to be back in action by the time training camp opened later in the summer. But the Patriots would owe him $12.5 million for that final year of his services. By releasing him, Belichick would keep the team under the cap. Plus, Law, who was still one of the top cornerbacks in the league, would be free to sign with another team for even more money.

Law was hobbling his way through an airport in late February when he got a call from one of Belichick's assistants. Propped up on his crutches in the middle of a concourse, Law listened as the assistant told him the team was going in another direction and had decided to cut him.

In the back of his mind, Law knew this was just business. Still, to get the news the way he did felt so cold that he fumed. Deep down, he was hurt. He'd always wanted to retire a Patriot. It felt like he'd been kicked out of the family. When Belichick called later on and attempted to smooth things over, Law didn't want to hear it.

Robert Kraft was home when he received a call from Bruschi in the early evening on March 8. Kraft could tell from Bruschi's voice that he was down.

"I called to tell you I'm retiring," Bruschi said.

"I know, Tedy," Kraft said softly.

Kraft had been on bedside vigil with Bruschi in the hospital. He'd also been briefed by the doctors. The last thing he wanted was for Bruschi to be thinking about playing football again. He told him to focus on his health, his wife, and his children.

Bruschi couldn't help feeling guilty, as if he'd somehow let Kraft down. Privately, he'd always viewed Kraft as a father figure. Kraft would have a beer with Bruschi and talk about aspects of life outside of football. Kraft would routinely ask about the well-being of Heidi and the children. He knew their birth dates. And on Thanksgiving, Kraft was the one asking

Bruschi whether he preferred white meat or dark meat. Bruschi wanted to keep playing for him.

The next morning, Bruschi had his wife drive him to the stadium so he could clean out his locker and talk to Belichick. For years, Bruschi had wished that Belichick would be more expressive. *Come on, man,* he'd think, *give me a shoulder bump or something.* Even when Bruschi was hospitalized, Belichick called instead of visiting. But eventually, Bruschi came to realize that Belichick did indeed care about him but just had a different way of showing it. And Bruschi had been around long enough to see the benefit in Belichick's arm's-length relationship with players.

"Ask any of Bill's players if they've ever had pizza and beer with Bill Belichick," Bruschi said as a rhetorical statement. "Deep down inside, all those players know what I know—if I don't do my job, I'm out of here. That clears up a lot of drama. It isn't, 'Man, I thought you were my friend. We've had dinner together. We've had beers together. You've witnessed the birth of my children.' All the things that personal relationships have."

But Bruschi was about to turn the tables on Belichick by being the one to tell him that he was finished. It was a conversation Bruschi wanted to have face-to-face.

Belichick was behind his desk when Bruschi walked in and took a seat opposite him. After some small talk, Bruschi said, "What I really came here to tell you is that I'm not going to be here for you next year. I'm going to retire."

Belichick listened intently. Then he said, "Have you ever thought of just taking the year off like Mark Fields did?"

Fields was a linebacker on the Carolina Panthers who had sat out the 2003 season after being diagnosed with Hodgkin's disease. Bruschi saw his situation differently.

"No," Bruschi said. "I still have to deal with this heart procedure, and I can barely walk. A year off isn't going to help me. I've made up my mind. I'm retiring."

Belichick didn't press. He wished Bruschi the best and said the team was there for him if he needed anything.

Bruschi asked if it would be okay for him to rehab at the stadium.

"Absolutely, Tedy," Belichick said. "You'll always be welcome around here."

Bruschi felt himself starting to lose his composure. The sense that his football days were over was sinking in. He stood, shook Belichick's hand, and headed out. By the time he got to the minivan, he was a mess. Heidi got out and put her arms around him.

"What's wrong, Daddy?" TJ asked as Bruschi sat down between his sons in the middle seat.

"Daddy's just a little sad, buddy," Bruschi told him. "Just a little sad."

Tom Brady had been vacationing in Mexico when he got word of Bruschi's stroke. As soon as he got back to Boston, he drove to Bruschi's home, where he found his friend recuperating after his heart procedure. Bruschi was exhausted. His vision was still impaired. And there were bruises all over his body.

Brady didn't understand how something like this could happen. One moment they were mapping out the Patriots' three-peat. The next moment, his friend was trying to walk without stumbling.

Bruschi's life-altering experience came as Brady was dealing with his own new reality—extreme fame.

On April 16, 2005, Brady was greeted by loud cheers when he stepped onto the stage at Studio 8H in Rockefeller Plaza in New York, wearing jeans, a collared shirt, and a blue blazer. "Thank you very much," he began. "It's hard for me to believe I'm actually here tonight, hosting *Saturday Night Live*."

On cue, Brady looked directly into the camera. "I'm sure some of you are thinking at home—'He's not an actor,' which is true. But I am a professional athlete. And I'm used to performing live, under pressure, in front of millions of people. My team, the New England Patriots, has won three of the last four Super Bowls."

Robert Kraft could not have dreamed up a more ideal ambassador for his football franchise. In a city known for its sports legends, Brady had crossover appeal that had eluded Boston greats like Ted Williams and Larry Bird and Bobby Orr. One entertainment critic said of his *SNL* appearance: "Brady carries it off like Gary Cooper, which one can do when one is six feet four, model handsome, and actually proportioned like the Oscar statuette."

The same month that Brady danced and sang in skits with *SNL* comedians Seth Meyers and Kenan Thompson, he was also photographed by *GQ*, attended the *Vanity Fair* Oscar party in Los Angeles, appeared on ABC's *This Week with George Stephanopoulos* to discuss politics, and was a guest of honor at the White House Correspondents' Association Dinner in Washington. In the midst of all of this, Brady started dating actress Bridget Moynahan.

At twenty-seven, Brady had become the face of the NFL and was the game's brightest and most transcendent star. But with all of that light came a lot of heat. *Boston Globe Magazine* writer Charles P. Pierce started

interviewing Brady's family members, high school and college teammates, and Patriots personnel for a book about him called *Moving the Chains: Tom Brady and the Pursuit of Everything*. And in June, Brady sat down with *60 Minutes* correspondent Steve Kroft at Gillette Stadium to answer scores of probing questions for a segment that would air later in the fall.

Yet despite his success, Brady was still searching. Back in April when he was in New York for rehearsals leading up to his *SNL* appearance, he took the opportunity to study Lorne Michaels, the sixty-year-old creative genius behind the show. Michaels had been running *SNL* for thirty years. Watching Michaels work for a couple of days, Brady was looking for things that he could incorporate into his own approach: *What makes him tick? How does he continue to stay motivated? How does he keep the edge?*

Brady's edge was his humility, a virtue that is scarce in the hypercompetitive arena of professional sports. Even after becoming the center of attention, he remained beloved by his teammates and malleable to his coaches. During the spring of 2005, Brady signed a new six-year, $60 million contract that would take him through the 2010 season. At the time, Peyton Manning had a seven-year, $99 million contract, and quarterback Michael Vick had a ten-year contract worth $130 million. Neither Manning nor Vick had been to a Super Bowl. Brady's willingness to play for so much less than other top-tier quarterbacks freed up millions for the team to sign other great players. "The way the NFL works, the more you take, the less money other guys have," Brady said after signing his contract. "Other people need to get paid a lot of money too, because a lot of other people contribute."

Toward the end of the summer, when the offseason media blitz finally began to subside, writer Charles P. Pierce caught up with Brady at the Patriots training facility. "Do you mind having a book written about you?" he asked.

"To tell you the truth," Brady told him, "there's only one real problem I have with this. I don't know if I'm old enough for a book like this."

Pierce would later write: "It's an answer indicating that, despite his accomplishments, and despite all the extraneous celebrity sugar that's come his way, he will not be completed on anyone's terms but his own."

It was midnight when Robert and Myra Kraft arrived at the Louvre in Paris. The museum was dark and the public entrances were locked. Inside, director Ron Howard and actor Tom Hanks were about to start shooting *The Da Vinci Code*, a feature film that Howard had adapted from author Dan

Brown's international bestseller. As the Krafts approached a security check-
point, Brown greeted them with hugs and led them through the museum's
iconic glass pyramid to the set.

Kraft had read Brown's book shortly after it was published back in
2003. He liked it so much that he wrote to Brown and invited the author
to attend a Patriots game on October 5 of that year. For Brown, inviting
Robert and Myra to the Louvre for the first day of filming was a way of
returning the favor. When Kraft arrived on the set, Ron Howard and Tom
Hanks stopped what they were doing to say hello and congratulate him on
his third Super Bowl title. A number of cast members were huge Patriots
fans, including Howard's personal assistant, who invited Kraft to sit in the
director's chair.

But Kraft soon grew restless watching Hanks repeatedly perform the
same scene and deliver the same line over and over. After a while, Kraft
turned to Brown and whispered: "Wow, moviemaking isn't really a spectator
sport, is it?"

Eventually Kraft got back on his plane, and flew with Myra to London.
They were off to catch the final round of Wimbledon, followed by a visit to
Israel, where crowds chanted "DY-NA-STY" as Kraft stood alongside Israeli
finance minister Benjamin Netanyahu and hoisted the Lombardi Trophy
while dedicating the first football field in Jerusalem.

As Brady and Belichick had become two of the most visible sports per-
sonalities in America, Kraft's global profile as the owner and architect of one
of the most successful and financially profitable teams in the world had continued to grow. Months after the Patriots won their third Super Bowl, the
franchise reached a value of $1 billion, putting the team in very elite com-
pany. At that time, only three other sports teams worldwide were worth $1
billion—the British soccer team Manchester United and the NFL's Washington Redskins and Dallas Cowboys.

Just ten years earlier, the Patriots had been considered the worst team
in the NFL, both in terms of wins and losses and of financial stability. In the
decade since Kraft had taken over, the team's worth had increased by 445 percent, far outperforming the Dow Jones Industrial Average, the S&P 500, and
Nasdaq during that same period. By 2005, the team was debt-free, was generating nearly $250 million in annual revenue, was at full capacity with 62,000
season ticket holders, and had a paid waiting list of 50,000 more. Headlines
such as "Kraft-ing a Model Franchise" and "Krafts Turn Patriots into Financial Winners" appeared on the business pages of leading newspapers and in
finance periodicals. *Forbes* even put Kraft on the cover under the headline

"UNLIKELY DYNASTY" and declared: "Kraft has transformed the Patriots into one of the most valuable sports franchises in the world."

With all of the Patriots' success, Kraft found himself in positions that other NFL owners couldn't relate to. In the summer of 2005, Kraft accepted an invitation from Sandy Weill to travel to Russia with Rupert Murdoch and the CEOs of IBM, Intel, United Technologies, ALCOA, and International Paper to meet with President Vladimir Putin. Weill was attempting to stimulate commerce between the United States and Russia. Afterward, as the American business leaders posed for a group photo with Putin, Weill encouraged Kraft to show his Super Bowl ring to the Russian leader.

Kraft retrieved it from his pocket and handed it to Putin.

Putin admired the ring's size and its 124 diamonds. "I could kill someone with this ring," he said as he slipped it on his finger and made a fist.

Taken aback, Kraft said, "You could kill someone without it. You were the head of the KGB."

The group laughed.

As Putin removed the ring, Kraft put out his hand. But Putin slipped the ring into his own pocket.

Perplexed, Kraft looked at Weill, who subtly shook his head from side to side, signaling Kraft not to say anything. But Putin was stealing his ring. Kraft couldn't believe it.

Putin bade the group farewell and left with a number of his associates.

Days later, while Kraft was in Europe, word of the incident leaked. The Associated Press reported: "Russian President Vladimir Putin walked off with New England Patriots owner Robert Kraft's . . . Super Bowl ring." Within twenty-four hours, the story escalated into what the *Boston Globe* referred to as "an international incident." The Russian government took the position that the ring was a gift. Russia's leading business newspaper reported that although gifts to Russian presidents were normally kept in the Russian state treasury, Kraft's Super Bowl ring was deposited in the Kremlin library. Meantime, the Russian embassy in Washington declined to say whether a request had been made to return the ring.

Kraft soon got a call from the White House. The specter of Russia's president stealing jewelry from the owner of America's highest-profile sports team was detrimental to the already shaky diplomatic relations between the two superpowers. The Bush administration suggested it would be in the country's best interest if Kraft put an end to the controversy by stating publicly that he had intended the ring to be a gift.

But the ring had not been a gift. Kraft's name was inscribed on it.

Kraft wasn't happy. After hanging up, he begrudgingly decided that under the circumstances he would honor the Bush administration's request. Myra supported his decision. Later that day, Kraft issued a formal statement, acknowledging that he hadn't initially intended for the ring to be a gift, but had changed his mind when he saw how much Putin liked it. "At that point, I decided to give him the ring as a symbol of the respect and admiration that I have for the Russian people and the leadership of President Putin," Kraft said.

The incident was a barometer of just how visible the Patriots organization had become. And as a result of the episode, a Patriots fan club was formed in Moscow.

Kraft had barely gotten back from overseas when linebacker Ted Johnson came to see him at home. Training camp was about to start and Johnson had something he wanted to tell him face-to-face: after ten years with the Patriots, Johnson had decided to retire.

Over the course of his career, Johnson had torn his right biceps, torn his left biceps, broken his foot, undergone surgery on both shoulders, torn innumerable tendons, and sustained a number of head injuries. But he had never allowed physical ailments to keep him away from the field. Lately, however, Johnson had been experiencing more alarming symptoms—memory loss, depression, irritability, and insomnia, to name a few. So he'd gone to see a neurologist, who told him his symptoms were likely a result of concussions. He was advised that continuing to play football would subject him to serious and lasting health issues.

In the summer of 2005, public awareness about the long-term health implications of concussions was fairly limited. Chronic traumatic encephalopathy (CTE), the neurodegenerative disease caused by repeated head injuries, had not yet been publicly linked to an NFL player. And the first lawsuit against the NFL by retired players who had suffered repeated concussions was still six years off. But Johnson's doctor made the connection, and Johnson wasn't about to ignore his medical advice. Suddenly, the thought of absorbing another hit made Johnson feel physically ill.

Kraft was sobered by Johnson's prognosis and fully supported his decision to retire. He told him that the priority now was Johnson's health and his family, and Kraft pledged his support. To that end, he assured Johnson that he would receive the $400,000 roster bonus that he would have been entitled to if he played in 2005.

Johnson was grateful. That night, the two of them kicked off their shoes,

reclined in Kraft's living room with a couple of beers, and talked until midnight. The next day, the Patriots released an official statement from Johnson, which read, in part:

> It is with deep regret that I have decided to retire from football. The decision was not an easy one, but life sometimes has a timetable all its own. I can no longer ignore the severe short- and long-term complications of the concussive head injuries I have sustained over the years.

Johnson singled out the Krafts and thanked them for making him feel part of the Patriots family. He also acknowledged his teammates, his coaches, and the fans. He did not, however, mention Belichick.

Nonetheless, Belichick provided his own public statement on Johnson. "Ted informed me of his decision today and we had a good discussion," Belichick said. "Although his retirement is unexpected, we thoroughly respect his decision and support him as he moves on. It goes without saying, but Ted Johnson is a class act. He was a solid contributor to this defense and the New England Patriots organization his entire career. Ted's signature was a work ethic and toughness that were second to none. He retires a champion."

Belichick's relationship with Johnson had been contentious. Back in 2002, things got so bad between them that Johnson had cleaned out his locker, stormed out of the facility, and threatened to quit. "We went from I wanted out of there, I hated the man, I resented him, I was angry, hurt, disgusted, to being a captain the next year," Johnson said of that time period. "And honestly, we put it behind us."

But as Johnson stepped away from the Patriots, his views toward Belichick would harden.

twenty-six

LOSS

In team sports there is only one thing harder than building a dynasty—
sustaining it.

Since the 2001 season, when Tom Brady took over as quarterback,
the Patriots had ruled the NFL. Between 2001 and 2004, the team's cumula-
tive 57-16 record and .781 winning percentage were the best in the league.
All of that success had generated a lot of envy. In 2005, everyone would be
gunning for the Patriots. As one opposing scout put it: "They're going to see
everybody's A-game this year."

Belichick knew what his team was up against. He also knew he was heading into the 2005 season without some of the toughest enforcers on his notoriously physical defense. Ty Law was one of the best shut-down cornerbacks
in the game and had brought a sense of confidence and bravado to the team.
Roman Phifer was a punishing tackler who had missed just five games in four
years. And Ted Johnson was a quintessential 250-pound middle linebacker
who attacked blockers with reckless abandon, clearing the way for his teammates to have a clear shot at ball carriers. The three of them left a sizable void.

Then there was Bruschi. Over the summer, he'd worked tirelessly on
physical therapy and made a remarkable recovery. Dr. David Greer, the head
of his medical team at Massachusetts General Hospital, said there were no
medical reasons preventing him from returning to football. Bruschi had also
sought second and third opinions from other cardiologists and neurologists,
all of whom concurred with his primary physician. Still, Bruschi had decided
he would sit the year out and try to build up his strength for a comeback in
2006. His absence was immediately felt when training camp opened. The
overall drop-off on defense was significant.

Meanwhile, the offense looked stronger than ever. Tom Brady and Deion
Branch, in particular, appeared to have picked up right where they left off
at the Super Bowl back in February. During one three-day stretch of camp,
Brady and Branch connected on more than fifty pass plays.

But Belichick wasn't happy. After a morning practice session, he stopped Brady and Branch as they were walking off the field together.

"Look here, you two motherfuckers," Belichick barked.

Both players faced him.

"You've got fifty catches already," Belichick continued, looking at Branch and quickly turning to Brady. "Do not throw the ball to Deion anymore."

Brady tried to explain, but Belichick cut him off.

"Find somebody else to throw the ball to!" Belichick snapped.

The rest of the world may have been treating Brady differently, but Belichick made a point not to.

Frustrated, Brady didn't say anything more. When he returned to the field for the afternoon practice session, he found two defenders smothering Branch on every snap. For the next couple of days, Branch couldn't get open. The only way Brady could throw to his favorite target was after practice when they were alone.

"What's going on?" Branch said. "This is crazy."

Brady was pissed. But instead of openly complaining about Belichick, he channeled his anger onto the practice field, screaming at the offense to work harder. He didn't want to just beat Belichick's defense. He wanted to smash it.

On September 1, 2005, Tedy Bruschi gave an exclusive interview to Jackie MacMullan at the *Boston Globe*. It was the first time he talked in detail to a journalist about his stroke. In addition to describing the harrowing ordeal, he acknowledged that he planned to play again. But he ruled out playing in 2005. "I need time," he told MacMullan. "I think I've healed faster physically than I have emotionally."

When MacMullan asked whether Bruschi would entertain thoughts of returning in 2005, he said, "I'm telling you right now that's not going to happen."

The next morning, MacMullan's story, headlined "Bruschi Plans to Play Next Year," was the talk of New England. That afternoon, Belichick was in his office, preparing for the season opener against the Raiders, which was two days away. He was also looking to shore up his defense by striking a last-minute deal to add a linebacker to the roster. When Bruschi dropped by, Belichick invited him to have a seat.

Early that morning, Bruschi had met with Dr. Greer. They reviewed the results of Bruschi's latest echocardiogram. The results were stellar. Then Greer surprised him and Heidi by telling them that he had a perfect bill of health. The prognosis inspired Bruschi. After leaving the doctor's office, he

told his wife he no longer wanted to wait a year to play again. She supported his decision.

Rather than spelling all of that out in his meeting with Belichick, Bruschi simply told him he wanted to remain on the Physically Unable to Perform (PUP) list.

Belichick didn't see the sense in that. The only reason to keep a player on the 2005 PUP list was if he expected to return to the active roster in 2005.

"Let me get this straight," Belichick said. "There's still no way of you playing this year at all, right?"

When Bruschi paused, Belichick raised his eyebrows.

"I'm going to play this year," Bruschi said.

"I want to make sure we're on the same page here," Belichick said. "Are you telling me that going out there and picking up another linebacker this year would be the wrong move?"

"Yeah. That would be the wrong move."

Kraft was caught off guard when Bruschi showed up in his office and told him he'd just met with Belichick to let him know he planned to resume playing by midseason.

"Is Heidi on board with this?" Kraft asked.

Bruschi assured him she was. The echocardiogram results confirmed the conclusion of every doctor they'd been to see—that there was no medical reason to prevent him from playing football.

After listening patiently, Kraft said, "You have one more person to see."

Bruschi didn't follow what he meant.

Kraft told him about Dr. Matthew Fink, one of the country's leading experts on stroke and critical-care neurology. He was affiliated with the prestigious New York–Presbyterian Hospital/Weill Cornell Medical Center in New York City. Kraft insisted that Bruschi and his wife go to New York together to see him.

"With the important decisions in life, you measure nine times and cut once," Kraft told him. "This is one of those times."

Bruschi nodded.

"You can take my plane," Kraft said.

After winning the season opener, New England got roughed up a week later by the Carolina Panthers. In week three, the team suffered a big setback when

Rodney Harrison blew out his knee and was lost for the season. A week later, San Diego put up 41 points on the Patriots. Then Denver beat up on New England's defense. After six weeks, New England was 3-3 and the rest of the league smelled blood in the water.

Then word leaked that Bruschi would return in time for the Patriots' next game. The specialist in New York had confirmed that he was free to pursue a return to football. Bruschi and the Patriots thought word of his comeback would be viewed positively. Instead, it triggered intense criticism and sparked a national debate over whether someone who had suffered a stroke should be permitted to play football. Hall of Fame players weighed in against the idea. Newspaper columnists opined that Bruschi was being selfish and having a hard time walking away from fame. Boston's leading sports radio talk show hosts called the situation life-threatening. And ESPN's Tom Jackson wondered aloud how people would react if "we're watching some Sunday afternoon and something happens to Tedy Bruschi on the field. You tell me how the league and the Patriots are going to feel the moment that happens."

With all the scrutiny, team lawyers strongly advised Kraft to have Bruschi sign a waiver to shield the team from liability in the event that something went wrong. But Kraft decided against that approach.

In an effort to tamp down concerns, Bruschi's neurologist spoke to the press. "Tedy was neurologically normal or we wouldn't have let him play," Dr. Greer said. "While he could still get hit in the head and have a resultant stroke, that's no different than any other player." Regarding concerns that the device installed over the hole in Bruschi's heart could get dislodged by the violent collisions of the game, Greer said: "The heart is protected deep inside the chest cavity. And it exerts more energy on that device than would any chest blow."

On Bruschi's first day back on the practice field, Belichick spoke to the team. "There's going to be a lot of media interest in Tedy," he told his players. "And I'm going to advise you all not to comment on his health. I haven't even commented myself. The only person who should be commenting on the health of Tedy is Tedy."

Bruschi suspected his teammates had questions. The fact was that no professional football player had ever come back to play after a stroke. Nor had anyone ever played pro football with the device that had been inserted in Bruschi's heart. Plenty of people feared that a violent collision might cause Bruschi to die on the field. Nonetheless, on Bruschi's first day back, the linebackers coach started practice with a 9-on-7 drill that required him to knock heads at full-speed with a 240-pound fullback. It's considered the

most violent play a linebacker has to make. Bruschi went full speed. So did the fullback, planting his shoulder in Bruschi's chest. To Bruschi, it seemed like a loud explosion in his helmet. "Okay, I'm all right," he told himself. "I'm still here. Let's go."

Welcome-back signs and banners filled Gillette Stadium and 68,756 fans stood and roared as Bruschi ran out of the tunnel with his teammates for a Sunday night game on ESPN against the Bills on October 30, 2005. The Who's "Who Are You?" played through the public address system as Bruschi bounced up and down on the sideline, shadow boxing like Rocky, eliciting a chorus of "BROOOOO" that reverberated through the stadium. Briefly spotting his wife in the crowd, Bruschi waved, and she placed her hand over her heart.

Bruschi's return lifted his team. He played sixty-four of the game's seventy-seven defensive plays. He had forty-four hits and had seven tackles. The Patriots played their most spirited game of the season, beating Buffalo to improve to 4-3. And Bruschi became the first stroke survivor to return to a career in professional football. Just by stepping onto the field, he became an inspiration to stroke patients throughout the country.

In the locker room afterward, Belichick did something out of character.

"I'm going to break this one down," he said. "Let's go. Everybody up."

The players huddled around him the way they normally would around Bruschi after a game.

"I wanna know how we feel about having Tedy Bruschi back," Belichick said.

"OOOOOH, YEAH!" the team shouted.

Belichick then threw his arms around Bruschi.

It felt like a media circus was trailing the Patriots. A week after Bruschi's highly publicized return, Pulitzer Prize–winning author David Halberstam published a laudatory book on Bill Belichick, and Steve Kroft's complimentary profile on Tom Brady aired on *60 Minutes*. But neither Belichick nor Brady dwelled on past achievements. They cared only about what lay ahead—a *Monday Night Football* showdown in Foxborough with the 7-0 Indianapolis Colts. *Sports Illustrated* hyped the game by putting Manning and Brady on the cover and billing it: "THE DUEL."

In all six previous meetings, Brady and the Patriots had beaten Manning and the Colts. At the top of the broadcast, ABC announcer John Madden said all the pressure was on Manning and the Colts. "If you're going to be 'The

Man,' you have to beat 'The Man,'" Madden said. "And if you are going to be 'The Team,' you have to beat 'The Team.'"

Even with Bruschi back in the lineup, the Colts ran roughshod over the Patriots. The score was 40–21, dropping New England to 4-4. Afterward, Belichick and Brady were in no mood to talk. Belichick walked out of a post-game press conference after two and a half minutes. Brady stuck around for twenty seconds. The reality was that the pressure to win was far greater in New England than in Indianapolis or anywhere else. By winning three Super Bowls in four years, the Patriots had created unrealistic expectations— nothing short of a championship season would suffice. And the brunt of that load fell on the shoulders of the coach and the quarterback.

Late in the afternoon on November 19, 2005, Bill Belichick was going over the game plan for the following day's contest against the Saints when he got a call from his father, who had just gotten home from the Navy-Temple game in Annapolis. Belichick's father always called after Navy games. It was prac-tically a ritual. And Belichick never viewed the calls as interruptions. They were a welcome opportunity to talk shop with the man he idolized most.

Steve Belichick saw his first football game in 1924, and he fell in love instantly. After playing one season in the NFL in 1941, he spent the rest of his career as a coach and a scout. A lot of that time was spent at Navy. For nearly sixty years, he taught the game to thousands of young men. In all those years, Steve Belichick never garnered any public attention until he became known as Bill Belichick's father. But no title could have made him prouder.

Navy had blown out Temple that day. After discussing the game for a few minutes, Belichick thanked his dad for calling. Then he turned his focus back to the Saints. After midnight, Belichick received another call, informing him that his father had just died. Steve Belichick had been watching the USC– Fresno State game on television when his heart stopped. He was eighty-six.

Belichick had known this day would come and had thought about it in advance. But that didn't make it any easier. He revered his father so much that he once said if his father had been a fireman, he would have chosen firefighting for a career. He instead chose coaching as a profession because he was a coach's son. Football in the Belichick home had always been so much more than a game. It had been a way of life, a year-round endeavor to set your calendar by.

To Belichick, there was some poetic justice in the fact that his father had died while watching a football game. It was a fitting way to go.

Later that morning, Belichick notified Kraft.

Kraft assumed Belichick would be leaving immediately for Annapolis.

Belichick said he'd leave after the game.

"You should go now," Kraft told him. "Be with your mother."

"My dad would want me to coach this game," Belichick said.

Tom Brady was the only player who was told about Belichick's father before the game. Kraft felt he should know. To the rest of the team, that afternoon seemed like a typical Sunday at Gillette, but for Brady, it was different. "That was a heavy moment," he said. "I was in my twenties at the time. You don't think about your parents passing away when you're in your twenties. But Bill was in his fifties. He was at an age when that happens. It was an opportunity for me to grow, seeing how he handled it."

Brady went out and threw three touchdown passes, and the Patriots defeated the Saints 24–17 to improve to 6-4. In the locker room afterward, Belichick gathered the team.

"Look, on a personal note," Belichick said, pausing as he paced back and forth in the center of the room, "I coached this game today with a heavy heart. My dad passed away last night."

Some players stared at Belichick. Others looked at the floor. None of them were used to seeing him vulnerable.

"So I'm going to have to tend to some things personally in Annapolis," he continued. "Doesn't change anything we're doing. Let's start stringin' 'em together."

With a football in his hand, Kraft stepped to Belichick's side in the center of the circle.

"He found out in the middle of the night that his dad has passed," Kraft told the team. "We spoke this morning and I said if he wanted to leave, I knew everyone would understand. He said he knew his dad would want him to coach this game."

Belichick pursed his lips as Kraft continued.

"It's just a tremendous example of the commitment that he has to this team and what it means to him," Kraft said. "I'd like to dedicate this ball and give it to Bill in honor of the memory of his dad."

Belichick took the ball and looked at Kraft. "Thank you," Belichick said.

Amid applause from the players and coaches, Belichick and Kraft shook hands and embraced.

"Thank you," Belichick whispered. "Appreciate it."

Kraft nodded, took a step back, and locked hands with Belichick in a "bro" handshake.

The funeral was held three days later at the Naval Academy Chapel. Belichick delivered the eulogy.

"I know my dad felt, as important as football was, he fully understood what a midshipman's role was when he came here to serve, defend, and, if he had to, die for his country," Belichick told the audience. "He trained players to play football, to win, to beat Army, and to train to fight for their country."

Belichick paused amid his remarks and looked at his mother. When he was a little boy, she used to read to him a lot. She'd read aloud. And when there was a word that Bill didn't understand, she'd stop and explain it. The first book that Belichick had fallen in love with was *Winnie the Pooh*. He read it so many times that he wore the cover off. That was when his love for books began. So much of Belichick's quest for knowledge stemmed from his mother. And now that his father was gone, he was appreciating the profound impact his mother had on both him and his father.

"You were the real strength behind two coaches in this family," he told her. "And I love you."

Then he turned to say a final farewell to his father.

"Dad, may you rest in peace."

As Belichick sat back down, Kraft gently patted him on the shoulder. Days later, Kraft was in the visiting owner's box at Arrowhead Stadium, looking down on Belichick as he coached the Patriots against the Chiefs. New England lost in Kansas City. But Kraft wasn't focused on that. He was thinking about his own father, how much he had revered him, how devastated he had been when he passed, and how much he still missed him three decades later. From the time he was old enough to remember, Kraft had wanted nothing more than to impress his father. Even at sixty-four, he was still trying to be the man that would make his father proud.

In that respect, Kraft could relate to Belichick's decision to coach on the day after his father died and to return to coaching just days after his father was buried. At the funeral, one of the funniest memories of Steve Belichick had been shared by Rear Admiral Thomas C. Lynch, the superintendent of the US Naval Academy. Lynch had been a captain on the Navy football team when Steve Belichick coached there. He recalled being gathered around a television with his midshipmen teammates on October 22, 1962, when President John F. Kennedy informed the nation that he was ordering a naval blockade

around Cuba to counter the presence of Soviet missiles. Lynch said Coach Belichick had been furious. "Smoke was coming out of his ears," Lynch said at the funeral. "He said, 'Don't these people know we have Pitt this weekend?'"

While humorous, the story revealed a lot about the man who had the greatest influence on Bill Belichick. It also went a long way to explain Belichick's single-mindedness. Just as his father had, Belichick lived to coach. Such clarity of purpose is rare in any profession.

New England rallied to finish the season 10-6 and win the AFC East division for the third straight year. In the wild-card round of the playoffs, the Patriots defeated the Jaguars. The victory gave Belichick and Brady a perfect 10-0 record during the playoffs. No coach-quarterback tandem in league history had ever won ten straight postseason games. But a week later, New England's hopes of winning a third straight Super Bowl ended in Denver when the Patriots lost a hard-fought game to the Broncos. On Brady's last pass—a desperation heave in the closing seconds—he ended up flat on his back in the Broncos' end zone as the ball sailed into a defender's hands. No one bothered to help him up. And the fans took the opportunity to mock him.

The defeat marked the first time that Belichick and Brady had lost a playoff game since joining the Patriots. For a team that had gotten so accustomed to winning, the mood on the flight home was morose.

A few days later, Kraft invited Brady to take a trip with him and Myra to Israel. Kraft had been doing a lot of thinking about the future and how Brady fit into it. Just as Kraft put Belichick in a coaching class all by himself, Kraft was convinced that Brady was the rarest of football players, the likes of which the NFL had never seen. Kraft's assessment that Brady could one day become the greatest of all time had as much to do with Brady's personality as it did with his playing skills. In any event, Kraft intended to keep Brady in New England for a long time. And he wanted to take their personal relationship to another level.

Brady viewed the invitation to travel to the Holy Land with Kraft as a unique opportunity. He had grown up in a devout Catholic family, and his father had even considered becoming a priest. So Brady was eager to visit the birthplace of Christianity. Shortly after they touched down, Kraft took him to the Western Wall. Snaking his way through rows of wooden desks occupied by Jews studying ancient texts, Brady stepped to the wall and said a short prayer while Kraft prayed alongside him in Hebrew. Then, in keeping with tradition, Brady wrote a prayer on a scrap of paper, folded it up, and tucked it into a crevice in the wall.

It was a spiritually rich start to an unforgettable trip that included walks through the ancient streets of Jerusalem, visits to Christian holy sites, and discussions about the fact that Christians, Jews, and Muslims all considered the city holy. One day, Kraft took Brady to the football stadium he had built on the outskirts of the city, and Brady threw passes to Israeli children. On another day, Kraft arranged through the prime minister for them to get a private audience with some sharpshooters in the Israeli army. The meeting took place at a military base.

Boston-born Israeli soldier Avi Sandler and his fellow soldier Label Garelik were told by their commander that he wanted them to put on a weapons demonstration for a couple of distinguished American visitors. When Sandler and Garelik entered the firing range, they spotted two Americans wearing green army vests over their civilian attire. One of them was wearing sunglasses. The soldiers thought the guy in the shades resembled Tom Brady, but they couldn't imagine what he'd be doing in Israel. Then the man removed his glasses.

"Are you Tom Brady?" Sandler asked.

Brady nodded. The soldiers' jaws dropped.

"Do you want to play football with us?" Garelik said.

Brady smiled. "I don't mix business with pleasure," he cracked.

Minutes later, it was Brady's jaw that dropped as the soldiers fired a variety of weapons, including machine guns. Eventually, they handed rifles to Brady and Kraft and invited them to shoot. They warned Brady that his weapon would recoil against his throwing shoulder. But Brady didn't care. Shooting alongside the Israeli military was the highlight of the trip.

Later that night, Kraft took Brady to a rooftop bar in Jerusalem. Over drinks, the two men talked about Brady's relationship with Bridget Moynahan. Then he shared some personal anecdotes about his marriage to Myra and why they had remained together for more than forty years.

Brady took it all in. He couldn't help reflecting on the amazing life he was leading. Professionally, he got to dedicate his life to doing what he loved while working alongside the greatest football coach on the planet. At the same time, he had one of the world's most successful businessmen as a personal mentor. Belichick took Brady into dark rooms to look at film; Kraft exposed him to the Holy Land.

As the night wound down, Brady told Kraft, "It means a lot to me that you invited me here."

Kraft raised his glass.

twenty-seven
RELOAD

I t wasn't even April and a Boston sports columnist had already declared, "It's now official: The Patriots' offseason is a disaster."

After getting knocked out of the playoffs, the Patriots had decided not to re-sign two of the longest-tenured players in New England—linebacker Willie McGinest and kicker Adam Vinatieri. When Vinatieri joined the archrival Colts in March 2006, local sportswriters weren't the only ones who were dismayed. Fans were venting on talk radio and the Internet.

For New Englanders, the decision to part ways with the greatest clutch kicker of all time felt callous. Vinatieri had achieved folk-hero status and was second only to Brady in popularity. He was the team's all-time leading scorer and had nineteen game-winning kicks. Eighteen of those had been in the final minute or in overtime, including four in the postseason, two of which had won Super Bowls. The *Boston Globe* described his departure as a "kick in the teeth for the Patriots."

Initially miffed at Belichick, Vinatieri looked at the bright side. He would get to spend the rest of his career kicking indoors on a great team. After signing a five-year contract with the Colts, he didn't even bother notifying the Patriots.

"They had so many chances to sign me," Vinatieri said. "They chose to do what they did. There's no animosity on my part. I love the Kraft family. Bill Belichick is a great coach. I'll miss my buddies who are still in that locker room. I hated to leave, but when it's a business, sometimes you have to make tough decisions. They could have kept me. They didn't."

Belichick made another unpopular decision at the start of the 2006 season. After Deion Branch sat out training camp over a contract dispute, Belichick traded Brady's favorite receiver and close personal friend to Seattle for a future first-round draft pick. The loss of Branch was a mental drain on Brady. But he wasn't the only one who was frustrated by the move. "I don't think any of us envisioned something like this happening," said defensive end

Richard Seymour. "It took the air out of me. It really did. To not have number eighty-three in a Patriots uniform definitely hurts."

Still, New England was a force in 2006. Belichick had drafted kicker Stephen Gostkowski to replace Vinatieri, and convinced one of the game's all-time great linebackers, Junior Seau, to come out of retirement to shore up New England's defense. The Patriots went 12-4, won the AFC East division for the fourth straight year, and were on track to win another championship.

After blowing out the Jets in the wild-card round of the playoffs and knocking off the top-seeded San Diego Chargers in the divisional round, New England traveled to Indianapolis for the AFC Championship game. When the Patriots jumped out to a commanding 21–3 first-half lead, it looked as though they would go to the Super Bowl at the Colts' expense for the third time in four years.

At halftime, though, Adam Vinatieri rallied his new teammates by delivering a completely out-of-character tongue lashing in the locker room. With Manning leading the way in the second half, the Colts mounted the largest comeback ever in a conference championship game and stunned the Patriots 38–34.

The loss was by far the most devastating one to date in the Belichick-Brady era. "Like the kids who had had enough of being beaten up by the class bullies," NFL writer Judy Battista wrote, "the Colts fought back."

"I think everybody in this town needed it for their own reasons," said Vinatieri, who had kicked three field goals and accounted for twelve points. "My reasons may be different than their reasons, but we all had to beat New England."

Even in championship years, Kraft and Belichick would get together at the end of every season and address the same question: "What can we do to improve?" When they met shortly after the disappointing loss in Indianapolis, they could have concluded that the improvements the team needed to make for 2007 were only incremental. After all, they had ended up just four points short and sixty seconds shy of going to their fourth Super Bowl in six years. But Kraft and Belichick had long recognized that the Colts offense had more firepower than New England's. That disparity was more glaring than ever in the AFC Championship game. Specifically, the Patriots severely missed the sure hands of Deion Branch. When the game was on the line, Patriots receivers had dropped two key passes from Brady that could have led to a game-winning touchdown.

Belichick wanted to bring some top-flight receivers to New England. Kraft liked Belichick's thinking. But any effort to increase New England's offensive firepower would push the team over the salary cap. This led Kraft and Belichick to another question: Could they come up with more capital?

The conversation soon turned to Brady. He had by far the biggest salary on the Patriots' payroll. One way to free up some spending money would be to reduce Brady's annual salary, a move that would entail restructuring Brady's contract.

It would fall to Kraft to talk to Brady.

The last-second loss to Manning and the Colts was profoundly frustrating to Brady. But heading into the offseason, he had a lot more on his mind than football. Toward the end of the 2006 season, in late November, he had broken up with Bridget Moynahan. The couple "amicably ended their three-year relationship several weeks ago," a representative for Moynahan had told *People* magazine in December. But there was more to the story, and it would soon become public.

Later in December, right before Christmas, the twenty-nine-year-old quarterback agreed to go on a blind date with twenty-six-year-old Brazilian supermodel Gisele Bündchen. The date was arranged by a friend of Brady's who knew Bündchen and insisted that the two of them had a lot in common.

Brady and Bündchen met at Turks & Frogs, a Turkish wine bar in New York City's Greenwich Village neighborhood. At that point, Bündchen had been featured on more magazine covers than any other model and she was the face of twenty international brands from Dior to Versace. With an estimated fortune of $150 million, she was one of the richest women in the fashion industry. Brady, however, knew nothing about her wealth or the brands she represented.

Similarly, Bündchen didn't follow American football and knew nothing about Brady and his achievements. She knew more people in Hollywood than in sports. A year earlier, she had broken up with her longtime boyfriend Leonardo DiCaprio. Alone and in the midst of some serious soul-searching, Bündchen wasn't looking to enter into another serious relationship.

Fresh off the split with Moynahan, Brady wasn't eager to get into a new relationship, either. But he and Bündchen ended up talking for three hours that night. "I knew right away—the first time I saw him," Bündchen would later say. "I had to go home for Christmas, but I didn't want to leave. You

know that feeling of, like, you can't get enough? From the first day we met, we've never spent one day without speaking to each other."

After dating for two months, Brady and Bündchen vacationed together in Paris in February 2007. While they were there, *New York Post* gossip columnist Liz Smith reported that Moynahan was three months pregnant with Brady's child. Smith's column blindsided Brady, who had to explain to Bündchen that he was going to be a father. "I felt my world had been turned upside down," Bündchen later explained. "Needless to say, that wasn't an easy time."

With the tabloids having a field day as Brady and his family worked through a sensitive personal matter, Belichick faced a mounting series of public relations challenges of his own. Throughout the 2006 season, Belichick had been dogged by stories about his poor sportsmanship. Most of those stemmed from his feud with former assistant coach Eric Mangini. After coaching under Belichick for six years in New England, Mangini had left following the 2005 season to become head coach of the Jets. It was well documented that Belichick and Mangini did not part amicably. The first time they coached against each other in September 2006, New England won. Afterward, instead of extending the customary midfield handshake, Belichick essentially brushed by Mangini, looking away while reaching out his hand.

The press's reaction to Belichick's so-called "no-look handshake" was probably overblown. Nonetheless, with all eyes on him after the Jets upset the Patriots in Foxborough later that November, Belichick made matters worse when he failed to say anything as Mangini grabbed his hand and wished him well in another awkward postgame encounter. Then, while approaching Mangini through a sea of cameramen after the Patriots beat the Jets in the playoffs, Belichick shoved a *Boston Globe* photographer out of his way, knocking his camera into his face. The incident was captured on national television and prompted strong criticism from the press. "Here's Belichick's problem," wrote *Globe* columnist Brian McGrory, "and it has nothing to do with the fact that he dresses like he's from Appalachia and has the personality of a wet mop: He thinks he's above everybody else. . . . He believes three Super Bowl championships give him immunity against moronity. They don't."

Belichick called the photographer at home and apologized. He also spoke about the incident on the radio, saying, "I really didn't mean to hit him up high there. I was trying to just push him out of the way and get to Eric. It wasn't . . . it certainly wasn't called for, so I . . . I wish that hadn't happened."

A couple of weeks later, after losing the AFC Championship game to Indianapolis, Belichick drew more criticism for the way he brushed past Peyton

Manning, failing to congratulate him. "Here's a guy who goes down already on the short list as one of the greatest coaches in NFL history," said Bob Costas. "I would hope Bill Belichick's personal graciousness could approach his personal greatness as a coach."

At the same time, the tabloids in Boston and New York were publishing claims from a lawsuit filed by a construction worker in New Jersey who alleged that Belichick had an affair with his wife that had led to the breakup of their marriage. The man's wife had worked as a receptionist for the New York Giants when Belichick was the team's defensive coordinator. In court papers, she claimed her relationship with Belichick was platonic and referred to him as "a family friend." But in divorce depositions in November 2006 and January 2007, she testified that Belichick had been supporting her during her divorce, purchasing a town house for her to use and sending her monthly cash payments.

For Belichick, however, all of these issues paled in comparison to linebacker Ted Johnson's decision to go public with the fact that his life had spiraled out of control since his retirement seventeen months earlier. On February 2, 2007, two days before the Colts faced the Bears in Super Bowl XLI, Johnson appeared on the front page of the New York Times beneath the headline: "Dark Days Follow Hard-Hitting Career in N.F.L." The unsettling story detailed Johnson's addiction to amphetamines, his battle with depression, and his recent arrest for domestic abuse. "There's something wrong with me," Johnson told the Times. "There's something wrong with my brain. And I know when it started."

Johnson's chilling account read like an indictment, and he pointed the finger squarely at Belichick. Specifically, Johnson revealed that he had suffered back-to-back concussions in 2002. The first one occurred during a preseason game against the Giants in August of that year. Four days later, when the team returned to full-contact practice, Johnson was told by the team trainer to wear a red jersey, which notified teammates that he was not to be hit. But an hour into the session, Johnson was handed a blue jersey and told to put it on. Johnson told the Times he did so out of fear that he would otherwise lose his job. "This kind of thing happens all the time in football," Johnson said. "That day it was Bill Belichick and Ted Johnson. But it happens all the time."

According to Johnson, the first play that was called after he changed jerseys—"ace-ice"—required him to sprint four yards and hit a hard-charging blocker head-on. At the moment of the collision, Johnson saw stars, became disoriented, and was overcome by a warm sensation. Afterward, he

angrily told the trainer that he had suffered another concussion, which was later confirmed by a neurologist at Massachusetts General Hospital. Furious with Belichick, Johnson briefly quit the team.

On the same day that the *Times* story appeared, the *Boston Globe*'s Jackie MacMullan published an even longer, more graphic account of Johnson's concussions and their aftermath. Johnson told MacMullan about his heated confrontation with Belichick following the concussion he sustained in practice on August 14, 2002.

"I told him, 'You played God with my health,'" Johnson said. "'You knew I shouldn't have been cleared to play, and you gave me that blue jersey anyway.'

"Bill said, 'I had to see if you could play.' That's when I lost it. I told him, 'After all these years, you had to see if I could play?'

"Bill finally admitted, 'Hey, Ted, I fucked up. I made a mistake.'"

When MacMullan reached out to Belichick, he told her: "If Ted felt so strongly that he didn't feel he was ready to practice with us, he should have told me."

Belichick also told MacMullan that he remembered the contentious meeting with Johnson. "It was a watershed meeting for us," Belichick said. "We had a long conversation and we both tried to see the other's position.

"I'm sure in part of that conversation I apologized for things I said or did, as he did for his actions and his emotions following his decision to leave the team. If I made a mistake or hurt Ted in any way, I don't feel good about that.

"I felt as though we left that meeting saying, 'We've both made mistakes. Let's move forward and get on a higher level.' And that's what we did."

Since Johnson's retirement, more research about the dangers of concussions had come out, and the controversy over the league's handling of the situation was picking up steam. But the NFL had largely downplayed the situation. By deciding to speak out during Super Bowl weekend, Johnson helped change that. "We are very concerned about the issue of concussions, and we are going to continue to look hard at it and do everything possible to protect the health of our players," the league said in a statement to the *Times*. And on the day before the Super Bowl, Gene Upshaw, the executive director of the NFL Players Association, held a press conference and said: "If a coach or anyone else is saying, 'You don't have a concussion; you get back in there,' you don't have to go, and you shouldn't go. You know how you feel. That's what we tried to do throughout the years, is take the coach out of the decision making. It's the medical people that have to decide."

The airing of Johnson's ordeal was a particularly sobering moment for Belichick and the franchise. During Johnson's ten-year career, he had epitomized the Patriot Way. He'd been a team captain who garnered the respect of his teammates, many of whom, including Tedy Bruschi, Willie McGinest, Larry Izzo, and Roman Phifer, showed support for him.

Shortly after the dust settled, Belichick sat for an extraordinary interview with *Boston Globe* feature writer Bella English. English did not cover sports. When she arrived at Belichick's office, he told her right up front: "The first thing I'd like to come out is that this is not something I initiated." When she questioned what difference that made, he said, "I wouldn't want anyone to think . . . this is some type of campaign trail."

English asked Belichick about all of the controversies from the past year that involved him. He answered some of them. He said it had been a mistake to shove the photographer. He insisted that he and Peyton Manning had become friends since the brush-off after the AFC title game. And he volunteered that he and his wife had divorced. Asked about his relationship with his players, he said, "Some of them I love. I can't say I love fifty-three guys. I respect all of them, and I hope they respect me."

None of Belichick's players spoke to English. Team captains Mike Vrabel and Tedy Bruschi did not to respond to requests for comment. Kraft was the only person from the Patriots organization who spoke on the record to English. Asked about Belichick's reputation for being terse—or worse—with the media, Kraft focused on his coach's positive qualities.

"One of the reasons I like him as a coach and human being is that he is never boastful and self-important," Kraft said. "He's not a phony, and to me, at this stage of my life, that's important. I'll say this: I've never known him to lie to me. He might not tell me something, but he's never told me a lie." Pausing, he added: "I'm not saying he's always forthcoming."

English asked Kraft about the tabloid account of Belichick's role in the New Jersey divorce case. Kraft said he hadn't spoken to Belichick about it. "I also try not to sit in judgment of anybody," Kraft told her, "because no one knows anyone's personal life. All I can say is I think Bill's main focus after football matters are his children, and I have a great deal of respect for that."

English also talked to her former colleague Michael Holley, who had spent two years with Belichick while writing his 2005 book, *Patriot Reign*. Holley knew Belichick better than any Boston journalist. He told English: "Even the guy who hates his guts will tell you he's a great coach. He's not interested in being buddies with them, and they're not interested in being buddies with him. All they expect from him is, 'Give us a chance to win.' I

don't think people would say Bill Belichick is a great man. He's a great *coach*. He's an *interesting* man."

English's wide-ranging profile on Belichick appeared on March 4, 2007. The next day Belichick made a trade for Miami Dolphins receiver Wes Welker and signed him to a five-year contract worth $18 million. Two days later, Belichick signed Philadelphia Eagles wide receiver Donté Stallworth to a six-year contract worth $30 million. Welker was a highly talented kick and punt returner who had just started to establish himself as an effective receiver in Miami. Stallworth could flat-out fly. The addition of Welker and Stallworth to the roster instantly transformed New England's offense.

Belichick wasn't done, though. He had something far more audacious in mind. He wanted to go after the most electrifying and enigmatic player in the NFL—Oakland Raiders wideout Randy Moss. A self-described "freak of nature," Moss stood six feet, four inches tall, ran the forty-yard dash in 4.25 seconds, and possessed a fifty-one-inch vertical leap. He was so difficult to cover one-on-one that teams devised "Moss Rules" to defend him. Even that was useless. When double covered, Moss could simply outrun and outleap everyone. He was hands-down the most talented receiver in the league.

But the Patriots had no room left under the salary cap to sign Moss. In an effort to create some space, Kraft talked to Brady and the two of them worked through the night to restructure his contract. Brady agreed to reduce his $6 million salary in 2007 to $720,000 in exchange for a $5.28 million signing bonus. He also received a $2.9 million boost to his 2009 base salary. Although the changes to Brady's deal helped, New England still couldn't afford Moss—he had $21 million coming to him over the final two years of his contract with Oakland. However, Moss was very disgruntled and wanted out of Oakland.

Additionally, the Raiders had just hired a new coach, Lane Kiffin, who was the youngest head coach in modern NFL history. At thirty-one, Kiffin wasn't exactly experienced with making trades, and Belichick was the master. He offered Oakland a fourth-round draft pick in the 2007 draft in exchange for Moss. Knowing Moss wanted out, Kiffin figured it was the best he could do. Raiders owner Al Davis went along, recognizing that at least he'd be off-loading $21 million from his team's books.

There was one more hitch. Belichick was only going to offer Moss a one-year contract with a base salary of $2.5 million. That represented a $6 million pay cut. It was up to Belichick to close the deal.

The first day of the 2007 NFL Draft had ended hours earlier, but at 3:30 a.m. in Foxborough on Sunday, April 29, Belichick was still working the phones. He placed a call to Randy Moss.

It was 2:30 a.m. in Houston, and Moss was entering a nightclub with friends when his cell phone started buzzing and he answered it.

"Hi, Randy. This is Bill Belichick."

"Man, get the hell out of here! Who the *hell* is this?"

"This is Bill Belichick."

"You're shittin' me, man," Moss said before ending the call.

Moments later, Belichick called again.

"Randy, this is Bill Belichick."

"I don't want to hear that, man. Now who is this *really*?"

"No, Randy, this is Bill Belichick."

Moss finally paused and realized it really was Belichick.

Belichick waited.

"Coach, I apologize," Moss said.

Taking no offense, Belichick got to the point. "Randy, the Raiders want to trade you," he began. Belichick went on to inform Moss that he had struck a deal that would bring him to New England, and Raiders owner Al Davis had tentatively approved it. There were a few conditions. The big one was that Moss would have to accept a hefty pay cut.

It turned out that Moss was willing. He had made plenty of money in his career. The one thing he craved was a Super Bowl championship, and New England gave him the best chance to get one.

Belichick explained that he also had to pass a physical. And the physical had to be completed by the time the second day of the draft got under way later that day.

"I'll cut to the chase," Belichick said. "Al Davis said if you're not up here by ten a.m., the trade is void."

Fortunately for Moss, he had his own private plane. He hung up and immediately started high-fiving his friends and hugging random people in the nightclub.

"*What* is going *on*?" one of his friends asked.

"I'm getting ready to be a Patriot," Moss said.

Robert Kraft fully appreciated what the addition of Randy Moss could mean to New England's offense. By pairing him with Brady, the Patriots would be unstoppable. Kraft also couldn't get over the terms—all New England had to

give up was a fourth-round draft pick. Belichick had basically gotten away with grand larceny.

Kraft's only concern was Moss's reputation. Since entering the league, Moss had pleaded guilty to a misdemeanor after bumping a traffic officer with his vehicle and been fined multiple times for behavior that ranged from squirting a referee with a water bottle to verbally abusing corporate sponsors on the team bus. His most notorious incident was pretending to pull down his pants and moon Packer fans at Lambeau Field after scoring a touchdown for the Vikings during a nationally televised playoff game in 2005. After the league fined him $10,000, Minnesota traded him to Oakland a month later.

Belichick downplayed all the media reports about Moss's extracurricular behavior. The only thing that mattered, Belichick felt, was whether Moss could fit into the Patriots' team culture. And Moss answered that question to Belichick's satisfaction when he agreed to waive his contract in Oakland to play for New England. More than anything, he wanted a championship.

Still, Kraft told Belichick he wanted to meet face-to-face with Moss as soon as he completed his physical.

Kraft was sitting behind his desk when Moss was ushered into his office. Moss took the empty chair beside Jonathan Kraft on the opposite side of Robert's desk. After exchanging pleasantries, Kraft leaned forward, put his elbows on his desk, clasped his hands, and said, "Look, I know how great you are." Then Kraft pointed at the Patriots logo on his shirt. "This logo is synonymous with the Kraft family. Anyone who comes to New England really carries our family name."

Moss nodded.

"You can't moon the crowd or hump the goalpost like you did in Minnesota," Kraft continued. "Because if you do that, I don't care what Belichick says. I'm cutting you."

Moss nodded again.

"I just want you to know that," Kraft said. "And I want to say it up front. Because this is my family name."

There were a few moments of awkward silence.

"I want to be part of the Kraft family," Moss began, before expressing how grateful he was to be in New England. The conversation stretched for thirty minutes and covered everything from family to business. At the end, Moss emphasized how badly he wanted to play for Belichick, how much he was looking forward to playing with Brady, and how excited he was about being a Patriot. Then he stood, walked around to Kraft's side of the desk, and hugged him. "Thank you, Mr. Kraft," he said.

"All right," Kraft said softly, patting him on the back.

After Moss left, Robert turned to Jonathan.

"What do you think?" Robert said.

"He's smart," Jonathan said. "He's really smart. I like him. I like him *a lot*."

"I like him, too," Robert said.

But the meeting that really got to Moss was his encounter with Myra Kraft. Moss knew of her reputation as a philanthropist and an advocate for women's rights. When Moss saw her in the Patriots' front office, she approached him with a smile.

"Mrs. Kraft," Moss said, "regardless of what you heard about me—"

She cut him off. "I know. I know. We've done our homework on you. I'm just glad you're here." Then she leaned forward, craned her neck, and kissed him on the cheek.

Moss was moved. Up to that point, he had always viewed football as strictly a man's sport. Myra had changed his thinking.

In the first team meeting that Randy Moss attended, he sat next to Donté Stallworth. Both newcomers, they wondered what to expect. Belichick started off by talking about the AFC Championship loss to Indianapolis that had ended the previous season. He mentioned how they had blown a 21–3 lead. Then he proceeded to show video footage of every mistake the team had made in the second half. One of the mistakes was an errant pass by Brady.

"What kind of fucking throw is this?" Belichick barked. "I can get fucking Johnny Foxborough from down the street to make a better *fucking* throw than this."

"Oh, my God!" thought Moss.

"Holy shit!" thought Stallworth. "Is this real?"

Moss and Stallworth discreetly glanced at each other. "Uh-oh," Moss whispered. "What have we got ourselves into?"

Brady was in the front row, showing no expression, taking notes. He didn't necessarily like being singled out and berated in front of his teammates. No player did. But everyone was susceptible to Belichick's withering critiques, and Brady didn't want to be treated any differently than his teammates.

Nonetheless, Brady was different. And every one of his teammates knew that. He was the highest-paid player on the team, the most accomplished quarterback in the NFL, a fifth son to the owner, and the leader of the most successful franchise of the decade. Off the field, he was the most famous

football player in America, and he was in a romantic relationship with the woman that *Rolling Stone* had declared the "Most Beautiful Girl in the World." That summer alone, Gisele had been on the covers of *Vanity Fair*, *Vogue*, *Cosmopolitan*, *Harper's Bazaar*, and *W*. Meantime, Brady's ex-girlfriend gave birth to their son Jack near the end of training camp. With all that Brady had going on, his teammates admired his focus and viewed him as the ultimate leader. So anytime newcomers witnessed Belichick's calling out Brady, it had a jarring effect.

Belichick's penchant for demanding selflessness, discipline, and strict attention to detail was rooted in the military environment he had grown up in. "By the time I got out of high school, that's all I had known," Belichick said. "I didn't have a perspective on selfish players or guys who didn't want to do what they were supposed to do. That didn't exist at the Naval Academy and it didn't exist at Annapolis. When you grow up that way and that's all you see, then it influences you and it influences your philosophy because it's all you know."

Although he could have done without the name-calling and intimidation techniques, Brady's willingness to submerge his ego and submit to Belichick's militaristic methods were an essential ingredient to the Patriots success. Brady's malleability set the standard. By not rebelling or complaining, he set the tone for every newcomer who joined the Patriots. "That was our first initial football meeting with Bill Belichick," Moss said. "And for him to just call out Tom Brady . . . The accountability factor played a big role, knowing that if he held Tom Brady to a higher standard, everybody else better get in line or you're gonna get shipped out of there."

"That day," Stallworth said, "we learned the truth about New England: if Tom Brady was getting it, no one was safe."

All Brady was thinking about was getting back on the field with these new receivers. He felt reborn.

twenty-eight

TRANSCENDENCE

The Patriots opened the 2007 season like racehorses coming out of a starting gate. Standing in the tunnel in Giants Stadium while waiting to be introduced before the first game against the Jets, Brady couldn't wait to unleash. Running back Kevin Faulk pulled receiver Donté Stallworth aside. "Stay away from Brady before we walk out," Faulk warned. "He's gonna head-butt the shit out of you. He's too fired up." Moments later, Brady screamed: "Let's fuckin' go!" and hammered his helmet into Stallworth's helmet, knocking him back. "Shit!" Stallworth thought. "This dude is *serious.*"

On the first drive, Brady marched the offense ninety-one yards on twelve plays, capping the drive off with a touchdown strike to Wes Welker. Moss was open all day, catching nine passes for 183 yards. At times it seemed like the Patriots were toying with the Jets. On one play, Brady audaciously launched a pass fifty-one yards through the air into triple coverage. Moss caught it in stride and glided into the end zone for a touchdown. New England won going away, 38–14.

But the behind-the-scenes gamesmanship between the Jets and Patriots quickly overshadowed what had transpired on the field. In a conspicuous move that would have far-reaching repercussions, Jets coach Eric Mangini decided to call out Bill Belichick for violating a rule in the NFL's *Game Operations Manual*. The rule prohibited teams from using video recording devices on the field during games. It was intended, in part, to prevent the filming of opposing defensive coaches as they used hand signals to communicate which defense to play on each snap. Unlike offensive coaches, who communicate plays to the quarterback through an in-helmet communication device, defensive coaches signal plays in from the sideline.

It was common practice to try to decipher an opposing team's defensive signals. For example, a Patriots scout seated in the press box could look through binoculars at a Jets coach while whispering into a handheld audio

recorder—"four minutes remaining second quarter, second-and-five, left hand to shoulder, back down to knee, up to hat." That was permissible. But a year earlier, the league had issued a memo specifically reminding teams that the rulebook forbade capturing that same kind of information with a video camera.

Mangini suspected that Belichick was ignoring the memo. During the first half of the Jets game, twenty-six-year-old Patriots video assistant Matt Estrella had been stationed behind the Patriots' bench with a camera that was aimed at the Jets' sideline. Right before halftime, Estrella left the field and was heading to the Patriots' locker room when he was stopped by Jets security personnel. Estrella's camera and film were confiscated, and he was led to an office occupied by law enforcement officials, who were on site to police the stadium.

Mark Briggs, the Patriots' security chief, came to Estrella's aid. A no-nonsense former military officer, Briggs demanded the return of the tape. When Jets officials pushed back, the argument got so heated that a couple of state troopers stepped in to deescalate the situation.

Right before the start of the second half, Briggs called up to the visiting owner's suite and told the Krafts what was going on. A short while later, Ray Anderson, the NFL's executive vice president of football operations, showed up in the Krafts' suite. Anderson, a Harvard-trained lawyer, had written the memo about videotaping. He briefed Robert on what had transpired in the first half and reported that NFL security had taken possession of the tape and was transporting it to NFL headquarters in New York for review.

Anderson's briefing caught Kraft off guard. As soon as the game ended, Kraft sought out Belichick in the locker room.

"Bill, are we fucking taping?" he asked.

Belichick stared at him blankly.

One year earlier, forty-seven-year-old Roger Goodell had been chosen to succeed Paul Tagliabue as NFL commissioner. Five other candidates from outside the league had been under consideration. It had taken five rounds of voting by the NFL's thirty-two owners before Goodell obtained the necessary two-thirds needed under the league's bylaws. Kraft had lobbied for Goodell, placing calls to owners who were on the fence about supporting him. Kraft made a straightforward case—the NFL is a very complicated business; the commissioner has thirty-two bosses; the steep learning curve would make it all but impossible for someone to come from the outside and be able to start

running things on day one; Goodell was a known quantity who had trained internally under Tagliabue; Goodell was the most qualified for the job.

In the months leading up to the vote, Kraft had hosted Goodell at his home and spent many hours talking to him about league initiatives. No owner had developed a closer personal and working relationship with Goodell than Kraft, so the Jets' accusation against the Patriots put Goodell in an awkward position. Two days after the season opener, his office issued a statement confirming that an investigation was under way and that a decision on whether the Patriots had violated league rules would be forthcoming.

But the Patriots' image was already taking a hit. The headline in Wednesday morning's *Boston Herald* read: "Pats, Lies and Videotape." The brunt of the criticism was directed at Belichick. A banner headline in the New York *Daily News* read: "MANGINI BUSTS PATS' BELITRICK." "If Bill Belichick is indeed guilty in SpyGate," wrote *Daily News* columnist Gary Myers, "then Roger Goodell must not play favorites with a three-time Super Bowl–winning coach. . . . If Belichick set up the spy ring, it means he cheated, and cheaters must be disciplined."

Belichick promptly issued a one-paragraph statement, acknowledging that he had already talked to the commissioner but had not yet been notified of the league's ruling. "I want to apologize to everyone who has been affected, most of all ownership, staff, and players," Belichick said. "Following the league's decision, I will have further comment."

His statement did nothing to quell the controversy. When Belichick showed up in the Patriots' media room later that day for his weekly press conference to discuss the team's upcoming game against the San Diego Chargers, he was greeted by fifteen television cameras and a contingent of national media that hadn't come to discuss football. After fielding fourteen straight questions about videotaping, Belichick was exasperated. "Are there any questions about the Chargers?" he said. "Anything about the football game?"

Belichick was under siege. The following day, the headline in *USA Today* read: "Pats coach faces NFL discipline for signal stealing." And the paper's sports columnist Christine Brennan wrote: "Secretly videotaping the opposing sideline to try to steal the signals of rival defensive coaches is wrong." CNN and other cable channels were treating the situation as if it were akin to a political corruption scandal. *New York Times* columnist Dave Anderson wrote: "The biography of the Patriots' owner, Robert K. Kraft, in the team's 2006 media guide, brags that the three-time Super Bowl champions 'are often

referred to as a model franchise.' But no longer. It now appears to be a model fraud, a model cheat." Influential sports columnist Tom Pedulla chimed in: "Nothing less than the pride and prestige of the Patriots is at stake."

Even players from rival teams that had lost championship games to New England jumped into the fray. Without citing any evidence, Pittsburgh Steelers receiver Hines Ward insisted that the Patriots had known the Steelers' plays in advance during the AFC Championship game in 2002. "They knew a lot of our calls," Ward said. "There's no question some of their players were calling out some of our stuff." Similarly, members of the Philadelphia Eagles team that had lost the Super Bowl to New England questioned whether they had lost due to cheating. And the San Diego Chargers' reigning NFL MVP, running back LaDainian Tomlinson, whose team had been knocked out of the previous year's playoffs by New England, said, "I think the Patriots actually live by the saying, 'If you're not cheating, you're not trying.'"

Kraft was furious. His franchise's reputation was being tarred with a broad brush. Suddenly, everything the Patriots had achieved over the past decade was being called into question. Kraft talked to Belichick about the situation.

Belichick didn't deny that a league rule had been broken. They had in fact videotaped the Jets sideline during the first half. But the taping, he insisted, had zero bearing on the outcome of the game. For Belichick, it was simple—this was a "thing" because the Patriots were involved.

Kraft agreed that the issue was being overblown. But that didn't change the fact that impermissible videotaping had occurred. "This isn't what we're about," he told Belichick.

Belichick's actions stemmed from his obsession with knowing everything there was to know about his opponents. Kraft, meantime, viewed the team as a public extension of his family and resented when anybody did anything that put his franchise in a bad light.

After Kraft calmed down, he asked Belichick why he'd do such a thing.

"On a scale of one to one hundred, how much does this help?" Kraft asked.

"One," Belichick said.

"Then you're a real schmuck," Kraft said.

On September 13, Goodell fined Belichick $500,000. It was the largest fine levied on a coach in league history.

"This episode," Goodell wrote, "represents a calculated and deliberate attempt to avoid longstanding rules designed to encourage fair play and promote honest competition on the playing field."

While acknowledging that New England's taping had had no impact on the game's outcome, Goodell nonetheless also fined the Patriots organization $250,000 and stripped the team of its first-round draft pick in 2008.

The penalties were unprecedented. No team had ever lost a first-round pick as a punishment. And no franchise or coach had ever been disciplined for improper videotaping.

The harshest penalty, however, was delivered in the court of public opinion. Following Goodell's ruling, the *New York Daily News* declared: "IT'S OFFICIAL: Bill Belichick, one of the most successful coaches of the modern sports era, is a convicted cheater."

On the field, Eric Mangini and the Jets were no match for Belichick and the Patriots. But the decision to report Belichick—and the manner in which the Jets did so—had scarred Belichick and the Patriots franchise in a much more personal and lasting way.

Although it would do nothing to mitigate the damage, Belichick issued a second, more lengthy apology. "Once again, I apologize to the Kraft family and every person directly or indirectly associated with the New England Patriots for the embarrassment, distraction and penalty my mistake caused," he said in a formal statement. "As the commissioner acknowledged, our use of sideline video had no impact on the outcome of last week's game. We have never used sideline video to obtain a competitive advantage while the game was in progress.

"Part of my job as head coach is to ensure that our football operations are conducted in compliance of the league rules and all accepted interpretations of them. My interpretation of a rule in the constitution and bylaws was incorrect."

Prior to the Patriots game against the Chargers, Brady was asked by the San Diego press corps if he had a response to LaDainian Tomlinson's accusation that the Patriots were cheaters. "If I had a response to everything that people said about me or us, then I'd be busy all freaking day responding to things," Brady said. "I think part of the great thing here is we control what we can control. That's our attitude and our work ethic and our preparation."

Brady held his tongue. So did his teammates. Meanwhile, Belichick got pilloried all week long. One Boston columnist even dragged Belichick's

deceased father into the fracas, writing: "What would Steve Belichick say about his son's fall from grace?" But Belichick continued to preach one message in practice: Focus. Focus. Focus. And in his press conference heading into the Chargers game, Belichick practiced what he preached.

> REPORTER: Would you care to comment on people suggesting that this has happened in the past?
> BELICHICK: All my focus is on the San Diego Chargers. Just working to get ready for that team.
> REPORTER: Do you want to address the fans?
> BELICHICK: We're movin' on to San Diego. That's what I'm addressing.
> REPORTER: Can you explain how you misinterpreted the rule?
> BELICHICK: It doesn't matter. We're movin' on.
> REPORTER: Are you able to pay a half-million dollars in installments, or do you have to pay it up front?
> BELICHICK: Just thinkin' about the Chargers.

The players modeled their behavior after Belichick's.

Gillette Stadium felt purposely hostile. When Tom Brady took the field for pregame warm-ups, Eminem's "Lose Yourself" pulsed from the sound system.

No more games, I'ma change what you call rage
Tear this motherfuckin' roof off like two dogs caged

Silent and steely eyed, Brady glared at Chargers players as he jogged past them. Bruschi had a death stare, too, as did Vrabel and Seymour and Izzo and every other player who had toiled to win those three Lombardi Trophies that critics had been trying to tarnish all week long. And newcomers like Moss and Welker and Seau, who had never tasted what it was like to win a championship, suddenly found themselves in an emotionally charged atmosphere as sixty-eight thousand raucous fans holding signs like "In Bill We Trust" were on their feet, roaring and clapping when Belichick took the field. Everyone was so amped up that it felt like a playoff game. After a week of tumult, it was time for New England to deliver a message to the rest of the league.

On the Patriots' first possession, Brady essentially went into the two-minute offense and threw on every play, completing six of seven passes. The

seventh resulted in a touchdown. Less than three minutes into the game, the Patriots were in the end zone, Brady was punching the sky with his fist, Minutemen were firing muskets, and New Englanders were reveling.

"It's almost as if the Patriots said, 'We don't need any cameras,'" NBC announcer Al Michaels said over the noise. "I guarantee there are none being trained on San Diego's coaches tonight."

On the Chargers' first play, the Patriots intercepted the ball. Minutes later, the Patriots kicked a field goal. Then on the Patriots' next drive, Brady threw a touchdown pass to Moss. Brady jogged off the field and without saying a word patted Belichick on the butt. By halftime, the Chargers were down 24–0. Despite the whirlwind of distractions around the team, the players flawlessly executed Belichick's game plan. The Patriots went on to win 38–14 for the second straight week. As the final seconds ticked off the game clock, Brady walked up to Belichick on the sideline, put his arm around him, finally cracked a smiled, and let him know the team had his back.

In the locker room afterward, Bruschi huddled everyone up. "How do we feel about kicking butt and having the greatest coach in the league?" he shouted. The "Ooohhh, yeahhhhh," could be heard outside the locker room.

As soon as the game was over, New England faced a new wave of criticism. *Fox NFL Sunday*'s Jay Glazer had gotten his hands on the seized Patriots video from the Jets game that had been under lock and key at NFL headquarters. Fox aired it hours before the Patriots-Chargers game, and the controversy was reignited. Embarrassed and angry, Roger Goodell launched an investigation into his own office, trying to figure out who had leaked the video. Meanwhile, Goodell also opened a follow-up investigation into the Patriots, dispatching league officials to Foxborough in response to claims that Belichick's staff had taped other teams prior to 2007. The Patriots cooperated with the investigation. And within days, the league announced: "All tapes, documents and other records relating to this matter were turned over to the league office and destroyed, and the Patriots have certified in writing that no copies or other records exist."

Goodell never revealed what was on the additional tapes that were turned over by the Patriots. But his decision to destroy them prompted a backlash against him and the Patriots. Colts president and GM Bill Polian led the charge, insisting that teams that were filmed deserved to see the tapes. "We had every reason to believe we were one of the teams taped," Polian said, "and as a result we felt we had the right to know what had been done to us, the scope and nature of it."

Goodell's actions also got the attention of US senator Arlen Specter, the

ranking Republican on the Senate Judiciary Committee. In his view, Goodell had destroyed evidence of the Patriots' misdeeds. "That requires an explanation," Specter told the *New York Times*. "The N.F.L. has a very preferred status in our country with their antitrust exemption. The American people are entitled to be sure about the integrity of the game. It's analogous to the C.I.A. destruction of tapes. Or any time you have records destroyed."

Specter's decision to insert himself into the situation took the controversy to another level.

Thriving on the siege mentality that had enveloped Foxborough, the Patriots throttled the Bills in week three, 38–7. No team in NFL history had ever begun a season by scoring 38 points in three straight games. Yet Belichick continued to ramp up the intensity in Patriots practice sessions. During two-minute drills one afternoon in week four, Brady and Moss failed to connect on a simple five-yard-out pattern. The next day, Belichick showed film of the play to the entire team. Then he unloaded.

"Are you fucking kidding me?" Belichick bellowed. "I have my fucking All-Pro wide receiver and my All-Pro quarterback and you cannot complete a five-yard out? Tom, I can get the local high school quarterback if Johnny Foxborough isn't available to come and complete a fucking five-yard out."

The more Belichick pressed, the harder his team played. In the Patriots' locker room, the players wore white T-shirts with the words "I EAT IT" on the front and "HUMBLE PIE" on the back. Brady and Moss loved the camaraderie.

It also helped that outside of New England, critics continued to take shots at Belichick and the Patriots over Spygate. The louder those voices got, the more the Patriots took it out on their opponents.

Week four—Patriots 34, Bengals 13.

Week five—Patriots 34, Browns 17.

During a radio interview in Boston, Brady said, "We're trying to kill teams. We're trying to blow them out if we can."

When New England visited Dallas in week six, both teams were undefeated. Billed as a potential Super Bowl preview, the Patriots-Cowboys contest ended up being the most-watched regular season NFL game since 1996. With more than twenty-nine million viewers tuning in, the Patriots offense stole the show. At times, Brady operated as if he were a boy and Cowboy Stadium were his playground. In one instance during the fourth quarter, Brady called a new play in the huddle. It had been designed especially for Moss and had been

added to the playbook only days earlier. Unsure of what route he was supposed to run, receiver Donté Stallworth looked at Brady as the huddle broke.

"Tommy, what do you want me to do?" Stallworth asked.

"Just go deep," Brady said.

On the snap, Stallworth ran ten yards at half speed. Then, just as the defender came up on him, Stallworth took off in a full sprint. Under pressure
and seeing that Moss was covered, Brady spotted Stallworth, stepped up, and
let it fly, hitting Stallworth perfectly in stride for a sixty-nine-yard touchdown completion.

When Brady and Stallworth reached the sideline, they looked at each
other and laughed. "We essentially drew up a play in the sand while the clock
was running," Stallworth said.

Brady threw five touchdown passes, tying a franchise record, and New
England thumped Dallas 48–27.

After the Dallas game, Brady appeared on the cover of *Sports Illustrated*
under the headline: "YES, THAT GOOD." Brady was having the season of
his life. The addition of Welker, Stallworth, and Moss had put Brady and the
offense on pace to set a slew of records. Under Brady's tutelage, Welker was
blossoming into the best slot receiver in the league, and he was leading the
team in receptions. Stallworth was thriving under Brady's ability to impro-
vise. And Moss was leading the league in touchdown receptions.

Yet Belichick continued to needle Brady. In front of the entire team,
Belichick told Brady that if he weren't so worried about his next *GQ* cover
shoot with Gisele, perhaps he'd do better. And Belichick frequently reminded
Brady that he could always go down the street to Foxborough High and get
"fucking Johnny Foxborough" to throw a better ball.

In week seven, Brady completed twenty-one of twenty-five pass attempts
for 354 yards and six touchdowns and the Patriots beat Miami 49–28.

In week eight, the Patriots annihilated the Redskins 52–7.

With each game, the Patriots made a bigger mockery of the notion that
filming hand signals had had anything to do with their dominance. The
games were so lopsided that teams started accusing New England of running
up the score. Against the Redskins, for example, the Patriots twice went for it
on fourth down late in the game, once when they were up 38–0, and a second
time when they were leading 45–0. Both times, New England kept the drive
alive by getting a first down and then went on to score a touchdown. When a
reporter questioned Belichick's decisions in the postgame press conference,
he bristled: "What do you want us to do?" he snapped. "Kick a field goal? It's
38–0. It's fourth down. We're just out there playing."

Under scrutiny for two solid months and having no patience for ill-informed questions, Belichick's tone toward the press had become increasingly dismissive and confrontational. In return, the media stepped up its characterization of him as a villain, referring to him as "Bill BeliCheat," "Darth Belichick," and "Bill Voldemort."

"I don't care what everybody else thinks," Belichick said at a press conference. "I can tell you what this team thinks. We expect to win every week."

Kraft was more sensitive to what everybody else thought. He was particularly protective of the team's brand and therefore took a more diplomatic approach in his interactions with the press. But he fully backed Belichick and had no intention of asking him to change his approach. He had hired Belichick to win, not to be a media darling.

On one hand, Kraft hated the fact that his franchise's reputation had taken such a beating in the aftermath of the Jets' spying complaint. But he didn't hold that against Belichick. Of course he would have preferred that Belichick had been more scrupulous. But in his view, the real culprit behind the drumbeat of complaints about the Patriots was the team's remarkable success. In a league that was hardwired to facilitate parity, the Patriots had figured out a way to separate themselves from the pack. The lion's share of the accusations being levied against them were motivated by jealousy and envy. The NFL was a ruthlessly competitive business, Kraft reminded himself. Success required mentally tough people. And Belichick personified mental toughness.

Kraft's attitude toward Belichick was informed by past experience. In the early days of his ownership tenure, Kraft had endured plenty of stressful situations due to Bill Parcells's difficult personality and coaching style. But Parcells had never delivered a Lombardi Trophy. With Belichick, Kraft had a coach who prepared more thoroughly, worked more relentlessly, and won more consistently than any coach in the game. His personality was complicated. But the greatest leaders tended to be the most complex people. In Belichick's case, his thick skin, while at times unattractive, was vital to his greatness.

At the halfway point of the 2007 season, the Patriots were the scariest team in the NFL and they were on pace to go down in history as one of the most dominant teams of all time. Kraft's advice to Belichick was simple: "Keep doing what you're doing."

When the 8-0 Patriots went to Indianapolis to face the 7-0 Colts on November 4, 2007, the *New York Times* called it "one of the most eagerly anticipated regular-season games in at least a decade." Never in NFL history

had two undefeated teams met so late in the season. Thanks in large part to the Brady-Manning factor, the Patriots-Colts rivalry was the league's richest. And after Manning had finally managed to lead his team past the Patriots in the previous year's AFC Championship game en route to the Colts' first Super Bowl title, plenty of people around the league thought they might have been witnessing the end of one dynasty and the start of another.

For the first time all season, New England fell behind early and trailed throughout the game. Down by ten points with just under ten minutes to play, Belichick stalked the sideline, shouting at his players: "Sixty minutes! Sixty minutes! You understand me?"

Moments later, Brady completed a fifty-five-yard bomb to Moss, followed by a touchdown pass to Welker. On the Patriots' next possession, it took Brady just three plays to put his team back in the end zone. In less than a five-minute span, the Patriots had scored fourteen points to defeat the Colts 24–20 and improve to 9-0. Afterward, Belichick was asked about the prospect of his team going undefeated.

"I don't care about all that," he said. "It's just one game."

Brady echoed Belichick. "We're 9-0, but none of this matters," Brady said. "What matters is January."

For the second time in four weeks, a Patriots game had set an audience record, drawing 33.8 million viewers, making it the highest-rated Sunday afternoon regular season NFL game. And although Belichick tried to downplay it, he knew full well that after beating the Colts, the question that would loom over the rest of the season was whether his team could remain perfect. Only one team—the 1972 Miami Dolphins—had managed to go an entire season without losing a game, and that was at a time when teams played a fourteen-game schedule. No team had gone undefeated since the league had switched to a sixteen-game schedule in 1978.

Every player in the Patriots' locker room wanted to be the first team to go 16-0. And every team remaining on the Patriots' schedule was determined to stop them.

The Patriots had become such a ratings bonanza for the networks that the NFL moved the Patriots-Bills game originally scheduled to air on CBS at 1 p.m. on Sunday, November 18, to the 8:00 p.m. prime-time slot on NBC. Earlier that day, receiver Terrell Owens had caught four touchdown passes in the Cowboys' 28–23 victory over the Redskins, helping Dallas improve

to 9-1. Prior to the game in Buffalo, Brady approached Moss in the Patriots locker room.

"Did you see that Terrell Owens scored four touchdowns?" Brady said.

Moss hadn't heard. But he immediately wanted to top Owens.

So did Brady.

"Let's throw the ball tonight," Moss said.

When Brady and Moss took the field to warm up, it was cold and the wind coming off Lake Erie was whipping through Rich Stadium. Not exactly ideal throwing conditions. But Belichick walked up to Brady and said, "We're still gonna throw the ball."

Brady nodded.

At the eight-minute mark of the first quarter, Brady threw a touchdown pass to Moss. At the start of the second quarter, Brady threw another touchdown pass to Moss. Eight minutes later, Brady threw another touchdown pass to Moss. Then, with ten seconds left in the first half, Brady threw his fourth touchdown pass to Moss, putting the Patriots up 35–7. As they reached the sideline, Belichick walked up to Moss, chuckled, and said, "You're done."

After Owens had caught four touchdowns in one game, Moss had promptly bested him by catching four in one half. The Patriots dominated every phase of the game and went on to win 56–10 to reach 10-0.

The next day in the team meeting, Belichick showed film of every mistake that the Patriots had made against Buffalo and tore into his players. "Whether you are Tom Brady or the fifty-third man on the roster," said Pro Bowl offensive lineman Dan Koppen, "you leave that team meeting feeling like you lost the game."

Belichick was seeking nothing less than perfection.

The entire sports world was swept up in the Patriots' quest for an undefeated season. With one week remaining, the Patriots were 15-0. The New York Giants were the only team that stood between them and the first 16-0 season in history. The two teams were set to meet in Giants Stadium on Saturday, December 29. The game was scheduled to air exclusively on the NFL Network, the league's new premium cable channel that reached just thirty-five million households nationwide. But interest in the game was so high that Congress sent a letter to the NFL, threatening to reconsider the league's antitrust status if it didn't open up coverage of the game to all American households through commercial networks. The league responded by announcing that it would

simulcast the game on CBS and NBC. It would be the first time in history that an NFL game would be shown on three networks. "We have taken this extraordinary step because it is in the best interest of our fans," Roger Goodell said in a statement.

The hype leading up to the game was unprecedented for a regular season game. NFL Network aired more than sixty hours of pregame programming. The number of media credentials was second only to those issued for a Super Bowl.

Standing on the brink of history, Tom Brady and Bill Belichick shared a moment alone on the field during warm-ups.

"We're as ready as we're gonna be," Belichick said.

Brady nodded.

"Good day to throw," Belichick said.

Brady smiled. "Isn't it always?"

"Yeah."

With the stadium packed with more than seventy-nine thousand fans, the Patriots were greeted with boos as they took the field. Minutes later, the Giants struck first to go up 7–0, electrifying the crowd.

Trailing 7–3 in the second quarter, Brady lofted a pass toward the back corner of the end zone. Moss out-jumped a defender to put the Patriots up 10–7. With the touchdown, the Patriots set the all-time record for points scored in a single season, at 561. When Moss got to the sideline, Belichick stopped him.

"That was another good example right there of you going up and getting the ball," Belichick said.

"Right."

"Instead of you letting it come all the way down," Belichick said.

"Yes."

"When there's any space and you can go up and get it," Belichick said, "I think you should go up and get it."

"Right," Moss said.

Fittingly, the game was the most entertaining contest of the entire season. Every time New England went ahead, New York regained the lead. With New York up 28–23 in the fourth quarter, Brady launched a sixty-five-yard touchdown pass to Moss to put New England on top to stay. For Moss, it was his twenty-third touchdown reception of the season, breaking Jerry Rice's all-time record. For Brady, it was his fiftieth touchdown pass of the season, breaking Peyton Manning's all-time record. The Giants Stadium crowd was stunned. The entire Patriots defense leaped off the bench, fists in the air.

It was a magical, historical night in East Rutherford. On the same field where the Jets had accused the Patriots of cheating seventeen weeks earlier, the Patriots dynasty reached new heights by beating the Giants 38–35 in a game for the ages. More than 34.6 million viewers tuned in, making it the most watched television show since the Oscars ten months earlier.

After the final play, Brady quietly raised his right arm and extended his index finger. Finally, Belichick smiled. "I love it," he said, walking off the field, head held high, surrounded by cameras.

twenty-nine

INCONSOLABLE

N ew England rolled through the playoffs, knocking off Jacksonville in the divisional round and San Diego in the AFC Championship. By the time the Patriots reached Glendale, Arizona, for Super Bowl XLII on February 3, 2008, they were 18-0 and widely regarded as the greatest team in NFL history.

They had the best player—Brady had thrown for 4,806 yards and been named NFL MVP for the first time.

They had the best coach—Belichick had been named NFL Coach of the Year.

They had the highest-scoring offense in the history of the league, with 589 regular season points, including twelve games where they had scored thirty or more.

They had the best receiving corps—Wes Welker tied for the league lead in receptions with 112, and he and Moss had combined for thirty-one touchdown catches, the most for a duo in NFL history.

And the team had an unprecedented average margin of victory of twenty points per game.

The only question remaining was whether the Patriots could top off the greatest season in NFL history by winning the Super Bowl. In a scenario that could not have been better scripted by a Hollywood film studio, the New York Giants, a team that had lost six games and wasn't even supposed to be in the Super Bowl, managed to upset two heavily favored teams in the playoffs to set up a rematch with New England. No team had played the Patriots tougher than the Giants had in the epic thriller that had ended the regular season. When the Giants arrived in Glendale, the entire team was dressed in black, sending a message to the Patriots that it was time for their funeral.

During Super Bowl week, Belichick put his team through a punishing practice. He also hammered home the theme he'd been emphasizing all season long: finish. Way back in training camp Belichick had introduced the

concept of finishing team meetings, finishing practice drills, finishing plays, and finishing games. The idea had arisen from the team's failure to finish off the Colts in the second half of the 2006 AFC Championship game.

To end the season 19-0, the Patriots would need to finish off the New York Giants one more time.

Two days before the Super Bowl, Roger Goodell held a news conference in Phoenix. In his remarks, he acknowledged having recently received a letter from Senator Arlen Specter. The senator wanted Goodell to appear before the Senate Judiciary Committee to explain why he had destroyed the six videotapes turned over by the Patriots back in September. Goodell explained to the media that the tapes—a few from the 2007 preseason and a few from the 2006 regular season—had not established that the Patriots had violated any rules. And after the leak of the Jets' sideline footage, Goodell had decided to destroy the six tapes to avoid the risk of further leaks.

"We wanted to take and destroy that information," Goodell said. "They may have collected it within the rules, but we couldn't determine that. So we felt that it should be destroyed."

That evening, Robert and Jonathan were en route to the commissioner's annual party when they got an urgent call from Stacey James, the team's head of communications. James informed them that the *Boston Herald* planned to run a story the following morning that accused the team of secretly taping the St. Louis Rams' final pregame walk-through—a noncontact session where a team goes through its plays at a slower pace—at the Louisiana Superdome prior to Super Bowl XXXVI in February 2002.

"That's complete bullshit!" Jonathan said.

"Stacey," Robert said, "tell the *Herald* there is zero truth to that. And tell them they would be running the story at their own peril."

Minutes later, James called back. The reporter, he said, was going forward.

"Then tell the reporter," Jonathan said, "he has to make an editor available to hear our side before printing such a serious allegation."

The Krafts immediately called their attorney, Dan Goldberg. During the commissioner's party, Jonathan and Goldberg spent an hour on the phone with an editor at the *Herald*, who indicated that his reporter's story was well sourced. Kraft assured him that the story was false, and that the team would be prepared to offer a sworn affidavit stating that the Rams had not been taped prior to the Super Bowl. After an hour of wrangling, a lawyer for the *Herald* joined the conversation. At that point, Goldberg cut to the chase.

"If you run that story, it will be libelous," he said. "And we will end up owning the *Herald*."

The next day, the *Herald* ran the story. The claim that a Patriots video staffer had illegally filmed the Rams prior to the Super Bowl was attributed to one unnamed source. The incendiary allegation immediately went viral. By the end of the day, ESPN.com had its own headline, "Report: Source claims Patriots taped Rams before Super Bowl."

So on the eve of the Super Bowl, the Patriots faced another controversy. "It's a serious allegation and I hope it's not true," said former Rams head coach Mike Martz. "Obviously if there is enough substance to it the league should look into it." Former Rams quarterback Kurt Warner told ESPN that he agreed.

Belichick fumed. In thirty-four years of coaching he had never seen a tape of another team's practice. The story in the *Herald* wasn't true. But with less than twenty-four hours left to get ready for the Giants, he was determined not to let himself or his team get distracted by the charges.

However, that wasn't going to be easy. The league indicated it would investigate the new claim and even had members of the Patriots football staff, including vice president of player personnel Scott Pioli, come to the league's hotel to undergo interviews on the allegation on the eve of the Super Bowl.

Kraft was incensed. Later that day, he had the team issue an official statement: "The suggestion that the New England Patriots recorded the St. Louis Rams' walkthrough on the day before Super Bowl XXXVI in 2002 is absolutely false."

When the Super Bowl was over, the Patriots organization intended to launch an investigation of its own—into the *Boston Herald* and its reporting methods.

From the Patriots' perspective, Super Bowl XLII was strange from the outset. The Giants held New England scoreless in the first quarter. After the Patriots scored a touchdown on the first play of the second quarter to go up 7–3, neither team scored again until the eleven-minute mark of the fourth quarter, when quarterback Eli Manning threw a touchdown pass to David Tyree to put the Giants on top 10–7.

No other team had managed to hold the Patriots' high-powered offense to a mere touchdown so late in the game. Much of the Giants' success stemmed from the confidence they had obtained in the 38–35 loss to the Patriots a month earlier. "Psychologically, even though it was a loss, that last

regular-season game worked to the positive to an unbelievable degree," one Giants official said. "Literally, walking off the field that night, our guys were saying to themselves and each other, 'If we play those fuckers again, we're going to beat the shit out of them.'"

Through the first three quarters of the Super Bowl, the Giants defense had relentlessly pressured and pounded Brady, while simultaneously shutting down Moss and brutalizing ball carriers with punishing hits. Wes Welker was the only player the Giants hadn't been able to corral.

When the Patriots took possession on their own twenty-four-yard line with under eight minutes to play and down by three points, Brady and his teammates were on the ropes. Then Brady went to work. Completion to Welker. Completion to Moss. A run for nine yards. Completion to Welker. Completion to Faulk. Completion to Welker. Completion to Moss. Completion to Faulk. Suddenly, the Giants couldn't stop the Patriots. And on third-and-goal from the Giants' six-yard line, Brady hit Moss for a touchdown. Just like that, with 2:42 to play, New England had reclaimed the lead, 14–10.

As he'd done so many times in his career, Brady had orchestrated a last-minute, come-from-behind scoring drive. On the Patriots' sideline, linebacker Tedy Bruschi grabbed linebacker Junior Seau and told him: "One stop!" All the Patriots had to do to finish a perfect 19-0 season and capture a fourth Lombardi Trophy was to stop the Giants on one final drive.

The first opportunity to end the game came when the Giants faced fourth-and-one with 1:40 to go. But New England couldn't hold them, and the Giants gained just enough yardage to keep the drive alive.

Then, with 1:20 to play, Manning threw an errant pass that went right through the fingers of Patriots defensive back Asante Samuel; the Patriots' most sure-handed defender dropped what would have been a game-ending interception.

On the next play, Manning dropped back to pass and was immediately engulfed. Defensive end Jarvis Green grabbed Manning by the back of the jersey, holding him in place as Richard Seymour simultaneously got a hand on Manning. Seymour was about to pull Manning down when offensive lineman Shaun O'Hara reached out in desperation and grabbed Seymour by the throat. "I said, 'Screw it,'" O'Hara would later admit. "I was squeezing his trachea as hard as I could and not letting go."

The officials missed O'Hara's illegal hold, which forced Seymour off Manning. And despite Green's grasp, Manning broke free before the referee blew his whistle. Scurrying out of the scrum, Manning launched the ball forty-five yards downfield. Patriots defender Rodney Harrison and Giants

receiver David Tyree simultaneously leaped for it. Inexplicably, with Harrison draped all over him, Tyree fully extended his arms and pinned the ball against the top of his helmet with one hand as he was falling backwards through the air. Despite Tyree's crashing to the ground, the ball never dislodged from his helmet.

The "Helmet Catch," as it would famously be called, seemed to defy gravity, keeping the Giants' drive going and putting them in position to score. To beat the greatest team in NFL history, Eli Manning and David Tyree had combined for what NFL Films' Steve Sabol called "the greatest play the Super Bowl has ever produced."

The Patriots were stunned. And a few moments later, the defense looked exhausted and beaten as Manning tossed a routine pass to a wide-open Plaxico Burress to put the Giants ahead 17–14.

Just twenty-nine seconds remained on the clock when Tom Brady and the offense trotted onto the field. After an incomplete pass and a sack, the Patriots were backed all the way up to their own sixteen-yard line with nineteen seconds on the clock. Facing third-and-twenty, Brady decided to air it out. With Moss streaking down the left side of the field, Brady rolled to his right to buy himself an extra couple of seconds, then took a few steps forward and let it fly. His perfect spiral traveled sixty-eight yards through the air and reached Moss's hands at the same moment that a defender outstretched his hand between Moss's to break up the play. Like the season, the remarkable pass fell inches short of perfection.

The Giants prevailed 17–14.

The cheering from Giants fans inside University of Phoenix Stadium was deafening. New York had delivered a blow to New England's soul. Utterly demoralized, Robert and Jonathan Kraft dreaded the locker room scene. In silence, they rode the elevator down from the suite level and started down a corridor beneath the stadium. Finally, Robert broke the silence.

"We need to go find John and Steve and say congratulations," he said.

Jonathan looked at his father. "*Really?*"

John Mara and Steve Tisch owned the Giants. The thought of going out on the field to find and congratulate them wasn't appealing. Nor was it customary. It wasn't as if the owners of the Rams, Panthers, or Eagles had sought the Krafts out after the Patriots had beaten them in the Super Bowl. And Jonathan Kraft suddenly had a more acute appreciation for why losing owners didn't seek out winning owners after a Super Bowl—losing the biggest game

in American sports is a colossal letdown; all you want to do is bury your face in your hands and leave the building.

But Robert was serious. The Patriots had just been through a season in which they had been accused of cheating and subsequently gone on to win eighteen straight games fair and square. Now that a team had beaten them fair and square, Kraft felt it was imperative that he extend his hand to the victors.

Jonathan trailed his father onto the field, through a mass of euphoric Giants players and fans who were reveling in the fact that they had beaten the Patriots. Confetti rained down. The Krafts felt like shit.

They finally reached John Mara and Steve Tisch, who were stunned to see them.

Kraft extended his hand.

Meanwhile, in the Patriots' locker room, Wes Welker was crying inconsolably. Randy Moss bawled. Linemen and linebackers wept. The scene and sounds of pain and misery were overwhelming. Belichick looked around and knew he had to say something. On the inside, he was as torn up as his players. But he stood, with a pained expression on his face, and took full responsibility for the loss.

"We didn't prepare you guys well enough," he told his team. "And that falls on me. . . . And I'm really sorry for that."

The players were so demoralized that words—even apologetic ones from Belichick—failed to ease the pain.

Stewing over his team's loss, Kraft craved an explanation for what went wrong. But he hadn't seen or heard from Belichick after the Super Bowl. Finally, four days after returning from Arizona, Kraft was in his office with Jonathan late in the afternoon when Belichick walked in, a stoic expression on his face.

"How do you feel?" Kraft said.

"Let's just say I haven't gone to the top of any tall buildings since Sunday," Belichick said.

Kraft looked at him quizzically. "Bill, I'm not sure I understand what that means."

Jonathan filled in the blank. "It means he would jump," he chimed in.

It was a long winter in Foxborough. The depressing ending to the greatest season in franchise history had cast a pall over the team. But Kraft and Belichick still had loose ends to deal with from Spygate. Given the dominance of the Patriots' season, the controversy around the taping of the Jets had faded from the public's consciousness. But the *Boston Herald*'s report alleging a far more egregious offense of taping a Super Bowl opponent's practice session

had rekindled the controversy and helped fuel the Senate Judiciary Committee inquiry being led by Arlen Specter. Roger Goodell believed there was no merit to the *Herald* report. Nonetheless, the commissioner was unhappy with the way Belichick had responded to the league's findings in the case involving the Jets. Specifically, Goodell had expected Belichick to be more forthcoming about his role in the sideline taping back in September.

In an effort to put the matter to rest once and for all, Goodell wanted Belichick to come to the league meetings and apologize to the owners and coaches.

Belichick didn't see the point. Nor was he particularly in the mood to revisit the situation, especially in the aftermath of the most devastating loss of his career. The last thing he wanted to do was talk to a group of owners in suits who viewed him as an ill-mannered coach who dressed like a slob, in hooded sweatshirts with cut-off sleeves. Belichick didn't care what they thought. He wore his hood like a crown, and he didn't see the need to rehash something that he considered a moot point.

But Kraft persuaded Belichick to do it.

Kraft wasn't eager to revisit the situation, either. But the aftermath hadn't hurt only the Patriots. The league's reputation had taken a hit, too. So in Kraft's mind, the Patriots needed to demonstrate contrition. Taking a short-term hit by doing what was in the league's best interest, he believed, would accrue to the Patriots in the long term.

On April 1, 2008, Kraft and Belichick attended the league meetings at The Breakers Palm Beach. In a ballroom, they addressed owners and head coaches. When Kraft spoke, he choked up. Talking in personal terms about his family, he told his colleagues that he viewed the NFL like his second family. He looked around the room and apologized. And he promised that his franchise would never do anything in the future to embarrass the league. Moved, the audience clapped when Kraft sat down.

When Belichick spoke, it was clear from his disposition that he wasn't eager to be there. Nor was the audience particularly hospitable. A lot of owners and team officials were bitter toward him. Part of their disdain was rooted in the fact that Belichick simply won more than anyone else. They also saw him as arrogant. His curt delivery didn't help. When Belichick reiterated what he had said months earlier in his public apology—that he had misinterpreted the rule about taping—the tension in the room was palpable. Not one owner or coach believed that Bill Belichick had misunderstood a rule.

Goodell, in particular, was not pleased with Belichick's presentation. He

subsequently told football writer Peter King: "I was given assurances that he would tell his side of the story. He went out there and stonewalled the press. I feel like I was deceived." Belichick responded by telling King: "I did not make any assurances about thoroughly discussing the subject publicly. I said I would address it following the league's review. I then did that in a way I thought was appropriate. I don't think that was deceptive."

After meeting with league officials, Belichick spoke to the media and was given an opportunity to point the finger back at the Jets. "Do you think the Jets were doing the same things when they played you?" a reporter asked.

"You'll have to talk to the Jets," he said.

"Do you get angry when people say the titles are tainted?"

"I know what the truth is," Belichick said. "Everybody is entitled to an opinion. I can't control what everybody thinks."

A little over a month later, the Patriots were prepared to sue the *Boston Herald* for libel. But after consulting with their attorneys, the Krafts decided to accept the *Herald*'s offer to provide a significant amount of free advertising, a promise to permanently remove the reporter at fault from the Patriots beat, and to issue a public apology that included an admission of wrongdoing. On May 14, 2008, the *Boston Herald* acknowledged that the bombshell story about the Patriots' illegally filming the Rams prior to the Super Bowl was false. The full-, front-page apology read: "SORRY, PATS." The full, back page read: "OUR MISTAKE." Inside, the paper wrote:

> On Feb. 2, 2008, the *Boston Herald* reported that a member of the New England Patriots' video staff taped the St. Louis Rams' walk-through on the day before Super Bowl XXXVI. While the *Boston Herald* based its Feb. 2, 2008, report on sources that it believed to be credible, we now know that this report was false, and that no tape of the walkthrough ever existed.
>
> Prior to the publication of its Feb. 2, 2008, article, the *Boston Herald* neither possessed nor viewed a tape of the Rams' walk-through before Super Bowl XXXVI, nor did we speak to anyone who had. We should not have published the allegation in the absence of firmer verification.
>
> The *Boston Herald* regrets the damage done to the team by publication of the allegation, and sincerely apologizes to its readers and to the New England Patriots' owners, players, employees and fans for our error.

The *Herald*'s admission and apology got very little attention outside of Boston. For years to come, members of the Rams' Super Bowl team would cite the original story and insist that the Patriots had cheated.

Could have. Should have. Would have. Those phrases ran through Kraft's mind every time he thought back to the Super Bowl loss to the Giants. He had no doubt that the coaches and players were thinking the same thing. Winning every game except the last one is agony. You never really get over it.

Concerned about long-term damage to his team's psyche, Kraft was searching for something to brighten their outlook—something unrelated to football, something out of the ordinary, something uplifting. He figured he knew just the person to call.

The Krafts had known Elton John since the eighties. Every summer, Robert and Myra would fly to Elton's home in England to support his annual fund-raiser for his AIDS foundation. Over the years, they had become so close that Elton had begun to look upon Kraft like a brother and as one of his closest friends. When the Krafts planned their forty-fifth wedding anniversary celebration in the summer of 2008, they asked Elton to play at their party. In addition to inviting more than five hundred of their closest friends, the Krafts invited the Patriots players and coaches, along with their wives. They held the event at Gillette Stadium.

On a warm summer night, one end of the field was arranged like an upscale restaurant, with white tablecloths, waiters in tuxedos, colorful floral arrangements, fine wine, and a stage with a grand piano. A video montage of the Patriots' 2007 season played on a giant screen as a parade of guests took their seats: Donald and Melania Trump. Les and Julie Moonves. Shari Redstone. Roger and Jane Goodell. Paul and Chan Tagliabue. Sandy and Joan Weill. The presidents of Harvard, MIT, Massachusetts General Hospital, and the Dana-Farber Cancer Institute. The CEOs of Fidelity, Pepsi, BankBoston, Gillette, Staples, MGM, and Reebok. The owners of the Red Sox, Celtics, and Bruins. Brady and Gisele. The Bruschis. The Seymours. The Wilforks. Belichick.

Myra and Robert took the stage. After Myra welcomed the guests, Robert took the mic. "We don't get together enough just to celebrate good times," he said. "Not to raise money for a charity. Not for some ulterior motive. But just to celebrate. We have a lot of things to celebrate."

Elton walked onstage and started playing the hits: "Love Lies Bleeding," "The Bitch Is Back," "Tiny Dancer," "Levon," "Rocket Man." As he performed,

the transformation that Kraft had brought about in Foxborough seemed more pronounced than ever. Once a sleepy New England hamlet, the town thirty miles southwest of Boston had become a hub of power and influence. In addition to being the new epicenter of the NFL, it was the place where heads of state and captains of industry went to be entertained. A future president and first lady of the United States sat at one table. Nearby, the CEOs of America's television networks sat with their spouses. The greatest coach in NFL history sat at another. The top model in the world had come all the way from Brazil and, now engaged to the most popular athlete in America, was about to join the Patriots family. All of them were being serenaded by one of the greatest entertainers on the planet.

Pausing between numbers, Elton acknowledged that he was a huge Patriots fan. Then he paid tribute to Robert and Myra. "This is their song," Elton said. "It's always been their song." His fingers played the opening notes to "Moon River." As he started to sing, a scene from *Breakfast at Tiffany's* appeared on the giant screen in the stadium. Everyone watched as Holly Golightly stepped out of a yellow taxicab on a Manhattan street and approached the Tiffany's storefront. Myra cried as the memories came rushing back. As the song ended, clips from the film were replaced on the screen by a black-and-white picture of Robert and Myra on their wedding day.

Sitting beneath the stars on the field where he normally performed, Brady couldn't help reflecting as he glanced at Myra and Robert. They had influenced his life. And he admired their marital relationship. It reminded him a lot of what he had seen growing up in his own home—a husband and a wife, complementing, supporting, and respecting each other. He turned and smiled at Gisele. At thirty years old, he was looking forward to marriage.

Elton wasn't through.

"I want to put it on record that this team had the most amazing season last year," he said. "To go eighteen and zero is an incredible achievement. And I know you probably think, 'Well, it was a disappointing end.' But disappointments always come in life. We're not guaranteed anything. And sometimes you can't always get what you want. But I was so damn proud of you last year.

"This," Elton continued, "is for the team, the coach, and the organization. Go Patriots!"

He launched into his eighties hit "I'm Still Standing."

The Patriots opened the 2008 season at home against the Chiefs on September 7. Expectations were off the charts. Coming off the 2007 season,

everyone from fans to NFL prognosticators to the oddsmakers in Las Vegas had New England favored to win the Super Bowl. The offense hadn't lost any key players and the defense had added linebacker Jerod Mayo, a first-round draft pick out of Tennessee whom Belichick expected to be an immediate impact player.

On the Patriots' second possession, Brady stood in the pocket, looking to his right for Randy Moss. As Brady stepped up to throw, he never saw Chiefs safety Bernard Pollard—nicknamed "the Bone Crusher"—blitzing from his blind side. Just as Brady released the ball, transferring all of his weight to his left leg, Pollard, who had been knocked down, lunged from the ground, crashing his helmet into the side of Brady's left knee. Screaming violently, Brady crumpled to the turf, clutching his knee.

"He was in a lot of pain," Pollard would later say. "When you hear a scream, you know that."

With 7:27 remaining in the first quarter, an eerie silence blanketed Gillette Stadium as medical staff surrounded Brady at midfield. Moments later, with a man under each arm, Brady hobbled off the field and was led to the locker room. He never returned.

Fifteen snaps into the 2008 season, all bets were off on New England's getting back to the Super Bowl. With backup quarterback Matt Cassel leading the way, the Patriots scratched out a win against Kansas City. But the postgame press conference was all about Brady. Asked about his condition, Belichick was vague. Asked whether he thought Pollard's hit was dirty, Belichick made his point. His players, he said, were always taught that it's their responsibility to hit the quarterback above the knees and below the shoulders.

Late that afternoon, Brady was lying in bed at his Boston home, his left knee elevated, tears in his eyes. He was in pain. His season was over. Staring up at the ceiling, he felt replaceable. He had been hit. The ref blew the whistle. He got taken off the field. Another quarterback took the field. The twenty-five second play clock started. And the game resumed without him. It was a depressing reality.

Remarkably, Brady had been playing football for thirteen years at this point—five at Michigan and eight in New England—without missing a game due to injury. Since taking over for Drew Bledsoe early in 2001, he had started 128 consecutive games, a virtual eternity in the NFL. Heartbroken and bewildered, he struggled to come to grips with the uncertainty of his future.

After about an hour, Gisele led two visitors into the bedroom. Robert and Myra had come straight from the stadium. Kraft took one look at Brady

and nearly lost his composure. He had never seen Brady so vulnerable, so sad. Without saying a word, he bent over and hugged him.

In the back of his mind, Kraft couldn't help wondering if Brady would ever play again.

That night, Kraft kept his fears to himself. He promised Brady he would do everything in his power to help him through the difficult days ahead. "We're with you," he told his quarterback.

"You're family," Myra added. "We take care of family."

The next day, medical tests revealed that both the anterior cruciate and medial collateral ligaments in Brady's left knee were torn. Surgery was required.

That afternoon, Belichick faced sixteen television cameras and a throng of national and local print reporters.

"We feel badly for Tom," Belichick said. "Nobody's worked harder and done more for this team than Tom. . . . He played one position. He played it well. There'll be someone else playing that position now."

thirty

ALLOW ME TO REINTRODUCE MYSELF

I n early October, Tom and Gisele flew with Robert and Myra to Los Angeles, where renowned orthopedic surgeon Dr. Neal ElAttrache operated on Brady's knee at the Kerlan-Jobe Clinic. After the operation, Brady remained in LA for follow-up procedures and rehab.

Back in New England, Belichick tried to maintain business as usual. "As a team we all just have to do our jobs," he told his players.

In Brady's absence, Belichick's approach didn't change. But the results did. Although backup quarterback Matt Cassel performed admirably, his second start resulted in a blowout loss at home to Miami, snapping New England's twenty-one-game regular-season winning streak. Over the ensuing ten weeks, New England lost four more times, slipping to 7-5.

With his team struggling, Brady returned to Foxborough in late November to start rehabbing at the Patriots facility. But Belichick didn't want Brady attending games. "Every time we throw an incompletion, the camera will go to you on the sideline," Belichick told him. "And we don't need that." Brady agreed. Instead, he watched the games on television from his Boston home. It was a weird experience. Eventually, he went back to LA to resume working out there.

Despite winning the final four games and ending up 11-5, the Patriots failed to make the playoffs for the first time since 2002. The team simply wasn't the same without Brady. And with Brady lying low and the team remaining tight-lipped about his progress, the question that would permeate throughout the league during the offseason was whether he would be the same quarterback when he returned. In any event, the loss of the NFL's reigning MVP for the entire 2008 season prompted the league to institute the "Brady Rule," a new provision to better protect quarterbacks.

Under the new rule, defensive players were prohibited from lunging at a quarterback's legs.

On February 1, 2009, Brady woke up at the home he and Gisele Bündchen shared in LA. It was Super Bowl Sunday and the Steelers and Cardinals were set to face off in Tampa. Itching to play, Brady telephoned his knee surgeon and a few other friends and had them meet him at the football field on the UCLA campus. Five months had passed since Brady's operation, and he'd been working out and throwing for a few months. But on Super Bowl Sunday he wanted to throw to guys who were running routes. On a deserted field, Brady ran. Brady jumped. Brady put torque on his knee. It felt liberating.

During his time away from the team, Brady had had plenty of time to contemplate his situation and ponder his future. In a profession where a player's average career length was less than three years, Brady had already logged nine seasons. At age thirty-one, he was getting up there in years for an NFL player. But during the downtime, he convinced himself that he had only hit the halfway point of his career, and he determined that he was going to play another ten years and not retire until he was forty-one. He couldn't figure out why he'd ever want to do anything else. What could compare? Jumping out of airplanes? Bungee-jumping off cliffs? Flying to the moon? Nothing he could think of sounded even close.

The only thing that really mattered to Brady besides playing football was raising his one-year-old son and getting married. And the time away from the game helped crystallize his plans on that front. On February 26, 2009, he married Gisele in a private, low-key ceremony in Santa Monica. From Bündchen's perspective, Brady was a perfect match. She had been raised in a large Catholic family, and her parents had been married for thirty-seven years. "He's very close to his family," she said. "He's Catholic. His parents have been married forty years. He's got a pure heart." She saw marriage as "loving someone you want to grow with, share with them, share the same values, the same feelings about things, the same beliefs." She considered Brady a soul mate.

As far as Brady was concerned, marrying Gisele was the best thing that had ever happened to him. She understood him. She accepted him. And she fully appreciated the commitment level that was required to be the best in the world at something. With her at his side, Brady believed he could achieve his goal to be a peak performer into his early forties.

After the wedding, Brady called Wes Welker and Randy Moss so they could start throwing together. They moaned and groaned that they were just coming off a long season and needed some downtime. Brady wasn't interested in hearing any of that. He wanted to make up for lost time.

Heading into the 2009 NFL Draft, Belichick had a conversation with Rick Gosselin, a football writer for the *Dallas Morning News* who was known for his expertise on analyzing draft picks. Belichick respected Gosselin.

"A kid you might want to take a look at is this quarterback out of Kent State," Gosselin told Belichick. "I don't think he can play quarterback, but I've heard he's a pretty good player."

The quarterback at Kent State was Julian Edelman, a lefty who stood just five feet ten inches tall and weighed under two hundred pounds. By NFL standards, he was a shrimp. His official draft report described him as "too small and unconventional" and raised questions about his durability. Scouts referred to him simply as "an unknown."

Belichick decided to take a look for himself. He watched a bunch of game film and was particularly struck by Edelman's performance against Ohio State during his senior year. Kent State got killed in that game, but Edelman played like a man possessed. Despite having no blocking to speak of and being half the size of Ohio State's defenders, Edelman ran wild. Even after his team fell behind by four touchdowns, he fought for every last yard and continued to play every down as if the game were on the line. Belichick loved his tenacity.

"What would we do with Julian?" he asked his staff. "Is he a receiver? Is he a punt returner? Is he a defensive back? Is he maybe a guy that just can play multiple positions in the kicking game?"

Nobody in the Patriots organization knew the answer. The good news was that no one else in the league was particularly interested in a tiny, left-handed quarterback out of Kent State. On draft day, everyone overlooked him. In the seventh round, Belichick chose him with the 232nd overall pick.

The Patriots chose ten players ahead of Edelman, including safety Patrick Chung and offensive tackle Sebastian Vollmer in the second round. It was clear before they arrived where Chung and Vollmer would fit in. But when Edelman got to Foxborough, Belichick wasn't certain what to do with him. During rookie camp, he watched Edelman catch punts. It was clear that he didn't know what he was doing. Belichick approached and asked if he'd ever fielded punts. Edelman hadn't. "Here's how to do it," Belichick

said, giving him a quick tutorial. He coached him on how a ball spins and breaks and so forth.

Edelman promised to work hard.

Rookie quarterback Brian Hoyer went undrafted in 2009. After New England traded backup quarterback Matt Cassel following the 2008 season, Belichick signed Hoyer for next to nothing in hopes that he might develop into a serviceable backup for Brady. On Hoyer's second day in Foxborough, he attended his first team meeting. He was awed to be in the presence of Brady, Moss, and Welker. Then the lights went off and the film came on. First up was a play involving Brady's throwing thirty yards downfield to Welker. The pass was incomplete.

"Brady, how long have you been playing?" Belichick said. "You're trying to force the ball to this midget down the field and the running back is wide open on a five-yard hitch? It's first down. Take the gain and move on."

Like other newcomers before him, Hoyer was both stunned and intimidated.

But Brady was just thrilled to be back at work. Being on the receiving end of Belichick's barbs meant life was returning to normal.

After nine years together, Belichick and Brady had an uncanny relationship. Outside the game, they rarely spoke. On the football field, however, they were on such a high plain that they had their own language. They'd spent so much time together in one-on-one meetings, team meetings, film sessions, practices, and high-pressure game situations that they often knew each other's thoughts and were virtually always on the same page.

Being separated throughout the entire 2008 season had reminded both of them just how much they had missed what could easily have been taken for granted. Besides an unmatched commitment to winning, the main thing Brady and Belichick had in common was that there was literally no place in the world where the two men were more comfortable being themselves than on a football field.

Moments before the start of the first preseason game, on August 13, 2009, Brady was standing next to Belichick on the sideline at Lincoln Financial Field in Philadelphia during the singing of the national anthem. Brady had a lot on his mind—this would be the first time for him to test his surgically repaired knee. As soon as the anthem ended, Belichick turned to him.

"About the only thing I can cheer for in Philadelphia is the national anthem," Belichick quipped.

The crack brought a smile to Brady's face.

Belichick smiled, too. "It's good to have you back out here," Belichick said.

"It's good to be back," Brady said.

Preseason games don't matter in the standings. They are important, however, for sorting out who makes the final roster at the start of the regular season. Rookies, in particular, are tested and scrutinized. Prior to the start of the exhibition game in Philadelphia, Belichick learned at the last minute that star slot receiver Wes Welker would be sitting out due to a minor injury. Belichick turned to rookie Julian Edelman, whose size, speed, and sure hands were remarkably similar to Welker's.

With so much focus on Brady and his return, it went virtually unnoticed that his first pass completion—a six-yard quickie—was to Edelman. The rookie ended up being Brady's favorite target that day, leading all receivers with five catches. But it wasn't until a punting situation that Edelman turned heads.

Normally, Welker returned punts, and Belichick had asked Edelman to handle that responsibility as well. In the second quarter, Edelman fielded a punt on the Patriots' twenty-five-yard line. With a host of tacklers bearing down on him, he changed directions so quickly that players lunged and missed him. Then he turned upfield, accelerated, and raced seventy-five yards for a touchdown that electrified the crowd.

As Belichick watched Edelman leave everyone in the dust, he thought of New York Yankees slugger Lou Gehrig. In the summer of 1925, Gehrig was an unknown player riding the Yankees bench. When Yankees first baseman Wally Pipp was forced to sit out a couple of games due to a minor injury, Gehrig stepped in. At the time, Pipp was a star slugger who had twice led the American League in home runs. But Gehrig played so well so fast that he never went back to the bench. The Yankees ended up cutting Pipp at the end of the season. Gehrig went on to play his entire career with the Yankees. In seventeen seasons he was on six World Series championship teams and he earned the nickname "the Iron Horse" for his durability, playing in 2,130 consecutive games. He went down in history as the greatest first baseman of all time. Pipp, on the other hand, became a forgotten man.

While Edelman's teammates jumped all over him in the end zone, Belichick walked over to Welker on the sideline.

"You ever hear of Wally Pipp?" he asked.

"Wally what?" Welker said.

"Wally Pipp," Belichick repeated.

"Nah-ah," Welker said.

"You never heard of him?" Belichick pressed.

"Nah-ah," Welker said.

"Well, he played first base before Lou Gehrig."

"Oh, okay."

"Lou Gehrig played like 2,300 straight games."

Welker was finally catching on. "The Little Man," Welker said, referring to Edelman's nickname.

"That might be a punt-return story," Belichick told him.

After the game, a pack of reporters crowded around Edelman's locker. It was the first time the press had really paid attention to him. When asked to comment on his touchdown run, the rookie borrowed a page from Brady's playbook, deflecting credit to his teammates.

"I have a lot to learn," Edelman said. "That play—the punt return—everyone just executed the play the way we designed it to be. One thing led to another. Totally a team effort. The blocks were there. They did their job. I did mine."

If Belichick had been grading Edelman's response, he would have assigned an A-plus. The kid even managed to work in a reference to Belichick's Do Your Job mantra.

"I'm there when Coach needs me," Edelman continued. "If someone goes down, players have to step up, fill voids. All I was doing was trying to help the team."

The headlines the next day were all about the fact that Brady's return to NFL action had gone without incident. But there was no denying that the Patriots appeared to have found a diamond in the rough when they picked Julian "Little Man" Edelman out of Kent State with the 232nd overall pick in the seventh round of the NFL Draft.

When Brady took the field before the season opener against the Bills on September 14, 2009, Jay-Z was rapping the opening lyric, "Allow me to reintroduce myself." Those words certainly were fitting for Brady. But they were also apropos for the team in general. During the offseason, the roster had undergone dramatic turnover. Belichick had traded linebacker Mike Vrabel and cut linebacker Larry Izzo. Safety Rodney Harrison had retired. Tedy Bruschi had retired during training camp. And days before the Bills game, Belichick

unexpectedly traded All-Pro defensive end Richard Seymour to the Raiders. Those six players had been what was left of the core of the defense during the team's Super Bowl run. For the previous eight years, they had been the captains on the field and the leaders in the locker room, defining what it meant to be a Patriot.

The team that Belichick fielded for the season opener was virtually unrecognizable from the one that had built the dynasty. Of the fifty-three players on the Patriots roster, only six of them had won a Super Bowl in a Patriots uniform. A crop of new players—Jerod Mayo, Rob Ninkovich, Patrick Chung—were stepping into leadership roles and embracing the Patriots' culture. But the lion's share of the roster was comprised of young players and newcomers that faced a big learning curve.

Brady and Belichick, however, were heading into their tenth season together. With Brady under center in a regular season game for the first time in a year, Belichick thought he looked understandably hurried in his first couple of pass attempts. One fell incomplete to Kevin Faulk and another sailed past Laurence Maroney. As Brady came to the sideline, Belichick met him.

"Tom, look," he said. "Just settle down, buddy. Step into the throw."

"I'm hitting them *right in the hands*," Brady said.

"That throw to Kevin out here?" Belichick said.

"I got drilled when I threw it," Brady said.

"All right," Belichick said. "The one to Maroney?"

"It was in his *hands*," Brady insisted.

"It was over his head," Belichick said.

"Oh, that one," Brady said.

"Yeah. Just step into it. Okay?"

It didn't take long for Brady to regain his form. At the end of the game, Buffalo led by six. With time running out, Brady orchestrated a drive that he capped off with a last-minute touchdown pass. New England won 25–24.

Five weeks into the season, Belichick railed in a team meeting that the Patriots were the only team in the league at that point without a single passing play for more than forty yards. "We have no big plays!" he yelled.

In the next game against Tennessee, Brady responded by throwing five touchdown passes—in the second quarter—setting an NFL record. New England went on to win 59–0. In the locker room afterward, Belichick told the team: "I can't talk about 'no big plays' anymore. I guess that shut me the fuck up."

While Brady and Belichick were in sync, as the 2009 season wore on, they both recognized that the team wasn't up to par. They struggled to beat top-tier teams. Particularly concerning was the way they were losing—by surrendering big plays late in games and by making mental mistakes. In the eleventh week of the season, New England was getting blown out in New Orleans when Brady and Belichick stood together on the sideline in the final minutes, looking up at the scoreboard, which read Saints 38, Patriots 17.

"Boy, I tell ya, we got a long way to go," Belichick said.

"We got our ass kicked," Brady said.

"We just have no mental toughness. We can't play the game we need to play."

"You said it," Brady said.

"Gonna have to find a way to be a tougher team when we get on the road," Belichick said.

"They kicked our ass," Brady said.

"They sure did," Belichick said. "I just can't get this team to play the way we need to play. It's so fucking frustrating."

"We do it in spurts," Brady said. "We just don't do it for four quarters."

The season was a slog. But Brady had reason to celebrate. In early December, Bündchen gave birth to a boy and named him Benjamin. At the same time, New England went on a three-game winning streak and won the AFC East division title with a 10-6 record. Despite a broken finger, some bruised ribs, and a bruised shoulder, Brady had started every game and was leading one of the best offenses in the league. A lot of that was due to Welker. He had developed into the most productive receiver in the NFL. He led the league in receptions with 123, and he led the Patriots with 1,348 receiving yards. In addition to being Brady's favorite target, Welker's effectiveness made it harder for teams to double-team Moss, who had hauled in eighty-three catches for 1,264 yards.

Just in time for the playoffs, Brady and the offense had jelled. But on the fourth play of the Patriots' opening drive in the final regular season game, Welker's left knee buckled when he went to make a cut after catching a pass from Brady. Writhing in pain, Welker had to be carted off the field. He had suffered the same knee injury as Brady had, tearing his ACL and MCL.

Without Welker, New England lost to Houston. After the game, Kraft drove Brady home. The drive gave them time to talk. That night, Brady emailed Kraft: "Just want to say thank you for the ride home. I really appreciate all that you do for me and the support and love you have always showed me. I always enjoy being with you and around your family. . . . I know we all

feel bad about Wes, but we're gonna find a way to win this regardless. On to Baltimore."

One week later, on January 10, 2010, the Patriots hosted the Ravens in the wild-card round of the playoffs. On the first play from scrimmage, Ravens running back Ray Rice ran eighty-three yards for a touchdown. Seventeen seconds into the contest, New England trailed 7–0. On the Patriots' third play, Brady got hit from behind and fumbled. Minutes later, Baltimore scored again. Before the end of the first quarter, the Patriots trailed 24–0. They never recovered.

With Welker watching from Kraft's suite on a pair of crutches, Baltimore double-teamed Moss and roughed him up every time he came off the line of scrimmage. And Ray Lewis harassed, taunted, and pounded Brady. The Ravens routed New England 33–14. It marked the first time that the Patriots had lost a playoff game at home under Belichick. It was also the first time that New Englanders had booed their own team during the Belichick-Brady era. After the game, Brady said, "I'd have been booing us, too, the way we played."

The consensus in New England was that the Patriots' epic run had come to an end. In the nine years since Brady had taken over as the starting quarterback, the Patriots had the highest winning percentage in the NFL. They had won more division titles and conference championships than any other team during that period. They had also produced the only perfect sixteen-game regular season in history. But against the Ravens, the Patriots looked lifeless. The franchise had never been so thoroughly humiliated on their home turf. The harsh reality was that it had been five years since the Patriots had won a Super Bowl.

"It was great while it lasted," wrote *Boston Globe* columnist Dan Shaughnessy, "but even a pigheaded Patriots pigskin buff must acknowledge that the dynasty is over."

History supported that conclusion. In the history of the NFL, only the San Francisco 49ers dynasty had lasted more than a decade. The Niners had won five Super Bowls over a fourteen-year span from the early eighties to the mid-nineties. The Pittsburgh Steelers dynasty of the seventies lasted less than a decade. And in the nineties, the Cowboys dynasty quickly imploded after winning three Super Bowls in four years.

Belichick was intimately familiar with the history. He was the one head coach who had been around long enough to have coached against the seventies Steelers, the eighties 49ers, and the nineties Cowboys. And he was

convinced that the Patriots weren't done yet. Nor was he ready to call it quits. At age fifty-seven, he planned to coach well into his sixties. Like Brady, he had trouble seeing himself doing anything outside of football.

On the morning after the brutal loss to Baltimore, Belichick got up before dawn and drove to the stadium in the dark. As he parked his car in the empty lot outside Gillette Stadium and stepped into the frigid air, he was already thinking about what the team needed to do to improve. He was encouraged by the fact that some of the youngest players on the Patriots roster showed promise. Julian Edelman, in particular, had again stepped in for Wes Welker and displayed that he was capable of being a key contributor going forward.

In Belichick's view, Edelman had been the best player on the field against the Ravens. He played that game the way he played the Ohio State game when he was at Kent State. The play that stood out to Belichick was the one Edelman had made late in the game. With victory well out of reach, he had caught a screen pass on fourth-and-ten, broken five tackles, and fought his way to a first down.

Heading into the 2010 NFL Draft, Belichick was determined to find more players with that same degree of intensity and determination. Over the next couple of months, he zeroed in on his targets. Then, on April 22, 2010, Commissioner Roger Goodell stood at the lectern at Radio City Music Hall on the first day of the draft and announced: "With the forty-second pick in the 2010 NFL draft, the New England Patriots select Rob Gronkowski, tight end, Arizona."

thirty-one

NO PLACE LIKE HOME

R ob Gronkowski stood six feet six inches tall and weighed 265 pounds. A hulking figure in a tight-fitting gray suit, the twenty-year-old wrapped one arm around his mother and one arm around his father as they formed a huddle with Gronkowski's four brothers backstage in the greenroom at Radio City Music Hall. Swaying and chanting in unison, the Gronkowski family was celebrating as a team. As soon as the commissioner announced his name as the newest member of the Patriots, the tight end known simply as "Gronk" choked back tears, telling his mother how much he loved her and thanking his father for being such a great example.

Moments later, Gronkowski gave the rowdy audience in the jam-packed hall a first glimpse of what type of individual the Patriots had just chosen. Rather than following the draft-day tradition of walking onstage holding his new team's jersey, Gronkowski came out clutching a Patriots helmet. The move riled up the predominantly New York crowd and brought a smile to Goodell's face. After shaking the commissioner's hand, Gronkowski energetically greeted NFL Network commentator Deion Sanders and faced the cameras.

"How fired up are you, big fella?" Sanders said, smiling. "You grabbed me and almost dislocated my shoulder just now."

"Man, I'm so *fired up*, man," Gronkowski said. "This is a great organization. It's awesome. I'm going to have one of the best quarterbacks ever throwing me the ball. This is the greatest moment of my life, man. This is unbelievable."

Then his family came onstage, formed a circle around him, and started chanting, "Gronk! Gronk! Gronk!" He put on the helmet, clenched his fists, flexed his arms, and started screaming. The unprecedented celebration was so exuberant that the Patriots coaching staff had to call Gronkowski's cell phone to tell him to get off the stage so the commissioner could announce the next pick.

Belichick considered Gronkowski a shot in the dark. He hadn't played much as a freshman at Arizona. He had caught just forty-seven passes his sophomore year. And he had missed his entire junior season due to back surgery. Then he entered the draft. So in terms of a track record, there wasn't much to go on. But Gronkowski had an NFL body and great hands, and he could block. "You're gonna love him," his college coach assured Belichick. "All he cares about is winning."

Winning consumed Belichick. Since 2001, the Patriots had won 121 games, including three Super Bowls. Photographs from every Patriots victory in the Belichick era decorated the many hallways of Gillette Stadium. But during the 2010 offseason, every single picture was taken down. When a reporter asked why, Belichick simply said, "Walls needed painting."

There was more to it than that. The biggest lesson that Belichick had learned in all his years of studying football history was that the game was constantly changing. Belichick's idols were guys like legendary Cleveland Browns coach Paul Brown, an innovator who started his pro career in the forties. Brown was the first coach to use game film to scout opponents, he developed the modern face mask, and he invented the draw play. Like his idol, Belichick was an innovator. For the Patriots to remain on top, Belichick believed he had to constantly adapt. Heading into the 2010 season, he planned to introduce a new offensive scheme built around a double tight end formation.

Traditionally, teams used one tight end on offense. The only time a second tight end would be on the field was in short-yardage situations when an extra blocker was needed. But Belichick planned to go with two tight ends on virtually every play. And instead of having his tight ends line up in a three-point stance with the offensive lineman, he planned to put them out wide like slot receivers and wide receivers, making them primary targets. The prospect of having a giant like Gronkowski lined up as an outside receiver would present all kinds of match-up problems for a defense.

Two rounds after drafting Gronkowski, Belichick surprised everyone by drafting another tight end—Florida's Aaron Hernandez. Hernandez was considered even more athletic than Gronkowski and was looked upon as the best tight end prospect in the draft. But the rest of the league had shied away from picking him because of his negative pre-draft report. It warned of his low self-esteem, emotional immaturity, and numerous off-the-field problems. Among other things, Hernandez had been suspended for failing a drug test and had been caught smoking pot on multiple occasions. At the NFL scouting combine, he had told teams that his drug use had started after his

father unexpectedly passed away when Hernandez was a high school junior. But Florida's coach Urban Meyer had told Belichick that Hernandez was a good kid and an extremely hard worker, and prior to the draft, Hernandez had sent a letter to the Patriots saying he was willing to take a biweekly drug test throughout his rookie season and return some of his salary if he ever tested positive. "I ask you to trust me when I say you have absolutely nothing to worry about when it comes to me and the use of recreational drugs," Hernandez wrote.

The Patriots weren't worried about pot. The more practical concern was Hernandez's age. Just a few months beyond his twentieth birthday when the Patriots drafted him, Hernandez became the youngest player in the entire NFL. But as soon as Hernandez arrived in Foxborough, he demonstrated a great work ethic and a desire to meet the organization's high standards. Belichick was convinced he was talented enough to make an immediate impact as a rookie. And by pairing him with Gronkowski, New England might end up with the youngest, most dynamic tight end duo in the league.

Tom Brady was aggravated. Despite his successful comeback season following knee surgery, some of the most respected sportswriters in Boston were whispering that he was starting to look "very pedestrian." And they were pointing to the disastrous season-ending playoff loss to Baltimore as evidence that Brady had started to show his age in 2009. "We all know what we saw," wrote *Boston Globe* columnist Bob Ryan, "and what we saw was an inconsistent quarterback who had his good days and his so-so days, and then, in the end, a truly awful day in the biggest game of the year. Manning reigns supreme now, and the new flavors of the month are named Rivers, Brees, and Romo. Brady suddenly has a lot of catching up to do."

Criticism and doubt from so-called experts who didn't really understand what made Brady tick had always been an external source of motivation for him. But what really frustrated Brady in the summer of 2010 was the uncertainty of his future. He was heading into the final year of a six-year contract that called for him to earn $6.5 million for the 2010 season. When the contract was negotiated in 2005, both sides understood that by 2010, Brady's base salary would be way below his market value. The intention had always been to strike a new deal before the 2010 season.

Kraft and Brady started talking numbers shortly after the season-ending playoff loss to the Ravens back in January. Brady made it clear that he wanted to remain a Patriot for years to come, and Kraft assured him that he wanted

the same thing. But after some back-and-forth, they decided that neither of them felt comfortable negotiating with each other. They agreed to leave that to Belichick and Brady's agent, Don Yee.

But Belichick hadn't shown much urgency to work on a new contract for Brady. From his standpoint, any serious contract discussions were premature until the Patriots had a better handle on what the new labor deal would like between NFL owners and the NFL players' union. With the current collective bargaining agreement set to expire, it was unclear how much salary cap space the Patriots would have under the new CBA.

It didn't help that Belichick had never taken a personal interest in Brady the way Kraft had. Brady recognized that Belichick treated all of his players the same way. That was how he did business. Nonetheless, Brady was a relationship person. And he'd been Belichick's most productive Patriots player and the one most responsible for executing Belichick's game plans. So from a business standpoint, it would have been beneficial to cultivate a relationship that went beyond X's and O's. It also would have made sense to reward the employee who had the most responsibility and who had been the most productive for the franchise. But that wasn't how Belichick operated.

When Brady showed up for training camp in late July, he tried to shift his focus strictly to football. The Patriots had a receiving core that included Moss, Welker, Edelman, and newcomers Gronkowski and Hernandez. Brady had done his homework on the rookies. From day one, he pushed them hard.

Both Gronkowski and Hernandez were intimidated. It was unnerving enough to be standing in a huddle with Moss and Welker while Belichick looked on. But on top of that, to have Brady barking at them like a drill sergeant was overwhelming. Every time Gronkowski or Hernandez made the littlest mistake, Brady hammered them.

Gronkowski was convinced that Brady didn't like him. And the longer camp went on, the more Gronkowski started thinking that he didn't particularly like Brady. At one point, when Gronkowski couldn't answer one of Brady's many interrogating questions about where he was supposed to be on a particular play, Brady told him, "I just won't throw to you anymore."

Belichick didn't say a word. He liked it when Brady rode the rookies. The good ones would catch on. The ones who didn't wouldn't be around long.

Gronkowski was miserable.

Kraft knew that Brady had wanted to sign a new contract before training camp. He also knew that Brady felt underappreciated by Belichick. And Kraft

understood why. From the day Brady had arrived in Foxborough as a rookie in 2000, he had looked up to Belichick and had done everything he could to earn his approval. After ten years, three Super Bowl titles, a 16-0 regular season, and a gritty return from knee surgery, Brady was still the first one to the facility in the morning and the last one to leave at night. He never stopped working like a quarterback who was fighting to make the team. For all those reasons, Kraft was eager to sign Brady to a four-year contract extension.

At the end of the first week of August, Belichick gave the players a couple of days off before the team's first preseason game. Kraft emailed Brady and invited him to the Cape to play a round of golf. After a few hours on the course, they went back to Kraft's summer home, where they met up with Jonathan. Over lunch, the three of them discussed Brady's future. Brady said that he had no plans of slowing down. He was in the best condition of his life. He was committed to winning more championships. And he reiterated that he wanted to finish his career in New England. But he was worried that Belichick might not want him much longer.

As Kraft listened, he knew he faced a complicated challenge. On the field, Belichick and Brady were the greatest coach-quarterback tandem in the league. There was no close second. For a decade the two of them had viewed the game through the same unique lens. But at some point, their views were destined to diverge. Part of Belichick's genius was his rigorous analytical approach, which suggested that Brady's best years were probably behind him and that his remaining years as an elite quarterback were undoubtedly numbered. Brady, on the other hand, was an outlier who was built—physically and mentally—to defy the NFL's actuarial age charts. In addition to being in exceptional condition, Brady's knowledge of the game was growing with each passing year.

When it came to Belichick's coaching methods, Kraft never weighed in. He recognized the brilliance behind Belichick's method of treating the team's biggest star the same way he treated the fifty-third man on the roster. If anything, Belichick rode Brady the hardest, which made it easier to get everyone else to buy in to the team-first mentality. At the same time, Kraft recognized how vital Brady was to the success of Belichick's approach. Despite being the most accomplished quarterback in the league, Brady was forbearing enough to endure Belichick's methods. Peyton Manning never would have endured what Brady had. Nor would have John Elway or Brett Favre or Dan Marino or Aaron Rodgers.

The trick was to figure out how to keep Belichick and Brady together for the long haul without stepping on Belichick's toes or putting Brady in a position where he felt trapped.

Kraft looked across the table at Brady. "You've done more for this franchise than any other player," he said. "I want you to be our quarterback for as long as you decide to play football. I love you like a son. You know that."

Brady nodded.

Kraft leaned in and made him a promise—he would never interfere with Belichick's coaching decisions, but if it ever got to a point where Belichick didn't want him as his starter, he would allow Brady to go out and find another team to play for. If that happened, Kraft told him, they'd discuss it together, shake hands, and agree on a solution. Brady had earned that.

Brady thanked him.

The more immediate issue, Kraft insisted, was to get a contract done.

Brady agreed. But now that the start of the regular season was just weeks away, he figured that Belichick would be too busy to restart talks with Don Yee.

Kraft didn't disagree.

Brady turned to Jonathan. "Would you work with Don on this?"

The question caught Jonathan off guard. He never got involved in player negotiations and had no desire to, but this was Tom. "I'm good if RKK is," Jonathan said.

Robert concurred.

Later that night, Robert emailed Brady, thanked him for coming to the Cape, and expressed his love.

"I had a great time and there is no place I would have rather been," Brady wrote back. "I hope you know how much I respect you and admire you and look up to you."

Don Yee was a breath of fresh air in the world of sports agents. He had no ego. He was not motivated by money. He was always cordial. And his calling card was his integrity. Yee was also a pragmatist. When it came to the NFL, he viewed it as the ultimate Darwinian environment, and he considered Bill Belichick the ultimate practitioner within that environment. To Yee, what made Belichick so superior to every other coach was his single-minded focus on winning, with no sentimentality for anyone or anything. As far as Yee was concerned, Brady had spent ten years playing for the best coach, the most influential owner, and the best franchise. Looking around the league, Yee couldn't think of another franchise quarterback who had had a smoother, more successful run with an organization.

Yee appreciated that a key ingredient to Brady's happiness in New England was his unusually close relationship with Kraft. But in Yee's mind, this

was not the time for sentimentality. The situation called for realism. Brady had just turned thirty-three. He was one year removed from reconstructive knee surgery. On paper, he was fast approaching the end of the line. Appreciating how Belichick operated, Yee was determined to structure a contract that protected his client from becoming expendable. That was his mind-set when Jonathan Kraft reached out to him two days after Brady's lunch with the Krafts on the Cape.

Kraft and Yee established a good rapport. But they had different ideas on how to proceed. Kraft suggested a long-term contract for Brady. Yee preferred a shorter-term deal. When Kraft indicated that the Patriots were prepared to offer a lucrative contract that kept Brady in Foxborough through age thirty-six, Yee countered that he didn't want the contract to exceed three years. Ideally, Yee preferred a two-year deal. His point was that four years is practically a lifetime in the NFL. By the time Brady turned thirty-six, he'd be a middle-aged man. A lot of personal and professional circumstances could change. Most important, Belichick might not want him to play for his team by that point. A shorter contract would offer Brady more control over his future while giving Bill the flexibility he desired in player deals, especially ones involving older players.

Kraft emphasized that the Patriots didn't want to go through another contract negotiation with Brady in two years. They preferred to do a four-year deal that met Brady's desires.

But Yee held out for a three-year agreement. He had dealt with Belichick enough to know that when it came to high-priced veteran players, he was prone to trade or cut them heading into the final year or two of a contract. A shorter contract insulated Brady against that probability.

Throughout the month of August, Yee and Kraft continued to go back and forth. By the end of the month, Kraft had provided enough assurances to protect Brady that Yee had come around to the idea of a four-year contract. But the two sides were still far apart on Brady's compensation. Yee was looking for $80 million, averaging out to $20 million per season. The Patriots were stuck at $64 million, averaging out to $16 million per year. Yee's number would make Brady the second-highest-paid player in the league behind Peyton Manning. The Patriots number put Brady behind five other quarterbacks, none of whom were remotely close to him in terms of success and achievements.

Brady had had enough. On August 26, he emailed Robert at 1:43 a.m. "We've been dealing with these negotiations for seven months," he told Kraft. "I'm trying to get ready to play a season, and I don't want to think about

my future past this weekend. I told Don last night that I'm tired of talking about it. If we can't get something done by the start of next week, we will move forward with no deal.

"There is certainly no place I'd rather be than here, or person I'd rather play for than you. But I have also worked my ass off and will continue to work my ass off. And frankly, the offers I've seen recently are not something I'd accept, considering what we've accomplished and will continue to accomplish. I feel a bit angry and frustrated that you don't see it the same way. . . . I'm sure you think it's fair. But for me it does not work. . . .

"There is no person I respect more than you. You are someone I've leaned on for the last ten years to guide me in the most important decisions in my life. And for that I am forever grateful and feel privileged to be here and be part of your family. I will always wish you the best and have loved every second I have been here since I was drafted ten years ago. I apologize for the long email. Sleep well. Tom."

After reading that, Kraft couldn't sleep. Brady, he feared, was thinking of leaving.

The reality was that Kraft didn't disagree with Brady. But like Belichick, Kraft had been hoping that the league's new labor deal would get worked out before finalizing Brady's contract. Tired of waiting, Kraft composed a lengthy email response. In it, he said all the things that Belichick would never say, and he explained why the negotiations were taking so long. But he acknowledged Brady's frustrations.

"Speaking as a sixty-nine-year-old man (who thinks he's twenty-eight), where there won't be hard feelings, there will be great sadness and rupture internally that will never be able to be repaired if we are not mutually smart enough to solve this," he wrote. "I think it is also important to say that ten years from now, what we're laboring over will seem like minutia in the big picture."

Later that afternoon, Brady wrote back to Kraft. "I appreciate your heartfelt reply," Brady said. "I hope you don't feel as if I'm unappreciative. And I hope I will be here for as long as you want me here. I'm looking forward very much to what's ahead. Thank you. Lots of love. Tommy."

Randy Moss was frustrated about his contract situation, too. One week before the start of the regular season, he decided to go public with his displeasure.

"When you've done so much and put so much work in, it kind of feels like I'm not wanted," he told a CBS Sports reporter on September 6. "I'm

taking that in stride and playing my final year out, and whatever the future holds is what it holds, but it's kind of a bad feeling—feeling not wanted. It's not like my production has gone down. I'm speaking from an individual standpoint. I don't know about Tom or whoever else's contract."

Moss added: "I'm a little older and understand the nature of the business—the older you get the more your skills supposedly diminish. But I think I'm getting wiser in how to use my physical skills. That's the frustrating part—when you put so much heart and desire into things and feel like you're not wanted."

Belichick wasn't pleased. Neither was Kraft. Patriots players were schooled not to air grievances in public. Contract negotiations, in particular, were like family matters—sometimes messy, but always kept in-house. Brady knew this better than anyone. In ten years' time he had never once voiced publicly his frustrations. Nonetheless, when Moss did it, Brady understood where he was coming from, and he made a point to let him know publicly what he had often told him in private.

"There's only one Randy Moss that will ever play this game," Brady told the press when asked about Moss's comments. "He's the greatest, probably, downfield receiver in the history of the NFL. Those catches that he makes, where you guys see he runs sixty-five yards down the field, you throw it and he just runs and catches it. That's impossible to do."

The preseason ended with Brady and Moss still in limbo.

Jonathan Kraft and Don Yee had invested a solid month on Brady's contract negotiations. It was up to Robert and Brady to close the deal. The day after Moss went public with his grievances, Kraft called Brady. Yee wanted $80 million. The Patriots were offering $64 million. Kraft suggested they split the difference and settle on $72 million for four years. At $18 million per year, Brady would become the highest-paid player in league history based on average annual salary.

Brady enthusiastically agreed.

A couple of days later, Brady got up early, made himself a green smoothie, kissed his wife good-bye, and left their home in the Back Bay section of Boston before six thirty. The season opener against the Bengals was three days away and Brady couldn't wait to get to the stadium. Practice wasn't until early afternoon, but he planned to get in early to work out, study film, and sign his contract, the wording of which had been finalized over the previous forty-eight hours.

With the smoothie resting in his lap, Brady eased his black Audi S8 down a

familiar back alley, eventually coming to an intersection. The light was green. As he pulled out, he suddenly spotted a minivan to his left, barreling at him.

Frightened, Brady swerved.

The van smashed into Brady's car, flipped over, and landed upside down. Shattered glass and car parts went flying. A woman walking her dog near the intersection fell over backward. Two passengers were trapped in the van.

"What the fuck just happened?" Brady said to himself.

Shaken up and covered in smoothie, Brady staggered out of his car.

The toppled woman with the dog stood up. "Oh, my God!" she said. "Are you okay?"

"I think so," Brady said.

"Call 911," she said.

Brady reached for his phone. Minutes later he was in the back of an ambulance, being examined by paramedics. His car was totaled, and first responders were using the Jaws of Life to extract the occupants from the other vehicle. Brady appeared to be in a state of shock.

"Just relax," a paramedic told him.

"I'm good," Brady said. "I've got to get to work."

The driver and passenger in the van were in serious condition and were rushed to the ER. Refusing a trip to the hospital, Brady stepped out of the ambulance and walked away from the scene. When he came through the door of his home a few minutes later, it was clear that he'd been through something.

"What happened?" his wife cried.

"I just got in an accident," he said.

She threw her arms around him, and Brady let go of his emotions.

An hour later, Brady drove to the stadium in a different car. He worked out. Then he practiced as if nothing had happened.

When Kraft learned of the accident, he was shaken up. And when he saw pictures from the crash scene, he considered it a miracle that Brady had walked away. The reality was that if Brady didn't have such exceptional peripheral vision and hadn't swerved, the outcome could have been dramatically worse.

Upon arriving at the stadium, Brady went directly to the front office to sign his contract. Then he went straight to watch film. There was no celebrating or handshakes. It was time to get to work. The season was starting.

Minutes into the 2010 season, Randy Moss streaked downfield, drawing double coverage, and Brady threw underneath to a wide-open Aaron Hernandez, who raced forty-five yards to the Bengals' fourteen-yard line. Two

plays later, Brady dumped a short screen pass to Welker, who got behind Gronkowski, who plowed a defender out of the way, enabling Welker to dart into the end zone. The two plays perfectly integrated the rookie tight ends with the elite veteran receivers, previewing Belichick's new offensive game plan. The Patriots jumped out to a 31–3 lead and went on to demolish the Bengals.

New England's romp landed Brady and Moss on the cover of *Sports Illustrated* under the headline "SERIOUS FUN: Tom Brady and the Pats Take Care of Business (as Usual)." But the atmosphere in Foxborough was far more intense than fun. Toward the end of the game, Gronkowski had caught his first touchdown pass from Brady. Screaming at the top of his lungs and chest-bumping his teammates, Gronkowski quickly calmed down when a stern-faced Brady approached him in the end zone, showed no emotion, and gave him a soft fist bump that seemed to convey, *There's a lot more work to do.*

Immediately following the game, Moss walked up to the lectern in the press room and announced: "I want to let you know, let the fans—the *real* fans of New England—know that I'm not here to cause any trouble, I'm here to play the last year out of my contract." Then, without being prompted by a question, he sounded off on his contract situation. "I don't want to take away from the win," he said. "But before the season gets started—I don't want to be in week ten, week eleven, or week twelve, talking about a contract."

Moss acknowledged that his comments were going to land him in hot water with Belichick. When a reporter asked the status of his relationship with Kraft, Moss simply said, "Fair."

Belichick and Kraft talked about the situation. They were on the same page. Three weeks later, New England traded Moss to Minnesota for a third-round draft choice.

"In this business," Belichick said, "there are complex and often difficult decisions, but it is my responsibility to make them based on what I feel is best for our football team, in both the short term and long term."

The Patriots were 3-1 at that point and led the league in points scored. But the abrupt dismissal of Moss caught people off guard around the league. The loss of a Hall of Fame–caliber receiver from the roster would significantly handicap most offenses. But the Patriots weren't built like other teams. New England's roster was loaded with young, up-and-coming talent on the offensive side of the ball. More important, the ethos under Belichick had long been "Next man up." The idea was that no one was irreplaceable.

Six days after Moss left, Belichick pulled off an unexpected trade with Seattle that brought veteran receiver Deion Branch back to New England.

Brady hated to see Moss go. But he was elated to get Branch back. After

just three days of practice with his old team, Branch suited up against the Ravens on October 17. Despite the fact that New England was running a new offense, Branch nonetheless caught a team-high nine passes and scored a touchdown. The crowd gave Branch a spirited welcome-back ovation that brought tears to his eyes.

New England beat Baltimore in overtime to improve to 4-1.

On October 31, the Patriots hosted the Vikings. So three weeks after being traded, Moss returned to Foxborough. Earlier that week, the NFL had fined Moss $25,000 for refusing to grant postgame interviews. A couple of hours before the game, Moss spotted Robert and Myra Kraft on the field.

Kraft had been disappointed in some of the things Moss had said and done in his final months in New England. But he liked Moss a great deal, and he appreciated the contribution he had made to the franchise. As Moss approached, Kraft extended his hand, told him he missed him, and said he'd always be part of the Patriots family.

Moss was contrite.

Then he turned to Myra. "Thank you for letting me be part of something special," Moss told her.

Myra smiled and put her arms around him.

New England manhandled Minnesota, improving to 6-1 and establishing itself as the team with the best record in the league. Minnesota fell to 2-5. At the end of the game, the Patriots crowd gave Moss a long standing ovation. The outpouring of support reminded him how much he had loved playing in New England. With tears in his eyes, he jogged off the field.

After a quick stop in the Vikings locker room, Moss walked into the Gillette Stadium media room wearing a black Boston Red Sox cap and addressed the press.

"I got fined twenty-five thousand dollars for not talking to you all," he began. "Me, personally, I really don't care. At the same time, for the league to fine me twenty-five thousand dollars, I'm not going to answer any more questions for the rest of this year. If there's going to be an interview, I'm going to conduct it. I'll answer my own questions."

Pausing, he took a deep breath. "I really haven't had a chance to talk to the guys," he continued. "So this is no disrespect to the Minnesota Vikings and their organization. The [Patriots] captains—Wilfork, Tommy Boy, Mayo, Kevin Faulk—I miss them guys, man. I miss the team. . . . It was hard for me to come here and play. It's been an up-and-down emotional roller coaster all week. . . . I just want to tell the guys I miss the hell out of them. Every last helmet in that locker room."

He paused, trying to keep his composure. "Coach Belichick gave me an opportunity to be part of something special," he continued. "That's something I take to heart. I'm stuck for words. There's a lot of memories here. To the New England Patriots fans, that ovation at the end of the game really felt heartwarming.

"I can't say enough about this team and this organization. I'm going to go ahead and end this interview. I don't know how many more times I'm going to be up here in New England. But I'm going to leave the New England Patriots and Coach Belichick with a salute, man."

Moss raised his hand to his cap like a soldier. "I love you guys. I miss you. I'm out." He walked away from the lectern and disappeared behind a curtain.

The next day, Minnesota cut him.

In his eleventh season, Brady was more fiery than ever. In a midseason game in Pittsburgh, he screamed at his offensive linemen on the sideline after the team failed to get a first down in a short-yardage situation. Later, on a quarterback keeper, Brady rambled four yards, taking on three tacklers and enduring a head-on collision to score a touchdown, putting his team up 23–3. Frustrated Steelers piled on top of Brady, prompting Patriots linemen to start pulling guys off of him. A fight broke out. Whistles blew and flags flew. When Brady finally emerged from the pile, he walked to the back of the end zone, let out a primal scream, and fired the ball into the ground, inciting the Pittsburgh crowd and pumping up his team.

The Pittsburgh game was also a breakout performance for Gronkowski, who caught three touchdown passes. With a lot of help from Wes Welker, Gronkowski had been working overtime learning how to run his routes precisely the way Brady liked them. Three weeks later, Gronkowski had a mistake-free game against the Jets on *Monday Night Football*, and the Patriots won 45–3 to improve to 10-2.

Thinking Brady would finally start to ease up on him in practices, Gronkowski was surprised when Brady tore into him a couple of days after the Jets game when the tight end failed to run a simple ten-yard pattern with exact precision. Brady was so furious that Gronkowski thought he was going to throw a punch. Gronkowski had reached his limit. No matter what he did, it seemed he couldn't satisfy Brady. Fed up, he wanted to get in Brady's face.

But a week later in Chicago everything changed when Brady called the same play that Gronkowski hadn't run with precision in practice. This time, Gronkowski ran it exactly as Brady had insisted: With a linebacker draped

all over him, Gronkowski turned around, and Brady's pass was perfectly placed in the only space where Gronkowski could catch it. He hauled it in for a touchdown. After that, Brady never treated him like a rookie again. And Gronkowski finally figured Brady out—he didn't want his rookie tight ends to be good; he wanted them to be the greatest in the league.

New England beat the Bears 36–7.

Other than a loss in week two to the Jets and a fluke midseason loss to the Browns, the Patriots were unstoppable in 2010. The offense, in particular, was machinelike. During the final eight weeks of the season, New England scored more than thirty points in every game. Welker led the team in receptions. Gronkowski and Hernandez combined for eighty-seven catches and sixteen touchdowns. And Brady had been nearly flawless, throwing a league-high thirty-six touchdown passes and just four interceptions, giving him the highest quarterback rating in the NFL.

One year after the Patriots dynasty had been declared over, New England finished with a league-best 14-2 record and was the odds-on favorite to win the Super Bowl. But in the first round of the playoffs, the Patriots were stunned by the Jets. After beating New York by more than forty points a few weeks earlier, New England lost 28–21 at home on January 16, 2011. Jubilant Jets players celebrated by dancing on the Patriots logo and doing somersaults at midfield.

The next day was cold and dreary in Boston. Brady and Bündchen went for a walk along the Charles River with their one-year-old son. Brady was melancholy.

"How are you?" Bündchen said.

"I'm not great," he told her.

"Why?" she said.

"I'm just thinking about that stupid football game last night," he said.

Over the previous ten years, the Patriots were the only team in the NFL without a losing season. Still, Brady took season-ending playoff losses particularly hard. After working so hard to get to 14-2, it was a huge downer to get knocked out by an inferior team.

"You'll overcome it," Bündchen told him.

"This little squirt helps me," he said, finally cracking a smile. "Look at him."

Brady's perspective was changing.

thirty-two
THE PASSING

I n March 2011, Robert and Myra Kraft traveled to Israel. They brought along NBC sportscaster Al Michaels, a close family friend. While in Jerusalem, they attended a football game at Kraft Family Stadium, with a Patriots logo at midfield and an Orthodox Jew refereeing with tallit fringes coming out from under his T-shirt and payot. The adult recreational football league that Kraft had helped form was the only Israeli sports league that included Palestinian players. Michaels marveled at the sight of Jews and Palestinians playing on the same team. It was a perfect example, Kraft told him, of what he loved most about sports—its power to bring people together.

Kraft also visited a number of his Israeli businesses in the area, where he had long employed Palestinians from the Gaza Strip and the West Bank. Accompanied by an American television news crew, Kraft called on American and Middle Eastern entrepreneurs to join him in helping to create jobs in the West Bank, Gaza, and Israel. "I'm rooting for a lasting peace in this area of the world," he told reporters.

The press portrayed Kraft's visit as a business trip. But his primary motive for going to the Holy Land was much more personal. Unbeknownst to anyone outside the family, Myra was battling cancer. That spring she had told Robert she wanted to go to Israel before she became too weak to travel. Forty-seven years earlier, they had honeymooned in Jerusalem, and ever since then, Myra had visited the city regularly. She considered it her home away from home, and she longed to see it one last time.

While the Krafts were in the Middle East, the protracted labor negotiations between the NFL and the NFL players' union broke down back home. The two sides could not come to terms on a new collective bargaining agreement. The owners locked out the players from team facilities, bringing league operations to a halt. In response, Tom Brady, Peyton Manning, and Drew Brees filed an antitrust suit against the NFL on behalf of all players. The two sides were so far apart that the start of the 2011 season was in jeopardy.

As soon as Kraft returned to the United States, he received a call from DeMaurice Smith, the head of the NFL Players Association. Former Patriots quarterback Drew Bledsoe had assured Smith that if there was anyone who could break the impasse, it was Kraft. Smith asked Kraft if he'd help broker talks between the two sides.

Kraft agreed to step in. His first move was to suggest getting the lawyers out of the process and to commence face-to-face talks between a small contingent of players and owners. Both sides agreed to a series of meetings. At the first one, Kraft reminded everyone that countless people around the country—from team and stadium employees to outside vendors—depended on the NFL for their livelihood. Millions more planned their calendars in the fall around NFL games. "Football is part of Americana," Kraft said. "The only issue is how do we get football back?"

Over a three-month period, the small group of players and owners worked toward a resolution. During that time, Myra was hospitalized. Kraft shuttled between the hospital and the meetings, never missing a session. By that point, the owners and players were aware that Myra was gravely ill. They were also aware that Myra insisted on her husband's attending the negotiations. His presence strengthened everyone's resolve to forgo the bickering and work together on resolving their differences.

When it became clear in July that there was nothing more the hospital could do, Myra was transferred back home, where she received hospice care during her final days. Anchored to her bedside, Kraft rubbed Myra's feet for hours and rested his head in her lap, telling her how much he loved her, and whispering the lyrics to her favorite song. "Oh, dream maker, you heart breaker, wherever you're goin', I'm goin' your way."

On July 20, 2011, Myra died at home. She was sixty-eight.

Kraft wept.

Tom Brady was vacationing with his family in Costa Rica when he woke up suddenly in the middle of the night with a bad feeling that something had happened. In the dark, he reached for his phone. There was a text from Kraft's chief of staff, Al Labelle: "Myra passed away."

Brady broke down. Over the summer, he had spent many days with Robert at Myra's side in the hospital. A couple of times, Brady had even slept at the hospital just to keep Kraft company and help get him through the ordeal. Brady knew how badly Kraft hated to be alone. It was the reason he brought Myra everywhere he went. He would be lost without her.

Brady packed his bags and flew back to Boston. When he arrived at the synagogue on the day of the funeral, Brady was escorted to a private room in the back that was reserved for family members. With tears in his eyes, Kraft buried his head in Brady's chest and whispered, "Where's my partner?"

Brady put his arms around Robert and held him tight.

The funeral was packed. DeMaurice Smith and Roger Goodell—adversaries in the labor talks—came together. Corporate titans sat with volunteers who worked at the many charities that Myra had sponsored in the city of Boston. Past and present Patriots players filled the pews.

"Who else but Myra Kraft could bring together such an eclectic gathering of Jews and non-Jews, black and white, blue collar and white collar, players and owners?" Rabbi Wes Gardenswartz said to the mourners.

A cantor serenaded them with a rendition of "Moon River." Each of Myra's sons eulogized her. When Jonathan spoke, he recounted the time his mother had stood up to a white police officer in Johannesburg, South Africa, and demanded that he arrest her along with the black South Africans he was apprehending. "My mother went through life looking at the world through empathetic eyes," Jonathan told the audience. "My father didn't make any significant decisions without talking to her first. She chose to be a life partner to my father, and he sought her counsel on everything."

Afterward, Robert leaned into the back of the hearse and kissed Myra's coffin.

Following Myra's burial, shiva—a seven-day period of mourning—commenced. For days, mourners visited the Kraft home to pay their respects. One of the first people to show up was Randy Moss. He had flown across the country to hand-deliver a condolence card. He signed it: "Randy Moss Kraft." Tearing up, he told Robert how much he was going to miss Myra.

During shiva, the NFL owners and players agreed to a new collective bargaining agreement. Kraft left his home for a few hours and flew to Washington for the announcement. At a press conference, Indianapolis Colts center Jeff Saturday faced a throng of reporters. Saturday had helped lead the negotiations on behalf of the players. Flanked by a number of his colleagues and a few of the owners, Saturday announced the historic deal.

"A special thanks to Myra Kraft, who even in her weakest moment allowed Mr. Kraft to come and fight this out," said Saturday, choking up. He turned to Kraft. "Without him," he continued, "this deal does not get done. I don't want to be dramatic in any way, but he is a man who helped us save

football and we're so grateful for that. We're grateful for his family and for the opportunity he presented to get this deal done."

Saturday put his arm around Kraft and pulled him close. "Thank you very much," Saturday told him. "We really appreciate it."

Fighting back tears, Kraft tucked his head into Saturday's chest. "It means a lot," Kraft whispered.

There are five phases of mourning in Judaism. The first stage is despair. Kraft felt like he was never going to make it to the second phase. After forty-eight years of marriage, he suddenly felt empty and lost. His closest friends would call and try to get him to go out for dinner. But he didn't feel like leaving the house. Usually irrepressibly optimistic, Kraft was depressed.

Brady visited him regularly during the summer. Being around Brady made Kraft recognize that his only hope of making it through the grief was to be around the team. So he spent as much time as he could at the stadium. The players had decided they wanted to dedicate the 2011 season to Myra. Kraft decided to have her initials, *MHK*, stitched into the Patriots' uniforms. It would be the first time that the name of an owner's wife appeared on an NFL uniform. On short notice, Goodell approved the idea.

It was official—the 2011 season would be played in honor of Myra.

In 2010, Brady had played so nearly perfectly that he became the first unanimous choice for the Associated Press NFL Most Valuable Player Award since the news organization had begun using a nationwide panel of media members who cover the league to choose the honoree. Brady had received all fifty votes. On the day the award was announced, he had sat for an interview with NFL Network analyst Michael Lombardi. "You scored 518 points," Lombardi said. "You led the league in scoring. How can you make the Patriots offense better next year?"

It was a good question. But for Brady, it wasn't a new one. Throughout his career, he'd always been driven by the quest to go from best to even better. One reason he maintained a competitive edge over his opponents was that he never felt he had mastered quarterbacking; there was always room for improvement. Belichick had the same mind-set toward coaching. When his teams won by large margins, rather than celebrate, he'd zero in on little mistakes that needed to be eliminated before facing the next opponent. The key was to never become complacent, either as an individual or as a team.

By the time the 2011 season opened on *Monday Night Football* in Miami on September 12, Belichick had made adjustments to the offense that were intended to make it even more potent than it had been the prior year. On their second offensive series, the Patriots went without a huddle. With Brady calling plays on the fly, it took him just over three minutes to drive the offense seventy-eight yards before throwing a touchdown pass to Gronkowski.

Teams typically resort to a no-huddle offense when they are behind and time is running out. Against Miami, Belichick used it for almost the entire game. By doing so, he took the play-calling responsibility away from the coaching staff and put it solely on Brady, enabling him to survey the defense at the line of scrimmage and make adjustments based on what he saw. At one point, when New England was on its own one-yard line, Brady recognized that Miami was going to blitz. Standing in the shotgun formation, he called a quick pass play to Welker, who caught the perfectly timed throw and raced ninety-nine yards for a touchdown that tied an NFL record. The Dolphins' defense was on its heels and exhausted all night. Brady had the most prolific performance of his career, throwing for 517 yards. Dating all the way back to the 1950s, there had only been four instances when an NFL quarterback had thrown for that many yards in a game. New England won 38–24.

A week later, in New England's home opener, Belichick went with the no-huddle offense again. This time, Brady threw for 423 yards, and the Patriots beat the Chargers 35–21 to improve to 2-0. After just two games, Brady had thrown for almost a thousand yards. And while Welker remained his favorite target, the biggest change in the Patriots offense was the emergence of Gronkowski and Hernandez. Through the first two games, Gronkowski caught ten passes for 172 yards and three touchdowns, and Hernandez hauled in fourteen passes for 165 yards and two touchdowns. That was unprecedented production from the tight end position.

Teams just didn't know how to defend against two big, athletically gifted tight ends who were on the field at the same time. Gronkowski was so strong that he simply ran people over. In a game against the Redskins, he fully extended himself while diving to catch a pass at midfield. Before a defender could touch him, he leapt to his feet and began to run with the ball. One defender jumped on his back while another slammed full speed into Gronkowski's legs and latched on to his waist. He dragged both defenders ten yards before shrugging them off. He lumbered twenty more yards, staying upright after being submarined in the ankles by a third defender, and eventually was taken down by a fourth defender after gaining fifty yards on the play. As for

Hernandez, he tended to make defenders miss. He was nearly impossible to cover one-on-one, and once he got the ball in the open field, he was hard to corral.

During a dark time for Kraft, the two tight ends were a welcome bright spot. One was loud and fun-loving; the other was quiet and kept to himself. Gronkowski made thunderous spikes when he scored and had become a viral sensation on social media. After he posed shirtless for pictures with a college friend's girlfriend, who was wearing his jersey, Gronkowski subsequently learned that his friend's girlfriend was an adult-film star with a significant following on Twitter. When she posted pictures of herself with "Gronk," he found himself in unwanted headlines, such as "Porn Star Calls Rob Gronkowski 'A gentleman,'" and "Get the Gronk Party Started." He went to Kraft and apologized for any embarrassment he had caused the franchise. Kraft appreciated his remorse, but he wasn't concerned. Gronkowski always had his family around him. And he had an infectious upbeat personality that permeated the locker room. After the Twitter episode with the porn star, Kraft patted him on the back, and told him to keep his chin up. "You're on the New England Patriots now. Things like that will be taken out of context because we are in the public eye. So just watch out for yourself."

Hernandez was much more low-key and never had any family around. But he had observed how Kraft was always surrounded by his sons, and that they frequently kissed their father on the cheek. Hernandez started kissing Kraft on the cheek every time he saw him. And he told Kraft how lucky he felt to be a Patriot and to be wearing Myra's initials on his jersey.

In 2011, Aaron Hernandez's college teammate Tim Tebow was the biggest story in sports. After the Broncos began the season 1-4, the starting quarterback was benched in favor of Tebow. An outspoken evangelical Christian, Tebow led the Broncos on a historic winning streak that *Sports Illustrated* called "amazing," "incredible," "mind-blowing," and "incomprehensible." In an eight-week span, Denver won seven games. In six of those games, Tebow orchestrated last-minute comebacks, including three in overtime. Genuflecting after touchdowns and openly crediting Jesus Christ for his success, Tebow had become the most discussed and controversial figure in sports. *New York Times* columnist Frank Bruni dubbed him "the mile-high Messiah."

With Tebow Mania at a fever pitch and the Broncos on a six-game winning streak, the 10-3 Patriots traveled to Denver for a showdown at Mile High Stadium. CBS aired the game in more markets than any other game in

2011, and it drew the highest ratings of any regular season game on the network since the Patriots-Colts game in 2007. When Tebow scored the game's first touchdown, he ignited the crowd with his end zone celebration and his fist-pumping along the sideline. Just over two minutes later, Brady threw a thirty-three-yard touchdown pass to Chad Johnson. After Denver built a 16-7 lead, Brady threw a touchdown to Hernandez. Then Brady ran one in on a quarterback keeper. Tebow couldn't keep pace. Hernandez caught nine passes for 129 yards. New England pummeled Denver 41–23, ending Tebow's streak of heart-stopping finishes and elevating the Patriots to the best record in the NFL.

"We're gonna meet again," Brady told Tebow afterward. "I've got this feeling."

At the start of the 2011 season, Patriots offensive lineman Matt Light commissioned renowned artist Brian Fox to paint a tribute to Myra Kraft. It was intended to be a surprise gift for Robert. All the players and coaches pitched in. Fox had previously painted portraits of Jackie Robinson, Keith Richards, Muhammad Ali, and Jim Morrison. For this special occasion, he painted a huddle of Patriots reaching upward toward the initials *MHK*.

On Christmas Eve, the Patriots came from behind to beat the Dolphins at Gillette Stadium. After the game, Light presented the painting to Kraft. Surrounded by his players, Kraft was moved to tears. He had the portrait placed in his office.

A week later, the Patriots played the final game of the regular season at home against Buffalo. New England needed a win to clinch the top seed in the playoffs. But in the second quarter, the Bills went up 21–0. Before halftime, Kraft told Al Labelle to go to his office, retrieve the painting, and put it on an easel in the center of the Patriots' locker room. When the team came in for halftime, every player saw the painting. No one said a word. In the second half, the Patriots scored forty-nine unanswered points.

When the Patriots got the ball back with 1:30 to play, Belichick sat his starters and sent in backup quarterback Brian Hoyer and the rest of the second string to run out the clock. Gronkowski approached and asked to go back in. He was seven yards shy of setting the all-time record for receiving yards by a tight end. Belichick sent him out for one more play, and Hoyer tossed him a twenty-two-yard pass, giving him 1,327 receiving yards on the season. Gronkowski also set a new NFL record for touchdown receptions by a tight end, with seventeen.

It had been that kind of year for New England. The team finished 13-3, giving them the best record in the AFC for the second year in a row. Brady had improved on his MVP season from a year earlier, throwing for a career-high 5,235 yards, surpassing his record-setting total back in 2007. Wes Welker led the league in receptions with 122. Hernandez and Gronkowski were the most productive tight end tandem in NFL history, combining for over 2,200 yards and twenty-four touchdowns. And Belichick became the only coach in league history with at least thirteen regular season wins in five different seasons.

But heading into the playoffs, Belichick reminded his team that it was now a one-game season. They had worked hard for an entire year to get back to the same position that they had been in twelve months earlier when they had lost to the Jets in the first round of the playoffs. This time they'd be facing red-hot Tim Tebow and the Broncos. While the Patriots enjoyed a first-round bye due to being the top-seeded team, the Broncos had defeated Pittsburgh in the wild-card round when Tebow threw an eighty-yard game-winning touchdown pass in overtime. His heroics had made him the talk of the country and cast an unusually bright spotlight on his rematch with Brady and the Patriots on January 14, 2012, in Foxborough.

Four years had gone by since the Patriots last won a playoff game. For most teams, four years without a playoff victory was the norm. But for the Patriots in the Belichick-Brady era, a four-year drought was a novelty. On the night before the Broncos game, Belichick challenged his players to "do your job," and "play as a team."

The national spotlight was on Tebow. But Brady was the star. On the first drive, he went with the no-huddle offense, and he put Hernandez in the backfield as a running back. Brady completed a pass to Gronkowski. Then Hernandez ran the ball for forty-three yards. Then Brady threw a touchdown to Welker. Less than two minutes into the game, New England led 7-0. By halftime, Brady had thrown five touchdown passes, the most in NFL postseason history. Three of them were caught by Gronkowski, tying him for the most touchdown catches in a half in NFL postseason history. On the Patriots' first drive of the second half, Brady threw his sixth touchdown pass, to put New England up 42-7. This one went to Hernandez, who ran to the sideline after scoring, looked up toward the owner's box, and saluted Kraft.

"The rout is on," said CBS announcer Jim Nantz. He and color analyst Phil Simms were in agreement that they were witnessing the greatest, most dominant playoff performance of Brady's twelve-year career. Tebow was an afterthought. The Patriots destroyed the Broncos 45–10.

Afterward, Brady's influence on Gronkowski was evident when a CBS sideline reporter corralled them for a postgame interview on the field.

"What's it feel like to come out and hang forty-five points up, throw for six touchdowns, and three of them to this guy?" the reporter said to Brady.

"Well, the skill guys had a great day," Brady said, downplaying his role. "The offensive line blocked great. There was good execution. There's definitely things that we could have done better."

Done better? The reporter tried to get Brady to take some credit.

"It sounds rhetorical," Brady said. "But it's all about next week."

As Brady spoke, Gronkowski listened intently, studying his mannerisms and the way he deflected praise. When the reporter turned to him, Gronkowski followed Brady's lead.

"Gronk, three touchdowns," the reporter said. "And a couple of them were pretty nice catches. How's it feel?"

"It's a one-game season," Gronkowski said. "We played well. The offense played great. The whole defense played great."

"Hernandez," the reporter said. "Talk about how you two play off each other."

"Hernandez is a beast," Gronkowski said. "I love playing with him. I just can't wait to get back out there together this week."

After Brady's performance against Denver, the *New York Times* declared him "the pre-eminent quarterback of his generation." The victory also gave Brady and Belichick their fifteenth postseason win together, pushing them past the mark set by the Steelers' coach-quarterback tandem of Chuck Noll and Terry Bradshaw in the seventies. On January 22, 2012, the Patriots were back in the AFC Championship game for the sixth time in eleven seasons during the Brady-Belichick era. Once again, they faced the hard-nosed Baltimore Ravens, the team that had dominated them in the playoffs two years earlier.

Prior to the game, Gillette Stadium resembled a homecoming. Kraft asked family friend Steven Tyler, of Aerosmith, to sing the national anthem. And Kraft invited former players Drew Bledsoe, Troy Brown, Ty Law, and Tedy Bruschi to come back to Foxborough, serve as honorary team captains, and sit with him and his family in his suite. After sitting beside Myra during every Patriots home game for sixteen years, Kraft had not gotten used to having an empty seat to his right on game days. For the AFC Championship, he asked Bruschi to take Myra's seat.

The Ravens were a much stiffer challenge than the Broncos had been. Led

by Ray Lewis, Baltimore's menacing defense battered New England, holding them to one rushing touchdown and three field goals through three quarters. With eleven minutes to play, the Patriots trailed 20–16 and Gronkowski had left the game after tearing the ligaments in his ankle. Facing a critical fourth-and-goal situation from the Ravens' one-yard line, Brady took the snap and vaulted over the linemen, breaking the plane of the goal line with the ball. While he was airborne and his back was exposed, Lewis speared Brady in the kidneys with his helmet. Brady flipped over and landed in a heap. Emerging from the pile, he spiked the ball, igniting the crowd. New England led 23–20.

But the Ravens drove downfield and got in position to tie the game and send it into overtime. With fifteen seconds left on the game clock, Ravens All-Pro kicker Billy Cundiff lined up for a thirty-two-yard field goal. In two years, Cundiff had never missed a field goal in the fourth quarter. But he inexplicably hooked this one wide left, sending Gillette Stadium into a frenzy.

In the owner's suite, former Patriots players were jumping up and down with Aerosmith's lead singer. Bledsoe slapped Jonathan Kraft's hands so hard he nearly knocked him over. Robert turned to Bruschi and the two men held each other tight. No one could believe that Cundiff had missed the kick.

"Myra blew it left," Kraft told Bruschi.

At the trophy presentation down on the field minutes later, Kraft was flanked by his sons, Brady, and Belichick as Jim Nantz turned the honors over to Drew Bledsoe. The fans chanted "DREW" as the quarterback told Kraft, "I love you," and kissed him on the cheek before handing him the championship trophy.

"I've got two cheeks," Kraft said. "Give me the other cheek."

Bledsoe kissed him again.

Kraft raised the trophy over his head.

"Mr. Kraft," Nantz said. "What a season. How fulfilling it is. And I know it's been emotional every step of the way, too."

Kraft paused. The last thing he wanted to do was break down on national television. "Well, I want to congratulate these great players and the coaches," he said. "They're a great brotherhood. They're a family."

As he spoke, the fans cheered and held up "MHK" and "WIN IT FOR MYRA" signs.

Cradling the trophy, Kraft continued, "All of you in this stadium are family. Thank you for the support you've given us this emotional year."

He touched the *MHK* pin on the lapel of his overcoat, kissed his fingers, looked heavenward, and smiled.

The Patriots were going back to the Super Bowl.

thirty-three

BREAKING BAD

I n the press conference following the AFC Championship game, Belichick listened as a reporter pointed out that he and Brady were the first coach-quarterback tandem in NFL history to reach five Super Bowls together. Belichick tended not to dwell on milestones. Asked if he felt a certain sense of satisfaction from what he and Brady had accomplished together, Belichick was calculated in his response. "Anything that's associated with winning, I'm proud of," he said. "There's no quarterback I'd rather have than Tom Brady. He's the best. He does so much for us in so many ways on so many different levels. I'm very fortunate that he's our quarterback and what he's able to do for this team. It's good to win with him and all the rest of our players."

By Belichick's standards, this was high praise. Typically, he didn't single out Brady. Even when served up questions specifically designed to get him to talk about his longtime partner, Belichick often demurred.

Brady had become conditioned to hearing more criticism than compliments. A few minutes later, he stood at the same microphone and beat himself up for not having played better. Downplaying that he had scored the game-winning touchdown, he focused on the fact that he had thrown a couple of interceptions. "As a quarterback, you never want to turn the ball over," Brady said. "You want to hit the open guys. You want to capitalize. I wish I would have done a better job of that today. . . . I'm glad we're moving on. I hope I can do better in a few weeks."

Later, a reporter asked Brady to talk about his relationship with his father. Trying not to get emotional, Brady said that his dad had been his childhood idol. Then he paused for a moment to reflect on his upbringing. "It's great to grow up in a house where you are supported by your mom and dad," he continued. "I certainly wouldn't be standing here if I didn't have the loving support of my parents and my sisters."

The coach-quarterback relationship is very much like a marriage. And in the hypercompetitive, ultra-stressful world of professional football, the Belichick-Brady marriage had endured the longest and produced the most success. What separated them from everyone else was their mental toughness. Belichick defined mental toughness as doing your best for the team when everything's not going right for you personally. Brady epitomized that definition.

Shortly after Belichick and Brady left Gillette Stadium following the Ravens game, New York Giants head coach Tom Coughlin stood in the visitors' locker room at Candlestick Park in San Francisco, where his team had just upset the 49ers in the NFC Championship game. Eli Manning had turned in a gritty performance, and Coughlin didn't need a journalist to prod him to talk about his quarterback.

"Eli's just so . . . so . . . reliable," Coughlin told *Sports Illustrated* writer Peter King. "Totally reliable. Trustworthy. Smart. Tremendously hardworking. Consistent as the day is long. What I love about him is, I know what he's doing three hundred and sixty-five days a year. He's doing something that will help us win football games."

The Patriots and Giants were headed for a rematch in Super Bowl XLVI in Indianapolis.

From a ratings standpoint, the NFL could not have scripted anything more compelling than a Super Bowl sequel involving the Giants and Patriots. The Giants jumped out to an early 9–0 lead before the Patriots' offense started clicking in the second quarter. Near the end of the first half, Brady threw a touchdown pass to put his team up 10–9. Then on the opening drive of the second half, Brady drove his team the length of the field again, connecting with Hernandez for another touchdown to put the Patriots up 17–9. In the end zone, Hernandez celebrated by pretending to crack open a bank vault, take the money, and toss it in the air. Walking off the field, Brady tapped the *MHK* patch on his jersey, looked up, and pointed to the sky. The season dedicated to Myra Kraft was headed for a storybook ending.

But after the Giants kicked two field goals to pull within two points, the Patriots' offense sputtered. With Gronkowski hampered by a gimpy ankle, the Patriots struggled to put the game away. Late in the fourth quarter, normally sure-handed Wes Welker dropped a pass that would have given the Patriots a decisive first down and made it virtually impossible for the Giants

to get the ball back in time to score. Instead, New England was forced to punt. And with 3:46 remaining and the Giants on their own twelve-yard line, Eli Manning jogged onto the field. The Patriots' defense faced a situation ominously reminiscent of the one they had encountered at the end of the previous Super Bowl against the Giants.

Methodically marching his team downfield, Manning completed a remarkable thirty-eight-yard pass to Mario Manningham, whose acrobatic, sideline reception drew comparisons to the Helmet Catch. Two and a half minutes later, the Giants scored to take the lead 21–17 with less than a minute to play.

With so little time to work with, Brady advanced his team almost to midfield before being forced to launch a Hail Mary pass sixty-eight yards through the air on the game's final play. After being tipped by Hernandez in the end zone, the ball fell to the ground just beyond Gronkowski's outstretched hands. For the second time in four years, the Patriots had lost a heartbreaker to the Giants in the final minute.

With confetti falling inside a raucous Lucas Oil Stadium, Robert Kraft stood alone in his suite, hands in his pockets, a blank expression on his face, staring straight ahead like a man looking into an abyss. Then, finally, he gazed up, as if searching for Myra. He had wanted this so bad for her.

The Patriots-Giants Super Bowl was the most-watched program in American television history, drawing 166.8 million viewers. More than half of the US population had watched at least some of the broadcast. The game also set the record for the most tweets per second during a sporting event. For more than a decade, games involving Tom Brady, Bill Belichick, and the New England Patriots had continued to captivate audiences. But the second devastating loss to the Giants left the impression that the sun might finally be setting on the Patriots' epic run.

"They have won three titles," observed *New York Times* football writer Judy Battista, "but none since the 2004 season, casting their dynasty into the distance while the Giants are the only repeat champion of the last five years."

Chin up, Belichick praised his players for their effort and credited the Giants for their hard-fought victory. Brady complimented Manning. "Eli made some great throws in the fourth quarter," he said, "and deserved to win. They did a better job than we did."

Brady added, "It always comes down to one or two plays in this game. If you make it, you're celebrating. If you don't, you don't sleep for a week. . . . But I'd rather come to this game and lose than not get here."

Kraft took the loss to the Giants hard. But the disappointment in losing a Super Bowl didn't compare with the pain of losing his wife. All season long he'd been going home to an empty house. Everything there reminded him of Myra. Being around the team had helped get him through the fall and early part of the winter, but once the season finally ended, his depression became more acute. He stopped taking care of himself. He wasn't sleeping. The most energetic person in the Patriots organization seldom came to work.

For twelve years, Kraft, Belichick, and Brady had been the everlasting constants in the Patriots' seemingly indestructible dynasty. Naturally, Belichick and Brady garnered most of the credit for what took place on the field. But within the organization, everyone from Belichick down to the players knew that Kraft was the ringleader. "The most important thing in any organization is the mental toughness of the owner," retired linebacker Tedy Bruschi said. "People talk about the players' mental toughness, but the owner has to have it more than anybody else."

Jonathan Kraft had been at his father's side through every up and down since Robert had purchased the team nearly twenty years earlier. But he had never seen his father struggle the way he had been since Myra's passing. Jonathan and his brothers feared they were losing him.

"You hear about couples married for fifty years," Jonathan said, "whose lives were totally intertwined, and when one loses their partner, the other doesn't want to live. They degrade very quickly."

Jonathan couldn't bear the thought of losing his father. Nor could his brothers. They each spoke to Robert separately in the spring of 2012, expressing their concerns, and stressing the importance of finding a path out of the deep mourning he was in. They reminded him that Myra would want him to recommit himself to his businesses, to reconnect with his friends, and to reinvest in the philanthropic work that the two of them had championed throughout their married life.

They also told their father that it was critical for him to find companionship. It was a sensitive subject to broach. But Jonathan made the case that Myra would want him to find happiness.

One of Kraft's closest friends told him the same thing, assuring him that

the last thing Myra would want was to see him sitting home alone, watching television with tears in his eyes.

In the summer of 2012, Kraft was introduced to thirty-two-year-old actress Ricki Lander. She lived in Los Angeles, where they met. On Lander's first trip back east to spend time with Kraft and get to know him better, he decided to take her to New York. Hoping to impress Lander, Kraft brought her to his apartment at the Plaza hotel. He hadn't been there in more than a year. After Myra's death, he had told Brady he was free to use his place whenever he wished. Although Brady and Bündchen had their own New York apartment, they took Kraft up on his offer and would stay at his place whenever they had out-of-town guests using their place.

Thinking his apartment was empty, Kraft brought Lander inside his unit and had her take in the view overlooking Central Park. Then he gave her a tour. When he opened the door to the master bedroom, they unexpectedly came upon a masseuse standing over a beautiful woman lying naked on a massage table. It was Bündchen, whom Kraft referred to as "G."

"G, I didn't realize you were here," Kraft said.

Bündchen didn't flinch. "Hello, Robert."

Flummoxed, Lander looked at Kraft.

"Don't worry," Bündchen said in her Portuguese accent. "He's friends with my husband."

Kraft smiled at Lander and turned up his hands. "Welcome to my life," he said.

The masseuse resumed, and Kraft led Lander back to the living room, where a framed picture of Kraft with Brady and Elton John was propped on a table.

Lander decided that Kraft was going to be a lot of fun to be around.

Kraft found her sunny disposition attractive. He ended up spending the rest of the summer with her.

Kraft's sons were encouraged.

Bill Belichick had two top priorities in the offseason: signing both of his star tight ends to long-term contract extensions. In 2011, Gronkowski and Hernandez had rocked the league. Each of them had played more than one thousand snaps in the same season, a remarkable achievement in the modern era. Gronkowski's outsized physique and freakish athleticism—he had a thirty-three-inch vertical leap to go along with the strength of an interior lineman—made him impossible to cover one-on-one. And there seemed to

be no limit to Hernandez's versatility—in the playoff game against Denver, the speedy tight end had lined up twenty-one times at running back. Both players had two years remaining on the contracts they had signed as rookies. Belichick decided to tear up those agreements in favor of new ones. He started negotiating with Gronkowski's agent first.

One issue that came up in Gronkowski's contract talks was his larger-than-life, off-the-field persona. After just two seasons, Gronk had developed a reputation as the Patriots' most colorful character and the league's top party animal. *Sports Illustrated* dubbed him "a patron saint of meatheads . . . the league's best hope and worst nightmare." After the AFC Championship victory over the Ravens, Gronkowski had been interviewed by a reporter for ESPN's Spanish channel, Deportes. Asked in both Spanish and English if he planned to celebrate, Gronkowski smiled and quipped, "Si, yo soy fiesta," which translates to: "Yes, I am party." The phrase was a viral sensation and earned Gronkowski the nickname "El Gronko."

Over the summer of 2012, Gronkowski was living up to his "I am party" reputation. He sang "Sexy and I Know It" onstage at a televised karaoke event in Boston. He cohosted *Access Hollywood Live*. He appeared on the dating show *The Choice*. He got into a wrestling match with his brothers on the red carpet at the ESPY Awards. And he posed naked for the cover of *ESPN The Magazine*. All of this was wildly out of character for the buttoned-up Patriots team, which Belichick ran like a military unit. But Belichick viewed Gronkowski as a harmless kid with a big heart inside an adult body. Gronkowski spent more time with sick children at Boston hospitals than any other player on the roster. He shaved his head to raise money for cancer research. And he donned Patriots pajamas and spent the night on the floor of a children's cancer unit, where he surprised the kids with presents and pushed them around in wheelchairs as if they were race cars. Plus, Gronkowski always had his family around, especially his father. They were best friends.

Then there was the bottom line—at twenty-three, Gronkowski was already the best tight end in the league. Belichick signed him to a six-year, $54 million extension. Averaging $9 million per year, the salary made Gronkowski the highest-paid tight end in league history.

Unlike Gronkowski, Aaron Hernandez maintained a very low profile. Other than his on-the-field exploits, he stayed out of the headlines. There were no tweets about his posing with a porn star or viral video clips of him showing off his bilingual skills or singing karaoke at a nightclub. Nor did he pose

shirtless in selfies with fans or appear nude on a sports magazine cover. It wasn't that Hernandez didn't have an off-the-field persona. He did. But he had worked hard to keep it hidden. When Belichick negotiated with Hernandez's agent, he was focused on the tight end's future, not his past. But by the summer of 2012, Hernandez's past had caught up with him.

Hernandez had been an eighteen-year-old freshman at the University of Florida when the television drama *Breaking Bad* went on the air in January 2008. Critically acclaimed as one of the greatest shows ever, the series centered on the fictional character Walter White, a depressed high school chemistry teacher who secretly turned to a life of crime, making and selling meth. His sidekick was Jesse Pinkman, an eighteen-year-old former student, who was lost and struggling to find his way when his teacher reentered his life and convinced him to become his partner in his meth operation. A tortured soul to begin with, Pinkman got in way over his head and eventually became a killer.

The trajectory of Hernandez's real life was eerily similar to Pinkman's fictional one. Unbeknownst to the Patriots, Hernandez had grown up in a turbulent home. His father, Dennis Hernandez, an imposing former football player whose nickname was "The King," had beaten him when he was a child. The abuse was often triggered by the smallest things. Sometimes Hernandez was beaten for no apparent reason at all. His father also had numerous brushes with the law, including an arrest for attempting to purchase cocaine from an undercover police officer.

Hernandez's mother had an arrest record, too. When Aaron was eleven, she faced charges for her role in an underground sports-gambling operation that she was allegedly operating out of the home. Although Hernandez's mother kicked her husband out of the house more than once, she repeatedly welcomed him back.

Afraid of his father and estranged from his mother, Hernandez spent his teen years with a group of peers who were petty criminals. Then, when Hernandez was sixteen, his father unexpectedly died. A year later, Hernandez left high school partway through his senior year to attend the University of Florida on a football scholarship. He was just seventeen. He later told his mother: "I was the happiest fucking little kid in the world, and you fucked me up. And I just lost my father, and I had to go to college and I had nobody."

By the time Hernandez left college and was drafted by the Patriots, his friends back home had graduated to more serious criminal activity involving illegal drugs, weapons, and violence. With his new NFL salary, Hernandez hired two of his hometown friends to be his "personal assistants." By the end

of the 2011 season, Hernandez was using drugs supplied by one of them, and he had become obsessed with guns. At one point during Hernandez's new contract negotiations, his agent, Brian Murphy, visited him at home. Attempting to impress on his client the idea that his new contract would cause people to respect him, Murphy nonetheless pointed out that a contract wasn't going to define Hernandez as a person. "No, no," Hernandez told his agent. "I get my respect through weapons." He then pulled out a firearm from his closet. Despite knowing that his client had serious issues off the field, Murphy didn't think it was his place to disclose that information to the Patriots.

On July 15, 2012, "Live Free or Die"—the first episode of the final season of *Breaking Bad*—aired on AMC. In it, Jesse Pinkman, Walter White, and an accomplice cover their tracks after murdering a drug kingpin. Coincidentally, hours after the episode aired, Hernandez was involved with his first murder. That night, Hernandez and his marijuana supplier, a friend named Alexander Bradley, went to Cure, a Boston nightclub. Inside, a stranger named Daniel de Abreu allegedly bumped into Hernandez and accidentally spilled a drink on him, then walked away without apologizing. Later, around 2:30 a.m., Bradley pulled up to a traffic light near Cure, and Hernandez spotted de Abreu and another man in the car beside them. The window in Hernandez's vehicle went down and five shots were fired into de Abreu's vehicle, killing de Abreu and passenger Safiro Furtado. Hernandez and his friend sped off.

By morning, the Boston Police Department had determined that the two victims were legal immigrants from Cape Verde who worked together at a local cleaning company. Neither of them had a criminal record. With no witnesses, no murder weapon, and no apparent motive, the police opened an investigation into the double homicide.

A little over a month later, Hernandez signed a $40 million contract extension with the Patriots on August 26, 2012. It included a $12.5 million signing bonus, which was the largest for a tight end in NFL history. Hernandez was just twenty-two.

The following day, the Patriots organization held its annual Kick Off Gala at Gillette Stadium. The annual fund-raiser raised millions for charity. At the event, Hernandez announced he was donating $50,000 to the Myra Kraft Giving Back Fund. He personally handed a check to Robert Kraft, hugged him, and kissed his cheek.

"You can't come here and act reckless and do your own stuff," Hernandez told the media that night. "You get changed by Bill Belichick's way. You get

changed by the Patriot Way. And now that I'm a Patriot, I have to start living like one and making the right decisions for them."

By this time, homicide detectives in Boston had obtained security-camera footage from inside the nightclub where the two drive-by-shooting victims had last been seen alive. While reviewing the tape, the lead detective was surprised to discover that he recognized one of the patrons. "There's Aaron Hernandez!" he said.

"Where?" his partner said.

"Right there!" the detective said, pointing him out.

They both got a kick out of the fact that Hernandez had happened to be in the club that night.

"Why don't we talk to Aaron?" the partner kidded.

"Ha," the lead detective said. "No, no."

The police had no reason to suspect Hernandez.

Neither did the Patriots.

The 2012 season began with Rob Gronkowski on the cover of the *Sports Illustrated* NFL preview issue, which predicted that the Patriots' tight end and his youthful counterpart, Hernandez, would be a key to thirty-five-year-old Tom Brady's becoming the first quarterback in NFL history to reach six Super Bowls. "He wants to play until he's forty," the magazine's scouting report said, "but the sands of the hourglass are pouring out."

The Denver Broncos were expected to be the team that challenged the Patriots for supremacy in the AFC. During the offseason, thirty-six-year-old Peyton Manning had joined the Broncos after being released by the Colts following multiple neck surgeries that had forced him to sit out the 2011 season. When the Colts opted to move on from their franchise player in favor of up-and-coming quarterback Andrew Luck, Manning chose to finish his career in Denver, where he felt he had his best chance of obtaining a second Super Bowl ring.

By 2012, Brady and Manning were universally regarded as the two best quarterbacks of the twenty-first century. Their twelve head-to-head encounters between 2001 and 2010 had fueled the Patriots-Colts rivalry. Brady had bested Manning in eight of those contests and gone on to win three Super Bowls compared to Manning's one. On October 7, 2012, Manning returned to Gillette Stadium with his new team. Brady and the Patriots prevailed 31–21, dropping the Broncos to 2-3. But thereafter, Manning led his team on an eleven-game winning streak to finish with the AFC's best record at 13-3.

Brady, meanwhile, led the Patriots to the second-best record in the AFC at 12-4. For the third consecutive season, the Patriots had one of the most prolific offense in the league, scoring 557 points and becoming just the second team in NFL history to score more than 500 points in three consecutive seasons.

But throughout the 2012 season, Gronkowski and Hernandez were banged up and seldom appeared in games together. Hernandez missed six games at the beginning of the year with an ankle injury. Gronkowski played the first half of the season with excruciating back pain. Then, a few weeks after Hernandez returned, Gronkowski broke his forearm in the tenth game of the season, forcing him to undergo surgery. Two weeks after Gronkowski went down, Hernandez injured his shoulder. Despite needing surgery, Hernandez played the remainder of the season. Still, Brady threw for nearly five thousand yards and threw the just eight interceptions. His favorite target remained Wes Welker.

On the field, Hernandez continued to impress, playing through pain and demonstrating a willingness to do everything the coaches asked of him. In the locker room, however, his behavior had become more and more erratic. Before the start of the 2012 season, the Patriots had signed free agent wide receiver Brandon Lloyd. On Lloyd's first day as a Patriot, he was heading into the locker room when Wes Welker tapped him on the shoulder.

"He's looking at me wide-eyed in my face," Lloyd told the *Boston Globe*, "and he says, 'Your locker is in between Gronkowski and Hernandez. I just want to warn you that he's [Hernandez's] going to talk about being bathed by his mother. He's going to have his genitalia out in front of you while you're sitting on your stool. He's going to have his towel and try to dry off in front of you while you're sitting at your locker. He's going to talk about gay sex. Just do your best to ignore it. Even walk away.'"

Lloyd became a critical part of the Patriots' offense. He caught seventy-four passes for 911 yards in 2012. But as the season progressed, Welker's warning about Hernandez rang true to Lloyd. "There would be swings where he would be the most hypermasculine aggressive individual in the room, where he'd be ready to fight somebody in fits of rage," Lloyd said. "Or he'd be the most sensitive person in the room, talking about cuddling with his mother. Or he'd ask me, 'Do you think I'm good enough to play?' So we had these moments where we'd get along well. But there were also these moments where he was ready to rage out on other players in the locker room."

Brady tried to be a steadying influence on Hernandez, encouraging him by example and through conversation to embrace the Patriot Way. But

Hernandez increasingly spent his discretionary time with his friends from nearby Bristol, Connecticut, some of whom were ex-cons. The Patriots players didn't know how deep Hernandez was in. But everyone in the locker room recognized that his friends were trouble. It reached a point where more than one player diplomatically asked Hernandez not to bring his friends around.

Brady was fired up. Gronkowski had returned to the lineup in time for the playoffs. With a surgically implanted metal plate that had been screwed into the bones of his forearm, Gronkowski put the Patriots' offense at full strength. But on the Patriots' eighth offensive play of the divisional-round playoff game against the Houston Texans, Gronkowski caught a pass and landed with all of his body weight on his forearm, refracturing it and ending his postseason. The starting running back also went down in the first quarter. The Patriots adjusted. Hernandez and Welker stepped up. And Brady threw for 344 yards and three touchdowns, leading the Patriots to a 41–28 victory.

The Patriots expected to head to Denver for the AFC Championship game. But Manning and the Broncos were upset at home by the Ravens in the divisional round. So for the second consecutive year, the Patriots hosted Ray Lewis and the Ravens in the AFC Championship game in Foxborough, on January 20, 2013.

Despite being without Gronkowski, the Patriots were favored and jumped out to a 13–7 halftime lead. In Brady's career, he was 68-0 at home after leading at halftime. But Lewis had declared before the game that he was retiring after the season. He was the emotional leader of his team, and his teammates knew that Lewis didn't want his career to end with a loss to the hated Patriots. In the second half, the Ravens' defense rallied behind Lewis and shut out the Patriots, and the Ravens' offense scored three touchdowns. With Patriots fans already flocking to the parking lots and his team trailing 28–13 in the final minutes, Brady nonetheless drove downfield. His final pass completion was to Aaron Hernandez with a minute and a half to play. Brady's next pass was intercepted, effectively ending the game.

On the Ravens' sideline, Lewis shed tears of joy while his teammates gloated. "The Ravens are going to the Super Bowl!" outspoken Ravens linebacker Terrell Suggs shouted. "The Ravens are going to the Super Bowl. Shut out in the second half! In Foxborough!"

Brady trudged off the field, head down.

In the Ravens locker room, Suggs kept up his tirade. "These are the most arrogant pricks in the world, starting with Belichick on down," he said to the press. But eventually, he walked back his statements. "What would this league be like without Twelve and the New England Patriots?" he said. "People don't like them because they win. They're a great team. And they have every right to be who they are."

thirty-four

MOVING ON

Back in the summer of 2010, Tom Brady had undergone a physical with the Patriots medical staff. He had just completed his first full season since undergoing reconstructive knee surgery, and the team wanted to see how his knee was holding up. Brady sailed through the exam, and in particular, his knee looked strong. Still, the team doctor had concerns about the long-term stability and health of Brady's knee. Those concerns were based almost entirely on metrics that suggested football players were highly susceptible to recurring injury in a reconstructed knee three years after the surgery.

By the summer of 2013, it was clear that those warnings didn't apply to Brady. Four seasons removed from knee surgery, he had started all seventy-one regular season and playoff games for the Patriots. And between 2010 and 2012 he had had three of the most prolific seasons of his career. He was now thirty-five, but instead of slowing down with age, he seemed to be getting stronger.

Brady's durability was hard for doctors to explain. Other than the knee injury that had forced him to miss the 2008 season, he had played twelve seasons without missing a game because of injury. In the NFL, that kind of streak was virtually unheard of. A big part of Brady's success was due to extreme lifestyle changes that he had begun implementing as far back as 2004 when he started seeing Alex Guerrero, a personal trainer who had studied traditional Chinese medicine before opening a rehabilitation practice in Los Angeles, where he worked on elite track-and-field athletes. Brady met Guerrero during training camp in 2004, when Guerrero was a personal trainer for Patriots linebacker Willie McGinest. During camp that year, Brady had elbow tendinitis, and it had reached a point where he couldn't throw without pain. He'd been through all sorts of traditional treatments—ice, heat, electrostimulation, chiropractic therapy, stretching. When nothing that the training staff tried worked, McGinest told Brady he knew a guy.

Desperate for pain relief, Brady called Guerrero, who determined that the true source of the problem wasn't in Brady's elbow. Rather, it was extreme tightness in his forearm and biceps, the muscular regions below and above his elbow. Despite Brady's high pain threshold, he nearly came up off the treatment table when Guerrero started manipulating the balled-up muscles in his arm. But after his first treatment, Brady experienced a dramatic reduction in elbow pain. After further treatments, he was throwing without pain.

Through those sessions, Guerrero suggested that Brady needed to elongate his muscles to make them more pliable. Traditional training for football players had long consisted of a great deal of weight lifting. But continual use of free weights, Guerrero explained, put tremendous wear and tear on the joints. The constriction and accumulation of muscle mass also made athletes more prone to muscle tears.

"Why doesn't everyone know about this?" Brady asked Guerrero.

It was a good question that went to the heart of how football players train and recover from injuries. By and large, professional football teams had been following the weight-lifting approach for decades because it was geared to increase strength and build muscle mass.

But Guerrero steered Brady away from weight lifting toward the use of ropes, bands, and exercise balls. He also implemented a more holistic approach to training that focused on hydration, nutrition, supplements, and cognitive fitness.

Brady had already embraced Guerrero's methods prior to his knee surgery. But after the surgery, Guerrero put him through an aggressive rehab program that enabled him to return to full strength faster than anticipated. At the same time, Brady stepped up his commitment to hydration—drinking a minimum of one hundred ounces of water per day, coupled with lots of electrolytes—and a strict diet that avoided sugar, caffeine, dairy products, bleached flour, and foods that cause inflammation, such as tomatoes.

Brady's effectiveness was so pronounced that teammates Wes Welker, Rob Gronkowski, and Julian Edelman started working with Guerrero, too. Edelman nicknamed him Mr. Miyagi, after the karate master in *The Karate Kid*.

Kraft was convinced that Brady still had some of his best years ahead of him. And after the 2012 season ended, he talked to Brady about another contract extension. By this point, Brady had one priority: winning more championships. He'd made a lot of money. He'd won a lot of awards. But the Patriots hadn't won a Super Bowl since 2004. Entering what seemed like the final phase of his career, Brady was determined to make a push for more rings.

With the same goal in mind, Kraft worked with Brady to extend his contract. Based on the deal signed in 2010, the two of them already had an understanding that it was helpful to both parties to sign long-term, guaranteed
contracts that were frontloaded with large signing bonuses to compensate
for lower average salary in the back-end years of the deal. Brady understood
that before the lower-salaried years of his contract kicked in, Kraft would
step in and once again restructure his contract. In the meantime, the Patriots remained under the salary cap and had more flexibility to sign other
players.

In keeping with that philosophy, in February of 2013, Kraft and Brady
agreed to restructure the remaining two years on Brady's 2010 contract and
take a sizable reduction in base salary in exchange for a five-year, $60 million
deal in which all of the money was guaranteed for injury. It was the highest
injury guarantee in the history of the NFL and included a $30 million signing
bonus. And by Brady taking a lower base salary, the Patriots had more cap
space to sign other key players who would improve the Patriots' chances of
winning more Super Bowl championships.

After signing the new contract, Brady posted on his Facebook page, "Just
win."

One of the players that Brady was counting on the Patriots to re-sign
was free agent Wes Welker. In 2012, Welker had once again led the team with
118 receptions and 1,354 receiving yards, making him the first player in NFL
history to have five one-hundred-catch seasons. Since joining the Patriots in
2007, Welker had caught 672 passes for more than 7,400 yards, leading the
franchise in both categories. Even Kraft had publicly stated that he wanted
Welker to be "a Patriot for life."

But Welker's relationship with Belichick was strained, and Belichick
decided he was willing to part with the thirty-one-year-old receiver. So on
March 13, 2013, Welker signed a free agent deal with the Denver Broncos.

Brady was extremely disappointed. So was Kraft.

After six years in Foxborough, Welker was relieved to get away from Belichick. "It was just kind of hard, one of those deals where you have to endure
him, put up with him," Welker told a reporter after he left town. "But he does
it to everybody. It's the way he is."

For Welker, the hardest part of leaving New England was leaving Brady.
He had caught more balls from Brady than any receiver in Patriots history.
He'd also learned a tremendous amount from Brady about how to be a pro-
fessional football player. Playing with him had been the highlight of Welker's

career. But it was on to Denver, where he'd be paired with Brady's rival, Peyton Manning.

On the same day that Welker joined the Broncos, Belichick signed receiver Danny Amendola to a five-year, $31 million contract.

Despite his frustration over various personnel moves by the Patriots, Brady had a lot to look forward to. In the spring, he and Guerrero became business partners and formed TB12 Inc., a Delaware corporation headquartered in Foxborough. The company's mission statement offered a "comprehensive and customized method that fosters accelerated injury recovery and performance longevity in a holistic and prevention-oriented way." Brady and Guerrero opened their first TB12 Performance & Recovery Center next door to Gillette Stadium, renting the space at Patriot Place from Kraft, who supported Brady in establishing his company.

For Kraft, the good news was that Brady was continuing to put down roots in New England.

It was a rough offseason for Rob Gronkowski. In January he had undergone a second surgery on his broken forearm. Shortly thereafter, he developed a staph infection, which required a third surgery to remove the infected hardware in his forearm and put in new hardware. By spring it was evident that the crack in his broken bone still hadn't healed, prompting doctors to take a piece of bone from his hip and paste it into the crack in his forearm.

The bone graft was the fourth surgery on Gronkowski's forearm in five months. Doctors warned that the situation had become career-threatening—his forearm would only withstand so much trauma before becoming permanently compromised. If he incurred another infection or any other complications that required another surgery, Gronkowski would likely be finished as a football player.

Afraid to do anything or go anywhere due to the fragile nature of his arm, Gronkowski curtailed all of his normal activities. No workouts. No running. No going out with friends. During this period, he was also diagnosed with a ruptured disc, which required back surgery.

Normally irrepressibly happy, Gronkowski was demoralized. But his mother was his mainstay, helping him through the infection, the surgeries, and the rehab. She managed his medications, made sure his IVs were changed regularly, and cooked a lot of meals for him. His father and brothers were a big support, too.

In contrast, Aaron Hernandez was mostly on his own when he flew to Los Angeles for shoulder surgery on March 27. The same surgeon who operated on Brady's knee operated on Hernandez. On the eve of the procedure, Brady texted Hernandez: "Good luck! I hope everything goes well. . . . love you my brother and hope to see you soon."

After the surgery, Hernandez remained in Southern California to rehab. Alex Guerrero continued to work with him. One week into the recovery period, Belichick texted Hernandez.

BELICHICK: Just checking in. Sounds like the surgery went well. Hope you are doing ok!! Let me know how things are going. Best, BB

HERNANDEZ: Surgery went well and I'm doing fine and have been with Alex and will continue to be with Alex until it's time to be back at OTAs! [Organized Team Activities.] Hope everything has been well on ur end. Can't wait to get healthy and be back on the field. Ttys ill be in touch.

But Hernandez was far from fine. As chronicled in a six-part *Boston Globe* Spotlight series titled "Gladiator: Aaron Hernandez and Football Inc.," he had become paranoid. Convinced that police suspected him in connection with the drive-by shooting in Boston, Hernandez was behaving erratically. A month before his surgery, he had flown to Florida, where he and Alexander Bradley, who had been in the car with Hernandez when the two men were gunned down in Boston, spent two nights partying at a strip club in Miami. They ended up arguing over the bill. Bradley would eventually testify that later on that night, Hernandez shot him in the face. Despite losing an eye and undergoing numerous surgeries, Bradley declined to identify the shooter to investigators. Sometime later, however, Bradley texted Hernandez: "U left me with one eye and a lot of head trauma. U owe for what u did."

Shortly after telling Belichick that he couldn't wait to get back on the field, Hernandez purchased an armored SUV for $110,000. He obtained more guns and ammunition. And he hired an ex-con to be his bodyguard.

Alex Guerrero, meanwhile, was steadily encouraging Hernandez to make the necessary changes in his life that would lead to happiness for him, his fiancée, and his baby girl.

"At the end of the day its all up to me to be a big enough man to make the changes!" Hernandez texted Guerrero. "U hit it on the head today which made me wake up and hopefully it woke me up enough to stay on a path

that I want to be on and not hit a wrong turn over time like I always have in the past!"

"I know you have it in you," Guerrero texted him.

While Hernandez was telling people he needed to make changes, a teenage jogger in North Attleboro, Massachusetts, discovered a dead body in an industrial park around 5:30 p.m. on June 17. The victim, a twenty-seven-year-old black man from Boston named Odin Lloyd, had been shot six times. Police officers found a set of keys in Lloyd's pocket. They belonged to a rental car that had last been rented to Aaron Hernandez, who lived less than a mile from where Lloyd's body was discovered. That night, police officers showed up at Hernandez's door and asked him about Lloyd and the rental vehicle. Agitated, Hernandez said: "What's with all the questions?" Then he stepped back inside his house, closed the door, and locked it.

The following evening, a squad of state and local police officers returned to Hernandez's upscale neighborhood. With a small crowd of reporters and neighbors gathered outside, investigators searched Hernandez's home, took photographs, and seized items. By that night, Hernandez's connection to the murder investigation was the top story in Boston.

The next morning, June 19, television news trucks were parked outside Gillette Stadium when Kraft arrived at 8 a.m. Informed that Hernandez was working out, Kraft went to the weight room. No one else was around. Kraft motioned for Hernandez to follow him into the deserted office of the team's strength and conditioning coach.

"I want you to look me in the eye," Kraft told Hernandez.

Hernandez met his gaze.

"Did you do it?" Kraft said.

"Mr. Kraft, I didn't do it."

Kraft stared at him.

"I'm completely innocent," Hernandez continued.

Kraft believed him.

"Did you know Odin Lloyd?" Kraft asked.

Hernandez said they knew each other socially.

The conversation lasted less than ten minutes. It ended with Kraft offering to help Hernandez find a lawyer, and Hernandez saying that his agent had already gotten him one. Then Hernandez hugged and kissed him.

Hernandez also met with Belichick, who asked him directly if he was involved in Lloyd's murder. "Absolutely not," Hernandez told him.

But when not facing Kraft or Belichick, Hernandez behaved like a man who knew his time was up. Earlier in the week he had run into Jonathan Kraft in the cafeteria.

"I have something I want to give you," Hernandez told him. "Come with me."

Kraft followed Hernandez to the locker room, where the tight end removed an envelope marked "Jonathan" from his locker and handed it to him.

"Open it," Hernandez told him.

Kraft ripped the seal and removed a photograph of Hernandez's little girl. Puzzled, Kraft looked up at Hernandez.

"Will you do me a favor?" Hernandez said. Before Kraft could answer, Hernandez continued. "When I'm in your office I see all the pictures of your kids. Will you put this in your office? I want you to think of her like your little girl."

Kraft nodded.

A week after Hernandez assured Kraft and Belichick he was innocent, authorities showed up at his home on June 26, read him his rights, and charged him in connection with the death of Odin Lloyd. Jonathan Kraft was working at his desk when he looked up and saw Hernandez on live television, hands behind his back, being escorted to a police cruiser by six plainclothes detectives. He immediately phoned his father in Israel.

"He's being arrested," Jonathan told Robert.

Floored, Robert didn't want to believe it.

"They're taking him out of his home in handcuffs," Jonathan said.

Robert's mind flashed back to something a member of Belichick's staff had said on the day that the team had drafted Hernandez: "Urban Meyer swears by the kid."

Robert and Jonathan conferenced in Belichick, who was on vacation in Croatia, and brought him up to speed.

"Do we know the facts?" Belichick asked.

Robert had no intention of waiting for the judicial process to run its course. The organization had been misled long enough.

"Guys," Jonathan said, "he's being arrested for murder! This is serious."

"We gotta cut him," Robert said.

Although he preferred more facts, Belichick agreed it was the right course of action.

Within an hour, the Patriots issued a statement announcing that Hernandez was no longer a member of the team:

A young man was murdered last week and we extend our sympathies to the family and friends who mourn his loss. Words cannot express the disappointment we feel knowing that one of our players was arrested as a result of this investigation. . . . At this time, we believe this transaction is simply the right thing to do.

The NFL also released a statement:

The involvement of an NFL player in a case of this nature is deeply troubling. The Patriots have released Aaron Hernandez, who will have his day in court. At the same time, we should not forget the young man who was the victim in this case and take this opportunity to extend our deepest sympathy to Odin Lloyd's family and friends.

That afternoon, Hernandez appeared in a packed courtroom and was arraigned on murder charges. Prosecutors said that Lloyd was killed execution-style. Video surveillance showed Hernandez exiting his vehicle in his driveway with a gun shortly after a night-shift worker at the industrial site heard gunshots coming from the area where Lloyd's body was found. Shell casings at the scene matched those found in Hernandez's vehicle.

Hernandez showed no emotion while listening to prosecutors outline the case against him. In three seasons, he had piled up more than two thousand yards and eighteen touchdowns. None of that mattered now. At twenty-three, his promising NFL career was over. He was facing a life sentence without parole.

The next day, the headline in the *New York Times* read: "Former Patriots Tight End Is Charged with Murder." Similar headlines appeared throughout the country. Network news anchors, cable news shows, and ESPN were all covering the story.

Kraft was mortified. Over the course of his lengthy business career, he had been lied to plenty of times. But he'd always had a good nose for dishonesty when he encountered it. It was embarrassing to Kraft to think that he had believed Hernandez right to the very end. And it was grossly disappointing that he had worn the Patriots uniform for three years.

Belichick was stung, too. He had drafted Hernandez, brought him into the fold, and offered him a record contract extension. In hindsight, those decisions were looking worse by the day. Within a week of Hernandez's arrest for the murder of Odin Lloyd, Boston authorities had connected Hernandez to the unsolved double homicide that had taken place outside the nightclub a year earlier. Hernandez's connection to three killings had cast a pall over the entire organization.

The situation still weighed heavily on Belichick when the team returned to Foxborough for the start of the 2013 training camp. On the first day of camp, on July 24, Belichick had a pained look on his face as he ran his hand through his hair and walked to the press room to face the media.

"I'm going to address the situation involving Aaron Hernandez today," he began. "I felt that it was important enough to do that prior to the start of camp. It's a sad day. It's really a sad day on so many levels. Our thoughts and prayers are with the family of the victim. . . . Having someone in your organization involved in a murder investigation is a terrible thing."

Belichick spent seven minutes discussing Hernandez. Belichick usually didn't spend seven seconds talking about players' off-the-field matters. But the Hernandez situation was unprecedented. It was the kind of thing that could destroy an organization's morale and send the team into a tailspin. He was trying to avoid that.

"It's time for the New England Patriots to move forward," Belichick said. "Moving forward consists of what it's always been here. To build a winning football team. To be a strong pillar in the community. To be a team that our fans can be proud of. That's what we're here for."

A short while later, he gathered his players and gave them the same message.

"It's time for the New England Patriots to move on," Belichick told them.

For four years, Julian Edelman had toiled as the Patriots' ultimate all-purpose player. He played defensive back. He played receiver. He returned kicks. And he returned more than seventy punts for nearly a thousand yards and set an all-time NFL record for average yards per return. He also tore his ACL and MCL one year and broke his foot another year. Through it all, Edelman's commitment and intensity level never ebbed.

With Welker's departure, Gronkowski's injuries, and Hernandez's arrest and dismissal, Edelman stepped into a starting role, alongside newcomer Danny Amendola, in 2013. In the season opener, when Amendola went down

with a groin injury, Edelman caught both of Brady's touchdown passes. Four days later, he caught thirteen of Brady's nineteen completions in a Thursday-night game against the Jets. In week three, Edelman led the team in receptions again. And in the Patriots' fourth game of the season, he racked up 118 receiving yards. By the time Rob Gronkowski returned to the lineup in late October, the Patriots were 5-1 and Edelman had emerged as Brady's primary target.

Gronkowski's presence was a boost. With Gronkowski getting stronger by the week, the offense was finally starting to gel when the 7-3 Patriots hosted the 9-1 Broncos in a Sunday night game at Gillette Stadium on November 24. The late-season contest between the two top teams in the AFC took on the feel of a playoff game. Before the kickoff, Broncos receiver Wes Welker was asked about his contentious relationship with Belichick. Reluctant to say too much, Welker made it clear that he was happy to have moved on. He attributed his reticence to say more on the subject to Belichick's lingering influence on him.

"When I'm answering questions from the Denver media," Welker said, "I'm not worried about what the Broncos' people are going to think. I'm worried about what Belichick will think. Isn't that crazy?"

In one of the coldest games ever played at Gillette Stadium, Peyton Manning led the Broncos to a 24–0 halftime lead. In fifty years, only six NFL teams had come back to win after falling so far behind.

But the Patriots scored thirty-one straight points in the second half to take the lead. Two plays exemplified the Patriots' comeback. One was a short pass to Edelman, where he zigged and zagged around two defenders before accelerating toward the goal line and leaping Superman-like into the end zone. The other was a catch in traffic by Gronkowski, who absorbed two big hits and bulldozed four defenders before lunging to the goal line.

The Patriots won in overtime, 34–31. It was the biggest comeback in Brady's career.

With Gronkowski back at full strength, the Patriots' dramatic victory over the Broncos solidified the two teams as the cream of the AFC. But one week later, a defensive player on the Cleveland Browns ran full speed and dove into Gronkowski's knee just as he planted his leg. The force of the blow flipped Gronkowski upside down, causing him to land with all of his weight on his head. He suffered a concussion and blew out his knee, both in the same play. After being carted off the field, Gronkowski ended up in the back of

an ambulance, heading to the hospital. He was dizzy. He was seeing spots. He was nauseous. And his knee was swelling up like a softball. His father sat beside him with a look of grave concern on his face. Heading for his sixth surgery in two years, Gronkowski feared his career was over.

The Patriots finished the season 12-4, and Julian Edelman became just the third player in team history to catch 100 passes for 1,000 yards. But Gronkowski's absence and the loss of other key players was felt in the playoffs. After dominating the Colts in the divisional round 43–22, the Patriots traveled to Denver for a rematch with the Broncos in the AFC Championship game. The Broncos led from the outset, building a 23–3 lead by the start of the fourth quarter. The Patriots were unable to rally and ended up losing 26–16.

For the second straight year, the Patriots had come up short in the AFC Championship game.

With the victory over the Patriots, Peyton Manning became the first quarterback to lead two different teams to the Super Bowl. But his bid to win his second Lombardi Trophy was denied when the Denver Broncos were crushed in Super Bowl XLVIII by the upstart Seattle Seahawks. Meantime, it had been nine years since the Patriots had won a Super Bowl. In the interval, the team had been to the playoffs every year except for the one that Brady missed due to injury. With Brady at quarterback, the team had been to five AFC Championships in eight years, and they'd appeared in two Super Bowls. No other team had come close to matching that level of consistent success. But the bottom line remained that Belichick and Brady had not won the Lombardi Trophy since the 2004 season.

The day after the loss in Denver, in a column titled "Championship Days Are All Over for the Patriots," the *Boston Globe*'s Dan Shaughnessy wrote: "Sunday's annihilation at Mile High was merely the latest demonstration that the Super Bowl championship days are long gone in Foxborough. . . . And the proverbial window is closing for Brady. . . . When they get to the end of next season, they will not have won a Super Bowl for ten years."

It wasn't the first time that Shaughnessy had declared the end of the Patriots dynasty. But this time around, plenty of other members of the media agreed with him.

Publicly, Belichick declined to speculate on the future. But he had long believed that veteran players got paid too much under the salary cap. And in terms of deciding when to move on from a veteran player, he felt it better to

be a year early than a year late. In determining that timetable, he looked at a lot of factors, including a player's injury history, age, statistics, and salary. When he looked at Brady, the numbers suggested a drop-off in performance. His 60.5 percent completion rate in 2013 was his lowest since 2003. His 25 touchdown passes were his lowest total since 2006. And his overall quarterback rating—87.3—hadn't been that low since 2003.

When it came to age, Brady would be thirty-seven by the start of the 2014 season and he'd be entering his fifteenth season. In modern history, only four elite quarterbacks—Joe Montana, John Elway, Dan Marino, and Steve Young—had played more than fifteen seasons. All four of them were thirty-eight in their final season.

Based on those numbers, Belichick figured it was time for a succession plan.

Kraft, on the other hand, didn't put as much stock in the numbers when it came to Brady. But he didn't disagree with Belichick's decision to start making contingency plans. Nor was he opposed to drafting a quarterback, especially since it was pretty clear that the team would be trading Brady's backup, Ryan Mallett, during the offseason. So the team needed another quarterback.

But Kraft was counting on Brady to be the Patriots' quarterback for years to come. With that in mind, he had recently suggested that Brady build a home in his Chestnut Hill neighborhood. Now that he and Bündchen had two children, Brady was ready to move from Boston to the suburbs. He and Bündchen bought a lot just down the street from Kraft and built a home. Kraft didn't want to do anything that would give Brady the impression that the team was preparing to move on from him.

On draft day, Kraft sat between Belichick and Jonathan in the Patriots' war room as the team prepared to select Eastern Illinois quarterback Jimmy Garoppolo in the second round with the sixty-second pick.

Belichick's assistant punched in Garoppolo's number and handed Belichick the phone.

"Hey, Jimmy, it's Coach Belichick," he said. "How you doing?"

With a solemn expression on his face, Kraft stared at Belichick.

"Congratulations," Belichick told Garoppolo. "We just made you a Patriot."

Belichick handed Kraft the phone.

"Jimmy, congratulations," Kraft told him. "Great to have you as part of our squad."

The selection got a lot of attention. It was the first time in his fourteen drafts as Patriots head coach that Belichick had used a second-round pick on a quarterback.

"We know what Tom's age and contract situation is," Belichick said afterward. "I don't think you want to have one quarterback on your team. I don't think that's responsible to the entire team or the organization."

Brady had always paid close attention to everything Belichick said. He was also intimately familiar with Belichick's track record of getting rid of high-priced veteran players before they began to display a drop-off in production and performance. For fourteen years, Brady had had a front-row seat as Belichick moved on from Bledsoe, Milloy, Law, Vinatieri, Seymour, Welker, and a lengthy list of other beloved players.

With the selection of Jimmy Garoppolo, the writing was on the wall. It gave Brady a lot to think about heading into the summer of 2014.

thirty-five

ON TO CINCINNATI

In the early morning hours of February 15, 2014, authorities in Atlantic City arrested Baltimore Ravens star running back Ray Rice. News of the arrest first appeared the following day in the *Baltimore Sun*. In part, the *Sun* reported:

> Casino security called officers to the Revel Casino at about 2:50 a.m. Saturday after a domestic dispute between Rice and Janay Palmer that was recorded by video surveillance, according to a statement from police. Footage appeared to show both parties involved in a physical altercation.
>
> Palmer was Rice's fiancée. Palmer was also arrested.

Rice's attorney described the incident as "a very minor physical altercation."

At the outset, no one would have expected that a so-called very minor dispute between a player and his fiancée at a casino would mushroom into the greatest crisis of Roger Goodell's eight-year tenure as commissioner of the NFL.

But days after Rice and Palmer were arrested, the gossip website TMZ released video that showed Rice dragging an unconscious Palmer from a casino elevator. Although the video did not reveal what had transpired inside the elevator, the authorities soon dropped the charges against Palmer and indicted Rice for felony aggravated assault. As a first-time offender, Rice promptly entered a pretrial diversion program designed to spare him jail time in exchange for satisfying terms of probation.

After the NFL looked into the matter, Goodell met with Rice over the summer and convened a disciplinary hearing. Upon becoming commissioner, Goodell had coined the phrase "protecting the shield" to explain his behavior anytime he had to do something unpopular, such as suspend

a player, fine a team, or take a tough stance against the players' union. The "shield" was a reference to the iconic NFL logo. His meeting with Rice convinced Goodell that the best way to protect the shield in this instance was to suspend him for two games.

But in light of the footage of an unconscious woman's being dragged from an elevator, the leniency of the penalty triggered instant outrage. The *Washington Post* accused Goodell of showing "a dearth of sensitivity that blows away his other lapses in discipline, judgment and compassion." *Sports Illustrated* football writer Don Banks called the two-game suspension "tone deaf" and said it "defies logic and explanation." And NPR pointed out that players caught smoking pot routinely faced four-game suspensions by the NFL. Women's groups and advocates for domestic violence victims protested, and the national advocacy group CREDO gathered more than one hundred thousand signatures on a petition calling on the NFL to do more about its domestic violence problem. "This is not an isolated incident," CREDO's political director said in a statement. "The NFL is perpetuating a culture that tolerates violence against women. Responsibility for that culture goes straight to the top—Commissioner Roger Goodell."

With the league under fire, Goodell apologized to NFL owners for his decision in the Rice matter, saying, "I didn't get it right." Although Goodell still chose not to increase Rice's penalty, he did institute changes to the league's Personal Conduct Policy, imposing a mandatory six-game suspension on any player found to have engaged in assault, battery, domestic violence, or sexual assault. The new policy also banished second offenders from the league for at least one year.

As soon as the new policy was announced, San Francisco 49ers defensive lineman Ray McDonald was arrested and charged with assaulting his pregnant fiancée. With McDonald facing indictment, neither the 49ers nor the NFL suspended him. Goodell said he couldn't levy any punishment until a full investigation was completed. Once again, the league faced a backlash. US House minority leader Nancy Pelosi, a longtime 49ers fan, called out her hometown team for allowing McDonald to play while facing such serious charges. But in this instance, Goodell's cautiousness proved judicious, as prosecutors soon dropped the charges against McDonald, citing insufficient evidence that a crime had occurred.

When the Patriots opened the 2014 season in Miami on September 7, Robert Kraft couldn't help being preoccupied by the public relations problem

confronting Goodell and the league. After his team fell to the Dolphins, Kraft flew to New York to meet with Goodell. The following morning, TMZ released video taken from inside the elevator in the Ray Rice incident. For the first time, the public saw Rice knock his fiancée unconscious with a blow to the face, causing her to crumple to the floor.

Appalled, Kraft immediately phoned Goodell and asked if he had known about the in-elevator video. Goodell assured him that he had not. The league was going to face an uproar.

The Ravens quickly terminated Rice's contract, and Goodell suspended Rice indefinitely. But calls for the commissioner to step down intensified.

"The NFL has lost its way," National Organization for Women president Terry O'Neill told ESPN. "The only workable solution is for Roger Goodell to resign."

With NFL owners under pressure to remove Goodell, Kraft lobbied his colleagues to stand by him. Kraft also went on *CBS This Morning* and defended Goodell's character. Charlie Rose pressed Kraft on whether the commissioner had known about the elevator video. "He had no knowledge of the video," Kraft said. "Anyone who's second-guessing that doesn't know him."

After his interview, Kraft telephoned CBS president Les Moonves and urged him to arrange a sit-down interview for Goodell with someone from CBS News so the commissioner could speak to the public and explain his actions.

"We need to get Roger on the air," Kraft said. "Right away."

Moonves agreed. The network had just paid $250 million for the right to broadcast eight Thursday night games that year. The first one was set to air in just forty-eight hours. And as fate would have it, the game featured the Ravens. Moonves said he'd call the news division.

Kraft hung up and briefed Goodell on his call with Moonves.

A few hours later, CBS's Norah O'Donnell arrived at NFL headquarters and sat down with Goodell.

"Do you wish you had seen this video before it was released by TMZ?" O'Donnell asked.

"Absolutely," Goodell said.

"Why?"

"Because when we met with Ray Rice and his representatives, it was ambiguous about what actually happened."

"What was ambiguous about her lying unconscious on the floor being dragged out by her feet?" O'Donnell asked.

"There was nothing ambiguous about that," Goodell said. "That was the result that we saw. We did not know what led up to that."

Goodell took responsibility for his mistakes. But right after the interview aired, the Associated Press reported that a copy of the elevator video had been sent to the league months earlier.

With the league's integrity in serious doubt, Goodell scrambled to try to restore public confidence. The next day the NFL retained former FBI director Robert Mueller to conduct an independent inquiry into whether anyone in the league had seen the in-elevator video prior to its public release and to scrutinize the league's investigation.

One day after Mueller commenced his investigation, a headline in the *New York Times* read: "N.F.L. Rocked Again as Adrian Peterson Faces a Child Abuse Case." Peterson, a running back for the Minnesota Vikings, was one of the biggest stars in the league. Authorities charged him with beating his four-year-old son with a tree branch.

At the same time, a bipartisan group of sixteen female US senators said they were "shocked and disgusted" by the elevator video and called on Goodell and the NFL to institute a zero-tolerance policy that sent a stronger message opposing violence against women. In a letter to Goodell, they wrote: "We are deeply concerned that the NFL's new policy announced last month would allow a player to commit a violent act against a woman and return after a short suspension."

In mid-September, Goodell held a press conference, in which he acknowledged that the entire situation had been bungled.

"I got it wrong on a number of levels, from the process that I led to the decision that I reached," Goodell said. "But now I will get it right and do whatever is necessary to accomplish that."

He started by suspending Adrian Peterson without pay for the entire season.

Kraft had been at Goodell's side throughout the tumult. But there was also trouble in Foxborough. Despite starting the season 2-1, the Patriots weren't playing well. The offense, in particular, was struggling. Speculation was rampant that the Belichick-Brady era had finally reached the end of the road.

On September 29, 2014, Kraft flew to Kansas City, where the Patriots faced the 1-2 Chiefs on *Monday Night Football*. He and Jonathan looked on as the Patriots' offense floundered and the Chiefs built a 17–0 first-half lead.

It was only the second time in the past eight years that the Patriots had been shut out in the first half of a game. And the Chiefs' 303 first-half yards were the most allowed by the Patriots in a first half since Belichick had taken over the team in 2000.

At halftime, Belichick told his team: "This second half is going to define our season. I wanna see what kind of football team we have."

The Chiefs poured it on in the third quarter, going up 27–0. Then, in the fourth quarter, with his team trailing 34–7, Brady threw an interception that was returned for a touchdown. With ten minutes remaining and the Chiefs up 41–7, Belichick took Brady out of the game.

Scowling, Brady sat alone on the bench, shaking his head, as an ESPN camera zeroed in on him.

"This is as frustrated as I've ever seen Tom Brady in watching him since 2000," said ESPN announcer Mike Tirico.

"They are clearly struggling as a football team," color analyst Jon Gruden said. "And he's struggling himself. And they've got a long way to go to solve their problems on offense."

Moments later, rookie quarterback Jimmy Garoppolo trotted onto the field to make his Patriots debut. He drove the team eighty yards in three minutes. On the final play of the drive, Garoppolo completed a sharply thrown pass to Gronkowski, who fought through four tacklers, steamrolling his way into the end zone. It seemed like a meaningless touchdown. But to Gronkowski, it was personal. After two years of severe injuries, he was fighting his way back from reconstructive knee surgery and trying to reestablish himself as Gronk, the tight end who broke tackles, dragged defenders, and scored touchdowns. His father was sitting in the stands at Arrowhead Stadium and had to wipe away a tear when Rob scored.

With time expiring, the Patriots got the ball one more time. Despite the game's essentially being over, receiver Danny Amendola decided to block a defender, who took offense. A fight ensued. Pissed, Amendola ripped the defender's helmet off and got flagged.

The final score was 41–14. It was the Patriots' worst defeat in eleven years.

But as Belichick walked off the field, he felt encouraged. His team could have mailed it in during the second half. They were way behind and knew they weren't going to catch up. They were on the road. The crowd was in a frenzy. Yet Amendola got in a fight and tore a guy's helmet off. Gronkowski powered through four tacklers to bulldoze his way to a touchdown at the end of the game. Even though the Patriots got smashed, they never gave up.

From Belichick's perspective, the team had responded to his halftime challenge. Even in defeat, they had shown him what kind of football team they were—one that wouldn't quit. That was the kind of mind-set that could indeed define the rest of the season.

But Belichick hinted at none of that when he took to the lectern for his postgame press conference. Stern and gloomy, he declared the obvious—the team needed to do better in every phase of the game.

A reporter brought up the fact that as soon as Garoppolo entered the game, the team marched down the field and scored a touchdown. "Will the quarterback situation be evaluated this week?" the reporter asked.

Incredulous, Belichick rolled his eyes and shook his head, as if to say, *Give me a fucking break*. He didn't bother answering the question.

It was around midnight when Brady trudged out of Arrowhead Stadium and boarded the team bus. The one thing he never wanted anyone to think was that there might be someone who could do his job better than he could. After the Chiefs game, he feared people were thinking that. Plopping down in a seat by himself, he pulled out his iPad and started watching film on the Patriots' next opponent, the Cincinnati Bengals. He studied them all the way to the airport. He continued studying them on the flight back to New England, and on the bus ride from the airport to Gillette Stadium.

When the rest of the team disembarked from the shuttle buses, got into their cars, and drove home to get some sleep, Brady entered the stadium a couple of hours before dawn and spent the rest of the night in a film room. Alone, he continued prepping for the Bengals. He never left. He never slept.

Later on Tuesday morning, Brady ran into the quarterback coach. "We're going to play well this week," Brady told him, "and I'm going to do everything I can for us to win this game."

Brady's most defining characteristics as a quarterback had never been his physical attributes. His keen mind, his fortitude, his fierce competitiveness, and his relentless quest for self-mastery were what separated him from everyone else in the game. What Brady did after the loss in Kansas City was the same thing he had done in 2004 after an embarrassing loss on *Monday Night Football* in Miami—stay at the stadium and study while everyone else went home and slept. The big difference was that this time around, Brady had ten additional years of experience under his belt and a young quarterback on his heels.

Tuesday's headlines were not kind. The back page of the *Boston Herald* read: "BAD TO WORSE." The front page of the *Boston Globe* sports section

read: "DOWN AND OUT." The *Globe* deemed the loss to the Chiefs one of "the most hideous performances of the Belichick/Brady era." The national media concurred.

When the team returned to the stadium for meetings on Tuesday afternoon, Belichick purposely avoided talking about the Chiefs game. Win or lose, whether by a wide margin or a narrow one, Belichick's approach was consistent—as soon as one game ends, you turn your full attention to the next one. Just as there was no benefit in resting on your laurels after a big win, there was nothing to be gained by dwelling on a big loss.

The following day, Belichick held his weekly press briefing to discuss the upcoming game against the Bengals. Instead, he got bombarded with questions about Brady. One by one, he cut them off.

"Bill, you mentioned Tom's age at the draft—"

"We're on to Cincinnati," Belichick said.

"Bill, do you think having a thirty-seven-year-old—"

"We're on to Cincinnati. It's nothing about the past. It's nothing about the future. Right now we're preparing for Cincinnati."

"Do you feel like the talent you have here is good?" a reporter asked.

"We're getting ready for Cincinnati," Belichick said.

"I'm just asking: Do you think you've done enough to help Tom Brady?"

"We're getting ready for Cincinnati."

Belichick wasn't interested in what the press cared about. The only audience he cared about was his players. And by stiff-arming the media, Belichick had reached his core audience.

"The second Bill said, 'We're on to Cincinnati,' every player said, 'Phew!'" said Rob Gronkowski. "As a player, I didn't want to talk about the Chiefs game. None of us did. By Bill doing what he did in that press conference, we could all just follow his lead and tell everyone, 'We're on to Cincinnati,' too. It was a great model after a big loss. Those four words were easy to use all week. Because you have to move on right away, and 'We're on to Cincinnati' gave us a way to do that."

Since the start of the Belichick-Brady era, the mood in New England had never been darker. In a week when the first case of Ebola was confirmed in the United States, the story dominating the news cycle was the plight of a 2-2 team and the future of its quarterback. "NOW OR NEVER: Only Way to Quiet Doubters . . . *WIN!*" read the banner headline in the *Boston Herald* on Sunday, October 5, 2014. It was accompanied by a photo of Brady with

his hands on his hips. That night, in a nationally televised game on NBC, the amped-up crowd in Foxborough held large red, white, and blue banners that said:

WE BELIEVE . . . TRUST BILL & TOM
WE STILL BELIEVE IN BRADY

With anger in his eyes, Brady walked up to Kraft on the Patriots' sideline shortly before kickoff and said: "We're gonna kick their ass."

Kraft wasn't worried. He'd been reading all the press reports about Brady's being washed up. There was no better way to stimulate Tommy's competitive juices, Kraft felt, than to write him off.

Kraft turned to Jonathan and said, "Tommy's going to have a big night tonight."

On the first play of the game, Brady zinged a twenty-yard completion. Then, after two running plays, he threw a thirty-yard completion. He barreled for a first down on a fourth-and-one play, and jawed with the linebacker who tackled him. Playing angry, the Patriots finished off the eighty-yard, ten-play drive with a punishing run for a touchdown. As Brady jogged to the sideline, Belichick greeted him with a fist bump and a pat on the butt.

On the Patriots' next possession, Brady connected with Gronkowski on a twenty-seven-yard pass play. The completion marked a major personal milestone for Brady, making him just the sixth player in NFL history to throw for more than fifty thousand yards. As the public address announcer pointed out the achievement and Brady's image appeared on the stadium's jumbo screen, the fans started chanting "BRAY-DEE, BRAY-DEE, BRAY-DEE."

The crowd was still chanting when Brady hustled to the line of scrimmage, took the next snap, and fired a touchdown pass to put New England up 14–0.

Gillette Stadium erupted.

Brady celebrated in the end zone with his teammates. They handed him the ball to spike. Brady then handed it to Edelman, who tossed it back to Brady, who tossed it back to Edelman, who tossed it back to Brady, who spiked it. Chants of "BRAY-DEE, BRAY-DEE, BRAY-DEE" thundered through the stadium as Aloe Blacc played on the public address system: "Go ahead and tell everybody, I'm the man, I'm the man, I'm the man."

"Tom Brady, at least in the first quarter, playing the role of Mark Twain," quipped NBC announcer Al Michaels. "'Reports of my death have been greatly exaggerated.'"

Brady never let up, completing twenty-three of thirty-five passes for 292 yards and a pair of touchdowns. The Patriots rolled to a 43–17 drubbing of the Bengals, handing them their first loss of the season. As the final seconds ticked off the game clock, Brady and Belichick stood side by side on the sideline. Brady smiled. Belichick extended his hand. And Brady shook it. Since 2001 when Brady had taken over at quarterback, the Patriots had won 161 games. For Belichick and Brady, very few were more satisfying than this one.

With eye black running down his cheeks, Brady was all smiles as he entered the locker room after the game. Kraft greeted him with a bear hug.

"We needed that," Brady told him.

"When you said 'We're gonna kick their ass,' I knew," Kraft said.

"That was awesome," Brady said.

As soon as all of the players were in the locker room, Belichick called them together.

"We're certainly not big on individual stats around here," Belichick began. "But fifty thousand yards, Tom."

The players cheered and clapped as Brady stepped forward and Belichick handed him the game ball.

Brady wrapped his arms around Belichick, patting him repeatedly on the back.

"BRAY-DEE! BRAY-DEE! BRAY-DEE!" the players chanted.

Brady held the ball above his head, as if tipping his cap.

"Pretty good," Belichick said. Then he paused, drowned out by the noise. "Pretty good for a sixth-round draft choice," Belichick finally barked.

"Not bad," Brady said.

Belichick extended his hand and Tom shook it as the chanting continued.

"It's all because of you guys," Brady said. "I fuckin' love you guys. You guys know that. I love you all."

He spiked the ball, bringing the cheering to a crescendo.

Despite being the team leader, Brady was not one to break the team down in the locker room after games. Over his fourteen-year career that had never been his style. But amid the outpouring of emotion, he felt inspired.

"C'mon," Brady said, motioning them to come closer. "Let's break it down."

The players all put their hands in the center of the circle. With Belichick's hand touching his, Brady yelled: "TEAM on three. One. Two. Three."

"TEAM!" everyone shouted.

"Great job, man," Belichick said to Brady. "Great job."

After all the players congratulated Brady one by one, he returned to his locker, where Kraft was waiting.

"You know what?" Kraft whispered in his ear. "You deserve it."

"We all do," Brady told him.

"Yeah, we all do," Kraft said. "But what you've done for this team . . ."

The loss to the Kansas City Chiefs proved to be one of the most important games of all to the Patriots dynasty. It reignited Brady, propelling the thirty-seven-year-old quarterback to new frontiers that no one thought possible. It provided an opportunity for Belichick to do some of the wisest coaching of his career. And it refocused a team that was losing its edge. Belichick's "On to Cincinnati" mantra charted the course. But Brady was the one behind the wheel for the Patriots. More than anyone, he set the pace and determined the team's ultimate destination. Although none of his teammates knew that he had spent the night at the stadium following the loss to the Chiefs, all of them fed off his drive.

"I love football," said Gronkowski. "But Tom loves football to another power. It's inspiring to all of us."

After trouncing the Bengals, the Patriots went on a roll, winning their next three games, setting up a contest with the Denver Broncos, the team with the best record in the league. It marked the sixteenth time that Brady and Manning went head-to-head. In the second quarter, Brady rifled a touchdown pass to Edelman to put the Patriots up 13–7. Minutes later, Edelman returned a punt eighty-four yards for a touchdown, firing the ball into the stands and sending the stadium into a frenzy.

Screaming, Brady ran all the way from the bench to the opposite corner of the field to head-butt and congratulate Edelman in the end zone. When Edelman got back to the bench, he wasn't sure if he'd been seeing things. He turned to Brady. "Were you in the end zone after my punt return?" Edelman said.

Brady smiled. "You're my guy. That was an unbelievable play."

Brady and the Patriots played with much more emotion than Manning and the Broncos, and the game was never close. With his team up 37–21 in the fourth quarter, Brady threw a pass over the middle of the field that was off target. Gronkowski leaped and snagged it out of the air with a one-handed, behind-the-back catch as two defenders closed in on him. "Dude, that was unbelievable!" Brady told him. "How the fuck did you catch that?"

Gronkowski had taken it personally when skeptics were going after Brady

at the start of the season. His way of protecting Brady was to play with more determination than ever. Similarly, Edelman would do anything for Brady. With the aid of his two favorite targets, Brady outdueled Manning for the eleventh time. The Patriots beat the best team in the league 43–21 to improve to 7-2.

In the locker room afterward, Belichick tore into his team. "We got a long way to go," he said. "I'm just tellin' ya. Seven games isn't going to win anything in this league. It's just not enough! It's not anywhere near enough!"

Two weeks later, the Patriots traveled to Indianapolis to face the red-hot Colts in a nationally televised Sunday night game. Again, the Patriots ran away with the game. Late in the fourth quarter, Gronkowski had had enough of the trash-talking from Colts defensive back Sergio Brown. When Brady called a run play on the Colts' goal line, Gronkowski cleared a path for the ball carrier by blocking Brown. After the ball carrier crossed the goal line and the referee raised his hands to signal a touchdown, Gronkowski continued to block Brown, driving him ten yards out of bounds, plowing him into a television cameraman, and planting him on his head. Flags were thrown and the fans inside Lucas Oil Stadium rained down boos as the replay on the jumbo screen showed Gronkowski manhandling Brown like a rag doll. NBC broadcasters Cris Collinsworth and Al Michaels were cracking up on the air. "Gronk over there, stirring it up like it's a nightclub," Collingsworth said.

Two minutes later, Gronkowski caught a pass from Brady, broke a tackle, stiff-armed another would-be tackler, swatted away a third tackler, outran two defenders, and leaped over two more defenders as he crashed into the end zone for a touchdown.

"Gron-*kowski*!" shouted Al Michaels. "Like a runaway truck."

"Oh, man!" said Collinsworth. "How do you tackle that guy?"

The play epitomized the return of Gronkowski and the dominance of the Patriots. After embarrassing the Colts 42–20, the Patriots went on to finish the regular season with a 12-4 record, earning the top seed in the AFC play-offs. Since the humiliating loss to the Chiefs in week four, the Patriots had gone 10-2 and averaged just over thirty-two points per game. And after all the changes in player personnel, a new nucleus of stars had formed around Brady. Edelman's 197 total receptions in 2013 and 2014 were the third most in the NFL, and Gronkowski was named the 2014 NFL Comeback Player of the Year.

The Patriots were primed for another Super Bowl run.

Robert Mueller delivered his report on the Ray Rice incident to the National Football League on January 8, 2015. Mueller had found no evidence that anyone in the league had seen the in-elevator video prior to its release by TMZ. Nonetheless, Mueller concluded that the league had had a copy of the criminal complaint, which charged Rice with "striking [Palmer] with his hand, rendering her unconscious." The league also had a copy of the grand jury indictment, which described behavior "manifesting extreme indifference to the value of human life."

"That information did not provide the graphic detail that the in-elevator video depicted," Mueller wrote, "but it should have put the League on notice that a serious assault had occurred and that it should have conducted a more substantial independent investigation."

The NFL owners were embarrassed.

"This matter has tarnished the reputation of the NFL due to our failure to hand out proper punishments," said New York Giants owner John Mara and Pittsburgh Steelers owner Art Rooney II in a joint statement.

Two days after the release of Mueller's report, the Patriots hosted the Baltimore Ravens in the divisional round of the playoffs. Under Belichick, the Patriots were 12-3 in playoff games at home. Two of those losses were against the Ravens, the one team that wasn't intimidated by coming into Gillette Stadium.

The Ravens raced out to a 14–0 first-quarter lead, stunning the Patriots. After Brady rallied his team to tie the game, the Ravens scored two more touchdowns. Halfway through the third quarter, the Patriots trailed 28–14.

With the game slipping away and the offense struggling to move the ball, Belichick used an offensive formation that no defense had ever seen in an NFL game. The Patriots normally used five offensive linemen—a center, two guards, and two tackles, all wearing numbers between 50 and 79. Players with those numbers are generally not eligible to be pass receivers except in the rare situation in which the player declares himself eligible to the referee, who in turn notifies the defense. After a Patriots lineman got injured, Belichick replaced him with backup tight end Michael Hoomanawanui, who wears number 47. Belichick had him line up as the left tackle. Then Belichick stacked all of his other receivers on the right side of the line of scrimmage. Under the rules, since there were no receivers to the left of Hoomanawanui, he became an eligible receiver. And since he wasn't wearing a number between 50 and 79, he was not required to declare himself eligible to the referee. But the Ravens didn't pick up on what the Patriots were doing. They were confused.

On the snap, Hoomanawanui ran downfield. Thinking he was an ineligible receiver, the Ravens failed to cover him. Brady threw a quick strike to him and Hoomanawanui barreled downfield for a sixteen-yard gain.

The Ravens were so flummoxed by the play that Brady ran it once more. Again, Hoomanawanui was wide open and picked up another fourteen yards.

Enraged, Ravens coach John Harbaugh stormed onto the field, yelling at the officials and drawing a penalty for unsportsmanlike conduct. The Ravens insisted the formation was illegal. But it wasn't.

Moments later, Brady threw a touchdown pass to Gronkowski, who spiked the ball, igniting the crowd, shifting the momentum, and trimming the deficit to a touchdown.

On their next possession, the Patriots called another play that they had never used in a game. Brady threw a backward pass to Julian Edelman, which made the pass a lateral, making Edelman eligible to throw the ball after catching it. He launched the ball to a wide-open Danny Amendola, who raced fifty-one yards for a touchdown that tied the game at 28. The play, known as "double-pass," completely fooled the Ravens. Edelman had never thrown a pass in his entire pro career.

The Ravens responded with a drive that resulted in a field goal to go up 31–28.

But Brady orchestrated another late fourth-quarter drive, and with five minutes left, he lofted a twenty-three-yard pass that fell perfectly into the hands of Brandon LaFell as he crossed the goal line to put the Patriots up 35–31. It was Brady's forty-sixth postseason touchdown pass, breaking Joe Montana's all-time record and sending Gillette Stadium into a frenzy.

Moments later, the Patriots intercepted Ravens quarterback Joe Flacco to seal the victory. For the fourth straight year, the Patriots were headed to the AFC Championship game.

The bad blood between the Ravens and Patriots spilled over after the game.

Coach Harbaugh criticized the Patriots' play calling, saying, "it was clearly deception." He added: "It's not something that anybody's ever done before. They're an illegal, trick type of thing, and I'm sure that the league will make some adjustments and things like that."

"Do you consider that cheap or dirty?" a reporter asked in a follow-up question.

"I'm not going to comment on that," Harbaugh said, thereby insinuating that the play was indeed cheap or dirty.

When told of Harbaugh's deception remark, Brady wanted to lash out. Instead, he smiled. "Maybe those guys gotta study the rulebook and figure it out," he said. "We obviously knew what we were doing. I don't know what's deceiving about that."

The Ravens were livid.

On January 18, 2015, the Patriots hosted the Colts in the AFC Championship game. One day prior, the Colts equipment manager had emailed Colts general manager Ryan Grigson and told him that an assistant coach from the Baltimore Ravens had called and complained about the Patriots. The email read, in part:

> As far as the gameballs are concerned it is well known around the league that after the Patriots gameballs are checked by the officials and brought out for game usage the ballboys for the Patriots will let out some air with a ball needle because their quarterback likes a smaller football so he can grip it better, it would be great if someone would be able to check the air in the game balls as the game goes on so that they don't get an illegal advantage.

Grigson forwarded the email as an "FYI" to two members of the NFL's Football Operations Department, adding, "all the Indianapolis Colts want is a completely level playing field. Thank you for being vigilant stewards of that not only for us but for the shield and overall integrity of our game."

The league contacted the Colts and asked if they had any specific source for such a serious allegation. The Colts produced none, citing only "chatter throughout the league."

Under NFL rules, balls must be pressurized between 12.5 and 13.5 pounds per square inch (PSI). Apprised of the Colts' concern, the head referee said he'd ensure that all of the standard pregame protocols for ball security were followed.

The Patriots jumped out to a 14–0 lead. Then in the second quarter, Colts linebacker D'Qwell Jackson intercepted Brady. Saying he wanted the ball for a souvenir, Jackson took it to the Colts' sideline and gave it to the assistant equipment manager. A member of the Colts equipment staff inserted a pressure gauge in the ball, a violation of league rules that the team would later admit. Insisting the intercepted ball was underinflated, a short while later, GM Ryan Grigson entered the NFL's suite at Gillette Stadium and told

league vice president of football operations Troy Vincent: "We are playing with a small ball."

As the first half ended, Belichick's chief of staff, Berj Najarian, was told that the league needed all of the Patriots' game balls. With no idea why, Najarian gathered up the footballs and turned them over. During halftime, league and game officials met in the dressing area of the officials' locker room. In an uncoordinated, chaotic effort led by one of the league officials who had received Grigson's email the night before, the group started hurriedly testing the balls' air pressure.

Using two pressure gauges, the officials checked New England's eleven game balls first. According to both gauges, the balls were slightly below the 12.5 minimum PSI requirement. But none of the balls registered the same reading on both gauges. For instance, ball number 7 registered 11.85 PSI on one gauge and 12.30 on the other gauge.

The officials only had time to check four of the Colts' balls. According to one gauge, all four were at or above 12.5. On the other gauge, three of the four balls registered below the 12.5 threshold at 12.15, 12.30, and 12.35, while one registered at 12.95.

The officials added a few ticks of air to all of the underinflated balls and returned to the field. In the second half, Brady came out firing and the Patriots outscored the Colts 28–0. By the early part of the fourth quarter, the Patriots led 45–7. Belichick pulled Brady from the game and replaced him with Jimmy Garoppolo. As Brady came off, the fans cheered wildly as the stadium played Aloe Blacc's "I'm the man / I'm the man / I'm the man," and the jumbo screen showed Brady pumping his fist and shouting: "Let's go."

The early-season blowout to the Chiefs and the "sky is falling" mindset that it had triggered in New England were ancient history. Brady and Belichick were heading back to the Super Bowl for a record sixth time. No quarterback had ever been to six Super Bowls. And no coach had ever won twenty-one playoff games.

The atmosphere in Gillette Stadium was carnival-like as the players celebrated and a stage was erected for the presentation of the AFC Championship trophy. Earlier in the day, former Patriots head coach Pete Carroll had coached the Seattle Seahawks to victory in the NFC Championship game. With snow starting to fall in Foxborough, Jim Nantz asked Belichick to comment.

"Jim," Belichick said, hoisting the trophy, "I only have one thing to say. We're on to Seattle."

thirty-six
THE ENVY OF THE LEAGUE

T he Patriots' victory over the Colts was one of the most lopsided AFC Championship games in recent history. Sports columnist Bob Kravitz covered the game for WTHR, the NBC affiliate in Indianapolis. After the game, Kravitz went to the Colts' locker room. When he returned to the press box at Gillette Stadium to retrieve his cell phone, he discovered a text message from a contact asking Kravitz to call him. While driving back to his hotel, Kravitz placed the call and got a tip that had the potential to stir up a tsunami of controversy on the Patriots. At 12:55 a.m., Kravitz tweeted: "Breaking: A league source tells me the NFL is investigating the possibility the Patriots deflated footballs Sunday night. More to come."

Overnight, plenty of sports journalists read Kravitz's tweet. Before dawn, the term *Deflategate* was gaining traction on Twitter. One journalist who saw Kravitz's tweet was *Newsday*'s Bob Glauber, the highly respected president of the Pro Football Writers of America. At 7:00 a.m., Glauber sent out his own tweet reporting that an NFL spokesman had confirmed that the league was looking into whether the balls for the AFC Championship game had been properly inflated.

Shortly after Glauber's tweet, Brady called in to Boston sports talk station WEEI for his weekly, Monday morning interview. He was caught off guard when he was asked about reports of underinflated balls. "I think I've heard it all at this point," Brady said. "That's the last of my worries. I don't even respond to stuff like this."

At first, Brady couldn't believe the claim. But right after his radio interview he received a text: "Call me when you get a second." It was from John Jastremski, the team's assistant equipment manager. Jastremski was responsible for preparing the game balls to Brady's liking. He was also the one who set the air pressure level in each ball before the balls were inspected by the game officials.

Less than a minute after getting Jastremski's text, Brady called him.

Jastremski was scared and perplexed. "No idea what happened," he told Brady.

Brady wasn't overly concerned. He'd known Jastremski since he'd started working as a ball boy for the quarterbacks twelve years earlier. Over the years, Jastremski had worked his way up in the equipment staff. Hardworking and conscientious, he took great pride in his job.

Jastremski had been particularly meticulous in the lead-up to the AFC Championship game. Roughly a week before the game, Brady had selected the twelve game balls and twelve backup balls. Jastremski then treated each one with leather conditioner and spent hours rubbing them by hand to break them in. At noon on game day, Brady had asked to see the game balls. They felt fine, but there was rain in the forecast. When Brady expressed concern that the oil from the leather conditioner might make the balls slippery when wet, Jastremski spent the next two hours removing the leather preservative from the balls, brushing them, treating them with dirt, and vigorously rubbing each ball while wearing leather-palmed gloves. Then he set the air pressure in each ball to 12.6 PSI and placed them on a trunk in the equipment room for Brady to review. Around 2:30, Brady returned and was pleased to find that the balls had a very different feel. After Brady chose the twelve that he preferred the most, Jastremski put them in a bag and placed the bag in the equipment room. Shortly after that, the referees inspected each ball, checked the air pressure, and certified that every ball was in compliance with NFL game-ball regulations.

Yet by halftime, eleven of the Patriots twelve game balls were apparently underinflated.

"Can't explain it," Jastremski told Brady.

Brady was confident that there had to be some logical explanation.

But Jastremski feared that the blame was going to come back to him.

Before hanging up, Brady tried to reassure him.

When Belichick arrived at the stadium Monday morning, he was shocked to learn that the league was launching an investigation into why his team's footballs had been below the 12.5 PSI threshold in the first half of the previous night's game. Kraft had been notified by the league in a formal letter. Kraft didn't like the fact that his team was facing another investigation. But he was confident it would lead nowhere.

Incredulous, Belichick told Kraft that in his entire time as head coach he had never talked to his staff or his players or game operations personnel about

air pressure in footballs. The notion that his team was somehow involved in altering footballs to gain an advantage sounded pretty far-fetched to him.

When Brady arrived at the stadium, he met with Kraft. Kraft told him that if he'd done anything wrong it would be best to just admit it. "We'll deal with it," Kraft told him. Brady assured him that he did not deflate any footballs. Nor did he instruct anyone else to deflate footballs below the level permitted by league rules. And he had no knowledge of anyone deflating balls below the level permitted by league rules.

It was clear to Kraft that neither Belichick nor Brady had any general knowledge of what happens to game balls once they are turned over to the officials for inspection prior to the game. Nor did either of them have any specific knowledge of what had happened to the game balls after they were inspected prior to the Colts game.

Kraft sent word to all Patriots staff to fully cooperate and be transparent with league investigators. He also instructed all full-time and part-time employees to make themselves available for interviews and to turn over communication devices upon request. The sooner this thing was put to bed, the better.

Later that morning, Brady checked in on Jastremski.

"You good, Jonny boy," he texted.

Jastremski was a working-class guy, unaccustomed to the limelight and overwhelmed by the prospect of being swept up in a high-profile controversy. It meant a lot to him to get a text like that from Brady. He let Brady know he was pretty nervous.

"You didn't do anything wrong, bud," Brady texted.

"I know. I will be all good," Jastremski texted.

Although the league had formally notified Kraft that his team was under investigation, the NFL made no public statement confirming or denying that an investigation was under way. But leaks from "league sources" to the media were rampant. Much of what was being written in the immediate aftermath of the AFC Championship game was conjecture. And some of the most inflammatory reports were fictional. Yet they were coming from highly respected journalists at mainstream media outlets. At 10:57 p.m. on Tuesday, ESPN's Chris Mortensen tweeted:

NFL has found that 11 of the Patriots footballs used in Sunday's AFC title game were under-inflated by 2 lbs each, per league sources.

Mortensen was the quintessential NFL insider with a stellar reputation. But his tweet was false—eleven Patriots footballs were not underinflated by two pounds. There was one ball that was underinflated by two pounds. Yet, within an hour of his tweet, the *Washington Post* ran the headline "Report: NFL Finds 11 of 12 Patriots Balls to Be Underinflated by Two Pounds." The *Post* story quoted yet another Twitter post from Mortensen:

NFL rules stipulate that balls for their games must be inflated to 12½ to 13½ pounds per square inch. Under-inflated balls are softer and potentially easier to throw and catch, which could have given the Patriots an advantage in the AFC championship game against the Colts, which was played in cold, rainy conditions.

The floodgates had opened, and the narrative was spreading that the Patriots had cheated against the Colts by using balls that were underinflated by two pounds. Right away, the Baltimore Ravens piled on. The CBS affiliate in Baltimore reported:

With the Patriots under investigation for possibly under-inflating balls in their playoff win against the Colts, sources said some on Baltimore's sideline believed there may have been irregularities with the kicking balls used in their AFC divisional playoff game at Foxborough, Mass., on Jan. 10.

Baltimore's kicking and punting units were not getting their normal depth and distance, and some believed the balls they were using may have been deflated.

If the tweet by Indianapolis sports columnist Bob Kravitz ignited the "Deflategate" controversy, Mortensen's tweet effectively poured gas on the fire. Within hours of Mortensen's tweet, Kravitz was back on Twitter:

If bob kraft is a true man of integrity he will take it out of the leagues hands and fire belichick. Not holding my breath.

Pats fans: give up the fantasy. Your brilliant head coach is also a cheat. 11 of 12 balls deflated. Must be the ball boys fault right?

If Roger Goodell has an ounce of integrity, and he's not spending all his time going to pre-game soirees at Kraft's mansion, he will not only fine Belichick and take away draft choices, but suspend the head coach for the upcoming season.

In New England, Kravitz was perceived as a tool in the hands of Colts owner Jim Irsay. But outside New England, Kravitz's calls for punishing the Patriots were embraced. By Thursday morning, January 22, "Deflategate" was trending on Twitter and had become the most talked about story in the country. Even the hosts of *The View* spent the morning expressing outrage toward the Patriots. Rosie O'Donnell argued that the Patriots should be disqualified from playing in the Super Bowl.

While O'Donnell opined, Belichick stepped to the podium in the media room at Gillette Stadium for his most anticipated press conference since he had addressed Aaron Hernandez's arrest eighteen months earlier. It infuriated Belichick that his team's exceptional season was being overshadowed by a media circus over air pressure in footballs. His team had been written off after the week four blowout in Kansas City. Since then they'd defied all the naysayers who had said the dynasty was over by finishing the season with the best record in the AFC, and they'd beaten two very good football teams in the playoffs to earn a ticket back to the Super Bowl. That, Belichick felt, should be the story.

"With regard to the footballs," he began sternly, "I'm sure that any current or past player of mine will tell you that the balls we practice with are as bad as they can be. Wet. Sticky. Cold. Slippery. However bad we can make 'em, I make 'em. And anytime that players complain about the quality of the balls, I make 'em worse. And that stops the complaining. So we never use the condition of the footballs as an excuse. We play with whatever or kick with whatever we have to use."

As he paused, camera shutters clicked rapidly.

"I think we all know that quarterbacks, kickers, specialists have certain preferences on footballs," he continued. "They know a lot more about it than I do. They're a lot more sensitive to it than I am. I hear them comment on it from time to time. But I can tell you—and they will tell you—that there is *never* any sympathy whatsoever from me on that subject. Zero!

"Tom's personal preferences on his footballs are something that he can talk about in much better detail and information than I could possibly provide."

Adamant and forceful, Belichick spent six minutes explaining that he had never once in his career asked anyone—players or staff—about the air pressure of footballs and he had no explanation for why the Patriots' game balls had been below the 12.5 PSI requirement in the first half of the Colts game.

As soon as he finished his remarks, he was bombarded with questions from reporters yelling over each other.

"I've told you everything I know," Belichick said, cutting them off.

"Coach, notwithstanding what you've said here today, there are a lot of people questioning your integrity—"

"I've told you everything I know," Belichick interrupted.

"—who say that you will win at any and all costs," the reporter continued. "What do you say to critics who are challenging your character, which seems to go well beyond the state of football?"

Belichick glared at him. "I've told you everything I know," he repeated.

"Coach," another reporter said, "I assume you've had conversations with Tom about this specific issue and what happened."

"I have no explanation for what happened."

"Coach, why do you think these controversies continue to follow you?"

"I don't have an explanation for what happened."

Brady wasn't originally scheduled to address the media on Thursday. But right after Belichick's press conference, he received an email from a personal assistant with an attachment titled "Deflated—BIA Between the Lines Report." It was a report generated by a Boston behavioral assessment firm. The firm had analyzed Brady's initial radio interview about underinflated balls and found that his answers gave the impression he had something to hide. "You should read this prior to any interviews you do about this," Brady's assistant told him. He added: "Belichick has really dropped this in your lap just now. Don't take this lightly."

All the speculation was starting to drain Brady. He told himself that he had to compartmentalize his emotions and focus on preparing for the Seahawks. The first step, he felt, was to answer the media's questions so he could move past the subject. So six hours after Belichick's press conference, Brady walked toward the media room with Patriots vice president of communications Stacey James, to hold his own press conference.

James had concerns about Brady talking to the press. There were more journalists at the stadium to question Brady than had been on hand after Aaron Hernandez was accused of murder. This wasn't going to be the usual group of Patriots beat writers asking football questions. The Patriots' media room had taken on the feel of the White House briefing room. It was packed wall to wall with network television reporters and print journalists from national publications. Cable stations were planning to break away from regularly scheduled programming to carry Brady's news conference live. CNN's Jake Tapper was standing by at his Washington studio and the network

was running a chyron on the bottom of the screen that read: "BREAKING NEWS—TOM BRADY TO SPEAK ANY MINUTE ON 'DEFLATE-GATE.'"

Anxious, James suggested he prep Brady before he entered the fray.

Brady thanked him and told him that wouldn't be necessary.

The prospect of facing a roomful of cameras and reporters didn't faze Brady. He had spent his life in a pocket being pursued by three-hundred-pound men intent on dismantling him. He routinely made split-second decisions with the clock running down and the game on the line. And he did it all in front of millions of people on national television. He was accustomed to high-pressure situations. Answering questions was not intimidating to him. Besides, he had nothing to hide.

Wearing sweatpants, a gray sweatshirt, and a Patriots pom hat, Brady entered the room and stepped to the lectern to the *rat-tat-tat* of camera shutters.

"Guys, how you doing?" he said, with his hands in his pockets.

Suddenly, his image was being projected on a jumbo screen in Times Square and on television monitors in airport terminals, hotel lobbies, and restaurants and bars throughout America.

"Obviously, I'd rather be up here talking about the Seahawks and preparing for the Super Bowl, which we've been trying to do for the last few days," he said. "But Coach Belichick addressed it with you guys this morning, and I wanted to give you guys the opportunity to ask the questions that you want. And I'll do my best to provide the answers that I have, if any. And we'll go from there."

With that, he opened the floor for questions.

"When and how did you supposedly alter the balls?" a reporter shouted over the questions of others.

"I didn't alter the ball in any way," Brady said calmly. He then explained the process that he goes through before every game in terms of selecting the game balls that he wants to use. And he stressed that once game balls are selected, the last thing he wants is anyone touching them, removing air from them, or adding air to them.

"Peter Alexander from NBC News. This has raised a lot of uncomfortable conversations for people around this country who view you—a three-time Super Bowl champion and a two-time MVP—as their idol."

Nodding, Brady looked Alexander in the eye.

"The question they're asking themselves," Alexander continued, "is what's up with our hero?"

Brady smiled.

"So can you answer right now—is Tom Brady a cheater?"

Brady chuckled, but he didn't find any of this funny. "I don't believe so. I feel like I've always played within the rules. I would never do anything to break the rules. And I believe in fair play. I respect the league and everything they're doing to try to create a very competitive playing field for all of the NFL teams."

"Tom," another reporter asked, "what do you say to the skeptics who say, 'Look, the Patriots have had violations before. How can we possibly believe what Brady and the coach are saying now?'"

"Well, everybody has an opinion," he said. "Everybody has the right to believe whatever they want. I don't ever cast judgment on someone's belief system. I think part of being in this position and being open for criticism is very much a part of being a professional athlete."

Pressed, he repeatedly said that he had no knowledge of anything being done to the footballs by anyone.

The press conference was the longest in Brady's career. He fielded sixty-one questions. His integrity was called into question. His motives were challenged. Through it all, he never took offense or became defensive. When given a chance to blast the league over leaks or to criticize the media for blowing the situation out of proportion, he refrained. As he left the microphone, he smiled, thanked the journalists, and waved.

"That was Tom Brady," said CNN's Jake Tapper, "quarterback of the New England Patriots, which will be going to the Super Bowl in a couple Sundays, admitting . . . nothing. He did not cheat, he said. He did not alter or deflate footballs in any way. He doesn't know what happened."

As soon as the press conference ended, pundits blasted Brady. Talk show host Mike Francesa spent a full hour on WFAN in New York lambasting Brady for "stonewalling," criticizing Belichick and Kraft, and blasting the NFL for not interrogating Brady prior to the Super Bowl. "The league should be ashamed of themselves," Francesa said.

After watching the press conference and his peers' reaction to it, journalist Charles P. Pierce, who had written a biography of Brady back in 2006, sympathized with the quarterback's predicament. "He sounded very much like a man explaining how he walked away from an airplane crash," Pierce wrote. Pierce was among a minority of reporters who saw the media's coverage of the situation as a "flatly hilarious" commentary on what he called "the journalism of moral frenzy."

The reaction to his press conference wounded Brady. Unlike Belichick, who was accustomed to being maligned and had the kind of temperament

that was more suited for dealing with it, Brady internalized personal criticisms. In that respect, Brady was very similar to Kraft. It was particularly painful to be characterized as a cheater, especially by his peers.

"I did not believe what Tom Brady had to say," former Jaguars quarterback Mark Brunell said on ESPN following the press conference. "Those balls were deflated. Somebody had to do it."

"It's obvious Tom Brady had something to do with this," Hall of Fame quarterback Troy Aikman told a radio station in Dallas. "For the balls to be deflated, that doesn't happen unless the quarterback wants that to happen. I can assure you of that."

On ESPN, Steelers Hall of Fame running back Jerome Bettis said: "I'm disappointed in you, Tom Brady."

"It's cheating," said former Steelers receiver-turned-announcer Hines Ward. "Regardless of how you may want to spin it, it helps Tom Brady, provides a better grip on the football, especially in bad weather conditions like rain."

During the first half of the Colts game, Brady completed just eleven of twenty-one passes for ninety-five yards, while throwing one touchdown pass and one interception. After the balls were reinflated during halftime, Brady's second-half numbers went way up. He completed twelve of fourteen passes for 131 yards, two touchdowns, and no interceptions. But by this point in the controversy, no one was looking at data.

Meantime, one of the most cutting comments came from Brady's upcoming Super Bowl opponent, the Seahawks' flamboyant defensive back, Richard Sherman. "I think people sometimes get a skewed view of Tom Brady," Sherman told reporters. "That he's just a clean-cut [guy], does everything right, never says a bad word to anyone. And we know him to be otherwise."

Roger Goodell had attended the AFC Championship game. But he had been unaware that questions had been raised about the air pressure in the Patriots' footballs until later that night. He was on his way home from Gillette Stadium when he received a phone call and was told "there was an irregularity with the footballs." *Irregularity?* Initially, Goodell didn't think much of it. But by later that morning, as bits and pieces of information were spreading like wildfire on social media, Goodell knew he had a problem on his hands.

For Goodell, whenever there was a league matter involving the Patriots he had to be just as concerned about perception as he was about substance. It was well known throughout the league that he and Kraft had an unusually

close relationship. Some NFL owners resented that. Further complicating matters was the often-unspoken but nonetheless pervasive jealousy through-out the league of Kraft and his team. While the NFL purposely designed strat-egies and policy to foster parity, the Patriots were on an unprecedented run of fourteen straight winning seasons, during which the team had made six trips to the Super Bowl. With a world-class quarterback who seemed deter-mined to beat Father Time, a genius coach whose thirst for winning seemed to increase with each championship, and an owner who managed to keep his star quarterback–coach duo together longer than any previous owner of a dynasty franchise, there was a lot to envy.

The bottom line was that Goodell knew how the rest of the league—and by extension, the league's fan base—felt toward the Patriots. So as soon as allegations were levied that the Patriots had manipulated the air pressure in footballs, the die was cast, both in New England and throughout the rest of the country. "If you lit up the country on that issue," Goodell explained, "you would have one color light in New England. The rest of the country would have a different color light."

That reality factored into Goodell's handling of the investigation and how his actions would be perceived by fans throughout the country. *They want to know,* he told himself, *that the league is being run fairly and that Rob-ert isn't going to get some benefit no one else is going to get.*

At the same time, Goodell didn't want to be unfair to Kraft by coming down harder on the Patriots just to prove that he wasn't being partial to a friend.

His job, he felt, was to play it straight down the middle.

That was going to be a lot easier said than done. At the outset, Goodell leaned heavily on the NFL's general counsel, Jeffrey Pash, to be the league's point person for the investigation. Pash reached out to prominent criminal defense attorney Theodore "Ted" Wells and asked him to conduct an "in-dependent investigation" for the league. Wells had defended Vice President Dick Cheney's former advisor Lewis "Scooter" Libby when he was accused of lying to the FBI. Wells had also represented former New York governor Eliot Spitzer when he was snared in a prostitution sting. The league hired Wells and his team from the law firm Paul, Weiss to investigate and render an opin-ion as to what might have caused the reduction in air pressure in the Patriots footballs during the AFC Championship game.

On Friday, a full five days after the Colts started clamoring behind the scenes for the NFL to look into the Patriots, the league finally issued a for-mal statement: "The investigation is being led jointly by NFL Executive Vice

President Jeff Pash and Ted Wells of the law firm of Paul, Weiss." In revealing for the first time that Pash and Wells were jointly investigating the Patriots and that nearly forty interviews with team personnel, game officials, and third parties with relevant information and expertise had already occurred, the league gave no indication on whether the findings thus far pointed to wrongdoing.

"The playing rules are intended to protect the fairness and integrity of our games," the league's statement said. "We take seriously claims that those rules have been violated and will fully investigate this matter without compromise or delay."

Impatient with the way the league was treating the Colts' claims, Kraft got proactive. The Patriots hired their own scientific experts and conducted a series of simulations designed to explain why balls that had initially been inflated to 12.5 PSI hours before the AFC Championship game could have been found to have less air by halftime.

It was all new territory for Belichick and his staff. But Belichick was intrigued by the simulation results, which revealed that if you inflate footballs to the league minimum 12.6 PSI in a warm, dry environment such as a locker room and then place them on a cold, wet field for up to two hours, the air pressure in the balls will drop slightly below the league minimum. This also helped explain why even the four Colts footballs that had been tested had been found to have a lower PSI at halftime than at the outset of the game. But since the Colts' balls had initially been inflated to a 13.0 PSI, per quarterback Andrew Luck's preference, the balls had lost air pressure by halftime and, according to one gauge, were slightly below the 12.5 PSI minimum.

After spending an inordinate amount of time studying the science of atmospheric pressure and temperature, Belichick decided to call an impromptu press conference on the Saturday before the team departed for Phoenix. Tired of being put on the defensive, he went on offense.

"This team was the best team in the AFC in the regular season," he told a large gathering of journalists in the Patriots' media room. "We won two games in the playoffs against two good football teams. The best team in the postseason—that's what this team is. I know that because I've been with them every day and I'm proud of this team.

"I just want to share with you what I've learned over the past week. I'm embarrassed to talk about the amount of time that I put into this relative to the other important challenge in front of us. I'm not a scientist. I'm not an expert in footballs. I'm not an expert in football measurements. I'm just

telling you what I know. I would not say that I'm Mona Lisa Vito of the football world, as she was in the car expertise area, all right?"

Reporters smiled at the reference to actress Marisa Tomei's character as an expert witness in the famous courtroom scene in *My Cousin Vinny*. Belichick loved that movie and had seen it dozens of times. But the attacks on his team had put him in no mood for humor.

"At no time was there any intent whatsoever to try to compromise the integrity of the game or to gain an advantage," he said. "Quite the opposite, we feel like we followed the rules of the game to the letter in our preparations, in our procedures, and in the way that we handled every game that we competitively played in as it related to this matter. We try to do everything right. We err on the side of caution. It's been that way now for many years. . . . We welcome the league's investigation into this matter."

His spirited defense of his team prompted a reporter to bring up Spygate.

"I mean, look, that's a whole 'nother discussion," Belichick said. "The guy's giving signals out in front of eighty thousand people, okay? So we filmed him taking signals out in front of eighty thousand people, like there were a lot of other teams doing at the time too, okay? But forget about that. If we were wrong, then we've been disciplined for that."

Later that night, the absurdity of the situation continued to spread across pop culture when the *Saturday Night Live* cold open featured a press conference at Gillette Stadium with comedian Beck Bennett playing Bill Belichick and Taran Killam playing Tom Brady. In the skit, they were both upstaged when a Patriots equipment manager joined the press conference and got into a tense exchange with a reporter that parodied the courtroom exchange between Jack Nicholson and Tom Cruise in *A Few Good Men*.

"You don't want the truth because deep down in places you don't talk about at Super Bowl parties, you *want* me on that ball. You *need* me on that ball," the equipment manager said.

"Did you deflate the balls?" the reporter pressed.

"I did the job I was told to do!" the equipment manager yelled.

"Did you deflate the balls?" the reporter shouted.

"You're damn right I did!"

When Kraft stepped off the plane in Phoenix for the start of Super Bowl week, it was all he could do to keep his composure. He'd had it with the way his team had already been convicted in the court of public opinion. He'd had

it with the leaks coming out of the league office. And he'd had it with the shots being taken at Brady's and Belichick's integrity. As soon as he reached the team hotel, Kraft called an unscheduled press conference.

"Given the events of last week, I wanted to take a minute to address the air pressure matter before we kick off this week's media availabilities," he said in a serious tone. "I have spoken with Coach Belichick. I have spoken with Tom Brady. I have taken the time to understand, to the best of my abilities, what goes into the preparation of game-day footballs and I want to make it clear that I believe *unconditionally* the New England Patriots have done *nothing* inappropriate in this process or in violation of NFL rules.

"Tom, Bill, and I have been together for fifteen years. They are my guys and they are family to me. Bill, Tom, and I have had many difficult discussions over the years and I have never known them to lie."

Kraft turned his focus to Goodell and delivered a warning.

"If the Wells investigation is not able to definitively determine that our organization tampered with the air pressure in the footballs," he said, "I would expect and hope that the league would apologize to our entire team, and in particular to Coach Belichick and Tom Brady, for what they've had to endure this past week. I am disappointed in the way this entire matter has been handled and reported upon."

Kraft was trying to shift the pressure off his team and onto the league.

The Seattle Seahawks were attempting to become the first team to win back-to-back Super Bowls since the Patriots had done it in 2003 and 2004. Tom Brady was playing for much more. After appearing in hundreds of NFL games, there had never been a game that Brady wanted to win more than Super Bowl XLIX. So much had been said about him. His father had encouraged him to answer through his play on the field.

In the first half, Brady set a Super Bowl record for completions in a half by completing twenty of twenty-seven attempts. The twentieth completion was a touchdown pass to Gronkowski with thirty seconds left in the half, to put the Patriots up 14–7.

But the Seahawks scored seventeen unanswered points in the second half and held a firm 24–14 lead early in the fourth quarter. No team had ever come back to win a Super Bowl when trailing by ten points in the fourth quarter. Plus, the Seahawks had the best defense in football. In the previous eight games, they had held teams to a combined seven points in the fourth quarter.

With just over twelve minutes remaining, Brady started a drive from the Patriots' thirty-two-yard line. Over the next four minutes, he drove his team

the length of the field with a pair of twenty-one-yard passes to Edelman before connecting with Amendola on a short touchdown pass to cut the Seahawks' lead to 24–21. Eight minutes remained.

A minute later, the Seahawks were forced to punt. Brady and the offense got the ball back on their own thirty-six-yard line. This time, Patriots fans chanted: "Bray-dee, Bray-dee!"

Brady stepped into the huddle. "We need a big championship drive," he told his teammates. "That's what we need."

Over the next five minutes, he picked apart the Seahawks' defense, completing nine consecutive passes. The last one was a three-yard touchdown strike to Edelman, putting the Patriots up 28–24 with 2:02 remaining on the game clock. Brady set the record for completions in a Super Bowl with thirty-seven and pulled off the most dazzling comeback of his storied career. And he was thirty-seven years old.

"That was a big-time play, Jules," Brady told Edelman. "Championship play."

"It don't mean nothin' unless we win it," Edelman said.

"We are gonna win it," Brady said.

But one minute later, Seahawks quarterback Russell Wilson threw a deep ball to receiver Jermaine Kearse. Leaping to make the catch, Kearse had the ball deflected by Patriots defensive back Malcolm Butler. Both Kearse and Butler crashed to the turf. As Kearse landed on his back, the ball caromed off his leg, hit his foot, hit his knee, and ricocheted off his hand as another Patriots defender leaped over him.

"And it's broken up," announcer Al Michaels said.

Still on his back, Kearse juggled the ball before grabbing it, rising to his feet, and starting to run toward the end zone.

"Holy . . . wow!" said announcer Cris Collinsworth.

"Did he come up with the *football*?" Michaels said.

Butler sprang to his feet and knocked Kearse out of bounds.

"Unbelievable!" Collinsworth said.

"Look at that," Michaels said as the instant replay appeared on television.

"How many different plays are the Patriots gonna have like this?" Collinsworth said. "Mario Manningham. David Tyree. And now Kearse! You've got to be kidding me. Not again."

On the Patriots' sideline, Brady stared up at the replay on the stadium jumbo screen, shaking his head in disbelief.

With 1:06 remaining, the Seahawks had the ball on the Patriots' five-yard line.

Belichick faced the same question he had faced at the end of the team's last Super Bowl appearance against the Giants: whether to let the Seahawks score right away in order to give Brady time to make a last-ditch effort to score.

On the snap, Wilson handed off to running back Marshawn Lynch, who bulled his way for four yards before being tackled eighteen inches from the goal line.

With less than a minute left and the clock ticking, Belichick thought about calling time-out. But he decided to let the clock run. It was the gutsiest call of his coaching career.

His decision seemed to unnerve the Seahawks' sideline.

The game clock went from 1:01 to 0:26 as Russell lined up in the shotgun formation and took the snap. Within one second, he fired a pass to a receiver running a slant route.

Malcolm Butler jumped into the passing lane.

"INTERCEPTED AT THE GOAL LINE by Malcolm Butler!" Michaels shouted.

Butler had the ball on the one-yard line.

"Unreal!" Michaels said.

The Patriots defenders piled on Butler.

The Seahawks players were stunned.

The stadium was in a frenzy.

Childlike, Brady jumped up and down on the sideline, screaming.

On a bang-bang play that would go down in the annals of football history as both one of the greatest NFL plays of all time and one of the worst play calls ever, Butler, an unknown rookie free agent out of West Alabama who had never made an interception as a pro, pulled the Patriots back from the brink of defeat.

Yet twenty seconds remained. Brady put on his helmet and trotted onto the field.

The Patriots were still in a precarious position. With the ball on the Patriots' one-yard line, Brady didn't have the option to simply take the snap and kneel down to end the game. That would result in a two-point safety and put the ball back in the Seahawks' hands. The Patriots were going to have to run a play and try to advance the ball.

As Brady stepped to the line of scrimmage, Belichick called time-out and Brady jogged to the sideline. In this critical moment, the competitive advantage of fifteen years' experience together was on display. They both were thinking the same thing—the Seahawks had an extremely aggressive defense.

And defensive lineman Michael Bennett was prone to jumping offside. In 2014 he led the league with ten offside penalties. Belichick wanted Brady to try to draw the Seahawks offside. Brady was on the same page.

The Seahawks crowded the line of scrimmage. Brady went with a hard count. Bennett jumped and made contact with a Patriots player. A flag was thrown. Belichick thrust his fist in the air. The five-yard penalty advanced the ball to the six-yard line. The game was effectively over.

With room to maneuver, all Brady had left to do was take two more snaps and take a knee each time. But on first down from the six-yard line, as Brady knelt, players started pushing and shoving. Linebacker Bruce Irvin slapped Gronkowski. Gronkowski clubbed him and then got into it with Michael Bennett. They ended up on the ground. A brawl broke out. Punches were thrown. Helmets were ripped off. Flags flew.

In the scrum, Brady remained on his knee, ball in hand, a scene of chaos around him. When the dust settled, Irvin was ejected, the Seahawks were assessed another fifteen-yard penalty, and Brady huddled his team one final time, screaming at his teammates to stay focused.

Then he took the final snap and knelt down.

As the Patriots players dumped a cooler of ice water on Belichick and ran onto the field in jubilation, Brady retreated toward the end zone to be alone. Down on one knee, he clutched the ball. No team had ever come from ten points behind in the fourth quarter to win a Super Bowl. To pull it off, Brady had orchestrated sixty-eight- and sixty-four-yard touchdown drives in what Peter King would later call "the greatest quarter of his life." Bowing his head, Brady was taking in the moment when he was suddenly interrupted by someone stepping into his personal space. Seeing the individual's cleats, Brady looked up and recognized Richard Sherman, who had vilified him earlier in the week. Preferring his privacy, Brady nonetheless stood and shook his hand.

"You're a great player," Sherman said.

Brady nodded.

thirty-seven

NEW ENGLAND VERSUS EVERYBODY

S tanding on the stage beside Gronkowski for the Lombardi Trophy presentation, Julian Edelman leaned over the railing and reached down to his father. "We did it, Dad," Julian told him. "We did it."

Crying and wearing his son's jersey, Frank Edelman reached up and grabbed his son's hand.

"I love you," Julian told him, choking up. "I wouldn't be here without you."

Belichick came up behind Edelman and wrapped his arms around him.

"Coach, thanks for bringing me to this moment," Edelman said, squeezing him.

"Thanks for doing this for *me*," Belichick said.

"You gave me the best year of my life," Edelman said.

"You know what?" Belichick said, taking a step back to look at Edelman and Gronkowski. "You guys went out there and won it."

Gronkowski nodded.

"It's a players' game," Belichick said.

"That's the best team win I've ever been a part of," Gronkowski said.

Edelman embraced Belichick again and said, "I'd do anything for you."

Written off at the beginning of the season, the Patriots had persevered through career-threatening injuries to key players, a grueling stretch of games, and withering scrutiny triggered by allegations from rival teams. Through all of the adversity, the Patriots had formed an unusually tight brotherhood, and they were brimming with raw emotion.

When Kraft reached the podium for the trophy presentation, Goodell was already in place, waiting to congratulate the team that his office was investigating. In the commotion, Kraft pulled NBC's Dan Patrick aside. "Can I have twenty seconds of airtime?" he said.

Patrick smiled. "Mr. Kraft," he said, "I think you deserve all the time you want."

Kraft had something he wanted to get off his chest, and he wanted to do it on national television. It was extremely satisfying that his team had won another Super Bowl after a ten-year interlude. And he was thrilled that the team had mounted a historic fourth-quarter comeback. Nonetheless Kraft couldn't help steaming when he considered how much the league had done to thwart his team's chances. The NFL had dispatched eight investigators to Foxborough and spent the entire week prior to the team's trip to Phoenix probing coaches and players and staff. At the same time, league officials had leaked false and incendiary information to the press, fueling a media frenzy. It was fuckin' ridiculous, Kraft felt. While the Seahawks prepared to play the Patriots, Belichick and Brady and the rest of the organization had to fend off an investigation concocted by rivals.

"Here to present the Lombardi Trophy to the New England Patriots," Patrick said, "the commissioner of the National Football League, Roger Goodell."

Booing drowned out his voice.

"Wow!" Goodell said, ignoring the noise. "What a night. Congratulations to both teams. But in particular, congratulations to the Patriots and their fans."

As soon as Goodell handed the trophy to Kraft, the boisterous booing instantly switched to euphoric cheering. Goodell faded into the background and Kraft faced the camera as Patrick held the mic.

"To all the Patriots fans out there," Kraft said, "wherever you are, this is our fourth Super Bowl championship in the last fourteen years. The first one we won I thought was pretty special because it happened at a unique time in our country when it meant a lot. I never thought another trophy could feel as special."

Kraft raised the Lombardi.

"But this one *ab-so-lute-ly* does!" he said.

Patriots fans cheered wildly.

"And every true Patriots fan understands it," Kraft continued. "I want to thank the great coaching staff and the players, because we are all Patriots. And tonight, once again, the Patriots are world champions."

Amid the cheering, Kraft passed the trophy to Belichick, who stepped to the microphone.

"I'm so proud of all these players," Belichick said, his voice cracking. "I love these players."

Belichick handed the trophy to Brady.

Patrick informed Brady that he had been named the Super Bowl MVP.

Mentally exhausted, Brady shrugged off the news. He'd just been through two of the most trying weeks of his career. His integrity had been impugned and he'd been widely mocked. "I want to thank my family and all my friends who supported me," he said, clutching the Lombardi Trophy as his eyes welled up. "All my teammates. I love you guys. This is for you guys."

When Dan Patrick informed Brady that by virtue of being named Super Bowl MVP he was the recipient of a new cherry-red, dual-cab Chevy Colorado pickup truck, Brady told him to give the keys to Malcolm Butler. The rookie, Brady insisted, deserved the truck.

It was a triumphant end to the most emotional season in the Brady-Belichick era. It had culminated with the two of them joining the Steelers' Terry Bradshaw and Chuck Noll as the only quarterback-coach tandem to win four Super Bowls. And Brady had become just the third quarterback with four Lombardi Trophies, tying him with Bradshaw and Joe Montana.

The Patriots-Seahawks game was the most watched broadcast in US television history. There were also 28.4 million tweets related to the game that were sent during the live telecast, making it the most tweeted Super Bowl ever. With a record number of Americans watching and engaged on social media, Brady had put on a Super Bowl performance for the ages—completing thirty-seven of fifty passes for 328 yards and four touchdowns. "It bolstered the argument that Brady, already on the list of history's best quarterbacks, is in fact the greatest of all time," declared *Sports Illustrated*. The *New York Times* called Super Bowl XLIX "quintessential Brady." And Patriots offensive coordinator Josh McDaniels told the press afterward: "I've been coaching for fourteen years, and I've never known anyone who has more mental toughness. It was a fitting end for him."

But when asked during his postgame press conference to assess his own legacy, Brady refused. "No, not going to do that," he said. "I've got a lot of football left."

On the day after the Super Bowl in Phoenix, a blizzard hit Boston, dropping more than a foot of snow. But that didn't stop city officials from breaking out the famous World War II–style amphibious duck boats and hosting a full-scale Patriots victory parade. Fans from all across New England flocked to downtown Boston, forming massive crowds lining the parade route and

proudly bellowing "Bray-dee, Bray-dee" and "Bill, Bill, Bill," while holding up signs that read: "DEFLATE THIS!"

Snowflakes blew through the air as construction workers at the Prudential Center attached a Patriots flag to a giant crane and lowered it over the parade's starting point. In the lead boat, Kraft fired up the crowd by pumping his fist while clutching the Lombardi Trophy. With Stevie Wonder's "Sir Duke" blaring from a sound system, the procession of boats on wheels moved down Boylston Street, through Copley Square, past Boston Common to Tremont Street, and on to City Hall Plaza. Fans reveled as Belichick donned a Patriots pom hat, Gronkowski danced, and Malcolm Butler bowed in acknowledgment of a salute from a throng of college students atop a mountainous snowbank.

Wearing dark shades and his Grizzly Adams beard, Edelman accepted a handmade sign—"YOU HAD ME AT HELLO"—from a young woman. Then he climbed onto the roof of his duck boat, removed his sweater, and hoisted a big flagpole. Wearing only a T-shirt, Edelman waved the Patriots flag as if he were leading a revolution. There was euphoria in the streets.

For Edelman, Gronkowski, Butler, and virtually every other player, it was their first parade in Boston. For Brady, it was his fourth. No longer young and single and carefree, Brady spent most of the duck boat ride with his arms tightly wrapped around his younger son, absorbing the moment.

Unlike his teammates, Brady had so much more on his mind, so much more on his shoulders, and so much more to balance. He was married to one of the most recognizable and successful women in the world. He had three children. He had his own company. He was the top player in the most popular sport in America. His celebrity status was on par with that of rock stars and Hollywood actors. And he was the target of the most intense NFL investigation in league history.

When the parade ended, Belichick headed to New York to appear on David Letterman's show, the players got on with their offseason plans, Kraft prepared to testify at the Aaron Hernandez trial, and Brady girded himself to fight for his reputation.

Ted Wells and his team had developed a working theory to explain the loss of air pressure in Patriots footballs in the AFC Championship game. The theory centered on two Patriots employees—equipment assistant John Jastremski and locker room attendant Patrick McNally.

Wells confirmed that the game officials had inspected the balls and certified that they were properly inflated approximately three hours before kickoff. Security camera footage outside the officials' locker room showed that McNally had removed the balls from the officials' locker room to bring them to the playing field shortly thereafter. En route, McNally stopped at a bathroom at the end of the stadium tunnel corridor. Approximately ninety seconds later, McNally emerged and continued onto the field, where he deposited the balls.

A physicist working as an expert witness for Wells concluded that the air loss in the Patriots' balls wasn't fully attributable to weather conditions and likely involved some human intervention. Wells considered the ninety-second bathroom pit stop as an opportunity for human intervention. But under questioning, McNally insisted he hadn't deflated the balls. He had entered the bathroom, he maintained, for the same reason that everyone else does.

Wells also interviewed the referee, who said that it was not protocol for McNally to take the footballs to the field without first notifying the officials. But a security guard stationed outside the Patriots' locker room told investigators that it was "routine for McNally to walk to the field with the game balls unaccompanied." A second witness corroborated the security guard's account.

McNally and Jastremski also turned over their text messages and emails. There was nothing in there to implicate them in the AFC Championship game. But earlier in the season, there had been a game against the Jets in which the referees had added air to the balls, inadvertently overinflating them. After that game, Jastremski had texted McNally: "The refs fucked us . . . a few of them [the balls] were at almost 16 (PSI)." Although it hadn't been Jastremski's fault, Brady had complained vociferously to him about how terrible the balls had felt. Jastremski had shared Brady's displeasure with McNally, who sarcastically texted back, "Fuck Tom," and encouraged Jastremski to "make sure you blow up the ball to look like a rugby ball so tom can get used to it before Sunday."

The texting banter between McNally and Jastremski was at times profane and often comical. In one text after the Jets game, McNally even jokingly referred to himself as "the deflator." But the reality was that McNally was a part-time game-day employee who had no responsibility over game-ball preparation. Nor did he have much opportunity to tamper with them, except perhaps during his bathroom pit stop. Under questioning by highly experienced lawyers accustomed to dealing with sophisticated, white-collar

criminal behavior, McNally and Jastremski were consistent—they had never deflated the game balls for the AFC Championship game.

Tom Brady had always taken the mantle of role model seriously. Way back in the early 2000s, when he had first experienced stardom, Brady had spent the better part of a week in New York City while rehearsing for his first appearance on *Saturday Night Live*. One evening, a couple of acquaintances invited him out for a night on the town. Young, single, and on top of the world, Brady figured: Why not? But at the last minute, he changed his mind. He could make a thousand good decisions, he figured, and if he made one bad decision, that would be the thing that people remember. He ended up spending that night alone in his midtown Manhattan hotel room.

Brady's decision that night was an example of why the NFL's biggest star had gone fifteen years without ever getting into trouble or doing anything in his private life that would bring embarrassment to his family, the Patriots franchise, or the league.

Ted Wells didn't know the story about Brady's spending the night alone in his hotel room. In fact, Wells didn't know Brady at all. But he'd been told that Brady had a great reputation and had been an exemplary member of the NFL community.

Days before he was scheduled to question Brady, Wells notified Brady's agent that he wanted to see his client's cell phone. Wells was particularly interested in any text messages, emails, or phone calls between Brady and Jastremski and between Brady and McNally dating back to September 2014.

When apprised of the request, Brady was willing to oblige, saying he had nothing to hide. But under the collective bargaining agreement, the league had no authority to compel a player to surrender his phone or its contents. When the league had investigated quarterback Brett Favre for texting lewd messages and photos of himself to a New York Jets employee, Favre had never turned over his phone. Even though Brady was willing to turn over his phone to help clear his name, his agent, Don Yee, strongly advised him to decline Wells's request. Brady's phone was full of personal communications. And the league, after all, had a terrible reputation for leaks. Brady took his advice.

On March 2, Yee emailed Wells and told him that his request had been considered. "However," Yee told him, "we respectfully decline."

Wells wrote back, encouraging Yee to reconsider.

On March 6, Brady met Wells and his team at Gillette Stadium. Yee and Brady's lawyer sat in. At the outset, Wells asked Yee if they had reconsidered.

"We respectfully decline," Yee told him.

Yee did not volunteer an explanation, and Wells did not seek one. Nor did Wells or anyone from the league inform Brady that he would be subject to punishment for not turning over his personal electronic communications.

But in his mind, Wells formed a jaded perception of Brady before he had even asked his first question. Wells would later say under oath of Yee's advice to Brady: "In my almost forty years of practice, I think that was one of the most ill-advised decisions I have ever seen because it hurt how I viewed his [Tom's] credibility."

The interview went smoothly. Brady answered every question and stated unequivocally that he had had no involvement in any effort to deflate balls. Nor did he know of any attempt to deflate balls by anyone else in the Patriots organization.

After interviewing Brady, Wells later stated: "He answered every question I put to him. He did not refuse to answer any question in terms of the back and forth between Mr. Brady and my team. He was totally cooperative."

At the same time, Wells had interviewed Belichick, who confirmed that he believed Brady had had nothing to do with altering game balls. Wells and his team hadn't interviewed anyone who suggested that Brady had had any involvement in or knowledge of an attempt to modify the air pressure in balls.

Yet Wells couldn't get past the fact that Brady wouldn't turn over his phone.

Aside from the league investigation and a jury convicting Aaron Hernandez of first-degree murder and sentencing him to life in prison without parole, spring was a time for the Patriots' brain trust to take stock of the fact that their unparalleled continuity had set them apart in the annals of NFL history. Since Brady had taken over at quarterback in 2001, the Patriots' winning percentage (.759) in the regular season had been the best in the NFL. The nucleus of that winning team—Robert and Jonathan Kraft, Bill Belichick, and Tom Brady—had fully formed when Brady was drafted, on April 16, 2000. It had been unimaginable then that a full fifteen years later, the four of them would be standing together at Boston's Fenway Park, each holding one of the four Lombardi Trophies they had won together.

Yet on April 13, 2015, the Red Sox public address announcer invited the opening-day crowd to welcome the four-time Super Bowl champions.

Suddenly, Robert Kraft, Jonathan Kraft, Bill Belichick, and Tom Brady emerged from behind a giant American flag draped over the Green Monster. Clutching their trophies, the four of them walked triumphantly from left field as U2's "Beautiful Day" played and Red Sox fans roared.

When they reached the infield grass, the brother of a Boston Marathon bombing victim handed Brady a baseball. As Brady stepped to the mound and prepared to deliver the ceremonial first pitch, the Krafts and Belichick formed a semicircle behind him. Brady's pitch landed in the glove of Red Sox star David Ortiz, who then ran to the mound and posed for pictures with the four other men as the Fenway faithful showered them with cheers and a long standing ovation.

In Boston, the Patriots were kings. Kraft was the city's most beloved sports team owner. Belichick was alongside legendary Celtics coach Red Auerbach as the best ever. And no athlete in any sport from any era was as beloved as Brady. More revered than Ted Williams or Larry Bird or Bobby Orr, he was now drawing comparisons to Paul Revere, and his popularity was becoming more on par with JFK's. The ongoing NFL investigation had only deepened New Englanders' allegiance to Brady and the Patriots.

Yet the stigmatization by those outside New England had wounded Brady in a visceral way. The whole experience had caused him to turn more inward, to shrink his circle, and to surround himself even more closely with family and his most trusted friends. The biggest star on the American sports scene yearned for privacy.

A week after revving up Red Sox fans at Fenway Park, Brady stayed behind when the rest of the team traveled to Washington to be honored by President Barack Obama. It was the first time that Brady had not attended a White House ceremony following a Super Bowl victory, and his reasoning was personal, not political. Among other things, his wife announced her retirement from the fashion runway that week. She did her final show in São Paulo. After twenty years in the industry, Bündchen said: "It's a privilege to be able to stop." At thirty-four, the highest-paid supermodel in history was moving on to pursue other interests, and Brady wanted to be there for her on such a momentous occasion.

Flanked by more than 125 Patriots players and personnel, President Obama lauded the team.

"Even those of us who have other teams we root for, the Patriots organization is as good of an organization as there has ever been in professional sports," he said. "To be able to maintain that kind of consistent excellence is a rare thing."

With a straight face, the president glanced over his shoulder at Belichick, who wore a suit and tie.

"I'm particularly grateful that coach decided to dress up today," he said.

Kraft grinned. The players cracked up.

"We had some scissors if he wanted to cut the sleeves off," Obama continued.

Belichick laughed.

"Formal hoodies are allowed," Obama said. The players loved the way the president ribbed Belichick. Moments later, Kraft presented Obama with a Patriots jersey. Then Kraft turned the podium over to Belichick.

"To be welcomed by President Obama so warmly, to have the opportunity, each of us, to shake hands with him and talk with him, exchange a greeting, it makes you feel about as patriotic as you could feel right now," Belichick said. "Just proud to be an American. Proud to be at the White House. Proud to be a New England Patriot."

After Belichick and the Patriots were punished for improperly filming the Jets in 2007, the NFL had lowered the burden-of-proof standard for investigating alleged violations of the league's Integrity of the Game policy. At Goodell's urging, the long-standing "clear and convincing evidence" requirement was changed to "preponderance of the evidence." Under the new standard, the league had to find only that there was more than a 50 percent chance—that it was "more probable than not"—a rule had been violated.

This change had major implications for the Deflategate investigation. On May 6, 2015, the NFL released the Wells report, a 139-page document that concluded it was "more probable than not" that equipment staff for the Patriots—McNally and Jastremski—had "participated in a deliberate effort to release air from the Patriots game balls after the balls were examined by the referee."

At the same time, despite no testimony from anyone indicating that Brady had instructed or even suggested that the equipment staff deflate balls below the 12.5 PSI limit, Wells concluded "it was more probable than not that Brady was at least generally aware of the inappropriate activities of McNally and Jastremski involving the release of air from Patriots game balls."

Generally aware? The players' union and Brady's agent were irate. No player in the history of the NFL had ever been disciplined for being generally aware of something. From the union's perspective, that would be akin to suspending a player for being generally aware that a teammate was taking

performance-enhancing drugs. But in this instance, the union felt, even that analogy didn't fit, given that Brady had said he *wasn't* aware of McNally's or Jastremski's doing anything improper.

With Wells's opinion in hand, Goodell was left to decide what, if any, punishment was appropriate. He started by fining the Patriots $1 million and taking away the team's first-round draft choice in 2016 and its fourth-round draft choice in 2017. He also required the Patriots to suspend Jastremski and McNally.

But Goodell saved his harshest punishment for Brady, suspending him for the first four games of the 2015 season, which amounted to a $2 million loss in salary.

Kraft was livid. In his view, Deflategate never would have amounted to anything if it weren't for Spygate. A past sin had given oxygen to a specious allegation about air pressure levied by a jealous rival. And the league had participated in the ruse. The most damning allegation of the entire Deflategate controversy was Chris Mortensen's claim that the "NFL has found that 11 of the Patriots footballs used in Sunday's AFC title game were under-inflated by 2 lbs each, per league sources." Someone with the NFL fed that incendiary information to Mortensen, which cast a shadow over the Patriots heading into the Super Bowl. One of the more salient conclusions in the Wells Report was that Mortensen's information was bogus. Only one Patriots ball was two pounds below the league's air pressure minimum, and it's unclear whether that particular ball even made it onto the field of play. Although the Patriots appealed numerous times to NFL general counsel Jeffrey Pash and those who worked for him to publicly set the record straight, they never did so. Not right after Mortensen's tweet. Not for two weeks leading up to the Super Bowl. Not even after the Wells Report was released. In the meantime, Brady's legacy had been stained.

The league's actions put Goodell directly at odds with Kraft. For years, Kraft had been Goodell's biggest advocate, starting with Kraft's efforts to help him become the commissioner and culminating recently in Kraft's spirited defense of him and his reputation during his handling of the Ray Rice incident. Now Goodell was treating Brady more harshly than he had initially treated Rice.

Instinctively, Kraft wanted to fight back. Some of his closest friends encouraged him to do just that. One of them, a CEO, gave Kraft some simple advice: "Tell Goodell to go fuck himself."

A couple of Kraft's sons who weren't involved with the team felt similarly. Their father, after all, had always gone out of his way to put the league first. He had facilitated the television contracts that had enriched the league and its owners. He had mediated the labor disagreement and brought the owners and players together to save both sides from a crippling lockout. And he had put his neck on the line to publicly defend Goodell after the release of the in-elevator video of Rice beating his fiancée. After all that, it felt like it was time for their father to take a page from the playbook of former Raiders owner Al Davis, who had taken the league to court on more than one occasion.

But Kraft had no interest in suing the league. Instead, the Patriots aggressively attacked the Wells Report, launching a website, wellsreportcontext.com, and publishing a twenty-thousand-word rebuttal to Wells's conclusions. Patriots lawyer Daniel Goldberg picked apart the scientific evidence cited by the league and called Wells's findings "incomplete, incorrect, and lack[ing] context." Goldberg also accused Wells of having manipulated evidence to make Brady look bad. At the same time, scholars at the American Enterprise Institute released a scathing report that took apart the scientists Wells had relied on for his findings.

Meantime, lampooning Goodell became a recreational sport in New England. Fans called in to radio talk shows and railed against him. Journalists shredded him. "Free Tom Brady" chants became common at Red Sox games. Even Massachusetts attorney general Maura Healey weighed in, saying, "I sure wish that the NFL would spend a tenth of the time that it's spending on this on issues of domestic violence and sexual assault. I'm just struck by the fact that somebody like Ray Rice gets a two-game suspension and Tom Brady, over deflated balls, is facing a four-game suspension. It doesn't add up for me."

Wells faced such a backlash that he took the extraordinary step of publicly defending his own credibility. Meantime, the players' union filed an appeal on Brady's behalf, challenging the four-game suspension. But under the collective bargaining agreement, the commissioner had the right to serve as the hearing officer. Goodell promptly appointed himself to be the arbitrator of Brady's appeal.

As the standoff escalated, Kraft began to question the wisdom in continuing such a public war of words with the league. It wasn't that he didn't want to fight. The problem was that the collective bargaining agreement gave the commissioner the power to act as judge and jury in matters of player discipline.

If he was going to go to battle, Kraft wanted to know that he could win. But in this case, the commissioner was essentially a czar. Goodell had all

the authority. Kraft could appeal. He could sue. But in the end, Goodell would prevail.

There were other factors to consider. The Patriots were a privately owned franchise. As the sole owner, Kraft had always embraced a philosophy of doing what was best for the long-term future of the organization, even if that meant taking a short-term hit. If he went after Goodell, Patriots fans would like it. But doing so would diminish Kraft's ability to work within the league, which was more valuable to him in the long run.

Reluctantly Kraft accepted Goodell's $1 million fine and the loss of draft picks. "I don't want to continue the rhetoric that's gone on for the last four months," he said in a public statement on May 19, 2015. "I'm going to accept, reluctantly, what he has given to us, and not continue this dialogue and rhetoric, and we won't appeal."

Brady was not happy. For him, this was personal. A new ESPN/ABC News national poll found that 54 percent of all fans and 69 percent of all avid fans believed that Brady had cheated. It galled Brady that the league was doing this to him.

"I could go out there for show and fight," Kraft told him. "But it won't make a difference because Goodell is the judge and the jury."

Brady had no intention of backing down. His reputation was on the line. Everything he'd ever accomplished was being called into question. And after spending more than $8 million and carrying out the most thorough investigation in the history of the NFL—with more than sixty witnesses interviewed over a five-month period—the league had not proved that *anyone* in the Patriots organization, much less Brady, had let air out of the footballs prior to the AFC Championship game.

The players' union filed a motion seeking to have Goodell removed as the arbiter of Brady's appeal. Goodell had previously recused himself from arbitrating Ray Rice's challenge to his suspension, and the union wanted nothing less for Brady.

"You cannot lawfully arbitrate a hearing in which you are a central witness," Brady's legal team argued to Goodell. "You cannot lawfully arbitrate a matter implicating the competence and credibility of NFL staff."

Undeterred, Goodell denied Brady's motion and insisted that he would hear Brady's appeal. He scheduled a hearing in July to determine whether Brady's four-game suspension should be reduced. Goodell also denied Brady's request to question the NFL's general counsel, Jeffrey Pash, over his

role in the investigation and his role in helping to write Wells's final report. Goodell told Brady that Pash could not be compelled to testify. Brady's request to see all documents pertaining to the league's investigation was also denied.

Brady was in the impossible position of trying to prove a negative. Goodell was in the unenviable position of judging the league's most accomplished player. At 9:30 a.m. on June 23, 2015, the two of them faced each other in a conference room at NFL headquarters. With twenty lawyers and a stenographer looking on, Goodell presided.

"We all know why we are here this morning," Goodell began. "This is in response to an appeal filed by Tom Brady."

Under oath, Brady answered direct questions.

"As you are sitting here today," his lawyer said, "I am going to ask you to be very clear. Did you ever give anyone any directions or instructions or authorization, anything, for the AFC Championship game that they should alter, change, lower the air pressure of footballs?"

"Absolutely not," Brady said.

"As you are sitting here right now, do you still believe Mr. Jastremski when he told you he didn't know anything about it and he didn't do anything?"

"Yes."

Prior to the hearing, Goodell had learned that Brady's phone had been destroyed after Wells had requested access to it. Goodell found that suspicious. Brady explained that every time his cell phone provider came out with a new model, he received one free of charge. It was a perk of being Tom Brady. And every time he traded in his phone for a new one, he gave instructions to destroy the old phone and the SIM card. It was a way to ensure that no one could get access to the personal information on it—contact information for many players in the league, family pictures, and so on. On four previous occasions, Brady had followed that safety precaution when upgrading to a new phone.

Brady's lawyer pointed out to the commissioner that the destruction of the phone had nothing to do with the investigation. In fact, it had been established that Brady had never texted, emailed, or called McNally. And all of Brady's electronic communications with Jastremski had been made available through Jastremski.

Goodell remained skeptical.

Brady's lawyer tried to put the matter to rest.

"Do you recall whether there was any discussion of deflation or pressure

or the Wells investigation or anything else that you recall in those text messages?" his lawyer asked.

"Absolutely not," Brady testified.

"Did you ever discuss with him any effort to conceal any deflation of footballs from investigators or anything else?"

"Absolutely not," Brady said.

Wells also testified. He explained that the league had paid his fee, that league attorney Jeff Pash reviewed and suggested edits to his report, and that Brady was polite and fully cooperated in his interview. Wells also explained that the biggest strike against Brady was the fact that he didn't turn over his phone.

"Not only did it hurt him in terms of how we evaluated his credibility," Wells testified, "but it put us in a hell of a spot because you have a person with this exemplary record and has done all these good things that people are saying, and yet they are conducting themselves in a fashion that suggests they are hiding something and may be guilty and not being forthcoming. So it was really hard to give them credit for the good stuff when he's basically looking you in the face and saying I'm not going to give you my phone."

The hearing adjourned at 8:27 p.m.

Based on the strength of Brady's under-oath testimony, the players' union and Brady's legal team were confident his suspension would be tossed out. But Goodell issued a twenty-page written decision upholding the suspension. Goodell also went much further in his accusations against Brady than Wells had in his original report. "Mr. Brady," Goodell wrote, "participated in a scheme to tamper with the game balls after they had been approved by the game officials for use in the AFC Championship Game."

Kraft was irate when he saw Goodell's ruling. The outcome didn't surprise him in the least, but the hard line he took and the defamatory wording he used—especially the way he branded Brady as a schemer—incensed Kraft. To him, it was incomprehensible that the league would attempt to destroy the reputation of one of its greatest players without any evidence that he did anything wrong.

Brady's agent, Don Yee, called the NFL's appeal process "a sham."

And the NFL Players Association blasted the entire process as "a kangaroo court proceeding, bereft of fundamentally fair procedures."

Anticipating a legal challenge from the players' union, the NFL took the extraordinary step of filing suit in a federal court in Manhattan, where league

lawyers asked a judge to certify that the commissioner had the power to arbitrate in Brady's case.

Brady, meanwhile, was sick and tired of trying to defend his reputation on the league's terms. He was ready to take the fight directly to Goodell. He authorized his lawyers to countersue the commissioner. In the suit, Brady and the players' union challenged Goodell's authority and sought to have the four-game suspension tossed out.

Back in Foxborough, Kraft convened a press conference at Gillette Stadium and went after the league's lawyers.

"I continue to believe and unequivocally support Tom Brady," Kraft said. "I, first and foremost, need to apologize to our fans because I truly believed what I did in May, given the actual evidence of the situation and the league's history on discipline matters, would make it much easier for the league to exonerate Tom Brady. Unfortunately, I was wrong."

Kraft had been banking on cooler heads prevailing and a deal being struck that would have enabled Brady's suspension to be lifted after he submitted to the league's appeal process. But Kraft was convinced that Goodell was being influenced by bad legal advice.

"I have often said, 'If you want to get a deal done, sometimes you have to get the lawyers out of the room,'" Kraft continued. "I had hoped that Tom Brady's appeal to the league would provide Roger Goodell with the necessary explanation to overturn his suspension. Now the league has taken the matter to court, which is a tactic that only a lawyer would recommend."

When training camp opened at the end of July, Bill Belichick was preparing to start the 2015 season with second-year quarterback Jimmy Garoppolo under center. Brady, meanwhile, was dealing with fallout from his appeal. Judge Richard M. Berman, who was presiding over Brady's lawsuit, refused to let either party submit evidence under seal. As a result, when the Players Association filed an amendment to its complaint, 1,400 pages of emails from Brady's Patriots account between September 2014 through March became accessible to reporters with a PACER (Public Access to Court Electronic Records) account. The hundreds of emails contained nothing incriminating, which was why the union wanted them admitted as evidence. But Brady's mundane communications about everything from the color of his pool cover to his golf outings to his tendency to refer to friends as "babe" became media fodder. On August 12, while Garoppolo was running the offense during practice in Foxborough, Brady entered a federal courthouse in New York and took a seat just a few

feet away from Roger Goodell. Approximately seventy-five reporters filled the courtroom as Judge Berman brought the proceeding to order. "I don't know what to make of that finding Tom Brady was at least generally aware of the activities of [Jim McNally and John Jastremski]," he said at the outset.

The NFL simply wanted Berman to rule that Goodell had the power to suspend Brady. But Berman questioned the fairness of the process that had led to Brady's suspension.

"What is the direct evidence that implicates Mr. Brady?" Berman asked NFL lawyer Daniel Nash.

Nash referred to the text message between McNally and Jastremski, as well as the phone calls between Jastremski and Brady. "Brady clearly knew about this," Nash insisted.

Unconvinced, Judge Berman repeated his original question.

Nash finally conceded that there was no "smoking gun" implicating Brady, but he argued that Brady's unwillingness to turn over his phone made it "clearly reasonable to infer" culpability.

Neither Brady nor Goodell testified before Berman. All of the judge's questions were fielded by the lawyers for each side. After the hearing concluded, Judge Berman spent hours in talks with both sides, trying to facilitate a settlement. But neither side was willing to budge.

On the morning of September 3, 2015, Judge Berman vacated Brady's four-game suspension. Citing "sufficient legal deficiencies" in the NFL's case against Brady and saying the league had "prejudiced" the Patriots quarterback, Berman concluded: "No NFL policy or precedent notifies players that they may be disciplined (much less suspended) for general awareness of misconduct by others."

It was a surprise legal victory for Brady and a resounding PR defeat for the league. "For His Arrogance in Tom Brady Ruling, Roger Goodell Pays the Price," the headline in the *New York Times* read. "Ah, Roger," wrote Michael Powell, "being king isn't what it used to be." The cover of *Sports Illustrated* featured a sketch of Brady standing triumphantly over Goodell in the courtroom, fists over his head, under the headline "ELATEGATE."

In New England, it was game on. The Patriots' official Twitter account tweeted a picture of Brady fist-pumping. Gronkowski tweeted a picture of himself with Brady on his back, accompanied by the words: "Let's go! This season to be one heck of another ride!! #PatsNation." And Kraft took the opportunity to praise Judge Berman.

"As I have said during this process and throughout his Patriots career, Tom Brady is a classy person of the highest integrity," Kraft said in a prepared

statement. "He represents everything that is great about this game and this league. Judge Richard Berman understood this and we are greatly appreciative of his thoughtful decision that was delivered today. Now, we can return our focus to the game on the field."

By afternoon, the governor of Massachusetts declared September 3 Tom Brady Day, oddsmakers in Las Vegas increased the odds on the Patriots' winning the Super Bowl, and the White House weighed in with President Obama's press secretary saying, "There is a lot of good-natured ribbing that is going on in fantasy football leagues."

Even Brady's rivals came out in support of the ruling.

"It's just guys getting justice, guys not being persecuted for things they didn't do, getting a fair trial of sorts," said Seahawks defensive back Richard Sherman. "A lot of times in this league, it's guilty until proven innocent sometimes. And it's good to see guys be able to get a fair trial. Unfortunately, it had to go so long."

Hours after Judge Berman handed down his ruling, Goodell announced that the NFL would appeal. But the appeal process would take months, and in the interim, the league said it would not seek a stay to stop Brady from playing.

Meantime, the NFL season was due to open with a nationally televised Thursday night game between the Steelers and the Patriots in Foxborough on September 10. It was tradition for the commissioner to attend the season opener, and Patriots fans came armed with signs taunting Goodell. But Goodell opted to skip the game.

In an elaborate pregame ceremony, the Patriots raised the fourth Super Bowl banner. In the game, Brady threw four touchdown passes, including three to Gronkowski, and at one point completed nineteen straight passes, setting a team record. The game was never in doubt. With the Patriots leading comfortably in the fourth quarter, sixty-six thousand fans started chanting: "Where is Roger?" It was so loud that it overwhelmed the broadcast.

"I gotta say," said NBC announcer Cris Collinsworth, "I agree with them."

"You know, if he came to the game tonight, where we gonna put him?" said Al Michaels.

"Right in the middle of that crowd," joked Collinsworth.

Michaels laughed. "Right."

At the outset of the 2015 season, Brady played some of the best football of his career and the Patriots were unbeatable. In week two, Brady completed

38 of 59 passes for 466 yards in a victory in Buffalo. A week later, Brady threw for 358 yards, completing 33 of 42 passes, and the Patriots thumped the Jaguars 51–17. Brady was in his own zone. Then *Boston* magazine published an exposé on Alex Guerrero titled "Tom Brady's Personal Guru Is a Glorified Snake-Oil Salesman." The hard-hitting piece reported that Guerrero had been sued by the Federal Trade Commission back in 2004 for claiming in an infomercial that a dietary supplement known as Supreme Greens could help cure and prevent cancer, heart disease, AIDS, and other ailments. While admitting no wrongdoing, Guerrero had settled the matter by paying a fine. On another occasion, Guerrero's company, 6 Degrees Nutrition, had been ordered by the FTC to discontinue selling a product called NeuroSafe. It was a drink that Guerrero said helped athletes recover from concussions. The magazine story led to a barrage of negative headlines about Guerrero, who was mocked in the Boston media as being a fake doctor.

Guerrero was humiliated. Brady was angry. And rather than lie low while controversy swirled around his best friend, Brady publicly defended him much more vigorously than he had defended himself during Deflategate. When a Boston radio host likened Guerrero's dietary supplement to "cancer quackery" and questioned Brady's judgment for going into business with him, Brady criticized the host for only knowing part of the story.

"When you say, well this sounds like quackery," Brady said, "there's a lot of things I see on a daily basis in Western medicine that I think—'Wow, why would they ever do that? That is crazy.'"

When the host pushed, Brady pushed back. "In the ten or eleven years we've been working together, he has never been wrong," Brady said. "I had doctors with the highest and best education in our country tell us, tell me, that I wouldn't be able to play football again. That I would need multiple surgeries on my knee from my staph infection. That I would need a new ACL, a new MCL, that I wouldn't be able to play with my kids when I'm older. Of course, I go back the next year and we win Comeback Player of the Year. I follow the next season and we win the MVP of that year. I've chosen a different approach, and that approach works for me."

Even when the host tried to move on from Guerrero, Brady kept on. "I wouldn't be playing today if it wasn't for what he's been able to accomplish with me," he said.

Belichick, meanwhile, wasn't thrilled about all of the attention being generated by Guerrero. Earlier in the year he'd been profiled in *Sports Illustrated* and the *New York Times Magazine*. Belichick particularly didn't appreciate Guerrero discussing how his methods often conflicted with those espoused

by the Patriots' training staff. "Everyone thinks I'm a kook and a charlatan," Guerrero told the *Times*.

The Patriots, meanwhile, steamrolled along. With a 4-0 record, the team returned to Indianapolis, where Lucas Oil Field was covered with signs calling the Patriots cheaters. A whole group of Colts fans wore orange T-shirts with a replica of a Wheaties cereal box with Tom Brady's image beneath the wording: "CHEATIES: The Breakfast of Cheaters." Feeding off the taunts, Brady led his team to another victory.

As the season wore on, it looked as though the Patriots were destined to go undefeated. With an 8-0 record, the Patriots trailed the Giants at MetLife Stadium 26–24 with 1:28 to play. On fourth-and-ten from the Patriots' twenty-yard line, Brady completed a twelve-yard pass to Amendola to keep the drive alive. Then he quickly completed three more passes to move the Patriots into Giants territory. With one second left on the game clock, Stephen Gostkowski kicked a fifty-four-yard field goal to win the game, 27–26. Brady had thrown for 193 yards in the fourth quarter. The Patriots were 9-0.

But Julian Edelman, the team's leading receiver, broke his foot in the Giants game. Two weeks later, the Patriots went to Denver with a 10-0 record to face the 8-2 Broncos on November 29. In a snowstorm, the Patriots led the entire way. Then, with just over two minutes to play, Gronkowski was carted off the field after taking a shot to the knee. The Patriots lost in overtime.

Besides the injuries to Edelman and Gronkowski, the Patriots also saw offensive tackle Nate Solder, receiver Danny Amendola, and running back Dion Lewis go down. Still, the Patriots managed to finish the 2015 season at 12-4, tying them with the Broncos for the best record in the AFC. The Patriots had the top offense in the league. The Broncos had the top defense. They met again in the AFC Championship game in Denver on January 24, 2016, in what would be the final head-to-head contest between Tom Brady and Peyton Manning. With a surgically inserted screw in his foot, Edelman returned to action and played in the game. Gronkowski also played. Brady outplayed Manning. But with less than a minute and a half remaining, Denver led 20–12.

Facing fourth-and-ten from the fifty-yard line, Brady threw the ball forty yards downfield to Gronkowski, who hauled it in with two defenders on him.

Then on fourth-and-goal with seventeen seconds left, Brady threw the ball to the back of the end zone, where Gronkowski leaped over a defender to make the catch for a touchdown, cutting the Broncos' lead to 20–18.

The season came down to a two-point conversion. Brady's pass to Edelman was broken up at the goal line.

Dejected, Brady congratulated Manning at midfield and wished him well. It was the last time the two would face each other in competition. Two weeks later, Manning would win his second Super Bowl, leading the Broncos over the Panthers. Then he retired.

At the end of the AFC Championship game, Belichick felt horrible about the outcome.

"Proud of our guys," he said afterward. "They fought right to the very end like they always do. . . . There's such a fine line today between winning and losing." Pausing, Belichick looked distraught. "Crash landing at the end of the season," he continued. "Like it usually is in the National Football League."

The Patriots had been to an unprecedented five consecutive AFC Championship games. But they were not returning to the Super Bowl.

thirty-eight

NO ONE KNOWS WHERE THE TOP IS

W hen Tom Brady entered the NFL at age twenty-two, his approach was a lot like a racehorse that speeds down the track wearing blinders. Brady's only focus then was playing football. But at thirty-eight, he was more like the guy who has seen how the sausage is made. Brady still loved football. But after seeing the behind-the-scenes business dealings and political machinations that went into the game, he could never look at football the same way again. He often wished he didn't know a lot of the things that he knew. They took away from the bliss of ignorance.

Despite all that Brady had been through, after the 2015 season he made up his mind that he wanted to continue playing until he was forty-five. It was, by any measure, an outlandish pursuit. Other than a small handful of kickers, no one had ever played in the NFL at that age. A few journeymen players had managed to hang on into their early forties. But Brady was no journeyman, and he wasn't talking about hanging on. He was convinced that he could continue to get better with age.

Part of Brady's thinking was influenced by his unique partnership with Alex Guerrero. Physically, Brady was considerably healthier and better conditioned at thirty-eight than he had been at twenty-two. So he wasn't worried about his body's holding up. Nor was he concerned about his mental toughness. Brady had always viewed football as a mental game, and his approach gave him a competitive advantage over younger, less experienced players, especially when it came to his preparation, his ability to recognize and exploit opponents' weaknesses, and his impermeability to pressure.

The one area that Brady had to continuously work at was the emotional aspect of continuing to show up year after year and mustering the will to do

what it takes to win championships. Already considered the greatest of all time, Brady couldn't look to other players for inspiration. He had to generate his drive from within. To sharpen his mental and emotional acuity, he looked to nontraditional sources. One was shaman Don Miguel Ruiz, whose spiritually inspirational book *The Four Agreements* was Brady's favorite. Another source of inspiration was an eighty-five-year-old sushi chef in Japan named Jiro Ono. Brady learned about Ono by watching a 2011 documentary called *Jiro Dreams of Sushi.*

Considered the greatest sushi craftsman in the world, Ono maintained a restaurant that seated only ten people beneath a subway station in Tokyo. His customers came from all over the world and paid upwards of four hundred dollars just to experience a fifteen-minute meal. Four of Ono's statements about his ambition to keep pursuing perfection at age eighty-five resonated with Brady and his own ambition to keep playing football into his mid-forties:

I do the same thing over and over, improving bit by bit.

There is always a yearning to achieve more.

I'll continue to climb, trying to reach the top, but no one knows where the top is.

When to quit the job that you've worked so hard for? I never once hated this job. I fell in love with my work and gave my life to it. Even though I'm eighty-five years old, I don't feel like retiring. That's how I feel.

Belichick knew how Brady felt about retirement. Belichick also knew the facts:

Brett Favre had played his last game at age forty-one. But in his later years, the quarterback had been a shell of his former self, retiring and unretiring multiple times, and missing large portions of seasons due to injuries.

Peyton Manning had lasted eighteen seasons and retired right after Super Bowl 50 in February 2016. But he had experienced a

pronounced drop-off in performance in 2015 and had missed a number of games due to injury. He had walked away at age thirty-nine.

Joe Montana, John Elway, Dan Marino, and Steve Young—the four most durable elite quarterbacks after Favre and Manning—had all yielded to age and injury and retired at age thirty-eight.

Brady was going to be thirty-nine at the start of the upcoming season.

Analytical and pragmatic, Belichick saw no precedent for what Brady intended to do. At the same time, Belichick knew it wasn't entirely up to him to set the length of Brady's next contract. The X-factor was Kraft and his relationship with Brady.

Kraft had no idea whether Brady could play until age forty-five. But it was clear to him that what Brady had done in his seventeenth season at age thirty-eight was phenomenal. Statistically, he was off the charts. His 402 completions that season were the most in his career. His thirty-six touch-down passes led the league. His seven interceptions gave him the lowest interception rate among all starting quarterbacks. And from a durability standpoint, Brady was like the Energizer Bunny. In 2015, Brady had started in all sixteen regular season games for the seventh consecutive year. Other than the year he had missed due to his knee injury, Brady had started in 223 straight regular-season games.

The way Brady was going, Kraft wasn't about to begin doubting him now. Nor did he want to get hung up speculating on whether Brady could play for seven more years. He preferred to instead focus on results. The bottom line for Kraft was that the Patriots had been to five consecutive conference championship games, an achievement that no other team had come close to pulling off in the salary cap era. Convinced that Brady and Belichick were most responsible for separating his franchise from the rest, Kraft focused on one thing—keeping them together for as long as possible.

With two years remaining on Brady's contract, Kraft and Brady talked at the start of the offseason. They agreed generally to a new deal that would keep Brady in New England through the 2019 season. By that point, Brady would be forty-two and would have played twenty seasons for the Patriots.

Jonathan Kraft and Don Yee hammered out the details, which called for Brady to receive a $41 million contract extension, including a $28 million signing bonus. Under the new deal, Brady would be paid handsomely in 2016

and 2017. But in years 2018 and 2019, Brady's base salary would drop to $1 million. The understanding was that Kraft and Brady would reconvene and adjust those numbers after the 2017 season.

In the meantime, Brady and Belichick were wedded for four more years. Brady signed his new contract on March 10, 2016.

A month later, a three-judge panel of the United States Court of Appeals for the Second Circuit issued a 2–1 decision reinstating Brady's four-game suspension in connection with Deflategate. Overturning the lower court's ruling from seven months earlier, the appeals court determined that Goodell had broad discretion to punish players and had not deprived Brady of fundamental fairness when he suspended him. "In their collective bargaining agreement," the majority wrote, "the players and the league mutually decided many years ago that the commissioner should investigate possible rule violations, should impose appropriate sanctions, and may preside at arbitrations challenging his discipline."

The court ruling once again put Goodell in the unenviable position of deciding whether to sideline the league's biggest ambassador. In 2015, league-licensed merchandise bearing Tom Brady's name had outsold all other NFL players', and according to Nielsen's celebrity index, Brady's "awareness" score was the highest among any player in the NFL. Brady was clearly the most popular man in the NFL. But Goodell's legal victory had established that Goodell was the most powerful man in the NFL. Brady's suspension would stand.

Over the summer, Brady considered making an appeal to the US Supreme Court. But his chances of prevailing there were slim. Besides, Brady was tired of the distraction. The legal wrangling had been going on for a year and a half. Enough was enough.

On July 15, 2016, Brady announced on Facebook that he would not pursue an appeal. Thanking Kraft, Belichick, the players union, his family, and the fans for their support, he wrote: "It has been a challenging 18 months, and I have made the difficult decision to no longer proceed with the legal process."

Kraft issued his own statement, which was much more critical of the league: "The penalty imposed by the NFL was unprecedented, unjust and unreasonable, especially given that no empirical or direct evidence of any kind showed Tom did anything to violate league rules prior to, during or after the 2015 AFC Championship game. What Tom has had to endure throughout

this 18-month ordeal has been, in my opinion, as far removed from due process as you could ever expect in this country."

Goodell's status as one of the most despised figures in New England sports lore was cemented.

With Brady sidelined, Belichick's mind-set was to move forward and not waste time thinking about something that was out of his control. Besides, he had a great deal of confidence in second-string quarterback Jimmy Garoppolo. Belichick had drafted him with the intention of having him eventually succeed Brady anyway. Backed by his coach and his teammates, Garoppolo shone in his first pro start. In a nationally televised Sunday-night game in Glendale, Arizona, on September 11, 2016, he led the Patriots to a 23–21 victory. Afterward, Belichick awarded him the game ball.

A week later in Foxborough, Garoppolo got off to a scintillating start, throwing three touchdown passes in the first seventeen minutes, putting his team up 21–0 over the Dolphins. But in the second quarter he was driven hard to the ground, injuring his shoulder. As Garoppolo left the game and was taken to the hospital, Belichick turned to third-string quarterback Jacoby Brissett. Just five months earlier, Belichick had drafted the athletic twenty-two-year-old rookie out of North Carolina State. Now Belichick had to rely on Brissett to run the offense. To take the pressure down a notch, Belichick relied mainly on running plays, shifting most of the offensive load to running back LeGarrette Blount, a workhorse who had been nicknamed "Blount Force Trauma" by his teammates.

Nervous, Brissett struggled to move the offense. The Dolphins came almost all the way back, and the Patriots barely escaped with the victory. Brissett guided them to an impressive win in week three. Blount carried the offense and earned NFL Player of the Month honors in September. Then the Patriots got shut out 16–0 by the Bills, at home on October 2. Under the circumstances, Belichick wasn't complaining. In Brady's absence the team had gone 3-1.

Brady had never gone on a vacation in September. But under the terms of his suspension, he was not allowed to be around the team or even have verbal contact with anyone in the organization. So Brady and Bündchen had packed their bags and taken a trip to the coast of Italy. It was an opportunity to get away.

While Brady was overseas, the paparazzi staked him out. Soon the *New York Post* published indiscreet pictures of Brady sunbathing. The pictures made the rounds on social media, and *Boston* magazine reported: "Tom Brady Sunbathed Nude in Italy During Vacation with Gisele." Julian Edelman thought the whole thing was pretty hilarious, and he wasn't going to let Brady live it down.

On Brady's first day back at work, he entered the locker room, and all of his teammates stared at him in silence. Brady's face turned red. Relishing the moment, Edelman grinned and started chanting: "Bray-dee! Bray-dee!" Laughing, his teammates joined in, putting a grin on Brady's face.

Brady was thrilled to be reunited with his team. Although it still galled him that he had been forced to miss four games, he didn't say a word about it to his teammates. Nor did he say much about anything. But his teammates could see from the fierceness in his eyes that Brady had something to prove.

"He always had this look in his eye," said running back LeGarrette Blount. "But it was different this time. It was like, 'They want to suspend me for four games for something I didn't do, we're gonna see who's gonna get the last laugh at the end of the season.'"

With speculation swirling about whether he'd be rusty or out of sync after being unable to practice for a month, Brady looked past fans and reporters in stony silence when he arrived at FirstEnergy Stadium in Cleveland on October 9. Signs depicting Brady's image next to the word "GOAT"—the acronym for Greatest Of All Time—were throughout the stadium. He completed his first pass to Edelman, his second pass to Gronkowski, and his third pass to newly acquired tight end Martellus Bennett. Of Brady's first fifteen pass attempts, the only two incompletions were the result of dropped balls. After his first drive resulted in a Patriots touchdown, the Cleveland crowd gave him a standing ovation.

The game was never close. Edelman and Gronkowski each had a huge day, and Brady threw three touchdown passes to Bennett. Throughout the game, fans chanted "Bray-dee" as he torched the Browns' defense, throwing for more than four hundred yards. The Patriots won 33–13. At thirty-nine, Brady hadn't missed a beat.

"Damn!" Patriots linebacker Dont'a Hightower said afterward. "I know that's TB. But you don't miss four games and just come out and throw for four hundred yards like that. Whatever he's on, I need to jump on that, too."

Even the Browns players were in awe. When the game ended, one Browns player after another approached Brady, told him how much they respected him, and expressed support.

A week later, a playoff-like atmosphere filled Gillette Stadium for Brady's first home game since his suspension. Tickets had sold for $1,000 each on the secondary market, the highest price recorded in 2016 for a regular season NFL game. Signs mocking Goodell and calling for "REVENGE" from "THE GOAT" were everywhere. Sixty-six thousand–plus thundered: "BRAY-DEE, BRAY-DEE, BRAY-DEE" as he and the offense took the field at the start of the game.

"Hey, Twelve," Edelman said in the huddle.

"Let's go," Brady said, tapping Edelman's fist.

Brady threw for 376 yards on the day and three more touchdowns. Gronkowski had a career-best 162 yards receiving. The Patriots crushed the Bengals 35–17 to improve to 5-1. When the game was over, Brady wasn't interested in celebrating. He wanted to bury every team on the schedule. And his teammates were all in.

In a strange way, Roger Goodell's efforts to avoid the perception of giving preferential treatment to the Patriots, by coming down so hard on Brady, had actually done a disservice to the rest of the league. The Patriots, a team that had never lacked for motivation, was now more than ever on a mission to destroy any team in their path and win a fifth Super Bowl. There would be nothing sweeter than making Roger Goodell present the Lombardi Trophy to Kraft, Belichick, and Brady.

Brady was doing his part. After four starts, he had thrown twelve touchdown passes and no interceptions. The Patriots had the most explosive offense in the league. And after routing the Bills in Buffalo 41–25 on October 30, the Patriots headed into a bye week with the best record in football at 7-1.

But the next day, Belichick unexpectedly traded Pro Bowl linebacker Jamie Collins.

"Holy shit!" thought Edelman upon hearing the news. "I can't believe that just happened."

Collins was considered by his teammates to be the best defensive player on the team. He was certainly the Patriots' most athletic defensive player.

All Belichick said to his players was that he was doing what was best for the team.

The move put a lot of players on edge.

"Everyone's looking around like, 'Am I next?'" Edelman said.

Brady, however, was a steadying influence. He didn't understand the trade any more than anyone else. But he'd seen this happen so many times

over the years that it was old hat. His approach was to focus on the things he could control and keep his eyes on the goal of winning another championship.

His teammates followed suit.

Robert and Myra Kraft bought a place in Palm Beach in the early nineties. Around the same time, Donald Trump was opening Mar-a-Lago nearby. Trump reached out and invited Kraft to play a round of golf. Then he invited Robert and Myra to Mar-a-Lago, where they viewed the property and soon developed a social relationship. Eventually, Trump started attending games in Foxborough. Over time, Kraft's friendship with Trump grew. When Trump married Melania Knauss in 2005, Kraft flew down to Palm Beach for the wedding on the night before the Patriots played in the AFC Championship game in Pittsburgh. And when Myra passed away in 2011, Trump and Melania attended her funeral. For about a year afterward, Trump called Kraft once or twice a week to check on him. That experience deepened the bond between them.

Through Kraft, Trump had also met Brady and Belichick and built friendships with them as well. In Brady's case, he met Trump in 2001, just as he became the starting quarterback. After Brady won his first Super Bowl in early 2002, Trump asked him to judge a Miss USA competition. By 2004, Trump would call Brady after watching his games on television and invite him to play golf. Over the years, they became friendly. When Trump became the presumptive Republican nominee to run for president in 2016, he wanted Brady to speak at the Republican National Convention. But Brady was uncomfortable with how polarizing politics had become. He politely turned Trump down. Political support, Brady felt, was different than supporting a friend.

Belichick took a different approach. As Trump's bruising campaign with Hillary Clinton wound down, Belichick wrote a letter of support to Trump during the Patriots' bye week in early November. On November 7, on the eve of Election Day, Trump was scheduled to speak at a rally in Manchester, New Hampshire. Beforehand, Trump's team contacted Belichick and asked if Trump could read his letter at the rally. Belichick had not composed the letter with the intention of having it shared publicly, so he asked the campaign not to read it. Instead he dashed off a new letter in time for the event.

That night, Trump invoked Tom Brady's name, drawing loud applause. Calling Brady a "great friend," Trump told the crowd that Brady had already voted for him in Massachusetts, where early voting was permitted. Trump

also claimed that Brady had told him that he could tell the New Hampshire crowd how he had voted. The crowd cheered.

Then Trump praised Belichick and read aloud his letter.

"So he writes, 'Congratulations on a tremendous campaign. You have dealt with an unbelievable slanted and negative media and have come out beautifully. You've proved to be the ultimate competitor and fighter. Your leadership is amazing. I have always had tremendous respect for you. But the toughness and perseverance you have displayed over the past year is remarkable. Hopefully tomorrow's election results will give you the opportunity to make America great again.'"

The audience roared.

"'Best wishes for great results tomorrow. Bill Belichick.'"

It was very unlike Belichick to inject himself into a political campaign, especially such a divisive one. That night, his letter to Trump became a top story in Boston and throughout New England. The news confused his players, all of whom were well schooled in Belichick's no-nonsense philosophy of avoiding anything that causes distractions.

The next day, despite Belichick's endorsement, Trump lost New Hampshire. But Trump won one of the closest, most polarizing presidential elections in US history. The Patriots were immediately inundated with calls from the press seeking an explanation for why Belichick had backed Trump. Suddenly, with his team heading into the biggest game of the season against the Seattle Seahawks, Belichick had a political controversy on his hands.

Against his wishes, Brady also got inadvertently roped into it when the *New York Times* and other media outlets questioned the veracity of Trump's claim that Brady had voted for him and that Brady had given him permission to say so at the New Hampshire rally. But Bündchen quickly put an end to that debate when one of her 15 million Instagram followers posted: "Gisele I heard you and Tom were backing Trump! Is that true??" Bündchen replied on Instagram: "NO!"

Belichick, who routinely stonewalled the press, decided to speak out. On the day after the election, he stepped to the lectern in the Patriots' media room for his weekly press briefing to discuss the upcoming game against the Seahawks. But at the outset he said he wanted to address the letter he had written to Trump two days earlier.

"Our friendship goes back many years," Belichick told the media. "And I think anyone that spent more than five minutes with me knows I'm not a political person. My comments are not politically motivated. I have a friendship and a loyalty to Donald.

"A couple weeks ago we had Secretary of State Kerry in our locker room," Belichick continued. "He's another friend of mine. And I can't imagine two people with more different political views than those two. But to me, friendship and loyalty are just about that. It's not about political or religious views. I write hundreds of letters and notes every month. It doesn't mean I agree with every single thing that every person thinks about politics, religion, or other subjects.

"I have multiple friendships that are important to me," he continued. "That's what that was about. So it's not about politics. It's about football. We've got a huge game this week against a great team and a great organization. And that's where it all is going forward—on Seattle."

"Coach," a reporter said, "were you happy or annoyed that Trump read the letter?"

"Seattle," Belichick said.

"Your team has always been good at keeping outside distractions on the outside," another reporter said. "Given the nature of this presidential race—"

"Seattle," Belichick interrupted.

". . . did you find it—"

"Seattle."

"Did you find it helpful to—"

"Seattle."

". . . talk to your players about this? Did any of your players talk to you about this?"

"Seattle."

"Any concerns about any locker room rancor as a result of this?" the reporter said.

Belichick glared at him. "Next," he said.

Patriots players who didn't support Trump weren't happy.

After Belichick's press conference, Brady got hit with Trump questions when he did his press briefing before the Seahawks game. He didn't want to get into anything political. He simply wanted to focus on winning. Plus, he didn't appreciate it when other people tried to dictate his narrative.

A reporter asked: "Why did you give Trump permission to talk about your political preferences at that rally in New Hampshire in front of a national audience?"

Aggravated, Brady paused. "Why did I give him permission?" he said, repeating the question. "So you're assuming I gave people permission?"

"Did you not give him permission to talk about your political preferences?" the reporter said.

Brady laughed. "I'm just going to talk about football this week."

Pressed, Brady smiled and said, "I talked to my wife. She said I can't talk about politics anymore. I think that's a good decision made for our family."

The Patriots hadn't faced the Seahawks since Super Bowl XLIX twenty-one months earlier. When they met in Foxborough on November 13, many NFL pundits thought the two teams might be headed for a Super Bowl rematch. The lead changed hands seven times in a back-and-forth game that once again came down to a last-second play from the one-yard line. Trailing 31–24 and facing a fourth-and-one situation with seconds on the clock, Brady threw to Gronkowski in the corner of the end zone. Gronkowski got tangled up with the defender, and the ball fell incomplete. No flag was thrown. The Patriots lost, falling to 7-2.

After the game, doctors found that Gronkowski had suffered a pulmonary contusion to his lung in the first half. He sat out the next game. Then Gronkowski returned to action two weeks later against the Jets. But after taking another big hit, he left the Jets game with back and leg pain. Days later, the Patriots announced that Gronkowski was undergoing back surgery for the second time and would be lost for the remainder of the year.

It was a big blow to the Patriots. Gronkowski had been on track to have a record-setting year in terms of production. In his absence, running back Le-Garrette Blount and receivers Chris Hogan, Danny Amendola, and Martellus Bennett all picked up the pace. But no one stepped up more than Edelman.

Earlier in the year, Edelman had written a children's book called *Flying High*. It was a story about a squirrel named Jules, a goat named Tom, and a wise owl that wears a headset and a hoodie. At one point in the story, the goat tells the squirrel: "You have to work hard. Working hard leads to success." The squirrel responds: "Please, please, please show me what to do!"

Brady and Edelman had had that kind of relationship from the time that Edelman first arrived in Foxborough. By 2016, they were the most dependable quarterback-receiver tandem in football. Brady targeted Edelman a career-high 159 times during the season and Edelman had a career-high 1,106 receiving yards.

The Patriots won their final seven games and finished the season with the best record in football at 14-2.

All season long, Belichick's mantra had been "No days off." In all his years in the NFL, he had never coached a harder-working group of players than the

2016 Patriots. Heading into the playoffs, the team's determination to outwork every opponent in their quest to win the Super Bowl hadn't diminished.

Brady, in particular, was pushing himself even harder than usual to achieve perfection. During the regular season he had completed more than 67 percent of his passes. The only time in his career when he'd had a higher completion percentage was in 2007, during the team's perfect regular season. More remarkably, in 2016, Brady threw only two interceptions in 432 pass attempts.

What most people didn't realize was that in 2016 Brady had something extra to play for—his mother, Galynn. She had been diagnosed with an aggressive form of breast cancer. Her treatment, which consisted of surgeries, chemotherapy, and radiation, had made it impossible for her to travel to any of Tom's games. But Brady had assured his mother that the Patriots were going to make it to the Super Bowl and that she was going to complete her chemo in time to be able to attend.

In the first round of the playoffs, the Patriots faced the Houston Texans, who came in with the top-ranked defense in the league. Brady connected with Edelman eight times for 137 yards, and the Patriots thrashed the Texans 34–16. But Brady threw two interceptions, matching his season total.

The Patriots were the first team in the Super Bowl era to reach the conference championship game six years in a row. But neither Brady nor Belichick was celebrating. Brady had thrown two interceptions and the team had made mental errors.

"We just didn't do enough," Brady told the press. "We're gonna have to play better than we did tonight on offense."

"Tom, you don't sound happy," a reporter said.

Emotionless, Brady credited the Texans' defense. "When you add our poor execution on top of that," he said, "and you add our turnovers on top of that, it doesn't feel great because we work pretty hard to play a lot better than we played."

Belichick painted an even bleaker picture. "We're gonna have to play better and coach better than we did tonight," Belichick said, "or there won't be much left in our season."

The Pittsburgh Steelers awaited.

On the day after attending President Trump's inauguration, Robert Kraft sat alone in his living room, watching news reports on television of millions of people throughout the world marching in the streets to protest

Trump's election. Whenever Kraft was home alone, his mind easily drifted to Myra. Kraft reached for his phone and started calling friends. One of the friends he called was Jon Bon Jovi. He reached him at his home in New Jersey. They started talking about the Patriots' chances against the Steelers the following day.

"Come on up, stay the night," Kraft told him. "You can come to the game with me tomorrow."

Unsure whether he felt like making the trek to Boston, Bon Jovi checked with his wife.

"Yes, you're going," she told him. "He's asking you personally to come so he's not alone."

Bon Jovi packed a bag and headed north. That night, Kraft hosted the CBS announcers and the broadcast crew at his home for dinner. After everyone left, Kraft and Bon Jovi kicked off their shoes, reclined in La-Z-Boy chairs, and turned on ESPN. With the volume muted, Kraft wanted to talk about Bon Jovi's successful touring company, his relationship with his sons, and his thirty-year marriage. Kraft was especially interested in the marriage.

The following morning, Kraft retrieved some fresh eggs from the free-range chickens he keeps on his property. After enjoying them for breakfast, he and Bon Jovi rode to the game together.

With the Patriots leading the Steelers 20–9 late in the third quarter, a sequence of plays epitomized the intensity the Patriots had displayed during the season. The Patriots were on the Steelers' nineteen-yard line when Brady handed off to running back LeGarrette Blount, who built up a head of steam before ramming into a Steelers tackler at the ten-yard line, driving him backward as four more Steelers converged on Blount. Legs pumping, Blount dragged five Steelers to the five-yard line. With Blount still on his feet, another Steeler jumped on the pile.

"Surrounded by six Steelers," said CBS's Jim Nantz. "Still going!"

Patriots players started pushing the pile from behind. Blount kept driving. The crowd was roaring.

"Can you believe this?" Nantz shouted.

Blount plowed his way almost to the goal line before being taken down.

"They finally stop him at the one," Nantz said. "My goodness! Took more than half the team with him."

"That play said it all," said Phil Simms. "The team with the passion and being physical is the New England Patriots."

Seconds later, Brady handed off to Blount again and he barreled in for the touchdown to put the Patriots up 27–9.

While Brady repeatedly punched the sky, Bon Jovi's "Livin' on a Prayer" started playing in the stadium. The crowd sang along. Then the jumbo screens showed Bon Jovi in Kraft's box, standing beside Gronkowski, singing the words to his own song. Gillette Stadium erupted and Bon Jovi started leading the crowd through the chorus.

While the stadium rocked, Edelman sat between Brady and Amendola on the bench. "My dad used to always tell me when I was a young boy, 'When you get 'em down, you break their fuckin' neck,'" Edelman said.

Amendola didn't know what to say. Brady was unfazed.

"I was twelve," Edelman continued. "That's why I am the way I am."

On the first play after the kickoff, the Steelers fumbled. Moments later, Brady threw a touchdown strike to Edelman to put the Patriots up 33–9, and the party was on in Foxborough. The Patriots were headed back to the Super Bowl to face the Atlanta Falcons.

For Brady and Belichick, it was their seventh trip there together.

For Kraft, it was his eighth Super Bowl, more than any other owner in the history of the NFL.

thirty-nine

LORD OF THE RINGS

As the Patriots ran onto the field before the start of Super Bowl LI at NRG Stadium in Houston on February 5, 2017, Tom Brady glanced up at his family's suite, held up his index finger, and pointed. Wearing a bandanna on her head and a TB12 jersey with "BRADY'S LADIES" emblazoned on the back, Galynn Brady looked down at her son. After a grueling round of chemotherapy, she was attending her first football game of the year. Brady was dedicating the game to her.

"If I yell at you," Brady told the head referee, "nothing personal."

"I know," the ref said, smiling and patting Brady's butt.

"You know me," Brady said. "I'm competitive."

Falcons quarterback Matt Ryan had just been named the 2016 NFL MVP. His team had scored 540 points in 2016, the most in the league that year. But the Falcons started slow. So did the Patriots. Neither team scored in the first quarter.

Then the Falcons scored two quick touchdowns to take a 14–0 lead in the second quarter. The Patriots looked shell-shocked. As the Falcons prepared to kick off, Brady stalked the sideline. "Hey, no fear!" he told his teammates. "No fear! Cut it loose."

With 2:48 left in the half and the Patriots driving, Brady threw a pass to Amendola. Falcons defensive back Robert Alford intercepted the ball at the Falcons' fifteen-yard line and started streaking toward the Patriots' end zone. The only man he had to beat was Brady. Brady lunged and missed, and Alford was gone.

From his knees, Brady watched Alford race eighty-two yards untouched for a touchdown. A few feet from Brady on the Patriots' sideline, Belichick grimaced in silence. "If we lose," Brady thought, "this will be the play that defines this game." He trudged to the bench. The Falcons led 21–0.

A couple of minutes later, the Patriots managed to kick a field goal right before the end of the half.

With the Patriots trailing 21–3 at the half, the mood in Kraft's suite was gloomy. Elton John and Mark Wahlberg were so discouraged they left early. John Legend and Chrissy Teigen didn't know what to say. Leon Black, the cofounder of private equity colossus Apollo Global Management and the chairman of New York's Museum of Modern Art, tried to comfort Kraft.

"Don't worry," Black told him. "You've had a great season and a lot to be proud of."

"Fuck that!" Kraft snapped. "We're still gonna win this game."

In the locker room, Belichick said the same things in the same tone that he'd been saying during halftimes all season long. His business-as-usual approach had a calming effect on the team. Meantime, Edelman exhorted his teammates, telling them it wasn't too late to come back. "It's gonna be a helluva story," he told them. LeGarrette Blount was busy telling himself that his team had the greatest quarterback of all time and the greatest coach of all time. As long as there was time on the clock, there was no lead they couldn't overcome.

At the start of the second half, Brady rallied his teammates on the sideline. "C'mon, boys," he said. "Let's see what we got now. Let's see what we got."

Belichick turned to offensive coordinator Josh McDaniels. "We'll be okay," Belichick told him. "Our guys believe. They will fight their asses off."

The Patriots squandered the first drive of the third quarter. The Falcons, meanwhile, drove down the field at will and put up another touchdown to go up 28–3. No team had ever come back from a twenty-five-point deficit in a Super Bowl.

Up in the owner's box, Kraft was worried. He turned to Jonathan.

"You think Tommy has given up?"

"No fuckin' way," Jonathan said.

"Do you think we can still win?"

"Possible," Jonathan said, pausing. "Not probable."

With 8:31 to play in the third quarter, Brady stalked the Patriots' sideline.

"Gotta play harder!" he barked. "Gotta play tougher. Harder. Tougher. Everything. Everything we got."

But the mountain seemed insurmountable. On the next drive, the Patriots struggled to get a first down. With his team facing a fourth-and-three from their own forty-six-yard line, Belichick felt he had little choice but to go for it. If the offense failed to convert and the ball was turned back over to the Falcons at midfield, the game was likely going to be over.

Brady lined up in the shotgun. Recognizing that the Falcons were in man-to-man coverage, he saw that a linebacker was on receiver Danny Amendola. It was a mismatch. Brady threw a seventeen-yard strike to Amendola for a first down.

Moments later, when Brady saw no one open, he tucked the ball under his arm and ran downfield for fifteen yards. Moments later, he threw a touchdown strike to running back James White. The Patriots missed the extra point. With two minutes to play in the third quarter, New England trailed 28–9.

"Let's go now!" Brady shouted at his teammates. "Let's go show some fight."

The Patriots entered the fourth quarter trailing by nineteen points. In NFL postseason history, there had been ninety-three instances when a team had entered the final quarter trailing by nineteen or more. In none of them had that team ever come back to win.

After a Falcons punt, the Patriots started the fourth quarter on their own thirteen-yard line. Following a long drive, the Patriots kicked a field goal to cut the lead to 28–12 with 9:44 remaining in the game.

A minute later, Dont'a Hightower strip-sacked Falcons quarterback Matt Ryan, forcing a fumble. The Patriots recovered on the Falcons' twenty-five-yard line.

Moments later, Brady threw a touchdown pass to Amendola, cutting the lead to 28–18 with six minutes to play. He immediately raised two fingers, signaling to his teammates that they were going for a two-point conversion rather than kicking the extra point.

Brady lined up in the shotgun. On the snap, Brady jumped up, acting as if the ball had been snapped over his head. But it had instead been snapped directly to James White, who crashed across the goal line, cutting the Falcons' lead to 28–20 with 5:56 remaining.

Upstairs, Jonathan turned to Robert and said: "Probable."

Down on the field, two referees looked at each other.

"Hey," one of them said, "this could get interesting."

"Yeah, it could," the other one said.

On the Patriots' sideline, LeGarrette Blount looked at Brady as if he weren't human. Ninety-nine-point-nine percent of the world would be so nervous, Blount figured. But Brady wasn't worried. The confidence in his eyes emboldened Blount.

On the ensuing possession, the Falcons drove deep into Patriots territory. With 4:40 to play, they had a first down on the Patriots' twenty-two-yard line. To put the game out of reach, all the Falcons had to do was take a little more time off the clock and kick a field goal.

But two plays later, the Patriots sacked Matt Ryan for a twelve-yard loss. Then the Falcons got called for a ten-yard holding penalty. Suddenly they were out of field goal range and facing a fourth-and-thirty-three situation. They punted.

Trailing by eight with 3:30 to go, the Patriots' offense needed to go ninety-one yards to have a chance to tie the game.

Brady's first two passes were incomplete. Facing third-and-ten from his own nine-yard line, he hit Chris Hogan on a sixteen-yard completion for a first down. Then, after another first-down completion, Brady threw a pass to midfield to Edelman, who was being covered by three defenders. One of them jumped up and deflected the ball into the air.

"Broken up," said Fox's Joe Buck.

As the four players collided and landed in a heap, the ball came down on one of the defensive player's legs. From his knees, Edelman lunged for the ball as it hit the player's leg.

"And the pass . . . is . . ." Buck said.

Landing, Edelman snatched the ball off the defender's leg, but instantly had the ball jarred loose as he hit the ground. Then he re-grabbed it as a defender wrapped an arm around his neck and spun Edelman onto his back.

"No sign yet," Buck said.

Rolling around and being wrestled by the defenders, Edelman sprang to his feet with the football in his arms.

"Edelman comes down with the football," Buck said. "They're saying it's a catch!"

The Falcons challenged the call. While the officials looked at the instant replay, the catch was shown in slow motion on the jumbo screens in the stadium. Edelman and one of the defenders stared up at the screen.

"I caught it," Edelman told him. "I swear to God."

"No way," the defender said, pointing at the screen. "Look at that."

"Watch," said Edelman.

"It's on the ground," the defender said.

"No," Edelman said.

In slow motion, the video replay showed less than an inch of space between the ball and the ground when Edelman snatched it out of the air.

"Oh, my God!" said Fox's Troy Aikman.

"That's incredible!" said Buck.

The officials confirmed the ruling on the field. "The receiver's hand is under the ball," he said. "The ball never hits the ground."

Edelman returned to the huddle. "Gotta believe, boys," he told his teammates. "Gotta believe."

After twice losing Super Bowls to the Giants on freak catches, Edelman's miracle grab had kept the Patriots' comeback drive alive. It was quickly dubbed "Jules' Robbery."

With 2:28 to go, the Patriots had a first down on the Falcons' forty-one-yard line.

On the Patriots' sideline, LeGarrette Blount turned to Dion Lewis. "We got Tom Brady," he said again. "We get into OT, it's over with."

On the next play, Brady fired a twenty-yard strike to Amendola.

"Wow!" said Buck. "In a season that started with a four-game suspension, Tom Brady is in a position now, with the ball resting at the twenty-one-yard line of Atlanta, to try and finish off this comeback."

Brady fired a thirteen-yard completion to James White, making it first-and-goal from the eight-yard line.

"Tom Brady, somehow," Buck said, "is over four hundred yards passing in this game."

"He's got four hundred ten!" said Aikman. "That's the second-most all time."

With the clock ticking, Brady again hit White, who was tackled at the one-yard line.

Brady hustled his team back to the line of scrimmage, called a running play, and handed off to White, who crossed the goal line with fifty-seven seconds left. Brady raised his arms, signaling touchdown. It was 28–26, Atlanta.

In need of two points to tie, Brady again held up two fingers.

He called a passing play. On the snap, Brady took one step back and quick-released to Amendola, who caught the ball and barely reached across the goal line for the score.

"This is a tie game!" shouted Buck. "Amendola for two."

"Don't ever count Tom Brady out," said Aikman.

The Patriots had scored twenty-five points in just over sixteen minutes. With under a minute to play, it was 28–28.

"This is just shocking," said Buck.

Brady had thrown for 246 yards in the fourth quarter.

"Best ever?" Buck said.

"The best ever in my book," Aikman said.

For the first time ever, the Super Bowl was headed to overtime.

The Patriots won the coin toss and elected to receive. The first team to score a touchdown would win. On the Patriots' bench, Edelman turned to Brady.

"Let's go score and win this thing," he said.

"We got this," Brady said.

"For your mom," Edelman said. "For your mom."

Brady nodded.

Staring down at Brady as he trotted onto the field, Kraft turned to Jonathan and said, "It's over." The two of them put on their suit jackets. Down on Atlanta's sideline, Falcons owner Arthur Blank stared hopelessly at Brady as if he were looking at the Grim Reaper.

Emotionless, Brady proceeded to throw five straight completions, advancing the Patriots to the Falcons' twenty-five-yard line. After a pass-interference call, the Patriots had a first-and-goal situation from the Falcons' two-yard line.

Moments later, Brady pitched it back to White, who fought through four tacklers and stretched the ball over the goal line.

"He's in!" Buck shouted. "Patriots win the Super Bowl! BRADY HAS HIS FIFTH! What a comeback."

With the crowd cheering and the confetti falling and pandemonium breaking out on the field, Brady dropped to his knees. The Patriots had scored thirty-one straight points in the final twenty-eight minutes to complete the greatest comeback in Super Bowl history. Physically and emotionally spent, Brady lowered his face to the turf as a pack of photographers and television cameramen surrounded him. "Back! Back!" a Patriots security official yelled. Motionless and silent, Brady stayed down for nearly a minute. Finally, Alex Guerrero knelt down and put his arm around Brady.

Collecting himself, Brady finally stood, and LeGarrette Blount hugged him. Then Belichick grabbed Brady and Blount.

"I love you guys!" Belichick shouted.

"Oh my God!" Brady said.

"I *love* you guys," Belichick said.

"I love you," Brady said in his ear. "We did it."

Soaked in sweat and clutching each other, Brady and Belichick had reached nirvana. Together, they had won five Super Bowl championships.

Grinning, Fox color analyst Terry Bradshaw stood between Roger Goodell and Robert Kraft for the trophy presentation. The overwhelming cascade of booing surpassed what Goodell had encountered in Glendale two years earlier after the Patriots had beaten the Seahawks.

"What a wonderful football game tonight," Goodell said, his voice drowned out by the fans. "That's what NFL football is all about."

The booing was so pronounced that Bradshaw and his colleague Michael Strahan had to work to keep a straight face. Behind Goodell, Brady stood next to Belichick, clearly cognizant of the fact that Patriots fans were voicing their displeasure with the commissioner.

"Robert, you know how hard these are to get," Goodell barked into the microphone.

Flanked by Jonathan, Kraft stared at Goodell.

"And this is your fifth under your leadership, Coach Belichick and Tom Brady," Goodell said.

Spotting his family at the bottom of the stage steps, Brady stepped down and hoisted and hugged his son. Then he took his daughter in one arm and put his other arm around Bündchen, pulling them close and kissing them. Bündchen wrapped her arms around him like a security blanket.

The booing continued unabated.

"What an unbelievable achievement for your organization," Goodell shouted to Kraft. "We're so proud of you. Take your Super Bowl trophy home to New England."

Running through Kraft's mind was the fact that all of those individuals in the league office who had tried so hard to discredit his team were only going to be more envious and jealous. The league had spent upward of $22 million on Deflategate, much of it on lawyers and appeals. What a waste!

But as Goodell handed Kraft the trophy and the booing instantaneously switched to cheering, Kraft shook Goodell's hand. No sense in holding a grudge, especially when you're holding the hardware.

As Kraft raised the trophy, the cheering was deafening.

Kraft continued to hold the trophy up high as Goodell shook Jonathan's hand and turned to leave the stage. Belichick stopped him. Goodell congratulated him, and Belichick shook his hand.

"Mr. Kraft," Bradshaw said, "what do you have to say to all your fans out there after the first four weeks of the season and your quarterback's not starting, and to find yourself in the greatest Super Bowl ever played, and you're the victor?"

Goodell was descending the stairs as Kraft took the microphone.

"Two years ago we won our fourth Super Bowl down in Arizona," Kraft began. "I told our fans that was the sweetest one of all. But a lot has transpired during the last two years."

Bradshaw grinned, and the fans roared.

"And I don't think that needs any explanation!" Kraft yelled.

Descending the steps, Goodell spotted Brady, who was still embracing his wife and children. Goodell approached and tapped him on the shoulder. Brady turned, and Goodell grabbed his right hand. "That was awesome," Goodell said.

Brady smiled earnestly.

The last time they'd been that close was in a federal courtroom.

"Congratulations," Goodell told him. "Great football game."

"Thank you," Brady said.

As Goodell turned to go, Bündchen kissed Brady again and squeezed him.

Onstage, Kraft held up the trophy again. "This is unequivocally the sweetest!" he shouted.

Backstage, Brady threw his arms around his mother, kissed her face, and pulled her in. "I love you," he whispered.

"Oh, my God!" Tom Brady Sr. said, tears in his eyes, as he hugged Bündchen.

Bradshaw called Brady to the microphone.

"Your mother, after eighteen months, she's here tonight," Bradshaw said. "You dedicated this game to her. She has got to be beyond herself right now."

Brady's eyes welled up. "Yeah," he said. "It's going to be a great celebration tonight." He paused and looked at the crowd. "Thank you to all our fans," he said, raising his voice. "Everyone back in Boston. New England. We love you."

The crowd roared.

"You've been with us *all year*!" he shouted, his expression turning intense. "We're BRINGING THIS SUCKER HOME!"

He raised the trophy.

The celebration in the Patriots' locker room was deafening. While players hugged and hollered, Kraft handed out Cuban cigars. Then he spotted Brady,

sitting alone on a stool at his locker. When Brady stood, Kraft put his hand on the back of his head and kissed him.

"I love you," Brady said quietly.

Brady's sixty-two passes, forty-three completions, and 466 passing yards were all Super Bowl records. He'd also set four career Super Bowl records: 309 attempts; 207 completions; 2,071 passing yards; and fifteen touchdown passes. He was also named Super Bowl MVP for the fourth time, another record.

In another part of the locker room, Alex Guerrero fielded a question about Brady from a *Sports Illustrated* writer.

"I don't think people believed us when we said Tom could play to forty-five or beyond," Guerrero said. "I still don't know if they believe it. But Tommy and I, we believe it."

forty

HEAVY IS THE CROWN

———

O n the morning after Super Bowl LI, Tom Brady and Roger Goodell were together in Houston for the MVP trophy presentation. Belichick joined them. With Brady and Belichick seated behind him, Goodell stood at a lectern, facing a large gathering of journalists.

"The two gentlemen that we have here have set new bars across the league," Goodell told the audience. "Five Super Bowl championships and four MVPs for Tom Brady, cementing his legacy as not just a Super Bowl performer but maybe one of the greatest players of all time. And this duo, Coach Belichick, with his success of five Super Bowls, cementing his legacy as perhaps the best coach of all time."

Goodell glanced back at them.

"And it's a great honor for us and for me personally to have both of these guys here this morning," Goodell continued. "Tom, come on up. Get your trophy."

All eyes were on Brady and Goodell as they shook hands and posed for photographs, jointly holding the silver football-shaped trophy. But those anticipating drama were disappointed. Both Brady and Goodell had moved on from Deflategate.

The far more important relationship dynamic in the room that morning involved Brady and Belichick. Hours after adding another notch to their championship belt, the two men who epitomized the Patriots' mantras "Do Your Job" and "No Days Off" were already turning their sights to next season and the vexing issues of Brady's age and his determination to play until he was forty-five.

The night before, Brady and Belichick had embraced and expressed love for each other in the immediate aftermath of an epic triumph. But during their relentless seventeen-year march to unprecedented heights, there had been a dearth of affection between them. They had long ago figured out that they didn't need to be friends to win together. Hours after their emotionally

charged moment on the field at NRG Stadium, it was time to get back to business as usual—Belichick wondering how much longer Brady could continue to play at such an elite level, and Brady wondering how much longer Belichick wanted him as his quarterback.

After giving Brady his trophy, Goodell invited him to say a few words.

Tired, Brady stepped to the lectern and asked the press if they had any questions. With Belichick looking on stone-faced, Brady spent ten minutes giving stock answers, crediting his teammates, complimenting his opponents, and expressing gratitude to his family and his coaches. But the last question of the press conference provided Brady an opportunity to say something that he hoped would get through to Belichick.

"Have you had a chance to reflect at the age of thirty-nine on what you've accomplished as unprecedented in team sports, anywhere?" a reporter asked.

"I don't feel thirty-nine," Brady began. "I hang out with a bunch of twenty-year-olds. So that makes you feel pretty young."

Brady grinned and the journalists laughed. But Brady was intensely serious about the way he trained and took care of his body. From his perspective, Belichick didn't appreciate how integral Alex Guerrero and the TB12 Method had been to the Patriots' two most recent Super Bowl victories. Without them, Brady wouldn't still have been playing. He wouldn't have been around to lead the extraordinary Super Bowl comebacks against the Seahawks and Falcons. Brady seized the chance the question gave him to indirectly talk to Belichick.

"I try to just take care of myself through learning, through a lot of positive and negative experiences with that," he said. "When you're in the locker room for seventeen years, you kind of learn what to do, and what *not* to do, and what works for you.

"I've found a unique way that's a little outside the box that's really worked," Brady continued. "I try to spread that message to a lot of other players because football is a demanding sport. It's a demanding sport on your body. Your body is your asset. If you are hurt all the time, football is no fun. When I was twenty-five, I was hurting all the time and I couldn't imagine playing as long as I did because if your arm always hurts and you can't throw, how can you keep playing? Now at thirty-nine, my arm never hurts. My body never hurts. Even after I get banged up, I know how to take care of it and jump on it right away so that I can feel good for a Wednesday practice. It really allows you to continue to improve because you can practice."

With that, Brady thanked everyone, tucked his silver football under his arm as if he were a ball carrier, and rushed out of the building.

There were fewer reporters and fewer cameras when Belichick stepped to the lectern. But he had something he wanted to say about Brady. "A lot of things were said about him this morning," he said. "They're all true. A great player. It's been a privilege to coach Tom for the last seventeen years, sixteen years as a starting quarterback."

He paused. "We have a great relationship," he continued. "We meet on a regular basis weekly. I can't think of a more deserving player than Tom to be the recipient of the accolades that he has this week, and particularly last night and today.

"He's our leader. He competes as well as any player I've ever coached. He's well prepared. He's got great poise. Great presence. May not always be perfect, but it isn't for any of us. Tom, like many of the players on the team, is the guy that fights to the end and competes to the end, and there's no player that I respect more than Tom."

Belichick's remarks were heartfelt and represented the highest praise that he'd ever paid a player. But Brady wasn't there to hear him.

Nobody understood the complexity of the Brady-Belichick relationship the way Kraft did after working with them for seventeen years. Kraft's connection to Brady was deeply personal. They lived down the street from each other. Their families spent time together and were close. The expressions of affection that Kraft and Brady shared through word and deed were routine throughout the year. Kraft's relationship with Belichick was different, but no less significant. Although they didn't socialize much and possessed very different leadership styles, Kraft and Belichick had the most efficient working relationship between an owner and a coach in the NFL.

In Belichick, Kraft saw the greatest genius to ever coach the game. Belichick's football IQ was off the charts, his commitment to the organization beyond reproach, and his resiliency in the face of adversity inspiring. The one thing Belichick hadn't quite figured out was how to treat an enigmatic football player who had become a world-famous icon. Brady had become the genius's conundrum.

In Brady, Kraft saw the greatest football player who ever lived. Sensitive as a poet and possessing the drive of a machine, Brady was wired so differently than other men on the gridiron. Nothing was going to stop Tom except

Tom. The only thing Brady hadn't achieved was something he could never obtain no matter how hard he worked—fatherly approval from his coach. Belichick was the only target the quarterback couldn't reach.

Yet, Belichick and Brady were magical on the field, and Kraft just wanted the show to go on. His hope was to keep Brady and Belichick on his payroll until both of them retired.

Jonathan Kraft agreed. While Jonathan looked at Brady like a brother and appreciated how much pressure he'd been under in Foxborough, he also recognized how Belichick's coaching philosophy had benefited Brady and the team. Keeping Brady and Belichick together for so long, Jonathan felt, was his father's greatest achievement as an owner. Behind the scenes, he did his part to help Robert.

Days after Brady's comments at the MVP press conference in Houston, Jonathan stood beside Robert on a balcony at Boston's City Hall, watching Belichick address thousands of fans packed into the plaza after the Super Bowl victory parade.

"They took no days off," Belichick told the crowd, referring to his players.

Then Belichick held up the Lombardi Trophy and uncharacteristically started chanting: "No days off. No days off." Belichick kept doing it until the crowd joined in.

Triggered by the chant, Jonathan stepped forward and took the microphone. Pointing at Belichick, he shouted: "Hey! How lucky are we to have this guy?"

The crowd roared.

"When he says, 'No days off,' he's in there *twenty-four-seven, three-sixty-five!*"

The crowd chanted: "Bill. Bill. Bill."

"We've been so fortunate," Jonathan continued. "Since 2001, we've won five Super Bowls. Think about it. Five! And the quarterback of each of those teams was Tom Brady."

Jonathan paused and looked over his shoulder, trying to find Brady. "Get Tommy!" he yelled.

Brady emerged from the back of the platform wearing a black trench coat and holding one of the team's Lombardi Trophies.

The crowd erupted.

Jonathan slipped into the background as Brady took his place beside Belichick. The two of them held up their trophies and the crowd went wild.

"One more!" Brady shouted to the crowd.

The crowd started chanting: "We want six! We want six! We want six!" It was music to Kraft's ears.

In the early morning hours of April 19, a Massachusetts corrections officer found former Patriots tight end Aaron Hernandez hanging naked from a makeshift noose in his cell. Hernandez was promptly transferred to a nearby hospital, where he was pronounced dead. Hours later, the Patriots were honored at the White House by President Trump. For Kraft and Belichick, it was their fifth time taking the team to Washington after winning a championship. But Brady didn't make the trip, choosing instead to be with his family. Sustaining the dynasty had become particularly weighty for Brady. On top of being the greatest in the world in his profession, he was dutifully raising young children and growing his business with Guerrero while being married to Bündchen, who was in her own right the greatest in the world at her profession. From a family perspective, it was a lot to balance.

When Brady had met Bündchen in 2006, he'd told her that he was going to play for ten more years and that he hoped to win more Super Bowls during that time. After the 2016 season, Bündchen pointed out that it had been ten years. Moreover, Brady's magnum opus performance against the Falcons in the Super Bowl put him at the pinnacle of his profession and firmly established him as the greatest quarterback of all time. It was the ideal moment, in Bündchen's view, for him to walk away from professional football. She was, as one friend put it, "dead serious."

But Brady was equally serious about playing longer. He had never felt healthier. And despite having won two Super Bowls in the previous three seasons, he was convinced he could continue to get better and continue to push the boundaries in terms of what an athlete could accomplish in midlife. Guerrero agreed.

"Two more to go," Brady told Bündchen.

While Brady and Bündchen spent the spring discussing how much longer he'd play, Brady agreed to cooperate with documentary filmmaker Gotham Chopra, who wanted to make a film about Brady's unique training regimen and his quest to play into his mid-forties. The film would be called *Tom vs. Time* and would air on Facebook. It was most unusual for Brady to participate in a project of this nature. But with so many journalists writing about him, Brady warmed up to the idea of taking control of his own narrative. And he had known Chopra for some time and had come to trust him.

By the spring of 2017, Brady and Chopra's work was under way. The scope of the film soon evolved into a more comprehensive look at the intersection between Brady's personal life and his football life. At one point during the offseason, Brady and Bündchen sat together for an interview with Chopra, who asked them about Brady's decision to keep playing.

"Football, as far as I'm concerned, is his first love," Bündchen told Chopra. With his arm around her, Brady laughed.

"It really is," she continued. "And it's like his main love, quite frankly."

Bündchen told Chopra what Brady had said about only playing ten more years when they first met. "But then he's like, 'No,'" she said.

"Still got a few more to go," Brady chimed in.

"Yeah," Bündchen told Chopra. "He said *that.*"

In a separate interview with Chopra, Brady acknowledged that football was his first love, which had begun when he was a little boy at Candlestick Park, watching his idol, Joe Montana. Maintaining that love, Brady said, was effortless "because it's so synonymous with my being."

"When I'm out on the field in front of seventy thousand people, I can really be who I am," Brady told Chopra. "If I want to scream at somebody, I can scream at somebody. That's probably why I love football so much. Because it allows me to be who I am in a very authentic way that is hard for me to be when I walk off the field."

In late spring, Bündchen sat for a lengthy interview with Charlie Rose for *CBS This Morning.* The interview was supposed to be about Bündchen's environmental activism and her efforts to combat global warming. But toward the end, Rose brought up Brady.

"Your husband said the other day that you wanted him to retire," Rose said. "*He* said that. Not me. And that he was going to play as long as he felt as good as he does now. Are you trying to get him to retire?"

"I just have to say as a wife, I'm a little bit," Bündchen began before pausing to provide the context that football is an aggressive sport. "He had a concussion last year," she continued. "He has concussions pretty much. We don't talk about it, but he does have concussions. And I don't really think it's a healthy thing for your body to go through. . . ." Pausing, she smacked her hands together. "You know, through that kind of aggression, like, all the time."

The beauty of Bündchen was her fearlessness and her honesty. She was also unabashed in openly expressing her love for her husband. She told Rose that she wanted to be with Brady when they were a hundred years old. "I know that he loves what he does and I will always support him," she said. "And I told

him, in my dreams I would like for him to, you know, maybe not do it for as long anymore just because I'm concerned. . . . I just want him to be healthy."

When the segment aired on May 16, CBS promoted Bündchen's comments about Brady's having had a concussion in 2016. The sound bite instantly caused a stir, trending on social media and sparking headlines on the Internet. As an unintended consequence of Bündchen's claim, the Patriots came under scrutiny. Under league rules, a player diagnosed with a concussion must be removed from competition, and his concussion must be reported on the team's official injury report. It was well established that Brady had not missed any action due to injury in 2016. Nor had the Patriots ever put him on the injured list with a head injury.

Attempting to defuse the situation, Brady's agent, Don Yee, quickly issued a statement, saying: "Tom was not diagnosed with a concussion last year." But his statement didn't indicate whether Brady had suffered a concussion.

The NFL then released a more complete statement: "There are no records that indicate that Mr. Brady suffered a head injury or concussion, or exhibited or complained of concussion symptoms."

However, the league also faced questions about its concussion protocol. As a result, the NFL and the NFL Players Association announced they would jointly review all Patriots game film from 2016, looking at every play involving Brady to determine whether he had sustained an undocumented head injury. As part of their inquiry, the NFL and NFLPA also sought access to Brady's medical records for 2016, which Brady and the Patriots granted.

For Brady, constant scrutiny had become like a heavy suitcase that he had to carry everywhere he went. Fiercely loyal to Bündchen, he fended off the media's attempts to bait him into discussing her comments. "I mean we go to bed in the same bed every night, so I think she knows when I'm sore, she knows when I'm tired, she knows when I get hit," he finally told a radio host. "We drive home together. But she also knows how well I take care of myself. She's a very concerned wife and very loving."

While the league and the union conducted their review, Brady took a trip to China and Japan with his elder son, Jack. It was a welcome respite. They visited the Great Wall and practiced martial arts, and Brady put on football clinics in Tokyo and Shanghai, where thousands of fans turned out with "GOAT" and "TB12" signs. It was an indication that Brady's popularity had become global.

Upon their return, Brady and his son visited Brady's parents at their San Mateo home, where Brady had grown up. One morning, while seated at the kitchen table with his son and his parents, Brady FaceTimed Kraft.

Kraft and Brady hadn't seen much of each other during the offseason. Like Brady, Kraft had been abroad. He had taken Jim Brown, Joe Montana, Roger Staubach, and fifteen other NFL Hall of Famers to the Holy Land on a historic trip in an effort to build unity throughout the league. And since returning from Israel, Kraft had been consumed with league matters. As a leading member of the NFL's compensation committee, he was working to extend Roger Goodell's term as commissioner and navigating his new employment contract through a complicated negotiation process. He was also advancing the league's effort to launch an LGBTQ outreach program for gay athletes.

But in the midst of all this, Kraft had hosted the entire Patriots team and coaching staff at his home earlier in the summer to present them with newly minted Super Bowl rings, each of which was encrusted with 283 diamonds to commemorate the team's historic comeback after being down 28–3. It was during that event that Kraft and Brady hatched a plan to do something special for Brady's mother when Brady returned from China.

Once his FaceTime connection was established, Kraft asked Brady: "Is Galynn there?"

Brady aimed his phone at his mother so Kraft could see her.

"How are you, sweetie?" Kraft said.

"How are you, Robert?" she said.

Kraft brought up the Super Bowl. "Tommy told me right before the game, 'This is the first game Mom and Dad are gonna be there. They haven't been there all year.'"

Galynn's eyes welled up.

"We talked about how we had to win the game in your honor because you've been such an inspiration to us," Kraft said. "So we want to give you a little present. Only players and coaches get this. But we wanted you to have it. So I hope you'll accept this little token of our appreciation."

Brady reached across the table and handed his mother a Super Bowl ring.

"Oh my goodness!" she said, feeling the weight of it. Smiling and crying, she slipped it on her finger. "That is . . . I love my gift."

"I know it's a little understated," Kraft joked.

"Hey, Robert," Tom Brady Sr. interjected. "That's so sweet. Thank you so much."

While Brady's father took the phone and talked with Kraft, Galynn came around to Tom's side of the table, put her arms around him, and repeatedly kissed him. Tears ran down Brady's face. His son Jack looked on, beaming.

Belichick spent his offseason doing what he did every offseason—evaluating players for the draft, planning for the upcoming season, and overhauling the Patriots roster. In a clinical fashion, he declined to re-sign running back Le-Garrette Blount, who led the team in rushing with over 1,100 yards and eighteen touchdowns. He also decided not to re-sign tight end Martellus Bennett, whose total of 701 receiving yards in 2016 was the second highest on the team. Both players signed elsewhere. In all, Belichick cut, waived, traded, or simply didn't re-sign nearly half of the players from the 2016 squad. In their place, he brought in a crop of new players through the draft, free agency, and trades. Among the new players were All-Pro cornerback Stephon Gilmore, running back Rex Burkhead, and receiver Brandin Cooks.

But the boldest decision Belichick made in the offseason was opting not to trade quarterback Jimmy Garoppolo. With Garoppolo and Jacoby Brissett behind Brady, the Patriots had the deepest, most talented group of quarterbacks in the league. And with so many teams looking for a top-tier starting quarterback, Belichick was getting a lot of overtures from teams interested in trading for Garoppolo.

Despite some tempting offers, Belichick had long considered Garoppolo the ideal successor to Brady. There was a reason why so many teams were offering a lot to pry Garoppolo out of New England. Young, athletic, and possessing a strong arm, he demonstrated poise and exhibited good leadership qualities.

Left to his own devices, Belichick would have preferred to move on from Brady and keep Garoppolo. That approach would have been consistent with Belichick's usual method of operation. After playing in 271 games, Brady had logged a lot of football miles. And no matter what Guerrero was doing for Brady, Belichick felt that Brady would sooner rather than later succumb to the laws of nature. Garoppolo, on the other hand, had virtually no wear and tear on his body and was just entering the prime years of his career. Barring serious injury, he could conceivably be the Patriots quarterback for ten years to come. But Belichick knew that Kraft would never let him trade Brady. So he didn't broach the subject.

Meantime, Garoppolo was entering the final year of his four-year contract. At the end of the 2017 season, he'd be a restricted free agent. Efforts to get Garoppolo to sign an extension with the Patriots were futile as long as Brady was still playing. Garoppolo and Brady had the same agent, and Don Yee knew that the Patriots couldn't afford to keep both quarterbacks. The Patriots were already on the hook with Brady for salary cap hits of $22 million in 2018 and $22 million in 2019. Once Garoppolo's contract expired in early

2018, he'd attract similar money on the open market. Belichick wouldn't be able to dedicate at least 30 percent of the team's 2018 salary cap to two quarterbacks. That possibility was as unrealistic as trading Brady.

Despite these realities, Belichick rejected all deals for Garoppolo in the spring and summer of 2017, choosing instead to keep his protégé in Foxborough for as long as possible. But barring an injury to Brady in 2017, Belichick knew Garoppolo's days were numbered. So he had decided not to seek a trade for Jacoby Brissett, who would likely ascend to the second-string slot when Garoppolo moved on. But when Julian Edelman tore his ACL in a preseason game in August 2017, Belichick had a change of heart toward Brissett.

The loss of Edelman for the 2017 season was a big blow. In 2016 he had led the team in receptions, receiving yards, and total yards. To fill the void, Belichick needed a receiver. So at the end of the preseason, he reluctantly traded Brissett to the Colts for receiver Phillip Dorsett.

The move meant that the Patriots were heading into the season with a forty-year-old quarterback and a backup quarterback who would likely be moving on.

At the start of training camp, the NFL and the NFLPA announced that they had concluded their summer-long review and found no evidence of Brady's having sustained a concussion or reported signs or symptoms of a concussion. The matter was closed. Meantime, Brady's age and the TB12 Method dominated the news coverage around the team during the preseason. When Brady turned forty in August, a radio host in Boston poked some fun at his diet, saying on the air: "Happy fortieth birthday hashtag Tommy Brady. Enjoy that avocado ice cream and a cake iced with organic hummus." And pundits were skeptical about his ability to hold up.

"The next eighteen months he will be at best middle of the pack," predicted ESPN's Max Kellerman. "He'll be average at best."

"Forty is normally the demarcation line for regression," another pundit said, "especially among professional athletes."

Alex Guerrero dismissed the doubters. "Forty's just a number," he told Brady. "It's just a number."

Belichick didn't listen to Guerrero. But he couldn't ignore what his training staff and his strength and conditioning coaches were saying about him. They were increasingly at odds with Guerrero, whose methods and advice often conflicted with theirs. The conflict came to a head in training camp

over the treatment regimen for Rob Gronkowski, who had undergone back surgery in the offseason. Gronkowski had fully embraced the TB12 Method and was rehabbing and training with Guerrero. Belichick felt the strength coach and team trainer had the best prescription to enable Gronkowski to have a healthy, productive season. But Gronkowski stuck with Guerrero. Belichick wasn't pleased.

As far back as 2013, Belichick had granted Guerrero access to meetings with the training staff. He had also given Guerrero sideline access and allowed him to fly on the team plane. These privileges had begun as a way to accommodate Brady. But little by little, the Patriots allowed other players to start seeing Guerrero for treatment. Belichick reluctantly went along with that, too. By the summer of 2017, more than a dozen of the Patriots' top players were relying on Guerrero for treatment. They included Edelman, Amendola, and linebacker Dont'a Hightower. But it was Guerrero's work with Gronkowski that was bringing the power struggle between Guerrero and the training staff to the fore.

The situation aggravated Gronkowski, who felt as though the team was questioning his commitment level simply because he had chosen to train differently. Belichick, meanwhile, was ready to send Guerrero packing. But Guerrero's connection to Brady limited how far Belichick could go.

Despite the loss of Edelman, the Patriots remained the presumptive favorites to return to the Super Bowl and once again win the championship. The headline on the cover of the *Sports Illustrated* 2017 NFL preview issue read, "THE PATRIOTS PROBLEM: Can The Unstoppable Dynasty Be Stopped?" The question was accompanied by an image showing a giant Brady with a bunch of tiny players from other teams attempting to crawl up his legs and arms.

The Patriots kicked off the 2017 regular season in a nationally televised Thursday-night game against the Chiefs. After avoiding Gillette Stadium for the previous two seasons, Roger Goodell returned for the season opener. Patriots fans finally got their chance to voice their opinion on his handling of Deflategate. And they were merciless. Thousands of fans wore aqua-blue T-shirts depicting Goodell as a clown. The fan website Barstool Sports had distributed an additional seventy thousand matching towels. The booing was so loud when Goodell entered the stadium that it interrupted NBC's pregame broadcast. The public address announcer had to remind fans of the stadium's policy prohibiting profanity.

The fans had little else to cheer them that day. The game was a blowout, with the Chiefs trouncing the Patriots 42–27. The Patriots' defense gave up 537 yards, which was the most allowed in a game during the Belichick era. Receiver Danny Amendola got knocked out of the game with a concussion. Gronkowski, in his first game back after his surgery, got nicked up. Brady, meanwhile, was hit and harassed all night.

After just one game, it appeared the 2017 season was going to be a slog.

forty-one
TENSION

T he Patriots rebounded in week two with a road win in New Orleans to improve to 1-1. Five days later, the team, along with the rest of the NFL, got pulled into a political maelstrom that no one could have seen coming. It threatened to divide the locker room and overshadow the season.

On September 22, President Trump spoke at a political rally in Huntsville, Alabama. In the weeks leading up to the rally, there had been a lot of press coverage about the fact that outspoken quarterback Colin Kaepernick was unemployed. Throughout the previous season, Kaepernick had knelt during the national anthem in order to draw attention to racial injustice and police violence. President Barack Obama had voiced support for Kaepernick's stance. A number of other players also knelt to show solidarity with Kaepernick. And his team, the 49ers, even pledged $1 million to organizations that combat racial and social inequality. But after the 2016 season, the 49ers did not re-sign Kaepernick, and no other team signed him as a free agent. Kaepernick felt that he was being blackballed by the NFL for his political activism.

Although kneeling during the anthem as a form of protest had fizzled out at the end of the previous season, Trump decided to weigh in on the subject while campaigning for one of Alabama's US senators.

"Wouldn't you love to see one of these NFL owners, when somebody disrespects our flag, to say, 'Get that son of a bitch off the field right now. Out. He's fired, he's FIRED!'"

The crowd cheered.

"You know, some owner is going to do that," Trump continued. "He's going to say, 'That guy that disrespects our flag, he's *fired*.' And that owner—they don't know it—they'll be the most popular person for a week. They'll be the most popular person in this country."

Instantly, the NFL had a problem on its hands.

The next morning, Goodell tried to diffuse the situation by issuing a nonconfrontational statement of support for the league's players. "The NFL and our players are at our best when we help create a sense of unity in our country and our culture," he said. "Divisive comments like these demonstrate an unfortunate lack of respect for the NFL, our great game and all of our players, and a failure to understand the overwhelming force for good our clubs and players represent in our communities."

Trump immediately fired back at Goodell on Twitter:

If a player wants the privilege of making millions of dollars in the NFL, or other leagues, he or she should not be allowed to disrespect . . .

. . . our Great American Flag (or Country) and should stand for the National Anthem. If not, YOU'RE FIRED. Find something else to do!

Later in the day, Trump tweeted again:

Roger Goodell of the NFL just put out a statement trying to justify the total disrespect certain players show to our country. Tell them to stand!

Trump's attack on the NFL was popular among his political base. But the slur he used to reference those who had knelt to protest racism was deeply offensive to players throughout the NFL. Athletes in other sports were upset, too. Hours after Trump's tweets, NBA star Steph Curry, whose Golden State Warriors had recently won the NBA Finals, told reporters he didn't want to go to the White House for the traditional ceremonial visit. Trump went back on Twitter and disinvited the entire Warriors team, which prompted LeBron James to call the president a "bum" and say: "Going to White House was a great honor until you showed up!"

In a span of less than thirty-six hours, the situation had spiraled out of control.

In the Patriots locker room, many players were hurt and angry over the president's actions, and they were searching for a way to respond. Earlier in the year, when the team had visited the White House to celebrate their latest Super Bowl victory with President Trump, half of the Patriots players had skipped the trip. At the time, team captain Devin McCourty said:

"I don't feel accepted in the White House." He and others were criticized for being disrespectful. After Trump's comments in Alabama, McCourty tweeted:

> Ppl said it was disrespectful not going to the White House. I'm sure they are quiet about us being called "sons of bitches."

Kraft empathized with McCourty and other players who felt similarly. Trump's characterization of them and their families was, in Kraft's view, wrong and hurtful. And between Belichick's public endorsement of Trump during his campaign and his own close friendship with the president, Kraft felt compelled to speak out. While the league and the rest of the NFL owners were trying to figure out whether to respond, Kraft issued a public statement hours before the Patriots hosted the Texans at Gillette Stadium on September 24:

> I am deeply disappointed by the tone of the comments made by the President on Friday. I am proud to be associated with so many players who make such tremendous contributions in positively impacting our communities.
>
> There is no greater unifier in this country than sports, and, unfortunately, nothing more divisive than politics. I think our political leaders could learn a lot from the lessons of teamwork and the importance of working together toward a common goal. Our players are intelligent, thoughtful and care deeply about our community and I support their right to peacefully effect social change and raise awareness in a manner that they feel is most impactful.

Prior to the game, Kraft also met privately with McCourty and fellow captain Matthew Slater. After listening to their viewpoint, he told them that he agreed with the sentiment of standing for the national anthem, but he disagreed with the president's language. Kraft mentioned the team's strong connection to the men and women serving in the armed forces and his preference that everyone in the organization continue to honor them by standing during the anthem. But he understood what the players were saying, respected their position, and recognized their right to take a knee. He told them he supported them and would stand behind whatever they chose to do prior to the game.

That afternoon, seventeen Patriots players knelt during the national anthem at Gillette Stadium. Many others, including Brady, locked arms. Some Patriots fans booed those who knelt.

Similar scenes played out in stadiums across the league. In some cases, entire teams knelt during the anthem. A number of teams chose to remain in the locker room until after the anthem. As the day wore on, more owners issued statements in support of the players. But it was Kraft's pointed words that instantly became a lead item in the *New York Times* as the president spent his Sunday raising the stakes by calling on Americans to boycott the NFL if the league didn't punish players for disrespecting the flag. "If NFL fans refuse to go to games until players stop disrespecting our Flag & Country," he tweeted, "you will see change take place fast. Fire or suspend!"

Against that backdrop, the Patriots struggled against an inferior team and trailed 33–28 with 2:24 to play. But Brady had a banner day, completing twenty-five of thirty-five passes for 378 yards. With twenty-three seconds left in the game, Brady threw his fifth touchdown pass on the day, capping off a furious comeback and giving the Patriots a 36–33 victory.

For weeks to come, players throughout the league knelt during the anthem. But after the Texans game, the Patriots players chose to show solidarity by standing together and placing one arm on a teammate's shoulder and one hand over the heart.

While the anthem controversy raged, Tom Brady released *The TB12 Method: How to Achieve a Lifetime of Sustained Peak Performance.* Published by Simon & Schuster, the book was nothing like the traditional memoir that top athletes tend to write at or near the end of a career. Rather, this was Brady's bible for delaying the aging process through his revolutionary approach to health and fitness. Instead of reliving glory days, he was advancing the TB12 Method and its core tenet—"pliability," which he described as training his muscles to become "long, soft, and primed." It was a concept that he hoped would reach the masses. "Pliability is not just for elite athletes," he wrote. "It's for anyone who wants to live a vital life for as long as possible."

Brady's book instantly shot to number one on the *New York Times* bestseller list, indirectly bringing further attention to Guerrero and his efforts to extend Brady's football career. Throughout the book, Brady made bold claims, particularly when it came to explaining how he'd been able to play

a violent game into his forties without succumbing to age or injury. In one passage, he wrote:

> The moment another player's helmet makes contact with my body, my muscles are pliable enough to absorb what's happening instantly. My brain is thinking only *Lengthen and soften and disperse* before my body absorbs and disperses the impact evenly and I hit the ground.

Through the first four weeks of the season, Brady exemplified what he was saying in his book. While the team had stumbled to a 2-2 start, Brady had been hit or knocked down twenty-six times, a disconcerting number for any quarterback, especially one who was forty years old. Nonetheless, Brady hadn't missed any snaps and was averaging 350 yards passing per game. Although the defense was struggling mightily—it had given up more than four hundred yards in each of the first four games and was ranked last in the league—the offense was averaging more than thirty points per game.

"If you want proof that pliability and the TB12 Method works," Brady wrote, "I'm it."

It was a message that had become impossible to ignore in the Patriots' locker room, where Brady's way of doing things continued to appeal more and more to his teammates. After an undermanned Patriots team squeaked out a victory in Tampa Bay in week five, Gronkowski returned in week six and caught two touchdown passes, helping the Patriots improve to 4-2.

In mid-October, quarterback Colin Kaepernick filed a grievance against the NFL and its owners, alleging they had colluded to keep him off the field because of the national anthem protests he had instigated a year earlier. "If the NFL . . . is to remain a meritocracy," said Kaepernick's attorney, Mark Geragos, "then principled and peaceful political protest—which the owners themselves made great theater imitating weeks ago—should not be punished, and athletes should not be denied employment based on partisan political provocation by the Executive Branch of our government." Meanwhile, the president's call for an NFL boycott was wreaking havoc. In the weeks following Trump's speech calling for NFL players to be fired for kneeling, nearly five hundred Russia-linked Twitter accounts had sent 2,623 NFL-focused tweets such as: "VIDEO: Trump SHREDS NFL Anthem Protesters!" and "Trump Supporters SACK NFL Commish Roger Goodell for Attacking Trump." The

Russians' attempt to exploit the kneeling controversy was so significant that it reached the attention of the Senate Intelligence Committee. "We watched, even this weekend, the Russians and their troll farms, their internet folks, start hashtagging out #TakeAKnee and also hashtagging out #BoycottNFL," said Republican senator James Lankford. "They were taking both sides of the argument this weekend . . . to try to raise the noise level of America and make a big issue seem like an even bigger issue as they are trying to push divisiveness in this country."

Polls showed that Americans were pretty evenly split between those supporting the president and those supporting the players. That spelled bad news for the league. With players on at least ten teams still kneeling on a weekly basis, a significant number of fans were turning away from the game. Attendance was down, television ratings were in decline, and league sponsors were getting rattled. Cowboys owner Jerry Jones, who had taken a knee with his entire team in the first game they played after the president's remarks, had since changed his tune and threatened to bench any player who knelt thereafter. A number of owners wanted the league to adopt Jones's approach, while the players' union argued such a move would only further alienate the players.

Facing an unprecedented political crisis, Commissioner Goodell took the unusual step of inviting a group of twelve players and eleven owners to NFL headquarters in October for a roundtable discussion. To signal the need to promote unity, players and owners sat in alternating seats around the table. Kraft sat between two New York Jets players.

At the outset, Goodell invited the players to speak first and to speak freely. Some of them wanted to discuss why Kaepernick hadn't been signed. But most of them wanted the owners to know that the players who had been kneeling were responsible citizens who loved their country, some of whom had family members who served in the military. They weren't protesting the flag or the anthem. They were calling attention to racism and police brutality in minority communities throughout America. Jets linebacker Demario Davis stood and spoke passionately to the owners. "You guys aren't supporting us," he told them. "And until you do, there's going to be an issue."

When Davis sat down, Kraft patted him on the leg and Falcons owner Arthur Blank nodded favorably, signaling his understanding. When it was the owners' turn to speak, they expressed concern that the business of professional football was under attack. After a while, Kraft interjected that everyone was dancing around "the elephant in the room . . . the kneeling."

"The problem we have is we have a president who will use that as fodder

to do his mission that I don't feel is in the best interests of America," Kraft told the group. "It's divisive and it's horrible."

Eagles owner Jeffrey Lurie agreed.

"We've got to be careful not to be baited by Trump or whomever else," Lurie said. "We have to find a way to not be divided and not get baited."

Goodell artfully steered the conversation back to the players' concerns.

All-Pro receiver Anquan Boldin quieted the room with a painful story about a relative of his being shot and killed by a police officer. Then he suggested that the best way to foster unity was for the owners to step up. "Letting people know it's not just the players that care about these issues, but the owners, too," Boldin said.

The meeting lasted three hours. Tough subjects were broached. And at one point, when it had become clear that everyone was tired, Kraft said to Demario Davis: "Can we just shut the fuck up and end this?" The comments caused Davis and his teammate to smile. The sight of two Jets players sharing a laugh with the Patriots owner momentarily lightened the mood and reminded everyone in the room that they were on the same side. Kraft gave Davis a fist bump.

Before adjourning, the group crafted a joint statement. It said, in part: "Today owners and players had a productive meeting focused on how we can work together to promote positive social change and address inequality in our communities."

The following day, Goodell met with all thirty-two of the owners in a hotel conference room in lower Manhattan. They discussed what had taken place in the smaller session with the players. Jerry Jones, who had not been present in the meeting with the players, stood and reminded everyone that he was the owner with the most seniority. Visibly angry over the situation confronting the league and the overall impact it was having on the bottom line, Jones pushed for a resolution mandating that all players be required to stand during the anthem. Others supported him, including Houston Texans owner Robert McNair. "We can't have the inmates running the prison," McNair interjected.

McNair's comment brought silence to the room.

Kraft disagreed with Jones's proposal and felt strongly that it would only deepen the divide. Leery of knee-jerk reactions in times of crisis, Kraft felt everyone would benefit from taking a step back. The situation, he suggested, would resolve itself through respectful, ongoing dialogue rather than mandates.

In the end, fewer than ten owners supported Jones and his proposal against kneeling. The matter was tabled.

Heading into the bye week, the Patriots were 6-2 and gaining momentum. Belichick liked his team's trajectory. But the clock had run out on his efforts to keep Jimmy Garoppolo in Foxborough. While Brady continued to defy the actuary charts by outplaying every quarterback in the league, Belichick had come to the realization that his well-contrived succession plan simply wasn't going to pan out.

With the trading deadline looming, Belichick worked out a deal with the 49ers. In exchange for Garoppolo, the Niners offered a second-round draft choice and agreed to release their backup quarterback, Brian Hoyer. The Patriots would need a backup to replace Garoppolo, and Hoyer had previously played in New England and knew the Patriots' system.

Before pulling the trigger, Belichick called Kraft and asked if he was okay with it. Kraft had hoped they could get more in return for Garoppolo. But at least Belichick was planning to trade him to an NFC team, ensuring that the Patriots would rarely face him in a game. He told Belichick he'd get right back to him.

Then Kraft called Jonathan to apprise him of Belichick's proposed trade. "What do you think?" Robert said.

"I think given what we hope is going to happen with Tom, it's probably the right thing," Jonathan said.

The Krafts were expecting Brady to play a few more years and retire a Patriot.

Kraft called Belichick back and gave him the green light.

On October 31, 2017, the Patriots announced that Garoppolo had been traded to San Francisco. The 49ers subsequently signed him to a five-year contract extension worth $137.5 million, making him the highest-paid player in the history of the NFL in terms of average salary per year.

Right after Garoppolo left town, a full close-up of Brady's face appeared on the cover of *ESPN The Magazine*. His hair and whiskers had been altered to appear gray, and slight wrinkles had been added to his forehead and around his eyes. "IS THE FUTURE OF FOOTBALL STARING US IN THE FACE?" the magazine provocatively asked. "MEET TOM BRADY, 2022 MVP. HE SAYS YES."

Brady had cooperated for the profile, which focused largely on his new book and his quest for pliability. Praising the "genius" efforts of Guerrero, Brady told the magazine that in his daily workouts, Guerrero's hands generated "50 newtons of force in a single finger," which enabled him to penetrate Brady's muscles and improve their elasticity.

The article also hinted at the conflict between Brady and Belichick over

Guerrero and quoted an unnamed friend of Belichick's saying: "There's a collision coming."

After the article came out, Belichick revoked Guerrero's sideline access during games and suspended him from flying on the team plane. He also told Guerrero that with the exception of Brady, he could no longer treat Patriots players at Gillette Stadium. Any other Patriots players who wanted to see Guerrero would have to do so across the parking lot at the TB12 facility. Belichick felt that in taking these actions he was removing a major distraction.

Brady was furious. He was doing everything humanly possible to help the team win another championship, and Guerrero was an integral part of his ability to perform. Revoking Guerrero's privileges came across like a repudiation of Brady himself. The whole scenario seemed petty.

But Brady wasn't about to get into a heated exchange with Belichick. That wasn't his nature. He was a tenacious competitor on the field. But when it came to interpersonal relations, Brady preferred to avoid conflict. He didn't like fighting. But he seethed.

While the tension between Brady and Belichick intensified, Kraft was dealing with an escalating feud between Jerry Jones and Roger Goodell. Back in August, Goodell had suspended Dallas Cowboys star running back Ezekiel Elliott for six games after his former girlfriend alleged that he had assaulted her on five occasions. The authorities had declined to bring charges. But the league had spent a year investigating the matter and concluded that there was "substantial and persuasive evidence supporting a finding that [Elliott] engaged in physical violence against [his girlfriend] on multiple occasions."

With Elliott denying the allegations, Cowboys owner Jerry Jones was so furious with the commissioner that he attempted to prevent the league from extending Goodell's employment contract. Jones started by threatening to sue the six members of the league's compensation committee. Besides Kraft, the other members included the owners of the Falcons, Giants, Chiefs, Texans, and Steelers. Kraft's committee responded by issuing Jones a cease-and-desist warning. But days later, on November 17, 2017, ESPN's *Outside the Lines* reported on a private phone call involving Jones, Goodell, and league general counsel Jeffrey Pash back in early August. During that call, Goodell had given Jones a heads-up that he was going to suspend Elliott. According to ESPN, while Goodell and Pash were huddled over a speakerphone, Jones lashed out, saying: "I'm gonna come after you with everything I have." Then

Jones referenced Deflategate and said, "If you think Bob Kraft came after you hard, Bob Kraft is a pussy compared to what I'm gonna do."

Three people were on that call. The fact that what was said got leaked to ESPN was an indication of just how badly relations between Jones and the commissioner's office had deteriorated. While Jones fought the league, his team floundered through another mediocre season. Kraft defended Goodell and worked with his fellow owners on the compensation committee to solidify a consensus to get Goodell's contract extended.

The Patriots, meanwhile, ground on as if they were impervious to everything going on around them. In November, they went on the road and crushed the Broncos 41–16 and the Raiders 33–8. December brought more of the same. By the time the Patriots reached Pittsburgh on December 17, they were 10-3 and the Steelers were 11-2. In a game that would determine which team secured home-field advantage in the playoffs, the Patriots trailed 24–19 with just over two minutes to play. During the ensuing seventy seconds, Brady drove the offense seventy-seven yards, thanks in large part to three big catches by Gronkowski. After the Patriots scored a touchdown with fifty-six seconds left on the clock to go up 25–24, Brady again went to Gronkowski on the two-point conversion, lofting a pass to the corner of the end zone. As the defender bounced off Gronkowski and fell to the ground, Gronkowski easily hauled in the pass. Pointing down at the defender and laughing, Gronkowski spiked the ball.

After the Patriots kicked off, Ben Roethlisberger completed a sixty-nine-yard pass that put the Steelers on New England's ten-yard line with thirty-four seconds remaining. On first-and-goal, Roethlisberger then completed a short pass to Jesse James, who appeared to score a touchdown when he lunged and extended the ball across the goal line, losing control of the ball as he hit the ground. While the scoreboard indicated that Pittsburgh had gone up 30–27 with twenty-eight seconds remaining, the officials reviewed the play and determined that the receiver "did not survive the ground," meaning he never had control of the ball. "Based on the rule, I think they made the right call," Tony Romo said on the air. "But it's just a *backbreaker* for Pittsburgh." Moments later, the Patriots intercepted Roethlisberger in the end zone to preserve the 27–24 victory.

With Gronkowski having one of the best years of his career, the Patriots improved to 11-3 and clinched the AFC East division title for the ninth straight year.

Two days after the Steelers game, the *Boston Globe* reported: "Belichick curbs privileges of Tom Brady's associate Alex Guerrero." Although the

development had happened earlier in the season, this marked the first time that word of the change became public. It immediately prompted thorny questions. At Belichick's weekly press conference, one day after the *Globe* story ran, the subject came up.

"How would you describe the dynamic with you and Tom, in terms of the working relationship?" a reporter asked. "Has anything changed this year?"

"Well, every year's different," Belichick said.

Belichick was a master at choosing his words. *Different*, in this instance, was how he chose to characterize his working relationship with Brady in 2017. The only fundamental difference between 2017 and every other year in their relationship was that Brady had established his independence. He had written his own book. He was making his own film. He had his own company. He had, for all intents and purposes, become his own brand. The ultimate team player was also a world-famous icon.

No matter how tightly Belichick held to his time-tested philosophy of treating every player on his roster the same way, Brady simply wasn't like anyone else. Everything about him—his achievements, his age, his fame, his training methods, his wife's global sphere of influence, and his relationship with the owner—forced Belichick to make accommodations for Brady that he'd never consider for anyone else.

On the field, Brady and Belichick continued to work their magic. But a virtual cold war existed between them. They didn't talk to each other. And they didn't talk about each other, especially to the media. Brady didn't see any upside to getting into it. For him, it would be like wading into mud. And once he engaged, he figured, he'd have to reengage. He was determined to avoid that when he attended his weekly press conference.

"How did you react when Bill Belichick told you he was going to restrict Guerrero's access?" a reporter asked.

"I don't really agree with your question," Brady said. "So I don't know what you're talking about. How do you know what he said?"

"So, are you saying the report about his access being restricted was—"

"I'm not saying anything," Brady cut in. "I mean, how do you say that he said anything? You don't know anything about that."

"Bill never told you that he was removing Alex from the sideline or the team planes?" the reporter pressed.

"Well, I have a lot of conversations with him," Brady said. "Those are private between he and I, and I don't think anyone knows what we talk about. Certainly I've never talked about it. He's never talked about it."

Another reporter chimed in: "The story with Alex, has any of that put any strain on your working relationship with Bill?"

"I just try to show up and do the right thing and try to win football games," Brady said, smiling. "I let my play do the talking."

On December 31, 2017, the Patriots closed out the regular season at home by beating up on the Jets to finish with the AFC's best record, 13-3. After the shaky 2-2 start, the Patriots had gone 11-1 the rest of the way. Despite subzero windchill temperatures in a game that was over by halftime, Patriots fans braved the weather and stayed to the bitter end, rooting for a team that continued to make history and push the boundaries of what anyone had dreamed possible.

It seemed that no team was capable of derailing the Patriots from another Super Bowl title. The biggest foes the Patriots faced were internal strife and relentless scrutiny. Five days after the regular season concluded, ESPN .com published a sensational story titled: "For Kraft, Brady and Belichick, Is This the Beginning of the End?" Alleging that the dynasty was "threatening to come undone the only way possible: from within," the story landed like a bomb in New England. The story's most incendiary claim was that Kraft had given a mandate to Belichick to trade Jimmy Garoppolo, which left Belichick "furious and demoralized" while leaving Brady feeling "liberated." The story ended with a provocative jab about the season-ending victory over the Jets. "It didn't look like Belichick's last regular-season game as the Patriots' head coach, but several coaches and staffers later remarked to one another that it felt as if it could be."

The story caused such an uproar that the Patriots took the unusual step of issuing a joint statement by Kraft, Belichick, and Brady:

> For the past 18 years, the three of us have enjoyed a very good and productive working relationship. In recent days, there have been multiple media reports that have speculated theories that are unsubstantiated, highly exaggerated or flat out inaccurate. . . . It's unfortunate that there is even a need for us to respond to these fallacies. As our actions have shown, we stand united.

As the agent for Brady and Garoppolo, Don Yee also issued a statement: "I don't really know what to say; it's tough to have a response since [the article] didn't appear to me to have one on-the-record quote. All I can suggest is, don't believe everything you read."

But ESPN's narrative didn't just stick; it spread like wildfire. Headlines like "Brady-Belichick-Kraft Rift Has Patriots on Brink of Implosion" appeared on sports pages and on websites. Football writer Peter King wrote: "The Patriots haven't been as angry about anything since the Tom Brady deflated footballs scandal. Apoplectic might be a better word."

Then, on January 11, the *New York Times* published "Tom Brady's Midlife Crisis," a feature story that stirred the pot even more by focusing on Guerrero's banishment. "Patriots Kremlinologists have been in a tizzy about whether Brady and Coach Bill Belichick are feuding—and whether that might imperil one of the N.F.L.'s greatest dynasties," the *Times* reported.

With his team in the eye of another media firestorm heading into the divisional round of the AFC playoffs, Belichick methodically put his players through the paces as if it were just another week at the office. Then Brady went out and completed thirty-five of fifty-three passes for nearly 340 yards against the Titans, Danny Amendola had the game of his life with eleven catches for 112 yards, and New England's defense set a club record by sacking Titans quarterback Marcus Mariota eight times. Machinelike, the Patriots ground out a 35–14 playoff victory.

The Patriots were headed to the AFC Championship game for a record seventh straight year. And for the seventh straight year, CBS had the most dominant team in America and the game's biggest star playing in the network's marquee game. In a year when the NFL's television rating had tumbled, the Patriots remained must-see television. Few people appreciated the juggernaut in Foxborough more than CBS president Les Moonves. From his perspective, the Patriots had been a godsend. Dating all the way back to the snow game against the Raiders in 2002, the Patriots had been the most reliable form of live entertainment the network had to offer.

After the Titans game, which Moonves and his nine-year-old son, Charlie, had watched from Kraft's box, Kraft led them to the locker room so he could personally congratulate the team. When Moonves went to Brady's locker to shake his hand, Brady noticed the boy staring up at him.

"Hi, Charlie," Brady said.

In awe, Charlie smiled.

Brady took off his wristbands and gave them to Charlie. Then he knelt down and gave him a hug.

Moved, Moonves turned to Kraft and shook his head.

Kraft looked at Brady and winked.

forty-two

THREADING THE NEEDLE

O n the Wednesday before the AFC Championship game against the Jacksonville Jaguars, the Patriots were practicing outside in the bitter cold. On a routine play, Brady handed the ball off to running back Rex Burkhead. In the exchange, the ball jammed back into Brady's thumb, hyperextending it with such force that the skin at the base of the thumb split open. With blood gushing, Brady let out a yell and rushed off the field, clutching his hand. Burkhead and his teammates looked on in stunned silence.

Minutes later, Dr. Matthew Leibman's cell phone rang. Leibman was the hand and wrist surgeon for the Patriots, Red Sox, and Bruins. He was having lunch outside Boston when Patriots assistant trainer Joe Van Allen reached him.

Van Allen was frantic. "Matt, we need you at the stadium right now," he said. "Brady hurt his hand. It's bad. It's bleeding."

"What happened?" Leibman said.

Van Allen quickly explained that Brady's thumb had somehow gotten jammed and bent backward during a handoff. "There's a pretty big laceration," he said.

"Is it his throwing hand?" Leibman said.

Van Allen said he'd text a picture.

Leibman hung up. Seconds later, the image was on his phone. It looked as though Brady's hand had been slashed by a blade. The base of his thumb was split wide open. The laceration was gaping.

"Holy *shit!*" Leibman said to himself.

In 99 percent of the cases where a hyperextended thumb results in a gaping laceration, there is also a fracture or dislocation involved. And the underlying ligaments and tendons are inevitably damaged as well.

Confident that Brady needed surgery, he called Van Allen back. "Does Tom just want to meet me at the hospital?" Leibman said. "Because we may go straight to the OR."

Van Allen said that the team really wanted him to evaluate Brady at the stadium. "Get here as quick as you can," Van Allen said.

"I'm on my way," Leibman said. "Give me fifteen minutes."

Leibman flew down the highway, confident that if he got pulled over all he'd have to do was tell the police officer, "Brady's bleeding and waiting for me." His bigger concern was the unnerving proposition of what he was about to do: operate on the throwing hand of the greatest quarterback of all time on the cusp of the AFC Championship game.

Distraught and awaiting the results of his X-ray, Brady lay on a stretcher in the medical treatment room at Gillette Stadium, his right arm outstretched, his hand wrapped in a towel. He feared his career was over, and his eyes welled up.

Alex Guerrero stood next to Brady's head. Guerrero was worried, but he tried to comfort Brady.

Scowling, Belichick stood off to Brady's side, next to trainer Jim Whalen.

Dr. Mark Price, the team's head doctor and chief orthopedic surgeon, stood opposite Belichick to Brady's right.

The room was eerily silent when Dr. Leibman entered.

"Hi, everybody," Leibman said. "How's everybody doing?"

No one responded.

"The good news is I just looked at the X-rays and they're clean," Leibman said. "There's no fracture and there appears to be no dislocation."

Still no one spoke.

Leibman sat down on a stool beside Brady and explained that he needed to examine his hand. Leibman removed the towel and looked at the wound. It was deep enough that he could see down to the bone and tendon. Brady grimaced as Leibman gently touched his thumb.

"It looks like the ligaments and the bone and the tendons are structurally intact," Liebman told Brady. Leibman turned to Belichick and the trainer. "I'm very surprised. Normally with a laceration like this, the bones get pulled in a way that they either break or you tear a ligament."

The tension in the room remained palpable.

"Guys, you don't understand," Leibman said. "This is a hyperextension loading injury causing a skin burst. The fact that there's no fracture or dislocation is amazing."

Leibman explained how rare it is to see someone endure such a high-energy injury without damage to the bone or dislocation. With all the hype

about Brady's pliability thanks to the TB12 Method, Leibman figured he'd lighten the mood by referencing it. Looking at Guerrero, he said, "I guess it's because Tom's thumb is so . . ." Then he glanced at Belichick and figured *pliable* wasn't the best word choice. "Flexible," he said.

Belichick glared at Brady.

No one smiled.

The only thing Brady cared about was whether he had a shot at playing on Sunday.

Leibman explained the realities of the situation: The game was four days away. Brady's hand needed surgery. After the procedure, skin takes a good eight to ten days to seal. If Brady were to fall on his hand or get hit on his thumb during that period, the surgical wound would blow open.

A discussion ensued about things they could do to protect his hand.

Dr. Price chimed in that another Patriots player had previously played in a game after getting stitches for a hand laceration.

To Belichick, the situation wasn't comparable. "Tom's the *quarterback*," he groused.

"We'll have to take it day by day and make a game-time decision on Sunday," Leibman told everyone.

Without saying a word to Brady, Belichick left the room. Whalen followed. Guerrero stayed with Brady while Leibman performed the procedure. Dr. Price assisted.

Telling himself *This is just another hand*, Leibman prepared to operate on Brady by numbing his thumb with numerous injections. Then Leibman irrigated the area around the bone and tendon, removing any grass or dirt particles from the wound. When it came time to realign Brady's skin and sew him up, Leibman told Brady he was going to use a larger caliber of thread than he would ordinarily use, since he knew the plan was to try to enable Brady to play in four days. For extra strength, he also used twenty-five sutures sewn in a crisscross pattern for maximum support.

After the procedure, Leibman dressed Brady's hand and applied a splint. Then he looked at Brady and Guerrero. "Right now, the concern is that the thumb is going to get very swollen and painful," he told him. "So you can't do any of your massage. You can't do any of your mobilization. We want to immobilize. Whatever you do, don't remove the splint."

Brady figured his season was over.

Leibman arranged for him to have an MRI later in the day just so he could be sure that there was no underlying damage to the joint.

As Leibman prepared to leave, Rex Burkhead entered the room with tears in his eyes.

"It's not your fault," Brady told him.

Burkhead was inconsolable.

"Don't worry," Brady told him as he put an arm around him. "I love you."

After Burkhead left, offensive coordinator Josh McDaniels and backup quarterback Brian Hoyer entered.

Dr. Price gave McDaniels the prognosis.

McDaniels turned to Hoyer and said, "You better get fuckin' ready."

At 3:18 p.m., the Patriots announced: "Tom Brady is with our medical staff and will not be available to the media today."

Belichick was notorious for remaining tight-lipped about player injuries. In this instance, it was particularly critical to keep a lid on Brady's situation. On the outside chance that Brady played on Sunday, Belichick didn't want the Jaguars to realize that he was vulnerable, especially in his throwing hand.

By 6:00 p.m., longtime Patriots beat writer Karen Guregian tweeted, "Tom Brady jammed his throwing hand at practice after accidentally being run into, according to a source. X-ray showed no structural damage." Thirty minutes later, NFL Insider Ian Rapoport tweeted, "This is my understanding, as well. Sounds manageable."

By evening, ESPN's Mike Reiss tweeted, "Source close to Brady: 'Hand should be OK.'" And the *Boston Herald* reported that Brady was expected to play on Sunday "barring an unexpected setback."

On Thursday morning, Dr. Leibman reviewed Brady's MRI. It confirmed that the bone hadn't been broken and that the ligaments were intact. However, the imaging revealed swelling at the joint or base of the thumb, indicating that the scope of the injury went beyond a bad laceration. Leibman drove to Brady's home later that morning to discuss the MRI. When he arrived, he found Brady had ignored his instructions: the splint had been removed, and Brady was gripping a football. And Guerrero was with him.

"I think I'm okay," Brady told Leibman.

"Listen, Tom," Leibman said. "We need to let this rest. We don't have that many days." Exasperated, Leibman then looked at Guerrero. It was absolutely critical, he said, that Brady wear the splint and keep his thumb immobilized. "Don't mess with it," he said.

"Matt, don't worry," Guerrero told him. "We got it."

That afternoon, Brady attended practice in full pads, but he didn't

participate. His teammates told reporters Brady "looked good." When he skipped his media session again, however, speculation mounted that his injury might be more serious than had originally been thought. "It's not a big deal at all," insisted Stephen A. Smith on ESPN. "It's a waste of time. It's a bogus story."

On Friday morning, Boston radio and television stations reported that Brady got four stitches. The Patriots listed Brady as "questionable" for Sunday's game on the team's official injury report. Then Belichick held his weekly press conference. Asked about Brady's status for Sunday, he said: "It's Friday."

A short while later, Brady entered the media room wearing a glove over his injured hand. The first question he faced was, "How's your hand?"

"Not talking about it," he said.

"Thumbs up or thumbs down for Sunday?" a reporter asked.

"We'll see," he said.

"What exactly happened on Wednesday?"

"I'm not talking about it."

With Guerrero at his side, Brady went to the Patriots' indoor practice facility known as "the bubble" and threw. The more he threw, the more he became convinced that he could play on Sunday.

When Brady told Leibman about his progress, Leibman told him: "Don't throw! You don't need to throw."

"I was just testing it out," Brady said.

"Stop testing it," Leibman said. "We'll test it on Sunday."

The Jacksonville Jaguars were an upstart team trying to complete a Cinderella season. Loaded with young talent, the Jaguars' defense was ranked number one in the AFC. Six of its defensive players were Pro Bowlers. Days before Brady injured his thumb, CBS had asked actor John Malkovich to film a commercial teasing the game. In the commercial, standing in front of an orchestra at the New England Conservatory of Music, Malkovich tossed aside the script and told the director: "You've overcomplicated this story. This is one of the simplest, oldest stories there is.

"It is the story of David versus Goliath," he continued, his voice rising in concert with the violins and bass strings. "The story of the mighty giant against the tiny underdog. And yet, what does football teach us? You always have a chance. Look at what . . . the Jaguars did only last weekend. . . . But now it's against the Patriots. You are fighting a giant.

"They don't have one Goliath," Malkovich railed. "They are two Goliaths. Brady! Belichick! Relentlessly! THE MACHINE . . . STOMPS . . . ON! It's that simple."

But it wasn't nearly that simple this time. Just four days after a surgery on his throwing thumb that took twenty-five stitches to close, Brady was compromised. He was also still in a lot of pain. On game day, Leibman could have given him a shot to numb up the area around the wound, but Brady declined, saying he didn't want to do anything that would limit his feel for the ball. The Patriots, meanwhile, insisted that Leibman be on the sideline in the event that Brady split open his hand and treatment was required during the game.

About five minutes prior to kickoff, Brady walked into the medical training room adjacent to the locker room, where Leibman was laying out his instruments.

Startled, Leibman stopped what he was doing.

Brady closed the door behind him, drew the blinds, and took a seat on a stool. Then he rested his chin on the training table. Staring ahead with a diabolical gaze, he extended his arm across the table, opened his hand, and calmly said: "Will you trim the tails of the sutures? I don't want them touching the ball."

Bewildered, Leibman sat on a stool on the other side of the table and faced him. The game was about to start. Everyone else was already on the field.

"Tom, I don't want to touch the sutures."

Brady explained that he didn't like the feel of the suture tails pushing against the bandage and pressing against the ball when he gripped it.

"Tom, my biggest concern is that the sutures are going to unravel and it's going to split open."

"I trust you," Brady said.

"I really don't want to touch them."

"You need to do it."

It was a negotiation that Leibman knew he was losing. He reached for a pair of suture scissors and peeled back the bandage over Brady's wound.

"Tom, we really shouldn't do this," he said.

"No, you need to do it."

There were two minutes to kickoff.

One by one, Leibman delicately snipped a millimeter off roughly twenty sutures on the exterior of the wound. Then he redressed Brady's wound.

Brady stood and gripped his ball. It felt much better.

"Thanks, buddy," he said.

"Good luck, Tom."

Brady walked out, his cleats click-clacking as he headed to the field.

On the Patriots' opening drive, Brady threw six passes and completed all of them. He ran the ball once and got popped. He also got sacked. On the sideline, Leibman winced, especially when one of Brady's linemen helped him up by gripping his throwing hand and pulling him to his feet. But Brady never flinched.

After the Patriots took a 3–0 lead, the Jaguars' defense shut them down, delivering one big hit after another. Then, with the Patriots trailing 14–3, Gronkowski stretched out in an attempt to catch a pass and took a brutal helmet-to-helmet hit. The play drew a personal-foul penalty for unnecessary roughness. And Gronkowski suffered a concussion and was lost for the game. It was starting to appear that Goliath was going down.

In the second half, things didn't improve for the Patriots. The Jaguars held a firm 20–10 lead with a little over twelve minutes remaining in the fourth quarter. All the Jaguars had to do was stop Brady one more time and muster a couple of first downs on offense to put the game away. But on the Patriots' next possession, it took Brady less than four minutes to drive the length of the field, completing five passes, three of which went to Amendola. The third one, a nine-yard touchdown strike, cut the lead to 20–17.

Two minutes later, the Jaguars punted. Then the Patriots punted. Then the Jaguars punted again. After a big return by Amendola, the Patriots had the ball on the Jaguars' thirty-yard line with 4:58 to play. Two minutes later, Brady zinged a spiral over the outstretched arms of two defenders on the goal line toward Amendola, who was streaking across the back of the end zone while being chased by two more defenders. Leaping while twisting his upper body backward against his forward momentum, he snatched the ball out of the air, managing to get his front foot down and then the toes of his second foot before falling out of bounds.

Gillette Stadium erupted. Brady's pinpoint pass and Amendola's acrobatic catch had given the Patriots a 24–20 lead. For the eleventh time in a playoff game, Brady had orchestrated a game-winning drive in the fourth quarter or overtime. But this time he'd done it at age forty with twenty-five sutures holding his thumb together. It was the kind of performance that would have been the defining moment for virtually any other quarterback.

But for Brady, thanks in large part to the secrecy shrouding the magnitude of his injury, it would go down as just another one of many great feats.

As the final seconds on the game clock ticked down, Belichick triumphantly raised his arms on the sideline. Brady, with a black bandage on his throwing hand, simultaneously raised his arms. Despite injury, controversy, strife, media scrutiny, and another seemingly insurmountable fourth-quarter deficit, Belichick and Brady were headed to the Super Bowl for the eighth time.

With a blizzard of confetti raining down on Gillette Stadium, Kraft made his way onto the field for yet another AFC Championship trophy presentation, on the twenty-fourth anniversary of the day he had purchased the team. Kraft was taking his franchise to the Super Bowl for an unprecedented ninth time.

As he took in the moment, Kraft looked at his sons and thought back to when he had sat with them in the stands in the seventies, dreaming about owning the team that he watched lose year after year. They'd come a long way. In the twenty-four years since he'd purchased the team, the Patriots had gone to the postseason nineteen times and suffered just two losing seasons, the last one being way back in 2000. Kraft's franchise was poised to win its sixth championship. Only legendary Chicago Bears owner George Halas had amassed six championships. But that was in the pre–Super Bowl era and it had taken Halas forty years. If the Patriots won this time, Kraft would have caught up to him in about half the time.

In an on-the-field interview with CBS, Brady downplayed his injury. "I've had a lot worse," he said. In the locker room, however, Brady tracked down Leibman, put his arms around him, and thanked him. "I thought this injury was going to be the end of my career," Brady told him.

One by one, players thanked Leibman. Then Robert and Jonathan thanked Leibman. But Leibman deflected all of the credit back on Brady.

"I still don't understand how he played," Leibman said. "It doesn't make any sense to me. He played with a surgical incision on his *throwing* thumb."

In his postgame press conference, Belichick was asked to talk about Amendola.

"Danny's a tremendous competitor," he told the press. "Danny's such a good football player. When you look up 'good football player' in the

dictionary, his picture's right there beside it. Doesn't matter what it is. Fielding punts. Third down. Big play. Red area. Onside kick recovery. Whatever we need him to do. He's just a tremendous player. Very instinctive. Tough. *Great* concentration. And made some big plays for us today."

"Bill," a reporter said, "just your thoughts on Tom Brady, all that went on outside the locker room, and throwing the way he did today."

Belichick's expression changed. "Yeah, well, what went on outside the locker room is all you guys," he said. "So you could tell me all about that. Inside the locker room, everybody prepared for the game. Tom did a great job preparing. I thought we all competed today and made enough plays to win."

"Bill, did anything have to change game-plan-wise because of Brady's hand?" a reporter asked.

Exasperated, Belichick took a long pause. Shaking his head, he finally said, "Not that I'm aware of."

"Can you just speak to the resourcefulness of Tom dealing with something like that midweek and then coming out and playing a huge game like that?" a reporter said.

"I mean, look," Belichick said. "Tom did a great job and he's a tough guy. We all know that. All right? But we're not talking about open heart surgery here."

forty-three
SHUTTLE DIPLOMACY

D riving home from the AFC Championship game, Bündchen asked Brady about Gronkowski's head injury and whether he'd be well enough to play in the Super Bowl. Brady called Gronkowski to check on him.

"How you doing?" Brady said.

"Man, you're an animal, dude," Gronkowski said. "Nice job."

"No, you're a fuckin' animal," Brady said. "Just so you know that."

"How you feelin', honey?" Bündchen said.

"I'm feelin' way better," Gronkowski said. "I just actually laid down for an hour and a half."

"That was a miracle of us winning without you out there," Brady said. "That was a fuckin' miracle."

"Dude, how does Danny get so good in the playoffs?" Gronkowski said. "It's unbelievable."

Brady laughed.

They were going to be facing the Eagles in the Super Bowl, and Gronkowski's presence would be critical. But his concussion was serious. And while he was determined to play, the Patriots' medical staff was proceeding with caution.

Ten days before the Patriots faced the Eagles in Super Bowl LII, the first installment of *Tom vs. Time* aired on Facebook, on January 25. It opened with Brady talking about his mentality.

"What are you willing to do and what are you willing to give up to be the best that you can be?" Brady said. "In the end, my life's focused around football. It always has been. It always will be, as long as I'm playing. I've given my body—everything, every bit of energy—for eighteen years to it. So if you're

going to compete against me, you better be ready to give up your life. Because I'm giving up mine."

In the series, Brady didn't talk about his relationship with Belichick or Belichick's coaching style. But Brady did discuss his relationship with his teammates and his own leadership style. In the third episode, which aired on January 30, he said, "My connection with them is through joy and love. It's not through fear. It's not through insults. That's not how I lead."

Belichick wasn't a fan of anything that focused so much attention on one player. He didn't like distractions, either. That the documentary was rolled out in the lead-up to the Super Bowl didn't please him. But Brady's role in the film was out of Belichick's hands. And that, more than anything, was at the heart of the matter—Belichick was used to tightly controlling his team, and Brady was displaying more and more autonomy.

Kraft didn't have any input in Brady's film, either. But he had no qualms about Brady's decision to participate in the documentary. Nor did he take issue with anything Brady had said on camera. On the day after the third installment aired on Facebook, Robert and Jonathan sat down with NFL Network's Andrea Kremer.

"Is there dysfunction in the organization now?" Kremer asked.

"No," Robert said.

"Zero," Jonathan added.

"You have tension," Robert said. "I think a certain amount of tension helps make great things happen."

"Dysfunction is when people take energy and use it to think about how to undermine other people," Jonathan said. "That does not happen here."

Kremer looked at Jonathan. "Can you envision a scenario when you're the one that has to tell Tom Brady it's time to retire as a Patriot?"

"I think Tom Brady's earned the right to make that decision when he wants to make it," Jonathan said.

On the night before the Super Bowl in Minneapolis, Brady was named the NFL's Most Valuable Player for the third time in his career. He had won the award previously in 2007 and 2010. But this one meant more. No NFL player had ever won the MVP award at age forty. The only other athlete in the four major men's professional team sports to be named MVP at age forty was baseball slugger Barry Bonds, whose achievement was clouded by allegations of steroid use. Brady had completed 385 of 581 passes for a league-leading 4,577 yards, along with thirty-two touchdowns and just eight interceptions.

One thing was apparent. Since Belichick had drafted Jimmy Garoppolo in 2014, Brady had found another gear. In the four years that Garoppolo was in Foxborough, Brady led the Patriots to three Super Bowls, at ages thirty-seven, thirty-nine, and forty. But winning the MVP trophy didn't motivate him. As Brady stood with his head bowed and his hand over his heart while P!nk sang the national anthem at US Bank Stadium in Minneapolis on February 4, 2018, he cared about only one thing—winning Super Bowl LII. He and the team were ready. The stitches were removed from his hand. At the eleventh hour, Gronkowski had completed the concussion protocol and been cleared to play.

But not far from Brady, Patriots defensive back Malcolm Butler had tears in his eyes during the anthem. Moments earlier he had been informed that he was being benched for the Super Bowl. Belichick had decided to start Eric Rowe, a rarely used second-string player who had made a grand total of fifteen tackles during the regular season. Butler was blindsided. He had been the defense's iron man in 2017, playing in 98 percent of the Patriots' defensive snaps and finishing fourth overall in solo tackles. And during the two playoff games, Butler had been on the field for every defensive play.

Mortified, Butler looked on from the sideline as Eagles quarterback Nick Foles immediately tested Rowe, repeatedly throwing in his direction and completing passes at will as Foles marched his team down the field. The Eagles kicked a field goal to go up 3–0.

After the Patriots kicked a field goal to tie the game, Foles again targeted Butler's replacement. Eagles receiver Alshon Jeffery beat Rowe for a thirty-four-yard touchdown reception to put the Eagles back on top.

Trailing 9–3 at the start of the second quarter, Brady completed a twenty-three-yard pass to receiver Brandin Cooks, who took a brutal helmet-to-helmet hit, knocking him out of the game with a concussion. After the loss of his only deep-threat receiver, Brady relied even more on Gronkowski and Amendola, picking apart the Eagles' defense with quicker, shorter passes. By halftime, he had already thrown for 276 yards. Yet the Eagles led 22–12.

The Patriots' defense was struggling to slow down the Eagles' offense. During halftime, Belichick was asked by NBC sideline reporter Michele Tafoya why he had not started Malcolm Butler and why Butler hadn't played a single snap in the first half.

"I made the decisions that gave us the best chance to win," Belichick told her.

In New England's first possession of the second half, Brady drove the Patriots seventy-five yards in 2:45. Brady threw five passes to Gronkowski,

who accounted for sixty-eight yards and hauled in a touchdown to pull the Patriots to within a field goal at 22–19.

But the Eagles drove right back downfield as Malcolm Butler's replacement missed multiple open-field tackles. "Butler's still on the bench," noted NBC's Al Michaels. "It's one of the stories of the game. It was a coach's decision. Bill Belichick telling Michele, 'We put the players in we think can best win the game.' Go figure. The big hero of three years ago with the interception of Russell Wilson only playing special teams tonight."

Moving the ball at will, the Eagles scored again to go up 29–19.

Brady countered by mounting another long drive, which he concluded with a touchdown pass to Chris Hogan. At the end of the third quarter, the Eagles led 29–26.

The Eagles tacked on a field goal at the start of the fourth quarter, increasing the lead to 32–26. Once again, the Patriots started on their own twenty-five-yard line. After three straight handoffs to Burkhead, Brady went to the air, connecting with Hogan. Brady followed that with three straight completions to Amendola. Then he threw another touchdown pass to Gronkowski, giving the Patriots the lead for the first time, at 33–32 with 9:22 to play. It was the third straight seventy-five-yard touchdown drive for the Patriots.

"Father Time has no idea where Tom Brady lives," Michaels said. "None."

It was up to the Patriots' defense to get a stop. But they couldn't. In a drive that chewed up seven minutes, Nick Foles completed eight of ten passes. The last one was a touchdown toss to put the Eagles back on top 38–33 with 2:21 to play.

After the Eagles kicked off, Brady trotted onto the field, confident the Patriots were going to win. The Eagles had been unable to stop the Patriots' offense all night. The Patriots had not punted the ball once in the entire game. Nor had they turned it over. And in Brady's thirty-eight pass attempts, the Eagles hadn't come close to sacking him.

But after completing a pass to Gronkowski to start the drive, Brady dropped back and was blindsided by Brandon Graham, who sacked him and jarred the ball loose in the process. The Eagles recovered. And just over a minutes later, the Eagles kicked a field goal to go up 41–33.

With fifty-eight seconds left, Brady stepped onto the field one more time. With the ball on the nine-yard line, the team had to go ninety-one yards. Brady's first three passes fell incomplete. On fourth-and-ten, Brady hit Amendola for a first down, keeping the drive alive. Then he completed two passes to Gronkowski. With nine seconds remaining, the Patriots were at midfield.

One of the greatest Super Bowls ever played would come down to the final play. And everyone in the stadium knew where Brady was going to throw it. He took the snap and maneuvered in the pocket, buying time for Gronkowski to sprint downfield. With a defender running at him, Brady launched a Hail Mary pass from his own forty-five-yard line. It soared sixty yards through the air. Amid five defenders, Gronkowski leaped. With guys draped all over him, he managed to get a hand on it as his arms were grabbed. The ball deflected off Gronkowski's helmet and his shoulder before a defender batted it away. As Gronkowski got hauled to the ground, the ball finally landed on the Patriots logo in the end zone, just out of Gronkowski's reach. He looked up at the official for a penalty flag. There was none.

Still seated where he'd been knocked down at midfield, Brady stared helplessly at Gronkowski. Both had given a Herculean effort. Brady had thrown for more than five hundred yards, the most ever in a Super Bowl. Gronkowski had caught nine passes for 116 yards and two touchdowns. Physically and emotionally exhausted, they both stood, removed their helmets, and trudged slowly toward the locker room as silver and green confetti rained down and the Eagles stormed onto the field.

Super Bowl LII had barely ended when Malcolm Butler was asked by a reporter if he had any idea why he hadn't been on the field for a single play on defense.

"They gave up on me," Butler told him. "Fuck. It is what it is."

Devastated, he added, "I don't know what it was. I guess I wasn't playing good or they didn't feel comfortable. I don't know. But I could have changed that game."

In his postgame press conference, Belichick refused to explain his decision. Asked if Butler was benched for a disciplinary reason, Belichick simply said, "No." Asked if it was strictly a football decision, he said, "Yes."

It was the second answer that left everyone scratching their heads, including Belichick's players. But none of them would comment.

"We don't talk," said defensive captain Devin McCourty. "It's a coach's decision."

The players weren't talking to the press. But they were talking among themselves. None of them was pleased about Butler's being held out of the game.

Some of Belichick's former players spoke out on social media. Patriots Hall of Fame cornerback Ty Law tweeted: "We need to get to the bottom of

this Malcolm Butler situation, I'm baffled about this one. We needed that man on the field." Former Patriots cornerback Brandon Browner was more direct, calling out Belichick in a series of tweets, including one where he said: "you were hurt/burnt where he was needed tonight .. #foolishpride."

Belichick's reputation for moving on from veteran players was well established. While many of his personnel moves over the years had been unpopular, they had almost always panned out in the Patriots' favor, consistently reinforcing the message that no individual player was above the team. But the decision to sideline one of the team's top defensive players in the team's ultimate game demoralized Butler and perplexed his teammates.

Moreover, the players that Belichick had counted on to fill Butler's position had not risen to the occasion. That had been obvious by halftime. Yet Belichick still refused to play one of the team's leading tacklers and best pass defenders in the second half, even as the Patriots' defense continued to have trouble tackling and covering receivers. For a coach so obsessed with winning, Belichick's handling of Butler was wholly inconsistent with his practical approach to game management. A less assured man might have felt the need to explain or defend his decision. But Belichick's hubris was part of what made him such a great coach, and many of his achievements would have been unthinkable without it.

Brady hadn't realized until after the game was over that Butler had been benched the entire time. Figuring Butler could use a lift, Brady telephoned him. The two of them had been close ever since Butler had helped win Super Bowl XLIX with his goal-line interception and Brady had rewarded him by giving him the Super Bowl MVP's Chevy truck. When Brady asked Butler what had happened this time, Butler didn't have an explanation. "Coach just decided something different," Butler told him.

Brady didn't get it. Butler was a great player. He had helped them win all season long. He could have helped them win the Super Bowl. He should have played.

Before hanging up, Brady reassured Butler, telling him he was appreciated.

Butler realized that he was finished in Foxborough. A free agent, he knew there was no way Belichick was going to re-sign him. After talking to Brady, he posted a classy message on Instagram, apologizing for using the *F*-word in his postgame interview, expressing appreciation to the Kraft family and his teammates and coaches for his time in New England, and assuring Patriots fans that he had not done anything during Super Bowl week to compromise

his team's chances of winning. "Although I wish I could have contributed more to help my team win, I have to get ready for the next opportunity."

Brady weighed in, saying: "Love you Malcolm. You are an incredible player and teammate and friend. Always!!!!!!" Many Patriots players, past and present, signed on to Butler's post with a like—Jimmy Garoppolo, Jamie Collins, Rob Ninkovich, Marcus Cannon, and LeGarrette Blount among them.

Belichick had no use for social media. But he kept apprised of what his players said on platforms from Twitter to Facebook to Instagram. While none of his current players were directly calling him out, it was clear that there was pent-up frustration. Still, he opted not to explain the Butler decision.

Kraft knew the 2018 offseason would be turbulent. That had been clear even before the Patriots lost the Super Bowl despite setting records for the most yards gained by a team (613) and the most points ever scored by a losing team (33). Brady's near-perfect performance and the offense's prolific production had exposed Belichick to withering scrutiny for benching Butler and refusing to say a word to anyone about his reasoning.

Besides the lingering resentment over the Butler situation, the Patriots had other personnel matters to address. Longtime defensive coordinator Matt Patricia had left right after the Super Bowl to become the head coach of the Lions. Longtime offensive coordinator Josh McDaniels was preparing to become the head coach of the Colts. Gronkowski had hinted after the game that he was contemplating retirement. Amendola was about to become a free agent and was at odds with Belichick over his worth to the team going forward. And Butler, one of Kraft's personal favorites, was certainly moving on.

But Kraft's paramount concern was the dynamic between Belichick and Brady. Belichick's decision to banish Guerrero from the sideline and the team plane in the middle of the 2017 season had been a tipping point. Kraft knew that Belichick's methods were grinding on Brady. He also knew that Belichick was tired of the exceptions that Kraft felt were necessary to accommodate a transcendent star. The differences of opinion between Brady and Belichick were more pronounced than ever. Kraft wanted to clear the air.

Two days after the Super Bowl, Kraft invited Belichick to have dinner with him at Davio's, a restaurant next door to the TB12 facility at Patriot Place. The conversation was productive. They covered a range of topics. Most important, Belichick agreed to a joint meeting with Brady and Kraft to discuss their working relationship going forward. Kraft suggested it take place at his home, and he said he'd reach out to Brady.

The next day, Brady was home, getting treatment. After another all-consuming season, he had a lot on his mind. As Guerrero worked on his body, Brady wondered, "What are we doing this for? Who are we doing this for? Why are we doing this?"

After eighteen years, Brady was asking himself difficult questions.

Bündchen was raising similar questions. Since retiring from the fashion runway, she'd been devoting a lot of time and energy to fight deforestation and educate world leaders on the impacts of climate change. She was serving as a goodwill ambassador to the UN's Environmental Programme, and Harvard Medical School had recently recognized her efforts by awarding her the Global Environmental Citizen Award. But there was so much more that she wanted to do around the world. Plus, the children weren't getting any younger, and Bündchen was eager for her and Tom to get more time together with them. Time was flying, and Bündchen was ready for the family to move out of the Boston area and get on with the next chapter of their lives.

Brady had a lot to consider when he agreed to go to Kraft's house to meet with Belichick. Kraft ushered them into his living room. Belichick took a seat on a chair to Kraft's right and Brady sat on a couch to Kraft's left. Hoping to facilitate some constructive dialogue, Kraft told them how important they both were to him. Belichick was diplomatic. Brady was respectful. But the distance between them was obvious. It occurred to Kraft that perhaps it was too soon to be having this conversation and that both sides might benefit from a little more time to wind down from the season. The meeting ended without getting to the heart of the matter.

Not long after that, Kraft invited Brady and Bündchen to his home for a "big picture" conversation about Brady's future. Seated in the living room, Kraft encouraged them to be candid.

Bündchen spoke first and passionately outlined how much her husband had done for the organization over the previous eighteen years. She also pointed out how ridiculous it was that after all these years, Belichick still treated Brady like "fucking Johnny Foxboro." It was bad enough to never voice approval. It was bullshit to still be dressing down the most accomplished quarterback in league history during team meetings and treating his personal trainer and best friend like some kind of outcast.

When the conversation shifted to the future, Brady and Bündchen indicated it was time for them to make some changes that were in the best interest of their family. Among other things, they were contemplating a change of scenery.

Kraft wasn't surprised by their feelings toward Belichick. He hadn't, however, expected to hear that Brady and Bündchen wanted to leave New England. Brady still had two years remaining on his contract. But the vibe Kraft was getting was clear—they were talking about the prospect of Brady's playing somewhere else. It was a lot to absorb.

Dating back to 2010, Kraft and Brady had a pact that they'd formed over lunch at Kraft's place on Cape Cod during Brady's prolonged contract negotiations. That year, Brady feared that Belichick might soon move on from him. He re-signed with the Patriots only after Kraft promised he'd protect Brady by stepping in and essentially allowing him to leave on his own terms if Belichick ever decided to trade him. Their unwritten understanding had been the key to keeping Brady in New England for so much longer than any other player who had played under Belichick.

But in this instance, Kraft wasn't inclined to let Brady walk away from the Patriots and play for another team. Belichick might have preferred Garoppolo at one time, but Garoppolo was gone. Belichick was counting on Brady's being the Patriots quarterback in 2018. So was Kraft. He explained that to Brady and Bündchen.

The conversation was a difficult one, and it ended without resolution.

The final episode in the six-part *Tom vs. Time* series was titled "The End Game." It aired on March 12, 2018. The opening scene featured Brady at home, sitting on his couch, facing the camera. An off-camera voice asked: "Sooooo . . . how are you feeling, man?"

"I'm feelin', um," Brady began before pausing to shake his head. "That's a loaded question."

Since the interviews in the segment were shot in the weeks after the Super Bowl, journalists carefully scrutinized every word for clues about Brady's thinking. The quote that got the most attention, however, came from Bündchen. "The last two years have been very challenging for him in so many ways," she said in the episode. "He tells me, 'I love it so much and I just want to go to work and feel appreciated and have fun.'"

But the most revealing thing in the episode was a comment by Brady that went largely overlooked. "This offseason is going to be about my family," he said. "They deserve it. There's more to think about than just me." It reinforced what he and Bündchen had tried to convey to Kraft.

The day after the segment aired, fallout from the 2017 season continued: Danny Amendola signed with the Dolphins. Amendola had been counting

on Belichick to give him an opportunity to re-sign with the Patriots. But when free agency started, Amendola quickly realized that Belichick wasn't going to get close to the two-year, $12 million offer from the Dolphins.

Initially, Amendola was disappointed. He'd been in New England for five years and had gone to three Super Bowls and won two rings. But as much as he hated parting with Brady and Edelman and Gronkowski, he looked forward to a fresh start in Miami. Playing for Belichick had been rewarding, but it had also been challenging. "It's not easy," Amendola told a reporter after he got to Miami. "He's an asshole sometimes. There were a lot of things I didn't like about playing for him. But I must say, the things I didn't like were all in regards to getting the team better. And I respected him."

Now that he was no longer playing for Belichick, Amendola felt more at liberty to say what he felt about a number of things that aggravated him. Belichick's handling of Malcolm Butler was chief among them. "I was out there putting my blood, sweat, and tears out on the field that night, and one of our best players wasn't on the field," Amendola told a reporter. "I hate to see a guy who worked so hard throughout the season not get a chance to play in the biggest game of the year and really get no explanation for it."

When Amendola's new deal was announced, Gronkowski posted on Instagram:

Stay lit, Be FREE, Be HAPPY. Your hard work, the way you play at your size, the pain you fought through, the hits you take and get right back up talking shit back. I appreciated it all. Congrats. Enjoy Miami kid.

Brady added: "Well said gronk!!!!"

Kraft knew that players weren't happy, especially Brady and Gronkowski. Considering Brady the key, Kraft invited him and Bündchen back to his home. He asked Jonathan to join them. In what ended up being another difficult conversation, Kraft didn't dispute Bündchen's characterization of Belichick's treatment of Brady. Nor did he excuse it. Kraft was willing to intervene and do things to accommodate Brady, such as getting Guerrero's privileges restored. But he wasn't inclined to let Brady out of his contract so he could go play for another team. When Kraft made his position clear, it was as if he had hit the lowest key on a piano. Silence filled his living room. On that note, Brady and Bündchen left without saying anything more.

As soon as they were gone, Kraft had a horrible, sinking feeling.

"I think I'm going to have to do something I thought I'd never do," he told Jonathan.

"Dad, I trust you'll do what's best."

Later that night, Kraft called Brady.

"Tommy," he said softly, "if you want to go, you can go."

The call was brief, the tone somber.

After hanging up, Kraft had trouble sleeping.

So did Brady.

For Brady, the decision was complicated. He had proven to himself that he could be the best in the game at age forty and he desperately wanted to see if he could continue doing it until he was forty-five. He had an estranged relationship with Belichick, but he had figured out how to navigate that. And he loved playing in New England. Over an eighteen-year span, he'd developed a powerful emotional bond with the region, the fan base, his teammates, and the Krafts. But his life had evolved, and he had so much more to consider besides what was best for him. As a forty-year-old husband and father, the most important thing to him was his relationship with his wife and his children.

For Kraft, it was simpler. Deep down he believed it was in Brady's best interest to finish his career in New England. The differences between Brady and Belichick had grown, but Kraft felt the situation was still manageable. The bigger issue was that Brady wasn't simply Tommy anymore. Rather, Brady had evolved into a man in full. As such, he had the wherewithal to recognize that he had weightier matters to consider than just his personal ambitions. Kraft took pride in the fact that Brady had become such a responsible husband and father and that those priorities were guiding his approach. Still, it felt like a favored son was leaving the family.

Overcome with sadness, Kraft tossed and turned all night.

The next day, Kraft called Brady back.

"Look, I know I told you that you could leave," Kraft said. "But I hope you don't."

"I'm not," Brady said.

"What?"

Brady had been talking with Bündchen about playing for two more years and remaining in New England.

"I don't want to go," Brady told Kraft. "I'll work it out on my end."

Kraft was shocked and relieved.

But Brady made it clear that he'd be making some changes going forward, starting with skipping the team's offseason training activities, known as OTAs, so he'd be able to spend more time with his family. Under league rules, OTAs were voluntary. But Belichick expected everyone to show up. Brady would be making other adjustments as well.

"I'll work it out with Bill," Kraft told Brady.

Brady was looking forward to having the offseason to travel more with his family and train on his own. Kraft, meanwhile, was determined to get Guerrero's privileges restored in time for the season.

Brady and Bündchen worked out an arrangement that would enable him to play two more seasons in New England. A short time later, *Vogue* writer Rob Haskell showed up at their Brookline home to interview Bündchen for a cover story about her environmental work around the world. It was a dark, rainy day and the wind was blowing when Haskell arrived. Having grown up in Brookline, Haskell was familiar with the dreary winters and inclement spring weather. Looking at Bündchen with her golden hair and tanned skin, he found it difficult to imagine her living there. He asked her about that.

"Why do I live here?" Bündchen told him. "It's called love. I love my husband."

Then she added: "But I'm not going to lie. Cold is not my flavor. I'm Brazilian. I'd rather live barefoot in a hut in the middle of the forest somewhere."

While Kraft was in discussions with Brady, Belichick decided to move on from Gronkowski. He worked out a deal with the Detroit Lions that would give the Patriots a first-round draft choice in exchange for Gronkowski. On April 22, Gronkowski was informed that he'd been traded. Pissed, he notified the Patriots that he wasn't going to Detroit. Instead, he would retire. He had one other message for the team—Brady was the only quarterback he'd ever play with.

Belichick nixed the deal with the Lions.

Two days later, Belichick and Gronkowski met. They reached an understanding that Gronkowski would return and play in 2018. The Patriots also added some incentives to Gronkowski's contract.

On any other team, Gronkowski would be the biggest star. Arguably, he was the leading celebrity in the NFL after Brady. They were the greatest quarterback–tight end duo in league history, giving the Patriots a virtually unstoppable one-two punch. Together they had connected on eighty-seven touchdown passes, including twelve in the postseason. Their on-the-field

synergy had led to a deep bond of trust between them. Off the field, Gronkowski revered Brady and admired his lifestyle choices. Through their friendship, Gronkowski had also come to trust and rely on Guerrero and his treatment and training methods. Brady and Gronkowski had shared some of the same frustrations, especially throughout the 2017 season.

A week after Gronkowski refused to go to Detroit, Brady was interviewed by sportscaster Jim Gray at the Milken Institute Global Conference in Beverly Hills, California. Brady and Gray were friends. And Gray had watched the *Tom vs. Time* series and was aware that Bündchen had talked about her husband just wanting to be appreciated.

"In any relationship, particularly one that's been successful and had such a long run, whether it's a friendship, a marriage, or a working environment, there's going to be peaks and valleys," Gray said. "So when Gisele says 'feel appreciated,' this brings to mind Coach Belichick and Mr. Kraft. Do you feel appreciated by them? And do they have the appropriate gratitude for what you have achieved?"

Brady grinned. "I plead the Fifth," he said.

The audience laughed.

"Man, that is a tough question," Brady continued.

"Your wife seems to indicate . . ." Gray said.

Brady was diplomatic. "I think everybody in general wants to be appreciated more at work," he said. "The people that I work with are trying to get the best out of me. So they treat me in a way that they feel is going to get the best out of me."

Back in 2015, when he was being accused of deflating footballs, Brady once said, "I don't think a lot of people know personally who I am. They may know what they think I may be, or what they see on the TV screen when I'm exposed publicly to them. For people who may think they know, or have snippets of who I am, you can attack that person. That's part of being a public figure."

Those same sentiments applied to Belichick. He was even more misunderstood than Brady. Going all the way back to his days as an assistant coach with the New York Giants, he'd been portrayed as cold and emotionless, a coach who kept his players at arm's length and had no personal connection to them. But Belichick was much more sensitive than he ever let on. While it was true that he possessed the discipline of a drill sergeant when it came to personnel decisions, he didn't relish that part of his job. And nothing hurt

him more than the feeling that his players didn't like him. Belichick loved his
players, and he wanted to be loved by them. There was no place in the world
he'd rather be than on a practice field or on the sideline during a game, surrounded by players. In that environment, he demonstrated how he felt about
them by the way he pushed them. And he pushed his best players—the ones
he admired most—the hardest. There was nothing he wouldn't do to prepare
them to become champions. He knew his players considered him "an asshole" at times. Yet it still stung to hear it.

For Belichick, leadership came with a price. So did winning. His coaching style put extreme pressure on everyone around him. He intimidated
people. That was by design. He believed that those who couldn't handle the
pressure from him wouldn't be able to handle the pressure it took to win
championships in the NFL.

Neither Brady nor Gronkowski attended OTAs at the end of May. Asked
about their absence, Belichick refused to discuss it. A little over a week later,
the league slapped Julian Edelman with a four-game suspension for violating
the NFL's performance-enhancing-substance policy. After missing the entire
2017 season due to knee surgery, Edelman would be forced to sit out the first
four games of the 2018 season.

Since his injury, Edelman had been rehabbing and training with Guerrero. As soon as the suspension was announced, Guerrero faced questions.
He issued a statement:

I've known Julian since his rookie year and he is a phenomenal athlete who takes his training seriously—it's disappointing to hear today's news. Elite athletes sometimes work with multiple coaches and
health professionals as part of their training. Here at our facility, we
take a natural, holistic, appropriate and, above all, legal approach to
training and recovery for all of our clients. And anyone who would
suggest otherwise is irresponsible and just plain wrong.

As Edelman's suspension made headlines, Kraft began a series of conversations with Belichick about Brady and Guerrero. Going in, Kraft knew
why Belichick had personal issues with Guerrero. But Kraft viewed Guerrero
pragmatically. He recognized that Guerrero did something for Brady and his
psyche that no one else could. Whether his unconventional methods were
valid didn't necessarily matter to Kraft. What mattered was that Guerrero
gave Brady confidence. Brady's performance year in and year out was the best

evidence of Guerrero's value to the organization. The bottom line was that no one else had ever been NFL MVP at age forty.

At the same time, Kraft recognized that Guerrero was loyal to Brady, not Belichick. And when Guerrero criticized the training staff, he was further undercutting Belichick's authority and causing discord. That had to be stopped.

Eventually, Kraft got Belichick to understand that if he could clearly articulate some reasonable rules for Guerrero, Kraft would explain them to Brady. At the same time, Kraft got Brady to understand that if Guerrero would abide by Belichick's rules, there was undoubtedly a middle ground that would enable Guerrero to get his privileges back.

With Kraft mediating, Belichick agreed to allow Guerrero back in the locker room on game days to help Brady with his pregame ritual. But he did not want Guerrero back on the sideline. Kraft proposed that Guerrero be allowed to watch the games from an on-site location, such as the locker room. Belichick agreed. The big sticking point was traveling with the team. Belichick really didn't want Guerrero on the team plane. But that was really important to Brady.

Kraft made it clear to Guerrero that in order to have a chance of restoring his travel privileges, he could not overstep his boundaries. That meant never calling out Patriots trainers and strength and conditioning coaches, even if he thought that what they were doing was wrong. And it meant supplementing the team's efforts, not critiquing them.

"You get to work with Tom," Kraft told him. "But please know your place."

Belichick still preferred not to have Guerrero on the team plane in 2018. But Kraft had made a strong case that it was in Brady's best interest, which meant that it was ultimately in the team's best interest. In the rare instances when they didn't agree, Belichick recognized that Kraft was the owner and he respected the owner's wishes.

So Guerrero was back on board.

After the most tumultuous offseason in the Belichick-Brady era, training camp was like a family reunion. Back from his yearlong hiatus due to injury, Edelman was zipping around, looking more fit than ever, and cracking jokes about Belichick's wardrobe and Brady's age. Still carrying a chip on his shoulder over the proposed trade to Detroit, Gronkowski showed up burning to have a big year. Brady had Bündchen and the kids with him. At one point, while Brady knelt near some of his teammates, Bündchen knelt

beside him, their hands touching each other as their children roamed nearby. Tanned and wearing shorts and sunglasses, Kraft walked the field, encouraging Edelman to keep his chin up, calling Gronkowski "big fella," catching up with Brady, kissing Bündchen on the cheek, and talking with Brady's children. Even Guerrero was around. And Belichick was right at home, barking out instructions and sizing up players. Throughout camp, he liked what he was seeing. Everyone was working hard. They were fiercely competitive. And they had a roster rich in seasoned veterans.

At the end of camp, a reporter asked Belichick: "What was the reasoning for allowing Alex Guerrero back on the team plane for travel?"

"I'm not going to get into all of the responsibilities of all of the people in our organization," Belichick said. "We'd be here for a month going through all of that."

It was back to business as usual. The Patriots were ready to make another quest for a Super Bowl.

forty-four

WE'RE STILL HERE

After losing back-to-back road games to start the season 1-2, the Patriots returned to Foxborough for what felt like a must-win game against the Dolphins on September 30. Just over seven minutes into the contest, Tom Brady completed a thirteen-yard pass to wide receiver Josh Gordon near the Miami goal line. The crowd gave Gordon a rousing ovation. It was his first catch in a Patriots uniform. An immensely talented receiver who'd spent most of his career with the Cleveland Browns, Gordon had been suspended multiple times for substance abuse. Those suspensions had kept him off the field for much of the previous four years. At the start of the 2018 season, the NFL cleared the receiver to return to football, and Belichick decided to give him a shot in New England. When Gordon got to Foxborough, he quickly discovered that it was nothing like Cleveland. He felt as though he had joined the military—but he also felt like he had been adopted into a stable family. The rigid structure and the sense of belonging were exactly what he needed. Moments after he was tackled at the Dolphins' three-yard line, the Patriots kicked a field goal to go up 3–0, and then they were off to the races.

Up in the owner's box, Robert Kraft was hosting Secretary of State Mike Pompeo. With the Patriots leading 38–0 late in the fourth quarter, Kraft took Pompeo to the Patriots' locker room. It was empty and silent when they entered. Kraft was showing Pompeo around when Rob Gronkowski emerged from the training room; he had exited the game earlier in the quarter. Barefoot and wearing a T-shirt and Under Armour pants, he had an oversized ice bag taped around his lower leg. Blood was visible through the ice. "Oh, hi fellas," Gronkowski said, flashing a smile.

Surprised to see Gronk, Kraft looked at his ice pack. "Is it your Achilles?" he asked.

"No, not the Achilles," Gronk told him. "It's my lower leg. I've got some kind of lump. It's pretty big."

"It happened today?" Kraft said.

"Actually, it happened last week in Detroit. I got kicked."

"We need you Thursday," Kraft said, referring to the upcoming game.

"I'll be ready," Gronkowski said.

"We're playing the Colts," Kraft said. "They started the stupid Deflategate thing. We have to kill the Colts."

"Definitely," Gronk said.

Kraft then introduced Pompeo. Moments later, the game ended, and the Patriots swarmed into the locker room. Belichick went straight to Gronkowski. "You all right?" he asked.

"I'm all right," Gronk told him.

Belichick patted him on the arm.

Brady went to Gordon's locker, congratulated him for getting off to a good start in his first game, and hugged him. As Belichick called the team together, Brady led Gordon to the center of the room. They were standing right behind Kraft and Pompeo when everyone knelt for the Lord's Prayer. Kraft reached for one of Gordon's hands. Pompeo took Gordon's other hand. On bended knee and sandwiched between the owner and the secretary of state, Gordon bowed his head.

After the prayer, everyone stood and Belichick paid tribute to Kraft, informing the team that the victory over the Dolphins marked his three-hundredth career win as an owner, making him the fastest owner in the one-hundred-year history of the NFL to achieve the rare milestone. The players gave Kraft an ovation as Belichick handed him the game ball. Deflecting the credit to the players and coaches, Kraft said, "I hope we're together for four hundred."

"*Four hundred*?" Gronkowski said.

Everyone laughed.

From the start of the 2018 season, Bill Belichick loved the attitude and camaraderie he saw among his players. They had the potential to be the first team of the twenty-first century to make it to three straight Super Bowls. But Belichick never hinted at that with the players. Instead, he kept reminding them that no one expected them to be very good in 2018. Everyone, he insisted, was counting them out, writing them off as past their prime.

Four days after beating the Dolphins, the Patriots hosted the Colts in a nationally televised Thursday-night contest at Gillette Stadium on October 4. Coming off his four-game suspension for using a banned substance, Julian Edelman made his return. Due to the knee injury that had forced Edelman

to miss the prior season, it had been 606 days since he'd last played in a game. On the Patriots' first play, Brady threw to Edelman for a nine-yard gain. Two minutes later, Brady went to him again, and then a third time. New England scored on the drive to take a 7–0 lead. Edelman ended up making seven catches on the night. Gronkowski, despite his nagging lower-leg injury, added six for seventy-five yards. And late in the game, Brady threw a thirty-four-yard touchdown pass to Josh Gordon to put the game away. It was Brady's five-hundredth career touchdown pass. The Patriots won 38–24.

With Brady, Edelman, and Gronkowski in the lineup together for the first time since November 2016, the Patriots boasted the most star-studded offensive trio in the league. They were also the oldest. Edelman, at thirty-two, was in his tenth season. Gronkowski, at twenty-nine, was in his ninth. Then there was Brady, who was forty-one. Combined, the three of them had logged thirty-eight NFL seasons, all in New England. The question that loomed over Foxborough was whether a team with aging veterans in such key positions could keep pace with the younger rivals threatening to finally overtake New England for supremacy in the AFC. Under Belichick, the Patriots were an old-school football team in a league full of exceptionally talented young players and new offensive schemes designed to exploit those talents. The biggest threat was the Kansas City Chiefs, led by twenty-three-year-old quarterback Patrick Mahomes and the fastest receiving corps in football. A week after beating the Colts, the Patriots hosted Mahomes and the Chiefs at Gillette Stadium. Kansas City entered the game with a 5-0 record and the top-ranked offense in the conference.

Brady and Mahomes both put up big numbers, and the teams were tied at 40–40 with seconds to play. As time expired, Stephen Gostkowski kicked a twenty-eight-yard field goal to win the game and hand the Chiefs their first loss. The Patriots were on a midseason roll, and by early November they had improved to 7-2. But on November 11, they got blown out in Tennessee, losing to the Titans 34–10. Gronkowski didn't play due to injury, and Edelman was knocked out of the game. Brady took a beating, and at one point twisted his knee awkwardly. The Patriots hadn't lost so decisively since early in 2014.

Four weeks later in Miami, the Patriots led 33–28 with seven seconds to play. The Dolphins had the ball on their own thirty-one-yard line. Expecting Miami to throw a desperation Hail Mary pass, Belichick sent Gronkowski in to play defense, stationing him as the deep man to take advantage of his height. But instead of throwing deep, Dolphins quarterback Ryan Tannehill completed a short-range pass over the middle to a receiver, who lateraled the ball to another receiver, who lateraled the ball to running back Kenyan Drake.

With some fancy footwork, Drake eluded tacklers and broke into the open field. By the time he reached Gronkowski, the speedy back had a full head of steam. Flat-footed, Gronkowski dove and missed as Drake raced by him and into the end zone to win the game. The play, which came to be known as the "Miami Miracle," marked the first time in NFL history that a game ended with a touchdown involving multiple laterals. The loss dropped the Patriots to 9-4. But it was the way they'd lost that sparked hysteria in New England. The sight of Gronkowski diving hopelessly as a much younger player dashed by him crystalized what the critics had been saying about the Patriots: the rest of the league had finally caught up to them. Belichick, meanwhile, was widely criticized for replacing the much faster safety Devin McCourty with Gronkowski on the final play of the game.

The following morning, during a radio interview, Belichick said, "Look, it's the National Football League. Nobody died. Got a big game this week against Pittsburgh. We have a two-game lead in the division. There's a lot of football left in the season."

Belichick wasn't panicking. The way his team lost was unfortunate, but at the end of the day, it was one loss. He told his players that the important thing was to get ready for the Steelers. The team had a great week of practice. On the day before the game, Kraft flew to Pittsburgh to attend the Bar Mitzvah of Max Aaron Shachner, a young man whose family belonged to the Tree of Life synagogue. Seven weeks earlier, a man had stormed into the synagogue during Shabbat morning service and opened fire with an AR-15 assault rifle while shouting anti-Semitic statements. He killed eleven people and wounded six. Shachner's Bar Mitzvah was the first since the mass shooting. The synagogue was packed when Kraft slipped in unnoticed and took a seat in the third row. Partway through the service, the rabbi informed the worshippers that there was a special guest in attendance and invited Kraft to say a few words. The worshippers were stunned to see the owner of the Patriots step to the lectern and read from the Torah in Hebrew. Kraft delivered a message about unity and talked about the need for Steelers fans and Patriots fans to join together to oppose anti-Semitism. Then he stepped away from the podium, reached into his suit pocket, and removed four tickets to the next day's game and presented them to Shachner for his Bar Mitzvah gift. When Kraft sat down, a man seated behind him tapped him on the shoulder, thanked him for coming, and handed Kraft a black kippah with the Steelers' red, blue, and yellow logo sewn on the back. The man had placed a yellow six-pointed Star of David over the logo.

The next day, the Patriots lost 17–10 in Pittsburgh, falling to 9-5. The last time they'd lost back-to-back games in December was in 2002. NFL analysts openly speculated that New England was running out of gas and had little chance of getting back to the Super Bowl.

Days after the Steelers game, Josh Gordon announced on Twitter that he was stepping away from the football field to focus on his mental health. "I would like to thank Coach Belichick, Mr. Kraft, as well as countless others in the Patriots organization for their continued support," he said. Later that day, the NFL suspended him indefinitely for again violating the league's substance abuse policy. At the time, Gordon led the team in receiving yards. His departure was yet another blow to the team.

Despite how bad things appeared from the outside, Belichick focused on the fact that his players had shown great resilience all season long. Gronkowski and Edelman had fought through injuries. The defense continued to show improvement as the season wore on. Most important, the players' commitment never waned. The loss to Miami would have sent plenty of teams into a downward spiral, especially after following that up with an emotionally deflating loss like the one in Pittsburgh. But the Patriots' roster was full of seasoned veterans who had long ago adopted Belichick's credo that you had to have a short memory to succeed in the NFL. Those who dwelled on losses and mistakes couldn't adequately prepare for the next challenge.

About thirty minutes before the start of the final regular-season game at home against the Jets on December 30, 2018, Belichick was bundled up in a winter coat, hands in his pockets, looking on as his team concluded pregame warm-ups. Alone in his thoughts, Belichick turned to leave the field and head to the locker room when Brady approached. Belichick and Brady hadn't spoken a great deal during the season, and the two of them typically kept to themselves during their pregame rituals. But in this instance, Brady intercepted Belichick, extended his hand, and looked him in the eye.

Without saying a word, Belichick nodded, grabbed hold of Brady's hand and squeezed it while reaching around Brady with his other hand and patting him on the back. The brief encounter was a quintessential Belichick-Brady moment—the two greatest minds in the league communicating without speaking. Then Brady let go, turned, and trotted with his head up toward the outstretched hands of fans reaching over the wall behind the Patriots' bench. Head down, Belichick walked behind him. Both men disappeared down the stairs and into the tunnel.

Belichick and Brady seemed to have an innate sense of synchronicity every time the end of the calendar year arrived. The Patriots demolished the Jets 38–3 that afternoon to finish the regular season 11-5, winning the AFC East division title for the tenth consecutive year and securing a first-round bye in the playoffs for the ninth straight time.

The mood in the locker room was more workmanlike than celebratory. Edelman's annual playoff beard was in full growth. There was a clear sense among the veteran players that they were fortunate to be in a position to compete for another title.

"All right, men, congratulations," Belichick said, calling the team together. "Winning today means we won this week. That's what winning today means."

The message was clear: it was playoff time. What happened in the regular season was history. From here forward, it was a one-game season.

Right after the Jets game, Robert Kraft flew to New York to meet with Jay-Z at his apartment that night. Although the national-anthem protests from the previous season had subsided, a great deal of residual damage remained. Colin Kaepernick's stance and the protests that stemmed from it had exposed a glaring disconnect between NFL owners and the African American community, which represented an important segment of the league's fan base. As one of Kaepernick's outspoken supporters, Jay-Z had announced earlier in the year that he wouldn't perform at the Super Bowl. Rihanna subsequently turned down an invitation from the league to perform at halftime, citing her desire to show solidarity with Kaepernick. Cardi B., Usher, Mary J. Blige, and other hip-hop artists followed suit. With a little over a month to go until the Super Bowl, the NFL had lined up pop-rock band Maroon 5 to perform at halftime, but not a single hip-hop performer would participate.

Kraft knew how Patriots players felt about the situation, and he wanted to help repair the damage that had been done and find a way to build a meaningful bridge between the NFL and the hip-hop community. For Kraft, the issue had become personal. One of his closest friends was Philadelphia 76ers co-owner Michael Rubin, who had introduced Kraft to rapper Meek Mill a few years earlier. Back in 2007, when Meek was nineteen, he was convicted and sent to prison after a police officer testified that Meek had pointed a gun at him. By the time Kraft met Meek, he was out on probation, and his music career was thriving. But in 2017, Meek was sent back to prison for two to four years for violating his probation. Shortly after Meek was locked up,

the officer who had accused him ten years earlier signed a sworn affidavit admitting that Meek had never pointed a gun at him. Still, the judge presiding over Meek's case refused to release him. In an effort to help free Meek and clear his name, Kraft visited him in prison. Sitting opposite Meek, who was wearing an orange jumpsuit, Kraft listened as he explained what it was like to grow up a black man in America. Meek had spent most of his adult life, he said, in jail or on probation for something he didn't do. When a young black man points a gun at a cop, he told Kraft, he doesn't get arrested—he gets shot.

Seven days after Kraft visited Meek in prison and held a press conference in Pennsylvania to denounce the way the system had treated him, Pennsylvania's highest court granted Meek's bail request. Shortly thereafter, his firearm conviction from a decade earlier was overturned. Meek's experience had a profound impact on Kraft. As a result, Kraft agreed to join Meek and partner with Michael Rubin and Jay-Z, both of whom had been instrumental in helping Meek clear his name, to raise $100 million and form a foundation that would address discriminatory probation and parole policies in the criminal justice system.

Kraft and Jay-Z were on the verge of announcing their foundation when they met to discuss the league's handling of the social-justice issues raised by Colin Kaepernick's protests. At the outset, Jay-Z told Kraft that he wasn't happy with the NFL. He also let him know that the NFL had underestimated the staying power of hip-hop music. In a frank discussion, Kraft acknowledged that the league needed help educating itself about the criminal justice system and the plight of young African American men. By the end of the night, Kraft offered to facilitate a three-way, face-to-face meeting with him, Jay-Z, and Roger Goodell. Jay-Z accepted the invitation. The meeting was set to take place the following week at Jay-Z's home in Los Angeles.

When Kraft flew home the next day, he stopped by the stadium. It was New Year's Eve and few people were around. When Kraft got home, he telephoned Belichick and the two of them talked shop for half an hour. Then Kraft kicked back in his recliner and reflected on the fact that he and Belichick had been talking on the phone to each other nearly once a day for twenty years. Feeling melancholy and suddenly realizing that he was home alone on New Year's Eve for the first time in his life, Kraft called Brady and got his voice mail.

"Tommy, RKK here. I was down at the stadium. Thought I might see you because the doors of your locker were open. Anyhow, wanted to wish you and G and the beautiful family a wonderful, beautiful, happy New Year. May

nineteen be even better than eighteen for us. And also wanted to tell you that you were awesome yesterday. The way you spread it around, the way you were in the pocket. We're so lucky to have you. Thank you. Love you."

As Kraft put down his phone, he thought about the fact that eight months earlier, when he had invited Belichick and Brady to his home to talk, it was unclear whether they would be together for the 2018 season. Now it felt as if something extraordinary was about to happen.

In the Belichick-Brady era, the Patriots had never faced such low expectations heading into the playoffs. For the first time since 2009, New England had won fewer than twelve regular-season games. All five losses in 2018 were to teams that weren't good enough to qualify for the playoffs. Gronkowski was a step slower. Brady and Edelman had gotten dinged up in the latter part of the regular season. Gordon was suspended. Opponents didn't view the Patriots as the same daunting team that had been to three of the previous four Super Bowls.

As New England took advantage of the bye week to rest and recuperate, Kraft flew to LA with Goodell to meet with Jay-Z. Before heading to Jay-Z's place, the two men walked from their hotel in Beverly Hills to a nearby restaurant for breakfast. As they made their way down the street, a pedestrian recognized them and asked: "You two guys are still friends?"

Kraft and Goodell looked at each other and smiled. Over the previous twenty years, they'd been through a lot together—the negotiations with Massachusetts officials that prevented the Patriots from moving to Connecticut; the construction of a new stadium; Spygate; the labor lockout; the Ray Rice incident; Deflategate; Jerry Jones's attempt to topple Goodell; President Trump's tweets. All of these things tested and ultimately strengthened their friendship. Neither of them would admit it publicly, but the bond between them was tighter than any other relationship the commissioner had with an NFL owner.

That bond was critical in the discussion with Jay-Z. In the eyes of the hip-hop community, Goodell was seen as the mouthpiece of billionaire owners who turned a blind eye to the racial injustices in the criminal-justice system that Colin Kaepernick had called attention to with his kneeling. As a result, Goodell had no standing in the hip-hop community. Kraft, on the other hand, had spent a lot of time with Meek Mill. And through that friendship, he had met other artists. "He's been to the recording studio with me and ten

or twenty of my guys," Meek explained. "These guys come from the ghetto. Robert had never been around these type of guys. But he had his feet up and was just chilling and naturally engaging with them the way friends do."

Jay-Z and Meek were close friends, and they both viewed Kraft as an ally. In turn, Kraft vouched for Goodell, who acknowledged missteps by the NFL and pledged his commitment to making changes. It was a conversation that laid the groundwork for a historic alliance between the NFL and Jay-Z's entertainment company, Roc Nation. It would take months to iron out the details, but later in 2019, Goodell and Jay-Z announced a partnership that enabled Roc Nation to oversee the selection of the Super Bowl halftime performers and produce the halftime show. In return, the NFL made a financial commitment to Roc Nation and a coalition of players to fight social and racial injustice.

On January 13, 2019, the Patriots hosted the 12-4 Los Angeles Chargers in the divisional round of the playoffs. Belichick generally preferred to start the game on defense, but when his team won the coin toss, he elected to receive the kickoff. It was a not-so-subtle message to the visitors that the Patriots were going on the offensive. Brady loved the call. Moments later, he delivered his own message, leading his team on a fast-paced, fourteen-play drive that culminated in a touchdown. Then the Patriots proceeded to score again, and again, and again, and again. It was only the second quarter and the Patriots were up 35–7. The Chargers didn't know what hit them. The game was over by halftime.

The Patriots' sheer domination of a talented Chargers team surprised a lot of NFL analysts. Brady had one of the most prolific playoff performances of his career, completing thirty-four of forty-four passes for 343 yards. Edelman was unstoppable, catching nine passes for 151 yards. And the Patriots' defense manhandled San Diego's offense.

The victory put the Patriots in the AFC Championship game for the eighth straight year. Normally, Brady liked to avoid the cameras when the game was over, preferring instead to get straight to the locker room, and he almost never focused on statistics. But when the final gun sounded, he made a beeline for CBS's sideline reporter, Tracy Wolfson. Before the camera started rolling, Brady made sure she was aware of the eight straight championship appearances. Moments later, when the camera was on, she said to him: "You mentioned it's your eighth straight AFC Championship game.

And it's a rematch against Kansas City. This time, though, in Arrowhead. What can we expect?"

"It'll be a good game," Brady said. "They're a good team. We played them earlier this year. I know everyone thinks we suck and can't win any games. We'll see. It'll be fun."

The "everyone thinks we suck" comment was Brady's way of taking control of the narrative. Although the Chiefs would be favored to win at home, the reality was that no one truly thought that the Patriots sucked. But Brady, like Belichick, thrived on slights. So, in this case, he manufactured one, and his teammates glommed onto the notion. "People think we suck," Edelman said after the game, echoing Brady. And when a reporter asked Gronkowski about Brady's comment, he said, "We've been hearing that kind of stuff for years now. We laugh at it and keep moving forward."

Belichick was anticipating frigid weather for the AFC Championship. To prepare his team, he planned to have them practice outside all week long. And he went out of his way to make the conditions as miserable as possible, doing things like icing balls to make them harder to throw, catch, kick, and punt. Beyond that, he kept his focus on what he could control. For three straight weeks his team had hammered opponents. They were peaking at the right time. But it was going to take near-perfect execution on both sides of the ball to beat the Chiefs at home.

On game day, while the Patriots warmed up, Robert Kraft could see his breath as he stood at the edge of the tunnel at Arrowhead Stadium. Suddenly, Joe Montana and his wife, Jennifer, approached. The Chiefs had invited them to attend the game. Jennifer hugged Kraft, and the three of them reminisced about their trip to Israel together eighteen months earlier. After wishing them well, Kraft watched as Montana stepped onto the field and Chiefs fans showered him with applause. To Kraft, it felt unnatural to see Montana at Arrowhead to cheer on the Chiefs. Montana was a San Francisco 49er. He was the soul of the 49ers' dynasty. The fact that he'd played his final two years in Kansas City had never sat right with Kraft. That would be like Brady leaving the Patriots to play his final two seasons elsewhere. He couldn't fathom that.

A few minutes later, Brady approached Kraft, removed his helmet, and kissed him on the cheek. Brady couldn't wait to get going. Patrick Mahomes was the NFL's brightest new star. In just his second season, he'd passed for

over five thousand yards and thrown fifty touchdowns, earning him NFL MVP honors at age twenty-three. He was more athletic than Brady, could run much faster than Brady, and had a cannon for an arm. But Brady was out to prove that he and his team were still the best.

"We're gonna get this one tonight," Brady told Kraft.

No team had stopped the Chiefs' offense in 2018. They had scored thirty points or more in all but four games. But the Patriots' defense managed to shut out the Chiefs in the first half. Meanwhile, Brady marched the Patriots up and down the field. With twenty-seven seconds to play in the first half, he threw a twenty-nine-yard touchdown strike to Phillip Dorsett to put New England up 14–0, silencing the crowd. On the sideline, Edelman got in Brady's face. "Nice ball!" Edelman screamed. "Nice fuckin' ball. You're too fuckin' old! You're too old!"

The Chiefs finally scored a touchdown in the third quarter. Still, New England clung to a 17–7 lead heading into the final quarter. But on the second play of the fourth quarter, Mahomes threw a touchdown pass to cut the lead to 17–14. Then, with just under eight minutes to play, he threw another touchdown pass to put his team on top 21–17. The momentum had clearly swung.

The Patriots, however, responded with a long touchdown drive, reclaiming the lead at 24–21 with a little over three minutes to play. A minute later, the Chiefs countered with another touchdown to go back up 28–24. The fourth quarter had turned into a shootout, and the Chiefs' offense was suddenly unstoppable. CBS's Tony Romo commented on the air that Brady was going to have to do something pretty extraordinary to get the Patriots back to the Super Bowl.

With 1:57 to play, Brady took the field. The Patriots had the ball on their own thirty-five-yard line. In the huddle, Brady looked his teammates in the eyes. Every one of them believed they were going to score. On the first play, he rifled a twenty-yard completion to Edelman. Then he hit Chris Hogan for eleven yards. It was first-and-ten on the Chiefs' thirty-four-yard line. After a couple of incompletions and a Chiefs penalty, Brady dropped back and lofted a twenty-five-yard pass down the sideline to Gronkowski, who leaped and brought the ball down at the four-yard line. On the next play, Rex Burkhead barreled into the end zone. With thirty-nine seconds left on the clock, New England was up 31–28.

But Mahomes needed just twenty-five seconds to drive his team into field goal range. With eleven seconds left, the Chiefs kicked a thirty-nine-yard field goal to tie the game and send it to overtime.

Up in the visiting owner's box, Robert and Jonathan Kraft watched as Patriots special teams captain Matthew Slater, whom Belichick had dispatched to midfield for the coin toss, called heads. The referee flipped the coin into the air, and it landed heads up. The Patriots were getting the ball first.

Kraft's longtime chief of staff, Al Labelle, had seen this scenario many times. Labelle turned to the security staff and said with a stern expression, "Time to get ready to go."

"Now?" one of the newer security personnel asked. "They just barely did the coin toss."

"Yeah," Labelle said. "And we won it."

It took Brady less than five minutes to march the offense seventy-five yards in thirteen plays. Edelman and Gronkowski accounted for fifty of those yards. When Rex Burkhead crossed the goal line on a two-yard run to win the game 37–31, Brady pulled off his helmet and leaped into his teammates' arms. The Patriots were heading to the Super Bowl for the third straight year and for the ninth time in the Belichick-Brady era. An astounding sixty-four million viewers had watched one of the most dramatic endings to an AFC Championship game in league history. As a mob of television cameramen circled Belichick and Brady on the field, they grabbed hold of each other.

"Could we have done that any other way?" Brady said jubilantly.

"Nope," Belichick said.

The next day, Brady's picture filled the back page of the *New York Post*, along with the headline "PUBLIC ENEMY NO. 1: Tom Brady makes Super Bowl *again*."

The Patriots arrived in Atlanta on January 28, 2019, to begin preparations for Super Bowl LIII against the Los Angeles Rams. Two days later, Robert Kraft was in his hotel suite atop the Ritz-Carlton when Goodell notified him that President Trump was scheduled to sit for an interview on CBS's *Face the Nation* on the day of the game. With the NFL in the midst of trying to forge a partnership with the hip-hop community, Goodell was hoping the president wouldn't bring up the anthem protests in his interview. Kraft called Trump and left a message. A few minutes later, Kraft's phone rang. A receptionist at the White House said she had the president on the line.

Kraft and Trump talked for twenty minutes. Toward the end of the call,

Kraft broached the subject of the president's upcoming television interview. Trump assured him that he had no intention of bringing up the flag and the anthem protests. Kraft texted Goodell and let him know.

Later that night, the Krafts hosted a private dinner for the CBS broadcast team at Ray's in the City in downtown Atlanta. Twelve CBS executives and crew members took their seats around a large rectangular table. Robert sat between Jim Nantz and CBS Sports president Sean McManus. Jonathan, Tony Romo, Tracy Wolfson, and Evan Washburn sat across from them. At the outset, Kraft expressed his appreciation for his lengthy partnership with the network, and he talked about the long-standing tradition of having intimate dinners with the CBS broadcast team during the playoffs each year. Over the next couple of hours, the group shared stories from the twenty-year span since CBS had acquired the rights to televise AFC games back in the late nineties.

As the night wound down, Jim Nantz rose to his feet and tapped a spoon on his glass. Once everyone had quieted down, he gave a heartfelt speech about what it had been like working with the Patriots over the past two decades. "You treat us like we're part of your family," Nantz said. "I've never experienced such kindness in this business. Thank you, Robert."

McManus led the applause. Then he rose, signaled for the restaurant manager, and asked for the check.

"We got it," Kraft said.

"Let me pay for it," McManus said.

"But it's already paid for," Kraft said.

"But we'd like to get this one," McManus said.

"But it's already paid for," Kraft repeated. "You can get it next time."

At thirty-three, Rams coach Sean McVay was the youngest head coach in the NFL. Fit, well-dressed, dating a model, and living in LA, McVay was a sharp contrast to Belichick. His team's overall record of 15-3 was tops in the NFL in 2018. The Rams had a stifling defense and a prolific offense that had averaged thirty-three points per game during the regular season. McVay's team was loaded with young, elite players.

On the eve of the game, Belichick met with his team. "You know what we need tomorrow night?" he said, pausing for effect. "Everything you've given me all year."

As Belichick spoke in a deliberate, measured tone, Brady made a mental note. Belichick's words provided a sense of security to the Patriots. He had

reminded them that everyone simply needed to do their jobs and fight for sixty minutes. If they did that, they'd win.

On the Rams' opening drive, the Patriots defense punished quarterback Jared Goff, throwing him and his receivers off their game. But the Rams' defense was equally aggressive. The game turned into an extremely physical contest. At one point in the second quarter, Gronkowski sustained a hit to his quad that resulted in the deepest thigh bruise of his career. The severity of his injury, which would ultimately cause his leg to swell up and require doctors to drain a liter of blood from the affected area, wouldn't be discovered until well after the game. In the meantime, he stayed on the field.

After three quarters, the Patriots and Rams were tied 3–3. It was the first time in Super Bowl history that neither team had scored a touchdown heading into the final quarter. Belichick felt that the tempo and the mounting pressure were to his team's advantage. With 9:49 to play, the Patriots took possession at their own thirty-one-yard line. Exhausted, Brady strode slowly toward the huddle, where he looked at Gronkowski and Edelman. Gronkowski was in tremendous pain. Edelman, who was having one of the best games of his life with nine catches for 128 yards, was amped up. "Let's do this," he said.

On the first play of the drive, Brady hit Gronkowski for an eighteen-yard gain. Then he hit Edelman for thirteen yards. Rex Burkhead ran through a hole for a seven-yard pickup. After just three plays, the Patriots were thirty-one yards from the end zone. Gronkowski lined up on the outside. On the snap, he sprinted straight down the field. Brady lofted a touch pass. With a defender hanging on him and two more running toward him, Gronkowski laid out. The ball was perfectly thrown and landed in his outstretched hands as he crashed to the turf at the Rams' two-yard line. Patriots fans in Mercedes-Benz Stadium rose to their feet. Moments later, running back Sony Michel scored on a two-yard run, and Tom Brady punched the sky. With seven minutes to go, the Patriots had finally broken through to go up 10–3.

On the Patriots' sideline, Belichick grabbed his defensive coaches. "We got about fifteen calls left in this game," he told them. "Let's get 'em right. Let's just know what we're gonna call here. Make sure we get the right personnel in the game."

Then Belichick rallied his defensive players, admonishing them to stay within the plan.

The Rams mounted their best drive of the game. With four and a half minutes to go, they were on the Patriots' twenty-seven-yard line when Goff threw toward the end zone. Stephon Gilmore leaped and intercepted the ball

on the four-yard line. As New England players shouted along the sideline, Belichick immediately consulted with offensive coordinator Josh McDaniels. Backed up against their own goal line, the Patriots had no margin for error. And they needed to get first downs to run down the clock and preserve the victory.

"What do you think, Josh?" Belichick said. "They're looking tired."

McDaniels agreed. He wanted to avoid pass plays and pound the ball up the middle with Sony Michel.

Belichick told McDaniels it was his call.

After getting the play from McDaniels, Brady huddled the offense. "Listen up," he told his teammates. "If we ever get a choice, we don't want to go out of bounds."

"Do *not*," Edelman added.

"No penalties," Brady continued. "And let's just knock the shit out of them. Let's go."

After a one-yard run, Michel got the ball again and burst through a big hole for a twenty-six-yard gain. Brady handed it to him two more times. Then Brady handed off to Rex Burkhead, who ran for another twenty-six yards. On the drive, Brady never passed the ball. The Patriots stayed on the ground, and New England's offensive line wore down the Rams' defensive front. After Michel was stopped inches from a first down on the Rams' twenty-four-yard line, Brady called a time-out and headed to the sideline. With 1:16 remaining, New England faced a fourth down.

As McDaniels and Belichick debated what to do, Brady interjected: "Why don't we just kick the field goal? It's a forty-yarder."

"We're good on the field goal," McDaniels chimed in.

But Belichick was still mulling it over.

"It's a forty-yarder," Brady said to Belichick. "The game's over."

"All right," Belichick said. "Let's go."

As the field goal unit took the field, Tony Romo and Jim Nantz pointed out that a field goal would seal the victory for the Patriots. As the ball left Gostkowski's foot, Nantz made the call. "It . . . is . . . good!"

Mercedes-Benz Stadium erupted.

"Six titles," yelled Romo. "Nine appearances."

The Patriots were up 13–3 with a minute to play. Belichick was about to become the oldest coach to win a Super Bowl, and the only coach with six titles. Brady was about to become the only player in NFL history to win six Super Bowls. As Brady thrust his fist in the air on the Patriots' sideline, a CBS camera zoomed in on him.

"Enjoy it, folks," Romo said. "You're never, ever gonna see it again."

"Not in our lifetime," said Nantz.

As the confetti began to fall, Edelman was informed that he'd been named Super Bowl MVP. Overwhelmed, he looked for Brady. "Hey, Tommy," Edelman yelled. "Come here. I love you."

"Love you, dude," Brady said.

Brady and Edelman were hugging when Belichick approached.

"You guys did awesome," Belichick said, putting his arms around both of them.

"Love you, coach," Edelman said.

"Where's RKK?" Brady said. "Let me get to RKK."

Kraft made his way through the sea of media and embraced Brady.

Belichick found Gronkowski, who was in tremendous pain.

"You're a helluva player," Belichick told him.

"You're a helluva coach," Gronkowski replied.

"We're a helluva team," Belichick said.

"We found a way," Gronkowski said. "Keep on grindin.'"

"That's it," Belichick said.

The Pittsburgh Steelers had been the only franchise with six Lombardi Trophies. It had taken the organization thirty-four years to win that many. The Patriots had just won their sixth title in eighteen years. Unlike the Steelers, the Patriots won all their championships after the league expanded to thirty-two teams and adopted changes intended to create parity, namely free agency and a salary cap. But the most remarkable aspect of New England's epic run was the inexplicable surge in the dynasty's sunset years. After a nine-year championship drought between 2005 and 2013, the Patriots had gone to four of the five most recent Super Bowls and won three of them. Struggling to put the magnitude of the Patriots' achievement in perspective, ESPN analyst Steve Young spoke to Belichick on the field right after the game and compared his coaching feat—securing a sixth title by holding the high-powered Rams to a field goal—to the Mona Lisa and the Sistine Chapel. "This has got to be the highest moment, the Everest," Young said.

In a metaphorical sense, Young was right. In the context of athletics, the Patriots' achievements under Belichick and Brady stood out like the works of Leonardo da Vinci and Michelangelo in the world of art. Echoing the

sentiment, the February 11, 2019, issue of *Sports Illustrated* pronounced the Patriots the "Greatest of All Teams."

Roger Goodell gripped the Lombardi Trophy and congratulated Robert and Jonathan Kraft, pointing out that they had won their first championship seventeen years earlier. As Patriots fans booed the commissioner, Robert patted Goodell's arm and Jonathan smiled at him for being a good sport. "Incredible organization," Goodell told them. "The Patriots are Super Bowl champs once again." He handed Robert the trophy.

"Truly an unprecedented accomplishment, managed by exceptional players and coaches," Kraft said. "But there is one constant throughout this whole eighteen years. Two men who are the best ever at what's been done in the history of the NFL—Bill Belichick and Tom Brady. Through their hard work and great leadership, I'm honored to say for the sixth time: We are all Patriots. And once again, the Patriots are world champions."

Standing behind Kraft, Belichick held his granddaughter in his arms while Brady held his six-year-old daughter Vivian in one arm and kept his free hand on the shoulder of his middle child, Benjamin. When they met in 2000, Belichick was a young father and Brady was fresh out of college. Now Belichick was a grandfather and Brady was a middle-aged dad. The sports world had watched them grow old together through the prism of football.

"We're still here," Belichick told Jim Nantz.

Then Nantz turned to Brady, whose daughter was pointing up at the streamers and confetti falling from the sky. "For all those fans out there, what will motivate you to come back?" said Nantz. "How will you reset and do it all over again?"

Brady faced the crowd. "Look at this," he said, his daughter smiling and laughing in his arms. "How could this not motivate you?"

Then Vivian put her arms around her dad's neck and squeezed.

"This is what it's all about," Brady said.

Epilogue

P oet Henry Wadsworth Longfellow said, "Great is the art of beginning, but greater the art is of ending." Endings can be hard to see coming, and even harder to accept when they arrive. That's especially true when it comes to sports dynasties. The greatest dynasties of all time—the New York Yankees of the Joe DiMaggio and Mickey Mantle eras; the Boston Celtics of the Bill Russell era; the Montreal Canadians of the Guy Lafleur era; the San Francisco 49ers of the Joe Montana era; and the Chicago Bulls of the Michael Jordan era—left a huge void when they died out.

The New England Patriots of the Tom Brady era are in the pantheon of greatest sports dynasties. No team in the twenty-first century formed a deeper emotional connection with its fans—or aroused more passionate disdain from opposing fans—than the Patriots under Robert Kraft, Bill Belichick, and Tom Brady. Together, they created a golden era of football that started in the year of the 9/11 terror attacks and continued for two decades. If the Patriots' dynasty had behaved like its football predecessors in Green Bay, Pittsburgh, and San Francisco, the run in Foxborough would have ended much sooner, perhaps as early as 2010 or 2011. But Kraft's biggest achievement as an owner was keeping Belichick and Brady together for so long. They needed each other to reach heights that had previously seemed unimaginable. For Belichick and Brady, the 2018 season was their magnum opus. When they walked off the stage in Atlanta in February 2019 with their sixth Lombardi Trophy, it was the football equivalent of the Beatles leaving the studio after recording *Abbey Road*. Although the Fab Four would end up releasing one additional record and didn't officially break up until the following year, their final musical masterpiece was behind them when they crossed the street on August 8, 1969.

Similarly, after winning a sixth championship, Kraft, Belichick, and Brady stayed together for one more year. But their swan-song season in 2019 was filled with the kind of frustrations and challenges that are unique to having

occupied the top of the mountain for so long. Nonetheless, the Patriots got through it without the public or private acrimony that so often accompanies breakups. And in the end, the parting scene was a testament to the character of the men who built the dynasty and the depth of the relationships forged between them.

The first clue that 2019 was going to be a trying year for the Patriots came early on. Less than three weeks after Super Bowl LIII, authorities in Jupiter, Florida, held a press conference and announced that Robert Kraft was among two dozen men who were being charged with soliciting prostitution inside a day spa where police had been conducting video surveillance. Kraft was in Los Angeles for the Oscars when he was blindsided by the news. The Patriots released a statement: "We categorically deny that Mr. Kraft engaged in any illegal activity." But as the *New York Times* reported in a front-page story on February 23, 2019, "Mr. Kraft is the most prominent name to emerge in the case, and the charges represent an embarrassing spectacle for a man who has become one of the most powerful owners in American sports."

"Embarrassing spectacle" was an understatement. Kraft's case made international headlines. Even President Trump was asked to weigh in during a press briefing in the Oval Office. For Kraft, it was the most humiliating situation of his life. Tom Brady happened to be in Los Angeles when the news broke. He was there with Gisele, who had an event to attend. Recognizing that Kraft was no doubt mortified, Brady reached out to him. Then he and Gisele chose to fly home with Kraft. The flight gave Brady and Kraft plenty of time to talk one-on-one. Over the years there had been many occasions when Brady had felt alone during difficult situations and turned to Kraft for support and advice. This time the roles were reversed. As Kraft's plane touched down on a small private airfield outside Boston, a TMZ camera crew was waiting near the chain-link fence that surrounded the hangar. Brady knew what it felt like to have cameras trained on him amid controversy. He also knew that whatever he did in the ensuing moments would go viral. As he and Kraft stepped off the plane, Brady purposely stayed at Kraft's side, walking him to his car as the cameras clicked. Then he hugged Kraft and told him he loved him.

Kraft struggled to keep his composure. "Tommy," he said, "you are . . ." His voice trailed off.

Brady didn't need an explanation.

Within weeks, prosecutors made an offer to Kraft to drop the case against

him in exchange for his paying a fine, performing community service, and admitting that if the case went to trial, the prosecutors would prevail. While his lawyer pointed out that this would make the matter go away expeditiously, Kraft rejected the deal, saying he wouldn't admit to something he didn't do.

Two months later, in May, after reviewing the underlying search warrant that the police relied on to conduct video surveillance inside the spa, the judge presiding over the case determined that the evidence was "seriously flawed" and deemed it inadmissible. The judge then dismissed the case against Kraft and the other defendants. Prosecutors subsequently appealed the judge's ruling. The appeal would languish in the courts, and was still pending in the spring of 2020.

While all of this was playing out, Rob Gronkowski made a surprise announcement. "I will be retiring from the game of football today," he said on Instagram on March 24. "I'm so grateful for the opportunity that Mr. Kraft and Coach Belichick gave to me when drafting my silliness in 2010. My experiences over the last 9 years have been amazing both on and off the field. . . . Now it's time to move forward. . . . Cheers to all who have been part of this journey, cheers to the past for the incredible memories, and a HUGE cheers to the uncertainty of what's next."

Gronkowski's retirement shocked the Patriots and created an instant hole in the heart of New Englanders. A larger-than-life figure in the truest sense, he was one of the most beloved athletes to ever perform in the greater Boston area. He was also Brady's wingman. His departure signaled that a changing of the guard was underway in Foxborough. For Gronkowski, the decision was straightforward. The 2018 season had been the most satisfying of his career. It had also been the hardest to endure. His inability to walk after the Super Bowl had a lot to do with his decision to step away from the game. The hit that he sustained to his quad in the first half triggered internal bleeding that caused his leg to swell up like balloon. In his hotel room in Atlanta that night, Gronkowski was in so much agony that he was in tears and unable to sleep. The pain and the sleeplessness continued for days.

"I was not in a good place," Gronkowski explained in the summer of 2019. "Football was bringing me down, and I didn't like it. I was losing that joy in life . . . I was dealing with pain. I needed to walk away because I needed to do what was best for myself."

In August 2019, Brady turned forty-two. Determined to play a twentieth season in New England, he signed a one-year contract extension right after his birthday. But he and Kraft agreed that after the 2019 season, Brady would be a free agent. That was what Brady wanted. And in Kraft's mind, Brady had earned that after leading the team to nine Super Bowls and winning six of them. The deal generated immediate speculation about whether the 2019 season would be Brady's last in New England. Questions about Brady's future would dominate the narrative surrounding the team.

Heading into the first game of the regular season, the Patriots signed controversial receiver Antonio Brown. The Patriots' acquisition of the game's most talented and troubled receiver stunned the league. Belichick was convinced that Brown could help the team make another championship run, and that he would conform to the Patriots' system. Brady was thrilled by the prospect of throwing to the most talented wide receiver to come to New England since Randy Moss. And Kraft figured that the addition of Brown might be enough to persuade Brady to remain in New England beyond 2019 and finish his career as a Patriot.

But the day after Brown arrived in Foxborough, a federal lawsuit accusing him of sexual assault was filed in Florida. Later that week, Brown played his first game with the Patriots in Miami and caught a touchdown pass from Brady, helping the team beat the Dolphins 43-0. The day after the game, *Sports Illustrated* published an extensive report that included allegations from a second woman who claimed that Brown had abused her. Brown denied all of the accusations. But after the story ran, he sent threatening text messages to one of his accusers. One of the texts included photos of his accuser's children. The day after the texts were made public, the Patriots decided to cut Brown. For Robert Kraft, putting children in a text was beyond any explanation that Brown or his agent might have offered. Brown lasted less than two weeks in New England.

Meanwhile, the Patriots marched to an 8-0 start against a weak schedule. While the Patriots' defense was dominant, the offense struggled. The only receiver that Brady could consistently count on was thirty-three-year-old Julian Edelman, who ended up having arguably the most prolific year of his career with one hundred catches for 1,117 yards and six touchdowns. Yet midway through the season, Brady said that he was "the most miserable 8-0 quarterback in the NFL." Rumors surfaced that Rob Gronkowski might come back in time to help the team make a playoff run. Although he had announced his retirement, under league rules he had until November 30, 2019, to decide whether he wanted to return to action. Plus, he still had a year remaining on

his contract. Kraft even talked to him to let him know how much the team missed him and hoped he'd return.

But Gronkowski stayed retired, and the Patriots went 4-4 over the second half of the season. Although New England won the AFC East division for the eleventh straight season, they sputtered at the end of the regular season. Then, in the wild-card round of the playoffs on January 4, 2020, they hosted the Tennessee Titans, a team coached by Mike Vrabel, the former Patriots linebacker who had been one of Belichick's favorite players during the early years of the dynasty. Trailing 14–13 with fifteen seconds to play, the Patriots were backed up on their own one-yard line. The impossible situation summed up the 2019 season. On the snap, Brady dropped back deep in his own end zone and threw to one of his newest receivers. The ball deflected off his hands and into those of defensive back Logan Ryan, a former Patriots player who returned the interception for a touchdown to put the Titans up 20–13 and end New England's season. Fans had hung signs throughout Gillette Stadium pleading with Brady to come back for one more year. In his postgame press conference, he was peppered with questions about whether he'd be back in 2020.

"Who knows what the future holds?" he said. "We'll leave it at that."

Tom Brady's contract with the Patriots voided at 4:00 p.m. on Tuesday, March 17, 2020. That evening at 6:20, Brady texted Kraft: "Hi there. Hope you're doing well. Are you in Chestnut Hill? Would love to see you in person if possible. I'm corona-free."

A week earlier, with the coronavirus beginning to spread in the United States, Governor Charlie Baker had declared a state of emergency in Massachusetts. Kraft had been self-quarantining in his home since the first confirmed cases were reported in Boston.

"Yes, I'm still here, dealing with a cough," Kraft texted. "I'm infection free. But trying to be corona free. So no hugging. Need to do social distancing."

"What's better?" Brady texted. "Tonight or tomorrow morning? Whichever you prefer. Just let me know. We will adhere to all CDC guidelines."

"Great, let's do tonight," Kraft texted. "Tell me when it's good."

Brady said he could be there in thirty minutes.

Kraft thought Brady was coming to tell him that he'd decided to play another season with the Patriots.

When Brady arrived, he parked in his customary spot—right outside the front door to Kraft's home. Kraft ushered him inside and they sat six feet

apart in the living room where they had met so many times before. After Kraft asked about Brady's family and they talked briefly about the virus, Brady brought up what he had come to discuss. Looking Kraft in the eye, he told him that he wasn't returning to the Patriots for another season. He would be happier, he explained, and it would be better for him to move on.

Kraft was overcome with sadness.

And as Brady tried to further explain his decision, he broke down.

After a long pause, Kraft told him he understood. There was no need for any further explanation.

Brady wiped his eyes. "This is hard," he said.

They wanted to hug each other, but they resisted.

"I'm sitting here thinking that when I met you twenty years ago," Kraft said, "you were this skinny beanpole college kid with peach fuzz on your chin."

Brady smiled. Now he was a global icon.

"You've matured so beautifully," Kraft said, his eyes welling up.

Tears streamed down Brady's cheeks.

The two of them spent the next hour reminiscing. Then Brady wanted to call Jonathan, who was in Aspen, Colorado. Robert dialed his number and put the call on speakerphone. When Brady told Jonathan that he was leaving, he got emotional again. "You're like a brother to me," Brady said. "I love you."

Half a continent away, Jonathan removed his glasses and wiped his eyes. "I feel the same way," he said. "I love you too."

After hanging up with Jonathan, Robert and Tom took a moment to collect themselves. It was time to call Belichick. Throughout their twenty-year partnership, Kraft, Belichick, and Brady had rarely been in the same room together. Normally, it was Kraft in a room with one of them, functioning as a bridge.

Kraft called Belichick at home. When Belichick picked up, Kraft said, "Bill, I'm with Tommy. He's got something he wants to tell you."

Kraft stepped away so Brady could be near the phone.

Brady thanked Belichick for being such a great mentor and coach, and told him he was leaving.

Belichick told him how much he admired and respected him, both as a player and as a man. "Tom," he said, "you're the greatest quarterback of all time. But you're an even greater person."

As Brady and Belichick spoke, Kraft marveled at the way the two of them were handling the situation. Breakups—especially when egos are involved—are almost always messy. But this one wasn't. A professional relationship

between the two biggest stars in the football orbit had gone as far as it could go. After twenty years together in the crucible of greatness, they had reached the end of the road. More than anything, Belichick and Brady sounded relieved. They closed by expressing once more their respect and admiration for each other.

After Brady hung up with Belichick, he and Kraft talked for a few more minutes. Then Kraft walked him to the door. Instinctively, they made a move to embrace, but stopped themselves. There would be no hug. No kiss on the cheek. Standing six feet apart, both men had tears in their eyes. "I love you, Robert," Brady said.

"I love you, Tommy," Kraft replied.

Brady turned, got in his car, and stepped on the gas.

Alone in the doorway, Kraft waved as Brady's taillights disappeared in the darkness. Thirty minutes later, sitting alone in his house, Kraft texted Brady: "Love you more than you know for being so classy in everything you do. Your parents should be so proud. I love them for creating you. You are truly one of a kind."

Acknowledgments

This book was made possible by exceptional access to the Patriots organization and, more specifically, the people profiled in these pages. I'm grateful to them for their time, their hospitality, and, most important, their trust. So I'll begin by thanking those who allowed me to see, hear, and tell their stories: Robert Kraft; Jonathan Kraft; Tom Brady; Drew and Maura Bledsoe; Tedy Bruschi; Roger Goodell; Paul Tagliabue; Leigh Steinberg; Chad Gifford; Rob Gronkowski; Dr. David Berger; Mel Karmazin; Richard Karelitz; Jon Bon Jovi; Sean McManus; Dr. Matthew Leibman; Deion Branch; Don Lowery; Andy Wasynczuk; Lee Johnson; and Sandy Weill. I also appreciate the many others who granted interviews for this book.

Behind the scenes, there were many who helped arrange and facilitate my reporting. I can't name them all, but I'm especially grateful to Stacey James, Anne Noland, Robin Glaser, Al Labelle, Jane Lydon, and Ed Fraioli with the Patriots, all of whom were exceptionally professional and treated me with kindness; Deborah Pugliese and Corey Harrison in commissioner Roger Goodell's office; Anson Christian in Paul Tagliabue's office; Scott Fisher in Sean McManus's office at CBS Sports; Rob Gronkowski's brother, Dan; Jon Bon Jovi's personal assistant, Aaron Lassin; Michael Rubin, for facilitating my interview with Meek Mill; and Bill Hofheimer at ESPN, for facilitating my interviews with Tedy Bruschi and Randy Moss.

I am indebted to the folks at NFL Films in Mount Laurel, New Jersey, where I spent days looking at film and listening to audio from more than forty of the games featured in this book. I'm especially grateful to Chris Barlow for his friendship, to Ken Rogers for helping me decipher dialogue, and archivist Chris Willis for being so resourceful and letting me camp out in his office. Likewise, Matt Smith at Kraft Sports Productions provided me access to hours of video footage from everything from Elton John's anniversary performance for Robert and Myra Kraft in 2008 to countless other events and moments that I requested.

At the *Boston Globe*, former sports editor Don Skwar shared valuable insights and went to great lengths to locate and retrieve Will McDonough's first-person account "An Inside Look at Parcells-Kraft: Here's How They Came to the Breaking Point in a Tumultuous Year." For my purposes, this was a monumentally important piece of journalism that was no longer available through the newspaper's website or archives.

At the *Hartford Courant*, editor Rick Green provided me with a workstation where I printed and culled through hundreds of stories about Connecticut's attempt to bring the Patriots to Hartford. The *Courant*'s archive was a critical resource for the Hartford chapter in the Patriots saga.

Governor John Rowland's former attorney, Brendan Fox, and former lobbyist, Jay Malcynsky, granted interviews that were critical to enabling me to re-create the dialogue and scenes involving key meetings between the governor and the Krafts.

Richard Lapchick at the Center for the Study of Sport in Society was instrumental in the sections of the book that dealt with race. When I worked for him in the 1990s, he assigned me to research and help write an annual report on the racial composition of front-office executives and head coaches in the National Football League, Major League Baseball, and the National Basketball Association. That experience helped shape my approach to the Patriots' hiring practices in *The Dynasty*.

Natalie Tysdal and Kathy Redmond entrusted me to write about their painful experiences at the University of Nebraska in the 1990s, which helped form the backdrop to what I wrote in this book about the Patriots' decision to cut Nebraska draft choice Christian Peter.

For the section of the book that deals with Robert Kraft's involvement with Labrador Linerboard mill in Newfoundland, I'm indebted to Jane Crosby and her daughter Ches, who dug up old journal entries and photographs that helped me understand that time period. Similarly, I'm grateful to Dan Kraft for all the time he spent educating me about International Forest Products. And I'm indebted to Richard Karelitz for helping me to get my arms around the legal nuances in Robert Kraft's acquisition of Sullivan Stadium and his purchase of the Patriots franchise.

One of the privileges of working on this book was that I got to meet and become friends with author Dan Brown, who did me the honor of editing one of my passages.

In June 2019 I traveled to Israel with Robert Kraft and fifteen current and former Patriots players, including Drew Bledsoe, Scott Zolak, Ty Law, Vince Wilfork, Andre Tippett, Joe Thuney, Stephon Gilmore, Nate Ebner, Isaiah

Wynn, David Andrews, Stephen Gostkowski, Julian Edelman, Kevin Faulk, and Jerod Mayo. Most of the players were accompanied by a spouse or family member. A week in the Holy Land with them enabled me to see and gain a deep appreciation for the spiritual side of each of these individuals. I'm particularly grateful to Vince Wilfork for helping to baptize me in the River Jordan.

Andre Tippett befriended me during this project and helped show me the ropes. Some of the most enjoyable moments along the way were talking with him about religion, music, race, food, and relationships.

Many journalists at the *Boston Globe*, *Boston Herald*, *Sports Illustrated*, the *New York Times*, ESPN, and a multitude of other publications and news organizations spent years covering the Patriots. I read thousands of articles and more than twenty-five books in preparation for writing *The Dynasty*. While it's not practical to mention every journalist whose work influenced mine, there are a few whose exceptional reporting and insights were particularly helpful: Michael Holley, whose books *Patriot Reign*, *War Room*, and *Belichick and Brady* were among the first publications I read before starting my research; veteran reporter Tom E. Curran, who has been on the Patriots beat for as long as I've been a journalist; Will McDonough, especially for his reporting on the Patriots' ownership prior to Robert Kraft and his writings on the relationship between Robert Kraft and Bill Parcells; Peter King and his features on Bill Belichick, Robert Kraft, Tom Brady, Roger Goodell, and the Patriots in *Sports Illustrated* and Monday Morning Quarterback; Jackie Mac-Mullan's special features on Ted Johnson, Bill Belichick, Robert Kraft, and Tedy Bruschi; Charles P. Pierce's book *Moving the Chains*; Nunyo Demasio's great reporting in *Parcells: A Football Life*; Ian O'Connor's authoritative biography of Bill Belichick; Steve Kroft's *60 Minutes* interview with Tom Brady in 2005; *The Brady 6* by NFL Films; the six episodes about the New England Patriots from the NFL Films series America's Game; *Bill Belichick: A Football Life* by NFL Films; Bella English for her story "After a Bruising Year, Belichick Opens Up"; Armen Keteyian's insightful sit-down interviews with Bill Belichick for CBS's *The NFL Today* and CBS News; the extraordinary *Boston Globe* Spotlight Team six-part series on Aaron Hernandez reported by Bob Hohler, Beth Healy, Sacha Pfeiffer, Andrew Ryan, and editor Patricia Wen; Glenn Stout and Richard A. Johnson's book *The Pats: An Illustrated History of the New England Patriots*; the Super Bowl coverage by Michael Silver and Greg Bishop in *Sports Illustrated*; Mike Reiss for his sound insights and observations; *Boston Globe* columnists Bob Ryan and Dan Shaughnessy; Judy Battista and Ken Belson for their exceptional coverage of the NFL in the *New*

York Times; and Don Van Natta and Seth Wickersham for their in-depth coverage of the NFL for *ESPN The Magazine*.

Gotham Chopra's fine work in the Facebook documentary *Tom vs Time* was most helpful. And I'm especially grateful to Alex Guerrero and his staff for such exceptional treatment at the TB12 Performance & Recovery Center in Foxborough while I worked on this book.

I'm fortunate to have a small circle of extremely talented and trustworthy colleagues: my editorial consultant, Dorothea Halliday; reporter Tim Bella; transcriber Jill Benedict; fact-checker Kelvin Bias; and video editor Christine Dupree. Jeff Katz and Justin Lindsey were great sounding boards, as were Armen Keteyian and B. J. Schecter.

My agent, Richard Pine, is one of my best friends and most trusted confidants. I owe a lot to him and his great team at InkWell Management, especially Eliza Rothstein. I'm extremely fortunate to have Jofie Ferrari-Adler as my editor. He's smart, sensitive, and a dear friend. Jon Karp, the CEO of Simon & Schuster, believed in this project from day one and provided sound guidance at the outset. I'm immensely fortunate to have the trio of Pine, Ferrari-Adler, and Karp to advise me at this stage of my career.

The rest of the team at S&S has been stellar: editor-in-chief Ben Loehnen, editorial director Lauren Wein, associate publisher Meredith Vilarello, editorial assistant Carolyn Kelly, production editor Benjamin Holmes, and publicists Jordan Rodman and David Kass, as well as Brigid Black, Alison Forner, Julianna Haubner, Elizabeth Hubbard, Morgan Hoit, Felice Javit, Gregg Kulick, Allie Lawrence, Jeff Miller, Amanda Mulholland, Sydney Newman, and Lewelin Polanco.

Finally, there's my family. I could not have written this book without the enduring love and support of my wife, Lydia, who epitomizes what Alexander Hamilton referred to as the "best of wives, best of women." Our son Tennyson, a third-year law student at UConn, was immensely helpful on this project as a researcher, as a second fact-checker, and in cataloging the book's source materials. Our daughter Maggie May, a high school senior, spent dozens of hours watching documentaries from NFL Films and noting the places where there was dialogue that I needed for the narrative. Our son Clancy, a musician and technology whiz, helped with backing up digital files. And our youngest daughter, Clara Belle, relieved my guilt by telling me time and time again that I was a "great dad" despite the fact that I was almost never around for the two-year period that I spent working on this book.

Notes

Much of the information in this book is based on over 250 interviews with team executives, coaches, players, players' wives, team doctors, lawyers, bankers, league officials, network television executives, sports agents, politicians, entertainers, and others. I conducted multiple interviews with more than fifty of these individuals. There were also a number of people who were interviewed off the record or on background. While their input was invaluable, none of those individuals are quoted in this book. I'm particularly grateful to those who spoke on the record, including Dr. Ken Anderson, Bill Belichick, Dr. David Berger, Peter Bernon, Senator Tom Birmingham, Drew Bledsoe, Maura Bledsoe, Jon Bon Jovi, Tom Brady, Deion Branch, Dan Brown, Tedy Bruschi, Steve Burton, Steve Comen, Jane Crosby, Kevin Faulk, Brendan Fox, Anne Gifford, Chad Gifford, Roger Goodell, Mark Gottfredson, Rob Gronkowski, Frank Hawkins, David Hill, Lee Johnson, Richard Karelitz, Mel Karmazin, Armen Keteyian, Dan Kraft, Jonathan Kraft, Josh Kraft, Robert Kraft, Senator George Jepsen, Al Labelle, Ken Langone, Richard Lapchick, Dr. Matthew Leibman, Don Lowery, Jay Malcynsky, Jerod Mayo, Willie McGinest, Sean McManus, Don McPherson, Frank Mendes, Meek Mill, Les Moonves, Randy Moss, Brian Moynihan, Rupert Murdoch, Jeffrey O'Brien, Bill Parcells, Carmen Policy, Brian Rolapp, Michael Rubin, Dan Salera, Phil Satow, Jeff Saturday, B. J. Schecter, Leigh Steinberg, Paul Tagliabue, Dr. Elsie Taveras, Andre Tippett, Natalie Tysdal, Sandy Weill, Bianca Wilfork, Vince Wilfork, Andy Wasynczuk, Steve Young, Amy Zolak, and Scott Zolak.

I also had access to thousands of pages of legal documents, business records, emails, text messages, journal entries, reports, and minutes from phone calls and meetings.

In instances where I describe scenes, I interviewed at least one person who was present or had firsthand knowledge of what took place. Where I've reconstructed dialogue, I interviewed at least one person who was a party

to the conversation, and in many cases I spoke to multiple parties who were present. Quotes from press conferences and legal proceedings primarily come from video footage, transcripts, and, in some instances, previously published works. Almost all of the dialogue from games—on the sideline, in the huddle, in the locker room—is based on video footage and audio recordings provided by NFL Films or the New England Patriots. I also relied on network broadcasts from CBS, ESPN, NBC, ABC, and Fox.

In the narrative when someone is said to have "thought," "felt," or "believed" something, I obtained that point of view directly from the individual or from a source with direct knowledge of the individual's conclusions. In an effort to remain true to the language and jargon of the main characters, I used their words and phrases even when they aren't directly quoted, thereby preserving the flavor of their speech as much as possible.

I began working on this book in the summer of 2018. Initially, my purpose was to explore how the New England Patriots became the most dominant American sports team of the twenty-first century. I wanted to get inside the engine room, so to speak, and see how this winning machine was built. I was particularly interested in how the team managed to stay on top for so long, especially once everyone else was gunning for them. Once I started writing, I decided to tell the story from the points of view of owner Robert Kraft, head coach Bill Belichick, and quarterback Tom Brady—the three individuals most responsible for the team's success. But there were many other people, most notably Myra and Jonathan Kraft, who also played vital roles in this story. I tried to reflect their points of view as well.

The scenes and dialogue depicted in the first and last chapter of this book are based on my personal observations—in other words, I was there and simply reported what I saw and heard. But most of this story is based on firsthand accounts of those who built the Patriots organization and ran the team. *The Dynasty* represents my best-faith effort to depict the truth according to what I saw, heard, and learned.

In every chapter, I relied first and foremost on interviews. For example, in the prologue, which consists of a series of scenes at Massachusetts General Hospital, I focused on six individuals—Drew and Maura Bledsoe, Dr. David Berger, Robert Kraft, Tom Brady, and Bill Belichick. I interviewed all six of them. Rather than listing who I interviewed for each chapter, these notes contain references to the primary and secondary sources that supplemented my reporting.

chapter one END GAME

I observed firsthand the scenes and dialogue depicted in this chapter.

Antonio Brown's "good force" quote is from his Raiders press conference on March 13, 2019.

Information about Brown's feuds with the Raiders is from Grant Gordon's article "Antonio Brown Upset by Raiders Fines over Absences" in NFL News, September 4, 2019.

"I wouldn't hire Belichick" is from "Here's What Experts Thought of the Patriots Hiring Bill Belichick in 2000," Boston.com, January 27, 2019.

chapter two BOBBY

Most of the information in this chapter was provided by the Kraft family and childhood friends of Robert Kraft.

Information about the song "Moon River" is from the IMDB page on *Breakfast at Tiffany's* and the Grammy Awards website.

chapter three FATHERS AND SONS

I relied on business records, email correspondence, personal correspondence, and photographs. The Crosby family in Newfoundland also provided journal entries, pictures, and other correspondence. Richard Karelitz also provided important background on the legal and financial aspects of this chapter.

For information about the first football game at Schaefer Stadium, see "Foxborough Stadium History—1971," in Patriot News, September 9, 2001; and Upton Bell's essay "The Night the Carburetors Died" in Glenn Stout and Richard A. Johnson's book *The Pats: An Illustrated History of the New England Patriots* (New York: Houghton Mifflin Harcourt, 2018).

For information about the Labrador Linerboard mill, see "Labrador Linerboard," Heritage Newfoundland & Labrador, 1998.

President Nixon's price freeze was reported by R. W. Apple Jr. in "Nixon Freezes Prices for up to 60 Days, Then Will Establish Phase 4 Controls; Farm Prices, Wages, Rents Unaffected," *New York Times*, June 14, 1973.

Information about the projected value of the Victory Tour was taken from "1984 Michael Jackson Tour," *Newsweek*, July 15, 1984.

For information about the Sullivan family's financial problems and involvement with Michael Jackson and the Victory Tour, see John Steinbreder's "The $120 Million Fumble," *Sports Illustrated*, March 14, 1988.

For additional information about Chuck Sullivan's financial losses from the Victory
Tour, see Michael Rezendes, "NFL Approves Sale of New England Patriots to
Reebok's Chairman," *Washington Post*, May 26, 1988; and Craig Barnes, "NFL
Approves Conditional Sale of Pats," *South Florida Sun-Sentinel*, May 26, 1988.

chapter four THE LONG GAME

I conducted interviews with representatives from Bain & Co. and the Center for the
Study of Sport and Society for this chapter. I also relied on business records,
court records, and bankruptcy records.

For background information on Martina Navratilova, I relied on her autobiogra-
phy, *Martina*, written with George Vecsey (New York: Knopf, 1985).

For information on Billy Sullivan's financial woes, I relied on reporting in the *Boston
Globe* and *Boston Herald*, as well as Steinbreder's "The $120 Million Fumble."

For an example of the press identifying Kraft as a leading contender, see Jackie Mac-
Mullan, "Kraft Pursues Stadium," *Boston Globe*, July 30, 1988.

Information on Chuck Sullivan's stadium debt taken from Barnes, "NFL Approves
Conditional Sale of Pats."

For information on Victor Kiam's purchase of the Patriots, see Stout and Johnson,
The Pats.

For Victor Kiam's self-introduction, see Remington commercial from 1979. See also
Jayson Blair, "Victor Kiam, 74, Entrepreneur Who 'Bought the Company,'" *New
York Times*, May 29, 2001.

For Victor Kiam's due diligence, see Mike Felger, *Tales from the New England Patriots Sidelines: A Collection of the Greatest Patriots Stories Ever Told* (New York:
Sports Publishing, 2017).

For information about Victor Kiam's interest in moving the Patriots to Hartford,
see "Victor Kiam, New Owner of the New England Patriots," United Press International, November 5, 1988.

For information about the terms of Victor Kiam's purchase, see "Kiam Buys Controlling Interest in Patriots," *Los Angeles Times*, July 29, 1988.

For information about bids for Sullivan Stadium, see Paul Harber, "Kraft, Karp
Secure Sullivan Stadium," *Boston Globe*, November 23, 1988.

For information about Chief Justice Gabriel's decision to award Sullivan Stadium
to Kraft, see Harber, "Kraft, Karp Secure Sullivan Stadium."

See also Victor Kiam, *Going for It* (New York: Signet, 1987).

For information about the Lisa Olson incident, see Frederick Waterman, "Owner
Backs Players in Sexual Harassment Dispute," United Press International, September 24, 1990; Frederick Waterman, "Reporter Describes Patriots' Sexual

Harassment," United Press International, September 27, 1990; Thomas Rogers, "Kiam Apologizes after Joking about the Olson Incident," *New York Times*, February 7, 1991; and Leigh Montville, "Season of Torment," *Sports Illustrated*, May 13, 1991.

"Pouring gasoline on a campfire": Howard Kurtz, "Herald Calls Foul on Patriots," *Washington Post*, September 26, 1990.

boycott Lady Remington razors: Warner Hessler, "A Call to Boycott Any Product by Tasteless Kiam," *Daily Press*, February 9, 1991.

Tagliabue hired Harvard Law School professor: Thomas George, "Patriots and 3 Players Fined in Olson Incident," *New York Times*, November 28, 1990.

Kiam wisecracked: Rogers, "Kiam Apologizes after Joking about the Olson Incident."

NFL statement regarding Victor Kiam's remarks provided by Paul Tagliabue's office.

chapter five LEVERAGE

For information about Robert Kraft's purchase of New England Television Corp., see "Kraft Named President of N.E. Television," *Boston Globe*, February 15, 1987; and Jack Thomas, "Channel 7's New Team Shows Extra Confidence," *Boston Globe*, April 24, 1987.

For information about the NFL taking control of the Patriots, see "SPORTS PEOPLE: PRO FOOTBALL: N.F.L. Is Reported to Control the Patriots," *New York Times*, October 15, 1991.

For information about James Orthwein's ownership, see "Offer Made to Buy Patriots," Associated Press, March 16, 1992; "SPORTS PEOPLE: PRO FOOTBALL: A Deal Is Reached on Sale of Patriots," *New York Times*, March 21, 1992; and Vito Stellino, "St. Louis Expansion Boss Buys Patriots," *Baltimore Sun*, March 21, 1992.

On hiring Bill Parcells, see Terry Price, "Patriots Brass Is Super Excited to Land Parcells," *Baltimore Sun*, January 22, 1993.

For the Michael O'Halloran quote on Bill Parcells, see Bill Burt, "The Parcells Factor: The Day when Patriots Fortunes Changed Forever," *Eagle-Tribune*, January 21, 2018.

"Robert very much wanted": Jeff Howe, "The Inside Story of How, 25 Years Ago, Robert Kraft Improbably Bought the Patriots," *Athletic*, January 18, 2019.

"A tribal whirl of street-corner life and sports": Tom Mulvoy and Bill Griffith, "Globe's McDonough dies at 67," *Boston Globe*, May 28, 2003.

"could get you a papal blessing": Allen Greenberg, "Will McDonough 1935–2003," *Chicago Tribune*, January 11, 2003.

For information about the William McDonough and Raymond Clayborn incident, see Dave Kindred, "Writers Arise," *Washington Post*, September 15, 1979;

"Clayborn Fined $2,000 by N.F.L.," *New York Times*, October 3, 1979; and Kevin Sherrington, "In 1979 Former UT and NE Pats Star Clayborn Found Out in Painful Way That Media Can Truly Be Hard-Hitting," *Dallas News*, May 28, 2016.

McDonough had initially introduced Parcells to Orthwein: Bill Parcells with Nunyo Demasio, *Parcells: A Football Life* (New York: Crown Archetype, 2014).

NFL owners unanimously voted: Bill Plaschke, "Carolina Is NFL's Newest: Pro Football: The Charlotte Group Is Awarded One of Two New Franchises. Decision on Second Is Delayed," *Los Angeles Times*, December 27, 1993.

NFL owners voted 26–2: Frank Litsky, "PRO FOOTBALL: N.F.L. Expansion Surprise: Jacksonville Jaguars," *New York Times*, December 1, 1993.

a strongly worded letter: Greg Garber, "Orthwein Warns NFL to Keep Out of Patriots Sale," *Hartford Courant*, December 6, 1993.

chapter six SOLD!

his best shot: Howe, "The Inside Story of How, 25 Years Ago, Robert Kraft Improbably Bought the Patriots."

"I can't tell you what to do": Ibid.

"Get on a plane": Ibid.

That's when Kraft knew: "Kraft Fought to Stay in the Game," *Boston Globe*, February 21, 1994.

It was Metcalfe: David Hunn, "Walter Metcalfe, a Deal Maker, a Builder," *St. Louis Post-Dispatch*, January 3, 2016.

1.6 million shares: Margie Manning, "Orthwein Cuts A-B Holdings," *St. Louis Business Journal*, December 21, 1997.

"Thank you all for coming": Press conference announcing the sale of the Patriots from James Orthwein to Robert Kraft, Ritz-Carlton, Boston, January 21, 1994.

chapter seven MEET THE NEW BOSS

"that we know today": Thomas George, "FOOTBALL: N.F.L.'s Free-Agency System Is Found Unfair by U.S. Jury," *New York Times*, September 11, 1992.

"should have fired": Ron Borges, "Kraft Has New Craft to Master," *Boston Globe*.

"There are five hundred": Don Pierson, "Cowboys' Jones, Johnson at It Again," *Chicago Tribune*, March 23, 1994; Todd Archer, "Now 30 Years in with Cowboys, Jerry Jones as Enthusiastic as Ever," ESPN, February 25, 2019.

A leading football writer: Parcells and Demasio, *Parcells*.

For additional information about Bill Parcells's insults of Drew Bledsoe, see Parcells and Demasio, *Parcells*.

One of them said: George Kimball, "For Kraft, Win's a Ball," *Boston Globe*, September 19, 1994.

"I've never given": Ibid.

"I got emotional": Ibid.

chapter eight THIS GUY IS DIFFERENT

youngest quarterback ever: Terry Price, "BLUE DREW: What's Happened to the $42 Million Man?" *Hartford Courant*, December 12, 1995.

Parcells didn't understand: Parcells and Demasio, *Parcells*.

Ozzie Newsome: 100 Greatest Game Changers: 59: Ozzie Newsome (video), NFL.com.

"He didn't want me to be the show": Parcells and Demasio, *Parcells*.

"the Rooney Rule": Charlotte Carrol, "What Is the Rooney Rule? Explaining the NFL's Diversity Policy for Hiring Coaches," *Sports Illustrated*, December 31, 2018.

chapter nine NOT SO FAST

Robert Kraft announced: Patriots news release.

"I can't even": Terry Price, "Bledsoe Becomes Highest-Paid in NFL," *Hartford Courant*, July 21, 1995.

"The bonus baby": Chad Millman, "4 New England Patriots," *Sports Illustrated*, August 1, 1996.

"some mechanical problems": Ibid.

Footage of the September 17, 1995, 49ers-Patriots game provided by NFL Films.

Even the television announcers: Television broadcast of the game provided by NFL Films.

"The doctor said": Terry Price, "Parcells: Bledsoe Won't Miss a Game," *Hartford Courant*, September 19, 1995.

"He was well enough": Terry Price, "Bye Week a Blessing, Especially for Bledsoe," *Hartford Courant*, September 18, 1995.

"We will probably rest him": Price, "Parcells: Bledsoe Won't Miss a Game."

"Players play": Ibid.

shouldn't be expected to play: "Ailing Bledsoe to Miss Game," Associated Press, September 27, 1995.

"With the number of games": Terry Price, "Bledsoe Isn't Himself," *Hartford Courant*, October 15, 1995.

"He's my starting quarterback": Ibid.

James Orthwein had said: Press conference announcing sale of Patriots to Kraft, January 21, 1994.

in 1994 alone: E. M. Swift, "Another Gusher Year for Jones," *Sports Illustrated*, December 12, 1994.

Kraft called out the governor: Ron Borges, "Kraft Weighing Patriots' Future; Current Level of Financial Losses Too High to Sustain, Owner Says," *Boston Globe*, January 29, 1995.

"There are other residents": Richard Kindleberger, "Kraft Gets Rebuffed on $35m Road Bill," *Boston Globe*, February 1, 1995.

"The state is not around": Scot Lehigh, "Hurdles for Kraft Found on Hill; Top Legislators Balk at Money for Patriots," *Boston Globe*, February 6, 1995.

Flattering headlines: Jackie MacMullan, "Kraft Now a Star in His Own Right," *Boston Globe*, September 2, 1995.

"They're playing poker": Ibid.

Referring to it as: Joan Vennochi, "Clueless in Foxboro," *Boston Globe*, January 5, 1996.

even the sportswriters: Dan Shaughnessy, "If We Don't Build It, Then Let Them Go," *Boston Globe*, December 27, 1995.

Parcells called Kraft: Transcript of Proceedings via Conference Call, January 28, 1997, Los Angeles, California.

Without showing it: Parcells and Demasio, *Parcells*.

chapter ten SHE

Dialogue among McDonough, Kraft, and Parcells in this chapter is largely based on Will McDonough, "An Inside Look at Parcells-Kraft: Here's How They Came to the Breaking Point in a Tumultuous Year," *Boston Globe*, 1997.

For information about Christian Peter's criminal record, see Jeff Benedict, *Public Heroes, Private Felons: Athletes and Crimes against Women* (Boston: Northeastern University Press, 1997).

the NFL was starting to face scrutiny: Ibid.

he didn't want to profit: Peter King, "Patriot Games: New England Fumbled When It Drafted Christian Peter and Tried to Recover by Cutting Him Loose," *Sports Illustrated*, May 6, 1996.

a press release: Patriots News, "Patriots Release Rights to Fifth-Round Draft Choice Christian Peter," April 24, 1996.

"For about twenty-four hours": Parcells and Demasio, *Parcells*.

she called it "disgraceful": "Patriots Owner Scolds Parcells," Associated Press, August 28, 1996.

The AP also asked: Ibid.

At Parcells's next press conference: Dialogue with reporters taken from video footage provided by NFL Films.

a television reporter cornered Kraft: Interaction taken from video footage provided by NFL Films.

Despite admitting afterward: Nick Cafardo, "Patriots Erase 22-Point Deficit to Beat Giants," *Boston Globe*, December 22, 1996.

"You showed me": Parcells and Demasio, *Parcells*.

chapter eleven THE TROUBLE WITH CONTRACTS

That morning, the Boston Herald: Parcells and Demasio, *Parcells*.

"Imagine": Ibid.; McDonough, "An Inside Look at Parcells-Kraft."

"Listen": McDonough, "An Inside Look at Parcells-Kraft."

Information about the confrontation among Parcells, Kraft, and McDonough largely comes from McDonough, "An Inside Look at Parcells-Kraft."

Dialogue on makeshift stage after the Patriots' victory over the Jaguars comes from video footage provided by NFL Films.

"Be here at nine thirty": Parcells and Demasio, *Parcells*.

Unable to sleep: Ibid.

Bledsoe quote on his relationship with Parcells taken from Rick Reilly, "Following the Leader: With Coach Bill Parcells Showing the Way, the Patriots Beat the Jaguars for the AFC Championship," *Sports Illustrated*, January 20, 1997.

Belichick later confided: Michael Holley, *Patriot Reign: Bill Belichick, the Coaches, and the Players Who Built a Champion* (New York: HarperCollins, 2004).

the press had deemed him: Ned Zeman, "The Last Straw: The Browns' Cold-Fish Coach, Bill Belichick, Is Unpopular in Cleveland, Where He Did the Unthinkable—He Cut Bernie Kosar," *Sports Illustrated*, November 22, 1993.

"as sentimental as a traffic ticket": Reilly, "Following the Leader."

"I see these faces": Ibid.

chapter twelve NEW ENGLAND VERSUS NEW YORK

"If Mr. Parcells": Taken from then NFL commissioner Paul Tagliabue's January 29, 1997, administrative decision regarding the Parcells-Kraft contract dispute.

Kozol tried to talk him into: McDonough, "An Inside Look at Parcells-Kraft."

"I'm speaking now to the Jets": Parcells and Demasio, *Parcells*.

"It's not about power": Taken from video footage provided by NFL Films.

"For better or worse": Bill Reynolds, "For Better or Worse, It's Kraft's Show Now," *Providence Journal*, February 4, 1997.

"Why doesn't Bob Kraft": Dan Shaughnessy, "With This Job Comes Someone to Watch Over Him (Closely)," *Boston Globe*, February 4, 1997.

the league issued: NFL press release, February 4, 1997.

They had talked: McDonough, "An Inside Look at Parcells-Kraft."

"a kid in need of some Ritalin": Bob Ryan, "Kraft Should Deal Instead of Squeal," *Boston Globe*, February 5, 1997.

"Kraft goes down in history": Dan Shaughnessy, "He Doesn't Look so Crafty Now," *Boston Globe*, February 6, 1997.

a response from Kraft: Shirley Leung, "Kraft Remark Called Unfair to S. Boston," *Boston Globe*, February 4, 1997.

"I have received two hundred calls": Ibid.

"He has never impressed me": Ibid.

Tagliabue scheduled a hearing: Paul Tagliabue to Robert Kraft and Leon Hess, letter, February 7, 1997.

A copy of the handwritten letter from former president George H. W. Bush made available by Paul Tagliabue.

"I just want to be": Parcells and Demasio, *Parcells*.

chapter thirteen YOU KNOW ME

On a hot, sunny afternoon: Richard Turner, "NBC: The Road to 'Tap City,'" *Newsweek*, January 26, 1998.

The description of the atmosphere at Foxboro Stadium during the "Tuna Bowl" is based on video footage provided by NFL Films.

"I love you, too": Parcells and Demasio, *Parcells*.

under the headline: Richard Sandomir, "CBS Guarantees Billions to Get N.F.L. Back," *New York Times*, January 13, 1998.

chapter fourteen DEAR JOHN

Content about Governor Rowland's various press conferences taken from Channel 8, ABC Connecticut affiliate, video footage.

For Tom Finneran's position on a stadium in Boston, see Greg Garber, "Brought to You by Kraft," *Hartford Courant*, November 20, 1998.

Paul Cellucci issued a warning: Mike Allen, "Rowland Offers the Patriots a New Stadium in Hartford," *New York Times*, November 18, 1998.

Finneran hit back hard: Derrick Jackson, "Finneran Scores Touchdown for Massachusetts," *Boston Globe*, November 20, 1998.

"This is a historic day": Tom Puelo, "Touchdown!" *Hartford Courant*, November 19, 1998.

"*The Patriots are coming*": Ibid.

published a full-page letter: Copy of publication provided by the Patriots.

For Rowland's reaction to Kraft's decision to back out of the Hartford stadium deal, see Will McDonough, "Patriots Owner Had a Terrific Deal, but He Goes Other Way for Much Less," *Boston Globe*, May 1, 1999.

"*You can expect legal action*": Taken from video footage from Channel 8, ABC Connecticut affiliate, and Tina Cassidy, "Threat of Lawsuit Tied to Query from Patriots," *Boston Globe*, May 2, 1999.

"*I'm a New York Jets fan now*": Taken from video footage from Channel 8, ABC Connecticut affiliate, and Tim Rohan, "Hartford's White Whale: How the Patriots Almost Became Connecticut's Team," *Sports Illustrated*, January 23, 2017.

Regarding the eventual resignation of Governor Rowland, see Mark Pazniokas and Christopher Keating, "Resignation: Rowland Remains Unapologetic," *Hartford Courant*, June 22, 2004.

Regarding the eventual resignation of House Speaker Finneran, see Katie Zezima, "Massachusetts Is Getting New Speaker," *New York Times*, September 28, 2004.

After being snared: John Lender, Christopher Keating, and Edmund Mahony, "In Shadow of Probe, Rowland Leaves as WTIC Talk-Show Host," *Hartford Courant*, April 3, 2014.

Finneran pleaded guilty: Erin Ailworth, "After Five Years, Finneran Set to Leave WRKO," *Boston Globe*, May 30, 2012.

The banner headline: Mike Swift, Christopher Keating, Greg Garber, and Matthew Daly, "Dear John . . . ," *Hartford Courant*, May 1, 1999.

"*Shame on Robert Kraft*": Jeff Jacobs, "The Patriots Owner Is Slicker Than a Greased Pig," *Hartford Courant*, May 1, 1999.

the Boston Globe *editorialized*: Scot Lehigh, "'Whining Millionaire' Becomes 'Public Hero,'" *Boston Globe*, May 1, 1999.

Even Globe *sports columnist*: McDonough, "Patriots Owner Had a Terrific Deal."

at the Boston Harbor Hotel: Greg Kruppa, "Kraft, Finneran Act Like Pals at Luncheon," *Boston Globe*, May 14, 1999.

behind closed doors: Will McDonough, "Krafts' Optimism Building; Patriots Owner Eyes New Stadium in 2001," *Boston Globe*, May 29, 1999.

chapter fifteen GETTING BELICHICK

Will McDonough was a primary source: Parcells and Demasio, *Parcells*.

Parcells met with Belichick: Ibid.

"*I've been waiting*": Steve Gutman to Paul Tagliabue, letter, January 7, 2000.

Parcells balled it up: Parcells and Demasio, *Parcells*; and Ian O'Connor, *Belichick: The Making of the Greatest Football Coach of All Time* (New York: Houghton Mifflin Harcourt, 2018).

Robert Kraft announced the dismissal: Patriots press conference, January 3, 2000.

Parcells looked at Belichick: O'Connor, *Belichick*.

"a perfect pass": Rich Cimini, "Inside Bill Belichick's Resignation as the Jets' Coach 20 Years Ago," ESPN, January 1, 2020.

"Why don't you go talk": Ibid.

"By contract arrangement": Taken from video footage provided by NFL Films, dated January 3, 2000.

"If you feel that undecided": Parcells and Demasio, *Parcells*; and Bill Belichick's January 4, 2000, press conference announcing his retirement as head coach of the Jets.

"A deal's a deal": O'Connor, *Belichick*.

"He tried to tell me": Bill Parcells and Will McDonough, *The Final Season: My Last Year as Head Coach in the NFL* (New York, William Morrow, 2000).

Mickey Corcoran: O'Connor, *Belichick*.

As Belichick's workout was winding down: Cimini, "Inside Bill Belichick's Resignation."

Gutman stepped to the lectern: Bill Belichick's January 4, 2000, press conference.

"He's not going to coach": Parcells and McDonough, *The Final Season*.

The headlines in the New York papers: Parcells and Demasio, *Parcells*.

"duplicitous pond scum": Kevin Mannix, "Price Ain't Right," *Boston Herald*, January 5, 2000.

Modell was on record: Zeman, "The Last Straw."

Modell went further: Peter King, "Robert Kraft Made a Mistake and Turned It Into a Dynasty," *Sports Illustrated*, January 30, 2017.

notified the league in a letter: Jeffrey Kessler to Jeffrey Pash, letter, January 11, 2000.

Belichick testified: Paul Tagliabue, decision regarding Belichick's grievance against the Jets, January 21, 2000.

Parcells replied: Ibid.

Kessler argued: "Belichick Files Antitrust Suit," Associated Press, January 25, 2000.

"Hopefully, this press conference will go": Judy Battista, "Jets and Patriots Make Deal for Belichick," *New York Times*, January 28, 2000.

chapter sixteen TOMMY

Some of the information in this chapter was sourced from Charles P. Pierce, *Moving the Chains: Tom Brady and the Pursuit of Everything* (New York: Farrar, Straus and Giroux, 2006) and NFL Films, *Year of the Quarterback: The Brady 6*, 2011.

Carr called him: Pierce, *Moving the Chains*.

two categories: Stout and Johnson, *The Pats*.

"Produces in big spots": Ibid.

chapter seventeen **BUILDING THE CORE**

"This is an unpleasant thing": Patriots press release, May 1, 2000; Mike Freeman, "PRO FOOTBALL: NOTEBOOK: Grier's Career Finishes in New England as Reign Starts," *New York Times*, May 7, 2000.

The New York Times *reported*: Ibid.

"Kraft assured me": Michael Felger, "Bill Won't Wait," *Boston Herald*, January 29, 2000.

a simple two-sentence statement: "Patriots Sign Rookie Draftees Antwan Harris and Tom Brady," Patriots press release, July 14, 2000.

"Who in the hell": Michael Holley, *War Room: The Legacy of Bill Belichick and the Art of Building the Perfect Team* (New York: HarperCollins, 2012).

"you really run a five-point-oh": O'Connor, *Belichick*.

"I can't stand it!": Taken from video footage provided by NFL Films.

The Niners had high expectations: *Year of the Quarterback: The Brady 6*.

"Giving up a number one": Bob Duffy, "War Is Over: Patriots Hire Belichick; Mixed Reviews from Around League," *Boston Globe*, January 28, 2000.

"I am in a way surprised": Ibid.

"A number one is": Ibid.

"Bill Parcells killed Bob Kraft with kindness": Steve Serby, "Parcells Gets Best of Kraft Again: Tuna Knows How to Pull Bob's String," *New York Post*, January 28, 2000.

"snookered": Ted Sarandis, WEEI.

"worth the tariff": Karen Guregian, *Boston Herald*, January 28, 2000.

"In my mind": Nick Cafardo, "Crime, Punishment, and Law: Kraft Addresses Patriots Issues," *Boston Globe*, January 27, 2001.

chapter eighteen **IN AN INSTANT**

"I have expressed over and over": Patriots press conference, March 7, 2001.

"I came up here": Bill Parrillo, "30 Years Later, Bob Kraft Owns All the Best Seats," *Providence Journal*, April 2, 2001.

after undergoing a stress test: O'Connor, *Belichick*.

Belichick's singling out Brady for praise in training camp was taken from video footage provided by NFL Films.

"Good afternoon": NBC broadcast.

chapter nineteen CHANGING PLACES

"We used to call him Doom": Ken Rodgers, *The Two Bills*, NFL Films.

Bryan Cox put it more succinctly: Christopher Price, "Bryan Cox on the 2001 Hit That Started the Patriots Dynasty," WEEI Sports Radio Network, January 31, 2017.

He once advised his friend: Holley, *War Room*.

"Cool-hand Tom": Nick Cafardo, "Something Special: Brady-Led Rally Erases Mates' Earlier Errors," *Boston Globe*, October 15, 2001.

"Next question": Patriots press conference, November 20, 2001, video footage provided by NFL Films.

Ron Borges accused Belichick of lying: Ron Borges, "There's a Risk Factor at Work for Belichick," *Boston Globe*, November 22, 2001.

chapter twenty THE PERFECT STORM

"We're gonna get this one": Video footage provided by NFL Films.

"Three by one": Video footage provided by NFL Films.

Al Davis was furious: *Tuck Rule*, NFL Films, October 2017.

had anticipated the backlash: Ibid.

chapter twenty-one WE ARE ALL PATRIOTS

Statistics at the top of chapter twenty-one were provided to author by CBS Sports via email on May 21, 2019.

Descriptions of the Pittsburgh Steelers game are based on video footage provided by NFL Films.

Postgame descriptions are based on video footage provided by NFL Films.

For information about the NFL's decision to ask U2 to perform at the 2001 Super Bowl halftime show, see *U2's "Beautiful Day" & Super Bowl XXXVI Halftime Show Helps Heal America after 9/11*, NFL Films.

Dialogue from U2's pre-Super Bowl press conference taken from video footage provided by NFL Films.

"Tonight, the dynasty is born": Video footage provided by NFL Films.

The description of U2's halftime performance is based on *U2's "Beautiful Day" & Super Bowl XXXVI Halftime Show*.

"the best coaching job": Rob Fleder, *Sports Illustrated Great Football Writing* (New York: Liberty Street, 2012).

The interaction between Brady and Belichick in the hotel room after the Super
  Bowl is based on Michael Silver, "Pat Answer: Following the Lead of Their
  Transformed Coach and Oh-So-Cool Quarterback, the No-Name Patriots Stun
  the Rams in Super Bowl XXXVI," *Sports Illustrated*, February 11, 2002.

chapter twenty-two GROWING PAINS

The New York Times *called*: Thomas George, "On Final Play, Patriots Claim the
  Super Bowl," *New York Times*, February 4, 2002.
Belichick turned to Brady: NFL roundtable interview when Brady was added to the
  NFL 100 All-Time Team, December 27, 2019.
"A football team": "Bledsoe Heads to Buffalo for 2003 pick," ESPN, April 21, 2002.
Charlie Weis explained: Albert Breer, "Five Belichick Protégés Explain His Two De-
  cades of Patriots Success," *Sports Illustrated*, January 31, 2019.
the emotional detachment: Peter King, "A League of Their Own: The Patriots
  Marched to an NFL-Record 19th Straight Win by Overwhelming the Dolphins
  in a Classic Display of the Brand of Football that Makes Bill Belichick's Team So
  Special," *Sports Illustrated*, October 18, 2004.
"a simply gratuitous effort": *Rodney Harrison: A Football Life*, NFL Films, September
  23, 2016.
"I just had never seen": Ibid.
"I had to bring Rodney": Ibid.
"The NFL is a cold business": Ty Law, "Letter to My Younger Self," *Players' Tribune*,
  January 17, 2019.
Kevin Mannix called: O'Connor, *Belichick*.
"I'm not as fully committed": Peter King, "Surprise! Surprise!" *Sports Illustrated*, Sep-
  tember 15, 2003.

chapter twenty-three ALL IN THE FAMILY

"Bill yelled at us": Ken Rodgers and Mike Viney, *3 Games to Glory II*, NFL Films, 2003.
"He was flat wrong": Ibid.
"It's like pornography": Michael Silver, "Cool Customer: Fresh Off a Storybook Sea-
  son in Which He Quarterbacked the Patriots to a Super Bowl Victory at Age
  24, Tom Brady Is Learning to Cope with the Blitz of Newfound Fame," *Sports
  Illustrated*, April 15, 2002.
As linebacker Mike Vrabel put it: King, "A League of Their Own."
Players were looking at each other: Rodgers and Viney, *3 Games to Glory II*.

"Great game!": Ken Berger, "Pats' Nasty Hits KO Colts: Physical 'D' Takes Away Indy's Game," *New York Newsday*, January 18, 2004.

"Let's put this week in perspective": Michael Silver, "Fight to the Finish: New England and Carolina Went Toe-to-Toe, but Tom Brady Kept His Cool and Led the Patriots to Their Second NFL Title in Three Years," *Sports Illustrated*, February 9, 2004.

"Fuck you": Holley, *Patriot Reign*.

chapter twenty-four LEAGUE OF THEIR OWN

Michael Powell called the exposure: Colin McEnroe, "Naked Coverup," *Hartford Courant*, February 8, 2004.

MTV Networks blamed: Bill Carter and Richard Sandomir, "Pro Football: Halftime-Show Fallout Includes F.C.C. Inquiry," *New York Times*, February 3, 2004.

The description of the scene at Boston City Hall Plaza on February 3, 2004, is based on video footage provided by Kraft Sports.

called to testify: Subcommittee on Energy and Commerce hearings regarding the Broadcast Decency Enforcement Act of 2004, February 11 and 26, 2004.

For information about Howard Stern's firing, see "Howard Stern's Radio Show Is Suspended by Clear Channel," *Bloomberg News*, February 26, 2004.

"Think how long it's been": King, "A League of Their Own."

chapter twenty-five A DAY IN THE LIFE

"The way the NFL works": Tom Brady, interview by Steve Kroft, part two, *60 Minutes*, November 4, 2004.

"Brady carries it off like Gary Cooper": David Kamp, "The Best There Ever Was?" *GQ*, August 10, 2005.

Charles P. Pierce caught up: Pierce, *Moving the Chains*.

value of $1 billion: Monte Burke, "Unlikely Dynasty: Robert Kraft Has Used Business Sense and a Fan's Blind Faith to Turn Once-Laughable New England Patriots into One of the Richest Franchises in Sports," *Forbes*, September 19, 2005.

Forbes *even put Kraft on the cover*: Ibid.

The Associated Press reported: "Russian President Gets Super Gift from Patriots Owner," Associated Press, June 29, 2005.

"an international incident": Donovan Slack, "For Putin, It's a Gem of a Cultural Exchange: Kraft Hands over Super Bowl Ring," *Boston Globe*, June 29, 2005.

For information about Ted Johnson's physical and neurological injuries, see Alan Schwarz, "Dark Days Follow Hard-Hitting Days in N.F.L.," *New York Times*, February 2, 2007.

For general information about the cultural awareness of CTE, see Mark Fainaru-
    Wada and Steve Fainaru, *League of Denial: The NFL, Concussions, and the Battle
    for Truth* (New York: Crown Archetype, 2013).
"It is with deep regret": Patriots press release, July 28, 2005.
"Although his retirement is unexpected": Ibid.
"We went from": O'Connor, *Belichick*.

chapter twenty-six LOSS

As one opposing scout put it: Paul Zimmerman, "New England Patriots: Never Mind
    That Both Coordinators and a Pair of Starting Linebackers Had to Be Replaced.
    Nothing Seems to Rattle the Two-Time Defending Champs," *Sports Illustrated*,
    September 5, 2005.
"I need time": Jackie MacMullan, "Bruschi Will Try to Return: After Checking With
    Doctors, Linebacker Confirms Bye Week Is Perfect Time," *Boston Globe*, Octo-
    ber 15, 2005.
Bruschi had met with Dr. Greer: Tedy Bruschi and Michael Holley, *Never Give Up:
    My Stroke, My Recovery, and My Return to the NFL* (Hoboken, NJ: John Wiley &
    Sons, 2007).
a laudatory book: David Halberstam, *The Education of a Coach* (New York: Hachette
    Books, 2005).
Sports Illustrated *hyped*: *Sports Illustrated*, November 7, 2005.
"on a personal note": Video footage provided by NFL Films.
For Belichick's eulogy, see O'Connor, *Belichick*.
The first book: Bill Belichick, CBS Sports interview, October 3, 2005.
"You were the real strength": O'Connor, *Belichick*.
"Dad, may you rest in peace": Ibid.
For Rear Admiral Thomas C. Lynch's anecdotes about Stephen Belichick, see
    O'Connor, *Belichick*.
The description of the scene between Tom Brady and Israeli soldiers is based on
    Lazar Berman, "In Super Bowl Matchup, Pats Have Israel Connection Covered,"
    Times of Israel, February 1, 2015.

chapter twenty-seven RELOAD

"It's now official": Carl Bialik and Jason Fry, "Vinatieri Leaves Patriots Behind, Fuel-
    ing Wrath in New England," *Wall Street Journal*, March 22, 2006.
For Adam Vinatieri's quotes on leaving the Patriots, see Jackie MacMullan, "Vin-
    atieri Shunned Patriots," *Boston Globe*, August 10, 2006.

"I think everybody in this town": O'Connor, *Belichick*.

a representative for Moynahan: Mark Dagostino, "Tom Brady, Bridget Moynahan Split Up," *People*, December 14, 2006.

Brady and Bündchen met at: Nora Princiotti, "The Patriots' Offseason Has Been Fun to Watch," *Boston Globe*, February 7, 2020.

"I knew right away": Leslie Bennetts, "And God Created Gisele," *Vanity Fair*, March 30, 2009.

While they were there: Charlotte Triggs, "Tom Brady 'Excited' about Ex's Pregnancy," *People*, February 20, 2007.

Bündchen later explained: Gisele Bündchen, *Lessons: My Path to a Meaningful Life* (New York: Avery, 2018).

The description of Bill Belichick shoving a *Boston Globe* photographer is based on Brian McGrory, "Candid Camera," *Boston Globe*, January 9, 2007.

"Here's Belichick's problem": Ibid.

For Bob Costas quote, see Bella English, "After a Bruising Year, Belichick Opens Up: Patriots Head Coach Admits He Made Some Mistakes," *Boston Globe*, March 4, 2007.

For information about Belichick's alleged affair, see Susan Edelman, "'Sugar Daddy' Belichick," *New York Post*, February 25, 2007.

Johnson appeared on the front page: Schwarz, "Dark Days Follow Hard-Hitting Days in N.F.L."

Jackie MacMullan published: Jackie MacMullan, "'I Don't Want Anyone to End Up Like Me': Plagued by Post-Concussion Syndrome and Battling an Amphetamine Addiction, Former Patriots Linebacker Ted Johnson Is a Shell of His Former Self," *Boston Globe*, February 2, 2007.

For Ted Johnson's description of his heated confrontation with Bill Belichick in August 2002, see MacMullan, "'I Don't Want Anyone to End Up Like Me.'" Ian O'Connor describes the dialogue between the two men slightly differently; see O'Connor, *Belichick*.

Belichick sat for an extraordinary interview: English, "After a Bruising Year, Belichick Opens Up."

"Some of them I love": Ibid.

"One of the reasons": Ibid.

English also talked to: Ibid.

For dialogue between Randy Moss and Bill Belichick, see O'Connor, *Belichick*; Ryan Wilson, "Randy Moss Explains Why He Cursed Out Bill Belichick after Trade to Pats," *CBS Sports*, November 2, 2016; Randy Moss, interview by New England Sports Network, July 16, 2018; "Apparent Leg Injury Ends Randy Moss's

Workout Early," Associated Press, August 1, 2007; and author interview with Randy Moss.

Rolling Stone *had declared*: *Rolling Stone*, September 2000.

"no one was safe": "The Lead: Antonio," *The Peter King Podcast*, NBC Sports, September 9, 2019.

chapter twenty-eight: TRANSCENDENCE

Running back Kevin Faulk pulled: Zach Braziller, "Beware of a Fired-Up Tom Brady," *New York Post*, May 2, 2020.

The headline in Wednesday morning's: Tom Pedulla, "Pats Go on the Defensive: Videotaping Incident Raises Questions of Integrity," *USA Today*, September 13, 2007.

"If Bill Belichick is indeed guilty": Gary Myers, "Super Stupid HC Must Pay," *New York Daily News*, September 12, 2007.

the headline in USA Today: Tom Pedulla, "Belichick Apologizes, Waits: Pats Coach Faces NFL Discipline for Signal Stealing," *USA Today*, September 13, 2007.

Christine Brennan wrote: Christine Brennan, "Cheating No Shock, Given Its History," *USA Today*, September 13, 2007.

columnist Dave Anderson wrote: Dave Anderson, "A Model Franchise Sprouts a Blemish," *New York Times*, September 13, 2007.

Tom Pedulla chimed in: Pedulla, "Belichick Apologizes, Waits."

Hines Ward insisted: Pedulla, "Pats Go on the Defensive."

Following Goodell's ruling: Rich Cimini, "Spygate Slams on Bill: Half-Million Reasons for Belicheat to Scowl," *New York Daily News*, September 14, 2007.

Belichick issued a second . . . apology: "Statement from Patriots Head Coach Bill Belichick," Patriots press release, September 13, 2007.

"What would Steve Belichick say": Peter Gelzinis, "Coach Betrays Father's Legacy," *Boston Herald*, September 14, 2007.

players wore white T-shirts: Larry Weisman, "A Clash of Styles; It's Dungy's Cool Confidence vs. Belichick's War Games as Colts Face Patriots," *USA Today*, November 2, 2007.

the media stepped up its characterization: Mike Bianchi, "Game Embodies Battle of Good versus Evil: Tony Terrific Taking on Bill BeliCheat," *Orlando Sentinel*, November 3, 2007.

For the quote from former senator Arlen Specter, see Greg Bishop and Pete Thamel, "Senator Wants N.F.L. Spying Case Explained," *New York Times*, February 1, 2008.

"What do you want us to do?": Christopher L. Gasper, "Patriots Humiliate Redskins in 52–7 Drubbing," *Boston Globe*, October 29, 2007.

an audience record: Statistics provided by CBS Sports.

Belichick walked up: Video footage provided by NFL Films.

Belichick stopped him: Ibid.

chapter twenty-nine INCONSOLABLE

"We wanted to take and destroy": "Senator Wants to Know Why NFL Destroyed Patriots Spy Tapes," ESPN, February 1, 2008.

he had never seen a tape: Bill Belichick, press conference, April 1, 2008.

one Giants official said: O'Connor, *Belichick*.

O'Hara would later admit: Ibid.

"I was given assurances": Peter King, "The Man of the Hour," *Sports Illustrated*, February 7, 2011.

"I did not make any assurances": Ibid.

"You'll have to talk to the Jets": Belichick, press conference, April 1, 2008.

The description of the scene with Elton John is based in part on video footage from Kraft Sports.

"He was in a lot of pain": "Brady to Have Season-Ending Knee Surgery, Will Be Placed on IR," NFL News, September 9, 2008.

His players, he said, were always taught: Dan Shaughnessy, "A Perfectly Miserable Development," *Boston Globe*, September 9, 2008.

"We feel badly for Tom": "Brady to Have Season-Ending Knee Surgery."

chapter thirty ALLOW ME TO REINTRODUCE MYSELF

For Gisele Bündchen's quote and insight, see Bennetts, "And God Created Gisele."

Belichick had a conversation with Rick Gosselin: Hayden Bird, "Bill Belichick Credits a Sportswriter for Helping Him Find Julian Edelman," Boston.com, February 4, 2019.

"Brady, how long have you": Jenny Verentas, "The Tale of Tom Brady and Johnny Foxborough," *Sports Illustrated*, January 18, 2017.

Belichick turned to him: *Bill Belichick: A Football Life, Part I*, NFL Films.

The conversation between Wes Welker and Belichick is taken from *Bill Belichick: A Football Life, Part I*.

"I have a lot to learn": Chris Forsberg, "Edelman Gets off to Fast Start; Rookie's Debut Is One to Remember," *Boston Globe*, August 14, 2009.

The dialogue between Brady and Belichick during the Buffalo Bills game is based on video footage provided by NFL Films.

The dialogue between Brady and Belichick during the Saints game is based on video footage provided by NFL Films.

"*I'd have been booing us, too*": Dan Shaughnessy, "In the End, They're Mere Mortals," *Boston Globe*, January 11, 2010.

"*It was great while it lasted*": Ibid.

chapter thirty-one NO PLACE LIKE HOME

they formed a huddle: Rob Gronkowski and Jason Rosenhaus, *It's Good to Be Gronk* (New York: Gallery Books, 2015).

"*We all know what we saw*": Bob Ryan, "Truth Hurts Regarding Brady," *Boston Globe*, January 11, 2010.

Brady was so furious: Gronkowski and Rosenhaus, *It's Good to Be Gronk*.

The description of the scene with Tom Brady and Gisele Bündchen along the Charles River is based on video footage from Gotham Chopra's documentary series *Tom vs. Time* (episode 4, "The Emotional Game"), Facebook Watch, 2018.

chapter thirty-two THE PASSING

Gronkowski subsequently learned: Gronkowski and Rosenhaus, *It's Good to Be Gronk*.

unwanted headlines: Olivia Vanni, "Porn Star Calls Rob Gronkowski 'A Gentleman,'" *Boston Herald*, October 25, 2011; Gayle Fee, "Get the Gronk Party Started!" *Boston Herald*, November 16, 2011.

that Sports Illustrated *called "amazing":* Sports Illustrated, December 19, 2011.

columnist Frank Bruni dubbed him: Frank Bruni, "Tim Tebow's Gospel of Optimism," *New York Times*, December 10, 2011.

chapter thirty-three BREAKING BAD

Coughlin told Sports Illustrated: Peter King, "Déjà Vu All Over Again," *Sports Illustrated*, January 30, 2012.

"*They have won three titles*": Judy Battista, "Giants Beat Patriots in Final Rally," *New York Times*, February 5, 2012.

Sports Illustrated *dubbed him:* Chris Ballard, "The Last Happy Man," *Sports Illustrated*, September 3, 2012.

Gronkowski smiled and quipped: Ibid.

he posed naked: Body Issue, *ESPN The Magazine*, July 2010.

For information about Aaron Hernandez's life and crimes, see *Boston Globe*'s Spotlight Team Bob Hohler, Beth Healy, Sacha Pfeiffer, Andrew Ryan, and editor Patricia Wen, "GLADIATOR: Aaron Hernandez and Football Inc.," a six-part series in the *Boston Globe*, and the accompanying seven-part podcast of the same name made with Wondery.

had beaten him: Bob Hohler, Beth Healy, Sacha Pfeiffer, Andrew Ryan, and editor Patricia Wen, "GLADIATOR: Aaron Hernandez and Football Inc.: Behind the Smile," *Boston Globe*, October 14, 2018.

For information about Hernandez's parents' criminal records, see "GLADIATOR: Aaron Hernandez and Football Inc.: Behind the Smile."

"I was the happiest fucking little kid": Geno McDermott, *Killer Inside: The Mind of Aaron Hernandez*, Netflix, January 15, 2020.

"I get my respect through weapons": "GLADIATOR: Aaron Hernandez and Football Inc.: Hail Mary," podcast, *Boston Globe* and Wondery.

The window in Hernandez's vehicle: "GLADIATOR: Aaron Hernandez and Football Inc.: The Patriot Way," podcast, *Boston Globe* and Wondery.

"You can't come here and act reckless": Chris Brodeur, "Connecticut Sports Decade in Review: The Rise and Fall of Aaron Hernandez," *Hartford Courant*, December 31, 2019.

homicide detectives in Boston: "GLADIATOR: Aaron Hernandez and Football Inc.: The Patriot Way."

"He wants to play until he's forty": NFL Preview edition, *Sports Illustrated*, September 3, 2012.

For Wes Welker's warning to Brandon Lloyd, see Bob Hohler, Beth Healy, Sacha Pfeiffer, Andrew Ryan, and editor Patricia Wen, "GLADIATOR: Aaron Hernandez and Football Inc.: Running for Glory, and for His Life," *Boston Globe*, October 16, 2018; "GLADIATOR: Aaron Hernandez and Football Inc.: Hail Mary," podcast.

"There would be swings": "GLADIATOR: Aaron Hernandez and Football Inc.: Running for Glory, and for His Life"; "GLADIATOR: Aaron Hernandez and Football Inc.: Hail Mary," podcast.

With a surgically implanted: Gronkowski and Rosenhaus, *It's Good to Be Gronk*.

"The Ravens are going to the Super Bowl!": Michael Vega, "After Uproar, He Calmed Down: Suggs Says He Respects Patriots," *Boston Globe*, January 22, 2013.

"These are the most arrogant pricks": Jim Hoban, "Shots from All Angles: CBS's Sharpe, Suggs Rip Patriots," *Boston Globe*, January 21, 2013.

chapter thirty-four MOVING ON

Edelman nicknamed him Mr. Miyagi: Jim McBride, "Exhibition Slate Announced," *Boston Globe*, April 12, 2018.

he wanted Welker to be: Erik Frenz, "Illustrating Life Without Wes Welker for Tom Brady and the Patriots Offense," *Bleacher Report*, April 5, 2013.

For Welker's quote on Belichick, see Tyler Conway, "Wes Welker Speaks Out on Difficulties Playing Under Bill Belichick," *Bleacher Report*, August 7, 2013.

For the text message from Tom Brady to Aaron Hernandez, see Bob Hohler, Beth Healy, Sacha Pfeiffer, Andrew Ryan, and editor Patricia Wen, "GLADIATOR: Aaron Hernandez and Football Inc.: A Killer in the Huddle," *Boston Globe*, October 17, 2018.

For the text messages between Bill Belichick and Aaron Hernandez, see "GLADIATOR: Aaron Hernandez and Football Inc.: A Killer in the Huddle."

For the text message from Alexander Bradley to Aaron Hernandez, see "GLADIATOR: Aaron Hernandez and Football Inc.: A Killer in the Huddle"; "GLADIATOR: Aaron Hernandez and Football Inc.: The Patriot Way," podcast.

an ex-con to be his bodyguard: Ibid.

For the text messages between Aaron Hernandez and Alex Guerrero, see Bob Hohler, Beth Healy, Sacha Pfeiffer, Andrew Ryan, and editor Patricia Wen, "GLADIATOR: Aaron Hernandez and Football Inc.: A Terrible Thing to Waste," *Boston Globe*, October 19, 2018.

Hernandez also met with Belichick: "GLADIATOR: Aaron Hernandez and Football Inc.: A Killer in the Huddle."

The next day, the headline: Bill Pennington, "Former Patriots Tight End Is Charged with Murder," *New York Times*, June 26, 2013.

For Bill Belichick's comments on Aaron Hernandez's arrest, see Bill Belichick, press conference, July 24, 2013.

"When I'm answering questions": John Breech, "Wes Welker on Playing for Bill Belichick: 'It Was Just Kind of Hard,'" CBS Sports, August 7, 2013.

in a column titled: Dan Shaughnessy, "Not Good Enough: Terrific Season, but Talent Just Isn't There," *Boston Globe*, January 20, 2014.

chapter thirty-five ON TO CINCINNATI

"Casino security called officers": "Ravens Running Back Ray Rice Arrested after Incident in Atlantic City," *Baltimore Sun*, February 16, 2014.

TMZ released video: "Ray Rice Cut, Then Suspended by NFL," ESPN, September 8, 2014.

"a dearth of sensitivity": Mike Wise, "Goodell Fails to Use the 'Shield' to Serve and Protect in NFL's Handling of Rice Situation," *Washington Post*, July 30, 2014.

Don Banks called the two-game suspension: "Was the NFL Too Lenient on Ray Rice?" WBUR Public Radio, July 31, 2014.

"I didn't get it right": Mark Maske, "NFL Gets Tough on Domestic Violence," *Washington Post*, August 29, 2014.

Ray McDonald was arrested: Gary Myers, "49ers' Defensive End Ray McDonald Arrested for Domestic Violence against Pregnant Fiancée," *New York Daily News*, September 1, 2014.

TMZ released video taken from inside: "RAY RICE; ELEVATOR KNOCKOUT: Fiancée Takes Crushing Blow (Video)," TMZ Sports, September 8, 2014.

"The NFL has lost its way": "NOW Wants Roger Goodell Out," ESPN, September 10, 2014.

"He had no knowledge": Robert Kraft, interview by Charlie Rose, *CBS This Morning*, September 9, 2014.

For interview dialogue between Norah O'Donnell and Roger Goodell, see *CBS This Morning*, September 9, 2014.

NFL retained former FBI director: John Breech, "NFL: Ex-FBI Director Robert Mueller Will Investigate Ray Rice Situation," CBS Sports, September 10, 2014.

For information about Adrian Peterson, see Steve Eder and Pat Borzi, "N.F.L. Rocked Again as Adrian Peterson Faces a Child Abuse Case," *New York Times*, September 12, 2014.

a bipartisan group: Marissa Payne, "Female Senators Call on the NFL to Institute a 'Zero-Tolerance' Domestic Violence Policy," *Washington Post*, September 11, 2014.

"We're on to Cincinnati": Bill Belichick, press conference, October 1, 2014.

The description of the Cincinnati Bengals game is based on footage provided by NFL Films.

"But fifty thousand yards, Tom": Video footage provided by NFL Films.

The description of the Denver Broncos game is based on video footage provided by NFL Films.

For more information about Robert Mueller's NFL report, see Robert S. Mueller III, "Report to the National Football League of an Independent Investigation into the Ray Rice Incident," WilmerHale, January 8, 2015.

"This matter has tarnished": Ken Belson and Steve Eder, "In Ray Rice Case, N.F.L. Chose Not to Ask Many Questions," *New York Times*, January 8, 2015.

Coach Harbaugh criticized: Sara Barshop, "John Harbaugh: Patriots Committed Deceptive, Illegal Substitutions," *Sports Illustrated*, January 10, 2015.

The email read, in part: email to Ryan Grigson, January 17, 2015, at 12:01:53 p.m.

"chatter throughout the league": Ted Wells, "Investigative Report Concerning Footballs Used during the AFC Championship Game on January 18, 2015," May 6, 2015.

"We are playing with a small ball": Troy Vincent testimony, "Key Points in Tom Brady's Documents on Deflategate," *Boston Globe*, August 5, 2015.

ball number 7: Wells, "Investigative Report."

According to one gauge: Ibid.

"We're on to Seattle": CBS broadcast, January 17, 2015.

chapter thirty-six THE ENVY OF THE LEAGUE

For quoted text messages in this chapter, see Wells, "Investigative Report."

he discovered a text: Bryan Curtis, "The Paranoid Style in Sportswriting," *Grantland*, February 11, 2015.

Kravitz tweeted: Bob Kravitz, tweet from @bkravitz, January 15, 2019.

Glauber sent out his own tweet: "Kravitz: Source Says NFL Investigating if Patriots Deflated Footballs in DeflateGate Scandal," WTHR, January 19, 2015.

For information about how Jastremski prepped the Patriots' footballs, see Wells, "Investigative Report."

"Can't explain it": Ibid.

Chris Mortensen tweeted: Chris Mortensen, tweet from @mortreport, January 20, 2015, 10:57 p.m. (The tweet was later deleted, and Mortensen acknowledged his handling of the tweet was a mistake.)

the Washington Post *ran*: "Report: NFL Finds 11 of 12 Patriots Balls to Be Underinflated by Two Pounds," *Washington Post*, January 21, 2015.

He fielded sixty-one questions: O'Connor, *Belichick*.

Charles Pierce's quotes come from Pierce's writing in "Brady, Belichick, and Great Balls of Fire: A Front-Row Seat for the Foxborough Farce," *Grantland*, January 23, 2015.

For Troy Aikman's quote, see Michael Hurly, "Tom Brady's DeflateGate Revenge Tour Includes Troy Aikman," CBS Boston, January 23, 2017.

For Hines Ward's quote, see Scott Stump, "Hines Ward: If Guilty in Deflate-Gate, Patriots' Punishment Should Be 'Very Harsh,'" *Today*, January 22, 2015.

For Richard Sherman's quote, see Cindy Boren, "Richard Sherman Rips Tom Brady, Deflates 'Clean-Cut' Reputation," *Washington Post*, January 22, 2015.

Pash reached out: Wells, "Investigative Report."

"The investigation is being led jointly": NFL statement, January 23, 2015.

The Deflategate cold-open sketch from season forty of *Saturday Night Live* aired January 25, 2015.

"*We need a big championship drive*": Peter King, "The Super Bowl Story, According to Tom Brady," *Sports Illustrated*, February 9, 2015.

chapter thirty-seven **NEW ENGLAND VERSUS EVERYBODY**

The description of the Lombardi Trophy presentation is based on *America's Game: The 2014 New England Patriots*, NFL Films.

"*Here to present the Lombardi Trophy*": NBC broadcast, February 1, 2015.

"*quintessential Brady*": Bill Pennington, "A Quarterback Measured Only by Titles Refreshes His Legacy with a 4th," *New York Times*, February 2, 2015.

"*I've got a lot of football left*": Ibid.

The description of the 2015 victory parade is based on news footage and video footage provided by the Patriots.

A physicist working: Wells, "Investigative Report."

"*routine for McNally*": Ibid.

"*The refs fucked us*": Ibid.

"*Fuck Tom*": Ibid.

He could make a thousand good decisions: Kamp, "The Best There Ever Was?"

"*In my almost forty years of practice*": Transcript of the arbitration hearing before NFL Commissioner Roger Goodell, June 23, 2015.

comparisons to Paul Revere: Bill Pennington, "How Tom Brady Became New England's Favorite Adopted Son," *New York Times*, February 1, 2019.

On Gisele's announcing her retirement, see Julie Miller, "Gisele Retires as a Runway Model," *Vanity Fair*, April 15, 2015.

For President Barack Obama's remarks, see the official transcript from April 23, 2015.

For Maura Healy's quote, see "Deflategate versus Domestic Violence Punishments: Priorities Out of Line, AG Says," WCVB, May 12, 2015.

"*We all know why we are here*": Transcript of arbitration hearing, June 23, 2015.

"*Mr. Brady . . . participated in a scheme*": Roger Goodell, final decision, July 28, 2015.

reporters with a PACER . . . account: Ben Volin, "E-mails Open a Window into the Life of Tom Brady," *Boston Globe*, August 6, 2015.

"*I don't know what to make*": Oral arguments, August 12, 2015.

For information about Judge Berman's decision, see "Decision & Order," United States District Court Southern District of New York, September 3, 2015.

"*Ah, Roger . . . being King isn't what it used to be*": Michael Powell, "For His Arrogance in Tom Brady Ruling, Roger Goodell Pays the Price," *New York Times*, September 4, 2015.

For the ELATEGATE cover, see *Sports Illustrated*, September 14, 2015.

"*It's just guys getting justice*": Bernie Augustine, "Seahawks' Richard Sherman on

Tom Brady and Patriots: It's Not Cheating If You Don't Get Caught," *New York Daily News*, September 10, 2015.

For the controversial story on Alex Guerrero, see Chris Sweeny, "Tom Brady's Personal Guru Is a Glorified Snake-Oil Salesman," *Boston Magazine*, October 9, 2015.

"this sounds like quackery": Mike Reiss, "In Different-from-Norm Radio Interview, Tom Brady Opens Up on 'His Calling,'" ESPN, October 12, 2015.

"Everyone thinks I'm a kook": Mark Leibovich, "Man Out of Time," *New York Times Magazine*, February 1, 2015.

The description of the attire worn by Colts fans is based on video footage provided by NFL Films.

chapter thirty-eight NO ONE KNOWS WHERE THE TOP IS

David Gelb, *Jiro Dreams of Sushi*, Magnolia Pictures, 2011.

For information about the Court of Appeals' reinstatement of Tom Brady's suspension, see Ken Belson, "N.F.L. Wins Appeal, and Tom Brady Has Little Recourse," *New York Times*, April 25, 2016.

Boston *magazine reported*: Matt Juul, "Tom Brady Sunbathed Nude in Italy During Vacation with Gisele," *Boston*, September 27, 2016.

The description of the scene of Tom Brady's first day off suspension is based on video footage provided by NFL Films.

"He always had this look in his eye": LeGarrette Blount, *America's Game: The 2016 New England Patriots*, NFL Films.

"I know that's TB": Don't'a Hightower, *America's Game: The 2016 New England Patriots*.

"Hey, Twelve": Julian Edelman, *America's Game: The 2016 New England Patriots*.

"Everyone's looking around": Ibid.

Trump asked him to judge: Mike Cole, "Tom Brady on Howard Stern Recap: What We Learned From QB's Interview," NESN, April 8, 2020.

he wanted Brady to speak: Ibid.

For Bill Belichick's letter to Donald Trump, see "Trump Reads Letter from Supporter Bill Belichick at Rally," CNN, November 7, 2016.

For information about how Tom Brady and Gisele Bündchen voted, see Alan Rappeport, "Did Tom Brady and Gisele Bündchen Back Donald Trump? She Says No, and He's Not Saying," *New York Times*, November 8, 2016.

Edelman had written: Julian Edelman and Assaf Swissa, *Flying High*, illustrated by David Leonhardt (Superdigital, 2016).

"My dad used to always tell me": Edelman, *America's Game: The 2016 New England Patriots*.

chapter thirty-nine **LORD OF THE RINGS**

The description of Super Bowl LI is based on video footage provided by NFL Films.
For Alex Guerrero's quote about him and Brady believing, see Greg Bishop, "Suspend Disbelief," *Sports Illustrated*, February 13, 2017.

chapter forty **HEAVY IS THE CROWN**

She was . . . "dead serious": Greg Bishop, "Hand of God Part II," *Sports Illustrated*, January 29, 2018.
"Two more to go": Chopra, *Tom vs. Time* (episode 5, "The Spiritual Game").
"Football . . . is his first love": Ibid.
"Your husband said the other day": Gisele Bündchen, interview by Charlie Rose, *CBS This Morning*, May 16, 2018.
"Is Galynn there?": Chopra, *Tom vs. Time* (episode 4, "The Emotional Game").
"Forty's just a number": Chopra, *Tom vs. Time* (episode 3, "The Social Game").
For the *Sports Illustrated* headline, see the September 4, 2017, issue.

chapter forty-one **TENSION**

"'Get that son of a bitch off the field'": Ken Belson and Julie Davis, "Trump Attacks Warriors' Curry. LeBron James's Retort: 'U Bum,'" *New York Times*, September 23, 2017.
For the NFL's statement in response to President Trump, see Belson and Davis, "Trump Attacks Warriors' Curry."
For information about President Trump's feud with Steph Curry and LeBron James, see Belson and Davis, "Trump Attacks Warriors' Curry"; Benjamin Hoffman, "Trump's Comments on N.F.L. and Stephen Curry Draw Intense Reaction," *New York Times*, September 23, 2017.
"I don't feel accepted": Deena Zaru, "Another Patriots Player Skipping White House Visit over Trump," CNN, August 16, 2017.
McCourty tweeted: "Devin McCourty, NFL Respond to Trump's Comments on League, Anthem Protests," NESN, September 23, 2017.
"I am deeply disappointed": Robert Kraft, statement, September 24, 2017.
it was Kraft's pointed words: "The Day the Real Patriots Took a Knee," *New York Times*, September 24, 2017.
"If NFL fans refuse to go": Abby Philip and Cindy Boren, "Players, Owners Unite as Trump Demands NFL 'Fire or Suspend' Players or Risk Fan Boycott," *Washington Post*, September 24, 2017.

Tom Brady released: Tom Brady, *The TB12 Method: How to Achieve a Lifetime of Sustained Peak Performance* (New York: Simon & Schuster, 2017).

2,623 NFL-focused tweets: Andrew Beaton, "How Russian Trolls Inflamed the NFL's Anthem Controversy," *Wall Street Journal*, October 22, 2018.

"VIDEO: Trump SHREDS": Ibid.

"Trump Supporters SACK NFL": Ibid.

attention of the Senate Intelligence Committee: Devlin Barrett, "Lawmaker: Russian Trolls Trying to Sow Discord in NFL Kneeling Debate," *Washington Post*, September 27, 2017.

For Senator James Lankford's comments, see Barrett, "Lawmaker: Russian Trolls Trying."

Jerry Jones, who had taken a knee: Benjamin Hoffman and Ken Belson, "Here's What Every N.F.L. Team Did during the National Anthem on Sunday," *New York Times*, October 2, 2017.

threatened to bench: Ken Belson, "Goodell and N.F.L. Owners Break from Players on Anthem Kneeling Fight," *New York Times*, October 10, 2017.

For information about the roundtable discussion between NFL owners and players, see Seth Wickersham and Don Van Natta Jr., "Standing Down," *ESPN The Magazine*, November 13, 2017.

"You guys aren't supporting": Ibid.

"the elephant in the room": Ken Belson and Mark Leibovich, "Inside the Confidential N.F.L. Meeting to Discuss National Anthem Protests," *New York Times*, April 25, 2018.

"baited by Trump": Ibid.

"We can't have the inmates": Wickersham and Van Natta Jr., "Standing Down."

For the magazine cover with Tom Brady's aged face, see *ESPN The Magazine*, November 13, 2017.

Brady told the magazine: Tom Junod and Seth Wickersham, "Tom Brady's Most Dangerous Game," *ESPN The Magazine*, November 13, 2017.

"[Elliott] engaged in physical violence": Austin Knoblauch, "Cowboys' Ezekiel Elliott Suspended Six Games by NFL," NFL News, August 11, 2017.

threatening to sue: Ken Belson, "N.F.L. Denies Jerry Jones's Call for Special Owners Meeting," *New York Times*, November 16, 2017.

a private phone call: Don Van Natta Jr. and Seth Wickersham, "Roger Goodell Has a Jerry Jones Problem, and Nobody Knows How It Will End," *ESPN Outside the Lines*, November 17, 2017.

"Bob Kraft is a pussy": Ibid.

"Belichick curbs privileges": Bob Hohler, "Belichick Pushing Back on Brady's Guru: As Players Seek Guerrero's Alternative Treatment, Coach Curbs His Privileges," *Boston Globe*, December 20, 2017.

a sensational story: Seth Wickersham, "For Kraft, Brady and Belichick, Is This the Beginning of the End?" ESPN, January 5, 2018.

"The Patriots haven't been as angry": Peter King, "Monday Morning Quarterback."

For *New York Times* article, see Joe Drape, "Tom Brady's Midlife Crisis," *New York Times*, January 11, 2018.

chapter forty-two **THREADING THE NEEDLE**

At 3:18 p.m.: "The Times of Hand," *Sports Illustrated*, January 29, 2018.

His teammates told reporters: Ibid.

On Friday morning: Ibid.

For the John Malkovich commercial, see "Teasing John Malkovich," CBS Sports, aired January 21, 2018.

chapter forty-three **SHUTTLE DIPLOMACY**

The description of the scene where Tom Brady and Gisele Bündchen call Rob Gronkowki is based on video footage from Chopra, *Tom vs. Time* (episode 6, "The End Game").

The description of Super Bowl LII and all dialogue is based on the NBC broadcast of the game and video footage from NFL Films.

"They gave up on me": Mike Reiss, "Malcolm Butler Says Patriots Never Gave Him Reason for Not Playing in Super Bowl LII," ESPN, March 14, 2018.

Ty Law tweeted: Ty Law, tweet from @officialTyLaw, February 5, 2018.

For Brandon Browner's tweets, see Mark Dunphy, "Brandon Browner Posted a Rant on the Patriots' Benching Malcolm Butler," Boston.com, February 5, 2018.

For Malcom Butler's Instagram statement, see Nicole Yang, "Malcolm Butler Posts Statement on Super Bowl LII Benching," Boston.com, February 6, 2018.

Brady wondered: Chopra, *Tom vs. Time* (episode 6, "The End Game").

For information about Danny Amendola's decision to leave the Patriots, see Mike Reiss, "Now a Dolphin, Danny Amendola Says Patriots' Contract Offer Fell Significantly Short," ESPN, April 13, 2018.

Gronkowski posted: Mark Dunphy, "Rob Gronkowski Tells Danny Amendola to 'Stay Lit' in Instagram Tribute," Boston.com, March 14, 2018.

Brady added: Mike Giardi, "Did Gronk, Brady Send Coded Message in Instagram Notes to Amendola?" NBC Sports, March 14, 2018.

Vogue writer: Rob Haskell, "Glorious Gisele," *Vogue*, July 2018.

"Why do I live here?": Ibid.

For Jim Gray's interview, see "Lord of the Rings: A Conversation with Five-Time Super Bowl Champion Tom Brady," Milken Institute, YouTube, May 22, 2018.

Brady once said: Kevin Valkenburg, "Tom Brady's Big Reveal," ESPN, January 22, 2016.

chapter forty-four WE'RE STILL HERE

I observed firsthand the scenes and dialogue depicted in this chapter.

For information about the synagogue shooting, see Campbell Robertson, Christopher Mele, and Sabrina Tavernise, "11 Killed in Synagogue Massacre," *New York Times*, October 27, 2018.

Jay-Z had announced: Cindy Boren, "Jay-Z Reportedly Turns Down Offer to Perform at the Super Bowl Halftime Show in February," *Washington Post*, September 20, 2017.

Goodell and Jay-Z announced a partnership: "Jay-Z's Roc Nation Entering Partnership with NFL," NFL News, August 13, 2019.

Index

About the Author

JEFF BENEDICT is the bestselling author of sixteen nonfiction books, including the #1 *New York Times* bestseller *Tiger Woods*, with Armen Keteyian. He has also been a special-features writer for *Sports Illustrated* and the *Los Angeles Times*, and his essays have appeared in the *New York Times*. His stories have been the basis of segments on *60 Minutes, CBS Sunday Morning,* HBO's *Real Sports with Bryant Gumbel,* the Discovery Channel, *Good Morning America, 48 Hours, 20/20,* the NFL Network, NPR, and ESPN's *Outside the Lines.* He is also a television and film producer. He lives with his wife and four children in Connecticut.